Excel 2000 Developer's Handbook

Excel 2000 Developer's Handbook™

Marion Cottingham

SYBEX®

San Francisco • Paris • Düsseldorf • Soest • London

Associate Publisher: Amy Romanoff
Contracts and Licensing Manager: Kristine O'Callaghan
Acquisitions & Developmental Editor: Melanie Spiller
Editor: Suzanne Goraj
Project Editor: Dann McDorman
Technical Editor: Steven Hansen
Book Designer: Kris Warrenburg
Graphic Illustrator: Tony Jonick
Electronic Publishing Specialist: Grey Magauran
Project Team Leader: Leslie Higbee
Proofreader: Richard Ganis
Indexer: John S. Lewis
Companion CD: Ginger Warner
Cover Designer: Design Site
Cover Illustrator/Photographer: David Bishop

SYBEX is a registered trademark of SYBEX Inc.

Developer's Handbook is a trademark of SYBEX Inc.

Screen reproductions produced with Collage Complete.
Collage Complete is a trademark of Inner Media Inc.

The CD Interface music is from GIRA Sound AURIA Music
Library © GIRA Sound 1996.

TRADEMARKS: SYBEX has attempted throughout this book to
distinguish proprietary trademarks from descriptive terms by following the capitalization style used by the manufacturer.

The author and publisher have made their best efforts to prepare
this book, and the content is based upon final release software
whenever possible. Portions of the manuscript may be based upon
pre-release versions supplied by software manufacturer(s). The
author and the publisher make no representation or warranties of
any kind with regard to the completeness or accuracy of the contents herein and accept no liability of any kind including but not
limited to performance, merchantability, fitness for any particular
purpose, or any losses or damages of any kind caused or alleged
to be caused directly or indirectly from this book.

Library of Congress Card Number: 99-62859
ISBN: 0-7821-2328-7

Manufactured in the United States of America

10 9 8 7 6 5 4 3 2 1

*To my mother and my sons, Steven and Alan, for
their support*

ACKNOWLEDGMENTS

Thanks to my working colleagues in the Computer Science Department at The University of Western Australia for their continued support throughout the writing of this book, especially to Dr. Richard Thomas and Dr. Ryszard Kozera for their friendship and encouragement. Special thanks to those involved in the Leadership Development for Women program—in particular to Professor Craig Atkins of the Botany Department, who gave me the courage and confidence to seek my goals.

I would like to thank Bill Adler of Adler and Robin Books Literary Agency for his encouragement and for assigning me to Martha Kaufman Amitay, agent and friend, who brought me together with Sybex.

I would like to thank Sybex developmental editor Melanie Spiller for having faith in my ability to write this book. She became my friend and confidant and kept me going with her wonderful stories throughout the earlier chapters.

Thanks to the project editor Dann McDorman for keeping me on my toes and getting this book out in such a timely fashion. I would like to thank the editor, Suzanne Goraj, for being a great source of support in the twilight hours and for her excellent editing and enthusiasm from start to finish. I would also like to thank the technical editor Steve Hansen for the comments and suggestions that have made this into a better book. Special thanks go to Leslie Higbee and Grey Magauran, who put these words onto the printed page.

Lastly, I would like to thank Microsoft for including me in their Office 2000 beta test program and for producing such powerful software that's a joy to write about.

CONTENTS AT A GLANCE

TABLE OF CONTENTS

INTRODUCTION

Spreadsheet software has had the same effect on adding machines as word processing packages have had on typewriters. Electronic spreadsheets became more common when IBM PCs became affordable enough for most companies to buy their first computers. Earlier computers had been either mainframes costing over a million or what were termed "minicomputers," which were also quite pricey for the smaller companies. In a way, computers were seen as a kind of status symbol; at that time, no one ever dreamed of having a personal computer at home.

Both mainframes and minicomputers required a special temperature-controlled, dust-free room all to themselves. Even so, many companies got caught up in the computer revolution of the '70s and '80s. When PCs and spreadsheets were introduced, companies were looking for a way to computerize everything that was done manually—and a four-day workweek was being predicted (disappointing that this never happened).

Companies usually computerized their payroll system first. Once that was established and working smoothly, the next thing was the account ledgers. These were normally huge, heavy books in which someone in authority meticulously wrote every conceivable monetary transaction—in two places. At the end of each month (and fiscal year), these ledgers had to balance. As often as not, they didn't, and all of the entries and calculations had to be rechecked until they did! This process was very stressful for the poor soul who had to do it, as the upper management was usually sitting waiting for the news of their profit or loss. Many a hole has been erased through a ledger sheet in the course of "balancing the books"—and the process was made more difficult by the accumulating total column that was present in most of these ledgers. To fix one mistake could require numerous changes.

When they were introduced, electronic spreadsheets were little more than an eraser-free way to keep track of all those monetary transactions and manipulate them, but—gee!—they had an accuracy never before achievable with the manual system. They allowed the profit or loss figure to be retrieved at any time the management requested it. And the ledgers were guaranteed to be accurate—after all, "computers don't make mistakes."

The first version of Microsoft Excel was introduced in 1985 and provided only simple row and column arithmetic—a far cry from what it is today. Excel has long been the leading graphical spreadsheet. Its popularity is due to the powerful features that make information easy to present in a meaningful way. In addition to numerical calculations, Excel can produce flow charts, tables, and even Web pages. Using your imagination and artistic flair, you can achieve some stunning results.

In 1993, Excel 5 was released. It was the first Microsoft Office application to incorporate Visual Basic for Applications (VBA) based on Microsoft Visual Basic, which had become a very successful programming environment for developing Windows applications. Visual Basic was one of the new visual languages introduced in the '90s that made developing Windows applications much easier and quicker, with the focus on reusable code modules.

Until then, there had been a tendency for companies to stick to programming languages that they had been using for years. Traditionally, these were COBOL, Fortran, and C. Their staff had the expertise in these languages, and management had invested lots of time and money developing software applications for their own use in these languages.

Over the years, several new languages have come and gone with little effect on the popularity of these traditional languages. However, the new visual languages have taken the software development industries by storm—or should I say hurricane! They were so breathtakingly powerful that companies were eager to re-engineer their software in the new languages. There are over four million copies of Visual Basic in use today.

In 1994, Microsoft announced to the world that its goal was to make Visual Basic the macro language for all of its applications. Microsoft later incorporated customized versions of VBA into all of its Office applications, starting with the Office 97 suite. Although VBA is slightly different in each application, there are lots of features that remain the same. This makes learning VBA extremely valuable, as your skills can be transferred between applications.

Excel is the world's leading spreadsheet program, providing features for

- handling numbers and text
- adding formulas and functions to automatically carry out calculations
- forecasting future budgets based on scenarios

- laying out data in different ways using PivotTables
- representing values in a chart
- publishing worksheets and charts on the Web

You're probably familiar with some of these features already. But Excel's best feature is often ignored or shied away from, even though it's unbelievably practical and can save you heaps of time. That feature is VBA.

What Can You Do with VBA?

With the help of VBA, you can automate just about anything except entering data into cells. After you've successfully coded a task using the VBA language, it's guaranteed to perform correctly and reliably every time you use it. Think how much time you'll save merely running your code instead of going through the same sequence of actions over and over again. With VBA, many tasks are completed with just one mouse click—you can't beat that. No doubt about it, Excel's VBA resources can save you lots of time and frustration. Can you imagine how much easier your workload will be when you've automated all your repetitive worksheet tasks?

As you progress through this book and build up your experience, you'll get more and more ambitious and find lots of tasks that can be automated. In fact, you'll probably concentrate more on the visual appearance of your worksheets when you know you only need to set them up once. Better still, you'll know the best way to go about automating tasks.

Just about any task you perform manually with Excel can be automated using a macro coded in the VBA language. You can develop the code for a VBA macro yourself, or you can let Excel do it for you. The act of creating a macro can be automated simply by recording the actions you do while performing a task. You don't even need to know the code is there, far less have to understand it. After you've accomplished creating a few macros and you see how simple it actually is, you're guaranteed to get curious—you'll want to go one step further and learn how to make adjustments to your existing macros. Once you can do that, you're well on your way to writing your own macros from scratch.

What is computer programming, anyway? The moment you wrote your first formula, you were already programming your computer. This book takes you by the hand and gently leads you deeper into the realm of the mysteries of computer programming. You don't have to be a guru to do it, and you'll be amazed at just how easy it is!

What's in This Book?

This book will take you through the practical steps required to create powerful and time-saving VBA macros in Excel 2000. Our focus will be on automation and reusing the reusable as ways to save time, increase productivity, and produce some amazing output.

The book is divided into seven parts:

Part I, "Referencing Cells in Excel VBA," shows you how to record your first macro and introduces you to the concept of classes of objects, toolbox controls, and Visual Basic Editor components. You'll see how to run macros using shortcut keys and in response to specific events.

- Chapter 1 reviews the referencing styles for cells and introduces you to the objects, properties, methods, and events in VBA macros. You'll learn how to record your first macro, view it using the Visual Basic Editor, and run it using a shortcut key.

- Chapter 2 introduces the Control Toolbox and the methods for adding controls to your worksheet and changing their properties. You'll see how to communicate with comments and control tips.

- Chapter 3 looks at the various components that make up the Visual Basic Editor and shows you how to view macros in the code window. You'll learn how to run your macros from code in response to a particular event.

Part II, "Naming Formulas, Functions, and Constants," explains how to use formulas and functions in worksheets and in code. It describes the importance of naming cells and introduces constants. You'll see how to use a TextBox control and validate input as it's being entered.

- Chapter 4 describes formulas and functions and how to use arithmetic operators in Excel worksheets and VBA code. You'll see how to code a macro that displays a message box and reports errors, and how to call a macro from a command button.

- Chapter 5 demonstrates the importance of names and how they overcome problems with external references and increase the understandability of VBA code.

- Chapter 6 covers worksheet constants and how these can be changed from inside a macro. The TextBox control is introduced for data input, and you'll see how to write code to validate any characters entered.

In Part III, "Macro-izing Styles from Toolbars," you'll learn all about formats and styles and how to save time by writing a macro to apply them. It will show you how to customize toolbars, menu bars, and command bars and how to use them to call your macros. You'll see how to align and position controls on a User-Form and how to use the Visual Basic Editor debugging facilities.

- Chapter 7 describes how to apply formats and styles to your workbooks, both manually and automatically, from a macro.

- Chapter 8 describes how to create a toolbar and use it to call macros. You'll see how to use the debugging features available in the Visual Basic Editor.

- Chapter 9 covers all you need to know about printing the information from your workbook.

- Chapter 10 introduces UserForms and explains how to display them from a macro. You'll also learn how to develop a graphical user interface (GUI) by aligning and positioning controls on the UserForm.

- Chapter 11 illustrates how to build custom command bars and menu bars.

Part IV, "Data Handling and Protection," covers handling files containing workbooks or data, viewing your data using charts, and protecting your data.

- Chapter 12 discusses how to handle files containing workbooks and data from VBA code.

- Chapter 13 covers all you'll need to know about charts and how to generate them from a macro by setting the properties of the various components.

- Chapter 14 discusses data security methods including protecting workbooks and hiding data, and describes Excel's auditing (cell reference–tracking) features.

Part V, "Web Publishing," illustrates how to set hyperlinks and publish worksheets and charts on the Web.

- Chapter 15 shows you how to construct hyperlinks from a cell, a graphic, or a toolbar button.

- Chapter 16 illustrates how to publish a worksheet on the Web.

- Chapter 17 shows you how to publish a chart on the Web.

Part VI, "Automating Blueprints and Scenarios," shows you how to create templates and covers the powerful *what-if* features of Excel.

- Chapter 18 shows you how to create templates that save you time.

- Chapter 19 describes how to create PivotTable and PivotChart reports using the Wizard, and how to filter data according to particular criteria.

- Chapter 20 describes Excel's Goal Seek feature for what-if analysis and shows how to build a data table. You'll see how to goal-seek with data tables and charts, and even interactively from a macro.

- Chapter 21 demonstrates the features of the Scenario Manager and the Solver.

Part VII, "Help," shows you how to use Visual Basic Editor's on-line help facility and how to provide the same level of help for users of your applications.

- Chapter 22 describes the Visual Basic on-line help facility and how to run its code samples. You'll also see how to control the Office Assistant.

- Chapter 23 shows you how to provide help, via UserForms, to the users of applications you've developed. This help ranges from a ToolTip to the full-blown compiled online help facility. You'll also see how to add a What's This button to your UserForm.

- Chapter 24 wraps up the book with a grand finale—a fun section on making the Office Assistant entertain you—and shows you how to enhance worksheets by replacing titles with WordArt objects.

Finally, the appendices provide easy reference tools to help you find the Excel information you need—when you need it.

- Appendix A lists all the ASCII symbols in handy table format.

- Appendix B contains a brief description of objects used throughout the book, the collections they belong to, and some of their properties, events, and methods.

Who Should Read This Book?

This book assumes that the reader is already a casual user of Microsoft Excel and has performed basic tasks such as opening and saving workbook files, viewing worksheets, and entering simple formulas and data. The material builds on this knowledge, making the reader aware of all of the features and tools available in Microsoft Excel 2000 to automate repetitive tasks.

What's on the CD?

The CD-ROM that accompanies this book contains all of the numbered code listings from the book. This allows you to quickly access the code without having to enter it—just transfer any macros to the Visual Basic Editor, which will let you run them and then try out any changes you want to make. Also included on the CD are evaluation copies of some poweful utilities that will be sure to make developing your Excel applications much easier!

PART I

Referencing Cells in Excel VBA

CHAPTER

ONE

1

Cell References

This chapter quickly takes you through the A1 and R1C1 styles of cell referencing offered by Excel, showing you how to create cell references in formulas using both the relative and absolute referencing modes. It's important to understand how these work before you begin to create formulas in macros.

Visual Basic for Applications (VBA) is an object-oriented system, so this chapter also gives an overview of what objects, properties, methods, and events actually are and how they all work together to offer a powerful way to develop VBA macros that can be used time and time again.

I'll show you how to write a few simple formulas in VBA and take you through the steps of recording your first macro, viewing it in the Visual Basic Editor, and running it using a shortcut key. I'll even give you a few tips on how to streamline your recorded macro code to make it more efficient and easier to understand.

Quick Recap on Cell Referencing Styles

In general, formulas perform calculations on values stored at other cells, which are identified by cell references. A cell reference can refer to a single cell or a range of adjacent cells in

- the same worksheet as the formula

- a different worksheet in the same workbook

- a worksheet in another workbook

NOTE   Cell references that refer to cells in other workbooks are called *external* references.

Referencing Styles

Microsoft Excel provides both the A1 and R1C1 styles for cell references, but only one of these styles can be used in a workbook at any one time. You can tell from the column headings which style is currently in use: letters are used for the A1 style and numbers are used for the R1C1 style. To change to the R1C1 style:

1.   Choose Tools ➢ Options to open the Options dialog box shown in Figure 1.1.

2. Select the General tab and check the R1C1 Reference Style check box.

3. Click OK to return to the worksheet, which will now display numerical column headings.

NOTE   When you switch styles, Excel automatically updates the cell references in all the formulas throughout the workbook.

FIGURE 1.1:

Changing to the R1C1 reference style

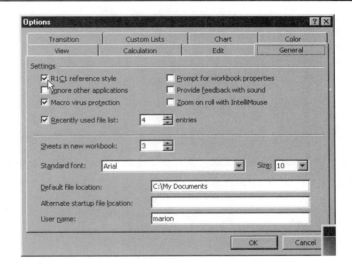

The R1C1 Reference Style check box allows you to toggle between styles, so to change back to the A1 style simply leave this check box blank.

Relative and Absolute Referencing Modes

When you use the relative referencing mode, cell references in formulas will refer to cells at positions relative to the cell containing the formula. With the absolute referencing mode, they refer to specific cells using row and column headings.

The difference between the two referencing modes is best explained by thinking about how you would give someone the directions to your home. You could give them your address, which would be equivalent to using the absolute referencing mode. Or you could tell them you live on the second street on the left in the third house on the right, which would be equivalent to using the relative referencing mode. Giving them your address will always get them to the same house, whereas the other way is dependent on where they are.

In cell references, this difference becomes apparent when you start copying formulas, as absolute addresses always refer to the same cell and relative addresses are updated to maintain the same relativity.

Both relative and absolute modes can be used in the same cell reference. Start entering your formula into the Formula bar, and immediately after entering a cell reference, repeatedly press the F4 function key. This last entry will be updated at each depression of the F4 key in the following (cyclic) sequence for cell A1:

   A1 $A$1   A$1 $A1

or for cell RC:

   RC   R1C1   R1C   RC1

If you want to try this out for yourself, remember that cell references must be in the current style. Thus, the A1 style can only be used when column headings are letters and the R1C1 style can only be used when they're numbers.

TIP

To change from relative to absolute referencing mode (or vice versa) when entering a formula, select the cell to be referenced and repeatedly press the F4 key until the cell reference has the required mixture of modes.

The A1 Style for Cell Referencing

The A1 reference style refers to cells using a column letter in the range A–IV and a row number in the range 1–65536. This section describes how this style of cell reference is handled in both relative and absolute modes.

Relative References in the A1 Style

The relative reference mode is based on the notion that the cells referenced in a formula are positioned relative to the cell containing the formula. This means that when you drag the formula to copy it to adjoining cells, the cell references in each copy of the formula are updated to maintain the same relationship as the original formula. For example, Figure 1.2 shows cell C1 containing the formula referring to other cells in the same row:

   =A1 + B1

FIGURE 1.2:

Absolute and relative cell referencing modes for the A1 style

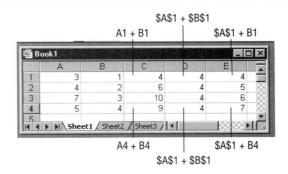

Any formula can be copied to adjacent cells by dragging the fill handle (black square in bottom-right corner, as shown below). Drag-copying cell C1 down to cell C4 will not only copy the formula but will update the cell references in the new formulas, making them also refer to cells in their own row. The formula in cell C4 thus becomes:

    =A4 + B4

Fill handle

Our example demonstrates what happens to relative references when formulas are copied to cells in the same column. In a similar way, when you drag the fill handle horizontally across cells to copy formulas along rows, the column letters will be updated with relative references.

References are not restricted to being in the same row or column. If A2 is a cell reference in the formula contained in cell D4, it refers to the cell two rows up and three columns to the left. Drag-copying this formula to D5 will change this reference to A3 and drag-copying it to E4 will change it to B2 to maintain the same relative positions.

Absolute References in the A1 Style

The absolute referencing mode refers to a cell with its column and row headings both preceded by a $ sign to distinguish them from cells referenced using the relative referencing mode.

The absolute reference is based on the assumption that when you refer to the value at a specific cell, the cell reference will still refer to that same cell no matter where the formula is copied to. For example, Figure 1.2 shows cell D1 containing the formula $A$1 + $B$1. When this is drag-copied down to D4, nothing changes—all cell references still refer to cells A1 and B1.

Absolute and Relative Modes in the A1 Style

As you saw in the example shown in Figure 1.2, cell E1 contains the formula

    $A$1 + B1

where one cell reference is specified in the relative referencing mode and the other in the absolute mode. It's also possible to have a cell reference specified using a mixture of modes. For example,

    $A1

will always refer to cells in column A but the row will be updated to maintain its relative position to the row containing the formula. For instance, if the cell reference $A1 appears in a formula contained in cell D3 that is drag-copied to cells in the same column, all the cell references will start with $A (absolute mode) to refer to cells in column A but the 1 (relative mode) will be changed to two rows above the current row in each copy. If the formula is drag-copied along the same row, none of the formulas are updated.

Table 1.1 lists the variety of ways that the relative and absolute cell references can be written for the A1 style of cell referencing. The table includes references for ranges of adjacent cells as well as ranges of nonadjacent cells.

T A B L E   1 . 1 :   Relative and Absolute Addressing Modes for the A1 Style

Relative	Absolute	Cell or Range of Cells
C5	$C$5	The cell in column C and row 5
B2:F5	$B$2:$F$5	The range of cells in columns B through F, and in rows 2 through 5
D:D	$D:$D	All cells in column D
3:3	$3:$3	All cells in row 3
2:6	$2:$6	All cells in rows 2 through 6

Continued on next page

TABLE 1.1 CONTINUED: Relative and Absolute Addressing Modes for the A1 Style

Relative	Absolute	Cell or Range of Cells
1:1,3:3,5:5	$1:$1,$3:$3,$5:$5	All cells in rows 1, 3, and 5
A:A,B:B,C:C	$A:$A,$B:$B,$C:$C	All cells in columns A, B, and C
B2:D5,F2:H4	$B$2:$D$5,$F$2:$H$4	All cells in range B2 through D5 and F2 through H4

The R1C1 Style for Cell Referencing

The R1C1 reference style uses row and column numbers to uniquely identify a cell. To change to the R1C1 style, choose Tools ➤ Options and click the R1C1 Reference Style check box in the General tab (Figure 1.1). The worksheet column headings will change from letters to numbers, making it easier for you to specify cells in this style.

Relative References in the R1C1 Style

Relative references are defined by their relative positions from the cell containing the formula—for example, R[1]C[2] refers to the cell one row down and two columns to the right. Row and column numbers can also be negative, with R[-1]C[-1] referring to the cell one row above and one column to the left. If the number is omitted altogether, Excel uses the same row or column as the formula. Figure 1.3 shows the worksheet at Figure 1.2 with the referencing style changed to the R1C1 style.

FIGURE 1.3:

Absolute and relative cell referencing modes for the R1C1 style

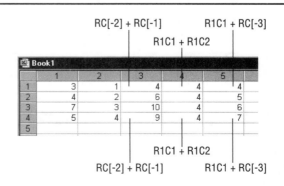

Notice how the formulas at cells C1 through C4 have now all been updated and contain the same references:

```
=RC[-2]+RC[-1]
```

In fact, copies of all R1C1 style references are always exactly the same, with relative references (brackets) evaluating to different results according to the position of the cell containing the formula and the values in the cells it references.

NOTE   When an R or C occurs in a cell reference without any number being specified, Excel uses the same row or column as the cell containing the formula.

Absolute References in the R1C1 Style

Absolute references refer to cells by their actual row and column numbers as defined by the worksheet's row and column headings. To distinguish them from relative references, no brackets are used, as you see here:

```
R2C1
```

Absolute and Relative Modes in the R1C1 Style

An R1C1 cell reference can be specified using both modes. For example,

```
R1C[2]
```

will always refer to cells in the first row, but, to maintain the relativity, the column used will always be two to the right of the column containing the formula.

NOTE   With the A1 reference style, the cell references in a formula change when the formula is copied to another cell. With the R1C1 reference style, all copies of a formula are exactly the same.

Objects, Properties, Methods, and Events in VBA

Before you start using VBA to create macros, let's take a quick look at the bits and pieces that make up Excel Visual Basic for Applications and how they all fit together. VBA is an object-oriented environment that provides a large collection of objects, each with its own sets of properties and methods. The sheer number of these can be overwhelming, but luckily you don't actually need to know very much to get started. (See Appendix B for a listing of the objects used in this book and information about their collections, properties, events, and methods.)

An object and everything needed to create it, display it, make it respond to user events, destroy it, etc. are all encapsulated in a single *class* named after the type of object it contains. Classes can be thought of as blueprints for creating other objects of the same type—for example, all TextBox objects will behave in the same way because they're using the same code encapsulated in the TextBox class. In other programming languages, you can usually group related data items together and refer to them collectively using a single name such as Employees or Products, but in the object-oriented methodology this is taken one step further, by allowing executable code to be part of the type which is now referred to as a class.

Properties and methods are said to be *members* of the class. Properties are the attributes of an object that determine how it looks, including text formatting, color, size, etc. Methods are the procedures (sets of coding statements that perform a specific task) that an object needs to perform its roles, including procedures to create and destroy the object, and event procedures that determine how the object interacts with a user.

Objects

In an object-oriented system, just about everything is an object. In Excel VBA, an object is any element of the application, such as a cell, a worksheet, any controls placed in a worksheet, a workbook, a chart—in fact, your Excel application itself is an object. Other objects include ranges of cells, cell borders, panes, pivot tables, scenarios, styles, trend lines… the list goes on. Each class of object has its own set of properties, methods, and events.

When you add an object to your workbook, an *instance* of that class of object is created and assigned the default property values as defined in the class. By default, instances of the same class are named using the class name followed by a sequential number. Every instance of the same class has its properties initialized to the same default values, except for the Name property. Because VBA assigns default values to anything that needs a value, you don't actually need to know very much about VBA to get started. So don't worry if you feel a bit lost at this stage; things will become clearer once we progress.

Properties

A property is an attribute of an object that describes how it looks (such as its size, color, and position) or how it behaves (such as whether or not it's resizable, visible, or enabled, or whether it can refer to another object). When you create an object, Excel executes the procedure for creating an instance of that object. This procedure, which is stored in the object's class, assigns the default values for all the properties, thus allowing you to use the object immediately. You may want to change a few properties, but you'll find they're mostly set to what you require anyway, so you won't need to update very many of them. To assign a new value to a property in VBA macro code, you simply create an assignment statement that, on the left side, specifies the object by name and (separated by a period) the property, and, on the right, indicates the new value. For example, the following assignment statement sets the name of the worksheet from the default name of Sheet1 to the new name Accounts:

```
Sheet1.Name = "Accounts"
```

A worksheet's Name property appears in the tab at the bottom of the worksheet. You'll find that the Name property is included in lots of other classes.

Methods

A method is an action that can be performed on an object. Methods are carried out by executing the method's procedure, which is a member of the object's class. The format for calling a method is to name the object followed by the method, separating the two with a period. For example, to use the Protect method to protect the worksheet object named Sheet1 against modification, you would write:

```
Sheet1.Protect
```

Events

Each time the user makes an interaction with a particular object in your workbook, an event is instigated. Each class of object has its own group of events that it can respond to. For example, a workbook has a NewSheet event that's executed whenever the user adds a new worksheet, and a worksheet has a SelectionChange event that's executed whenever the user selects another cell or range of cells. Excel provides the first and last lines as the skeleton of each event procedure; it's up to you to write the code for each event you want to respond to.

How Objects, Properties, and Methods Interact

When you add a new worksheet to your workbook, a `Worksheet` object is created by a member procedure in the `Worksheet` class. This new `Worksheet` object will be created with all its properties set to default values (for instance, its `Name` and whether it uses the A1 or R1C1 style), and it will be ready to use immediately. You'll be able to apply any of the class's built-in methods to it, such as `PrintOut` and `Save`, and write the code to respond to any of its events, such as `SheetCalculate` and `Open`.

When a Property or Method Returns an Object

When a property or method returns an object, the properties and methods of that object can be accessed as if you had actually specified the object itself. For example, let's consider the following line of code:

```
Workbooks("Book1").ActiveSheet.Name = "Expenses"
```

The `Workbooks("Book1").ActiveSheet` part returns a `Worksheet` object containing the active worksheet in Book1. The `Name` property that follows belongs to the actual `Worksheet` object rather than to the `ActiveSheet` property. So if `Sheet1` is the active worksheet, this assignment statement is equivalent to:

```
Sheet1.Name = "Expenses"
```

The original statement is more general, as it allows any active worksheet to be assigned the new name, whereas this statement uniquely identifies the worksheet as `Sheet1` and assigns the name to it whether or not it is the active worksheet.

The `ActiveCell` property returns a `Range` object. This property is a member of both the `Application` object (active application—i.e., Excel) and the `Window` object (active window) and returns the range of cells containing the active cell of the active window of the active application. It is coded in full as:

```
Application.ActiveWindow.ActiveCell.Borders.Color = vbRed
```

Because there is only one active cell at any particular time, the `ActiveCell` properties of the `Application` object and the `Window` object both refer to the same range of cells. Thus, this statement can also be written as:

```
ActiveWindow.ActiveCell.Borders.Color = vbRed
```

or

```
Application.ActiveCell.Borders.Color = vbRed
```

Also, because the Range object returned is unique, the ActiveCell property can even be written on its own:

```
ActiveCell.Borders.Color = vbRed
```

The Borders property is another property that returns an object. The Active-Cell.Borders part of this statement returns the Border object for the range of cells, which then has its Color property set to red. The vb prefix placed in front of Red is to distinguish it as a Visual Basic constant rather than a variable that has been declared in the code.

The object returned by the ActiveCell property is a Range object, so the Borders property sets the rectangular border for the group of cells defined in the Range object.

The statement

```
Application.ActiveWindow.ActiveCell.Borders.Color = vbRed
```

is most easily read starting from the right as "The color of the border of the range of cells containing the active cell of the active window of the application is set to red."

Ranges in Excel VBA

In Excel VBA, the Range object defines a cell or range of cells that can be assigned values and formulas in code and can be manipulated in the same way as worksheet cells are manipulated manually. For example,

```
ActiveCell.Borders.Color = vbRed
```

is equivalent to choosing Format ➤ Cells and updating the Color box in the Border tab of the Format Cells dialog box.

There is also a Range property that returns a Range object. The Range property enables you to refer to the cell or range of cells passed to it as an argument, but it is restricted to the A1 reference style, which can have any valid A1 style cell reference specified in the relative or absolute referencing modes.

```
Range("A1")
Range("$A$1")
```

The Range object class has more than 150 properties and methods encapsulated in it. Table 1.2 gives a description of some of these, which may already be familiar to you.

TABLE 1.2: Range Object Properties and Methods

Property / Method	Description
Application property	The application containing the range of cells—"Microsoft Excel"
Autofill method	Automatically fills the specified cells with the formula, values, formats, and other options from a given source
Borders property	Returns a **Borders** collection of the four borders of the specified range of cells
Clear method	Clears the values from an entire range of cells
Copy method	Copies the contents of the specified range of cells to the clipboard
Font property	The font used at the specified range of cells

Because the Range property returns a Range object, any properties and methods associated with a Range object can be set using the Range property. The following line of code shows the Range property being used to return the Range object that refers to cell A1; the Value property contains the value of cell A1:

```
Range("A1").Value
```

If cell A2 contains a formula, the result can be calculated using the Calculate method of the Range object returned by the Range property:

```
Range("A2").Calculate
```

You can also use the Range property to return nonadjacent ranges of cells and then assign the same value to all the cells in one line of code. This is particularly useful if you want to initialize the values in all the cells to zero:

```
Range("A3:B5,C3:D8").Value = 0
```

NOTE   Any valid A1 style cell reference that can be entered in a worksheet formula can be used as the argument in the **Range** property.

The Range property can also be used with two arguments that specify the cells at diagonally opposite corners of a range of cells. For example, the following statement selects cells in the range A1:C4:

```
Range("A1","C4").Select
```

VBA Arguments

Arguments are passed to methods and properties that use their values to perform whatever tasks they're programmed to do, but each argument must be the type expected by the method so that it can perform its task correctly. Arguments can be numbers, text, and logical values (true or false).

Excel gives you two choices of how to pass arguments to a method:

- implicitly—list the arguments in the same order as the method expects them
- explicitly—name the arguments without having to worry about their order

As an example, let's consider the BorderAround method of the Range object, which sets the attributes for placing a new border around the outside of the range of cells specified. This method requires up to four arguments to specify the line's style and thickness, the ColorIndex property to allow its color to be specified using a number, and Color to allow its color to be specified using a Visual Basic constant.

Implicit Arguments

The BorderAround method places a rectangular border around a range of cells. It can be called as follows:

```
Call ActiveCell.BorderAround(LineStyle, Weight, ColorIndex, Color)
```

or

```
ActiveCell.BorderAround LineStyle, Weight, ColorIndex, Color
```

where LineStyle, Weight, ColorIndex, and Color have been set to valid values such as xlContinuous, xlThick, xlColorIndexAutomatic, and 0 (zero). Notice that when the arguments are enclosed in parentheses you need to start the statement with the Call keyword.

Explicit Arguments

Methods can also be called with the arguments explicitly named and assigned their values using a colon and equals sign (:=), as follows:

```
Range("A1:C7").BorderAround ColorIndex:=3, Weight:=xlThick
```

This code results in a thick red border being placed around the range of cells A1:C7, as shown below.

When you specifically name the arguments, you don't have to adhere to any particular order. This is especially useful if you want to assign values to only some of the arguments and know them by name already. As you'll see, explicitly naming the arguments makes your code more readable.

Skipping Arguments

There are lots of methods in VBA that have arguments but only some of them need to be passed values, as any missing arguments are automatically assigned default values.

When you pass arguments without naming them, Excel uses the commas as delimiters when it pairs off the arguments expected with the values being passed in the call. When it gets to the end of these values, it assumes that the remaining arguments are to be set to default values. For example, in the following statement the first and last arguments are missing:

```
Range("A1:C7").BorderAround , xlThick, 3
```

Notice how the comma is still included although the first value is missing so that the remaining values will still be lined up with the correct arguments. The last argument to be passed a value will be allocated to `ColorIndex`, and although there is no argument passed for `Color`, no further comma is required.

TIP   To call a method with some arguments not defined, replace each skipped argument with a comma.

Required Arguments

There are several methods that require some of their arguments to be assigned values, in which case the required arguments are always placed at the beginning of the argument list. The `ConvertFormula` method is one of these. This method converts the cell references in a formula from the A1 to the R1C1 reference style or vice versa, and can also change the mode. The syntax for this method is:

```
Application.ConvertFormula(Formula, FromReferenceStyle, _
ToReferenceStyle, ToAbsolute, RelativeTo)
```

The first two arguments are required, but the other three are optional and can be skipped.

The `Formula` argument requires a string containing the formula to be converted. The `FromReferenceStyle` and `ToReferenceStyle` arguments specify the style and can be set to the Excel constants `xlA1` or `xlR1C1`; if the `ToReferenceStyle` argument is skipped, the style remains unchanged. The `ToAbsolute` argument is used to change the mode and can be set to one of the following Excel constants: `xlAbsolute`, `xlAbsRowRelColumn`, `xlRelRowAbsColumn`, or `xlRelative`; if this argument is skipped, the mode remains unchanged. The `RelativeTo` argument is assigned a `Range` object that refers to a single cell.

NOTE	All the constants provided by Excel start with the prefix `xl`.

VBA's *Formula* and *FormulaR1C1* Properties

`Formula` and `FormulaR1C1` are properties of the `Range` object that can be used to assign or retrieve a formula to or from the cells specified as the argument in the `Range` method. The `Formula` property assigns and retrieves formulas in the A1 reference style and the `FormulaR1C1` property assigns and retrieves formulas in the R1C1 reference style. The following lines show these properties being set:

```
Sheet1.Range("A1").FormulaR1C1 = "=sum(R2C1:R4C1)"
Sheet1.Range("A1").Formula = "=sum(A2:A4)"
```

These properties can be used with any Range object, including those returned by properties and methods. For example, they can be used with the ActiveCell property as follows:

```
ActiveCell.FormulaR1C1 = "=R[-5]C[1]"
```

Since a formula can be a single value, the formula property can be used to assign a value to a cell.

VBA's *Value* Property

The Value property is used to assign and retrieve values to and from cells. It can be used instead of the Formula property to make your code easier to read and understand. When it's used to retrieve a value from a cell containing a formula, the result is evaluated before being assigned to the Value property.

VBA's *Cells* Property for Referring to Single Cells

The Cells property is used to refer to a single cell by returning a Range object. This property is independent of the current style for cell references set in the worksheet and works entirely in the absolute referencing mode.

The worksheet is treated like an array (a collection of items that can be referred to by a single name), with rows and columns accessed by numbers denoting their positions. The Cells property requires two arguments, the row number and the number depicting the column, even if the A1 style is in use and column headings are letters. For example, the following line of code shows this property being used to assign the value 5 to cell D2:

```
Sheet1.Cells(2, 4).Value = 5
```

You can also assign a formula to a cell using this property. The following code shows a formula being assigned to cell E2:

```
Sheet1.Cells(2, 5) = "=sum(R2C1:R4C1)"
```

If you're used to working with arrays in other programming languages, you'll find that this is the easiest way to assign values and formulas to a specific cell. The Cells property is not restricted to accessing cells in the entire worksheet; it can be used to access a cell from a range of cells defined in a Range object. When used with a range of cells,

```
Cells(1,1)
```

is the top-left hand cell in the range—this may not be cell A1.

Referring to Cells in Other Worksheets

The examples of cell references considered so far have referred to cells in the same worksheet as the formula they're used in. Cell references can also refer to cells located in other worksheets. Because the row and column headings are the same in every worksheet, if there are five worksheets then there will be five cells referred to as A1 in the workbook. So the worksheet's name must also be included as part of the cell reference to uniquely identify the cell required.

In a worksheet formula, the cell reference begins with the name of the worksheet followed by an exclamation mark (!) to let Excel know that the name belongs to a worksheet object. For example, a formula entered in the worksheet named Sheet2 that refers to cell A5 in the worksheet named Sheet1 would be:

```
=Sheet1!A5
```

VBA has a Sheets collection object containing all the sheets in the active workbook. It also has a Sheets property that's passed the name of a worksheet from this collection as an argument, in much the same way as the Range property is passed a range of cells.

The VBA macro code equivalent to the formula entered into Sheet 2 is:

```
Sheets("Sheet1").Range("A5")
```

The worksheet named Sheet1 is specified by the value passed as the argument to the Sheets property. The Range object returned by the Range property represents cell A5 specified by the argument.

If the worksheet's name contains any spaces, it must be enclosed in single quotes when it's entered into the formula. For example, if Sheet1 was changed to General Office Expenses, the formula must be entered as:

```
='General Office Expenses'!A5
```

In VBA macro code, all strings are enclosed in double quotes (") to distinguish them from code instructions and names of values (variables). The value passed to the Sheets property is a string denoting the worksheet's name and is already enclosed in double quotes, so spaces in the name make no difference. The code for this is:

```
Sheets("General Office Expenses").Range("A5")
```

Referring to Cells in Other Workbooks

You've seen how to refer to a cell in the active worksheet and in a different worksheet in the active workbook; now let's look at how to refer to a cell in any open workbook. To do this, the cell reference must include the names of both the workbook and the worksheet to uniquely identify the cell. The workbook's name is given first and is enclosed in square brackets to let Excel know that it's the name of a workbook. This is immediately followed by the worksheet's name, an exclamation mark, and the cell reference.

Suppose you're entering a formula in a workbook named Book2 and you need to access cell B4 in worksheet Sheet1 of workbook Book1. In this scenario, a complete cell reference would be:

```
=[Book1]Sheet1!$B$4
```

A cell reference that refers to a cell in another workbook is called an external reference and is restricted to using the absolute referencing mode.

VBA has a Workbooks collection object containing all the workbooks currently open and a Workbooks property that's called with an argument that identifies one of these workbooks. The macro code for the whole cell reference is:

```
Workbooks("Book1").Sheets("Sheet1").Range("$B$4")
```

where Book1 is the name of the Workbook object required from the Workbooks collection object and Sheet1 is the name of the Worksheet object required from the Sheets collection object. The Range object contains cell B4 from the worksheet in the workbook specified.

Referring to Complete Rows and Columns of Cells

To refer to all the cells in a row or column, use the Rows and Columns properties. The following line of code shows how to assign all the cells in column 1 to zero:

```
Sheet1.Columns(1).Value = 0
```

The Rows property assigns values to rows of cells in the same way.

The Rows and Columns properties can be used with any Range object to refer to cells in a row or column within that range of cells.

```
ActiveCells.Rows(1).Value = 0
```

assigns the value 0 to the cells along the top row of the range of cells.

If you use the Rows or Columns property without any argument, the value on the right of the assignment statement is assigned to all the cells in the worksheet. The following example shows how to assign zero to all the cells in a worksheet (please read the following warning before trying this out):

```
Sheet1.Columns.Value = 0
```

WARNING Using **Columns** or **Rows** to assign a property to all the cells in the entire worksheet will tie your PC up for a long time.

Using Labels as Cell References

The column and row labels in a worksheet are the labels you give to columns and rows of adjacent cells of data by entering the label text into cells along the top (column labels) or down the side (row labels) of the range of cells containing the data. This range can be situated anywhere in the worksheet. Labels can be used to refer to cells in a worksheet as an alternative to row and column headings. Don't get these two mixed up: Row and column *headings* are the letters and numbers assigned automatically to whole rows and columns by Excel, whereas row and column *labels* are limited to rows and columns within a range of cells.

To reference all cells within the same column or row of adjacent cells of data, you need only give the column or row label. To make this possible, row and column labels must be unique. For example, the formula below totals all the numerical information that it finds at adjacent cells in the column or row labeled January.

```
=SUM(January)
```

The column and row labels can also be used by Excel as the basis for defining names, which is discussed later in Chapter 5.

3-D Cell References

3-D cell references refer to the same cell or range of cells in several worksheets and are typically used to analyze data. Before defining a 3-D reference, first check that the workbook contains all the worksheets you want to include in your 3-D model of the data. To define your 3-D cell reference:

1. Select the cell to be assigned the formula.

2. Enter an equals sign (=) and the name of a function (such as SUM) that will use the 3-D cell reference, and then enter an open parenthesis.

3. Select all the worksheets required by clicking the tab for the first worksheet and, while holding down the Shift key, clicking the tab for the last worksheet. All the selected worksheets will appear highlighted and will be appended to your formula as the names of the first and last worksheets clicked separated by a colon (:) and both enclosed in single quotes (').

4. Select the cell or range of cells to be referenced from the first worksheet, and finalize the formula by adding the ending parenthesis and pressing Enter.

For example, the formula shown below was created by selecting C7 as the cell to be assigned the formula, then entering **=SUM** and selecting Sheet1, Sheet2, and Sheet3 before selecting the range of cells A7 through B8 from worksheet Sheet1. Excel will automatically remove the quotes around the names of selected sheets, and the final formula will appear as:

```
=SUM(Sheet1:Sheet3!A7:B8)
```

Cell References for Moving Cells

What happens to a cell reference when it refers to a cell that's changed its position depends on whether the absolute or relative referencing mode is used.

Absolute Referencing Mode

Cell references defined using the absolute referencing mode always refer to the original cell irrespective of where its contents have been moved.

Relative Referencing Mode

When a cell's contents are moved to a different location in the same worksheet, all the relative mode cell references are automatically updated to refer to its new location. For example, if you enter the following formula at cell B7:

```
=B4+B5+B6
```

and then move it by copying it to cell D4, it will change to:

```
=D1+D2+D3
```

When a cell is moved to a different worksheet (using cut and paste), the cell references to it are automatically extended to include the worksheet's name:

```
=Sheet2!R[-3]C[-2]+RC[-1]
```

When a cell is moved to a different workbook (using cut and paste), the cell references to it are automatically extended to include both the workbook and the worksheet names:

```
=[Book2]Sheet1!R[4]C[-1]+RC[-1]
```

Recording Cell References in a Macro

The easiest way to get started in VBA macro programming is to record your actions and look at the code Excel automatically creates for you. Let's record the actions it takes to enter a number into cell A1:

1. Choose Tools; if Macro isn't included in the menu list, pause the mouse button over the double Down arrows at the bottom of the drop-down list (as shown).

2. The drop-down list will expand as shown to include all of the Tool menu commands. Choose Macro ➤ Record New Macro to display the Record Macro dialog box (Figure 1.4).

FIGURE 1.4:

Record Macro dialog box

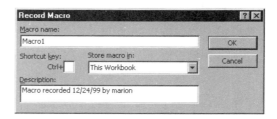

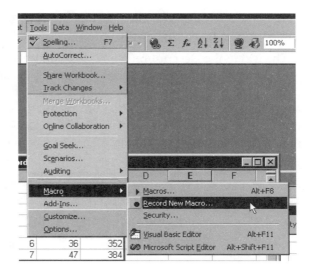

3. Click OK to return to the worksheet. The Stop Recording toolbar will now be displayed, and every action you make until you click the Stop Recording button (as shown) will be recorded.

4. Select cell A1.

5. Enter the number **123** followed by the Return key.

6. Click the Stop Recording button to finalize your macro.

All of your actions will have been recorded as Excel VBA macro code statements.

Record Macro Dialog Box

The Record Macro dialog box (shown in Figure 1.4) contains the information needed to create a new macro. The macro's name will automatically be defaulted to Macro#, where # is the next number in the sequence, and displayed in the Macro Name box. This name can be left as is, or you can overtype it with a new name that better describes the macro's function. A discussion on renaming macros is given later in Chapter 5.

The text in the Description box is defaulted to the string `Macro recorded` followed by the date and the name of the person recording the macro, both retrieved from Microsoft Windows. This can be left as is or updated to something more descriptive. I find the Description box useful for stating what the macro actually does, but when multiple users are involved it may also be important to know the name of the macro's creator and when the macro was created.

Mistakes Are Recorded Too!

Before you record your macro, it's best to plan what actions you're going to perform. Remember: If you make a mistake it will also be recorded, along with any actions you make trying to correct it. This will make your macros much longer than they need to be, and if left, your mistakes could follow you around for years. So it's probably best to repeat recording sequences of actions until you get them right. When you become more competent at writing macros, you'll be able to delete any excess code caused by recording mistakes and trying to fix them.

To View Your Macro

When you record your macro it's stored in a module attached to your workbook. VBA creates a new module when you record a macro for the first time after opening Excel. Any macros you record thereafter are appended to the same module until you close Excel again. Modules are objects and are given the default names `Module#`, where # is the next number in the sequence.

Macros are viewed in the Visual Basic Editor window. In this chapter, I'll just show you how to open this window; we'll get back to the Visual Basic Editor again in Chapter 3. The following steps show you how to open the code window to view your macro to see what's been recorded:

1. Choose Tools; if Macro isn't in the list of commands, click the double Down arrows to expand the drop-down list.

2. Choose Macro ➤ Visual Basic Editor (as shown) to open the Visual Basic Editor window, shown in Figure 1.5.

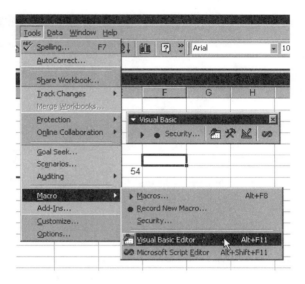

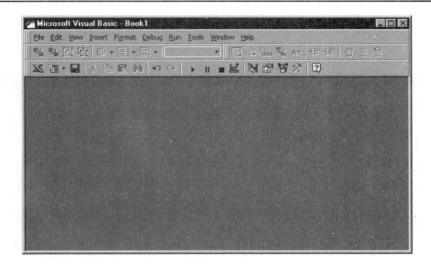

3. If the Visual Basic Editor window is empty (as shown), then choose View ➤ Project Explorer to display the Project window:

4. Click the plus (+) box next to Modules at the bottom of the tree to expand the Modules branch.

5. Double-click Module1 to open the code window displaying your macro, as shown in Figure 1.6.

FIGURE 1.6:

Code window for
Module1

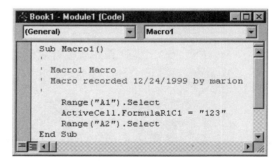

6. When you've finished viewing your macro, choose File ➤ Close And Return To Microsoft Excel to go back to your worksheet.

Listing 1.1 shows the recorded macro code. Let's go through this code and I'll show you how simple it is to understand.

LISTING 1.1

```
0    Sub Macro1()
1        '
```

```
 2        ' Macro1 Macro
 3        ' Macro recorded 12/24/99 by marion
 4        '
 5        '
 6        '
 7        Range("A1").Select
 8        ActiveCell.FormulaR1C1 = "123"
 9        Range("A2").Select
10   End Sub
```

ANALYSIS

Line 0 is the opening statement of the macro and it declares the macro as a subprocedure named Macro1.

Line 1 is a blank comment line.

Line 2 is a comment line that gives the macro's name, taken straight from the name entered in the Macro Name box in the Record Macro dialog box shown in Figure 1.4.

Line 3 is a comment line that is the description of the macro, taken straight from the Description box in the Record Macro dialog box shown in Figure 1.4. This description is also displayed at the bottom of the Macro dialog box, as shown in Figure 1.7.

Lines 4 through 6 are blank lines that Excel VBA puts in to remind you to add some comments about what the macro does.

Line 7 shows how Excel interpreted your action at step 3 when you selected cell A1. The Select property of the Range object is used to make cell A1 the selected cell; it also inadvertently becomes the active cell.

Line 8 shows the VBA code recorded for step 4, which uses the ActiveCell property to return the Range object containing cell A1 that the Formula-R1C1 property assigns the value 123 to.

Line 9 is the result of hitting the Return key immediately after entering the value, which updates the selected cell to the cell in the next row ("A2").

Line 10 is the End statement that marks the end of Macro1.

In VBA code, the comments start with a single quote character followed by whatever you want to put in the comment. When Excel is interpreting the code, it stops at the single quote character and proceeds to the next line of code, so comments do not affect the size of your interpreted code.

Streamlining Recorded Macros

Because recorded macros follow your every move, their code can often be streamlined to contain fewer statements to make them more efficient in both storage and execution time. For example, macros quite often include the last cell selected even though this is never used (Line 9 in Listing 1.1). This statement can be deleted without having any effect on the way the macro runs.

Often, two statements can be combined. In Listing 1.1, the selection and assignment done in Lines 7 and 8 could be reduced to the single statement

```
Range("A1").FormulaR1C1 = "123"
```

where the Range property identifies A1 as the cell to be assigned the value 123 using the FormulaR1C1 property, which allows both values and formulas to be assigned. In fact, your code would be easier to read and understand if the Value property was used instead of FormulaR1C1. Numerical values can be assigned as numbers or they can be enclosed in double quotes and assigned as a string; here I've opted to assign the numerical version. Making all these modifications changes lines 7 through 9 to:

```
Range("A1").Value = 123
```

Running Your Macro Using a Shortcut Key

One of the simplest ways to run a macro is to assign it a shortcut key. Keyboard shortcuts are familiar to most users of any Windows application. Excel makes setting this up very straightforward, even allowing you to use a key combination that already exists, making it override any previous combination while the macro's workbook is open.

The following steps show you how to assign a shortcut key to your macro:

1. Expand the Tools drop-down list and choose Macro ➢ Macros to display the Macro dialog box, shown in Figure 1.7.

FIGURE 1.7:

Macro dialog box

2. Click Options to display the Macro Options dialog box (shown).

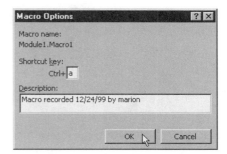

3. Enter a letter in the Shortcut Key box—I've entered an "a". You can edit the Description box to include the shortcut key. This new text will be displayed in dialog boxes instead of your original description, which will still remain in the opening comments of your macro.

To check whether your macro performs its task, delete the 123 value from cell A1 and enter your keyboard shortcut (such as my Ctrl+A). The value 123 should reappear in cell A1.

Ctrl+A is normally the keyboard shortcut used by Excel to select all the cells in the active worksheet. There is the danger in using such shortcuts that you'll forget a keyboard shortcut's new function and invoke your macro by mistake. This is even more likely to happen if the workbook is shared between several users.

WARNING Setting keyboard shortcuts to run your macro should be done with extreme caution, as you can override any previous Excel keyboard shortcuts. If other users access the workbook, they may invoke your macro by mistake.

Keyboard shortcuts provide only one way to run your macro. Many other ways are covered later in Chapter 8.

Changing Cell Reference Modes to Record VBA Macros

Cell references can be recorded using the absolute or relative referencing modes. To toggle from one to the other, click the Relative Reference button on the Stop Rec toolbar, shown in Figure 1.8.

FIGURE 1.8:

Relative Reference button

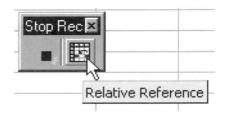

To demonstrate the difference these modes make when you record macros, let's record two macros that select the range of cells A1 through C5. We'll record the first macro using the absolute referencing mode and the second one using the relative referencing mode.

1. Open a new workbook.

2. Expand the Tools menu command and choose Macro ➤ Macros to open the Record Macro dialog box.

3. Click OK to accept `Macro1` as the name and return to the worksheet.

4. Select the range of cells A1:C5 and click the Stop Recording button.

To record the second macro, do steps 1 to 3 again and accept `Macro2` as the name for the second macro, then continue:

4. Click the Relative Reference button in the Stop Rec toolbar, shown in Figure 1.8.

5. Select the range of cells A1:C5 and click the Stop Recording button.

The two macros are shown in Listing 1.2 and Listing 1.3, followed by a discussion of their differences.

LISTING 1.2

```
0    Sub Macro1()
1        '
2        ' Macro1 Macro
3        ' Macro recorded 12/24/99 by marion
4        '
5
6        '
7            Range("A1:C5").Select
8    End Sub
```

LISTING 1.3

```
0    Sub Macro2()
1        '
2        ' Macro2 Macro
3        ' Macro recorded 12/24/99 by marion
4        '
5
6        '
7            ActiveCell.Range("A1:C5").Select
8    End Sub
```

ANALYSIS

Let's just consider the difference between these two macros. They are both recordings of the same actions, but Macro1 uses absolute cell references and Macro2 uses relative cell references.

Line 7 in Macro1 shows the range being selected using the Range object. The active cell is not taken into account at all, so the result is that the same range of cells is always selected.

Line 7 in Macro2 shows the range being started from the active cell. For example, selecting cell D5 to make it active and then running Macro2 causes cell A1 to be matched with cell D5 and the range D5 through F9 to be selected.

Changing the Cell Referencing Style to Record VBA Macros

The macros recorded in the previous section were both in the A1 style of cell references. If you change your workbook to the R1C1 style, you'll find that the macros recorded are exactly the same as those recorded in the A1 style, as the Range object only handles A1 style references.

Summary

This chapter gave you an overview of the A1 and R1C1 cell reference styles and the relative and absolute referencing modes. It covered how to refer to cells in the same worksheet, in different worksheets, and in different workbooks.

Here I introduced you to the concepts of

- classes of objects
- properties as attributes of objects
- methods as actions that an object can perform
- passing arguments to properties and methods
- events that occur when a user interacts with an application

I also showed you how these all interact together in the VBA object-oriented programming system.

You should now know about a few of the objects often used in recorded Excel VBA macros and should be able to

- refer to a range of cells by passing an argument to the Range property of the Range object

- refer to a worksheet in the Sheets collection object by passing its name as an argument to the Sheets property
- refer to a workbook in the Workbooks collection object by passing its name as an argument to the Workbooks property
- use the Formula, FormulaR1C1, and Value properties in assignment statements
- use the Cells property as an alternative to the more traditional A1 and R1C1 styles
- access whole rows or columns in your code and assign values to them all in a single statement
- use labels to access rows or columns in a range of cells
- record a macro, view it using the Visual Basic Editor, and run it using a keyboard shortcut key
- streamline code in recorded macros

CHAPTER
TWO

Communicating with Comments

This chapter discusses comments, ToolTips, and ControlTipText as a means of communicating with users in both Excel worksheets and VBA macro code. Although the messages they convey are communicated in different ways, all of these techniques serve the same purpose in that they provide some helpful information to their users. For example, comments can be attached to worksheet cells or can be made even more dynamic in a VBA macro.

Excel has grown in sophistication over the years, and the complexity of the data it models has grown with it. Often, multiple users are involved in working with these complex models, so it has become increasingly important to have extra information attached to worksheet cells for users to communicate among themselves.

This chapter discusses shared workbooks and combining comments with highlighted changes for greater clarity. The Control Toolbox will be introduced and a description of the Label control given along with some of its properties.

Worksheet Comments

A comment is text that you can attach to a cell to provide critical information or explanatory remarks about the cell's contents. Comments are useful for alerting users about changes to data or formulas, and for explaining why these changes were made. A comment can be simply general information about the contents of the cell, especially if the contents differ from what is expected after you've checked everything thoroughly. Comments can also serve as reminders to check up on data items that may be incomplete or missing.

When workbooks are shared among several people, a history is often kept of any changes made, who made them, and when they were made. Comments can provide supplementary information such as why these changes were necessary.

In computer programming, it's been standard practice to put comments into the code to help readers understand what particular short sequences of code actually do, and coding macros using Excel VBA is no different. In VBA, a comment commences with a single quote; everything following on the same line is part of the comment.

Adding a Comment to a Worksheet Cell

When you add a comment to a worksheet cell, a triangle is displayed in the top-right corner to alert users of its presence. The comment will pop up if the mouse cursor is paused over that cell. In Excel a comment has two parts, the opening word(s) and the comment text, which are handled as two separate entities. The comment shown has the opening word "marion:" with no comment text.

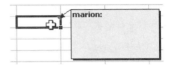

To display the comment and the triangle rather than just the triangle indicator, choose Tools ➤ Options and select the View tab from the Options dialog box. Select the Comment & Indicator option button as shown.

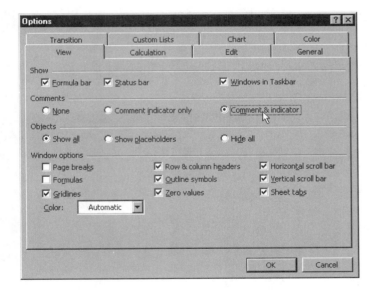

Specifying the Opening Word(s)

The opening word of a comment is the user name but can be changed to any text you like—at your peril! Before you change your user name, be aware that you'll also change the user name in other Microsoft Office applications—which is probably not what you want to do. For example, suppose you change the opening word to "Hi" and save a workbook. Excel will record that the workbook was last saved by the user named Hi. If you then save a document in Microsoft Word, that too will be recorded as being saved by Hi.

When any user creates a comment, Excel automatically adds that user's opening word(s) to their comment. This allows different users' comments to exist simultaneously in the same worksheet, with different opening words to identify the authors of the comments.

To reset the user name to the opening words that will be assigned to all future comments:

1. Choose Tools ➤ Options to open the Options dialog box, and select the General tab, shown in Figure 2.1.

2. The User name box at the bottom of the tab displays the opening word, and the default text is your name because it's most likely that you'll want to identify yourself to other readers of the comment. You can overtype this with the text you want.

3. Click OK to return to the worksheet.

FIGURE 2.1:

General tab of the Options dialog box

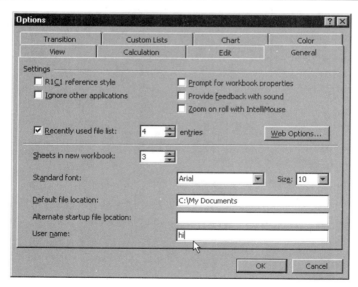

WARNING To change the opening words for a single comment, you must change your user name to the opening words required. As soon as you've finished entering the comment, you should change your user name back to what it was before saving your workbook if you want it saved in your name.

New opening words can be given to subsequent comments (by overtyping the original word inside the comment box) without affecting the user name. How to enter your comment text is given later in this chapter in the section entitled "Entering a Comment."

Editing Opening Words

By far the easiest way to change the opening words is to click on the comment box and then highlight them using a drag action of the mouse and overtype them with the words required. You can even just hit Enter and have no opening words at all. Editing the opening words carries no consequences as it doesn't change your user name—so it won't affect any other Microsoft applications.

The Comment Text

The comment text itself is normally different in each case, and is entered directly into the comment box. There are three ways to open the comment box for entering your comment:

1. Expand the Insert menu by clicking the double Down arrows at the bottom of the drop-down list, and choose Comment.

2. Right-click the cell you want to attach the comment to and select the Insert Comment command from the shortcut menu.

3. Click the New Comment button in the Reviewing toolbar (see Figure 2.2), or use the keyboard shortcut Shift+F2.

The Reviewing Toolbar

The Reviewing toolbar shown at Figure 2.2 contains icons for creating, editing, and deleting comments, and a few other reviewing tools. Some of the buttons toggle between two functions, depending on whether a comment exists already and whether comments are displayed or hidden.

New Comment   Attaches a comment box to the active cell, as shown in Figure 2.3, with the selection handles visible. The opening words will already be in place and the text-entry cursor will be blinking, ready for you to enter your comment text. As soon as the comment box is attached to allow text entry, the New Comment button's icon changes and its ToolTip becomes Edit Comment.

FIGURE 2.2:

The Reviewing toolbar

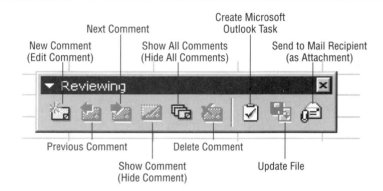

FIGURE 2.3:

Comment box containing comment

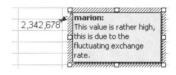

Previous Comment   Within each workbook, worksheets are ordered according to their tabs; within each worksheet, comments are sorted in ascending order based on their row number, and within each row in ascending order based on their column number. Clicking the Previous Comment button opens the comment box associated with the cell closest to but before the active cell. If the active cell's comment is the first comment in the worksheet, clicking this button will display the last comment in the previous worksheet.

Next Comment   Displays the next comment in the workbook. If the active comment is the last comment in the worksheet, clicking this button will display the first comment in the next worksheet.

Show Comment   Continuously displays the comment box attached to the active cell and changes the button to Hide Comment.

Show All Comments   Displays all the comments in the workbook and changes the button to Hide All Comments.

Delete Comment   Removes the comment(s) from the selected cell or range of cells.

Create Microsoft Outlook Task   Creates a Microsoft Outlook Task. Outlook is an information management package that is included in the Microsoft Office 2000 suite of applications and is not covered in this book. For more information about Outlook, see *Mastering Microsoft Outlook 2000* by Gini Courter (ISBN 0-7821-2472-0, Sybex, 1999).

Update File   Lets you update the workbook with the changes made by other users before you save your changes.

Send To Mail Recipient (As Attachment)   Allows you to send the workbook file as an e-mail attachment.

Comment Box

Because the comment box is classed as a drawing object, the selection handles will be displayed while you enter your comment, as shown in Figure 2.3. These handles allow you to adjust the comment box to suit the comment entered, as scrolling bars are not one of the features of comment boxes. Although you can enter a lot more text than the comment box can actually display, the user will only be able to view onscreen as much text as can fit into the pre-sized box. Users will have to print long comments to be able to read all the text.

WARNING   Adjust the size of the comment box to accommodate the comment text. Otherwise part of the comment may not be displayed.

Excel can do the adjustment for you. Simply right-click on one of the selection handles and choose Format Comment from the shortcut menu, then check the Automatic Size check box on the Alignment tab, as shown next.

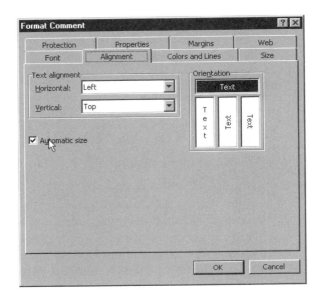

When you click OK and return to your worksheet, the adjustment will have been made.

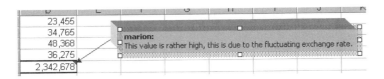

Entering a Comment

To enter your comment:

1. Choose Insert ➤ Comment to open the comment box shown in Figure 2.3.

2. Enter the comment as you would like it to appear in the comment box, using the sizing handles to adjust the comment box to fit the text if necessary.

3. Click anywhere on the worksheet outside the comment box to finalize your entry. Excel will attach both the opening words and your comment to the data contained in the cell.

NOTE   When you add a comment to a range of highlighted cells, the comment is attached to the active cell and will only be displayed when the pointer is paused above this cell.

Classifying Objects

Everything in Excel VBA is an object: workbooks, worksheets, ranges, toolbars—even Excel itself is an object.

Classes   For each type of object, there's a defined class that can be considered as the blueprint; it contains all the information and code required by that type. For example, the `Comment` class has properties to allow you to identify the author and state whether or not the comment will default to `Visible`, and it has methods to set the comment text and to delete it.

Some classes of objects can access objects belonging to other classes. For example, objects in the `Range` class can access any `Comment` objects that are attached to cells in their range. Accessing these other objects is usually done using properties with the same name as the object being accessed—for example, the `Range` object has the properties `Borders`, `Cells`, and `Comment` for accessing these classes of objects.

The benefit of using objects belonging to established classes is that you don't need to write any code and you can be sure that the methods are relatively bug-free so will not cause your macros to terminate abnormally with a runtime error.

Libraries   The number of different classes is huge and still growing, but luckily libraries have been created to make it easier for you to find the class you need when you're developing your macros. Some of the libraries presently available are Microsoft Office, Microsoft Excel, and VBA.

Formatting a Comment

When the selection handles are displayed around a comment box and you choose Format, the first item in the Format menu option's drop-down list changes from Cells to Comment (as shown) to allow you to format your comment.

Moving Cells Containing Comments

Comments can be attached to the data items stored in cells so that they will follow these data items as they are moved around the worksheet; if the data item is copied, the comment is also copied. Alternatively, comments can be anchored to a cell's position in the worksheet.

To control whether a comment moves with the data or stays at a specific cell, options are set in the Properties tab of the Format Comment dialog box, as shown in Figure 2.4.

FIGURE 2.4:

Format Comment dialog box

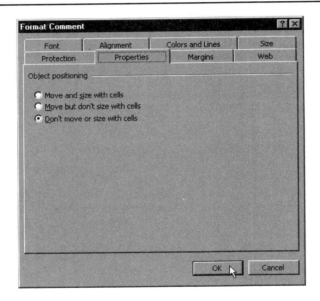

To display the Format Comment dialog box with all its tabs:

1. Display a comment box with its sizing handles. You can do this by clicking the New Comment button in the Reviewing toolbar or by selecting a cell with a comment attached and clicking the Edit Comment button.

2. Select the sizing handles of a comment box—otherwise the dialog box will only contain the Font tab.

3. Expand the Format menu options by clicking the double Down arrows and choose Comment. The Format Comment dialog box with all its tabs will be displayed.

The Properties tab allows you to choose whether you want the comment to move with the value of the cell it's attached to if the value changes its location in the workbook. The first two options will make the comment follow the value; the third option ties the comment to its current cell and that cell's position in the worksheet.

The first two options also allow you to specify whether you want the position of the comment to be adjusted to suit any change in the boundary positions of the cell it's attached to. Changes in boundary positions may be caused by adjusting the row heights or column widths of any cells in the same worksheet. In this case, the cell that the comment is attached to still remains at the same row and column position in the worksheet. If the comment box is set to Don't Move Or Size With Cells, the position of the comment box is static but the arrow will still point to the top-right corner of the same cell and will expand or contract to accommodate the cell's new position.

Recording the Action of Creating a Comment

The macro in Listing 2.1 is the result of recording the actions required to produce the comment shown at Figure 2.5.

FIGURE 2.5:

Attaching a comment to a cell

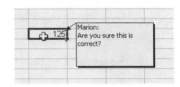

LISTING 2.1

```
0    Sub Macro1()
1        '
2        ' Macro1 Macro
3        ' Macro recorded to generate 3D comment
4        '
5
6        '
7        Range("D14").Select
8        Range("D14").AddComment
9        Range("D14").Comment.Visible = False
10       Range("D14").Comment.Text Text:= "marion:" & Chr(10)_
         & "Are you sure this is correct?"
11   End Sub
```

ANALYSIS

Line 0 indicates the start of the macro with the `Sub Macro1()` statement.

Lines 1 through 6 are comment lines for describing what the macro does.

Line 7 uses the `Select` method of the `Range` object returned by the `Range` property to select D14 and make it the active cell.

Line 8 uses the `AddComment` method to create a comment and attach it to the active cell.

Line 9 sets the comment's `Visible` property to `False` to make it hidden. The `Visible` property is one of the Boolean types, which can be set to either `True` or `False`.

Line 10 sets the text that's to appear in the comment box. The text argument has been recorded as three strings—the opening word (`marion:`), the newline character (`Chr(10)`), and the comment itself (`Are you sure this is cor-rect?`)—joined into one long string. In the Excel VBA programming language, the ampersand character (&) is the concatenation operator, which simply joins the end of one string to the start of the next. `Chr(10)` is a call to the function `Chr` with the argument 10. The `Chr` function returns the character specified by the character code 10 in the ASCII character set, which is the newline character. (See Appendix A for the complete ASCII character set.)

Line 11 marks the end of the macro with the `End Sub` statement.

NOTE   The `Chr` function is called with the ASCII code representing a character; that character will actually be sent to the output device when the string is processed. The output device could be a file, the display, or a printer. It's necessary to use this function for incorporating nonprintable characters such as new lines and spaces into output strings—there's simply no other way to enter them into your code.

NOTE   In Excel VBA, substrings are combined using the concatenation character (&). In Excel itself, there's a worksheet function called **CONCATENATE** that does the same thing to substrings in formulas.

Streamlining Adding Comments to Cells from a Macro

Writing your own macro to add comments to cells is easy in Excel VBA. The code in Listing 2.2 shows a streamlined version of Listing 2.1, with Lines 7 through 10 combined into a single line to attach a comment to cell C8 (as shown in Figure 2.5). Notice that you don't need to have the opening words if you don't want them.

LISTING 2.2

```
0    Sub Macro1()
1        '
2        ' Macro to add a comment to cell C8
3        '
4        Range("C8").AddComment "Are you sure this is correct?"
5    End Sub
```

ANALYSIS

Line 0 starts the macro.

Lines 1 through 3 are comment lines to describe what the macro does.

Line 4 uses the AddComment method to create a new comment, Are you sure this is correct?, without opening words. The new comment is attached to cell C8, which was passed as an argument to the Range property.

Line 5 is the end of the procedure.

When you add a comment to a cell, you can attach it to the value of that cell and follow it whenever it's moved. However, you must remember to manually update any references to cells in your macros before you run them again, as Excel doesn't attempt to incorporate these changes into the macro code. You can make this macro more general by changing Range("C8") to ActiveCell in Line 4 so that whatever cell is active will be the one to have the comment attached to it.

Dynamic Comments

You can make your comments more dynamic by writing a macro to create comments according to circumstances that you think may arise. Listing 2.3 contains such a macro and produces different comments depending on what value of sales are at cells D2 and D13 in the worksheet shown in Figure 2.6.

FIGURE 2.6:

Profit and Loss
worksheet with dynamic
comments

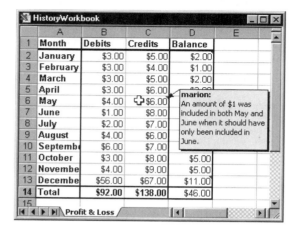

LISTING 2.3

```
0   Sub HandleComments()
1       '
2       'This procedure handles comments in the balance column
3       '
4       Range("D2").Select
5       If ActiveCell.Value < 4 Then
6           ActiveCell.AddComment "This is the slack period _
            after Xmas"
7       Else
8           ActiveCell.AddComment "We must have had a good _
            January Sale"
9       End If
10      Range("D13").Select
11      If ActiveCell.Value < 10 Then
12          ActiveCell.AddComment "This was a disappointing Xmas"
13      ElseIf ActiveCell.Value > 10 And ActiveCell.Value < 14 _
        Then
14          ActiveCell.AddComment "This was what was expected"
15          ElseIf ActiveCell.Value > 14 Then
16              ActiveCell.AddComment "WOW - this is a record!"
17      End If
18  End Sub
```

Line 0 is the start of the macro called HandleComments.

Lines 1 through 3 are for comments that give useful information about what the macro does.

Line 4 uses the Select method to make cell D2 (January's balance) the active cell so that the ActiveCell property can be used to refer to it in the rest of the code.

Lines 5 through 9 are an If...Then...Else... statement that checks the active cell's Value property (January's balance) against the number 4 and uses the AddComment method to attach the appropriate text to the comment. You'll meet up with If statements in Chapter 3.

Line 10 uses the Select method to make cell D13 active (December's balance).

Lines 11 through 17 are an If...Then...ElseIf... statement that has three different comments to assign according to whether December's balance is less than 10, in the middle range 10 to 14, or greater than 14.

Line 18 ends the macro.

3-D Comment Boxes

The comment box is really a drawing object, so its appearance can also be updated using the Drawing toolbar. You can have oodles of fun trying out different effects. Figure 2.7 shows a 3-D effect comment box.

Creating a 3-D Comment Box

The following steps show you how to create a 3-D comment box with the text shown in Figure 2.7:

1. If the Drawing toolbar shown at Figure 2.8 is not already displayed, click View ➢ Toolbars ➢ Drawing to display it.

2. Right-click D14 (the cell where the comment is to go) and choose Insert Comment from the shortcut menu.

FIGURE 2.7:

3-D comment box

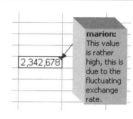

FIGURE 2.8:

The Drawing toolbar

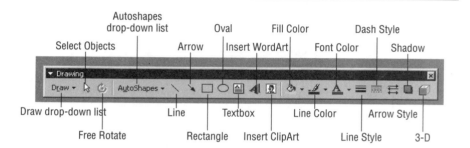

3. Enter the text **This value is rather high, this is due to the fluctuating exchange rate.**

4. Click the 3-D button in the Drawing toolbar and select the 3-D Style 2 button (second button on top row).

5. Click the selection handles of the comment box and choose Format ➤ Comment to display the Format Comment dialog box, shown in Figure 2.4. If Comment doesn't appear as the top item in the drop-down list under Format, click the selection handles and try again. Although the Comment menu option will appear if you expand the drop-down list, choosing Comment from this expanded list will only show the Font tab when the Format Comment dialog box is displayed.

6. Select the Properties tab and select the top option button, Move And Size With Cells.

7. Click OK.

8. Click anywhere in the worksheet outside the comment box to finalize your comment.

Printing Comments

Comments can be printed at the same position as they're displayed on the screen, or they can be printed at the end of the page after the worksheet. To print a comment either way:

1. Choose File ➢ Page Setup to display the Page Setup dialog box shown in Figure 2.9, and select the Sheet tab.

FIGURE 2.9:

Page Setup dialog box

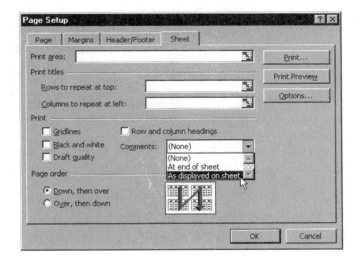

2. To print the comments at the same position they're displayed in the worksheet, select the As Displayed On Sheet item from the Comments drop-down list, and click Print. Figure 2.10 shows a worksheet with comments printed in this manner. To print all the comments in a worksheet, choose View ➢ Comments from the worksheet menu before printing from the Page Setup dialog box. Figure 2.10 shows a worksheet with comments printed in this manner. To print a selected comment, right-click the cell containing it and choose Show Comment from the shortcut menu. More than one comment can be selected at a time.

FIGURE 2.10:

Print Comments As Displayed On Sheet option

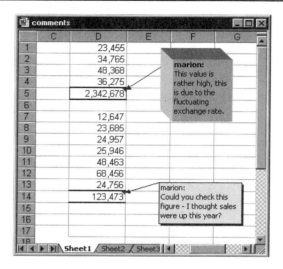

3.   To print the comments at the end of the worksheet, repeat step 1 and select the At End Of Sheet item from the Comments drop-down list. Your worksheet will be printed as usual, followed by a list of all the comments in the worksheet whether or not they are displayed on the screen. The comments will be printed in the following format:

> **Cell:** D5
> **Comment:** marion:
> This value is rather high, this is due to the fluctuating exchange rate.
>
> **Cell:** D14
> **Comment:** marion:
> Could you check this figure - I thought sales were up this year?

After you've printed your comments, you'll probably want to hide them again. You can hide individual comments by right-clicking the cell a comment is attached to and choosing Hide Comment from the shortcut menu. You can hide all the comments on display in one hit by choosing View ➤ Comments to toggle between displaying and hiding.

NOTE   The only way to see a long comment that overflows its comment box is to print it using the At End Of Worksheet option.

Editing a Comment

There are four different ways to edit an existing comment:

1. Click the Edit Comment button on the Reviewing toolbar (Figure 2.2). The New Comment button on the Reviewing toolbar toggles between New Comment and Edit Comment depending on whether or not the selected cell has a comment attached to it.

2. Right-click the cell the comment is attached to and choose Show Comment from the shortcut menu.

3. Expand the Insert menu command drop-down list and choose Edit Comment.

4. Use the keyboard shortcut Shift+F2.

Deleting a Comment

You can delete comments one at a time, you can delete all the comments attached to a range of cells, or you can delete all the comments attached to the workbook.

Deleting a Single Comment

Right-click the cell that has the comment attached and choose Delete Comment from the shortcut menu.

NOTE   Comments cannot be deleted using the Delete or Backspace key.

Deleting Selected Comments

1. Select the cells or range of cells containing the comments you want to remove.

2. Choose Edit ➤ Clear ➤ Comments (as shown) to delete all the comments in the selected range of cells.

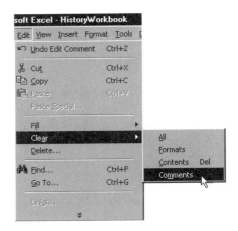

Selecting All Comments

1. Choose Edit ➤ Go To to display the Go To dialog box shown in Figure 2.11.

FIGURE 2.11:

Go To dialog box

2. Click Special to display the Go To Special dialog box, shown in Figure 2.12, and select the Comments option button.

3. Click OK to return to the worksheet, which will now have all the cells containing comments highlighted to show they're selected.

FIGURE 2.12:

Go To Special dialog box

Cycling Through Comments

The Next Comment button on the Reviewing toolbar (Figure 2.2) allows you to jump from comment to comment starting from the active cell and moving down the worksheet in a left-to-right direction. When you get to the last comment, a message box will ask you if you want to go back to the beginning (as shown below). Clicking OK displays the first comment in the worksheet.

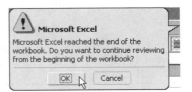

The Previous Comment button does much the same thing, but cycles in the opposite direction. When you get to the first comment the exact same message box is displayed, but clicking OK this time displays the last comment in the worksheet.

One Name or Another

When you open Excel, it creates a workbook called Book1 containing three worksheets called Sheet1, Sheet2, and Sheet3; the worksheets can be referred to by these names in both worksheet formulas and VBA macros. However, there are actually two names for each worksheet—the name that appears on its tab and is used in worksheet formulas, and the name that's used to refer to it in VBA macro code. When you rename worksheets, these two names may no longer be identical. To demonstrate this, let's change one of the names in the worksheet's Properties window. The following steps show you how to rename a worksheet:

1. Create a new workbook and save it as HistoryWorkbook.

2. Enter the values shown in Figure 2.13 into Sheet1.

FIGURE 2.13:

HistoryWorkbook

	A	B	C	D
1	Month	Debits	Credits	Balance
2	January	$3.00	$5.00	$2.00
3	February	$3.00	$4.00	$1.00
4	March	$2.00	$5.00	$3.00
5	April	$3.00	$6.00	$3.00
6	May	$4.00	$7.00	$3.00
7	June	$1.00	$8.00	$7.00
8	July	$2.00	$7.00	$5.00
9	August	$4.00	$6.00	$2.00
10	Septembe	$6.00	$7.00	$1.00
11	October	$3.00	$8.00	$5.00
12	Novembe	$4.00	$9.00	$5.00
13	Decembe	$56.00	$67.00	$11.00
14	Total	$91.00	$139.00	$48.00
15				

Sheet1

3. Choose View ➤ Toolbars ➤ Control Toolbox to display the toolbox shown in Figure 2.14.

FIGURE 2.14:

Control Toolbox containing worksheet controls

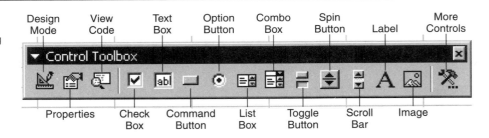

4. Click Properties (the second button) to display the Properties window for Sheet1, then click the second Name and enter **Profit & Loss** as shown in Figure 2.15. This will change the name on the worksheet's tab.

FIGURE 2.15:

Worksheet Properties window

You may have noticed that Figure 2.15 shows a worksheet's Properties window with two Name properties, each set to different names. The first Name (in parentheses) is the name used to refer to the worksheet object in Excel VBA code. The second Name is the name that Excel will use to refer to this worksheet in formulas and is the one shown on its tab. The first name must conform to what a valid name is in the Excel VBA language, and the second needs only to meet the much lighter restrictions enforced on it by Excel. For example, you might want to call the worksheet Profit & Loss or 1999–2000—but both of these names would be unacceptable in the VBA language because of the spaces and the dash. Names are handled in more detail in Chapter 5.

Control Toolbox

The controls available from the Control Toolbox shown in Figure 2.14 make Excel VBA a powerful visual programming system. The icons in this toolbox represent the controls that are widely used in Microsoft Excel, and most of these tools will already be familiar to users of any Microsoft Windows application. These controls can be added directly to worksheets and chart sheets.

NOTE   Visual programming systems provide sets of tools, enabling applications to be developed visually by clicking and dragging icons.

Control Toolbox Buttons

Design Mode   Puts Excel into Design mode and renders all of the controls in your worksheet inactive. This allows you to click on controls without them responding to your click. While in Design mode, this button appears depressed. If you want to delete any controls from a worksheet or change the value of any of their properties, you must be in Design mode.

Properties   Displays the Properties window with the list of properties for the worksheet (shown in Figure 2.15) or for the control that currently has the focus, which is denoted by visible sizing handles.

View Code   Opens the Visual Basic Editor and displays the code window showing the first and last lines of the primary event procedure for the active object. Each control has a primary event procedure that will open first for that control in the absence of any other event procedure containing code. To return to the Excel worksheet, select the File ➤ Close And Return To Microsoft Excel menu option.

CheckBox   Enables the user to select zero or more items from a group of check boxes. This control is also useful to indicate whether items are True or False, or to answer yes or no to questions. Although similar in function to the Option-Button control, you can check more than one check box at a time.

TextBox   Initialized with an empty string; allows users of the application to enter data using the keyboard.

CommandButton   When clicked, will appear to move as if physically pressed and then will respond in the way determined by the Click event procedure code. It's often used in applications with its caption set to OK; the user clicks on it if they want to continue to run the application.

OptionButton   Used in groups that allow selection of only one item per group. Choosing a new option automatically clears the previous one selected from the group. Initially, the first option button in the group will be selected unless the Value property of another option button in the group has had its Value property set to True beforehand.

ListBox   Enables the selection of one or more items from a list.

ComboBox Combines a text box and a list box, providing the user with the option of entering text into the text box or selecting one or more items from the list box. The ComboBox allows these two controls to communicate with each other.

ToggleButton Remains pressed in when clicked and is released when clicked again. ToggleButton1 shown below remains pressed in whereas ToggleButton2 is in the released state.

SpinButton Used with another control to increment or decrement numbers. The two main events associated with this control are SpinUp and SpinDown, with one of them being generated repeatedly while the mouse button is depressed.

ScrollBar Allows vertical scrolling to provide easy access to items in a long list. It can also be used to indicate quantity when the Min and Max properties are set to appropriate values to define some range.

Label Displays text assigned to its Caption property. This control is meant for display only and can't be updated directly by users of the application.

Image Contains a picture that can be stretched to fit the size of the Image control.

More Controls Displays a list containing lots of other controls that you can add to your Toolbox. The controls available on your PC will depend on the software installed.

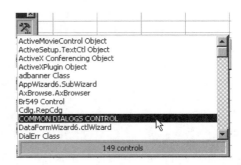

Each type of control is a class of object that encapsulates its own set of properties, events, and methods. When you drag and drop a control onto your worksheet, Excel creates an instance of that class of object. You can have as many instances of the same class as you like, and each instance will have the same set of properties initialized to the same default values except for the Name. These properties can then be updated for each control individually to suit your requirements.

Most of these controls react visibly to some event, such as being clicked by the mouse. For example, a Button object will appear to move as if pressed in, an Option Button object will toggle a black dot visible or invisible, and a Text Box object will display a vertical line cursor for text entry. All these reactions are controlled by procedures inside their respective classes.

Adding Controls to a Worksheet

A control is placed on a worksheet by clicking its icon in the Control Toolbox, moving the mouse cursor to the position required on the worksheet, and sizing the control with a drag-and-drop action. There are several ways of displaying the Control Toolbox:

- Choose View ➢ Toolbars ➢ Control Toolbox.
- Click the Control Toolbox button in the Visual Basic toolbar.
- Right-click any toolbar and select Control Toolbox from the shortcut menu.

When you select a control's icon in the Control Toolbox, Excel will automatically go into Design mode. In this mode, your controls will remain deactivated to allow you to position and size them on the worksheet. To make any adjustments to them at a later stage, you can put Excel into Design mode by clicking the Design Mode button in either the Control Toolbox or the Visual Basic toolbar. You can then drag and drop and resize all the controls you want, but when you've finished designing your worksheet you must remember to click the Exit Design Mode button to return to the normal Excel operating mode. Your controls will then be activated and will respond to mouse clicks in the usual way.

Adding the *Label* Control

The Label control displays text that can't be updated by the user while the application is running. The text that's displayed is stored in the Caption property, which is set at design time by updating it in the Properties window or setting it in your VBA macro code.

Figure 2.16 shows a worksheet containing five Label controls, with the Properties window listing the properties for the Label control named Label1. The Down arrow for the SpecialEffect property has been clicked to display the drop-down list of settings available. The Caption property for each Label control has been set to the name of the special effect assigned to its SpecialEffect property.

FIGURE 2.16:

The settings available for the SpecialEffect property of the Label1 control

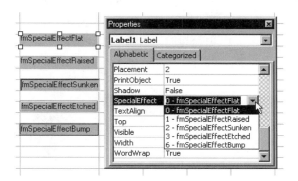

Naming Controls

When you place controls in your worksheet, Excel VBA gives them default names based on what type of control they are, followed by a number depicting the order they were added, such as Label1, Label2, Label3... This is similar to the way default names are given to worksheets and workbooks. These default names serve their purpose, as they're guaranteed to be unique, but they don't really reflect the function of each control.

If you have 10 text boxes in your worksheet named TextBox1 through TextBox10 and each is used for data entry, it's better to rename these controls to something more meaningful than to leave them as they are. It's much easier to code your macros correctly if you use names that reflect the kind of data that they'll contain.

You don't need to change the Name properties of all controls. For example, suppose you've added 10 Label controls with default names Label1 through Label10, each lined up with TextBox controls to indicate what the user is expected to enter. If these labels are not referred to anywhere in the code, there is no need to change their names.

In the following example, a Label control is placed in the workbook and then renamed.

1. Open a new workbook and place a Label control in it. The text in the formula bar will change to

   =EMBED("Forms.Label.1","")

2. Right-click the Label control in the worksheet to give it the focus and to display the shortcut menu shown.

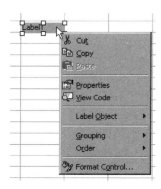

3. Choose Properties from the shortcut menu to open the Properties window (shown).

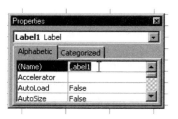

4. Overwrite Label1 with lblBalance at the first position against (Name). Using the prefix lbl for all label names makes it easy to identify labels as the type of object referred to by these names.

5. Press Enter or click outside the Properties box to finalize.

It's good programming practice to adopt naming conventions for control objects. Microsoft recommends that these be named with predefined prefixes that identify their types. The benefits of using naming conventions are that all objects for the same class of control object are listed next to each other in the Properties window and the macro code that refers to them is easier to read and understand.

Moving Controls

To move a control to a new position, place the mouse cursor inside it, press the mouse button and, while holding it down, drag the control to the position required (as shown). For you to be able to do this, the application must be in Design mode. A Design Mode button to toggle between modes is available in both the Control Toolbox and the Visual Basic toolbar.

Properties Window

Properties are the attributes that define an object's characteristics, such as its color, size, and position. They might also define how text should appear. Every object in Excel VBA has a set of properties associated with it, which you can view with their settings in the Properties window.

1. Select the Design Mode button from the Visual Basic toolbar or the Control Toolbox.

2. Right-click the control and choose Properties from the shortcut menu.

Properties can be set at design time by updating the values in the Properties window. Alternatively, properties can be assigned values in the code for updating during the execution of the application. In general, the syntax for this is

```
ControlName.Property = New Value
```

For example, resetting the Name property of the TextBox control from TextBox1 to txtGetAmount would be

```
TextBox1.Name = "txtGetAmount"
```

The prefix txt is recommended for text box names.

Whenever you create an instance of a control object by selecting it from the Toolbox and placing it in a form, its properties are automatically set to default values. The Properties window in Figure 2.16 shows the settings for a Label control object. The box at the top displays the Name of the object followed by its type. When you click any property it'll become highlighted, and if a Down arrow button appears you can click it and select an item from the drop-down list. Otherwise you can overtype the existing value with the one you require.

If two Label control objects exist, they'll have the same attributes in their property lists, but each can have its attributes set to different values. For example, the objects will be at different positions, so their Top and Left properties will differ; they may also be different sizes, so their Width and Height properties will differ too. This follows the object-oriented paradigm where objects are instances of the same class of objects but are allowed to have different attributes.

Don't think that you need to memorize all the properties of each control, as you'll probably only use a few of them. Let's take a brief look at some of the properties belonging to the Label class of object. Just to get started, I've listed quite a lot of properties here; you'll soon become familiar with most of them, as you'll meet up with them time and time again when you look at other control objects. Most properties have the same function in several controls.

Name What the Label control will be known as in code.

Accelerator Set to one of the letters in the Caption property (see **Caption**, below) to allow the label to be accessed using the keyboard. The accelerator letter will be displayed in the control's caption as an underlined character.

AutoSize Resizes the label control automatically so that it encompasses its Caption property.

BackColor Sets background color.

BackStyle Determines whether a label appears transparent or opaque.

BorderColor Sets color for the border.

BorderStyle Determines whether or not a border is displayed. If the border is required, it's drawn using the setting of the BorderColor property.

Caption   The read-only text displayed to the user.

Enabled   Determines whether the Label control is available for selection.

Font   Opens up the Font dialog box to allow you to change the font's style and size, as shown in Figure 2.17.

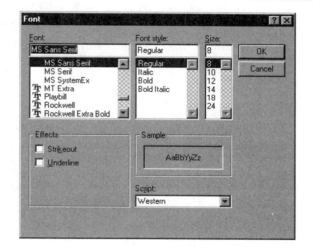

ForeColor   Sets the color of the caption text.

Height   Sets the height of the control, which can also be set by dragging and dropping the control's selection handles.

Left   Sets the distance between the left edge of the control and the worksheet containing it.

MousePointer   Redefines the icon for the mouse cursor when it's paused over the control. Clicking the arrow button provides a drop-down list for selection of the new cursor (as shown).

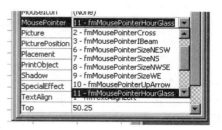

Picture   Allows you to specify a picture to put on the control, as illustrated by the What's New picture.

Placement   How an object is attached to cells; the options available are xlMoveAndSize, xlMove, or xlFreeFloating.

Shadow   Set to True or False depending on whether an object has a shadow.

SpecialEffect   Determines the visual appearance of an object. Figure 2.16 shows these options in action with a Label control.

Top   Specifies the distance between the top of the control and the worksheet containing it. This can also be set by dragging and dropping the control using its sizing handles.

Visible   Determines whether the Label control is displayed.

Width   Defines the width of the label, which can also be set using the selection handles.

WordWrap   If a label has its AutoSize property set to True, the WordWrap property determines whether the control should be expanded horizontally or vertically. If WordWrap is set to True, the expansion is done vertically by wrapping the caption text down to the next line if it becomes too long for the width. If WordWrap is False, the expansion is done horizontally and the caption may even be displayed as a single line.

Changing the *Caption* Property

The Caption property setting is the text that's displayed on a control. The caption text is for display purposes, so only those classes of controls that need to display text have this property. For example, the Caption property for a Label control is the label text; for a CommandButton control, it's the text that appears on the button. Not all classes of controls need to display text, so some classes, such as the SpinButton control, don't actually have a Caption property at all.

If you want to ensure that all the caption text will be displayed on a control, set the control's AutoSize property to True. This will adjust the width and height of the control to encompass the caption. To demonstrate the difference the AutoSize property setting makes, two command buttons were placed on a worksheet, the first one with the AutoSize property set to False and the second with it set to True:

Control Tips, ToolTips, and Comments

Control tips and comments both provide pop-up messages when the mouse pointer is paused, but not clicked, on a control or cell. Control tips and comments provide the same facility to users of your application as ToolTips provide for you when you're running Excel. ToolTips are the text that pops up when you pause the mouse pointer over toolbar items, etc., and are supplied by Microsoft to help you while you're running Excel. Control tips are supplied by you, and they'll pop up to help users while your application is running. Comments are attached to cells to provide information to users of an Excel worksheet.

When you develop a worksheet with lots of calculations and external references, it's a good idea to attach helpful comments to specific cells. If you've added any UserForms to your application, control tips could provide your users with the same kind of help that ToolTips provided for you. Control tips are specified by setting the ControlTipText property of control objects and are only available for controls added to UserForms (see Chapter 10).

A Mock Control Tip Using Comments

Controls placed directly onto Excel worksheets don't have the ControlTipText property like their counterparts placed on UserForms. The setting of the ControlTipText property is the text that pops up when you pause your mouse over a control. UserForms are dealt with in detail in Chapter 10, but are introduced here in order to make the comparison between them and the mock ControlTipText whose purpose you simulate using a comment.

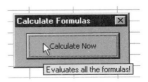

If you would really like to add ControlTipText to a control in your worksheet, the next best thing is to add a comment to the top-right cell that the control covers. Leave enough room for the red triangle to be displayed and for users to be able to position the pointer to pop up the comment.

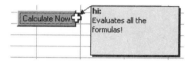

Assigning ControlTipText to a Control

The ControlTipText property serves the same purpose as the ToolTips that Excel provides. The ControlTipText property can be set in the Properties window at design time or it can be set or changed in your macro at runtime. To set it in the Properties window, you enter the text required next to the ControlTipText property.

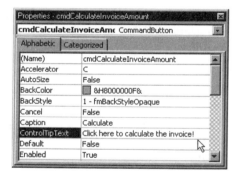

The ControlTipText can also be set in VBA code:

```
cmdCalculateInvoiceAmount.ControlTipText = "Click here to _
calculate the invoice!"
```

which shows the ControlTipText assigned to a command button named cmd-CalculateInvoiceAmount. This example depends on the control being on a UserForm rather than on a worksheet, as command buttons from the Excel Control Toolbox don't have a ControlTipText property. The result of setting the ControlTipText property is shown by displaying the UserForm and pausing the mouse pointer over the command button.

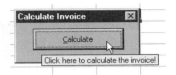

Comments in VBA Macros

Comments in the VBA programming language are completely different from the comments placed in worksheets. VBA comments are placed in the code to supply information to the person who is updating the code, rather than someone who is accessing the worksheet or running the macro.

A comment in code starts with a single quote (') character; the remainder of that line is dedicated to the comment. You can have any characters you like in a comment, as the Visual Basic interpreter skips the line when it gets to the quote. You'll see comments being used in macros throughout this book, so they really don't need any further explanation here.

Shared Workbooks

When a workbook is shared, several people will have read and write permission to it at the same time. To avoid any mishaps, the workbook's users must have set guidelines to avoid interfering with each other's changes. (This is one situation where you'd want users to keep their user names as the opening words of any comments they add.) You can easily tell if a workbook is shared, as the filename will have "[Shared]" after it on the title bar. To share a workbook:

1. Open the workbook you want to share and choose Tools ➤ Share Workbook to open the Share Workbook dialog box, shown in Figure 2.18.

2. Select the Editing tab and check the Allow Changes By More Than One User... check box. Note that only your name will appear in the Who Has The Workbook Open Now list, and your name will be followed by the word "Exclusive" in parentheses. Now that you've set the sharing property, when you open this dialog box again "Exclusive" will be omitted.

FIGURE 2.18:

Editing tab in Share Workbook dialog box

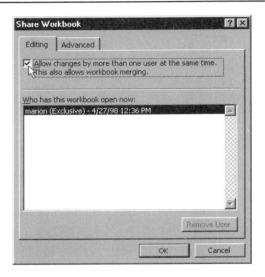

3.   Select the Advanced tab, shown in Figure 2.19.

FIGURE 2.19:

Advanced tab in Share Workbook dialog box

4.   Check the Keep Change History For option button and enter the number of days required in the Days box.

5. Click OK in the Share Workbook dialog box. If the workbook has never been saved before, the Save As dialog box will open to allow you to save your workbook. Otherwise you'll get the confirmation dialog shown.

The workbook will be saved and any changes made to it from that point on will be added to the change history. The title bar should now show the word "Shared" in brackets.

The options available in the Advanced tab (shown in Figure 2.19) and the Highlight Changes dialog box (shown in Figure 2.20) allow you to control every aspect of handling changes. The Advanced tab options allow you to set how long to keep changes, when to make changes, and how to resolve conflicts that occur between changes. The Highlight Changes dialog box options allow you to set when to start tracking changes, whose changes to track, what cells you want to track, and how you want to view the changes. More details of these options are given in the next two sections.

FIGURE 2.20:

Highlight Changes dialog box

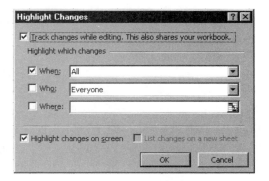

NOTE You won't be able to view or edit your macros while the workbook is shared, but you can still run existing macros and record new ones.

Advanced Tab Options

The options available in the Advanced tab allow you to specify how long to keep the changes, when to update the changes, and how to resolve any conflicts. Here's a brief description of each option:

Track Changes   Allows you the option of whether or not to keep the change history and, if kept, to specify how many days to keep it.

Update Changes   Gives you the option of when to update changes made to the workbook by other users. Selecting the When File Is Saved option button will update the workbook with the other users' changes when you save the workbook. Selecting the Automatically…option button will update the file with these changes at regular intervals, as specified in the Minutes box. Selecting this second button makes the two options below it available for selection, allowing you to decide whether or not to save your changes automatically at the end of each interval while you view any changes that may have been made by the other users.

Conflicting Changes Between Users   A conflict happens when two users try to change the same cell contents to different values. The two options here are for you to be notified of the conflict to allow you to intervene or for Excel to automatically accept the last change made.

Include In Personal View   Enables all users of the workbook to have their own personal print settings as set in their own Page Setup dialog box (shown in Figure 2.9) and their own filter settings for restricting the types of items displayed in the list.

Highlight Changes Dialog Box

To view the change history, you must select options in the Highlight Changes dialog box (shown in Figure 2.20) that allow you to specify the changes you want to track. The Track Changes While Editing… check box must be checked to make these options available. To display this dialog box, choose Tools and pause the mouse pointer until the drop-down list is expanded, then choose Track Changes ➤ Highlight Changes.

When checked, the Track Changes While Editing… check box turns on the change history feature; if the workbook is set up for exclusive use, Excel will automatically make it shared. When the Track Changes While Editing… check box is cleared again, the workbook will automatically be returned to exclusive use and all the highlighted changes will be lost.

Turning off tracking changes also turns off sharing, resulting in all the workbook's highlighted changes being lost.

Let's take a look at the When, Who, and Where check boxes.

When Check Box Enables you to select the starting time period for saving the changes. The choices are:

- All

- Since I Last Saved

- Not Yet Reviewed

- Since Date...

If you select the Since Date... option, the current date will appear in the When box. This can be overtyped with any date you require.

If you select the Not Yet Reviewed item from the list, you can review changes by choosing Tools ➤ Track Changes ➤ Accept Or Reject Changes to open the Select Changes To Accept Or Reject dialog box, shown below.

Clicking OK opens this dialog box and displays each change made, one at a time, allowing you to accept or reject each one. If you have already reviewed all of the changes, a message box is displayed to let you know.

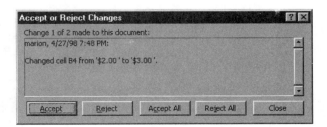

Who Check Box Allows you to identify the people whose changes you want to track and gives you the option of including yourself.

Where Check Box Allows you to track the changes for a range of cells. The Collapse Dialog button at the right of this box allows you to collapse the dialog box, making it easier to select cells from the worksheet using the mouse. Holding down Ctrl allows you to select several non-contiguous cells or ranges of cells scattered throughout the worksheet.

Viewing the Changes History

Before you try to view the history of the changes made to a workbook, ensure that the workbook has been saved—otherwise you won't be able to do step 4.

1. Choose Tools ➤ Track Changes ➤ Highlight Changes to display the Highlight Changes dialog box (shown in Figure 2.20).

2. Check the Track Changes While Editing… check box to share your workbook and make the options available to specify the changes you want recorded. These changes will be recorded in the change history, which includes only the changes recorded during past editing sessions.

3. Check the When check box and select All from the drop-down list.

4. Select the List Changes On A New Sheet check box to create a new worksheet called History, as shown in Figure 2.21. This check box is available for selection only if your workbook has been saved and you have checked the check box for Track Changes While Editing. The History worksheet contains column labels with filter arrows to help you find specific entries.

5. Click OK and save the workbook if prompted. The workbook will now display "Shared" after its name in the title bar.

The changes recorded in the worksheet's history include the date when the change was made, who made the change, what data was deleted or replaced, and how any conflicts were resolved (see Figure 2.22).

FIGURE 2.21:

History worksheet entries

Action Number	Date	Time	Who	Change	Sheet	Range	New Value	Old Value	Action Type
1	4/27/98	7:48 PM	marion	Cell Change	Profit & Loss	B4	$3.00	$2.00	
2	4/27/98	7:48 PM	marion	Cell Change	Profit & Loss	D8	$6.00	=C8-B8	
3	4/27/98	7:49 PM	marion	Cell Change	Profit & Loss	D8	=C8-B8		Result of reject

The history ends with the changes saved on 4/27/98 at 7:49 PM.

FIGURE 2.22:

Changed item marked by triangle on upper-left corner of cell

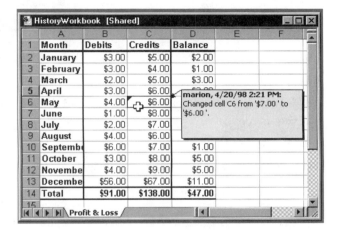

WARNING   Controls cannot be added to worksheets while they're in Shared mode. To return to Exclusive mode, you must stop tracking the changes and will lose any highlighted changes.

Combining Comments and Highlighted Changes

When a change is highlighted, a triangle is placed in the upper-left corner of the cell that was changed. When comments are added to cells containing these changes, another triangle is added to the upper-right corner of the cell. When the mouse pointer is paused over the cell, both the information about the update and the comment are displayed in the same box, as shown in Figure 2.23.

FIGURE 2.23:

Result of mouse pointer paused over cell with highlighted change and comment triangles

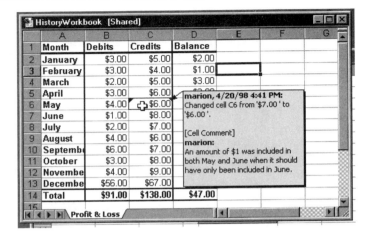

When you return to Exclusive mode, all the highlights disappear and the comments remain.

Stopping Tracking Changes

To stop tracking the changes:

1. Choose Tools ➤ Track Changes ➤ Highlight Changes to display the Highlight Changes dialog box (shown in Figure 2.20).

2. Turn off the Track Changes While Editing check box to make the workbook exclusive to you.

3. Click OK.

4. Click Yes to the message box about making the workbook exclusive to you (as shown).

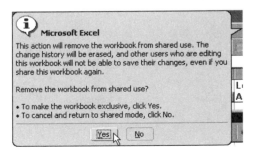

When you return to the workbook, "Shared" will have disappeared from the title bar and there will no longer be a History worksheet.

Passwords

A password can be used for protecting shared workbooks. The password has to be set before the workbook is shared. If the workbook is already shared, you've got to make it exclusive (losing all the highlighted changes), set the password, and then share the workbook again. Using passwords is described in full in Chapter 14.

Summary

Now that you've finished this chapter, you should be able to

- attach comments to cells using the menu options available in Excel
- use VBA's AddComment property to add comments from a macro
- know the difference between comments attached to a cell to provide information to the user and comments written in code to help the VBA macro developer
- identify the control objects available in the Control Toolbox and position them in worksheets
- add Label controls and set their properties in the Properties window at design time
- assign Label controls values in VBA macros while the application is running
- tell the difference between control tips, ToolTips, and comments
- work with shared workbooks, track changes made by other users, and view the changes history in the workbook itself or in the History worksheet

The Visual Basic Editor

The Visual Basic Editor is made up of various components that are briefly described in this chapter along with explanations of how they can be used to navigate around the editor. You'll see how to find your recorded macros and how to code a skeleton event procedure to run a macro in response to a user's action.

This chapter also discusses the Visual Basic Editor's powerful editing features that can automatically pop up helpful information as you enter your code. This takes the guesswork out of entering the names of any properties, methods, events, constants, and variables; it can even save you a few keystrokes, as you can select these names from the pop-up list instead of entering them via the keyboard. The Visual Basic Editor's automatic syntax and formatting features are described as well.

The `With` statement is introduced as a means of abbreviating your code and making it run faster. The various versions of the `If` statement are also given, along with some suggestions for when to use each one.

Creating Macros

There are two ways to create a macro: you can record your actions while you work with Excel worksheets or you can write your own macros from scratch using the Visual Basic Editor. You'll see throughout this book that writing your own macros unleashes a tremendous amount of power and flexibility compared to recording macros, but of course it's much easier to record macros than it is to write them.

In Chapter 1, you saw how to record your actions in a macro and view your macro using the Visual Basic Editor, and I promised to give you more details about the Visual Basic Editor when you got to this chapter. Let's start with Excel's Visual Basic toolbar, which provides shortcut alternatives to the frequently used macro-handling menu commands, including running the Visual Basic Editor.

The Visual Basic Toolbar

Excel provides the Visual Basic toolbar with seven buttons for fast alternatives to using its menu commands, and you've used some of these already. Figure 3.1 shows this toolbar with all of its buttons named.

FIGURE 3.1:

Visual Basic toolbar

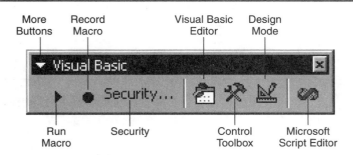

I'll run quickly through this list and briefly describe the function of each button and the menu commands it replaces.

More Buttons   Provides a shortcut menu that enables you to add and remove buttons and customize your Visual Basic toolbar. Shortcut for choosing View ➤ Toolbars ➤ Customize.

Run Macro   Opens the Macro dialog box, allowing you to select the macro you want to run from the list displayed (see Figure 1.7 in Chapter 1). Shortcut for choosing Tools ➤ Macro ➤ Macros.

Record Macro   Opens the Record Macro dialog box, allowing you to give your macro a name and a short description (see Figure 1.4 in Chapter 1). It then translates all subsequent actions into macro code instructions and adds them to the named macro, which is stored in a module. Shortcut for choosing Tools ➤ Macro ➤ Record New Macro.

Security   Opens the Security dialog box shown in Figure 3.2, allowing you to choose how to protect your PC against running macros that potentially could be contaminated with viruses. Shortcut for choosing Tools ➤ Macro ➤ Security.

Visual Basic Editor   Opens the Visual Basic Editor to allow you to view and edit your code, add UserForms and modules, and create new macros. Shortcut for choosing Tools ➤ Macro ➤ Visual Basic Editor.

Control Toolbox   Displays the Control Toolbox to enable you to add controls to your worksheet. Shortcut for choosing View ➤ Toolbars ➤ Control Toolbox.

Design Mode   Toggles on and off Design mode. When Excel is running in Design mode, you can add controls from the Control Toolbox directly onto your worksheet. Otherwise these controls will react to your clicks, making it impossible to resize them or move them around the worksheet. Alternative to choosing View ➢ Toolbars ➢ Exit Design Mode and clicking the single button available.

FIGURE 3.2:

Security dialog box

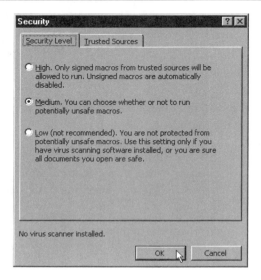

Microsoft Script Editor   Allows you to use the Web Scripting feature, which is not covered in this book. If you are interested in using Visual Basic for Web applications, see *Mastering Visual Basic 6* by Evangelos Petroutsos (ISBN 0-7821-2272-8, Sybex, 1998).

Recording a Macro Using the Visual Basic Toolbar

Let's use the Visual Basic toolbar buttons to record a macro that counts the number of nonzero entries in the range A1:A5:

1.   Open a new workbook and choose View ➢ Toolbars ➢ Visual Basic to display the Visual Basic toolbar (see Figure 3.1) if it's not already on display.

2.   Click the Record Macro button in the toolbar to start recording your actions. This button will toggle from a circle to a square, its ToolTip will change from Record Macro to Stop Recording, and the Record Macro dialog box will be displayed.

3. Click OK to return to your worksheet.

4. Enter the values at cells A1 through A5 as shown.

5. Enter the following formula in cell A6:

   =IF(A1>0,1,0)+IF(A2>0,1,0)+IF(A3>0,1,0)+IF(A4>0,1,0)+IF(A5>0,1,0)

   Each If part of this formula will evaluate to 1 if the contents of the cell referenced are greater than zero.

6. Set the top and bottom borders of cell A6 by choosing Format ➤ Cells to open the Format Cells dialog box.

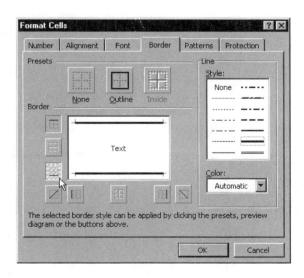

7. Click the Border tab and select the thick line from the Style box in the Line frame (shown highlighted), click the top and bottom border buttons in the Border frame, and click OK.

8. Enter the text **Number nonzero entries** into cell B6. Select the text to high-light it, and choose Format ➤ Cells to display the Format Cells dialog box containing only the Font tab (as shown).

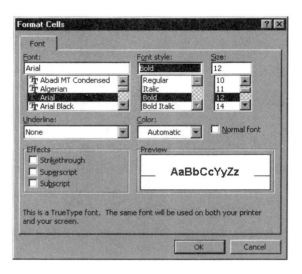

9. Select Bold from the Font style list and 12 from the Size list.

10. Click OK to return to the worksheet.

11. Click the Stop Recording button in the toolbar, and the button will toggle back to the Start Recording button.

Listing 3.1 shows the macro code recorded in response to these actions.

LISTING 3.1

```
0    Sub Macro1()
1        '
2        ' Macro1 Macro
3        ' Macro recorded 5/24/99 by marion
4        '
5        Range("A1").Select
6        ActiveCell.FormulaR1C1 = "4"
7        Range("A2").Select
8        ActiveCell.FormulaR1C1 = "0"
9        Range("A3").Select
```

```
10      ActiveCell.FormulaR1C1 = "5"
11      Range("A4").Select
12      ActiveCell.FormulaR1C1 = "4"
13      Range("A5").Select
14      ActiveCell.FormulaR1C1 = "1"
15      Range("A6").Select
16      ActiveCell.FormulaR1C1 = _
            "=IF(R[-5]C>0,1,0)+IF(R[-4]C>0,1,0)+IF(R[-3]C>0,1,0) _
            +IF(R[-2]C>0,1,0)+IF(R[-1]C>0,1,0)"
17      Range("A6").Select
18      Selection.Borders(xlDiagonalDown).LineStyle = xlNone
19      Selection.Borders(xlDiagonalUp).LineStyle = xlNone
20      Selection.Borders(xlEdgeLeft).LineStyle = xlNone
21      With Selection.Borders(xlEdgeTop)
22          .LineStyle = xlContinuous
23          .Weight = xlThick
24          .ColorIndex = xlAutomatic
25      End With
26      With Selection.Borders(xlEdgeBottom)
27          .LineStyle = xlContinuous
28          .Weight = xlThick
29          .ColorIndex = xlAutomatic
30      End With
31      Selection.Borders(xlEdgeRight).LineStyle = xlNone
32      Selection.Borders(xlInsideVertical).LineStyle = xlNone
33      Selection.Borders(xlInsideHorizontal).LineStyle = xlNone
34      Range("B6").Select
35      ActiveCell.FormulaR1C1 = "Number nonzero entries"
36      With ActiveCell.Characters(Start:=1, Length:=23).Font
37          .Name = "Arial"
38          .FontStyle = "Bold"
39          .Size = 12
40          .Strikethrough = False
41          .Superscript = False
42          .Subscript = False
43          .OutlineFont = False
44          .Shadow = False
45          .Underline = xlUnderlineStyleNone
46          .ColorIndex = xlAutomatic
47      End With
48   End Sub
```

ANALYSIS

Line 0 is the opening statement for Macro1.

Lines 1 through 4 are comment lines.

Line 5 uses the Select property of the Range object returned by the Range property to make A1 the selected (and active) cell.

Lines 6 through 14 show the VBA code recorded for step 3. Line 6 uses the ActiveCell property to return the Range object for the cell A1. The FormulaR1C1 property is assigned the contents of this cell, so this line places the value 4 into the active cell A1.

Lines 7 through 14 do the same thing as Lines 5 and 6, but with different cells and values.

Lines 15 and 16 show the VBA code recorded for the formula you entered at step 5. Line 15 makes cell A6 the active cell, and Line 16 uses the FormulaR1C1 property to assign the formula. Excel interprets the string being assigned as a formula when the equals sign (=) is the first character. Notice the underscore characters at the end of Line 16 and the line below it. This serves no purpose but to allow the statement to continue on to the next line. Although the string representing the formula is shown here conveniently spread over two lines, because it's a string it can't actually be cut using the underscore character—in reality, it must be placed on a single line to prevent a syntax error. However, you can split a long string into substrings and use the concatenation character (&) to join them together, in which case each substring can be placed on a separate line:

```
ActiveCell.FormulaR1C1 = _
    "=IF(R[-5]C>0,1,0)+IF(R[-4]C>0,1,0)" & _
    "+IF(R[-3]C>0,1,0)+IF(R[-2]C>0,1,0)+IF(R[-1]C>0,1,0)"
```

Line 17 makes A6 the active cell.

Lines 18 through 33 show the VBA code recorded for the actions you made at step 7. The settings made to the border were interpreted when we clicked OK in the Border tab to return to the worksheet. This block of code is really quite comprehensible and uses the With statements to identify the objects so that properties can be set without having to qualify them each time. (The With statement is described in the next section.) The two borders set are identified using the Excel constants `xlEdgeTop` and `xlEdgeBottom` and have their properties assigned to the values you selected in the Border tab of the Format Cells dialog box.

Lines 34 and 35 show the code recorded for your actions at step 8. Cell B6 is made the selected and active cell. The `FormulaR1C1` property is assigned the string `"Number nonzero entries"`.

Lines 36 through 47 are your actions at steps 9 and 10, when the settings were updated in the Font tab of the Format Cells dialog box.

Line 48 ends the macro, which is the VBA code recorded in response to clicking the Stop Recording button at step 11.

WARNING The underscore character allows you to split a code statement onto the next line but can't be used inside a string.

Let's take a closer look at the `With` statement before I show you how to view your recorded macro using the Visual Basic Editor (so don't delete it).

Using *With* Statement Blocks

The `With` statement acts as shorthand to perform a series of statements that can use the properties and methods of the designated object without having to qualify it at each instance. This not only saves you time when entering the code but it actually makes your code run faster. The properties and methods start with a period (.) so that they can easily be identified by the Visual Basic Editor as belonging to the object designated in the opening statement. Lines 21 through 25, 26 through 30, and 36 through 47 in Listing 3.1 are all examples of `With` statement blocks. If the `With` statement hadn't been used, Line 37 would read

```
ActiveCell.Characters(Start:=1, Length:=23).Font.Name = "Arial"
```
Lines 38 through 46 would also have to be extended to include the qualifier.

TIP All of the statements beginning with a period character (.) in a `With` statement block use the same object variable.

Nested *With* Statements

With statement blocks can themselves contain With statements. The qualifier used to replace the period character (.) is the object designated in the most recent With statement that hasn't been ended. For this reason, if the object designated in the outer With statement is required in the nested With statement, it must be fully qualified.

WARNING   Jumping in or out of With statement blocks without executing the opening and closing statements may cause your macro to terminate abnormally, give wrong results, or make your code behave unpredictably.

The Visual Basic Editor

You've already visited the Visual Basic Editor a few times to view recorded macros. The Visual Basic Editor also enables you to edit the macros you've recorded, create new ones, and run macros as if you'd run them from the Macro dialog box in Excel. The editor has powerful editing features that pop up information as you enter your code, removing the need to memorize the names of properties, methods, variables, and constants. It even displays the parameters for you as you enter a method or macro procedure.

Figure 3.3 shows the Visual Basic Editor with the code window, Properties window, and Project Explorer window all on display. Because these windows can all be reconfigured, the Visual Basic Editor may look different on your PC; some of the windows may be missing or you may have extra windows. Don't worry—the configuration is not important and windows can be opened and closed easily as you need them.

Opening the Visual Basic Editor

Let's look at four different ways to open the Visual Basic Editor without your macro being displayed:

- Clicking the Visual Basic Editor button in the middle of the Visual Basic toolbar (see Figure 3.1) displays the Visual Basic Editor as it was last configured, so the code window will be in the same opened or closed state it was in when you last closed the editor.

- Selecting the Tools ➤ Macro ➤ Visual Basic Editor menu command opens the Visual Basic Editor in the same state it was in when you last closed it.

- Selecting the View Code button in the Control Toolbox opens the Visual Basic Editor with the code window open and the `Worksheet_Selection-Change` event procedure on display.

- Using the keyboard shortcut ALT+F11 opens the Visual Basic Editor in the state it was in when last closed.

FIGURE 3.3:

Visual Basic Editor

Project Explorer Window   Code Window

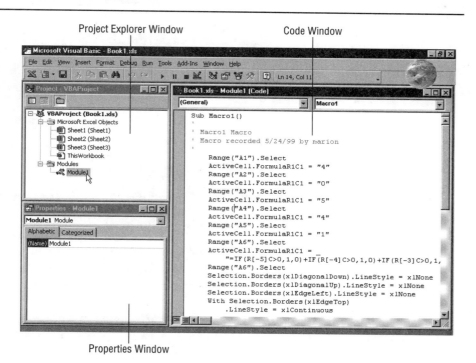

Properties Window

Once you become more proficient at Excel VBA you'll find your way around the editor without any difficulty, and opening the Visual Basic Editor without a code window on display will not cause any problems. But until you become more familiar, it's perhaps easier to open the Visual Basic Editor with the code window and your macro code already on display.

Opening the Visual Basic Editor Displaying Your Macro

Instead of opening the Visual Basic Editor and then trying to find your macro, you can open up the editor with your macro already displayed in an open code window. Let's look at how this is done:

1. Open the workbook containing the macro you recorded earlier for counting the number of zero entries (Listing 3.1).

2. Choose Tools ➤ Macro ➤ Macros to display the Macro dialog box (as shown).

3. Select the macro you recorded (Macro1).

4. Click the Step Into button to open the Visual Basic Editor with the code window open. The code window will be displaying the macro selected as shown in Figure 3.3, except that an arrow will have appeared at the first line:

The arrow means that your macro is running and has temporarily been stopped at the statement indicated by the arrow. Click the Reset icon (small black square in the toolbar) to stop running your macro and make the arrow disappear.

Visual Basic Editor Components

In this section, I'll show you the components that make the Visual Basic Editor so powerful. I'll take you on a brief tour describing the function of each component, and as we go you'll get an idea of the overall structure of the whole environment and how it all fits together. The components are:

- Menu Bar
- Toolbars
- Toolbox
- Properties Window
- Project Explorer Window
- Object Browser
- Code Window

Menu Bar

The extensive facilities that Visual Basic provides are accessible via a hierarchical menu system with 11 main menu options (as shown), each having a drop-down list of further menu options.

Visual Basic Editor Toolbars

The frequently used menu commands can also be accessed via buttons on one of the four toolbars that are listed when you choose View ➤ Toolbars (as shown). This section gives a brief introduction to some of the menu commands that have shortcut buttons on these toolbars.

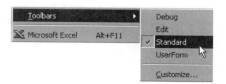

Standard Toolbar

The Standard toolbar, shown in Figure 3.4, offers the most features of all the toolbars available. It contains shortcuts to the most frequently used menu commands listed under the File, Edit, View, Insert, and Run menu options.

FIGURE 3.4:

Visual Basic Standard toolbar

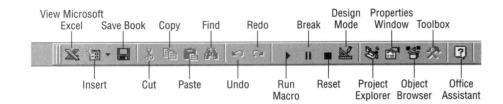

View Microsoft Excel   Returns to the Excel worksheet.

Insert   Clicking the Down arrow of this button displays a drop-down list of objects that you can add to your project (as shown). UserForm is the default initially, so it has its icon delegated to the toolbar; after you've inserted an object, the icon delegated is the last object inserted.

Save Book   Saves the complete Excel workbook and any macros and Visual Basic objects you've added.

Cut   Copies the selected control or text to the clipboard and deletes it from the project.

Copy   Copies the selected control or text to the clipboard without deleting it from the project.

Paste   Pastes the contents of the clipboard to the current position.

Find   Displays the Find dialog box to enable you to search for a string of text in the code.

Undo   Undoes the last edit.

Redo   Reverses the last undo action, provided no editing has occurred since.

Run Macro   Clicking this button runs your macro. If the code breaks for any reason, the ToolTip changes from Run Sub/UserForm to Continue (as shown) and an arrow is displayed at the line of code where execution stopped. If there are no errors in that line of code, clicking Continue will resume running your program from that point onwards.

Break   Temporarily stops an application running and puts it into Break mode, displaying an arrow at the line of code containing the breakpoint.

Reset   Resets the project when it has stopped, making it ready to run again. This is useful if your project has gone into Break mode because of a compiler error or if you just wanted to stop it running by inserting a break-point.

Design Mode   Toggles between Design Mode and Exit Design Mode. In Design mode, no code is run and user events are never processed, thus allowing you to resize and position your controls. The Exit Design Mode command reinitializes any module-level variables and turns Design Mode off, causing controls to respond to user events again.

Project Explorer   Displays the Project Explorer window (as shown later in Figure 3.15).

Properties Window   Displays the Properties window for the selected control (as shown later in Figure 3.11).

Object Browser   Displays the Object Browser dialog box listing the objects available (as shown later in Figure 3.16). These objects are the types, classes, methods, properties, event procedures, and constants provided by VBA and any other modules and procedures that you have included.

Toolbox   Displays or hides the Toolbox containing the controls you can place on UserForms (as shown later in Figure 3.9). This toolbox is only available for selection when a UserForm is active.

Office Assistant   Displays the Office Assistant to provide you with some help. There are various animated characters available for depicting the assistant, which can be viewed and set in the Gallery tab of the Office

Assistant dialog box (shown) by clicking the Office Assistant button to display the bubble and then clicking the Options button inside the bubble.

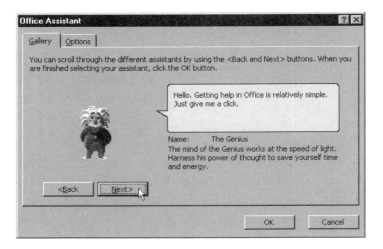

Edit Toolbar

The Edit toolbar, shown in Figure 3.5, provides shortcuts to menu items in the Edit drop-down submenu list. It also includes a Toggle Breakpoint shortcut from the Debug drop-down submenu list.

FIGURE 3.5:

Edit toolbar

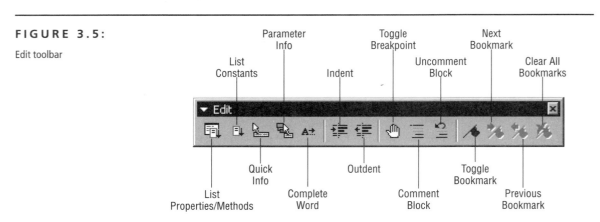

There are so many properties, methods, and procedures in VBA that at first you can become overwhelmed by the sheer volume. The Edit features partially help overcome this problem by providing lots of helpful pop-up information as you enter your code. I'll show you how to configure your Visual Basic Editor to make this happen automatically before describing the functions of the buttons in the Edit toolbar.

Making Pop-up Items Appear Automatically

Some of the pop-up editor commands can be set to happen automatically as you enter your code. These are set by choosing Tools ➤ Options and selecting the Editor tab, shown in Figure 3.6.

FIGURE 3.6:

Editor tab of Options dialog box

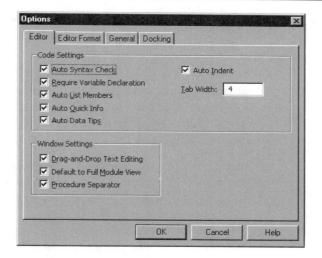

Checking the Auto List Members check box will automatically display a list of the functions, methods, and properties that are members of the class of object you're entering. Checking the Auto Quick Info check box displays a pop-up window with information about the function or method you're entering and its parameters. Clicking Auto Indent will automatically align code you enter to the same tab position as the previous line.

Edit Toolbar Buttons

List Properties/Methods   Displays a drop-down list of properties and methods for the class of object you're entering in the code window. This will work even if you're entering a property or method that returns an object—the list will contain the properties and methods for the returned object. The drop-down list for the worksheet named Sheet1 is displayed as shown when the period character (.) is entered. Notice how up-to-date this list is—even the procedure I'm coding is included!

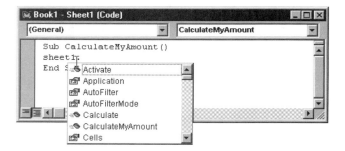

You can get Visual Basic to enter the property or method for you by double-clicking the entry in the list or by selecting it and pressing the Tab or Enter key. If you intend to move to the next line when you've inserted this item, it's quicker to press the Enter key instead of Tab, as this will both insert the item and add a new line.

List Constants   Displays a drop-down list of constants available for the property just entered. The list of valid constants for the Enable-Selection property (as shown) is displayed when the equals sign (=) is entered.

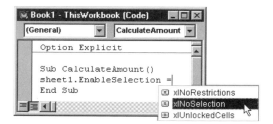

Quick Info   Provides pop-up information about variables, functions, methods, or procedures based on the location of the cursor (as shown below). In this example, the information given for Sheet1 tells you that it's a class, and for the constant tells you its value.

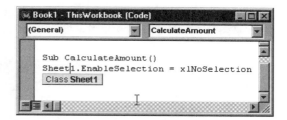

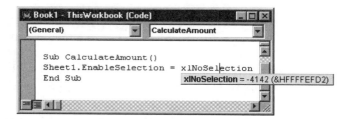

Parameter Info Displays information about the parameters required by the procedure just entered. The procedure can be one included in Excel VBA, one you've coded yourself, or a macro. For example, I created the procedure GetPersonalDetails:

The parameters for this procedure pop up when the open parenthesis character is entered, as shown below.

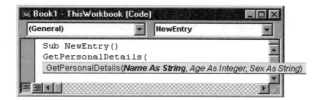

The Visual Basic Editor follows you as you enter your parameters and displays the parameter currently being entered in bold text, as shown.

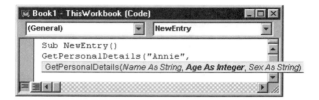

Complete Word   As you start to give meaningful names to items in your macros, these names can become quite long. The Complete Word feature is dual-purpose, serving as both a reminder of the names you've used and a fast method of entering code. The Visual Basic Editor will do its best to automatically complete the name you're entering. If there are several names beginning with the same string of characters as you've entered, the Complete Word feature displays a drop-down list of valid words (as shown). If there's only one name beginning with the same string, your word will be completed for you.

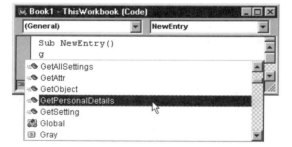

Indent   Allows you to insert tabs to where you want a line of code to start and causes all the subsequent lines you enter to align at the same tab position.

Outdent   Allows you to remove a tab from a line of code and causes all subsequent new lines entered to start at the new tab position.

Toggle Breakpoint   Toggles the current line of code on or off as a breakpoint. When the breakpoint is turned on, the line is displayed as highlighted; if the code is run, execution will stop temporarily at this line.

Comment Block   Makes the current line or group of selected lines into a comment by placing a single quote (') at the beginning of each line. This is useful if you want to run a macro without executing a block of code, as comments are ignored. The block of code can easily be reinstated using the Uncomment Block button.

Uncomment Block   Removes the single quote from the beginning of the current line or group of selected lines.

Toggle Bookmark   Adds a bookmark (placeholder) to the current line if it doesn't already have a bookmark, and removes the bookmark if it does.

Next Bookmark   Moves the insertion point to the next bookmark.

Previous Bookmark   Moves the insertion point to the previous bookmark.

Clear All Bookmarks   Removes all the bookmarks from the current project.

Debug Toolbar

The Debug toolbar (shown in Figure 3.7) contains shortcuts to menu commands that help you to debug your code. This toolbar is discussed in the "Debugging Features" section in Chapter 8.

FIGURE 3.7:

Debug toolbar

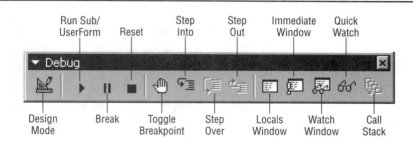

UserForm Toolbar

The UserForm toolbar (shown in Figure 3.8) contains shortcuts to the menu commands that are associated with UserForms. These shortcuts are covered in detail when UserForms are introduced in Chapter 10.

FIGURE 3.8:

UserForm toolbar

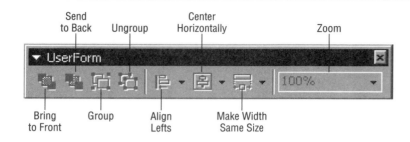

Toolbox

The Toolbox contains the controls commonly found in Microsoft Windows applications. Figure 3.9 shows the controls that the Visual Basic Editor automatically includes in the Toolbox for you.

FIGURE 3.9:

Toolbox

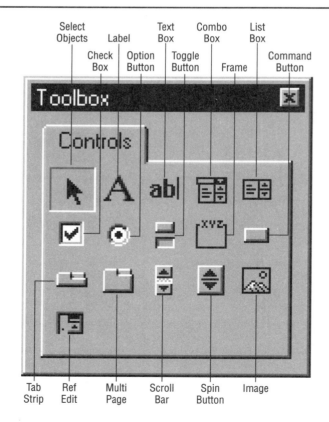

To view the Toolbox you must have a UserForm on display, so choose Insert ➤ UserForm, which will not only create a new UserForm but will also display the Toolbox. If for some reason the Toolbox isn't displayed, view the UserForm graphically (choose View ➤ Object) and then choose View ➤ Toolbox.

There are lots of other controls available that you can add to the Toolbox at the click of a button. To see the list of these additional controls and to add more controls to your Toolbox, right-click anywhere in the Controls tab of the Toolbox to display the Additional Controls dialog box, shown in Figure 3.10.

FIGURE 3.10:

Additional Controls
dialog box

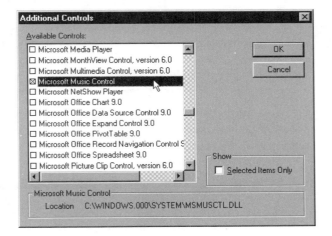

Click the check boxes of all the controls you want to add to your Toolbox. (In Figure 3.10, I chose the Microsoft Music control.) Click OK when you've finished your selection to close the dialog box. The Toolbox will now include icons for the additional controls you selected. (My toolbox now contains the Microsoft Music control, as shown below.)

Applications developed under Excel VBA can reuse any of the controls from the Microsoft Windows environment they're running under. Notice that the complete path name for the file containing the Microsoft Music control object that's displayed at the bottom of the dialog box (shown in Figure 3.10) is located in the Windows System directory. Because nearly all of the controls are reused from the Microsoft Windows or Microsoft Windows NT environments, the controls you've used in your application will look and behave exactly like the controls in other Microsoft Windows applications that you run on your PC—they are the same controls. When users move on to the next version of Microsoft Windows or Microsoft Windows NT, your application will metamorphose to suit!

WARNING   If your application uses any of these additional controls, there's no guarantee that the end user will have the same controls on their machines—you'll have to include them in your distribution disks.

The added benefit is that you can build complex applications in Excel VBA with lots of bells and whistles (and controls) and they'll still be surprisingly small in terms of their size.

Control Toolbox versus VBA Toolbox

The VBA Toolbox and the Control Toolbox available in Excel (shown in Figure 2.14 in Chapter 2) contain different sets of tools. Both toolboxes seem to have a lot of controls in common that appear at first glance to be the same. But these controls belong to different classes of objects that have their own sets of properties and that differ slightly.

Properties Window

The Properties window displays the list of some of the properties available for an object and the values assigned to each one; these can be updated as required. The Properties window shown in Figure 3.11 is for the `Worksheet` object called `Sheet1`. This is viewed by opening the Properties window for a UserForm (because it can be viewed graphically using View Object in the Visual Basic Editor) and then displaying the Project Explorer window (View ➢ Project Explorer) and clicking `Sheet1`.

Properties window for
Sheet1

Properties can be viewed in alphabetical order (Figure 3.11) or by category, as shown in the Properties window for command button CommandButton1.

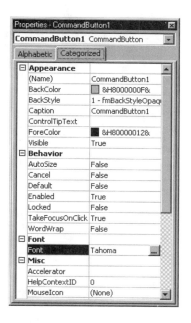

The Properties window lists all the properties that you can set during design time. However, there are a few properties that you can update only while your macro is running—these are not included in this window. To view all of the properties associated with a control or object, you must access the Object Browser or Excel VBA's online Help facility.

Let's use the Help facility, as it also gives you some information about the properties and methods, and frequently gives examples of how these are used in code. To access VBA's online Help:

1. Choose Help ➢ Microsoft Visual Basic Help to display the Office Assistant bubble, and enter **commandbutton control** in the box, as shown in Figure 3.12. Click Search.

FIGURE 3.12:

VBA's Office Assistant bubble

2. The `CommandButton` control item will appear as the first option in the list in the Office Assistant bubble. Click the round button beside it, as shown in Figure 3.13. The Microsoft Visual Basic Help window shown in Figure 3.14 will be displayed.

FIGURE 3.13:

Getting help with the CommandButton control in the Office Assistant bubble

FIGURE 3.14:

FIGURE 3.14:

Help window for Com-
mandButton control

3. The subjects printed in blue near the top of the window (SeeAlso, Example, Properties, etc.) can be clicked to get further information. For instance, click Properties to display the Topics Found dialog box (shown), which lists all of the properties associated with the CommandButton control.

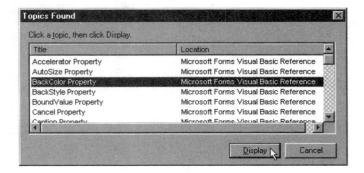

Project Explorer Window

The Project Explorer behaves in much the same way as the Windows Explorer or the Windows NT Explorer tree. Clicking the plus sign expands the list to the next level. Clicking the minus sign collapses the list to the item clicked. Double-clicking a module allows you to view the code it contains in the code window; double-clicking a UserForm displays the UserForm.

There are three ways to view the Project Explorer:

- Choose View ➤ Project Explorer in the Visual Basic Editor.
- Click the Project Explorer button on the Visual Basic Editor's toolbar.
- Use the keyboard shortcut Ctrl+R.

In Excel VBA, your workbook, worksheets, and macros are all considered to be items in a single project. The hierarchical structure in the Project Explorer window (shown in Figure 3.15) allows you to navigate directly to any of these project items.

FIGURE 3.15:

VBA Project Explorer window

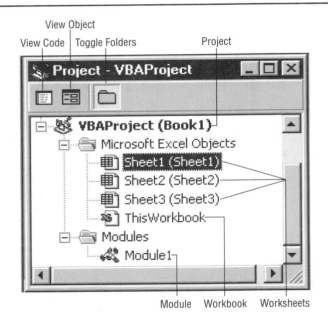

The View Code button at the top of this window opens the code window containing the code associated with the highlighted item. The View Object button reverses this by displaying the Object window containing the highlighted item in the graphical form, which can be a worksheet or a UserForm containing controls. The Toggle Folders button displays items contained in a folder, with or without displaying the folder itself.

Object Browser

The Object Browser, shown in Figure 3.16, lists all of the classes of objects available in your application. Selecting one of these classes changes the list on the right panel to contain the members of that class. In Figure 3.16, the `Application` object has been selected and the list on the right shows the members of the `Application` class. You've already used the `ActiveCell` property from this list extensively in your macros.

FIGURE 3.16:

Object Browser window

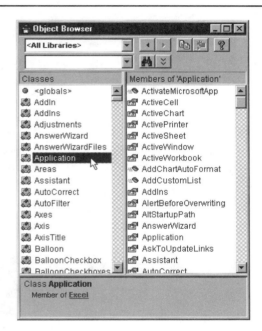

It's easy to guess what each object and its members are used for because they have meaningful names that are not abbreviated. The icon beside each member lets you know whether it's a property, a method, or an event. The list shown in the members list in Figure 3.16 contains three methods and numerous properties.

Code Window

The code window is where recorded macros are streamlined, new macros are created, and existing macros are edited. The Visual Basic Editor provides separate code windows for each of the items listed in the Project Explorer window. When you record a macro, your actions are transformed into VBA code and are placed in a `Module` object. The code window for `Module1` that contains the recorded macro named `Macro1` is shown here.

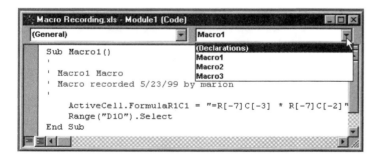

The title bar of the code window displays the name of the project, which is the name of the Excel workbook (I've called mine `Macro Recording`). The `xls` extension is displayed if the Excel workbook has been saved to a file—it won't be displayed if you've just created your workbook and haven't saved it yet. The extension is followed by the name of the module (`Module1`) and the word Code in parentheses.

You can view all the macros contained in the same module by clicking the arrow key in the right-hand box, as shown.

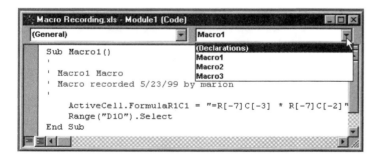

Clicking any of the macros in the drop-down list causes the code for that macro to be displayed in the code window. The button at the bottom-left corner of the code window allows you to display the current macro; the next button allows you to display all the macros in the current module.

Finding a Macro

When you record your macro, it's interpreted into VBA code and placed in a module named Module# that VBA creates for you if you haven't previously recorded a macro during your current session of running Excel. (The # is a number in the incremental numeric sequence.) All the macros you record during a single Excel session will be appended to the same module.

To find your macro, open the Project Explorer window and expand the Modules folder by clicking the plus box. Double-click the module required. This will be the one with the highest # number if you've just recorded your macro. Otherwise, you'll have to look for your macro in the other modules. The easiest way to find a macro when you have no idea which module it's in is to use the Visual Basic Editor's Find menu command to search for the text string representing the macro's name:

1. With the code window open, choose the Edit ➤ Find menu command to open up the Find dialog box, as shown. The Find dialog box allows you to define your search area as the current procedure (or macro), the current module, or the current project.

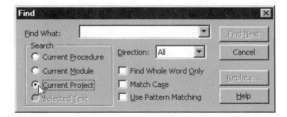

2. Enter the name of the macro you're looking for in the Find What box and select the Current Project option button in the Search frame so that the search area will incorporate all the items in your project.

3. Click Find Next to update the code window with the next instance of the search string.

4. Click Cancel to close the Find dialog box.

NOTE   You must have a code window open before you can display the Find dialog box. Closing the code window with the Find dialog box still on display will hide some of the Find command's features, so you must have a code window open to search for your macro.

Calling a Macro from VBA Code

You can write code to call a macro whenever a specific event procedure is triggered for a particular object. Suppose you want to initialize a range of cells to zero in the event that a workbook is opened. This requires a macro to do the initialization, so let's record the macro first and then I'll take you through the steps of how to call it. This macro will be executed in the event of the user opening the workbook.

Let's first record the macro to initialize cells in the range A1 through A5 in Sheet1 to zero:

1. Click the Record button on the Visual Basic toolbar.

2. Click OK in the Record Macro dialog box.

3. Select cell A1.

4. Enter the value 0 and press Enter.

5. Drag the fill handle from cell A1 to cell A5.

6. Click Stop Recording.

The code recorded for these actions is shown in Listing 3.2.

LISTING 3.2

```
0    Sub Macro1()
1        '
2        ' Macro1 Macro
3        ' Macro recorded 5/23/99 by marion
4        '
5        Range("A1").Select
6        ActiveCell.FormulaR1C1 = "0"
7        Selection.AutoFill Destination:=Range("A1:A5"), _
         Type:=xlFillDefault
8        Range("A1:A5").Select
9    End Sub
```

ANALYSIS

Line 0 is the opening statement.

Lines 1 through 4 are comment lines for information only.

Line 5 selects A1 as the active cell.

Line 6 sets the contents of A1 to 0.

In **Line 7**, the Selection property returns the Range object that's being assigned attributes in this statement. The AutoFill method assigns these attributes using the parameters Destination and Type. The Destination parameter defines the range of cells to be filled as A1 through A5. The Type parameter specifies the type of fill required. Excel selects this type for you based on the source range, which is the 0 at cell A1. In this example, notice how the parameters are passed. The following subsection discusses parameter passing in more detail.

Line 8 just selects the range A1 through A5 and could be deleted.

Line 9 is the end of the macro.

Parameter Passing in VBA Macros

In VBA, the parameters of a procedure can be explicitly identified or can be passed implicitly using the same order as the parameters listed in the procedure's declaration. For example, Line 7 in Listing 3.2 shows the AutoFill method being called with its two parameters passed explicitly:

```
Selection.AutoFill Destination:=Range("A1:A5"), _
Type:=xlFillDefault
```

This line could be rewritten to call the parameters implicitly as

```
Selection.AutoFill Range("A1:A5"), xlFillDefault
```

which is more in line with the way parameters are passed in other programming languages. When parameters are not explicitly defined, you need to take more care to specify them in the same order as the definition of the procedure being called.

Another variation of the same thing uses parentheses and explicitly defines the parameters:

```
Call Selection.AutoFill(Destination:=Range("A1:A5"), _
Type:=xlFillDefault)
```

Calling a Macro from an Event Procedure

Let's get back to the macro we've just recorded and call it when the workbook is first opened. We'll need to open the code window for the workbook module:

1. Click the Visual Basic Editor button in the Visual Basic toolbar to run the Visual Basic Editor.

2. Choose View ➤ Project Explorer to display the Project Explorer window.

3. Double-click ThisWorkbook to open the code window for this module, as shown in Figure 3.17.

FIGURE 3.17:

Code window for
ThisWorkbook

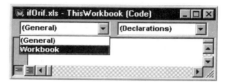

4. Click the arrow in the left box to see the drop-down list of objects and select the Workbook object, as shown in Figure 3.17.

5. The Open procedure will be displayed in the right-hand box. This won't always be the case if you've coded one of the other event procedures; you may have to click the right box arrow and select the Open procedure from the drop-down list as shown.

6. Enter the macro's name, **Macro1**, as shown, to execute the macro in the event of the workbook named ThisWorkbook being opened.

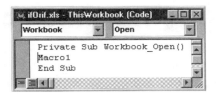

Let's extend this application by asking the users to enter some values if all the values are zero and by displaying the current total if they're not. This requires writing the actions to respond to the user in the event that the worksheet named Sheet1 is changed. Run the Visual Basic Editor and display the Project Explorer as before, and then follow these steps:

1. Double-click Sheet1 to open its code window.

2. Select Worksheet from the drop-down object list and SelectionChange will appear in the Procedure box.

3. Enter the code shown in Figure 3.18. As shown below, running this macro with the cell reflecting the sum as zero will display Please enter some values! in the adjoining cell; if the sum is nonzero, Current Total will be displayed. The variety of If statements available is described after the next section.

FIGURE 3.18:

Code window for the Worksheet_ SelectionChange event procedure

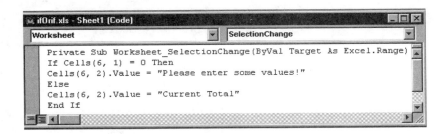

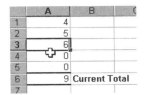

Automatic Syntax and Formatting Features

The Visual Basic Editor features automatic syntax checking and automatic formatting. The syntax checker scans each line of code as it's entered and, if an error is present when you hit the Return key, a message box is displayed providing immediate feedback, as shown.

If the message given is not sufficient, pressing the F1 key often provides an expanded explanation about the error:

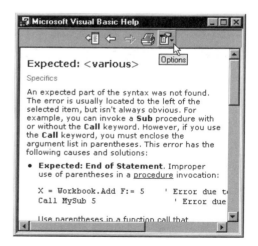

To access more Help information, click the Options button and select Show Tabs.

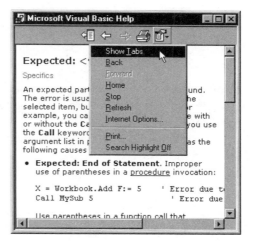

This will add the tabs shown into the Microsoft Visual Basic Help window.

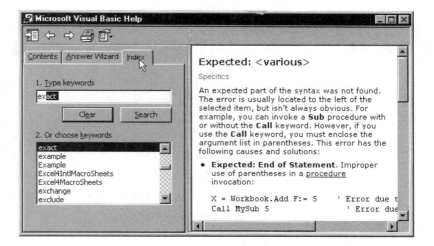

Code that's syntactically correct is translated into an internal format to speed up the translation during runtime. Although you'll find the automatic formatting feature a boon to begin with, more-experienced users sometimes find the syntax-checking facility distracting when entering code for the first time and prefer to turn it off. To do this:

1. From the Visual Basic Editor, choose Tools ➤ Options to display the Options dialog box.

2. Select the Editor tab.

3. Check the Auto Syntax Check check box in the Code Settings Frame (see Figure 3.6).

The Automatic Syntax Check feature not only checks for errors but also formats each line of code as it's entered. It changes your entry to match the case of reserved words, declared variables, and constants, as well as procedures. When it recognizes reserved words it changes their color to blue, signifying that you have entered the reserved word correctly. You may have noticed this already when you entered the code shown in Figure 3.18.

The words in most of your code start with a capital letter, but it's easier to enter all the characters in lowercase and let the automatic formatting feature capitalize the letters for you whenever required. This feature is particularly useful for verifying that certain words are actually part of the language and, when the case doesn't change, for identifying spelling mistakes.

Using *If* Statements in VBA Macros

The If statement allows us to conditionally execute a block of statements depending on whether an expression is True or False. In Excel VBA, the If statement can take several different forms. You already used the If...Then...Else and the If...Then...ElseIf versions of this statement in Listing 2.3 in Chapter 2, and the If...Then...Else again in the code just copied from Figure 3.18.

VBA offers a variety of If statements. This section looks at these and considers under what circumstances it's best to use one over the others.

Conditions

An If statement contains at least one condition, which can be a numeric or a string expression, that evaluates to True or False. The conditional expression is normally a comparison, which is computed to a value for the expression and then interpreted as True if it's nonzero or False if it's zero. When the condition is True, it executes the statement(s) following it.

Statements

An If statement contains at least one statement. If several statements are required, these can be placed on separate lines:

```
If A < 100 then
    B = A
    C = A * 1.4
    D = 40
    E = C - B
End If
```

Alternatively, statements can be separated by a colon character (:) and placed sequentially on the same line, as follows:

```
If A < 100 then
    B = A: C = A * 1.4: D = 40: E = C - B
End If
```

or they can even be part of a single-line If statement:

```
If A < 100 then B = A: C = A * 1.4: D = 40: E = C - B
```

Placing several statements in the same line generally makes the code harder to read and maintain compared to placing statements on separate lines, and should be done only in circumstances where the condition and statements are relatively simple.

If...Then Structure

The If...Then structure is used when one or more statements have to be executed conditionally. The syntax allows the structure to be used as a single line:

```
If  condition  Then  statements
```

or as a multiple line block:

```
If  condition  Then
    statements
End If
```

The statements are only executed if the condition is True. Otherwise execution jumps to the End If statement that defines the end of the structure or to the next statement where the single line structure has been used.

NOTE　　　The End If is not required when the If statement is on a single line.

If...Then...Else Structure

The If...Then...Else version of this statement is used when there are two or more blocks of statements and only one has to be executed conditionally. The syntax for two blocks of statements is:

```
If condition1 Then
    statements1
Else
    statements2
End If
```

Excel VBA tests the condition and if it's True, executes the statements1 block before jumping to the End If statement. The Else statement block is executed if the condition is False.

If...Then...ElseIf Structure

The If...Then...ElseIf version can be used when there's more than one condition to be tested:

```
If condition1 Then
    statements1
ElseIf condition2 Then
    statements2
        :
        :
Else        {optional}
    statementsN
End If
```

Excel VBA works its way through the conditions until it finds one that's True. It executes that True statement block before jumping to the End If statement. An Else statement block without a condition can be included as an option and will only be executed if all the other conditions are False.

Summary

After reading this chapter you should be able to

- display and hide toolbars
- use Visual Basic Editor toolbars
- open the Visual Basic Editor displaying your macro
- use the Visual Basic Editor's Toolbox and the Excel Control Toolbox
- code macros using the automatic syntax and formatting features available
- call macros from VBA code
- write event procedures
- open and close windows using the toolbars and menu commands
- view all the properties and methods available using the Object Browser
- use the Project Explorer to find macros

The chapter also covered how to call your macro from an event procedure that would be run in response to a user's action. The `With` statement was introduced along with a discussion of the benefits of using it to save time at both the code-entering stage and runtime. And the variety of `If` statements available in VBA was also discussed.

PART II

Naming Formulas, Functions, and Constants

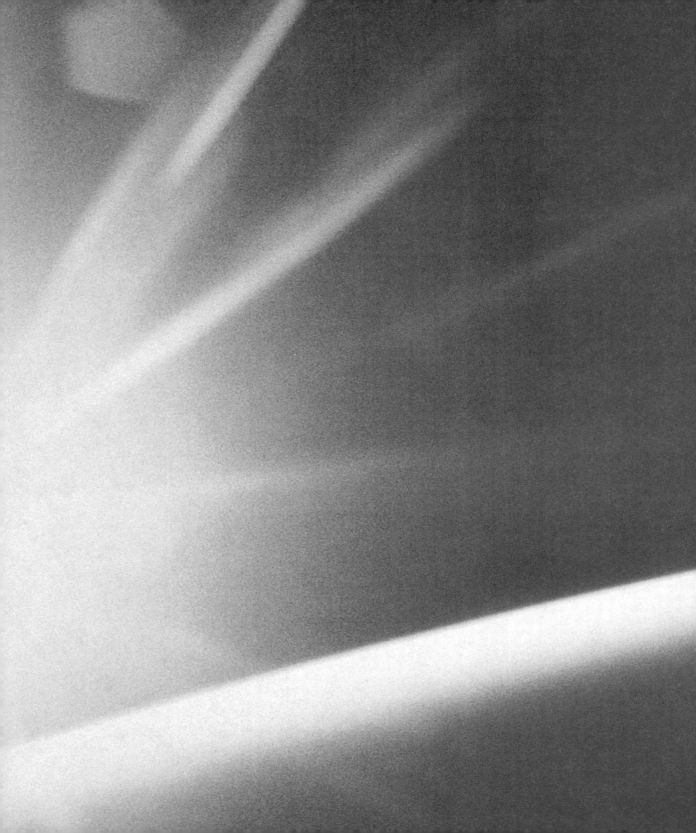

CHAPTER
FOUR

4

All About Formulas and Functions

This chapter looks at formulas and functions and how these are handled in macros. It highlights the difference between the arithmetic operators available for worksheet formulas and those available for VBA macros to help you avoid any pitfalls these may bring. It discusses the use of cell references and names in formulas and macros, and the consequences of restructuring worksheets.

We will look at Excel's rich reserve of built-in functions that allow you to avoid rewriting code that already exists. You'll see how to include these functions in macros and how to write your own macro functions so that they can be added to this reserve for future use.

You will also become familiar with some of the error strings that formulas display when something goes wrong, such as when Excel cannot calculate or display the results of a formula. These messages often don't mean a thing to the casual user. In this chapter, you'll see how to write macros for error prevention and reporting. You'll use command button controls as a way of running these macros, and message boxes as a means of communicating with the user.

The chapter finishes with a discussion on recursive programming and circular references.

Formulas and Functions

Formulas provide you with a powerful way of performing calculations and analyses on your data. A formula has a few basic characteristics:

- The first character is always an equals sign (=).

- The result is displayed in the worksheet cell.

- The formula bar displays a selected cell's current formula.

- The result changes automatically when you're working in Automatic calculation mode and the contents in any of the cells referenced by the formula change.

Entering a Simple Formula Let's create a new worksheet and enter a formula that adds the values stored in two other cells.

1. Open a new workbook and select cell A3.

2. Enter the formula **=A1+A2** in the formula bar. A zero may appear in cell A3 as soon as you hit the Enter key.

If A3 doesn't display a zero, it's because you're working in the Manual calculation mode. If A3 does contain a zero, you're working in the Automatic calculation mode; here, you can see your formula in action by entering values into cells A1 and A2 to change the value at cell A3 each time.

Manual versus Automatic Calculation Mode

Excel allows you to control when formulas are calculated by choosing one of the three calculation modes listed below:

- Automatic (by default)
- Automatic except tables
- Manual

Unless you've already changed the options, your formula will be calculated immediately if any of the values in the cells it references change. To change the calculation mode:

1. Choose Tools ➢ Options to display the Options dialog box, as shown.

2. Select the Calculation tab, and select one of the options shown in the Calculation frame. The option you choose will be the one used with all workbooks irrespective of whether they're new or they already exist.

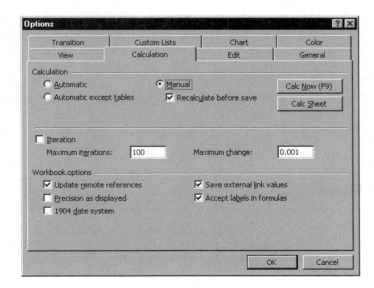

Often when you're working with a large model and you have a lot of data to enter, it's a good idea to run under the Manual calculation mode until all the data is in place. This speeds up the response time, and you don't get error strings popping up in formula cells to distract you.

If you're running Excel with the calculation mode set to Manual and a formula requires updating, the word "Calculate" will appear in the status bar as a reminder that you need to do this. You have two choices to recalculate your worksheet formulas:

- Press the F9 function key to calculate all formulas in all open worksheets, or Shift+F9 to calculate all formulas in the active worksheet; or

- Click either the Calc Now button in the Calculation tab in the Options dialog box to calculate all formulas in all open worksheets or the Calc Sheet button to calculate formulas in only the active worksheet.

Setting the Calculation Mode in a Macro

The calculation mode can be set to Manual in a macro to make sure that the word "Calculate" appears on the status bar—or perhaps you would like to place some other message in the status bar. The macro code shown in Listing 4.1 shows how to set the calculation mode to Manual and update the status bar. It uses a variable, `OriginalStatusBar`, to keep a copy of the status bar text before it's changed in the code, and copies this back into the status bar when it's finished.

This code is easier to develop if you use the automatic syntax and formatting features discussed in Chapter 3. When you enter the opening period character (.) in Line 1, a drop-down list of methods and properties for the `Application` object will be displayed. You'll find that most of the features you normally set using option buttons and check boxes in the pages of the dialog boxes (such as the settings in the Format Cells and Share Workbook dialog boxes) will be available in some drop-down list associated with some object. I'll discuss these in the analysis section at the end of the listing, along with an explanation of how I went about developing this block of code.

LISTING 4.1

```
0    With Application
1        .Calculation = xlCalculationManual
2        OriginalStatusBar = .StatusBar
3        .StatusBar = "Please wait while the data values are _
         checked!"
4    'code for checking data values goes here
```

```
5       .StatusBar = OriginalStatusBar
6    End With
```

ANALYSIS

Line 0 uses the `Application` object that represents the Microsoft Excel application that contains all the application-wide settings and options. The `With` statement (which was introduced in Chapter 3) is used to allow this object to be used without qualifying it.

Line 1 determines that when the period character (`.`) is entered, a drop-down list displays all the methods and properties available for the `Application` object. Since I want to set the calculation mode to Manual, I'll consider the three members—procedure `Calculate` and properties `CalculateBeforeSave` and `Calculation`—that have to do with calculations (as shown).

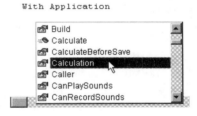

Since I want to set a property, and the `Calculation` property is the one I require, I double-click it and enter an equals sign (=). A drop-down list with the valid settings is displayed:

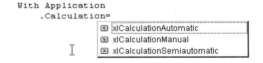

I double-clicked `xlCalculationManual` to add it to my line of code. When I hit Enter to start the next line of code, this line will automatically be formatted with spaces placed before and after the equals sign.

Line 2 assigns a copy of the text currently displayed in the Status Bar to my variable `OriginalStatusBar`, which I entered as the left-hand side of the assignment statement. After the equals sign, the right side starts with a period; since the status bar is also part of the `Application` object, the right side is the text in the status bar of Excel. This time the drop-down list contains only one `StatusBar` item, which (as I learned from the Help facility) sets or returns the text displayed in the status bar. Since this item was the required one, I double-clicked `StatusBar` to add it to my line of code.

Line 3 assigns text to the `StatusBar` property that asks the user to wait while data is being checked.

Line 4 is just a comment; when I continue developing this code later in the chapter I'll replace this comment with the error-checking code or a call to an error-checking macro.

Line 5 restores the status bar to the original text (copied at Line 2).

Line 6 ends the `With Application` code.

Naming a Formula

If you've got a formula that's required in several places throughout your workbook, it's a good idea to give it a name. That name, instead of the formula itself, can then be placed in cells. With this technique, you'll be less likely to make errors than if you retype the formula each time, and if the formula ever needs to be changed you'll only need to update it in one place. To name a formula:

1. Open a new workbook and enter the formula **=A1 + A2** in cell A3.

2. With cell A3 selected, choose Insert ➤ Name ➤ Define to open the Define Name dialog box (shown).

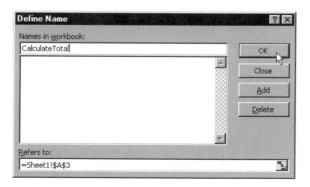

3. Enter the formula's name into the Names In Workbook box. The Refers To box will display the active cell (A3), qualified with the name of the worksheet that it belongs to (`Sheet1`). (Qualifying cell references is described in detail in the section "VBA's `Formula` and `FormulaR1C1` Properties" in Chapter 1.)

4. Click OK to finalize and return to your workbook. Now when you click cell A3, the formula bar will display the same formula but the Name Box on the left will display the formula's name.

Naming Formulas Not Allocated to a Cell

You can name a formula without having to attach it to any cell by choosing Insert ➤ Name ➤ Define to open the Define Name dialog box, entering the formula's name in the Names In Workbook box, and entering the formula itself into the Refers To box (Figure 4.1).

FIGURE 4.1:

Using the Define Name dialog box to name a formula

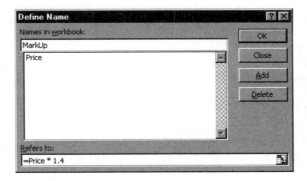

In this example, `Price` has already been defined in a worksheet, but the named formula `MarkUp` is not associated with any cells and can be referred to by name in any formulas throughout the workbook.

Recording the Naming of a Formula

Let's record our actions while we name a formula:

1. Open a new workbook and choose Record Macro from the Visual Basic toolbar to open the Record Macro dialog box.

2. Enter **NamingAFormula** in the Macro Name box, and **Recorded actions while naming a formula** in the Description box (as shown), then click OK.

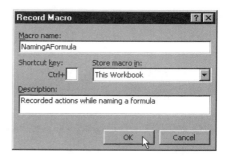

3. Choose Insert ➤ Name ➤ Define and enter **MarkUp** in the Names In Workbook box, and **=Price * 1.4** into the Refers To box (Figure 4.1), then click OK to return to the worksheet.

4. Click the Stop Recording button (square) in the Visual Basic toolbar.

Listing 4.2 shows how our actions were recorded in VBA code.

LISTING 4.2

```
0    Sub NamingAFormula
1        '
2        'NamingAFormula Macro
3        'Recorded actions while naming a formula
4        '
5        "
6        '
7        ActiveWorkbook.Names.Add Name:="MarkUp", _
8        RefersToR1C1:="=Price * 1.4"
9    End Sub
```

ANALYSIS

Line 0 opens the macro NamingAFormula; this name was retrieved from the Macro Name box in the Record Macro dialog box, where it was entered at step 2.

Lines 1 through 6 describe the macro, using the information entered into the Record Macro dialog box.

Lines 7 and 8 show the code for one statement. The underscore character (_) preceded by a space allows you to break one statement over two lines. Starting at the end of the line, =Price * 1.4 is assigned to the Refers-ToR1C1 argument of the Add function and MarkUp is assigned to its Name argument. Using these arguments, the Add function creates a Name object and adds it to the Names collection of the active workbook.

Line 9 ends the NamingAFormula code.

Excel Arithmetic and Comparison Operators

Excel provides a set of arithmetic and comparison operators for you to use in the formulas you enter into your worksheet. The VBA language also supports a set of arithmetic and comparison operators for use in macros. Although most of these operators perform the same function and give identical results in both sets, there is a slight difference in the results given by two of the operators. In this section I'll highlight these differences in detail, as you could go horribly wrong if you confuse these two nonidentical operators.

Using the Arithmetic Operators

The arithmetic operators supported in Excel worksheet formulas are listed in Table 4.1.

TABLE 4.1: Arithmetic Operators Available in Worksheet Formulas

Operator	Operation	Example
+	Addition	A1 + 5
−	Subtraction	B2−3
*	Multiplication	10 * C1
/	Division	A1/C1
^	Exponentiation	A1 ^ 3 (i.e., A1 cubed)
%	Percent (if placed after a number)	10%

The first five operators in Table 4.1 will yield identical results whether used in VBA macros or in worksheet formulas. However, the percent character is interpreted differently in formulas and macros.

Before the percent character's use in macros can be described, the two ways that macros represent formulas must be considered. Then we can review how the percent is interpreted in worksheet formulas, in recorded macros, and in macros that actually perform the formula calculations in their statements.

The Double Life of %

The percent character has been used in both Microsoft Excel and Microsoft Visual Basic for years, long before there was any thought that the two applications might ever merge or communicate with each other in any way. The percent character has always been an arithmetic operator in worksheet formulas, and it has always been a type-declaration character when used in the statements of a VBA macro. This can cause a few problems.

How Excel Formulas Interpret % The percent sign is an operator used in Excel formulas that divides the preceding number by 100. You can also have a percent sign immediately following a percent sign to divide by 10,000 (10K), and three percent signs to convert the number to millions. For instance, =5% gives a result of 0.05, and =1230654%%% gives a result of 1.230654.

Handling Formulas in Macros There are two ways of handling formulas in macros:

- Use the macro to place a string representing the formula into a worksheet cell (which is exactly what happens when you use Excel's recording feature).

- Code the formula so that the macro actually performs the calculations required in its statements.

The first method makes use of Excel's Automatic calculation mode, and the second method gives you control over when the formula will be run.

Recording a Macro Using % When it comes to recording the action of entering a formula containing a % operator, the formula you enter is stored as a string that will be assigned to the cell each time the macro is run. Because Excel VBA doesn't try to interpret the contents of strings, it's happy to record and run the code shown below, which simply assigns cell D8 the formula string.

```
Sub Macro1()
'
' Macro1 Macro
' Macro for % sign formula
'
    Range("D8").Select
    ActiveCell.FormulaR1C1 = "=5%"
    Range("D9").Select
End Sub
```

Letting Macros Calculate Using % When it comes to calculating a formula in a macro, the % sign takes on the role of being the integer type-declaration character. This means that when you use it at the end of a number or name of a numerical variable, you are simply stating that you want that number rounded to the nearest integer. So if I enter

```
a = 3% * 1
```

and hit Enter, the 3% will become the integer 3 and the % sign will disappear, leaving the line of code as

```
a = 3 * 1
```

Entering the decimal fraction 3.25 followed by % will generate an "Expected Expression" error, but assigning an expression that yields a decimal fraction (such as Temp% = 3.25 + 3) is acceptable, as the expression on the right-hand side is evaluated and then rounded to the nearest integer before assigning it to Temp. Values with fractional parts of 0.5 and below are rounded down; the rest are rounded up.

There are two operators available to VBA that are not available in simple worksheet formulas: an integer division operator (\) and a Mod operator (shown in Table 4.2). Although these are not supported in Excel, they can be emulated using the ROUND function with the number and 0 as the arguments for integer division and the MOD function for the Mod operator.

TIP   Ordinary division uses the forward slash, but the special rounding function of the integer division operator uses a backward slash.

T A B L E 4 . 2 : Operators Unique to Excel VBA

Operator	Operation	Example
\	Division	A1\C1 (where A1 and C1 are rounded to integers before the division, and the result is rounded to an integer afterward)
Mod	Mod	A1 Mod 5 (rounds the dividend [A1] and the divisor [5] and returns the remainder when the dividend is divided by the divisor)

Forward or Backward Division

The forward division operator (/) works in floating-point arithmetic and returns the same floating-point result whether used in a worksheet formula or a VBA macro.

The backward division operator is not supported in Excel formulas but is available in Excel VBA. The backward division operator rounds the dividend (the number to be divided) and the divisor (the number to divide by) before the division and the quotient afterwards—so it works entirely with integer values. The code below shows the results given by changing the division operator.

```
Temp1 = 30 / 4 'result is 7.5
Temp2 = 30 \ 4 'result is 7
Temp3 = 4.5 / 1.5 'result is 3
Temp4 = 4.5 \ 1.5 'result is 2
```

NOTE You can use the integer division operator in your VBA macros provided that it isn't part of a formula string you are going to place into a cell.

MOD or *Mod*?

MOD (Excel worksheet function) and Mod (VBA arithmetic operator) both require a dividend and a divisor and both return the remainder after the division as their result. The syntax when used in formulas is

```
MOD(31,5)
```

which gives a result of 1. The syntax when used in VBA code is

```
31 Mod 5
```

which gives a result of 1.

Both the MOD function and the Mod operator are based on the expression

```
= dividend -(divisor*INT(dividend/divisor))
```

The result of evaluating this expression may be different if the dividend and divisor have different signs. This is due to the different rounding methods used to compute the INT part of the expression.

Let's look at an example. Suppose the divisor and dividend are 7 and –2; the INT part evaluates to –3.5. In worksheet formulas this is rounded down to –4, whereas in VBA macros it's rounded up to –3. Substituting these values for the INT part of the expression in a worksheet formula gives us

```
= 7 - (-2 * -4)
```

which evaluates to –1, and for the expression in a macro gives us

```
= 7 - (-2 * -3)
```

which evaluates to 1.

Using Comparison Operators

Excel formulas and the Excel VBA language have the same set of comparison operators that compare the values of two expressions and produce the same logical result of True or False. These operators are:

=	Equals
>	Greater than
<	Less than
>=	Greater than or equal to
<=	Less than or equal to
<>	Not equal to

The two expressions involved in a comparison needn't be the same type, as Excel will try to resolve conflicting types when dealing with numeric types (Byte, Boolean, Integer, Long, Single, Double, Date, Currency, or Decimal) by performing a numeric comparison, and when dealing with string types by performing a string comparison. If one expression is empty, the comparison performed is based on the type of the other expression. If one expression is a string type and the other a numeric type, no comparison can be done and the comparison operator returns a Type Mismatch error.

If one expression is the Single type (32-bit floating point number) and the other the Double type (64-bit floating point number), then the Double expression is converted to Single before the comparison is performed.

Operator Order of Precedence

When more than one operator occurs in the same formula, Excel breaks it up into different parts for evaluation. Each part is evaluated in a predetermined order called *operator precedence*. Arithmetic operators are evaluated in the order shown in Table 4.3, with those operators at the top of the table having priority over those beneath them (e.g., percent is evaluated before multiplication). Operators in the same row are evaluated as they appear from left to right in the formula. For example, when multiplication and division (or addition and subtraction) occur together, they're evaluated from left to right.

TABLE 4.3: Order of Precedence

Operator	Function
^	exponentiation
%	percent
*, /	multiplication and floating-point division
\	integer division
+,−	addition and subtraction
=, <, >, <=, >=, <>	comparison

In applying the order of precedence to the expression

    6 / 2 * 3

the order of precedence is simply left to right because there's no higher or lower ranking for these operators. The expression evaluates as 6 divided by 2 equals 3, which multiplied by 3 equals 9. Applying the order of precedence to

    8 + 9 / 3 * 2

evaluates 9 divided by 3 equals 3, which multiplied by 2 equals 6, which can be added to the 8 to give 14.

Any parts of a formula contained in parentheses are evaluated before those outside, so parentheses are a useful technique for overriding operator precedence to get the result you want. In the example above, we could change the order of precedence by using parentheses:

```
6 / (2 * 3)
```

The expression would then be evaluated as 2 times 3 is 6, and 6 divided by 6 equals 1.

In the VBA language, integer division (\) is placed below the floating point division (/) and multiplication (*) operators in the pecking order but above the addition and subtraction operators. For example, the expression

```
Temp1 = 3 + 50 \ 9 / 2
```

is evaluated as 9 divided by 2 is 4.5, 50 divided by 4 (rounded for integer division) is 12, plus 3 is 15.

To Record or Not to Record (the Active Cell)

When you record your actions to enter a formula, the formula is recorded as a string that'll be assigned to the active cell (e.g., A1) each time the macro is run. If you want your formula to be placed always in the same cell, you must remember to start recording before selecting the cell and entering the formula. If you want your formula to be placed in whatever cell the user makes active before running the macro, then you must select the active cell before starting to record, recording only the formula.

For example, when I recorded entering the formula given in the macro below, I assumed that the formula would be required at whatever cell is currently active. I selected the cell to contain the formula before hitting the Record Macro button.

LISTING 4.3

```
0    Sub Macro1()
1        '
2        ' Macro1 Macro
3        ' coding for formula  B2 = C2 * 0.2
```

```
4         '
5         ActiveCell.FormulaR1C1 = "=R[-1]C[-1] - R[-1]C * 0.2"
6         Range("C4").Select
7    End Sub
```

ANALYSIS

Line 0 indicates the start of the macro with the Sub Macro1() statement.

Lines 1 through 4 are comment lines containing the name of the macro and its description. In the comment I've written the formula in A1 style, as I find that easier to read than the R1C1 relative referencing style that's coded in the macro. Both of these styles are discussed in detail in Chapter 1.

Line 5 uses the ActiveCell property to return the Range object representing the active cell—the cell selected by the user before running the macro. The FormulaR1C1 property of this Range object assigns the formula in the R1C1 style notation. Although the formula's cell references are in the R1C1 style when they are assigned inside the macro, the formula that will appear in the worksheet after the macro has ended will have its cell references specified in the current referencing style.

Line 6 changes the active cell to cell C4. This is the cell right below the cell we've just placed the formula into. This line could be deleted and the active cell left as the same before and after running the macro. (Streamlining macros is handled in Chapter 7.)

Line 7 marks the end of the macro with the End Sub statement.

NOTE Note how comments are coded in VBA: They start with a single quote and finish at the end of the line.

Using Cell References in Formulas

Cell references make formulas more powerful, as you can use data in multiple cells, worksheets, and even in workbooks. References can be used to identify single cells or a whole group of cells.

Cell Referencing Styles

The two styles available are the A1 and the R1C1 referencing styles (discussed in detail in Chapter 1). When you use cell references in a worksheet formula, you can enter them either via the keyboard or by selecting them with the mouse. You have a choice of absolute or relative referencing modes and can also choose whether to use the A1 or the R1C1 referencing style.

Changing Referencing Styles

To toggle between styles, check the R1C1 Reference Style check box in the General tab of the Options dialog box displayed when you choose Tools ➤ Options.

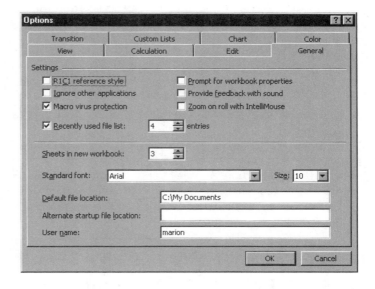

You can mix absolute and relative referencing modes as you enter a formula. For example, to enter the formula given below, I entered "=" to start off the formula, clicked cell A3, entered "+", clicked cell B1, and pressed the F4 key to switch cell B1 from the relative to the absolute referencing mode.

    =A3+$B$1

The first cell reference (A3) specifies the cell two rows down and in the same column as the active cell. The second cell reference ($B$1) specifies the cell B1.

You can't switch referencing styles in the middle of a formula; the Option command will be grayed, deeming it unavailable to be selected while your formula is being entered. However, you can toggle between the absolute and relative modes using the F4 function key. To do this, start entering your formula and, once you've typed a character or more, click the cell you want to reference. This will add a cell in the A1 relative referencing mode. Pressing the F4 function key will change your formula's reference to the $A$1 absolute referencing mode, and another F4 press changes it to A$1 mixed referencing mode. Pressing F4 yet again changes the mode to $A1. This sequence continues to cycle through at every press of the F4 function key.

If I change referencing styles, all existing formulas in the current workbook and any workbooks I open from that point onwards are automatically updated to the new style. For example, if I changed styles from the A1 style in the formula just shown, it would be replaced by the R1C1 style shown below.

    =R[2]C+R1C2

The cell reference A3 is converted to R[2]C, two rows down in the same column, and the second cell reference, $B$1, is converted to R1C2, row 1 column 2.

The absolute and relative referencing modes are preserved irrespective of any change of style.

NOTE   Notice how the A1 style of absolute references uses the dollar sign. Because of this, you cannot use dollar signs to represent currency inside worksheet formulas. You can set the format of the cell, row, or column to currency so that the result of the reference is shown in dollars.

Recording a Formula Containing Cell References

When it comes to recording cell references in a macro, you can control whether you want to use the absolute or relative referencing modes. The relative reference button for toggling this is the second button on the Stop Recording toolbar shown below.

If you want to write a more ambitious formula, be aware that certain ways of recording cell references can make formulas pretty incomprehensible. Consider the formula for calculating tax due in the example worksheet shown below. The following listing shows the formula recorded using the R1C1 style and the relative referencing mode.

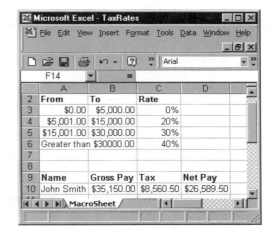

LISTING 4.4

```
0    Sub Macro1()
1        '
2        ' Macro1 Macro
3        ' coding for tax due formula
4        '
5
6        '
7        ActiveCell.FormulaR1C1 = _
8        " =IF(RC[-1]>R[-5]C[-1], ((R[-6]C[-1]-R[-7]C[-1]+1)* _
         R[-6]C)+ ((R[-5]C[-1]-R[-6]C[-1]+1)*R[-5]C)+(RC[-1] _
         -R[-5]C[-1])*R[-4]C, IF(RC[-1]>R[-6]C[-1], _
         ((R[-6]C[-1]-R[-7]C[-1]+1)*R[-6]C)+(RC[-1]-R[-6] _
         C[-1])*R[-5]C, _
         IF( RC[-1]>R[-7]C[-1], (RC[-1]-R[-7]C[-1])* R[-6]C)))"
9        Range("C11").Select
10   End Sub
```

I don't want to leave you scratching your head over the code above—you might decide just to close the book on me. Believe me, this is as bad as it gets! I'll be discussing Names in detail in Chapter 5, but I thought this example warranted a quick peek at the subject. You can greatly improve on the readability and understandability of such code by naming cells and substituting the relative cell references with their respective names, as in Listing 4.5.

LISTING 4.5

```
0    Sub Macro1()
1        '
2        ' Macro1 Macro
3        ' coding for tax due formula
4        '
5        ActiveCell.FormulaR1C1 = _
         "=IF(grosspay>Taxband3,((TaxBand2-TaxBand1+1)*TaxLevel1) _
         +((Taxband3-TaxBand2+1)*TaxLevel2)+(grosspay-Taxband3) _
         *TaxLevel3, _
         IF(grosspay>TaxBand2,((TaxBand2-TaxBand1+1)*TaxLevel1) _
         +(grosspay-TaxBand2)*TaxLevel2, _
         IF(grosspay>TaxBand1,(grosspay-TaxBand1)*TaxLevel1,0))) "
6    End Sub
```

Using names also gives us the benefit of being able to move cells around and restructure our workbooks without actually having to update any cell references hardwired into our macros. Imagine having to update the formula in Listing 4.4. The code would be very difficult to update correctly even if we only needed to insert an extra row in our worksheet.

Using Excel's Built-In Functions in Your Formula

You've seen how to handle formulas in your macros. Let's look at how to incorporate Excel's built-in functions into your formulas and how to create your own functions.

Calling Functions from Formulas

Excel provides a set of several hundred built-in functions, which include all the commonly used mathematical and statistical functions. These functions are tried and tested formulas that you can incorporate into your own formulas. In general, using functions will shorten and simplify your formulas and make it easier to get them right the first time.

Excel's built-in functions all have logical names, so it's easy to find the one you require. When you enter the first equals sign to tell Excel that you're about to enter your formula, the Name list at the left-hand side of the formula bar changes from the list of cell names to the list of the names of the 10 most recently used built-in functions.

When you select one of these functions, the Formula Palette opens with all the details you need to know before using that particular function. Let's look at the Formula Palette and follow the steps of entering a formula using this extremely helpful feature. The Formula Palette is opened when you use the Palette Function dialog box to delegate a function, or when you follow a click on the equals (=) button in the Formula bar with selecting a function from the Name box list.

Using the Paste Function Dialog Box

The Paste Function dialog box provides a list of categories to which functions have been delegated according to their type of functionality (see Figure 4.2). Selecting a category displays the names of the options that have been placed in that category. If you click any function's name, text is displayed along the bottom of the dialog box that provides the function's syntax, including any parameters required, and a brief description of what the function does.

To display the Paste Function dialog box, choose the Insert ➢ Function menu commands or click the Paste Function toolbar button.

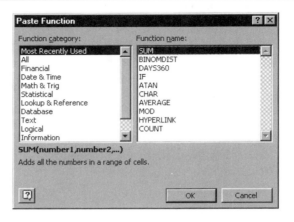

Using the Formula Palette

There are two ways to enter a function, the hard way and the easy way. Let's look at the easy way. The Formula Palette is really a must if you want to make full use of Excel's built-in functions. It takes the guessing out of trying to enter a function's name and its arguments, and can assist you in building a formula that contains worksheet functions. The example given below demonstrates how easy the Formula Palette is to use. It calls the SUM function to add the two values in cells A1 and A2 and places the result in cell A3.

Let's go through the steps required to enter this formula:

1. Place **5** at cell A1 and **4** at cell A2.

2. Select cell A3, where the formula will be entered and the results displayed.

3. Enter an equals sign or click the Edit Formula button on the formula bar (shown). This changes the Name list from the current cell's reference to the names of the built-in functions you've used recently.

4. Enter **100 +** after the equals sign in the Formula Bar.

5. Click the Down arrow in the Name box to display the list of functions, and select the SUM function, as shown. The Formula Palette dialog box will be displayed with the function's name appearing in the top-left corner, and a brief description of what the function does will be given below the entry frame.

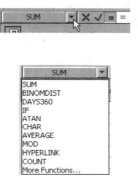

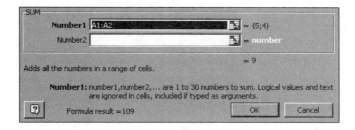

Notice how Excel is guessing ahead at what we're going to do. The A1:A2 cell reference automatically appears in the Number1 text box, and the light gray number at the end of the box has been replaced by {5;4}. The current function result 9 is given just below the bottom number, and the current result of the formula entered so far (Formula result = 109) is displayed along the bottom of the dialog box.

6. Click OK to close the Formula Palette dialog box and finalize entering the formula.

Did you notice that the Formula Palette had a Number2 text box? If you had selected it, a Number3 text box would have appeared. You can have a maximum of five text boxes displayed at a time on the Formula Palette, but when five text boxes are displayed a scroll bar appears down the right side to scroll down to box Number 30; this allows you to specify up to thirty cells or ranges of cells to take part in the summation or whatever other function you've selected.

Creating Your Own Function

You already know how to use functions supplied by Excel in the sense that you enter a name with the required set of arguments, and somehow the value required is automatically returned. Now we're going to have a look at Excel VBA functions. A VBA function is a series of statements that begin with the Function statement and finish with the End Function statement. In the following function I've included just one statement, but functions can be as long and complicated as you care to make them.

```
Function CalculateKilometers(NumberMiles)
    CalculateKilometers = NumberMiles * 1.6
End Function
```

A function can have a list of zero or more arguments, enclosed in parentheses so that you can pass the function any values it needs to use in its statements. As you can see from the example above, the name of the function is assigned the value that's returned. So every time I need to convert miles to kilometers, all I have to do is call my function and state the number of miles.

Creating your own function procedure is achieved using the Visual Basic Editor window. Let's create your first function by following the steps below:

1. Click the Visual Basic Editor button (choose View ➣ Toolbars ➣ Visual Basic if the toolbar is not already displayed).

2. Choose Insert ➣ Module to create Module1 and open the code window where you'll enter your function.

3. Enter the following lines of code:

```
Function AAAMine(Number1)
    AAAMine = (Number1 + 4) * 3.15
End Function
```

4. Choose the File ➣ Close And Return To Microsoft Excel menu command. You can save your workbook while in the Visual Basic Editor but you don't need to, as Module1 will still exist although you've closed the Visual Basic Editor; when you save your workbook in Excel, Module1 will be saved too!

5. Select the cell where the formula is required.

6. Enter an equals sign; the Names list will list the function names.

7. Click the arrow button and select the More Functions item from the bottom of the list. The Paste Function dialog box is displayed (see Figure 4.2).

8. Select All from the Function category list (or alternatively, select User Defined). Your function AAAMine will most likely be the first entry in the Function names because the list is ordered alphabetically.

You can now use your own function in the same way as any of the built-in functions. However, AAAMine is only attached to the current workbook and will not be included in the list of built-in functions in your other workbooks. To make it available to all workbooks created from this point forward, you must place it in a template. How to do this is explained in Chapter 18.

None of the macros you create are listed with the built-in functions because they start with Sub instead of Function. Try replacing the Sub with Function at the start of one of your macros and watch the Visual Basic Editor automatically change the last statement from End Sub to End Function to match your first statement. Your function's name will now magically appear in the Function name list; if you select All or User Defined in the Function category list, you'll be able to see it.

NOTE   You must use the word Function in the first line rather than Sub if you want your function to be added to the list displayed in the Paste Function dialog box.

TIP   It's a good idea to rewrite all your tried and tested functions in VBA so that you have them at your fingertips whenever required. You'll never be caught out again, trying to work out what that formula was that you used to know like the back of your hand. Do remember, though, to give them meaningful names, as it can be just as frustrating trying to find a formula you know you've already written.

Recording a Macro Containing a Built-In Function

Let's record a formula that calls the SUM function that we'll copy to adjacent cells by dragging its cell's fill handle. If you want to try this example, create a new workbook and enter the values at cells A1 through C13 (as shown).

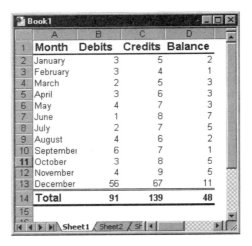

1. Click the Record Macro button in the Visual Basic toolbar to start recording.

2. Click OK on the Record Macro dialog box.

3. Select cell D2 and enter **=C2 - B2**.

4. Drag the fill handle of cell D2 to D13 to apply the formula to all months as well as to the total.

5. Enter the formula **=SUM(B2:B13)** at cell B14, and **=SUM(C2:C13)** at cell C14.

6. Click the Stop Recording button.

The totals should all be the same as those shown. I've styled my worksheet by increasing the font size of the column labels and the Total row label, and I've drawn a border to draw attention to the most important information in the worksheet. I've also opted not to have grid lines by unchecking the Gridlines check box in the View tab of the Options dialog box, available by choosing Tools ➢ Options.

To view the macro just recorded, choose the Tools ➢ Macro ➢ Macros command, and select the macro you just created from the list. Click Step Into to display the code shown in Listing 4.6.

LISTING 4.6

```
0    Sub Macro2()
1        '
2        'Macro2 Macro
3        'Macro to call the SUM function and drag the fill handle to copy
4        '
5        Range("D2").Select
6        ActiveCell.FormulaR1C1 = "=RC[-1]-RC[-2]"
7        Selection.AutoFill Destination:=Range("D2:D13"), _
         Type:=xlFillDefault
8        Range("B14").Select
9        ActiveCell.FormulaR1C1 = "=SUM(R[-12]C:R[-1]C)"
10       Range("C14").Select
11       ActiveCell.FormulaR1C1 = "=SUM(R[-12]C:R[-1]C)"
12   End Sub
```

ANALYSIS

Line 0 is the start statement for the macro.

Lines 1 through 4 are descriptive comments.

Line 5 uses the Select method to make D2 the selected cell and the active cell. There's a subtle difference between these two, which is discussed in the following section ("Can a Cell Be Selected But Not Active?"). This statement could just have easily used the Activate method, as only one cell was specified in the argument, like this: Range("D2").Activate.

Line 6 uses the ActiveCell property of the Application object to return the Range object representing the currently active cell (D2). FormulaR1C1 is the property of this Range object, which is used to assign the formula string in the R1C1 reference style.

Line 7 records the actions at step 3, when the fill handle for cell D2 was dragged down through cell D13. The code recorded for this fill uses the Selection property to return the currently selected range of cells in the active window (D2 through D13). Because these are cells, the object returned is the Range object defining the selected range of cells. The Auto-fill method belongs to the Range object; its general syntax is expression.AutoFill (Destination, Type), where Destination is the range of cells to be filled (D2:D13) and Type is the fill method (xlFillDefault). You can view the Excel constants for filling in the Object Browser by scrolling down to the xl constants and looking for those beginning with xlFill, as shown.

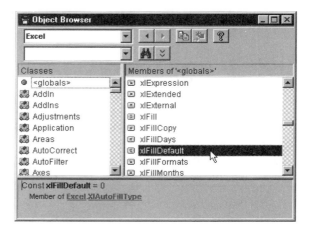

Line 8 is where cell B14 is selected and made the active cell, ready to receive the formula.

In **Line 9**, the FormulaR1C1 property is used to assign the string of text containing the formula, which includes a call to the SUM function; here this is recorded in the R1C1 style.

Line 10 is where cell C14 is selected and made the active cell, ready for the entry of our second formula.

Line 11 is where the formula calling SUM is entered again; it could just as easily have been dragged across from B14.

Line 12 ends the macro.

NOTE   The string representing a worksheet formula can contain any valid formula that can be entered into a cell, including single values, expressions, and calls to Excel functions.

Can a Cell Be Selected But Not Active?

The active cell is the one that receives the data when you start typing. The active cell is identified by a thick border and is unique in that only one cell can be active at any particular time.

When you select a single cell, it's both the active cell and the selected cell. But if you drag the mouse to extend this cell to a range of cells, the first selected cell (which remains unfilled, as shown) will still be the active one and all the other cells will just be selected cells.

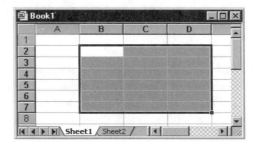

So an active cell is always a selected cell but a selected cell may not necessarily be the active one.

NOTE   If a range of cells is selected, then the active cell is always the first cell selected in the range.

Functions within Functions

As we've seen, functions are really just a series of statements that calculate some value. For this reason, a function can be substituted anywhere a particular value is required. Functions usually require one or more arguments for use in their calculations before they can return their value. In worksheet formulas, any function argument can be substituted by another function—provided, of course, that it returns the same type of value as the argument it replaces.

A function within a function is called a *nested* function. Let's look at one that uses the SUM function within the SUM function:

```
=SUM(1,2,SUM(3,4))
```

Excel allows a maximum of seven levels of nested functions in worksheet formulas. However, Excel VBA does not allow nested formulas at all and will give a compiler error if you dare to try.

Constructing Complex Worksheet Formulas

Constructing complex worksheet formulas to perform reasonably simple tasks can become quite complicated and likely to lead to errors. We have already looked at recording formulas, in the Tax Due example in the section "Recording a Formula Containing Cell References" of this chapter. I found this formula quite cumbersome to write and kept missing parentheses along the way. I started with just one If worksheet function, based on the syntax given below:

```
IF(logical_test, value_if_true, value_if_false)
```

This bit of code was extended to nest the second If function in the value_if_false part of the first If function:

```
IF(logical_test, value_if_true, IF(logical_test, value_if_true, _
    value_if_false))
```

I extended the code again to nest the third If function in the value_if_false part of the second If function. The structure of the formula ended up as follows:

```
IF(logical_test, value_if_true, IF(logical_test, value_if_true, _
    IF(logical_test, value_if_true, value_if_false)))
```

However, I'd find it quite time-consuming if I ever had to add a new level to the tax rates, as this would require a fourth nested If function in the value_if_false part of the third If function.

The main problem in building this formula is that all of the tax levels have to be considered simultaneously. Although I tried to build it in stages, I was really just adding to the complexity of the formula at each stage. The formula is shown next as it appears in the worksheet.

This formula could be formatted with line breaks to add to its readability.

Macro-izing Complex Formulas

We've already seen that formulas using names for cell references are much easier to understand. Well, the same goes for macros that you write yourself; in fact, using names makes the macros much easier to write too.

The macros shown in Listings 4.7 and 4.8 revisit our Tax Due formula example recorded in the section "Recording a Formula Containing Cell References" (Listings 4.4 and 4.5). They show two versions of how the same formula can be coded, by using references to cells or by using names to retrieve the values required, in the VBA language that evaluates the formula.

The macro code in Listing 4.7 uses the Cells property to reference cells and is comparable to the macro code in Listing 4.4, which uses the R1C1 cell reference style in a formula string assigned to the active cell. You'll see that it's not altogether unfathomable, and when you know that Cell(2,1) is just cell B1, this code becomes even more understandable. The macro in Listing 4.8, which uses the names to refer to values, should be compared to Listing 4.4, which also uses names.

LISTING 4.7

```
0    Sub CalculateTaxRates()
1    '
2    'CalculateTaxRates Macro
3    '
4    'the Tax Due formula (with cell references) coded in VBA
5    '
6    With Worksheets("Sheet1")
7    If (.Cells(10, 2).Value > .Cells(5, 2).Value) Then
8    'need all three tax rates
9        .Cells(10, 3).Value = (.Cells(4, 2).Value - _
         .Cells(3, 2).Value + 1) * .Cells(4, 3).Value + _
         (.Cells(5, 2).Value - .Cells(4, 2).Value + 1) * _
         .Cells(5, 3).Value + (.Cells(10, 2).Value - _
         .Cells(5, 2).Value) *  .Cells(6, 3).Value
10   Else
11       If (.Cells(10, 2).Value > .Cells(4, 2).Value) Then
12       'need first two tax rates
13           .Cells(10, 3).Value = (.Cells(4, 2).Value - _
             .Cells(3, 2).Value + 1) * .Cells(4, 3).Value + _
             (.Cells(10, 2).Value - .Cells(4, 2).Value) * _
             .Cells(5, 3).Value
14       Else
15       'need first tax rate
16             .Cells(10, 3).Value = (.Cells(10, 2).Value - _
               .Cells(4, 2).Value) * .Cells(5, 3).Value
17         End If
18     End If
19     End With
20   End Sub
```

ANALYSIS

Line 0 starts the macro named CalculateTaxRates.

Lines 1 through 5 are descriptive comments.

Line 6 is the With statement, specifying Sheet1 to be the worksheet being used. (The With statement is described in Chapter 3.)

Line 7 starts the If statement and uses the Cells property called with two arguments (row and column). The period (.) in front of Cells means that it's a member of the Worksheet object named Sheet1 specified in the With statement. The condition checks whether the gross pay is greater than the top tax rate.

Line 8 is a comment line giving information that will be helpful to maintain the code if the number of levels of tax rates changes.

Line 9 calculates the tax due, using the three rates, and assigns the value to cell C10.

Line 10, the Else keyword, marks the end of the If part if the condition is True, in which case execution jumps to the End If at Line 18. It marks the start of the Else part if the condition is False.

Line 11 is the inner If statement, with a condition to check whether the gross pay is greater than the second top tax rate.

Line 12 is a helpful comment.

Line 13 calculates the tax due and assigns it to cell C10.

Line 14 is the Else keyword marking the end of the inner If statement if the condition is True or the start of the Else part if it is False.

Line 15 is a helpful comment.

Line 16 calculates the tax due and assigns it to cell C10.

Line 17, the End If, marks the end of the inner If statement.

Line 18, the End If, marks the end of the outer If statement.

Line 19, the End With, marks the end of the With statement so that anything starting with a period (.) will no longer be linked to Sheet1.

Line 20, the End Sub, marks the end of the macro.

The macro shown in Listing 4.8 has the same structure as the macro in Listing 4.7, but names have been used as cell references to demonstrate how names can dramatically increase the understandability of a macro.

LISTING 4.8

```
0    Sub CalculateTaxRates()
1        '
2        'CalculateTaxRates Macro
```

```
3          'the Tax Due formula (with named values) coded in VBA
4          '
5          If (Range("GrossPay").Value > Range("TaxBand3").Value) Then
6              Range("Tax") = (Range("TaxBand2") - Range("TaxBand1") _
                   + 1) * Range("TaxLevel1") + (Range("TaxBand3") _
                   - Range("TaxBand2") + 1) * Range("TaxLevel2") _
                   + (Range("GrossPay") - Range("TaxBand3")) _
                   * Range("TaxLevel3")
7          Else
8              If (Range("GrossPay") > Range("TaxBand2")) Then
9                  Range("GrossPay") = (Range("TaxBand2") _
                       - Range("TaxBand1") + 1) * Range("TaxLevel1") _
                       + (Range("GrossPay") - Range("TaxBand2")) *
                   Range("TaxLevel2")
10             Else
11                 Range("Tax") = (Range("GrossPay") _
                       - Range("TaxBand2")) * Range("TaxLevel2")
12             End If
13         End If
14     End Sub
```

ANALYSIS

Line 0 starts our macro, called `CalculateTaxRates`.

Lines 1 through 4 are comments for information.

Lines 5 through 13 show how this macro utilizes the `Range` property using the names of cells as the argument rather than using cell references. The `If` used here is a statement in the VBA language and has the same functionality as the `If` function used in worksheet formulas, although syntactically different. (The VBA `If` statement is described in Chapter 3.) All these lines of code belong to the same `If` statement that has the following structure:

```
If Expression = True Then
    Statement
Else
    If Expression = True Then
        Statement
    Else
        Statement
    End If
End If
```

Only one of the three statements at Lines 6, 9, or 11 will be executed according to the GrossPay. The first statement (6) requires that Excel use all three of the tax bands, the second statement (9) uses two tax bands, and the last statement (11) uses only one tax band.

Line 14 ends the macro.

You can streamline this a bit further by simply referring to the data values by their defined names, as shown in the following code:

```
Sub StreamlinedCalculateTaxRates()
    '
    ' Macro1 Macro
    ' Macro recorded 2/16/98 by Marion Cottingham
        'formula coded in VBA
    If GrossPay > TaxBand3 Then
        Tax = (TaxBand2 - TaxBand1 + 1) * TaxLevel1 + _
                (TaxBand3 - TaxBand2 + 1) * TaxLevel2 + _
                (GrossPay - TaxBand3) * TaxLevel3
    Else
    If (GrossPay > TaxBand2) Then
        GrossPay = (TaxBand2 - TaxBand1 + 1) * _
        TaxLevel1 + (GrossPay - TaxBand2) * TaxLevel2
    Else
        Tax = (GrossPay - TaxBand2) * TaxLevel2
    End If
    End If
End Sub
```

As you can see, there's not a great deal of difference in the level of complexity or difficulty in reading this code compared to reading the recorded worksheet formula shown in Listing 4.5 that provides the same result. The point here is that writing macros is just about the same level of difficulty as writing worksheet formulas.

Compare these macros (Listings 4.7 and 4.8) with the macros in Listings 4.4 and 4.5, and you'll see that these are all implementations of the same formula. Notice how the three tax levels are handled individually at Lines 6, 9, and 11 in Listing 4.8, making it much easier to write the macro than the formula. The macro structure also makes it easier to handle changes, such as the introduction of another level of taxation.

What Happens if a Formula Is Moved?

If you move the formula to a different location, its cell references will be updated to reflect the move even if you moved it to a different worksheet or workbook.

The example below gives two versions of the same formula, before and after it was moved from Sheet1 to Sheet2. The original version of the formula as it appeared on Sheet1 is:

```
=RC[-2]+RC[-1]
```

When you move a formula to the same cell location in another worksheet, Excel updates all its cell references to ensure that they still refer to the same formula by including the worksheet's name as part of the reference, as follows:

```
=Sheet1!R[1]C[-2]+Sheet1!R[1]C[-1]
```

Moving things around in Excel is a dangerous occupation, as no doubt you are already aware. Naming cells seems the best way to avoid most of the problems, because a name always refers to the same data value no matter how or where you move these values. Cell names are definitely a must when writing your own macros, because none of Excel's automatic tracking features are available to update anything contained in your macro.

Calling a Macro Using a Command Button

You've seen how to run your macros using the Run Macro button in the Visual Basic toolbar: this opens the Macro dialog box with a list of all the macros that exist for the current workbook. Suppose you want to run a specific macro in one of your worksheets and you want to avoid the possibility of the user selecting the wrong macro from the list. One way to do this is to place a command button on your worksheet so that the required macro will be run whenever this button is clicked, without giving the user any choice of which macro to run.

Adding a Command Button to a Worksheet

The CommandButton control must be one of the most used controls in Windows applications. It is among the easiest possible ways for users to interact with your application. In this section, you're going to use command buttons to call the CalculateTaxRates macro shown in Listing 4.8. Let's start by placing a command button on your worksheet.

To bring up the Visual Basic toolbar, choose View ➤ Toolbars ➤ Visual Basic. Click the Control Toolbox icon in this toolbar to display the Control Toolbox that contains the Command Button icon.

Select the Command Button icon from the Control Toolbox and position and size it on your worksheet using a click-and-drag action. Try clicking the command button and watch it appear to move inwards as if pressed. This animated feature is handled automatically by the code encapsulated in the CommandButton class of your Windows application. If you want to respond to the click, you must enter code into the Click event procedure called CommandButton1_Click. But let's leave that for now and take a look at some of the well-used properties of the CommandButton control.

Handling *Command Button*'s Properties

The CommandButton control has many properties and methods. To view them, right-click the command button and choose Properties from the shortcut menu that pops up.

The Properties window is displayed, showing the settings for the `CommandButton` control with the default name `CommandButton1`. New values for these properties can be set by overtyping the old values or selecting a value from a drop-down list.

You don't need to know all the properties that belong to a control before you can use that control. In this section we're going to look at just three of them, the three properties you will most likely want to set.

Caption   The caption property is set to the text string you want displayed on the button. The default value is `CommandButton1`, so you really can't avoid setting it to something that better describes how it's going to react when it's clicked.

A standard feature in Windows applications is to give the user the ability to manipulate controls using the keyboard. Some users prefer this method of interaction and find it much quicker, especially if they're already using the keyboard for data entry. These users will be looking for an underlined character that they can use in combination with the Alt key to *click* the button.

NOTE   Shortcut keys are not case sensitive and the underlined character is not necessarily the first character in the word. There can't be two controls accessible simultaneously with the same shortcut key.

You can make your command button keyboard-selectable by setting the `Accelerator` property to the character to be used as the shortcut key. The Accelerator character will then appear underlined and your command button will be selectable by pressing Alt plus this character.

AutoSize The AutoSize property can be set to True or False. When set to True, the size of the command button will be adjusted to fit the entire Caption property's text. If set to False, and the caption's text is too long to fit into the command button, it will be truncated to fit.

Enabled The Enabled property can be set to True or False. When set to True, it enables the command button to respond to the user's clicks. If set to False, the command button appears dimmed and will not respond to clicks. The most likely reason to dim a button would be if some field in a dialog box needed to be filled in. You might think of other reasons as you're designing an application.

The Command Button's *Click* Event Procedure

Now you can think about writing the code for the actions required in the event of the user clicking your command button. The code is entered in a code window in the same way as you entered your macros. The macros were entered into a module; the event procedures are entered into the sheet where the events occur. To open the code window, right-click your command button and select the View Code command from the shortcut menu. This will open up the Visual Basic Editor and display the code window containing the first and last lines of the primary event procedure for the control with the focus, which just happens to be the Click event for your command button (as shown). Your command button has been given the default name of CommandButton1. Any code placed between these lines of code will be executed when someone clicks CommandButton1.

Running a macro from a command button looks very simple. Let's create a quick macro and try it out. Open a new worksheet and record a simple macro that enters the number 5 into cell A1. Remember to delete the 5 after the recording is finished so that you'll know if the macro has run and if it has given the correct result. (If you need a refresher on how to run a quick macro, see "Recording Cell References in a Macro" in Chapter 1.)

Now add a command button to your worksheet, right-click it, and choose View Code as before. The Visual Basic Editor opens and displays the code window for the `CommandButton1_Click` event procedure. This event procedure will run when the command button CommandButton1 is clicked. Enter your macro's name (I've used `Macro1`) as shown in the code below:

```
Private Sub CommandButton1_Click()
Macro1
End Sub
```

To run your macro from here:

1. Choose File ➢ Close And Return To Microsoft Excel. This will close the Visual Basic Editor and take you back to Excel and your worksheet.

2. Click the Exit Design Mode button from your Visual Basic toolbar to return to normal mode.

3. Click the command button you just created and watch while the `Click` event procedure runs and calls `Macro1` to display the number 5 in cell A1 as expected.

Macro-izing the Error Values Returned by Formulas

If Excel encounters any problems while trying to evaluate a formula, an error value will be displayed at the formula's cell. An error value is a string of characters that are meant to give you some indication of what went wrong. These strings are listed in Table 4.4, along with possible causes and solutions.

Error values all start with the number sign (#) followed by a short string of uppercase letters. Errors can happen for a variety of reasons; the most common errors include division by zero, the cell isn't wide enough to display the result, the cell referred to has been deleted, or the formula is doing something invalid such as using arithmetic operations on a text string (you cannot multiply a text string). This last error is usually caused by entering a name that doesn't belong to any cell, which may just be a simple spelling mistake.

The formulas themselves will be syntactically correct; otherwise Excel would have rejected them when they were entered.

If the cell containing the formula with the error is itself referenced in another formula, this other formula will also display an error value. This domino effect can trickle down the formula links, and in worksheets that contain several dependent formulas, it is often the case that one error can cause devastation with error values dotted all over the place. I'm sure you've experienced inserting a row or column and suddenly all these error values pop up—you hardly know where to start troubleshooting.

TABLE 4.4: Error Messages and Troubleshooting

Error Message	Possible Causes and Solutions
########	The numeric value has too many characters to be displayed. There are two possible solutions: Expand the cell or shrink the number. Try making the column wider to see the result. If this isn't roughly what you were expecting, you may have entered an extra figure in one of your data values. Or, reduce the number of characters in a cell by choosing Format ➢ Cell and selecting a new format from the Number tab.
#REF!	Cell reference is invalid. This often occurs after you've moved cells. The cells you move effectively delete the cells they are replacing. Cell references in any formulas that referenced the original cells will be updated automatically to invalid cells, and Excel will no longer be able to calculate the result for these formulas.
#VALUE!	Incorrect operands or arguments in functions. Check the values of cells referenced by the formula to make sure they are the correct type.
#NUM!	There is a problem with one of the numbers in your formula. The formula may be producing a very large or very small number that Excel cannot represent because of its size. Check that the function arguments are of the correct type.
#NAME?	The formula uses a name that Excel can't find. Check for correct spelling of the names of cell references, formulas, and functions. Check for quotation marks around a name, which indicate that it should be treated as a string. Make sure the named items all exist and have not been accidentally deleted from the worksheet. Check for a colon in the middle of cell references that identify a range of cells—without the colon, Excel will treat it as a name.

Continued on next page

TABLE 4.4 CONTINUED: Error Messages and Troubleshooting

Error Message	Possible Causes and Solutions
#DIV/0!	Division by zero. This error is often caused by blank cells, which Excel interprets as zero. Make sure none of the cells referenced in your formula refer to blank cells.
#NULL!	Reference to intersection of two disjointed areas. Check that you have entered ranges and cell references correctly, making sure that at least one cell is included in both ranges.
#N/A!	Value is Not Available to a function or formula. A cell referenced by the formula may contain the error, or you could be missing an argument to a built-in Excel function.

Creating a Macro for Error Prevention

In this section, you'll create a macro to give the user warnings when deletion of data will cause problems in formula calculations. You'll use a command button to run the macro and message boxes to display a warning whenever the user tries to delete data values that are referenced by a formula or tries to delete a formula cell. We haven't looked at message boxes yet, so we'll do that before we get into writing our macro.

Figure 4.3 shows the worksheet that we are going to use for our error-handling macros.

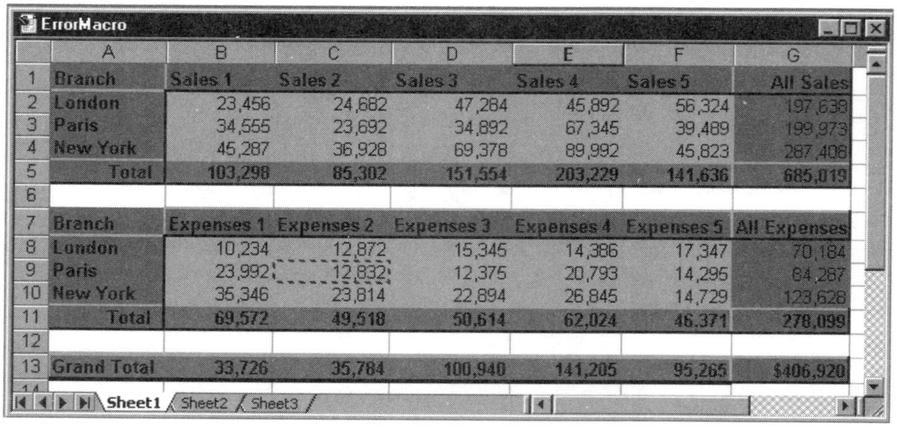

FIGURE 4.3:

ErrorMacro worksheet that demonstrates the error-handling macros

	A	B	C	D	E	F	G
1	Branch	Sales 1	Sales 2	Sales 3	Sales 4	Sales 5	All Sales
2	London	23,456	24,682	47,284	45,892	56,324	197,638
3	Paris	34,555	23,692	34,892	67,345	39,489	199,973
4	New York	45,287	36,928	69,378	89,992	45,823	287,408
5	Total	103,298	85,302	151,554	203,229	141,636	685,019
6							
7	Branch	Expenses 1	Expenses 2	Expenses 3	Expenses 4	Expenses 5	All Expenses
8	London	10,234	12,872	15,345	14,386	17,347	70,184
9	Paris	23,992	12,832	12,375	20,793	14,295	84,287
10	New York	35,346	23,814	22,894	26,845	14,729	123,628
11	Total	69,572	49,518	50,614	62,024	46,371	278,099
12							
13	Grand Total	33,726	35,784	100,940	141,205	95,265	$406,920

Customizing Message Boxes

The message box is a great way of communicating information to your user from a macro. You can display a message box on the screen that the user must respond to before continuing. The message can be just useful information or it can be a warning. You can even use a message box to give users some control over what the macro will do next.

TIP   Avoid using too many message dialog boxes in the same macro, as having to keep clicking to close these boxes may be a source of annoyance to users and will affect their perception of the usefulness and user-friendliness of your macros.

Using Message Boxes in Your Macro

A message box is just a variation of a dialog box that's displayed by the `MsgBox` function. The syntax for calling the `MsgBox` function is:

```
MsgBox(message[,buttons][,title][,helpfile, context])
```

Figure 4.4 shows a message box with some of these components labeled.

Message   The `Message` argument is the only one required, and is the string expression that appears inside the message dialog box. The other arguments are optional and are allocated default values if they're not specified.

Buttons   There are several different combinations of buttons that you can display in your message box, some of which are listed in Table 4.5. If no button combination is given, the default of a simple OK button is used.

FIGURE 4.4:

Message Box with the message "Hello"

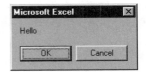

TABLE 4.5: Names and Values of Constants That Specify the Buttons Displayed

Constant	Value	Buttons Displayed
vbOKOnly	0	OK
vbOKCancel	1	OK, Cancel
vbYesNo	4	Yes, No
vbYesNoCancel	3	Yes, No, Cancel
vbAbortRetryIgnore	2	Abort, Retry, Ignore
vbRetryCancel	5	Retry, Cancel
vbCritical	16	Critical Message
vbQuestion	32	Warning Query
vbInformation	64	Information Message

Title   The title is the text you want displayed along the title bar of the message box. If not specified, this defaults to "Microsoft Excel."

Helpfile   The helpfile and context are discussed in Chapter 22; they default to the Help Assistant in Windows 98.

Calling the *MsgBox* Function

The GiveMessage1, GiveMessage2, and GiveMessage3 macros below provide three different ways of calling the MsgBox function. The first macro just calls the message box and takes no notice of the value it returns; the second macro assigns the return value to temp; and the third macro uses the Call statement and discards its argument. Although syntactically different, the first and third macros are equivalent.

The second and third macros both require that parentheses be placed around the arguments. All functions called in an assignment statement or called using the Call statement must have their arguments placed in parentheses.

Let's enter the three macros into a module:

1.   Open the Visual Basic Editor by clicking the Visual Basic Editor button on the Visual Basic toolbar or by choosing Tools ➢ Macro ➢ Visual Basic Editor.

2. Insert a module by choosing Insert ➤ Module to open the code window. Ensure that the Full Module View button is selected (second button from the left at the bottom of the window) so that you'll be able to see all three macros simultaneously after you've entered them.

3. Enter these three macros:

```
Sub GiveMessage1()
    MsgBox "Hello!", vbCritical
End Sub

Sub GiveMessage2()
    Temp = MsgBox("Hello again!", vbCritical)
End Sub

Sub GiveMessage3()
    Call MsgBox("Hello again, again!", vbCritical)
End Sub
```

4. Run `GiveMessage1` by placing the entry cursor anywhere in one of its lines and clicking the Run button (the first button in the Visual Basic toolbar). The Critical Message Box is displayed and the sound you've set as Critical Stop in your Windows environment will automatically sound. The Stop icon is automatically displayed when `vbCritical` is specified as the button. Similarly, the question mark icon is shown when the `vbQuestion` is specified, and the Information icon is displayed with `vbInformation`.

5. Your macro should stop running when you select a button in the message box.

6. Run the other two macros by repeating steps 4 and 5, placing the entry cursor somewhere within the macro you're calling.

Try creating other macros and make yourself familiar with the button selections shown in Table 4.5. It's much easier to use the automatic creation features that the `MsgBox` function offers than to try to get the same effect by other means.

Skipping Arguments

As mentioned above, only the first argument (the message) is required. You can stop there and let Excel default the rest for you. Excel VBA functions always list the required arguments first, followed by the optional arguments, so skipping arguments at the tail end of the argument list does not present any problems.

However, if you want to skip an occasional argument and be able to continue providing arguments later in the sequence, you must give Excel a clue as to what you are trying to do. Excel matches up the arguments using the commas as delimiters, so if you skip an argument but still put in its comma, Excel will be able to match everything up correctly and you'll get the result you want.

Formatting Your Message

Normally, when you format text you use non-printable characters such as the Entry character (formally known as the carriage return character). However, when you're writing VBA code, you can't enter an Entry character in the middle of a string, as this will cause a syntax error. Instead, you can use its ASCII character code as an argument to the Chr function, which returns a one-character string. (See Appendix A for the complete ASCII Character Set.) The useful ASCII codes to know are tab (9), space (32), and carriage return (13); the following shows how these are included in your message:

```
MsgBox "Click " & Chr(13) & Chr(9) & "Yes to continue" & _
Chr(13) & Chr(9) & "No to start again!", vbYesNo
```

The & character is used for concatenating (joining) strings, as explained in Chapter 2. The message box displayed when this statement is executed gives the user the Click Yes To Continue option.

Now you've become proficient at manipulating message boxes, so let's get down to the serious business of writing a macro for error prevention. Let's create a macro to prevent us from deleting values that will adversely affect values at other cells in the ErrorMacro worksheet shown in Figure 4.3. Listing 4.9 shows my version of the ReportPotentialErrors macro. This macro warns users if they try to cut the values at a cell that contains data required by formulas elsewhere in the worksheet or if they try to cut an empty cell.

LISTING 4.9

```
0    Sub ReportPotentialErrors()
1        '
2        'This macro is called when the user wants to cut the values at a
3        'cell or range of cells. The macro assumes no changes have been
4        'made to the worksheet since the macro was written and that
5        'all formulas are still in their original cells.
6        With ActiveCell
7            If .Column > 7 Or .Row = 6 Or .Row = 12 Or .Row > 13 Then
8                Beep
9                MsgBox "Cannot continue, there is no data here!"
10           ElseIf .Row = 5 Then
11               Beep
12               temp = MsgBox("This cell contains the formula =" _
                 & Chr(.Column + 64) & _"2 + " & Chr(.Column + 64) _
                 & "3 + " & Chr(.Column + 64) & "4." & Chr(13) _
                 & "Click Yes to continue and No to cancel.", vbYesNo)
13           ElseIf .Row = 11 Then
14               Beep
15               temp = MsgBox("This cell contains the formula =" _
                 & Chr(.Column + 64) & "8 + " & Chr(.Column + 64) _
                 & "9 + " & Chr(.Column + 64) & "10." & Chr(13) _
                 & "Click Yes to continue and No to cancel.", vbYesNo)
16           ElseIf .Row < 6 Then 'in Annual Sales group
17               Beep
18               temp = MsgBox("This will affect cells "_
                 & Chr(.Column + 64) & "5 and " & Chr(.Column + 64) _
                 & "13, G5 and G13." & Chr(13)_
                 & "Click Yes to continue and  No to cancel.", vbYesNo)
19           ElseIf .Row < 12 Then 'in Annual Expenses group
20               Beep
21               temp = MsgBox("This will affect cells " _
                 & Chr(.Column + 64) & "11 and " & Chr(.Column + 64) _
                 & "13." & Chr(13) & _
                 "Click Yes to continue and No to cancel.", vbYesNo)
22           ElseIf .Row < 14 Then 'in Grand Total group
23               Beep
```

```
24                    temp = MsgBox("This cell contains the formula =" _
                      & Chr(.Column + 64) & _"5 - " & Chr(.Column + 64) _
                      & "11 and should not be updated.", vbCancel)
25               End If
26               If temp = vbOK Then 'clear the selected cell or range _
                                     'of cells
27                    Selection.Clear
28               End If
29          End With
30     End Sub
```

ANALYSIS

Line 0 is the start of the ReportPotentialErrors macro.

Lines 1 through 5 contain descriptive information about the macro.

Line 6, the With statement, specifies that the active cell will be used.

Line 7's If statement checks that the active cell to be cut contains data.

Line 8 is the Beep statement that will emit the sound that is normally used as a warning.

Line 9 calls the MsgBox function to generate a message box displaying the string passed to it as an argument.

Line 10's ElseIf statement combines the Else and the If statements, allowing you to evaluate a new condition.

Line 11 is another Beep statement.

Line 12 calls the MsgBox function with a string made up of several substrings joined together using the concatenation operator (&). Notice how the Chr function is called with the argument Column + 64, which converts the column number to its alpha representation.

Lines 13 through 24 are Lines 10 through 12 repeated with different values and arguments.

Line 25 is the end of the If...then...ElseIf... statement.

Line 26 tests whether the MsgBox function returned the constant value of vbOK to indicate that the user clicked the OK button in the message box to agree to the cut going ahead.

> **Line 27**, the Clear method of the Selection property, is used to clear the active cell.
>
> **Line 28** marks the end of the If statement.
>
> **Line 29** is the end of the With statement.
>
> **Line 30** ends the macro.

Now I'll leave it up to you to call ReportPotentialErrors from a command button by following the steps shown in the section "The Command Button's Click Event Procedure" earlier in this chapter.

Creating a Macro for Error Reporting

You've just created a macro that provides users with warnings that might prevent them from accidentally deleting data referenced in a formula elsewhere in the worksheet. In this next section, we'll deal with the error strings that appear when these accidents occur. Let's try to be explicit in the message to the user as to what caused the error. The benefit of writing your own macro doesn't stop with helping the user through rough patches, but you can extend your reporting to warn of excessively high values or excessively low values so that the user can check these out. You could also report on any values that are missing.

The first thing your macro is going to check is that the value of the formula isn't one of the Excel error strings given in Table 4.5. Because we have to compare the value of the cell with the eight items in this table, we'll use the Select Case statement described below. We could have used an If...Then...Else statement, but the Select Case is a bit more efficient: it's easier to read, and if we use the If statement the value in the cell will have to be retrieved again for every test.

The next section describes the Select Case statement. After reading that, you'll be ready to write your own macro.

The *Select Case* Statement

The Select Case structure provides an alternative to the If...Then...Else statement for selectively executing a single block of statements. This is the preferred structure if the test expression in the If...Then...Else structure is the same and there are more than two expressions.

The Select Case structure works by evaluating a single test expression and comparing this value with the values at each Case in the structure. The syntax of the Select Case structure is:

```
Select Case test_expression
Case expression1
     statements1
Case expression2
     statements2

        . . .

Case Else
     statementsN
End Select
```

A Case Else block can be included as an option and will be executed only if the expression does not match any of the Case expressions. Case Else is commonly used for reporting errors.

The Select Case structure is preferable to the If...Then...Else structure because it is easier to implement and less error prone, and improves the readability of the code since each Case is represented individually by an expression.

You could write a macro to validate data entry. Such a macro would allow you to add further checks on the validity of data, such as whether the values used in the formula are in the correct range, or, if one cell contains nonzero data (such as quantity and price), to check that data is present at another specific cell.

LISTING 4.10

```
0    Sub ReportErrors()
1        '
2        'ReportErrors macro
3        '
4        'checks if the active cell contains an error message string
5        '
6        With Application
7        'check for error message
8        Select Case ActiveCell.Text
9        Case "#REF" _
             MsgBox "The formula at cell " & _
             Chr(ActiveCell.Column + 64) & _
             ActiveCell.Row & " contains an invalid cell _
             reference!"
```

```
10      Case "#VALUE" _
            MsgBox "The formula at cell " & _
            Chr(ActiveCell.Column + 64) & _
            ActiveCell.Row & " contains a function called _
            with arguments of the wrong type!"
11      Case "#NUM!" _
            MsgBox "There is a problem with one of the numbers _
            in the " & _"formula at cell " & _
            Chr(ActiveCell.Column + 64) & ActiveCell.Row
12      Case "#NAME?" _
            MsgBox "The formula at cell " & _
            Chr(ActiveCell.Column + 64) & _
            ActiveCell.Row & " uses a name that doesn't exist!"
13      Case "#DIV/0!" _
            MsgBox "The formula at cell " & _
            Chr(ActiveCell.Column + 64) & _
            ActiveCell.Row & " contains a division by zero!"
14      Case "#NULL!" _
            MsgBox "The formula at cell " & _
            Chr(ActiveCell.Column + 64) & _
            ActiveCell.Row & " contains a reference to the _
            intersection of two disjointed areas!"
15      Case "#N/A!" _
            MsgBox "The formula at cell " & _
            Chr(ActiveCell.Column + 64) & _
            ActiveCell.Row & " contains a value that's not _
            available!"
16      Case "" _
            MsgBox "The formula at cell " & _
            Chr(ActiveCell.Column + 64) & _
            ActiveCell.Row & " is empty!"
17      Case Else _
            MsgBox "The formula at cell " & _
            Chr(ActiveCell.Column + 64) & _
            ActiveCell.Row & " is OK!"
18      End Select
19      End With
20  End Sub
```

Line 0 is the start of the `ReportErrors` macro.

Lines 1 through 5 contain descriptive comments.

Line 6 is the `With` statement that allows the members of the `Application` object to be used without being qualified.

Line 7 is a comment.

Line 8 is the `Select Case` statement that will provide a message based on the contents at the active cell. Notice that I've used the `Text` property here rather than the `Value` property. The `Text` property is set to the string containing the error message; the `Value` property is set to the error number appropriate for the string.

Lines 9 through 15 display a message box if the active cell contains an error message.

Line 16 displays a message box telling the user the active cell is empty.

Line 17 is the `Case Else`, which is executed when none of the other `Case` statement conditions are `True`. This verifies to the user that the contents of the active cell are acceptable.

Line 18 ends the `Select` statement.

Line 19 ends the `With` statement.

Line 20 ends the `ReportErrors` macro.

Circular References

Circular references in formulas occur when one of the cell references refers directly or indirectly back to the formula cell. For example, if you enter the first formula below into cell A3 and the second one into cell B1, you'll get the circular reference warning shown.

```
=A1 * B1 + A2 * B2
=A3 * 2
```

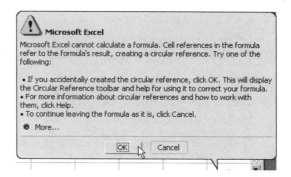

As you know, when Excel is in Automatic calculation mode, it tries to recalculate the value of formulas every time there's a change in the value of any cell referenced within the formula. In the example above, the cause of the circular reference is that the formula at cell A3 (=A1 * B1 + A2 * B2) contains a reference to cell B1 and the formula at cell B1 (=A3 * 2) contains a reference to cell A3. So if we changed the value at cell A1, the formula at cell A3 will be recalculated, causing the formula in cell B1 to be recalculated, causing the cell at A3 to be recalculated… forever. That is, it would if Excel didn't have any preventative measures.

If left to the default, Excel will not allow you to introduce circular references. However, there are some circumstances when you may want to have some recursion in your formulas. For example, suppose you need to compute factorials; this is best done by recursion. The following function is called with an integer as the argument:

```
0    Function Factorial (Number)
1        If Number < 2 Then
2            Factorial = 1
3        Else
4            Factorial = Factorial(Number - 1) * Number
5        End If
6    End Function
```

Suppose 3 is given as the argument evaluated. Factorial 3 is 3 * 2 * 1, which is 6. Now let's look at how this is done by recursively calling the Factorial function.

> **Call 1:** The first call to the function Factorial Number is set to 3. The condition in the If statement (Number < 2) is False, so the Else part is executed, which calls Factorial with (3 - 1).

Call 2: The second time through, the If condition is still False, so the Else part is executed again and calls Factorial with ((3 - 1)-1).

Call 3: The third time through, the If condition is True and returns 1 to Call 2.

Call 2: 1 is substituted for Factorial(Number - 1) and multiplied by Number (3 -1) to give 2, which is returned to Call 1.

Call 1: 2 is substituted for Factorial(Number - 1) and multiplied by Number (3) to give 6.

Recursive Programming Using Circular References

Most circular references are done by mistake, but sometimes you may be required to do some recursion intentionally. Excel will allow you to go around in circles for a finite number of times, called *iterations*. To set the number of iterations, choose Tools ➤ Options and check the Iteration check box in the Calculations tab. Enter the number of iterations required in the Maximum Iterations box. This number must be an integer, and up to 32,767 iterations can be specified.

Summary

This chapter has introduced you to formulas and functions. The important topics covered were

- how to enter formulas manually, record them in macros, and advance into Excel VBA macro programming where you had more control over the structure representing our formulas

- the difference that names made to our formulas, making them easier to read and understand, because they always reference the same data value even if the cell is moved

- the minor but critical differences in the arithmetic operators available for use in worksheet formulas and in VBA macro code

- how to use Excel's built-in functions and how to create your own

- how to use CommandButton controls and message boxes as interactive tools for your worksheets
- what error codes are and ways of preventing them and recovering from them
- use of the Select...Case statement in your error reporting macro

CHAPTER
FIVE

5

But Names Will Never Hurt Me!

Even if you're just a casual user of Excel, you've probably already used names for identifying workbooks and worksheets. So you've already realized the benefits of using names like `Expenses` and `Inventory` instead of `Book1` and `Book2`, and you've most likely organized all of your related worksheets into logical workbooks.

In this chapter, we discuss the naming hierarchy to enable you to go a step further and refer to cells in any workbook. The various features provided by Excel for creating names, defining names, applying names, using names, and moving names are described and macro-ized. You'll see how names can help in the maintenance phase and how they can overcome problems encountered using external references.

The `InputBox` function is introduced as a means of getting a single input string from the user. A small application is developed based on the `InputBox` function that allows two inputs—the cell reference and the name. This application uses a `Masked Edit` control, to reduce the risk of errors when the cell reference is entered, along with a text box and command buttons that are placed in a `User-Form` object to become the graphical user interface (GUI) for the application. The underlying event procedures are coded with validation checks.

Hierarchy of Names

There's an inherent hierarchy in Excel that affects how cell references and names refer to workbook data. This hierarchy has three levels:

- Workbook
- Worksheet
- Cell

Workbook Level Names

The workbook level is the highest in the hierarchy. A workbook's name is its full path name, including the drive letter, folder path, filename, and three-character extension (.XLS). A workbook's name therefore contains colons, spaces, and backslash characters—in fact, it can be any valid filename in Windows:

```
c:\Accounting Ledgers\Expenses.xls
```

It's easier to find data items if filenames are chosen to describe the data they contain. Filenames can contain spaces, allowing several words to be used. Excel's generous capacity for up to 218 characters in the path and filename gives you plenty of scope for creating descriptive filenames.

Excel abbreviates this path name to the filename and uses this abbreviation as the name that it displays in the title bar of the workbook. This abbreviation can be used in cell references with or without the .XLS extension.

A cell reference that refers to cells in another workbook is called an *external* reference. External references must include the name of the workbook inside square brackets, followed by the name of the worksheet followed by an exclamation mark (!), and the cell reference or name of the cells required. The external reference for a cell named MyCell in worksheet Sheet1 in workbook Book1 would be

```
[Book1.xls]!MyCell
```

I've used the default names and added the file extension .XLS to Book1. Excel will automatically add (or delete) this extension as required.

If there are any spaces in the workbook's name or the worksheet's name, the external reference must enclose both names in single quotes, as shown in the following example.

```
'1999 Profit & Loss.xls'!MyCell
```

Worksheet Level Names

The worksheet level is next in the hierarchy. To name a worksheet, double-click its name on the tab found near the bottom of the worksheet and overtype its old name with a new name. Worksheet names can contain almost any character, provided the full path name doesn't exceed 218 characters. Excel will filter out unacceptable characters such as the backslash and forward-slash characters. Names that begin with letters or underscore characters are used as is, but names starting with any other characters or containing spaces are treated as strings and require single quotes to delimit them.

To refer to cells in another worksheet in the same workbook, you only need to refer to them by name. If the name isn't unique to the workbook or if you're using cell references, you need to specify the name of the other worksheet followed by an exclamation mark and then give the cell reference or name. I'll refer to this combination as an *internal* reference, as such references are internal to the workbook. The internal reference for a cell named MyCell in a different worksheet than the active worksheet is given as =MyCell, where the name is unique to the workbook and =Sheet1!MyCell otherwise.

If the worksheet name contains spaces or starts with a character other than a letter or underscore, then the worksheet's name must be placed in single quotes (when referring to a non-unique cell name or cell reference), such as `'1999 Profit & Loss'!MyCell`. This name can be used anywhere in the workbook, but if you refer to it in another workbook you must also include its workbook's name. A worksheet can have the same name as the workbook that contains it: `'[1999 Profit & Loss.xls]1999 Profit & Loss'!MyCell`.

NOTE   If either the workbook name or the worksheet name contains spaces, they are both enclosed in single quotes in the cell reference.

Cell Level Names

Cell level names are at the lowest level of the hierarchy and only the cell name is required to uniquely identify a cell. Excel has a few simple rules that you must follow when you define cell names:

- A name can contain only the characters a–z (upper or lower case), the numbers 0–9, a period, or an underscore character.

- Names must begin with a letter or an underscore character.

- Names must be between 1 and 256 characters in length.

- Names cannot be a cell reference, such as A1, R1C1 or T$4.

NOTE   A cell name cannot contain a space character.

Table 5.1 shows a selection of valid and invalid names.

TABLE 5.1: Valid and Invalid Cell Names

Valid Names	Invalid Names
StockLevel	Stock Level (contains a space)
Profit1998	1998Profit (starts with number)
Tax	C10 (is the same as a cell reference)

Because spaces are not allowed in cell names, you'll have to improvise using underscore characters or mixing your cases for multiple word names. Using underscores is fast becoming obsolete and case mixing more prevalent—I've mainly used mixed cases throughout this book.

Your formulas and macros will be more readable if you use uppercase for the first letter of every word in multiple word names. This will also eliminate any ambiguities that arise—such as in `transferingoldvalue`, which could be interpreted as `TransferInGoldValue` or `TransferingOldValue`.

Using upper and lower case also acts as a double check when you're entering names in formulas or macros. If you enter names in lowercase and Excel recognizes them, it will automatically change them to the upper and lower case characters to match your definition. If they don't change, chances are you've entered them wrongly.

TIP   Use upper and lower case for names. Capitalizing the first letter in each word makes names easier to read. Entering names in lower case and letting Excel automatically reformat them for you enables you to pick up any names entered incorrectly.

Cell Identifiers

Worksheets often contain tabular data with column labels along the top and row labels down the left-hand side. In essence, every cell in that table can be uniquely identified by its row and column labels. These labels can be used to identify cells in formulas in much the same way as names can.

For example, suppose a company sets up a very basic accounting system containing three workbooks, one for income, one for expenses, and one for profit and loss figures. Let's start by creating the `Profit & Loss Statement` worksheet shown in Figure 5.1:

1. Create a new workbook, choose File ➢ Save As to open the Save As dialog box, and enter **Profit & Loss** in the File Name box. Rename `Sheet2` as Summary by double-clicking `Sheet2`'s tab and overtyping it with **Summary**.

2. Choose Tools ➢ Options, select the Calculation tab, and check the Accept Labels In Formulas check box at the bottom.

FIGURE 5.1:

Profit & Loss
Statement worksheet

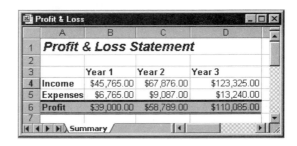

3. Enter the labels and values from cells A1 through D5 of the Summary work-sheet shown in Figure 5.1. Cell B4 can now be identified by either the row-column labels or the column-row labels combinations:

    Income Year 1

    Year 1 Income

4. Since these labels can be used as an alternative to cell references, enter the for-mula =**Income Year 1–Expenses Year 1** at cell B6 instead of entering =**B4–B5**.

5. Drag-copy the B6 formula by dragging the fill handle to include C6 and D6. Notice how Excel has updated the labels in the copied formulas to Year 2 and Year 3 in much the same way as it updates cell references.

In fact, this procedure can be streamlined even more: Because B4, B5, and B6 are in the same column, you can drop the column label and just enter =**Income–Expenses**.

Using the Create Names Dialog Box

Excel has a powerful feature that's really quite clever—you give it a selected range of cells that have row and column labels and it creates a collection of names based on these labels. The row labels can be along the top or the bottom of the table, and the column labels can be down the left-hand or right-hand side.

To create names from the labels in the Profit & Loss worksheet shown at Fig-ure 5.1, just follow the steps below and Excel will automatically create names based on the table's labels:

1. Re-enter the formula in cell B6 as =**B4–B5** and extend it to include cells C6 and D6.

2. Select cells A3 through D6.

3. Choose Insert ➣ Name ➣ Create to open the Create Names dialog box. The Top Row and Left Column check boxes will appear checked automatically because of the position of the labels (see Figure 5.2).

FIGURE 5.2:

Creating names
automatically
using labels

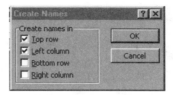

4. Click OK to define the names for the cells and to return to the active worksheet.

5. Select cell B6 and notice that the formula has not changed in any way: this is because you have to apply the names after you create them.

6. Choose Insert ➣ Name ➣ Apply to open the Apply Names dialog box (shown), select the names you want to apply, and click OK.

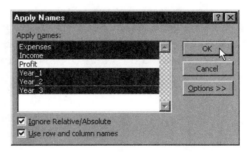

If another row or column is inserted into this range of cells, you'll need to remember to recreate these names.

TIP Create Names dialog box can be displayed using the keyboard shortcut Ctrl+Shift+F3 with a range of cells selected.

Recording a Macro to Create Cell Names

The macro below was recorded while performing steps 2 through 4 in the last example. Let's take a look at how Excel interpreted these actions into VBA code.

LISTING 5.1

```
0    Sub Macro1()
1        '
2        ' Macro1 Macro
3        ' Macro recording of using the Create Names dialog box
4        '
5        Range("A3:D6").Select
6        Selection.CreateNames Top:=True, Left:=True, _
            Bottom:=False, Right:= False
7    End Sub
```

ANALYSIS

Line 0 starts `Macro1`.

Lines 1 through 4 provide descriptive comments.

Line 5 was recorded while the range of cells A3 through D6 was selected at step 2. This has been coded using the `Select` method of the `Range` object, which changed the range of cells A3 through D6 to being selected.

Line 6 was recorded while the Create Names dialog box was displayed at steps 3 and 4. This was coded using the `Selection` property. This is equivalent to `Application.Selection`, but because the `Selection` property is used so frequently, Excel doesn't need to have the object qualifier specified explicitly. The `Selection` property identifies the range of cells in the `Range` object returned by the `Application` object. The `CreateNames` method from the `Range` object then creates the names based on the labels within this range of cells. Notice how the settings of the check boxes in the Create Names dialog box are used as arguments to the `CreateNames` method.

Line 7 ends the macro.

This macro will need the D6 updated if another year is included or another item added.

Create Names Method

The CreateNames method defines names based on the row and column labels in the range of cells that are currently selected. The syntax of the CreateNames method is:

```
expression.CreateNames(Top, Left, Bottom, Right)
```

where the expression is the range of cells, and the arguments can be True or False. Setting all the arguments to False will prevent any names from being created.

If you omit the arguments altogether, Excel guesses what names you want to create based on the labels available in the selected range of cells. This is just the same as using the Create Names dialog box shown at Figure 5.2 and clicking OK to accept Excel's check box choices.

Writing a Macro to Create Cell Names

Both the worksheet creation of names and the recorded macro examples have the drawback that they require some intervention if new rows or columns are inserted, or any row or column is deleted from the selected range of cells. Using the worksheet method, the range of cells could be moved around the worksheet and Excel would update the definitions automatically. Using the recorded macro method, the cell references were hardwired in so you would have to remember to manually update the range A3:D6 to reflect any changes made.

What's really needed is a macro that will work no matter how many rows and columns there are in a range of cells, and no matter how many cells are added or deleted. You don't want the outcome being dependent on a user remembering to recreate the names—they may not have the experience to do this and are more than likely to forget. The macro I'm about to show you is extremely adaptable—you only need to make one cell active in the table and it will create the names based on all the labels in that range irrespective of its size. Does that sound clever to you? Well, it's done with just one line of code!

LISTING 5.2

```
0    Sub CreateNamesFromLabels()
1        '
2        'Macro to create names from labels in the range of cells
3        'that includes the current cell.
4        '
```

```
5        ActiveCell.CurrentRegion.CreateNames
6   End Sub
```

Lines 0 through 4 start the macro and describe what it does.

Line 5 introduces the `CurrentRegion` property. The `ActiveCell` property identifies the active cell in the active worksheet. This is used by the `CurrentRegion` property, which propagates out from this cell to form the current region. The current region is the range of cells containing the active cell and all adjacent cells that contain values, bounded by blank rows and columns. This was the reason why row 2 was left blank in the `Profit & Loss` worksheet.

Line 6 ends the macro.

This macro shows the importance of being able to create your own macros rather than just recording them. Although this macro is more foolproof than the recorded one, it's still dependent on the user remembering to select an active cell in the range required before running the macro. A message box (introduced in Chapter 4) could be used here as a reminder to do this, but that still doesn't guarantee they'll actually do it.

What's needed is a dialog box similar to a message box but one that requires the user to enter the cell reference before being able to continue. Excel VBA provides an `InputBox` function that creates a dialog box containing a text box. Let's look at this `InputBox` function, then we'll get back to polishing off this macro in the section called "Finishing the `CreateNamesFromLabels` Macro."

Customizing Input Boxes in Macros

The input box is a great way to retrieve some text from a user. You can display your input box with a message or a question which the user must respond to, either by entering text as their reply or by clicking the OK or Cancel buttons. The message could be a question such as "What is your name?" or simply some prompt for a piece of information, such as a cell reference, that's required before your macro can continue to run. Figure 5.3 shows an input box that requires the user to enter the description of a stock item.

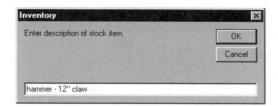

The input box is just a variation of the dialog box that is created and displayed using the InputBox function. It's similar to the MsgBox function you saw earlier in Chapter 4 in that it displays a dialog box for user interaction. Where the message box provides a message and does all its interaction with buttons, the input box prompts the user for information and provides a text box for them to enter their response before clicking the OK or Cancel buttons.

The syntax for calling the InputBox function is:

InputBox(*prompt*[,*title*][,*default*][,*xpos*][,*ypos*][,*helpfile*,*context*])

- prompt: The prompt is the only argument that is required by the InputBox function. This is simply a string expression containing up to 1024 characters that can be formatted using a carriage return (ASCII character 13), linefeed (ASCII character 10), or tab (ASCII character 9).

- title: This is optional, but if specified it's the caption displayed along the title bar of the input box. If it isn't specified, the default title "Microsoft Excel" is displayed.

- default: This is optional and is the text string that appears in the text box when the input box is displayed. The user can click OK to accept this text, or they can overtype it to whatever value they require.

- xpos, ypos: These are optional; if given, the xpos specifies the horizontal distance between the left border of the input box and the left edge of the screen and the ypos specifies the vertical distance between the top border of the input box and the top edge of the screen. Both the xpos and ypos measurements are in twips, which are the default units of measurement in the default coordinate system used by VBA for all dialog boxes and control objects that require screen coordinates. This default coordinate system has its origin placed at the top-left corner of the screen. Twips are device independent, with 1440 twips being equivalent to one inch, ensuring that the output will look the same irrespective of the resolution of the screen.

- `helpfile`, `context`: The `helpfile` and `context` are discussed in Chapter 22 and are defaulted to the Help Assistant in Windows 98.

As with the `MsgBox` function, you only need to specify the prompt and can omit any of the other arguments. Optional arguments skipped from the end of the argument list can simply be left out. But if you want to specify an optional argument after skipping some, you must insert a comma (`,`) delimiter for each optional argument skipped up to the one you want to specify. Remember that Excel uses these commas to match up the arguments in your call with those in the `InputBox` function.

Getting the Answer from the *InputBox* Function

The `InputBox` function returns the contents of its text box when the user presses the Return key or clicks OK. The zero-length empty string is returned if the user clicks Cancel.

The `GetStockDescription` macro given below provides an example of how the `InputBox` function is called from VBA code. This macro generates the input box shown in Figure 5.3. Only the first two arguments were given to specify the prompt and the caption on the title bar.

LISTING 5.3

```
0    Sub GetStockDescription()
1        '
2        'Macro to get a stock item's description from the user
3        '
4        StockItemDescription = Inputbox("Enter description of _
         stock item.", "Inventory")
5    End Sub
```

ANALYSIS

Lines 0 through 3 start the `GetStockDescription` macro and describe what it does.

Line 4 calls the InputBox function to display the input box shown at Figure 5.3. The string variable StockItemDescription is assigned the string hammer - 12" claw returned by the InputBox function when the user clicks OK or depresses the Return key.

Line 5 ends the macro.

Finishing the *CreateNamesFromLabels* Macro

Now that you know the details about the InputBox function, let's finish off the CreateNamesFromLabels macro shown in Listing 5.2. I'll show you how to extend this macro by including a call to the InputBox function that (we hope) will ensure that the user responds with the correct cell reference. This macro asks the user to enter a cell from the range of cells they want names created for, and continues by creating the names of cells in that range based on the row and column labels.

Let's be friendly to the user by having the text box display the cell reference of the active cell that is most likely to be the one required (Figure 5.4). This serves a double purpose, as it also lets the user know the expected style for their entry if they wish to change it. This is about as far as you can go in making your macro fail-safe; you can't do anything else but depend on the user giving a cell in the correct range.

LISTING 5.4

```
0    Sub CreateNamesFromLabels()
1        '
2        'Macro to create names from labels in the range of cells
3        'that includes the current cell.
4        '
5        UsersChoice = InputBox("Enter cell in range!", _
         "Create Names from Labels Macro", _
         Chr(ActiveCell.Column + 64) & ActiveCell.Row)
6        If UsersChoice then
7            Range(UsersChoice).Activate
8            ActiveCell.CurrentRegion.CreateNames
9        End If
10   End Sub
```

FIGURE 5.4:

Input box with cell reference already entered

ANALYSIS

Lines 0 through 4 start the `CreateNamesFromLabels` macro and describe what it does.

Line 5 uses the `Chr` function (see "Formatting Your Message" in Chapter 4) to assign the cell reference for the active cell to the default string that will be displayed automatically in the text box when the input box opens; all the user has to do is click OK to accept it. Alternatively, the user can enter a cell from another table. The variable `UsersChoice` is assigned whatever string the `InputBox` function returns from this text box. (That string needs to be a cell reference, so it should be validated—but I'll skip that for now and deal with it later in the section "Masked Edit Control.")

Line 6 tests whether the user actually made an entry in the input box, but doesn't go as far as testing whether the entry made is a valid cell reference. `UsersChoice` is considered to be `False` if it represents the empty string (string with no characters).

Line 7 uses the `Range` object to select the cell referenced by `UsersChoice`, and the `Activate` method designates it to be the active cell.

Line 8 uses the `ActiveCell` property to return the active cell, which is propagated outwards by the `CurrentRegion` property, until it hits blank rows and columns, to form the current region. The `CreateNames` method then creates the names based on the labels in this region.

Line 9 ends the `If` statement.

Line 10 ends the macro.

Name Box for Handling Names

You've just seen the Create Names dialog box create multiple names based on labels for ranges of cells containing values in tabular form. But often you may want to create only one name, or create names when the structure of your data is not in tabular form. Then you can use the Name box to create one name at a time.

The Name box is situated to the left of the formula bar and displays the name of the active cell, if it has a name; otherwise it displays the cell reference. The name of the active cell can be redefined by overwriting it in the Name box. (Remember to hit the Return key to finalize your definition. If you don't hit Return, the Name box will revert back to its previous contents.)

Click the Down arrow at the right of the Name box to display its drop-down list, which contains all the names that have already been defined in the active worksheet, listed in alphabetical order. Selecting a name from the drop-down list moves it into the top position in the Name box and highlights the cell it defines, making that cell the active one.

Take a look at the list of names in the Name box with your `Profit & Loss` worksheet active (as shown). In particular, look at how Excel has replaced the space in the column labels by an underscore character to make the names valid.

NOTE   When Excel creates a name based on a label, any space characters in the label are automatically replaced with underscore characters.

Recording a Macro for Adding a Name Using the Name Box

The following macro recorded adding the name `ProfitAndLoss` to the worksheet as a new definition for cell A1.

LISTING 5.5

```
0    Sub Macro2()
1        '
2        'Macro2 Macro
3        'Macro to name cell using Name Box
4        '
5        Range("A1").Select
6        ActiveWorkbook.Names.Add Name:="ProfitAndLoss", _
         RefersToR1C1:= "=~CA'Profit & Loss'!R1C1"
7    End Sub
```

ANALYSIS

Lines 0 through 4 start Macro2 and describe what it does.

Line 5 was recorded when cell A1 was selected.

Line 6 uses the ActiveWorkbook property to return the Workbook object. The Names property of this Workbook object is set to the Names collection; names from this Names collection are the names displayed in the Name box's drop-down list. The Add method adds the name assigned to its Name argument (ProfitAndLoss) and makes it refer to the argument assigned to its RefersToR1C1 property ('Profit & Loss'!R1C1). The exclamation mark (!) lets you know that Profit & Loss is the name of a worksheet, and you already know that RefersToR1C1 always works in the R1C1 reference style—the R1C1 is equivalent to A1.

Line 7 ends the macro.

Macro-izing Adding a Name

The following macro is just another version of the same thing, but this macro expects the active cell to be selected before it's called.

LISTING 5.6

```
0    Sub AssignNameToActiveCell()
1        '
```

```
2          'Macro to assign name to active cell
3          '
4          ActiveCell.Name = "ProfitAndLoss"
5     End Sub
```

Lines 0 through 3 start the `AssignNameToActiveCell` macro and provide descriptive information.

Line 4 uses the `ActiveCell` property to return the `Range` object identifying the active cell, then uses its `Name` property to assign the string `"ProfitAnd-Loss"`. Excel takes care of the rest for us by adding this name with the cell reference of the active cell to the `Names` collection for the active workbook.

Line 5 ends the macro.

This macro could be extended by calling the `InputBox` function at the start of the macro in the same way as the `CreateNamesFromLabels` macro. Doing so would ensure that the name was always explicitly defined by the user.

Duplicate Names in the Hierarchy

Worksheet level names override workbook level names if they're used in the worksheet where they are defined. Because names must be unique, when Excel creates names based on labels, these labels must also be unique. Let's continue to expand on your `Profit & Loss` example:

1.   On the Summary worksheet in the `Profit & Loss` workbook, add the labels and data values from A8 through D9, as shown in Figure 5.5.

2.   Select cells A8 through D9, then choose Insert ➤ Name ➤ Create to display the Create Names dialog box (shown in Figure 5.2). The Top Row and Left Column settings will be checked as before.

3.   Click OK.

In this example, there are four duplicate labels: `Year 1`, `Year 2`, `Year 3`, and `Profit`. When Excel tries to create the names based on these labels, it displays a message box for each duplication, asking if you want to replace the existing definition. The first message reported is shown at Figure 5.6. (Your message box may look somewhat different depending whether you are using the Office Assistant feature.) Clicking Yes deletes the first definition, leaving cells in the range A3:D6 without a name; clicking No cancels the current name definition, leaving the new cell without a name. Clicking Cancel aborts the naming process altogether and no more message boxes will be displayed.

FIGURE 5.5:

Extended Profit &
Loss worksheet

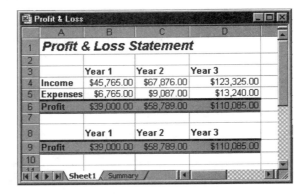

FIGURE 5.6:

Message box displaying
duplication warning

WARNING   Names must be unique, and because they are based on labels, the labels themselves must also be unique.

To avoid the duplicate names problem, let's move your two rows of summary information into a different worksheet:

1. Click Cancel to abort the process of creating names.

2. Rename Sheet1 as Profit & Loss (double-click Sheet1's tab and overtype with Profit & Loss).

3. Cut and paste the bottom two lines (A8:D9) from the Summary worksheet into the Profit & Loss worksheet (as shown in Figure 5.7).

FIGURE 5.7:

Profit & Loss worksheet

4. Select cells A1:D2 and choose Insert ➤ Name ➤ Create to display the Create Names dialog box (shown in Figure 5.2) with the Top Row and Left Column settings checked. Click OK.

5. Click Year_1 in the Name box drop-down list; cell B2 will be highlighted.

6. Click the Summary tab to return to the previous worksheet, and click Year_1 in the Name box list; the range of cells B4:B5 will be highlighted.

7. Select the Profit & Loss worksheet tab to make that the active worksheet.

8. Choose Insert ➤ Name ➤ Define to open the Define Name dialog box. You'll see that the worksheet's name has been listed beside the four names that Excel created from duplicate labels (see Figure 5.8). This is how duplicate names are defined in different worksheets.

NOTE   Defining two or more cells with the same name is allowed only if they belong to different worksheets.

FIGURE 5.8:

Define Name dialog box

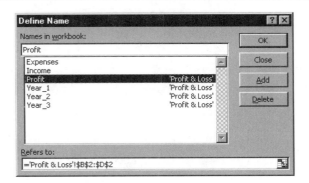

All of the names you've added to the active worksheet will appear in alphabetical order in the Name box drop-down list, with the last name entered taking pride of place in the Name box itself.

Creating Names with the Define Name Dialog Box

The Define Name dialog box can be used as an alternative to the Name box for defining names for cells, but it goes one step further: it allows you to define a name for a formula without the formula needing to be associated with any particular cell.

To Define One Name

It is possible to name a single cell even though it is inside a table. The following steps show how this is done.

1. Select the cell to be named.
2. Choose Insert ➤ Name ➤ Define to open the Define Name dialog box (see Figure 5.8).
3. Enter the new name into the Names In Workbook box to add the name to the alphabetically ordered list. The cell reference for the selected cell will be displayed in the Refers To box.
4. Click OK to return to the worksheet. The new name will now be displayed in the Name box.

To Define Several Names

If you have more than one name to define, it's much quicker to use the Add button to avoid having to keep reopening the Define Name dialog box. Replace step 4 of the steps listed in "To Define One Name" with the following steps:

4. Click Add.
5. Enter the first name into the Names In Workbook box.
6. Enter the cell reference for the cell you're naming in the Refers To box.
7. Continue to do steps 4 through 6 until all the names have been entered.
8. Click OK to return to the worksheet.

Keyboard shortcuts are available for defining names—for example, Ctrl+F3 will display the Define Names dialog box.

Recording a Macro to Define a Name

The following macro recorded the actions involved in naming a formula without it being entered into a cell. Because it isn't associated with a cell, its value won't actually appear in any cell. Such formulas are meant to be used by other formulas and macros, and often make them more understandable (in much the same way as does using names to define cells).

LISTING 5.7

```
0    Sub Macro3()
1        '
2        'Macro3 Macro
3        'Macro recorded for formula without cell
4        '
5        ActiveWorkbook.Names.Add Name:="TotalProfit", _
         RefersToR1C1:= _
         "=Profit Year_1 + Profit Year_2 + Profit Year_3"
6    End Sub
```

ANALYSIS

Lines 0 through 4 start the macro and provide descriptive information.

Line 5 uses the Add method to add a Name object to the Names collection with the name and the formula passed to it as arguments. The Names collection is identified by the Names property of the Workbook object. The Workbook object represents the active workbook, which is identified by the ActiveWorkbook property. Notice how the formula for adding the three years of profit is substituted for the cell reference in the RefersToR1C1 argument in the same way as when you entered your formula into the Refers To box in the Define Name dialog box.

Line 6 ends the macro.

Macro-izing Defining a Name

One of the benefits of writing your own macros is that you can make them as generic as you like—the more generic the better, as this increases their reusability. Let's write a macro that displays a UserForm as its means of interaction with the user. (UserForms are discussed in detail in Chapter 10.) I'll show you how to make this UserForm behave like a sophisticated Input Box that will retrieve the cell reference and the new name from the user and complete the cell definition for you. The following steps show how this is done.

1.   Open a new workbook and open the Visual Basic Editor.

2.   Choose Insert ≻ UserForm to create a new UserForm. As shown in Figure 5.9, the Toolbox should also appear, with controls that you can drag and drop onto your new form. If the Toolbox is not displayed, choosing View ≻ Toolbox in the Visual Basic Editor will display it.

FIGURE 5.9:

UserForm

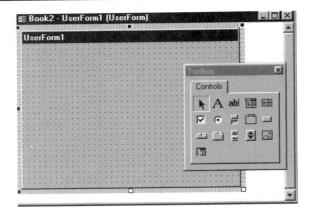

3.   Right-click anywhere on the UserForm and choose Properties from the shortcut menu (as shown) to open the Properties window for UserForm1.

4. Change the `Caption` property by overtyping `UserForm1` with **Naming A Cell** in the Properties window and watch your keystrokes being transferred to the title bar as you type.

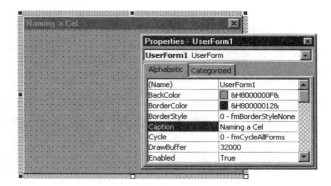

To make the macro fail-safe, you need to be sure that the user will enter a valid cell reference. You can do this by using a `Masked Edit` control instead of a text box for the cell reference entry. That way, the user is forced to enter an A1 style reference as a letter followed by a digit.

Masked Edit Control

The `Masked Edit` ActiveX control is similar to a text box control but has the additional feature of an input mask that can be set to ensure that characters of the correct type are entered into the box. The `Masked Edit` control is not one of the standard controls already in the Toolbox, but must be added to your Toolbox from the list of extra controls available to VBA. You only need to add this control once and it'll appear in your Toolbox thereafter. Let's extend your `Naming A Cell` example by adding a `Masked Edit` control to the Toolbox. To add this control to your Toolbox:

1. Right-click the Toolbox and choose Additional Controls from the shortcut menu. The Additional Controls dialog box, shown in Figure 5.10, will appear, displaying a list of all the controls that can be placed on a UserForm.

2. Check the check box for Microsoft Masked Edit Control, Version 6.0 and click OK. The dialog box will close and the `Masked Edit` control will be appended to the bottom of your Toolbox, as shown below.

FIGURE 5.10:

Additional Controls dialog
box

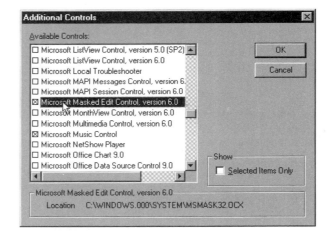

An input mask is defined by setting the Mask property of the Masked Edit control to a sequence of mask characters. The keystrokes entered by the user are checked against the corresponding character positions in the mask. If the character entered is not the correct type, a Validation Error is generated and the keystroke is rejected, with a Windows default sound played for emphasis.

The mask comprises a set of placeholders of specified types and literals. *Literals* are characters, such as $ and % (dollars and percentages), that are placed at specific positions to indicate that you want those actual characters to appear at those positions. The insertion point automatically jumps over these literals as characters are entered by the user.

The *Mask* Property

The Mask property defines an input mask, which is a sequence of mask characters that each define a type. The mask characters available and the types they represent are listed in Table 5.2.

TABLE 5.2: Mask Characters

Mask Character	Placeholder Type
#	digit
.	decimal point literal
,	thousands separator literal
:	time separator literal
/	date separator literal
\	allows mask characters to be marked as literals
&	character
A	alphanumeric
?	letter
Literal	considers all other symbols to be literals

Finishing the *Naming A Cell* UserForm

Let's continue developing the Naming A Cell UserForm. Your Toolbox should now contain a Masked Edit control; if it doesn't, you'll need to go back to the section called "Masked Edit Control" earlier in this chapter. To pick up where you left off:

1. Drag and drop two Label controls onto the UserForm and change their Caption properties to Cell Reference and Name, as shown in Figure 5.11.

FIGURE 5.11:

The Naming A Cell
UserForm

2. Drag and drop a Masked Edit control and position it beside the Cell Reference label.

3. Set the Masked Edit control's Mask property by right-clicking the control and choosing Properties from the shortcut menu. Next to the Mask property, enter ?# to restrict input to a single letter followed by a single digit.

4. Drag and drop a TextBox control and position it beside the Name label.

5. Drag and drop two CommandButton controls and update their Caption properties to OK and Cancel. Update their Name properties (the first entry in the Properties window) to OKButton and CancelButton—these will be the names they'll be known as in the macro. Set their Accelerator properties to O and C, to make these the access keys for these CommandButton controls. The O and the C will automatically appear underlined to let the user know they can be used in combination with the Alt key. The O can be in uppercase or lowercase, since there's only one O in OK. The C must be in uppercase to make the first c underlined as selectable; otherwise the second c will be underlined.

What you've done with the UserForm is developed the graphical user interface for what can now be called an application, since it's becoming a lot more than just a macro added to a workbook. The next step is to code the events that you want the application to respond to—I've chosen three that are described in the following sections.

Event 1: User clicks OK button.

In response to the OK button being clicked, make the cell specified in the Masked Edit control the active cell and define it by the name entered in the text box. The UserForm can then be closed. To code this, double-click the OK button on the UserForm to open the code window displaying the skeleton event procedure (Line 0 and Line 5 in Listing 5.8), then enter Lines 1 through 4 from the code shown in Listing 5.8.

An event procedure is like a macro, but it will be executed only in response to a particular user interaction (event) occurring. So, in general, event procedures can't actually be called in code like a macro or function but can be called from other event procedures in the same class module. The event procedures available for the different controls are predetermined by Excel VBA and are outside of your control.

LISTING 5.8

```
0    Private Sub OKButton_Click()
1        'user clicked OK
2        Range(MaskEdBox1.Text).Select
3        ActiveCell.Name = TextBox1.Text
4        UserForm1.Hide
5    End Sub
```

ANALYSIS

This event procedure is executed when the command button named OKButton is clicked.

Line 0 is the start of the OKButton_Click event procedure.

Line 1 is a comment.

Line 2 selects the cell reference entered in the Masked Edit box, making it both the selected and the active cell.

Line 3 defines the name entered into the text box as the name of the active cell.

Line 4 hides the UserForm named UserForm1 from the user.

Line 5 ends the event procedure.

Event 2: User clicks Cancel button.

The response required to the user clicking the command button named Cancel-Button is to ignore any input and hide the UserForm. CancelButton is included so that the user can retreat confidently, knowing that nothing has been changed.

Let's code the actions required for the response in the event that the user clicks the Cancel button. Double-click the `CancelButton` on the UserForm to open the code window displaying the skeleton event procedure (Line 0 and Line 3 in Listing 5.9), then enter Lines 1 and 2 shown in Listing 5.9.

LISTING 5.9

```
0    Private Sub CancelButton_Click()
1         'user clicked Cancel
2         UserForm1.Hide
3    End Sub
```

ANALYSIS

This event procedure is executed when the user clicks the command button with `Caption` property `Cancel`.

Line 0 starts the `CancelButton_Click` event procedure.

Line 1 is a comment.

Line 2 hides the UserForm from the user, disregarding any data entered by the user.

Line 3 ends the event procedure.

Event 3: User depresses Tab key in Masked Edit box.

If the user presses the Tab key in the Masked Edit box they'll expect the vertical entry cursor to appear in the text box, so let's not disappoint them. Double-click the `Masked Edit Box` control on the UserForm to open the code window displaying the skeleton procedure for the `Change` event. The `Change` event is the primary event for the Masked Edit box, just like the `Click` event is the primary event for command buttons. To respond to the Tab key being pressed, you must enter your response in the `KeyPress` event procedure. You can select the `KeyPress` event from the drop-down list that's displayed when you click the Down arrow in the Procedure box. Enter the code shown in Listing 5.10.

LISTING 5.10

```
0    Private Sub MaskEdBox1_KeyPress(KeyAscii As Integer)
1        If KeyAscii = vbKeyTab Then 'tab key has been depressed
2            'check valid cell reference
3        End If
4    End Sub
```

ANALYSIS

This event procedure is executed when the user depresses any keyboard key while the Masked Edit control has the focus. This control already has its Mask property set to accept a letter followed by a digit, but the mask won't stop the user from depressing the Tab key prematurely to move to the TextBox control unless you write the code to intervene.

Line 0 starts the MaskEdBox1_KeyPress event procedure.

Line 1 uses the vbKeyTab constant from the list of VBA KeyCodeConstants that can be viewed in the Object Browser, as shown. This constant is used to test whether the Tab key has been pressed. The Tab key is one of the nonprintable characters and has the ASCII code of 9.

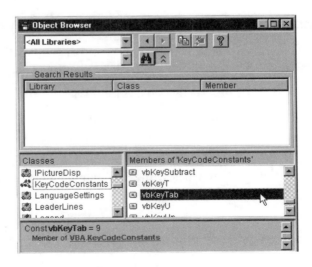

Line 2 is only accessed if the user has pressed the Tab key. I've put a comment here for now until it's clear what other validation is necessary elsewhere.

Line 3 ends the If statement.

Line 4 ends the event procedure.

Macro to Display the UserForm

Now let's create a macro that'll display your UserForm every time you run it. This macro has to be entered into a module before you can run it from your worksheet. Choose Insert ➢ Module to open the code window for Module1 and enter the code shown in Listing 5.11.

LISTING 5.11

```
0    Sub GetCellAndName()
1        UserForm1.Show
2        End
3    End Sub
```

ANALYSIS

This macro will be listed in the Macro dialog box that's displayed when you click Run Macro from the Visual Basic toolbar in Excel.

Line 0 starts the GetCellAndName macro.

Line 1 displays the UserForm on the screen. The UserForm sits there waiting for an occurrence of one of the three events that it has been coded to respond to.

Line 2 shows how the End statement is used to terminate the execution of your application.

Line 3 ends the macro.

When you're trying to make an application foolproof, you've got to think about the mistakes a user could make. In this application, what would happen if the user missed part of the cell reference or didn't enter any name in the text box? There are three ways the user can terminate the entry of the cell reference: by pressing the Tab key, by clicking the OK button, or by clicking in the text box. (Clicking Cancel is not considered here, as the text entered is disregarded when this happens so won't cause any errors.) The responses to the first two of these events are handled in the MaskEdBox1_KeyPress and the OKButton_Click event procedures. The third event is equivalent to pressing the Tab key. Terminating the name entry is achieved by clicking the OK button, so this should be handled in the OKButton_Click event procedure.

Because you have to validate the cell reference in both the MaskEdBox1_KeyPress and OKButton_Click event procedures, it's better to write a ValidateInput function and call it from both places. Because both of the calling procedures are local to the UserForm, you can enter the ValidateInput function in the General (object) Declarations (Procedure) section of UserForm1. There are three possible outcomes from the ValidateInput function: the cell reference is invalid (returns 0), the name is missing (returns 1), or the cell reference is valid and the name has been entered (returns 2). No checks have been included here to verify that the name is in fact a valid name in Excel terms.

Enter the ValidateInput function shown in Listing 5.12 into the General-Declarations section of UserForm1 and update the MaskEdBox1_KeyPress event procedure (insert Lines 2 through 6 from Listing 5.13) and OKButton_Click event procedure (insert Lines 2 through 6 from Listing 5.14).

LISTING 5.12

```
0    Function ValidateInput() As Integer
1        ' returns 0 if invalid cell reference
2        ' returns 1 if no name entered
3        ' returns 2 if cell reference and name are valid
4        If Right(MaskEdBox1.Text, 1) = "_" Or _
         Left(MaskEdBox1.Text, 1) = "_" Then
5            Beep
6            ValidateInput = 0
7        ElseIf TextBox1.Text = "" Then
8            ValidateInput = 1
9        Else
10           ValidateInput = 2
11       End If
12   End Function
```

ANALYSIS

Line 0 starts the `ValidateInput` function.

Lines 1 through 3 are comments providing information about the values returned by the function.

Lines 4 through 10 indicate that the `Text` property of the `MaskEdBox1` will be assigned to underscore characters, one for each mask character. This `If` statement uses the `Left` and `Right` functions to check whether either of the underscore characters still exists. If they do, this means that all or part of the cell reference is missing, which renders the cell reference invalid; then the function returns a zero by assigning a zero to the function's name. If the cell reference is valid, the `ElseIf` at Line 7 is executed. Line 7 checks whether the text box is empty, and if it is, returns 1; if it isn't, the `Else` part is executed and both the cell reference and the name are deemed to be valid, so the function returns 2.

Line 11 ends the `If` statement.

Line 12 ends the function.

Left and Right Functions

The `Left` and `Right` functions both have two arguments—a string and the number of characters to retrieve from the start (`Left`) or end (`Right`) of the string. They both return a string containing the substring required.

LISTING 5.13

```
0    Private Sub MaskEdBox1_KeyPress(KeyAscii As Integer)
1        If KeyAscii = vbKeyTab Then 'tab key has been depressed
2            If ValidateInput = 0 Then 'invalid cell reference
3                MaskEdBox1.SetFocus
4            ElseIf ValidateInput = 1 Then 'valid cell reference _
             but no name
5                TextBox1.SetFocus
6            End If
7        End If
8    End Sub
```

Lines 2 through 6, which were added to the original procedure, will place the entry cursor back in the Masked Edit box if the cell reference is invalid, or in the text box if the name hasn't been entered. The `SetFocus` method gives the focus to the control it belongs to, which automatically places the entry cursor into these controls.

LISTING 5.14

```
0    Private Sub OKButton_Click()
1        'user clicked OK
2        If ValidateInput = 0 Then 'invalid cell reference
3            MaskEdBox1.SetFocus
4        ElseIf ValidateInput = 1 Then 'no name entered
5            TextBox1.SetFocus
6        ElseIf ValidateInput = 2 Then 'valid cell reference and name
7            Range(MaskEdBox1.Text).Select
8            ActiveCell.Name = TextBox1.Text
9            UserForm1.Hide
10       End If
11   End Sub
```

ANALYSIS

Lines 2 through 6 check for any problems with the input before selecting and naming the active cell.

Advantages of Names for Maintenance

Chapter 4 demonstrated that names made formulas and macros much easier to read and understand. During the creation phase, names also make formulas or macros easier to write. When the creation phase is finished and your formula or macro goes into active service, it then enters into the maintenance phase of its life cycle. This phase is by far the longest; it continues for the duration of the formula's life, which could be several years. During this phase, your formula or macro may need to be updated several times.

Maintenance Example

To demonstrate the advantage of names in the maintenance phase, let's consider two companies that both need to record depreciation values of a piece of machinery they are purchasing. Each piece of machinery is to cost $10,000 and has an expected life of five years, after which it is expected to be sold as scrap for the residual value of $500.

By coincidence, employees at both companies enter the year the machinery was purchased in cell E4, the cost in cell F4, the expected life in H4, and the residual value in I4 (see Figure 5.12). A provision for depreciation is to be done annually, with the annual amount calculated by taking the scrap value from the cost and dividing the amount by the expected lifetime.

The first company enters the formula for evaluating the annual provision for depreciation per year in cell J4 as

```
=(F4-I4)/H4
```

with the formula for accumulating the amount depreciated entered in cell G4 as

```
= (YEAR(NOW( ))-E4) * (F4-I4)/H4
```

NOTE　　YEAR(NOW( )) calls the **NOW** worksheet function to return the serial number depicting the current date and time. The **YEAR** function uses this serial number to evaluate the current year.

Figure 5.12 shows the worksheet with these formulas already evaluated. The current year returned by the **YEAR** function was 1999; using the same values and formulas in any other year will yield different results.

FIGURE 5.12:

Depreciation workbook

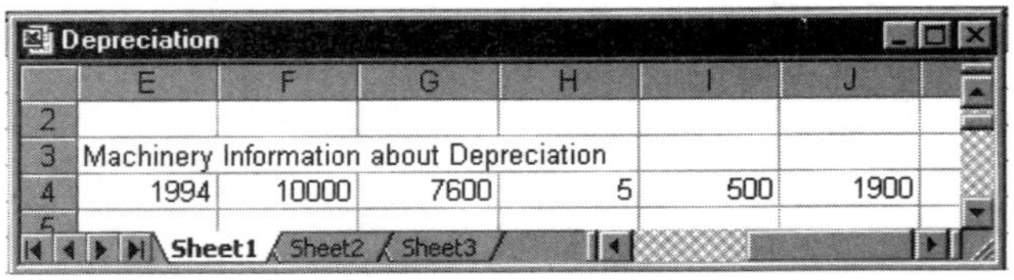

The second company names its cells, defining cells E4 through J4 as YearOf-Purchase, Cost, AccumulatedDepreciation, Life, ResidualValue, and Annual-Depreciation, respectively, and enters the annual depreciation formula in cell J4 as

```
=(Cost-ResidualValue)/Life
```

with the accumulated depreciation formula entered in cell G4 as

```
= (Year(Now( ))-YearOfPurchase)*(Cost-ResidualValue)/Life
```

This worksheet produces exactly the same results as the first company's.

At the end of the five years, the machinery is replaced by new equipment and both companies set about entering the new values to record the provision for depreciation for this new equipment. These new values are to replace the old machinery's values in the worksheet.

The first company has to search for the worksheet containing the information, then they have to track down the range of cells where the data values and formulas were entered. I'm sure this situation will be familiar to most of you—it sometimes feels like you're looking for a needle in a haystack. When they've found the data, they then have to work out what values to replace.

In the meantime, the second company has opened their workbook and selected the AccumulatedDepreciation name from the Name box drop-down list (as shown), which opens up the worksheet required and highlights cell G4.

The employee selects Cost from the Name box drop-down list and cell F4 is highlighted, ready for entering the cost of the new equipment. The new data values can all be entered in much the same way; using names to directly access cells clarifies what data values should be entered at individual cells.

Selecting Cells for Naming

The reasons behind naming cells are exactly the same as the reasons why you name workbooks or files. The names make it easier to organize your data and easier to find whatever you're looking for. But if you were to name every cell in your workbook it would defeat the purpose, as having so many names would make it harder to find any particular data value.

You may find it helpful to name cells referenced by more than one formula, provided they can't be identified using their row and column labels. Names could also be given to all cells containing formulas to save relentless searches through workbooks.

You should carefully choose meaningful names that reflect the data values they represent. A cell's name is meant to be much easier to interpret than its cell reference, so don't use cryptic names if you can avoid it. If you have difficulty in coming up with a name, ask yourself what you would search for in a list of names if you ever needed to access that data value again.

In years gone by, names were often limited in length so cryptic names were essential, but Excel now allows names to be up to 256 characters in length. So unpronounceable names like B4EOY should be a thing of the past and should be replaced by names that are spelled out in full, such as `BeforeEndOfYear`. However, if you're restricted to eight characters because of other software packages being used, you'll just have to do your best.

TIP   Call a spade a spade, then you'll be able to find the named data when you need it.

Direct Access to Named Cells

In Excel it's extremely easy to end up with heaps of numbers and quickly forget where specific formulas and data values have been placed. This is a big disadvantage if you need to update anything, as you may have to explore your whole worksheet cell by cell, looking for the formula or data value required.

There are obvious places you can look for formulas, but you can never really be sure. I've seen a worksheet containing a `Balance Sheet` with an item labeled `Discrepancy Funds` listed between `Bank Balance` and `Petty Cash`. The value next to `Discrepancy Funds` was the result returned by a formula that made sure that no matter what was entered in the other worksheet cells, the `Discrepancy Funds` value would be adjusted accordingly so the `Balance Sheet` would inevitably always balance. This is not the way to go.

You can avoid manually searching for formulas in your worksheet by letting Excel highlight them for you.

Highlighting All the Formula Cells in a Worksheet

I've already stressed how using names can make your formulas and macros easier to understand, but naming cells containing formulas also has the additional benefit of allowing direct access to the cells required. Simply choose Edit ➣ Go To to display the Go To dialog box containing a list of all the names that define cells in all the worksheets in the active workbook.

In the screen illustrated in Figure 5.13, the `Depreciation` workbook was opened before the Go To dialog box was displayed.

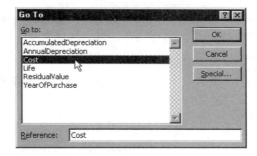

Selecting a name highlights the cell or range of cells associated with that name. This direct access provided by the Go To dialog box is the fastest way of accessing named cells in a large data model, especially one that's spread over several worksheets.

If you want to highlight all of the formula cells in your worksheet, click Special to display the Go To Special dialog box (shown at Figure 5.14).

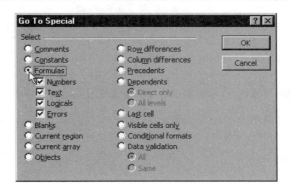

Select the Formulas option button to make the four related check boxes selectable. These check boxes select all the cells containing formulas that evaluate respectively to

- a number (Numbers)
- a text string (Text)
- True or False (Logicals)
- an Error Value (Errors)

The default is for all four check boxes to be selected. Click OK to return to the worksheet. All cells containing formulas will be highlighted, as shown in Figure 5.15, irrespective of whether the formula cell was defined by a name.

FIGURE 5.15:

Depreciation worksheet with both formula cells highlighted

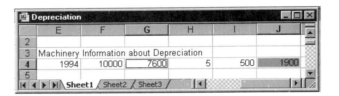

To highlight all of the cells containing data values, as shown at Figure 5.16, select the Constants option button from the Go To Special dialog box.

FIGURE 5.16:

Depreciation worksheet with cells containing constant values highlighted

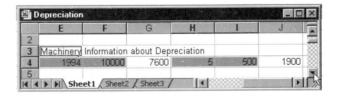

Applying Names to Formulas

After you've defined names for cells in your worksheet, you can apply them to any formulas you create. But what about existing formulas—wouldn't it be great if you could just change all their cell references to names? Well, this is easier than you'd think! You can tell Excel what names you want to apply and it will all be done for you.

The following steps show you how:

1. Open your Profit & Loss worksheet in the Profit & Loss workbook that you created in the section "Using the Create Names Dialog Box" earlier in this chapter.

2. Choose Insert ➤ Name ➤ Apply to display the Apply Names dialog box shown.

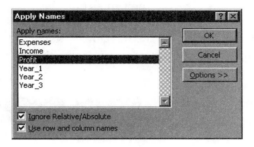

3. Select all the names you want to apply by holding down the Shift key and clicking the names required.

4. Click OK to apply the names to formulas in the active worksheet.

Clicking Options extends the Apply Names dialog box to provide extra facilities for applying names. The extended version offers a few extra features, as shown here.

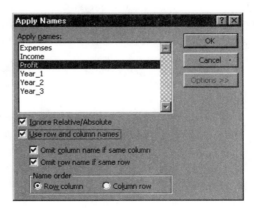

- The Ignore Relative/Absolute check box, if checked, replaces all references with their names irrespective of the referencing mode used for the cell reference. The Use Row And Column Names check box, if checked, will use the row and column names if the cells don't already have their names defined.

- The Omit Column Name If Same Column and Omit Row Name If Same Row check boxes determine whether both the row and column names should be included or just one of them. The option buttons in the Name Order frame allow you to specify the order when both row and column names are to be used.

To check whether the names have been applied correctly, select one of the cells containing a formula that references one of the named cells. The cell reference(s) should be replaced by the name(s) depicting the labels. Figure 5.17 shows cell B6 selected and the cell name replacing the cell reference in the formula bar.

FIGURE 5.17:

Result of names being applied to the formula at cell B6 in the Profit & Loss worksheet

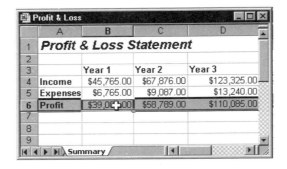

Only the row labels have been applied to this formula, because all the cell references that each formula contains belong in the same column. The same thing happens when all cell references in the formula belong to the same row.

1. Create a new workbook and call it Income by choosing File ➤ Save As to rename it.

2. Rename Sheet1 as Years 96-98 by double-clicking the Sheet1 tab and overtyping.

3. Copy the labels and values from cells A1 through D5, as shown in Figure 5.18. Insert the formula **=SUM(B3:D3)** at cell E3 and drag it down to cell E5 to give the totals shown.

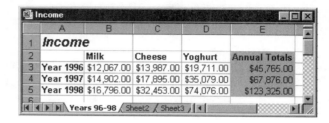

4. Choose Insert ➤ Name ➤ Apply. This time the Apply Names dialog box will only highlight the names you have just added, as shown.

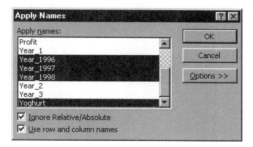

5. Click OK.

Select the cell containing the function and notice how both the row and column labels are used to replace the cell references, with =SUM(B3:D3) being replaced by =SUM((Year_1996 Milk):(Year_1996 Yoghurt)).

Applying Names to Formulas Using Macros

Applying names to the cell references in a formula unfortunately doesn't have any effect on the cell references in formulas that are coded in macros, only on the formula that appears in the formula bar.

Let's record what happens when you select a range of cells and choose the Insert ➤ Name ➤ Apply menu command. The macro recorded is shown in Listing 5.15.

LISTING 5.15

```
0    Sub ApplyNamesToIncome()
1        '
2        ' ApplyNamesToIncome Macro
3        ' Macro recorded to apply names to income worksheet
4        '
5        Range("A2:E5").Select
6        Selection.ApplyNames Names:=Array("Annual_Totals", _
             "Cheese", "Milk", "Year_1996", "Year_1997", "Year_1998", _
             "Yoghurt"), IgnoreRelativeAbsolute:=True, _
             UseRowColumnNames:=True, OmitColumn:=True, _
             OmitRow:=True, Order:=1, AppendLast:=False
7    End Sub
```

ANALYSIS

Lines 0 through 4 start the ApplyNamesToIncome macro and provide a description of what it does.

Line 5 selects the range of cells A2:E5.

Line 6 uses the Selection property to return the Range object that applies its ApplyNames method to apply the names to the cells in the selected range. The names are stored in an array in alphabetical order with row and column labels intermixed, as can be seen from the arguments passed to the Array function. The other arguments passed to the ApplyNames method are closely connected to the check boxes in the drop-down extended section of the Apply Names dialog box.

Line 7 ends the macro.

The Magic of Names on the Move

The fact that names are attached to data values also allows you to change the structure of data on your worksheet. Because names move with the data, any references to them in formulas or macros will still be correct after the move. This is true whether a name defines a single cell or a range of cells. Ranges of cells are a bit more complex and are discussed in detail in this section.

If you define a name for a range of cells, you can move it or insert or delete whole rows and columns and Excel will automatically adjust the cell references in the Range object to match—the name that you defined for that range will always reflect the current range. For example, suppose you define the name StockItems as representing the range

$A$1:$E$150

If the range is moved en bloc to

$G$2:$K$151

then the name StockItems will be redefined to match. If you then add a new stock item in row 12, StockItems will be redefined to

$G$2:$K$152

If you then delete six items of old stock, it will be redefined again to

$G$2:$K$146

and everything will continue to work correctly.

However, if you move a few cells out of the range, Excel will lose track of the cells that have moved. The name will still refer to the original range, which may have changed its boundaries to reflect any rows or columns deleted during the move.

External References

An external reference is a reference to a cell or range of cells in a different workbook than the one containing the reference. External references can take the form of a cell reference or a defined name.

Names Overcome Problems with External References

You already know that Excel updates the cell references contained in formulas as you move the cells they refer to around your worksheet. But Excel cannot update cell references in formulas that are in closed workbooks. This can lead to serious problems if you don't remember to open all the workbooks associated with any external references you have made.

Suppose you forget to open a workbook during a restructuring operation. When it's eventually opened, its cell references will refer to cells at their previous position. This is a risky practice, and, as Murphy's Law predicts, someone at some stage is going to open only one of the workbooks and move a cell that is referenced externally in another workbook.

You don't have to open the other workbooks if the external reference is in the form of a name, as names always refer to the same data value.

WARNING   If you need to work with more than one workbook at a time, then it is critical to use names for your cells.

External Reference Example

The following example illustrates the problems that can be encountered when using cell references, rather than names, for external references when working with multiple workbooks.

Suppose a company keeps an Expenses workbook containing worksheets for each department and updates it on a weekly basis. At the end of each month a workbook containing the profit and loss data is updated. This workbook contains external references referring to data in the Expenses workbook.

It's decided that after balancing the books on September 30th, the stationery expenses will be split into two items, photocopying and stationery. On October 1st, the Expenses workbook is opened and all the stationery figures updated so that stationery now takes up two rows of cells instead of one. At the end of the month, both workbooks are opened to do the usual end-of-month balancing of the books.

What happens at the end of October is dependent on whether the external references took the form of cell references or defined names. If names were used, then it would be business as usual. If cell references were used, then some of the data values picked up by the Profit & Loss workbook would have been taken from the wrong cells in the Expenses workbook—and someone will be burning the midnight oil!

Updating External References to Renamed Workbooks

When you open Excel you're automatically assigned an empty workbook, named Book1 by default. You can keep opening new workbooks by choosing File ➤ New and all their names will start with Book followed by a sequential number. You'll most likely want to rename all of these workbooks to better describe the data they contain. To change the name of a workbook:

1. Select the workbook to make it active.

2. Choose File ➤ Save As to open the Save As dialog box.

3. Enter the workbook's new name in the File Name box.

4. Click Save to return to your active worksheet.

Notice how the title bar of the active worksheet has now been updated to the name you've just entered.

You saw earlier in this chapter, in the section titled "Hierarchy of Names," that a workbook's name was included as part of an external reference. The question now is what happens to the external references if you happen to rename the workbook they reference? Well, Excel has thought of that one too—when you open the workbook containing the external reference to the renamed workbook, Excel will display the message box shown in Figure 5.19 to give you the opportunity to update your external references to the new name.

FIGURE 5.19:

Message box displayed when you are opening a workbook that contains external references

If you click the Yes in the message box, Excel will update all the external references to the workbook's new name, provided the workbook's name only changes once. If its name changes more than once, the File Not Found dialog box (Figure 5.20) will be displayed for you to select the current name of the workbook.

If you click the No button in the message box, the external references will be left as they are for you to deal with manually. This is easy to do; the following steps show you how.

1. Open the workbook with the formula containing the external reference and select the formula's cell to make it active.

FIGURE 5.20:

File Not Found dialog box

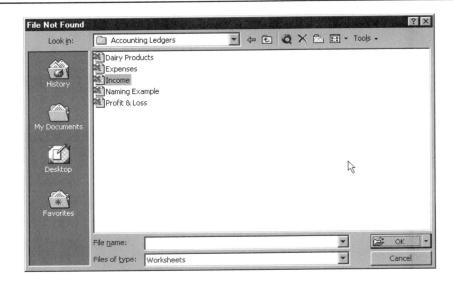

2. Choose Edit ➤ Links to open up the Links dialog box as shown in Figure 5.21.

FIGURE 5.21:

Links dialog box

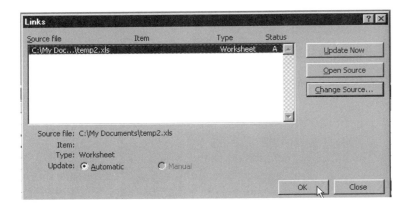

3. Click Change Source to open up the Change Links dialog box (see Figure 5.22), which displays all the workbooks in the current directory.

4. Select a workbook from the list.

5. Click OK to return to the active worksheet.

FIGURE 5.22:

Change Links dialog box

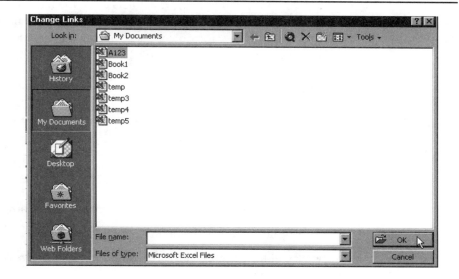

The external reference in the formula will now be updated to include the workbook's new name.

Summary

This chapter introduced you to the hierarchical structure of names and the features that Excel provides for naming ranges of cells, which included:

- Name box drop-down list, which displays all of the names that define cells containing data values or formulas on all worksheets in the active workbook. This allows direct access to named cells.

- Define Name dialog box, which allows you to define new names and indicate what they refer to. Formulas can be named without being attached to a cell.

- Create Names dialog box, which allows you to select row and column labels for Excel to use as a base for creating the names of cells in a selected range of cells. You not only recorded the actions to create names using this feature but you also created a macro from scratch using the CreateNames method.

- Apply Names dialog box, which lists all of the names defined in the active workbook to enable you to select the names you would like to apply to existing worksheet formulas. These names replace the cell references in all formulas in the active workbook.

You can now

- customize the `InputBox` function by calling it with different arguments
- retrieve the input the user entered into the Input Box dialog box displayed by the `InputBox` function
- code a macro to assign a name to the active cell
- create names from labels with an understanding of how
  - duplicate names are handled by Excel
  - Excel keeps track of the cell reference when rows or columns are added or deleted
- define names for cell references and for formulas not attached to specific cells
- overcome the problems caused by external references when workbooks are renamed
- develop a GUI using the `UserForm` object, along with the `Masked Edit`, `TextBox`, `Label`, and `CommandButton` controls
- code event procedures with the response to users' interactions
- open a `UserForm` object from a macro and allow it to interact with the user by executing its event procedures
- differentiate between cells that should be named and those that shouldn't
- go directly to named cells

CHAPTER

SIX

6

Using Constants

Constants allow you to give a value a meaningful name—and I hope Chapter 5 has already convinced you of the benefits of names. This chapter discusses constants in detail and how they're used in Excel worksheets and in VBA macro code. A macro for naming workbook constants is recorded and used as the basis for developing an application. I'll show you the steps involved in developing the application that updates a workbook constant by opening a UserForm from a command button placed in a worksheet and using a TextBox control as the means of getting a valid value from the user.

Then we'll move on to Excel VBA constants. I'll show you how to define constants and how to use the Object Browser to view your own constants as well as the built-in constants that are defined in the various libraries available to your application.

The scope of constants will be discussed, as will how you can determine the scope of your own constants by where you declare them. The chapter will also show you how to use the Object Browser to find the constants, properties, and methods that are all encapsulated in classes.

Using Constants in Workbooks

A constant in an Excel workbook is defined as a cell value that's not a formula or a value resulting from a formula. When the same constant is used in several places throughout a workbook, giving it a meaningful name and using this name instead of its value makes sense. If it changes, you'll only need to assign the new value to the constant and all the formulas containing its name will be changed automatically.

Naming a Workbook Constant

Constants in Excel workbooks are named using conventions similar to those used when naming formulas. The first character must be a letter or an underscore character; the rest of the name can be letters, numbers, periods (.), or underscore characters. Names can be up to 255 characters in length, but two constants in the same workbook can't have the same name because constants' names are all stored as a single collection.

To name a workbook constant:

1. Open a new workbook in Excel and choose Insert ➤ Name ➤ Define to open the Define Name dialog box, as shown.

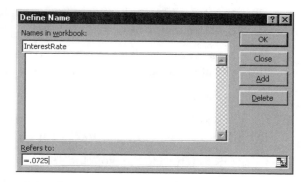

2. Enter the constant's name as **InterestRate** in the Names In Workbook box and the string **=.0725** in the Refers To box.

3. Click OK to finalize assigning the value .0725 to the constant.

4. Click cell D2 to make it the active cell.

5. Enter the string **=interestrate** into the formula bar and watch the value appear in the Formula Palette when you enter the last letter of the constant's name.

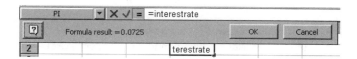

6. Click OK in the Formula Palette to end your formula. The value of the constant will now be displayed in cell D2.

NOTE   The Name Box drop-down list only includes names given to cells. Constants are named without attaching them to a cell, so they're not included in this list.

Updating the Value of a Constant in a Macro

You've just seen how to name a workbook constant; let's update its value and get Excel VBA to record our actions:

1. Click the Record Macro button in the Visual Basic Toolbox to open the Record Macro dialog box.

2. Enter **ChangeInterestRate** in the Macro Name box and **Macro to change the InterestRate's value** in the Description box. Click OK to begin recording.

3. Choose Insert ➤ Name ➤ Define to display the Define Name dialog box.

4. `InterestRate` will appear in the Names In Workbook list. Update the string in the Refers To box from =0.0725 to =0.07.

5. Click OK to return to the worksheet.

6. Click the Stop Recording button in the Visual Basic toolbar.

7. Click the Visual Basic Editor button in the Visual Basic toolbar to open the code window for `Module1`. If your `ChangeInterestRate` macro is not displayed, then click the Down arrow in the Procedure list and select it from the drop-down list. Listing 6.1 shows the recorded macro code.

8. Save your workbook as **ChangeInterestRateConstant**.

LISTING 6.1

```
0    Sub ChangeInterestRate()
1        '
2        ' ChangeInterestRate Macro
3        ' Macro to change the InterestRate's value.
4        '
5
6        '
7        ActiveWorkbook.Names.Add Name:="InterestRate", _
         RefersToR1C1:="=0.07"
8    End Sub
```

Lines 0 through 6 start the macro named from the entry you made in the Name box at step 2, then copies the text you entered in the Description box and makes it into a comment.

Line 7, the ActiveWorkbook property, identifies the workbook that's currently open. The Names property identifies the Names collection, and could have been used here with the same result if you'd left off the ActiveWorkbook object qualifier, as Excel would automatically assume that the Names property belongs to the active workbook. The Add method of the Names collection adds a name to the Names collection using the values passed to it by the Name and RefersToR1C1 boxes, which were both set during step 4.

Line 8 marks the end of the macro.

Updating a Constant's Value

Updating the value assigned to a constant will update all the formulas that refer to it by name. To demonstrate this:

1. Continuing with the ChangeInterestRateConstant workbook, enter the interest rate using the formula **=InterestRate** at cell A1 of Sheet1, cell B2 of Sheet2, and cell C3 of Sheet3.

2. Update the value of the RefersToR1C1 argument at Line 7 in Listing 6.1 from 0.07 to 0.085.

3. Run the ChangeInterestRate macro (choose Tools ➢ Macro ➢ Macros) and look at the cells updated at step 1—all your formula values will have changed to the new rate. Every time the interest rate changes, all you have to do is remember to update Line 7 of this macro.

This update can be made even simpler if the new interest rate is entered into a TextBox control placed on a UserForm and the contents of the text box assigned to the RefersToR1C1 argument in code (Line 7 in Listing 6.1). Let's take a quick look at the TextBox control and a few of its properties before we extend our macro into a full-blown application. (I'm using the term "application" here because extending the workbook in this way moves toward making the macro into an application within Excel VBA.) The application will consist of a collection of files that VBA's project management features will build as you add new controls from the Toolbox.

NOTE   VBA allows you to extend your Excel workbook into an application. To create an application, you use a project to manage the collection of files required by your application. A project will contain a file for each UserForm and Module you've added to your application and a project file that contains a list of all these files as well as any environment settings you've specified.

The *TextBox* Control

The TextBox control has two main purposes: to receive input from the user or to display information to the user. If used to receive input, any text entered must be verified to ensure that it's the expected type. Your program may terminate abnormally if the input is incompatible with the operations your code tries to perform.

Properties of the *TextBox* Control

The TextBox control has about 60 properties associated with it. In this section, I'll describe the five that I think you're likely to use most often.

Name   This is what the text box will be known as in code.

MultiLine   This property can be set to True or False. When set to False, it restricts the input to a single line. When set to True, it enables the input to take up as many lines as required by automatically starting a new line whenever the edge of the control is encountered. The MultiLine property is normally coupled with the ScrollBars property so that a scroll bar will be displayed when the input becomes too long for it all to be displayed in the text box.

ScrollBars   If the MultiLine property is set to True, then this property specifies whether or not a scroll bar will be added to the text box. The drop-down list of constants available for this property is shown here with their values.

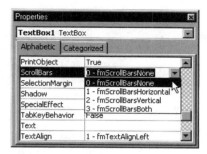

Text, Value   These properties both return the contents of the text box.

Naming Conventions for VBA Controls

When you start to develop more complicated applications with lots of controls, your code is easier to understand if you give your controls meaningful names. It's also useful if you can actually tell from the name what type of object or control the name refers to. The naming convention that Excel VBA has adopted is to have unique three-letter prefixes for all controls. Some of these prefixes are given in Table 6.1.

TABLE 6.1: Naming Conventions for Controls

Object	Prefix	Name
Check Box	chk	chkIncludeZeros
Combo Box	cbo	cboCurrency
Command Button	cmd	cmdCalculate
Image	img	imgLogoIcon
Label	lbl	lblName
List Box	lst	lstCurrentSelection
Option Button	opt	optColorRequired
Text Box	txt	txtInputName

> **TIP** Using prefix naming conventions for your controls means that controls of the same type will be listed together in the Object list in the code window.

Receiving Input to a Text Box

Now let's get on with extending the ChangeInterestRateConstant worksheet created earlier in the section "Updating the Value of a Constant in a Macro." We'll add a command button to our worksheet. When this is clicked, we'll display a UserForm containing a text box that's ready to receive the new interest rate. User-Forms are described in more detail in Chapter 10, so here I'll just show you how to add one to your application and display it on the screen.

Let's first add to our worksheet the command button that will be used to display the UserForm we're about to create:

1. Continuing with the ChangeInterestRateConstant worksheet created earlier in this chapter, drag and drop a CommandButton object from the Control Toolbox onto the worksheet. Command buttons are described in the section "Calling a Macro Using a Command Button" in Chapter 4.

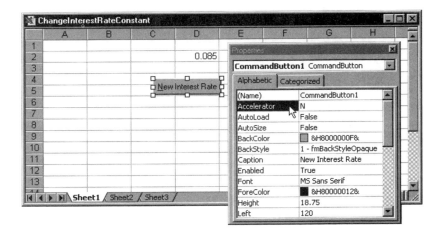

2. Still in Design mode, right-click the command button and choose Properties from the shortcut menu to display the Properties window. Set the Caption

property to **New Interest Rate** and the `Accelerator` property to **N** (as shown); the first N will appear underlined to let the user know that it's the shortcut key.

3. Double-click the command button to display the Visual Basic Editor with the `Click` event procedure displayed in the code window. Enter the statement **UserForm1.Show**. The following code shows the complete `Click` event procedure:

```
Private Sub CommandButton1_Click()
    UserForm1.Show
End Sub
```

This will display `UserForm1` (which we're about to create) whenever the command button is clicked or the Alt+N shortcut key combination is used.

4. Choose Insert ➤ UserForm to create `UserForm1` and display it graphically on the screen.

5. Right-click the UserForm, choose Properties to open the Properties window, and change the `Caption` property to **New Interest Rate**. This will appear character by character in the title bar of the UserForm, below.

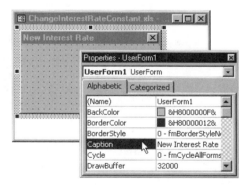

6. Click the UserForm and drag and drop a `TextBox` control from the Toolbox (choose View ➤ Toolbox if it is not already on display) onto the UserForm.

Since the user will be entering text into this text box, steps must be taken to ensure that only numerical data is accepted. Let's take a look at how each character can be validated as it's entered.

Validating Input to a Text Box

If a numerical string is required as input to a text box, each character must be validated as it's entered—that is, every time the user presses a key. Validation is therefore done in the KeyPress event procedure for the text box, which will also alert the user if a non-numeric key is pressed. Listing 6.2 gives an example of how the KeyPress event procedure could be coded for validating the characters input to TextBox1.

LISTING 6.2

```
0    Private Sub TextBox1_KeyPress(ByVal KeyAscii As _
     MSForms.ReturnInteger)
1        If KeyAscii < Asc("0") Or KeyAscii > Asc("9") Then
2            'input not numeric
3            KeyAscii.Value = 0 'cancel the character just entered
4            Beep                'alert the user to the error
5        End If
6    End Sub
```

ANALYSIS

Line 0 starts the event procedure that will be executed in the event of the TextBox1 control receiving the input character when the user presses a key. The Private keyword is placed at the start of this statement to prevent the event procedure being called from anywhere in the application. All event procedures are Private. The ByVal keyword is discussed in the next section.

Line 1 checks whether the key pressed is outside the 0…9 range of valid values. KeyAscii is the ASCII character code number for the key pressed; the Asc function is called with a single character string argument and returns the ASCII code, which is used for testing the condition. If the key pressed is valid, no action is required and the Text property of TextBox1 automatically receives the character entered when the End Sub statement is encountered.

Line 2 is just a comment.

Lines 3 and 4 are executed only when the user attempts to enter non-numeric characters. The character entered by the key press is cancelled by the assignment statement in Line 3 and doesn't appear in TextBox1, and the code at Line 4 emits a beep sound that alerts the user that the last character entered has been rejected.

Line 5 ends the If statement.

Line 6 ends the event procedure.

ByRef and *ByVal* Keywords

The ByRef keyword indicates that an argument is passed by reference using its address rather than its value. This allows a procedure to change the value of an argument and is the default way to pass arguments in Excel VBA.

In normal usage, the ByVal keyword is a way to pass a copy of the actual value of an argument instead of passing a reference to it. This means that the copy can be changed locally within the procedure and, when the procedure has finished executing, the copy will no longer be available and the original value passed as an argument will remain unchanged.

However, in the KeyPress event example in Listing 6.2, although KeyAscii is called by value its type is specified as the ReturnInteger object from the Microsoft Forms Object Model (MSForms). Here the ByVal keyword refers to the object's class rather than the method of argument passing. The object Return-Integer has a Value property that can be changed to produce the same results as if it had been called by reference.

Call by Value versus Call by Reference

When an argument is called using a variable's value, only a copy of the variable is passed to the procedure. The procedure can do anything to this copy but the variable's value will remain the same outside that procedure.

When an argument is called by reference, the procedure is passed the actual variable and any changes it makes will take effect outside the procedure.

Asc Function

The Asc function returns an integer number that corresponds to the ASCII character code for the first letter in the string that's passed to it as an argument. The ASCII character coding system can be viewed from the Visual Basic Editor as follows:

1. Choose Help ➢ Contents and Index to display the Visual Basic Reference.

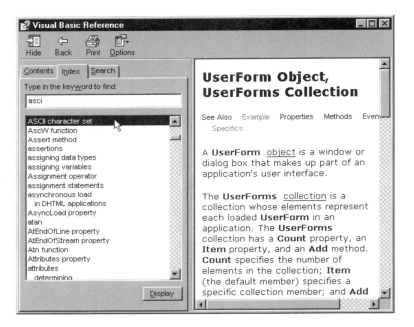

2. Select the ASCII character set entry from the Index tab list and click Display to display the Topics Found dialog box.

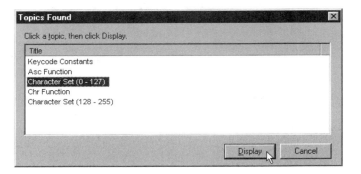

3. Select Character Set (0 - 127) from the list and click Display to view the characters represented by the ASCII codes 0–127.

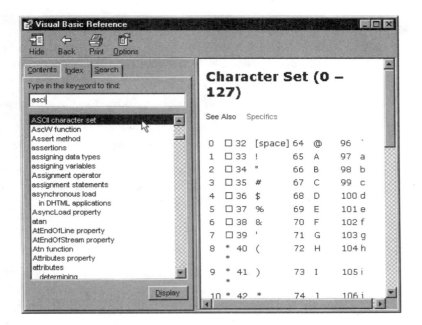

Beep Statement

This statement causes a tone to be sounded through the computer's speaker system. It is used extensively throughout all Microsoft Windows applications to alert users that they've done something unexpected or invalid.

Implementing the *Text Box* Control's *KeyPress* Event Procedure

Let's get back to our application development and implement the KeyPress event:

1. Double-click the text box to open the code window displaying the event procedure for the Change event. Select KeyPress from the drop-down list of event procedures.

2. Enter the code shown in Listing 6.2 to make sure that only numerical digits are entered.

NOTE   The KeyPress event occurs when any key that corresponds to an ASCII character is pressed. This event is used when you want to perform verification tests on characters or to process them in some way, such as changing their case.

---

3. Return to your worksheet by clicking the View Microsoft Excel button in the toolbar.

4. Exit Design mode by clicking the button in the Visual Basic toolbar.

5. Test your macro by clicking the New Interest Rate command button and making valid and invalid entries. Making an invalid entry should sound a beep and cancel the key pressed.

Customizing Data Entry

So far, the application has a command button on the worksheet that will display a UserForm containing a text box when clicked, and any characters entered will be validated. What's next? Adding a label beside the text box will let the user know what to enter and will add to the user-friendliness of the application. Additionally, as the application stands, nothing happens after the user has entered the interest rate, so a command button that the user can click when they've finished the entry is also needed.

What if the user clicked the worksheet button by mistake and doesn't really want to change the interest rate? Let's have another command button to allow them to backtrack and cancel their request. Figure 6.1 shows my version of the UserForm containing all its controls.

FIGURE 6.1:

New Interest Rate
UserForm

Now that we know what we want to do, let's finish off our application.

1. Add a `Label` control to the UserForm and change its `Caption` property to **Interest Rate**.

2. Add a `CommandButton` control and change its `Caption` property to **OK** and its `Accelerator` property to the letter **O**. When this is clicked, Line 7 of our `ChangeInterestRate` macro (see Listing 6.1) will be updated to the new interest rate.

3. Double-click the OK command button to open the code window displaying the skeleton code for the `Click` event procedure for `CommandButton1`. Enter **ChangeInterestRate** to call the macro, and on the next line enter **UserForm1.Hide** to return to the worksheet.

4. Next, we'll update the macro itself. Double-click `Module1` in the Project Explorer window (choose View ➤ Project Explorer if it's not already displayed) to open the code window displaying the `ChangeInterestRate` macro. Change the `RefersToR1C1` argument in Line 7 (Listing 6.1) to **UserForm1.TextBox1.Text/100**. The `UserForm1` object qualifier was needed here because `UserForm` objects and modules are two separate entities in your project.

5. Now let's give the user a chance to cancel without updating the interest rate. Add a second `CommandButton` control to the UserForm and change its `Caption` property to **Cancel** and its `Accelerator` property to **C**, as shown in Figure 6.1.

6. Double-click the Cancel button to open the code window displaying its `Click` event procedure. Enter **UserForm1.Hide** to close the UserForm and return to the worksheet. This has no effect on the original value of the `InterestRate` constant.

Test your application by running it and selecting the New Interest Rate button on your worksheet. Check whether your application responds to clicking either command button as expected. If you have any problems, compare your code with Listing 6.3.

LISTING 6.3

```
0    Private Sub CommandButton1_Click()
1        'OK button
2        ChangeInterestRate
3        UserForm1.Hide
4    End Sub
5
```

```
6    Private Sub CommandButton2_Click()
7         'Cancel button
8         UserForm1.Hide
9    End Sub
10
11   Private Sub TextBox1_KeyPress(ByVal KeyAscii As MSForms.ReturnInte-
ger)
12        If KeyAscii < Asc("0") Or KeyAscii > Asc("9") Then
13        KeyAscii = 0
14        Beep
15        End If
16   End Sub
```

If you're feeling rather ambitious, you can extend the text box KeyPress event to allow a decimal point and to restrict the value entered to being within the range 0...100.

Using Constants in Excel VBA

In Excel VBA, a constant is defined as a named item that remains unchanged throughout the execution of a program. This differs from the Excel worksheet definition of a constant, in which changes can take place at any time and constants really only remain the same until they are overwritten by another constant value!

In Excel VBA, constants can be

- *intrinsic* (or built-in) constants that are an integral part of Excel VBA and its controls for use with objects, methods, and properties

- *symbolic* constants that you create and assign values to in declaration statements in your code using the Const statement

Some data values never change, while others remain the same for numerous runs of an application and are updated very infrequently. All of these values should be declared as constants and their values stated literally wherever required throughout the code. Doing this makes the code easier to maintain, for if the values do change you only need to update them in one place rather than searching worksheets and workbooks for instances of where they were used—which in the end could introduce errors if you miss any instances.

Viewing VBA's Built-in Constants Using the Object Browser

Excel VBA has lots of built-in constants that you can use without having to declare them. You can view these using the Object Browser window in the Visual Basic Editor. These constants are listed in several different libraries, each of which has its own set of constants. These constants are qualified by giving them a prefix or their library reference to avoid any confusion that may arise if two or more libraries contain constants with the same name. Figure 6.2 shows the Object Browser with all of its components labeled.

FIGURE 6.2:

Object Browser

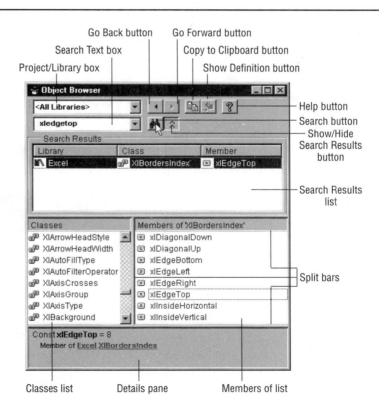

We will discuss the Object Browser components in more detail later in this chapter, in the section "Using the Object Browser."

Let's take a look at the intrinsic constants using the Object Browser:

1. Open a new workbook and click the Visual Basic Editor button.

2. Choose View ➤ Object Browser in the Visual Basic Editor.

You've already seen intrinsic constants in your recorded macros. Listing 4.1 in Chapter 4 uses xlManual to set the Calculation property of the Application object. Listing 3.1 in Chapter 3 has quite a few constants beginning with the prefix xl. The following lines of code belong to one of the With statements in Listing 3.1:

```
With Selection.Borders(xlEdgeTop)
    .LineStyle = xlContinuous
    .Weight = xlThick
    .ColorIndex = xlAutomatic
End With
```

The Borders class of object is in the Excel library and is found in the Object Browser by selecting the Excel library from the drop-down list in the Project/Library box and then by selecting the Borders class from the list in the Classes box. The Borders class members will be displayed in the Members Of list, which will now include "Borders" in its header label (as shown in Figure 6.3).

FIGURE 6.3:

Members of the Borders class displayed in the Object Browser

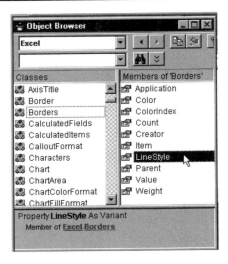

Let's take a look at how we can use the Object Browser to view all the constants available. The Details pane along the bottom of the Object Browser summarizes the details of the member selected. Selecting a library name from the Project/Library box drop-down list displays the name of the library, the path name where it's stored, and what kind of library it is. The Details pane for the Excel library is shown below.

Let's use the search feature of the Object Browser to find the x1EdgeTop constant, as shown in Figure 6.2:

1. Open the Object Browser and enter **xledgetop** into the Search Text box.
2. Click the Find button (binoculars) to start the search.

As illustrated in the Object Browser shot in Figure 6.2, the Search Results pane shows x1EdgeTop's Library (Excel), Class (x1BordersIndex), and Member (x1EdgeTop). The icon next to x1EdgeTop in the Members Of list indicates that it's a constant. Type, value, and object class appear in the Details pane.

Constants Qualified by Prefix

The names of constants are in mixed-case format, with a prefix of two lowercase characters to identify the object library that the constant belongs to. Constants that come from the Visual Basic and VBA object libraries are prefaced with vb, and those from the Excel object library with x1.

For example, Table 6.2 shows some of the constants from these two libraries.

TABLE 6.2: Some Built-in Constants from the VBA and Excel Object Libraries

Constant	Denotes
vbBack	backspace character
vbCr	carriage return character
vbKeyLButton	left mouse button
vbKey0	0 key
vbKeyF1	F1 function key
vbSunday	Sunday
vbFirstFullWeek	first full week of the year
xlEdgeBottom	bottom edge border of cell
xlEdgeTop	top edge border of cell
xlCalculationAutomatic	formula cells updated automatically
xl24HourClock	24-hour clock required
xl4DigitYears	4-digit years

Constants Qualified by Library Reference

Constants can be qualified by their library reference using the name of the library containing their definition followed by the name of the class where they're declared. For example, the MySheet1 constant shown highlighted in the Members Of box can be qualified in code in three ways:

- VBAProject.Sheet1.MySheet1

- VBAProject.MySheet1

- Sheet1.MySheet1

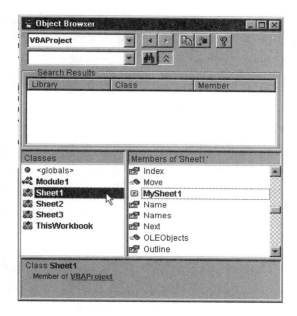

Naming a Constant in Excel VBA

In Excel VBA, the rules for naming a constant are the same as those for naming variables. The name must begin with a letter and cannot contain any spaces, periods (.), or any of the !, @, &, $, or # characters. It can be up to 255 characters in length, and two or more constants can't have the same name if their lifetimes overlap (see the section "Scope and Visibility of a Constant" later in this chapter).

You can't call any of your constants by the same name as any of the built-in constants. This is easy to avoid because your constants won't have any of the prefixes that built-in constants have to identify the library they belong to.

Const Statement

Symbolic or user-defined constants are defined using the Const statement. The definition of a constant resembles an equation, with its name followed by an equals sign (=) and then its value (which can be a number, a string, an expression, or another constant):

```
Const NumberHoursPerDay = 24
```

A constant's type can also be defined in the `Const` statement; if left out, VBA applies the type that is most appropriate to the value assigned to the constant:

```
Const Epsilon as Double = 0.0000001
```

Several constants can be declared in the same line, with each assignment being terminated by a comma:

```
Const Num1 = 1, Num2 = 2, Num3 = 3
```

Constants of different types can also be declared in the same line:

```
Const Pi as Integer = 3.14159, Psi as Double = 0.04
```

If you've got a lot of constants to declare, this is a good way of forming them into small logical groups. If you use the `Private` or `Public` keyword at the start of the line, it will apply to all the constants.

Declaring a Constant In a Procedure

Constants declared in any procedure are `Private` by default. Declaring them as either `Private` or `Public` will display a message box with the message `Invalid attribute in Sub or Function`.

Declaring a Constant In a Module

Any constant declarations outside procedures are considered to be module-level and are listed at the beginning of the declarations section of a module. Any constant declared in a module is `Private` by default unless declared otherwise. To override this, you can declare it as public by adding the keyword `Public` to the start of the statement. It's good programming practice to make everything explicit rather than relying on default values; bearing this in mind, the following program statements are for declaring a `Private` and a `Public` constant:

```
Private Const LastKey = "Z99999X"
Public Const Pi = 3.14159265
```

Private versus Public Constants are all `Private` by default but can be declared as `Public` provided the declaration is inside a module rather than a UserForm or a procedure. From the maintenance point of view, it's much better to declare a constant as `Private` if it's only used by procedures in the same module. This helps pinpoint what has to be checked for correctness if the value of that constant ever needs to be changed.

Scope and Visibility of a Constant

The scope (or lifetime) of a constant refers to its availability for use by other procedures and modules in the project. There are three levels of scope that a constant can have:

- procedure level
- `Private` module level
- `Public` module level

The level of scope that a constant has is dependent on where it is declared.

Procedure Level Scope

A constant declared inside a procedure is considered to be a local constant, and its lifetime lasts only while that procedure is running. All local constants are `Private`, although you can't declare them as such. Declaring a local constant as `Private` gives the runtime compilation error message `Invalid attribute in Sub or Function`, and declaring them as `Public` gives the compilation error `Constants, fixed-length strings, arrays, user-defined types and Declare statements not allowed as Public members of object modules` as soon as you've entered the declaration.

Public and Private Module-Level Scope

A module-level constant can be declared as `Public` to make its lifetime last as long as the program is running and make it available for use by all procedures in all modules in the project:

```
Public Const NewRate = 3.75
```

Alternatively, it can be declared as `Private` to limit its availability to only those procedures belonging to the same module:

```
Private Const MaximumMark = 80
```

NOTE   Excel VBA constants are all defaulted to being `Private` and can only be made `Public` if the declaration is inside a module rather than inside a UserForm or a procedure.

How the Compiler Handles Constants

When used instead of variables, constants not only make it easy to update values but also increase the speed of your running code—they're just so much more efficient. When your code is compiled, all of the constant names are replaced by their values. During runtime, the values declared as constants are all ready to be used immediately, whereas each variable's value has to be retrieved from its appropriate memory address.

Using the Object Browser

The Object Browser allows you to browse information about all of the objects in your current workbook, including the built-in constants and any custom ones you've included yourself. The information available is very extensive and includes:

- Classes: the definition of objects
- Properties: the attributes of objects
- Methods: the actions performed by objects
- Events: the events an object can respond to
- Constants: the names of values that never change during execution

Object Browser Components

The Object Browser is a dialog box that allows you to view the items in object libraries, type libraries, and classes. An object library includes all the information required to define the objects it contains, which are all stored in a single file with the extension .OLB. A type library can be included in an object library or can be a library in its own right. Classes define the properties (or attributes) that describe an object and the methods that dictate its behavior, including the event procedures that it can respond to. To keep the amount of detail to a minimum, only the event procedures that you've inserted some code into are listed in the Object Browser. (See Figure 6.2, the Object Browser with all components labeled.)

Project/Library box Clicking the Down arrow provides a drop-down list of the libraries available to the active project, as shown below.

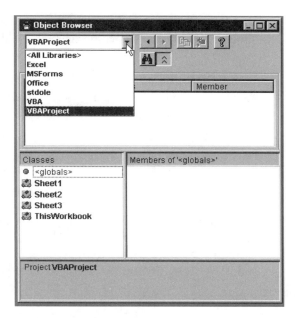

You can select a library from this list to view the objects that it contains, or you can use the default <All Libraries> to view the objects in all of the libraries.

Search Text box   Enter the string you want to find or select it from the drop-down list, then hit the Enter key (or click the Search button). The Search Text box list displays the last four search strings used since your project was opened.

TIP   Wildcard characters can be included in your search string to provide more versatility when the Object Browser is performing pattern matching during its search. The most used wildcards are * to represent zero or more characters and ? to represent a single character.

Go Back and Go Forward buttons   These allow you to jump back and forth between previous selections you've made in the Classes list and the Members Of list. When you open the Object Browser for the first time after opening Microsoft Excel, the <globals> item in the Classes list is the default class and will appear highlighted. Neither of these buttons will be selectable until you select another item from one of the lists. The Go Back button will become selectable when you make your selection and the Go Forward button will become selectable only after you've used the Go Back button.

Copy to Clipboard button   You use this button to copy the item you've selected from the Classes list, Members Of list, Details pane or Search Results box to the Clipboard so that you can paste it into your code.

Show Definition button   This button opens the code window when the selected item from the Classes or Members Of list contains code you've created (such as a macro you've written or recorded, or code you've inserted into an event procedure in a UserForm). Figure 6.4 shows this button when it's about to be clicked with the Module1 class selected and Macro1 the sole member displayed in the Members Of box. When clicked, this button will open the code window for Module1, displaying the code for Macro1. If there is more than one member in the Members Of box, you'll need to highlight your choice before clicking.

FIGURE 6.4:

Object Browser with the Show Definition button available for selection and the Module1 class selected

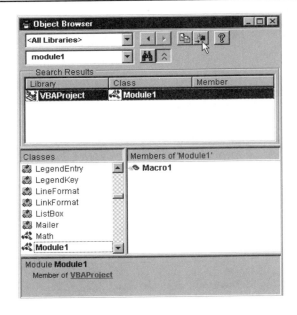

Help button   Use this button as an alternative to F1 to display online Help information for the selected item from the Classes or Members Of list.

Search button   Click this button to search the libraries for any class, property, method, event, or constant that matches the string entered in the Search Text box. Any matches found are listed in the Search Results pane.

Show/Hide Search Results button   Toggle this button to display or hide the Search Results pane that contains the items that match the string in the Search Text box (as shown in Figure 6.4 and Figure 6.5).

FIGURE 6.5:

Object Browser with the Search Results pane hidden.

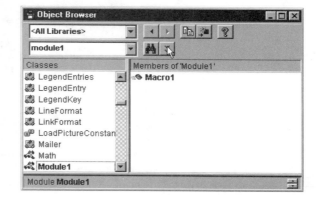

Search Results list   In the Search Results pane, this shows the names of the libraries, classes, and Members Of items that match the string in the Search Text box. The listed items will change if you re-run your search in a different project or library selected from the Project/Library drop-down list.

Classes list   This list contains all the classes in the project or library shown in the Project/Library box.

Members Of list   This list contains all the constants, properties, methods, and events of the class of object selected in the Classes list. Members that include code appear as bold text, as shown in Figure 6.6, and events not coded aren't listed.

You can arrange the Members Of list so that all the constants, properties, etc. are listed together in groups, as shown below.

FIGURE 6.6:

Object Browser showing
UserForm1 and its
members.

Notice how a strictly alphabetical list of members is rearranged by type after the Group Members option is clicked:

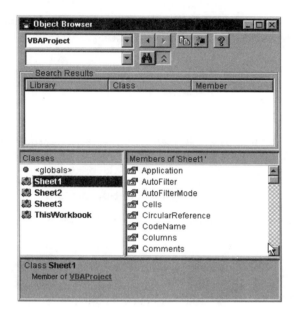

Details pane   Here you view the libraries, classes, and members resulting from a search, as shown in Figure 6.2 and Figure 6.5.

Split bar   Allows you to move the borders of the panes.

The *List Constants* Command

The List Constants command in the drop-down list of options under the Edit menu command is a great help for entering constants' names in code. It provides a pop-up list of available constants for setting the property just entered. The pop-up list for the FilterMode property of the Sheet1 object is shown here.

```
x = sheet1.FilterMode =
End Sub
```

This command also works for any function arguments that are constants. You can pop up this list manually by choosing Edit ➤ List Constants or you can have it pop up automatically when you enter an equals sign (=) after entering a property. To make it automatic, choose Tools ➤ Options and check the AutoList Members check box in the Editor tab.

Summary

This chapter covered all you needed to know about constants. You should now

- be able to name workbook constants
- be able to recognize built-in constants
- be able to define your own constants
- know the scope of a constant
- know how the compiler handles constants

You should be able to declare a constant

- as `Private` or `Public`
- with its type
- with several others in the same line of code

You should be able to use the Object Browser to view libraries and find constants contained in classes.

In VBA, you should know how to validate key presses as a user enters values into text boxes using the `Asc` and `Beep` functions, and how to display a UserForm in response to a command button being clicked.

PART III

Macro-izing Styles from Toolbars

CHAPTER

SEVEN

7

Formats and Styles for Automation

There's no doubt about it, formatting and styles can add pizzazz to your worksheet and can help immensely with the interpretation of the data being presented. Whether your worksheet is part of a report or part of a presentation, you can liven it up with a visually pleasing layout. Everyone knows that the data is the most important aspect of a worksheet, but its creator needs to ensure that the data can easily be interpreted correctly and that the important items stand out from the rest. Just looking at rows and rows of data in itself can be tedious and mind-numbing.

In this chapter, we'll look at the formats available and how these can be combined into styles. You'll see how to apply styles to automate the formatting of your Excel worksheets. It's important to understand how styles work so that you can use them in the most effective way! Not only do styles speed up the process of manually setting the formats of your worksheet, but they also have a huge impact on the length and readability of any macros you create for formatting cells.

I'll record a few macros along the way and show you the connection between the information you enter into the dialog boxes to set your formats and styles manually and the properties you use to do the same thing in code. At the end of the chapter, I'll show you how to create your own macro to color-code your data values.

What Are Formats and Styles?

Formats

Formats are the characteristics that determine how a cell (or range of cells) and its contents will be displayed. These include:

- the format for displaying numerical, currency, and date information, and the alignment of data within cells

- the font size and other textual characteristics that will be used to display the data

- the four borders of individual cells

- the color of flooded cells

- whether or not a cell is protected from being overwritten

Styles

A style is a collection of formats stored together as a single entity to give a particular range of cells the visual impact required. Styles are given names so that they can be referred to in worksheets and macros. Because styles are normally a combination of several formats, they're generally more efficient to use irrespective of whether you're setting them manually or in code.

Let the Formatting Begin!

Let's take a look at the different formatting attributes available and how these are set manually by entering them into boxes, by checking check boxes, and by selecting them from lists. I'll record some of my actions as I go to show you the strong correlation between the attributes you define in Excel and the properties you set in VBA macros that have the same function.

Formatting cells can be done in two ways:

- by selecting items from the Format Cells dialog box, shown in Figure 7.1, where the format properties are grouped into separate tabs

FIGURE 7.1:

Setting the format of the Number category in the Format Cells dialog box

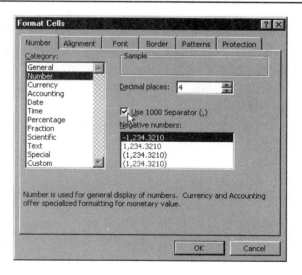

- by clicking the formats available in the Formatting toolbar (Figure 7.2) that's displayed by choosing View ➤ Toolbars ➤ Formatting

FIGURE 7.2:

Formatting toolbar

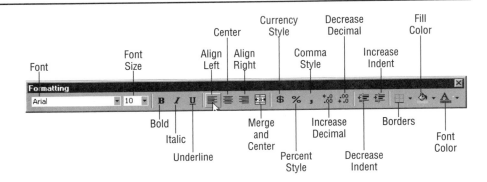

Let's take a look at the features for setting formats available in the tabs of the Format Cells dialog box and the equivalent shortcuts to frequently used features in the Formatting toolbar.

Displaying the Format Cells Dialog Box

If you're not a frequent user of the Format Cells dialog box, you should explore the features it offers before writing format statements in your macro code. Among other things, there are a lot of predefined cell formats that contain currency, dates, and numbers. You should make yourself familiar with these built-in formats so that you don't waste time recreating something that already exists.

There are three different ways to display the Format Cells dialog box:

- Click the cell to be formatted and choose Format ➤ Cells.

- Right-click the cell to be formatted and choose Format Cells from the shortcut menu.

- Click the cell to be formatted and use the keyboard shortcut Ctrl+1.

Number Tab This tab contains a **Category** box with a list of all the built-in number, date, time, and text formats as well as a few others (see Figure 7.3). When you open this tab, Excel examines the value in the active cell and highlights the nearest format to it in the Category list.

Number tab in the Format
Cells dialog box

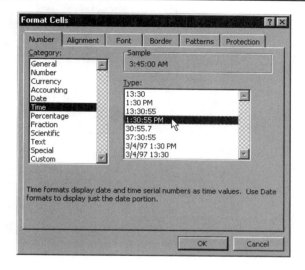

For example, before displaying this Format Cells dialog box I entered 3:45 into the active cell. Excel categorized this as a time value because of the colon (:), so when the Number tab was opened Time was already highlighted.

The **Sample** frame displays the value formatted to match the selected item in the **Type** list. You can customize any of these formats. I'll explain how to do this later in the "Customized Numbers" section.

Shortcuts to the frequently used number formats are provided by the Currency Style, Percent Style, Comma Style, Increase Decimal, and Decrease Decimal buttons in the Formatting toolbar.

Alignment Tab Figure 7.4 shows the Alignment tab, which allows you to set the alignment attributes of a range of cells.

Items in the **Horizontal** list (shown) in the **Text Alignment** frame allow you to specify how characters are aligned horizontally within a cell or a range of cells in the same row.

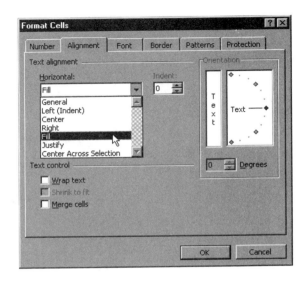

FIGURE 7.4:

Alignment tab in the Format Cells dialog box

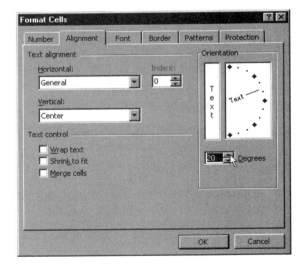

General Selecting General from this list uses Excel's default alignment properties, which align text entries to the left and numbers, dates, and times to the right.

Left Selecting Left aligns the contents with the left border of the cell, taking into account any indentation.

Fill   Selecting Fill from this list fills the selected range of cells by repeating the value in the leftmost cell to fill each empty selected cell (in the same row) border to border.

In the worksheet shown, cell A1 contains a minus sign (−) but has General selected from the Horizontal list, so only one minus sign is displayed. Cell A2 contains a minus sign and has Fill selected, so the minus sign is repeated to fill up the width of the cell. The fill only affects the displayed contents in a cell and doesn't have any effect on its true value, so cell A2 still only contains a single minus sign value after the fill. Cell A3 contains an underscore character (_); the range A3:B4 was selected before setting the Horizontal alignment to Fill, and you'll notice that only the selected cells in the same row were filled with this character. Note that although cell B3 appears to contain underscore characters, it doesn't actually contain an underscore value, so the Formula bar will remain empty if cell B3 is selected. Excel will keep a note that cells A4 and B4 should be filled and will repeat any values that are assigned to them in the future.

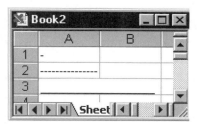

Justify   The Justify option displays the cell's contents as multiple lines of left- or right-justified text.

Center   The Center option centers the contents of a cell. To center the contents over a range of cells, you must ensure that the Merge Cells check box is selected in the Text Control frame.

Items in the **Vertical** list are quite straightforward, but they won't have any effect unless you increase the height of the row. The **Text Control** frame options allow you to specify whether text has to be wrapped to the next line or shrunk to fit in and whether or not to merge cells.

The **Orientation** frame options allow you to set an orientation angle for the contents of cells. In the example shown, the orientation is set to 20 degrees and the height of the row of cells is adjusted automatically to allow the contents of cells to be displayed at this angle.

The shortcuts available in the Formatting toolbar (shown) include horizontal alignment, merge, and indent.

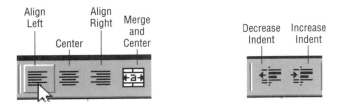

Font Tab   This tab allows you to choose the font to be used, including its size and style. The **Preview** box lets you see what the end result will be for your current selection (see Figure 7.5). The **Underline** box contains a selection of lines you can use to underline text, and the **Color** box allows you to select a color from a pop-up palette. The **Effects** frame allows you to strike through (or cross out) text or make it superscript (raised) or subscript (lowered).

FIGURE 7.5:

Font tab in the Format Cells dialog box

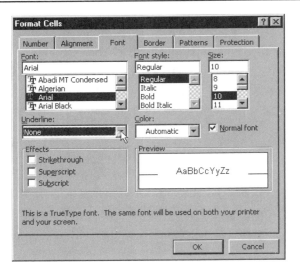

The **Normal Font** check box is a quick way of resetting everything back to its default values. This is useful when you're trying out new ideas in a trial-and-error process, as it ensures you can get back to a reasonable set of formats.

There are shortcuts available in the Formatting toolbar (as shown) for everything except the options in the Effects frame and the Normal check box.

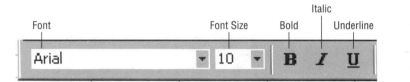

Font   Font Size   Bold   Italic   Underline   Font Color

TIP

The description along the bottom of the Font tab includes whether or not the font selected is a TrueType font. Printing worksheets with a font that's a TrueType guarantees the same results on any printer.

Border   The features in this tab allow you to set the four borders of a cell and display diagonal lines, as shown in Figure 7.6.

FIGURE 7.6:

Border tab in the Format
Cells dialog box

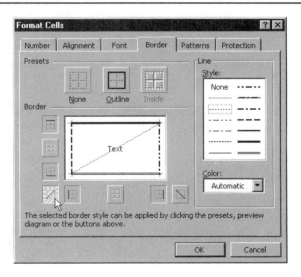

The **Presets** frame contains a None button that will restore the border formats to the default value—which is no border. The Outline button allows you to set the

borders of the outer perimeter of a range of cells; in the example below, these borders are shown as double lines. The Inside button allows you to set the borders of the inside cells of a range of cells, shown in the example as dashed lines.

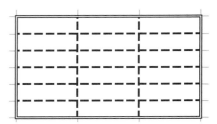

Line styles can be selected individually from the variety of styles available and can be colored. The preview box in the **Border** frame shows how the border and line style settings will appear when applied to a single cell.

The Toolbar button provides a shortcut to the selection of predefined border styles, as shown.

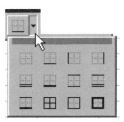

Patterns The Patterns tab shown in Figure 7.7 allows you to select the background color and pattern of a cell. The **Sample** frame displays the result of applying the current settings. You can resort to the default by clicking the No Color button, which also resets the pattern to none.

Only the **Color** frame in this tab is associated with a toolbar button to provide a shortcut to it.

FIGURE 7.7:

Patterns tab in the Format
Cells dialog box

FIGURE 7.7:

Patterns tab in the Format
Cells dialog box

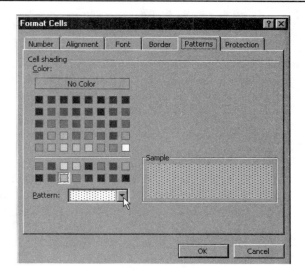

Protection   The options in the Protection tab shown in Figure 7.8 allow you to
lock the values in cells and to hide them. There are no preexistent toolbar shortcuts for this tab, but there's a Lock Cell toolbar button that you can add to an
existing toolbar. The section "Adding a Functional Button to Your Toolbar" in
Chapter 8 takes you through the steps of how to do this. The Lock Cell button is
the last one listed in the Commands box when you select Format from the Categories box.

FIGURE 7.8:

Protection tab in the Format Cells dialog box

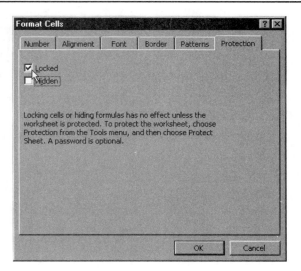

Formatting a Cell

Let's take a look at how the format settings in the different tabs inside the Format Cells dialog box can be changed in VBA macro code. We'll do this manually and record our actions. The following steps set at least one format property in each tab:

1. Create a new workbook and make sure the Visual Basic toolbar is on display.

2. Select cells A1 through F1.

3. Click the Record Macro button in the Visual Basic toolbar and enter **Using-FormatCellTabs** in the Macro Name box and **Recording setting formats in the tabs available in the Format Cells dialog box** in the Description box.

4. Click OK to return to the worksheet.

5. Choose Format ➤ Cells to open the Format Cells dialog box.

6. In the Number tab (Figure 7.1), select Text from the Category list.

7. In the Alignment tab (Figure 7.4), select Center from the Horizontal and Vertical boxes and enter **45** in the Degrees box.

8. In the Font tab (Figure 7.5), select Bookman Old Style from the Font list, Bold from the Font Style list, and 16 from the Size list.

9. In the Border tab (Figure 7.6), click the double line in the Line Style box and on the Outline and Inside buttons in the Presets frame.

10. In the Patterns tab (Figure 7.7), click the Down arrow in the Pattern box and select the dotted 6.25% Gray from the top-right corner of the pop-up patterns.

11. In the Protection tab (Figure 7.8), select the Hidden check box.

12. Click OK to finalize the formatting and return to the worksheet.

13. Click the Stop Recording button in the Visual Basic toolbar.

The range of cells in your worksheet will be formatted as shown below.

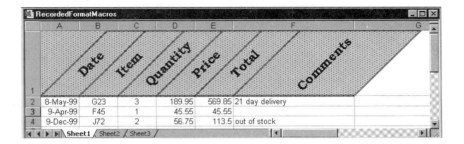

Recorded Macro for Formatting a Cell

Listing 7.1 gives the macro recorded in the previous steps to format a cell. Here you can see how these actions were translated into Excel VBA code and how the different tab topics are handled.

LISTING 7.1

```
0    Sub UsingFormatCellTabs()
1       '
2       ' UsingFormatCellTabs Macro
3       ' Recording setting formats in the tabs available in the _
        ' Format Cells Dialog Box
4       '
5       Selection.NumberFormat = "@"
6          With Selection
7             .HorizontalAlignment = xlCenter
8             .VerticalAlignment = xlCenter
9             .WrapText = False
10            .Orientation = 45
11            .AddIndent = False
12            .ShrinkToFit = False
13            .MergeCells = False
14         End With
15         With Selection.Font
16            .Name = "Bookman Old Style"
17            .FontStyle = "Bold"
18            .Size = 16
19            .Strikethrough = False
20            .Superscript = False
```

```
21              .Subscript = False
22              .OutlineFont = False
23              .Shadow = False
24              .Underline = xlUnderlineStyleNone
25              .ColorIndex = xlAutomatic
26          End With
27          Selection.Borders(xlDiagonalDown).LineStyle = xlNone
28          Selection.Borders(xlDiagonalUp).LineStyle = xlNone
29          With Selection.Borders(xlEdgeLeft)
30              .LineStyle = xlDouble
31              .Weight = xlThick
32              .ColorIndex = xlAutomatic
33          End With
34          With Selection.Borders(xlEdgeTop)
35              .LineStyle = xlDouble
36              .Weight = xlThick
37              .ColorIndex = xlAutomatic
38          End With
39          With Selection.Borders(xlEdgeBottom)
40              .LineStyle = xlDouble
41              .Weight = xlThick
42              .ColorIndex = xlAutomatic
43          End With
44          With Selection.Borders(xlEdgeRight)
45              .LineStyle = xlDouble
46              .Weight = xlThick
47              .ColorIndex = xlAutomatic
48          End With
49          With Selection.Borders(xlInsideVertical)
50              .LineStyle = xlDouble
51              .Weight = xlThick
52              .ColorIndex = xlAutomatic
53          End With
54          With Selection.Interior
55              .ColorIndex = 0
56              .Pattern = xlGray8
57              .PatternColorIndex = xlAutomatic
58          End With
59          Selection.Locked = True
60          Selection.FormulaHidden = True
61  End Sub
```

The Selection property is used throughout this macro to return the Range object that identifies the selected range. The cells to be formatted were selected before the record button was clicked rather than being hardwired into the code itself. This makes the macro more flexible, as each time it's run it will format whatever range of cells was selected rather than formatting the same range of cells each time.

Lines 0 through 4 start the UsingFormatCellTabs macro and its description.

Line 5 assigns the NumberFormat property for the selected range of cells.

Lines 6 through 14 assign all of the settings made to the Alignment tab (at step 7) to the properties of the selected range of cells. The With statement is used to avoid having to qualify each of these properties, which are instead prefixed with a period (.).

Lines 15 through 26 use the With statement to set the properties of the Font object without qualification. The Selection.Font part of this statement uses the Font property of the Range object to return this Font object for the selected cells. The properties are set in the body of this With statement to the values that were selected in the Font tab at step 8.

Lines 27 through 53 deal with the settings in the Border tab made at step 9. The Borders property of the Range object returns a Borders collection object containing the Border objects for the selected cells. Each border is identified by passing an Excel constant as an argument. The constants available are xlDiagonalDown, xlDiagonalUp, xlInsideVertical, xlEdgeLeft, xlEdgeRight, xlEdgeTop, and xlEdgeBottom, as shown in the macro. The line style and thickness and the color of borders are also specified using Excel constants.

Lines 54 through 58 deal with assigning the settings made in the Patterns tab to the Interior property of the selected Range of cells.

Lines 59 and 60 deal with the settings in the Protection tab.

Notice how all the settings from the boxes, drop-down lists, and check boxes have been translated into code and are often specified using Excel constants.

The items available in the Format Cells dialog box drop-down lists are set to pre-defined Excel constants.

To view the full set of member properties and methods available for the Range object, open the Object Browser (see the section "Using the Object Browser" in Chapter 6) and select Excel from the list of libraries in the Project/Libraries list and Range from the Classes list. The member properties of the Font and Border objects' classes can be viewed in the same way.

Customized Numbers

In this section, I'll show you how to create your own number format or how to modify any of the built-in formats by entering them into the Type box in the Number tab inside the Format Cells dialog box (Figure 7.3). The new format must be specified using format codes so that Excel will be able to interpret what's required. Let's take a look at these format codes, and then we can use them to create our own number format.

Format Codes

Using format codes, you can specify how you want to display numbers, time, dates, or text. You can define these with up to four parts, each separated by a semicolon (;). The first part defines the format codes for positive numbers, which must always be given; the other parts define the codes for negative numbers, zero values, and text, which are optional so can be omitted. Because Excel matches up the semicolons, if you want to skip any parts in the middle you must still enter the semicolon to mark the end of the omitted part.

TABLE 7.1: Some of the Format Codes

Format Code	Placeholder Type
#	digit or space
0	digit or zero

Continued on next page

TABLE 7.1 CONTINUED: Some of the Format Codes

Format Code	Placeholder Type
_	digit if non-zero, space if zero
.	decimal point literal
,	thousands separator literal
:	time separator literal
/	date separator literal
%	percentage

Creating Your Own Number Format

Let's create our own number formats. In this example, the format codes specified in step 6 can be adapted to make different formats. My format codes will display positive nonzero values in black, negative values in yellow, zero values as dashes (-), and empty cells as `missing`.

Follow these steps to create your own number format and record your actions in a macro:

1. Open a new workbook and enter the values shown at cells A1:D4. (Note that there is a space character in cell B2.) Enter the formula **=SUM(B2:D2)** at cell E2 and drag-fill it down to cell E4.

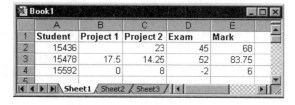

2. Select cells A2:D4 and click the Record Macro button in the Visual Basic toolbar to open the Record Macro dialog box.

3. Enter **CustomizedNumber** in the Macro Name box and **Recording actions involved in customizing a number** in the Description box. Click OK to start recording.

4. Choose Format ➤ Cells to open the Format Cells dialog box.

5. Select Custom from the Category list on the Number tab, as shown in Figure 7.9.

6. Enter the following format codes in the Type box:

    [Black]#00.00;[Yellow]#00.00;---;"missing"@

7. Click OK to return to the worksheet with the new formats applied. I've saved my workbook as `CustomizeNumber`, as shown in the title bar.

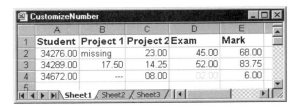

8. Click the Stop Recording button in the Visual Basic toolbar.

FIGURE 7.9:

Creating a new
Custom type

To view new number types that you've added to the list, choose Format ➤ Cells and scroll down the Categories list to Custom. The number types will be displayed in the list under the Type box and are ordered by the number of parts making up the format.

Macro for Customizing Numbers

Listing 7.2 shows the code recorded while creating our customized number in the last section.

LISTING 7.2

```
0    Sub CustomizedNumber()
1        '
2        ' CustomizedNumber Macro
3        ' Macro recorded actions involved in customizing a number
4        '
5        Selection.NumberFormat = "[Black]#00.00;[Yellow] _
         #00.00;--;""missing""@"
6    End Sub
```

ANALYSIS

Line 5 shows how the number format entered into the Type box of the Number tab is assigned to the selected range of cells in code.

Dressing Up a Worksheet

Formats can improve the appearance of your worksheets. As a quick demonstration, I've generated the same data in both of the worksheets shown in Figure 7.10.

The worksheet on the left has been generated using the default formatting properties. The one on the right has had some of the format settings changed to make the data more visually pleasing and easier to interpret. The column and row labels have been made bolder, and particular attention was paid to the cell containing the value representing the total, since this is what most people will be interested in when they look at the worksheet. The formats that were applied to get the effect shown in the worksheet on the right are listed below.

FIGURE 7.10:

The left worksheet uses Excel's default values and the right worksheet was reformatted for visual impact.

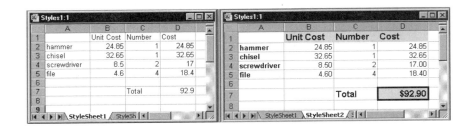

TABLE 7.2: Formats Applied to the Worksheet on the Right in Figure 7.10

Cells	Format
A1:D1	Arial, bold, 12
Columns A, B, C	width expanded to contain larger text
A2:A5	Arial, bold, 10
C7	Arial, bold, 12
B2:D5	number format - 2 decimal places
D7	currency, Arial, bold, 12, surrounding border set as thick line

In my opinion, the right worksheet has more visual impact than the one on the left and the data is much easier to interpret at first glance—your eyes are pulled towards cell D7. However, there's a price to pay: setting up the formatting for this worksheet took more time than entering the data.

Formatting any worksheet can take up a great deal of time, as it's really an artistic process and therefore very much a trial-and-error affair. There's no correct way to do it, and in the end it's how visually pleasing you think your document looks that really matters. You can save time by copying the format settings from another cell; I've described how to do this in the next section. Alternatively, you can save your artistic efforts as a style to speed up the formatting process when you want to repeat a particular effect (see "Why You Need Style!" later in this chapter).

Copying Formats between Cells

If a cell already exists with the formats you want, then it's quicker to recreate the same visual effect by copying the formats rather than setting them using the Format Cells dialog box. The example to demonstrate this is developed in three parts: Create Sheet1 with the formatted cells, create Sheet2 using the default format settings, then copy the formats from Sheet1 to Sheet2.

Part 1

Let's start off by creating Sheet1 with the formatted values shown on the right-side worksheet in Figure 7.10:

1. Create a new workbook and enter the values shown at cells A1:C5 in Figure 7.10 into Sheet1.

2. Enter the formula **=B2 * C2** into cell D2 and drag-fill it down to D5.

3. Enter **Total** in cell C7.

4. Enter the formula **=SUM(D2:D5)** in cell D7.

5. Format the cells in A1:D7 using the formats listed in Table 7.2.

Part 2

Let's enter values into Sheet2:

1. Enter the values shown below into cells A1:C5 and cell C7.

	A	B	C	D
1		Rate/Hour	Hours	Wage
2	Mary	25.75	42	1081.5
3	John	22.55	37.5	845.625
4	David	26.25	45	1181.25
5	Steven	20.75	40	830
6				
7			Total	3938.375
8				

Sheet2

2. Enter the formula = **B2 * C2** into cell D2 and drag-fill it down to cell D5.

3. Enter the formula = **SUM(D2:D5)** into cell D7.

Part 3

Now we're ready to copy the format settings from Sheet1 to Sheet2:

1. Select the range A1:D7 from Sheet1 (the source).

2. Choose Edit ➤ Paste Special and select Formats from the Paste Special dialog box.

3. Select the range A1:D7 in Sheet2 to finalize copying the formats.

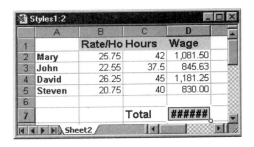

All you need to do now is adjust the width of column B to accommodate the length of its label, and column D so that the total wages can be displayed.

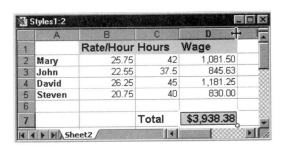

If you want to copy the formats to several different locations, then:

1. Select the range containing the cells you want to copy your formats to.

2. Choose Edit ➤ Paste Special and select Formats from the Paste Special dialog box.

3. Continue to select all the ranges required in this way until all your formatting is completed.

Conditional Formatting

Conditional formatting allows you to specify formats that will be applied to cells only under certain circumstances. This is useful for highlighting items that warrant attention when you're monitoring data values. In the following example, conditional formatting is applied to a value in a cell in the Profit & Loss Statement worksheet. Let's record our actions in a macro to see how they're interpreted into Excel VBA code:

1. Create a new workbook and enter the values in the Profit & Loss Statement shown in the Dairy Products workbook.

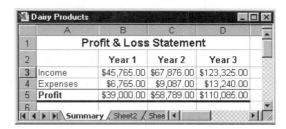

2. Click the Record Macro button to start recording. Click OK to accept the default macro name and description when the Record Macro dialog box is displayed.

3. Select cell C3 as the one to attach the conditional formatting to. Choose Format ➤ Conditional Formatting to open the Conditional Formatting dialog box, shown in Figure 7.11.

FIGURE 7.11:

Conditional Formatting dialog box

4. The first box will already display `Cell Value Is`; select `greater than` from the drop-down list in the second box, and the fourth box will disappear.

5. Enter **=$B$3 * 1.333** into the third box to define the condition.

6. To set the formatting that's to be applied if the condition is `True`, click the Format button in the Conditional Formatting dialog box to open the Format Cells dialog box.

7. Select the Font tab and change the Color box in the Font tab to white.

FIGURE 7.12:

Patterns tab in the Format Cells dialog box

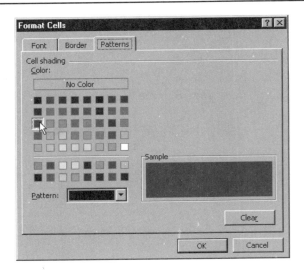

8. Select the red color in the Patterns tab (as shown in Figure 7.12) and click OK to return to the Conditional Formatting dialog box, which will now display the new formatting settings in its preview box as shown here:

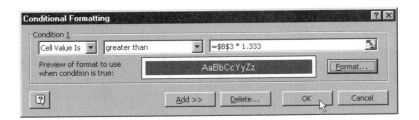

9. Click OK to return to the worksheet. The cell will now have adopted the new formats (as shown below).

10. Click the Stop Recording button in the Visual Basic toolbar.

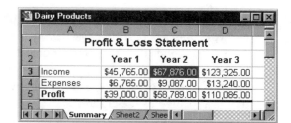

Save this worksheet, as we'll come back to it in our section on Excel's AutoFormat command later in this chapter.

Applying Conditional Formatting with a Macro

Listing 7.3 shows how the steps for applying conditional formatting were translated into VBA macro code.

LISTING 7.3

```
0    Sub ConditionalFormatting()
1        '
2        ' ConditionalFormatting Macro
3        ' Macro recorded the actions of applying
4        ' conditional formatting to a cell.
5        '
6        Range("C3").Select
7        Selection.FormatConditions.Delete
8        Selection.FormatConditions.Add Type:=xlCellValue, _
         Operator:=xlGreater, Formula1:="=$B$3 * 1.333"
9        Selection.FormatConditions(1).Font.ColorIndex = 2
10       Selection.FormatConditions(1).Interior.ColorIndex = 3
11   End Sub
```

ANALYSIS

Line 6 makes cell C3 the selected cell.

Line 7 applies the Delete method of the FormatConditions collection object of the Range object returned by the Selection property. The Delete method removes any existing format conditions from the collection. None of our actions deleted a conditional format; this is instigated by Excel to avoid any problems.

Line 8 creates a new `FormatCondition` object using the values assigned to its `Type`, `Operator`, and `Formula1` arguments, then uses the `Add` method of the `FormatConditions` collection object to add this new object to the collection. The `FormatConditions` collection object can contain up to three `FormatCondition` objects, each one being identified by an index number that is allocated as it's entered.

Lines 9 and 10 identify the `FormatCondition` required using its index value of 1 and assigns a value to the `ColorIndex` property of its `Font` and `Interior` objects.

Streamlining Selections in Macros

You'll have noticed that when you record macros Excel sometimes responds to your every move. The `ConditionalFormatting` macro in Listing 7.3 is no exception. In Line 6, the macro recorded cell C3 being selected as

```
Range("C3").Select
```

and in Line 7, the `Selection` property returned the `Range` object for C3 as

```
Selection.FormatConditions.Delete
```

Since Line 7 doesn't actually change the selection, these two lines can be streamlined into one as

```
Range("C3").FormatConditions.Delete
```

Shortening your macros not only saves space but also makes your code run faster, as there are fewer statements to interpret and execute.

Copying Conditional Formatting

What I'd like to do now is to make cell D3 adopt the same conditional formatting if its value is more than 33% larger than the value at C3. I can't use the fill handle, or the value will be copied too. You can use the Format Painter button from the standard Excel toolbar to copy conditional formatting as follows:

1. Select the source cell C3, since it has the conditional formatting you want to copy.

2. Click the Format Painter toolbar button.

3. Select the range of cells that includes both the destination cell and the source cell (C3:D3).

However, this will have made an exact copy of the condition in cell D3, which you'll need to change as follows:

1. Click cell D3 and choose Format ➤ Conditional Formatting.

2. Change the B in the third box (in the Condition 1 frame) to a C to associate the condition with the value in cell C3.

3. Click OK to return to the worksheet

Try entering different values into cells C3 and D3 to check whether your conditional formatting works.

Removing Conditional Formatting

You can set a maximum of three conditions for the conditional formatting associated with any cell, and these can each be removed individually. Let's remove the conditional formatting from a cell, recording our actions in a macro as we go along:

1. Click the Record Macro button to start recording.

2. Select the cell with the conditional formatting you want to remove.

3. Choose Format ➤ Conditional Formatting.

4. Click the Delete button to display the Delete Conditional Format dialog box as shown below.

5. Select the Condition 1 check box and click OK to return to the Conditional Formatting dialog box showing No Format Set. If you've set more than one condition, you can remove the others by checking their check boxes too.

6. Click OK to return to the worksheet with all of the conditional formatting deleted from the active cell.

7. Click the Stop Recording button in the Visual Basic toolbar.

TIP   To remove all formatting (including conditional formatting) and restore the default settings for selected cells, choose Edit ➢ Clear ➢ Formats.

Removing Conditional Formatting with a Macro

Let's look at how the actions for removing conditional formatting to a cell were actually recorded (Listing 7.4).

LISTING 7.4

```
0    Sub DeleteConditionalFormatting()
1        '
2        ' DeleteConditionalFormatting Macro
3        ' Macro recorded actions to delete conditional formatting
4        '
5        Range("C3").Select
6        Selection.FormatConditions.Delete
7    End Sub
```

ANALYSIS

Line 5 makes cell C3 the selected cell.

Line 6 uses the Delete method of the FormatConditions collection to remove all format conditions from the selected cell's collection.

The Delete method here deletes the single condition that was set. When more than one condition is set, those conditions are all deleted and any remaining conditions moved up to fill any gaps. Listing 7.5 shows the first of three conditions being removed.

LISTING 7.5

```
0    Sub DeleteOneFromThreeConditions()
1        '
2        ' DeleteOneFromThreeConditions Macro
3        ' Macro recorded to delete one from the
4        ' three conditions set
5        '
6        Selection.FormatConditions.Delete
7        Selection.FormatConditions.Add Type:=xlCellValue, _
         Operator:=xlBetween, Formula1:="11", Formula2:="19"
8        Selection.FormatConditions(1).Interior.ColorIndex = 34
9        Selection.FormatConditions.Add Type:=xlCellValue, _
         Operator:=xlBetween, Formula1:="20", Formula2:="50"
10       Selection.FormatConditions(2).Interior.ColorIndex = 19
11   End Sub
```

ANALYSIS

Line 6 deletes all three conditions that have been set in response to deleting the first condition.

Line 7 shows the original second condition being reinstated by adding it to the empty list of conditions, making it the first condition.

Line 8 shows the interior color being defined for the new first condition.

Line 9 shows the original third condition being added to the list of conditions to become the new second condition in the list.

Line 10 assigns the interior color to this new second condition, which is identified by the argument 2.

Excel's *AutoFormat* Command

Excel's AutoFormat command is a super-fast way of formatting a table that contains row and column labels. Let's use the Profit & Loss Statement worksheet you created earlier in this chapter in the Conditional Formatting example. The following steps show you just how easy this is:

1. Open the worksheet containing the `Profit & Loss Statement` in the `Dairy Products` workbook.

2. Select the range of cells that contain the labels and data (A1:D5).

3. Choose Format ➤ AutoFormat to open the AutoFormat dialog box, shown in Figure 7.13, and choose one of the styles displayed.

FIGURE 7.13:

The AutoFormat dialog box

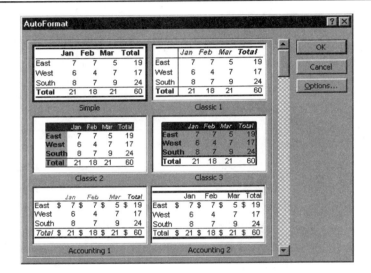

4. Click Options to expand the AutoFormat dialog box as shown in Figure 7.14, and try checking and unchecking some of the check boxes to see their effect.

5. Click OK to close the AutoFormat dialog box and apply the chosen format to your data.

The tables shown in Figure 7.15 give you an idea of some of the results you can achieve by applying the automatic formats to the `Profit & Loss Statement`.

FIGURE 7.14:

Expanded AutoFormat
dialog box

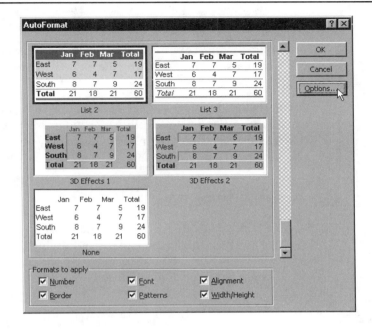

FIGURE 7.15:

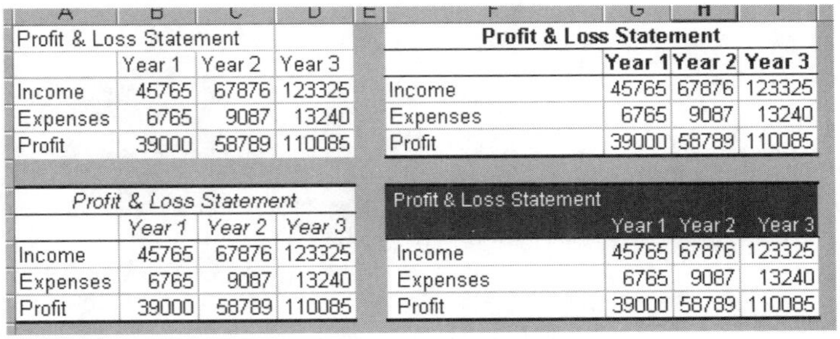

Four of the table style available in the AutoFormat dialog box list, with None (left) and Simple (right) at the top, Classic 1 (left) and Classic 2 (right) at the bottom.

Why You Need Style!

A style allows you to save all the formats you've applied to a cell as a single entity that can be reused over and over again. Applying a style is as quick as setting one format attribute, so if you find yourself setting the same combination of formats in several locations, it's more efficient to save them as a style.

Another advantage of using styles is that if you ever want to change any of a style's formats, all the cells using that style will immediately be updated to incorporate your changes.

Styles have advantages when it comes to writing macros, too. They improve readability and understandability by condensing your code, since applying one style containing multiple formats requires only one line of code—the same as required to set one format.

Excel's Default Styles

Excel provides a few default styles already set up to help you get started. You can use these as a basis for a new style by modifying the format attributes:

1. Choose Format ➤ Style to display the Style dialog box, shown in Figure 7.16.

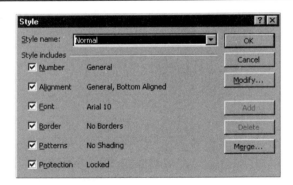

2. Select the Normal style from the list in the Style Name box. The Style Includes frame contains check boxes with their `Caption` properties set to the names of formatting elements followed by the values of some (but not all) of these attributes. For example, the Font check box gives the name and size of the font but doesn't say whether it's bold or italicized.

3. To demonstrate that these formats are retrieved from the Format Cells dialog box, click Modify to display the Format Cells dialog box, shown in Figure 7.17 with General selected from the Categories box in the Number tab. If

you compare this with Figure 7.16, you'll see that the Numbers check box has the attribute value of General.

4. Click Cancel to stop here, as we don't really want to change the Normal default style.

Notice how the captions next to the selected check boxes in the Style dialog box in Figure 7.16 match the various default options assigned by Excel and set in the tabs—they display the same format values.

FIGURE 7.17:

Format Cells dialog box showing the General category of number selected

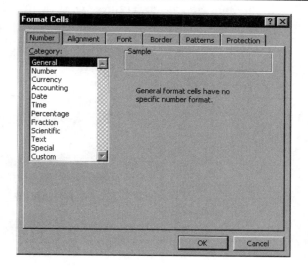

Fashion a Style of Your Own

When you create your own style, you can format it and then name it (style by example) or you can name it and then format it (style by definition). Either way, the formatting is achieved by setting values in the Format Cells dialog box. The next two examples illustrate both methods of creating your own style.

Style by Example

Excel can create a style based on a sample cell that's got the combination of formats you want. So if you've got a cell that you like the look of, you can save it as a style. In the following example, steps 1 through 10 format a cell, and steps 11 through 13 show you how to save these format settings as a style:

1. Enter the text **$1** at cell A1 and, with the cell still selected, choose Format ➤ Cells to open the Format Cells dialog box, which will be ready to change the format properties of A1 in the various tabs.

2. In the Alignment tab (see Figure 7.4), change the orientation to 45 degrees.

3. In the Font tab (Figure 7.5), change to Bookman Old Style, bold, 12.

4. In the Patterns tab (Figure 7.7), click any color.

5. In the Border tab (Figure 7.6), click double line style and Outline.

6. In the Number tab (Figure 7.18), click currency and leave the Symbol as $ and the Decimal Places as 2.

FIGURE 7.18:

Selecting Currency from the Number tab of the Format Cells dialog box

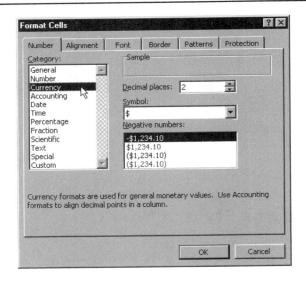

7. Click OK to apply the new formats to cell A1 and return to the worksheet.

8. Choose Format ➤ Row ➤ Height to open the Row Height dialog box:

9. Enter **41.25** in the Row Height box.

10. Click OK to set the height of the active row and return to the worksheet.

11. While the formatted cell is still selected, choose Format ➤ Style to display the Style dialog box (Figure 7.19).

12. Enter the name of your new style into the Style Name box. I've called mine "DollarSlant." Notice all the check box captions changing to the formats of the active cell as you enter your new style's name.

FIGURE 7.19:

Entering a style's name into the Style dialog box

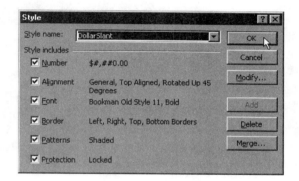

13. Click OK to define your style and return to the worksheet. The active cell should now be formatted in the new style (as shown).

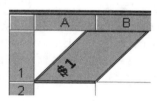

TIP	Choose descriptive names for styles, as this makes them easier to find when you're looking for them at a later date or when you've created your own library of styles.

Now every time you open the Style dialog box your style's name will appear in alphabetical order in the list, as shown in Figure 7.20.

Style dialog box with the DollarSlant style highlighted

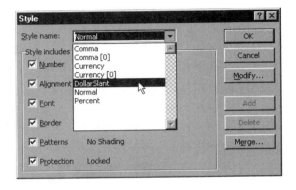

Style by Definition

Styles can also be created by naming them in the Style dialog box before defining their format settings. The following steps show how this is done:

1. Choose Format ≻ Style to display the Style dialog box.

2. Enter the name of the new style in the Style Name box.

3. Click Modify to display the Format Cells dialog box.

4. Select the formats required (repeat steps 2 through 6 in "Style by Example").

5. Click OK to return to the Style dialog box.

6. If you only want to define one style, click OK to apply the new style to your workbook and add its name to the Style Name list. If you want to define another style, click Add to add its name to the Style Name list for later use and select another style for the active cell.

7. Click OK to return to the worksheet.

This book is about automation and reusability, so if you already have a set of favorite styles it makes sense to reuse them. If you haven't, then you should consider creating some based on a worksheet you've already formatted or one you just like. You'll find it's worth the time and effort and you'll end up with a library of styles at your fingertips. Maybe you'll even consider spending a little time sprucing some of them up a bit now that you know how easy it is to do!

Saving a Style in a Macro

Listing 7.6 gives the macro for saving the style of the selected cell or range of cells. This code was recorded while steps 11 through 13 of "Style by Example" were performed.

LISTING 7.6

```
0    Sub SaveStyle()
1        '
2        ' SaveStyle Macro
3        ' Macro recorded actions for saving a style
4        '
5        ActiveWorkbook.Styles.Add Name:="DollarSlant"
6        Selection.Style = "DollarSlant"
7    End Sub
```

ANALYSIS

Line 5 adds the new name DollarSlant with the current format settings to the Styles collection in the active workbook.

Line 6, the Style property, returns a Style object and implicitly assigns its Name property to DollarSlant, which becomes the Style for the selected cell(s).

VBA's *Style* Object

Take a look at the list of members of the Style classes in the Excel library using the Object Browser. Some of the properties will already be familiar to you, as they are the same as the settings available in the Font tab inside the Format Cells dialog box, which are assigned to members in this class.

The Style object is an instance of the Style class, which contains all the format properties that can be set individually (such as Borders, Font, Locked, Name, Value, and WrapText) and has only one method (Delete). A Style object is returned by the Style property, which is a member of the Range object, so the code

```
Range("A1:B4").Style
```

returns a Style object. Therefore, you can specify any members of the Style class with this code, such as

```
Range("A1:B4").Style.Locked = True
```

Any property that returns a Range object can also be substituted for the Range keyword:

```
Selection.Style.Name = "NewStyleName"
```

Some of the properties of the Style object also return objects and so can be used to access member properties and methods of the object concerned. An example of this would be the Font property:

```
Range("A1:B4").Style.Font
```

which returns a Font object with properties that can be assigned values, such as:

```
Range("A1:B4").Style.Font.Bold = True
```

Applying a Style

So far, you've seen how to format cells and create new styles. All the hard work has been done; from this point forward, your life will be a little easier since you now only need to apply your styles. These four easy steps show you how:

1. Select a cell or range of cells you want to assign the style to.

2. Choose Format ➤ Style to display the Style dialog box.

3. Select the desired style from the list.

4. Click OK to apply the style to the selected cell(s).

In fact, you'll see in the next chapter how customized toolbars can be used to call macros that do the formatting for you—making life really simple!

Applying a Style with a Macro

The ApplyStyle macro (Listing 7.7) shows how the DollarSlant style saved in the SaveStyle macro (Listing 7.6) is applied to the selected cell.

LISTING 7.7

```
0    Sub ApplyStyle()
1        '
2        ' ApplyStyle Macro
```

```
3        ' Macro recorded actions to apply a style
4        '
5        Selection.Style = "DollarSlant"
6   End Sub
```

ANALYSIS

In **Line 5**, the selected cells are assigned the formats of the style named DollarSlant.

Merging Styles from Another Workbook

To copy a style from another workbook:

1. Open the workbook containing the style you want to copy from (the source).

2. Open the workbook you want to copy the style into (the destination), and choose Format ➤ Style.

3. Click Merge to display the Merge Styles dialog box (shown), which lists all the currently open workbooks except the active one (destination).

4. Select the source workbook from the Merge Styles From list. If the same style name appears in both the source and destination workbooks, you'll be prompted to confirm whether you want to proceed with the merge, in which case:

    •   Click Yes to overwrite all the styles in the destination with those of the same name in the source, or

    •   Click No to keep the styles with the same name in the destination workbook.

5. Click OK to return to the Style dialog box.

6. Click OK to return to the worksheet.

NOTE   The Merge Styles dialog box displays only the workbooks that are currently open. If only the active workbook is open, this list will be empty.

WARNING   During a merge of styles from several workbooks, you'll be prompted *only once* if two or more styles have the same name.

Making a Style Available to All Workbooks

So far we've saved styles in the active workbook, which means that all these styles will be available every time you open that workbook but unavailable when you open any other workbook. If you want a style to be available to all your workbooks, you've got to place it into Excel's default template. You do this as follows:

1. Open the workbook containing the style(s) you want to make available to other workbooks.

2. Open a new workbook.

3. Choose Format ➤ Styles to open the Style dialog box.

4. Click Merge to open the Styles Merge dialog box.

5. Select the workbook containing the styles that you want to make available in the Merge Styles From box.

6. Click OK to return to the Style dialog box. All styles from the workbook will now be listed in the Style Name list.

7. Click OK to return to the workbook.

8. With the new workbook active, choose File ➤ Save As to open the Save As dialog box.

9. **If you type "Book" in the File Name box, this will have repercussions for all future spreadsheets**, as this is the name for the default template used by Excel to create new workbooks. Enter **Workbook2** here. Although doing so

will prevent your styles from being automatically available to every workbook, you still have the option of selecting Workbook2 when you choose File ➤ New to create your workbook.

10. In the Save As Type box, select Template.

11. In the Save In box, select the `xlstart` folder (this can easily be found using Windows Explorer).

12. Click Save to return to the new workbook.

13. Close the workbook.

All the styles you've placed in the new workbook will now be contained in your Workbook2 template, which will be available for selection when you create any new workbook in the future by choosing File ➤ New. If you want to use these styles in workbooks that already exist, you must follow the steps given in the section "Merging Styles from Another Workbook" earlier in this chapter to add the new styles.

Changing Your Style

There are three different ways to change your style:

- If the style you want already exists, you can copy it.
- You can select a style that closely matches what you want and modify it by changing its formats as required.
- You can use styles available from another workbook (see "Merging Styles from Another Workbook" earlier in this chapter).

Changing by Example

To change the formats assigned to an existing style by reformatting a cell that uses that style:

1. Click the cell with the style you want to change.

2. Choose Format ➤ Cells and update the format properties as required in the tabs.

3. Choose Format ➤ Styles to open the Style dialog box.

4. Enter the exact name of the existing style you want to change in the Style Name box. You must enter the name using the keyboard rather than selecting it from the list to make the Add button available for selection.

5. Click Add to include the new style with the existing styles. Because you already have a style with the same name, you'll be prompted as shown below.

6. Click Yes to redefine the style and return to the Style dialog box.

7. Click OK to return to the worksheet.

Changing by Definition

These steps show you how to modify the formatting properties belonging to an existing style:

1. Select the cell with the style you want to modify.

2. Choose Format ➤ Style to display the Style dialog box.

3. Select the style to be modified from the list.

4. Click Modify to display the Format Cells dialog box.

5. Modify all the formatting properties as required.

6. Click OK to return to the Style dialog box.

7. Click OK to update the style with the new formats and return to the worksheet.

The active cell will now reflect these modifications, as will any other cells (in any workbook) that use the same style.

Deleting Your Style

They say if you keep something long enough it will come back into fashion—don't believe it! There is no doubt that you'll end up with a few styles that you've outgrown, or that have been superseded by others you've created as your expertise in Excel expands and your idea of what's visually appealing moves on.

Spring-clean and throw out all these old styles or you may end up using some of them by mistake. Deleting a style is much easier than creating one and is achieved in these four easy steps:

1. Open any workbook that contains the style and choose Format ➤ Style to display the Style Name dialog box.

2. Select the style you want to delete from the list.

3. Click Delete.

4. Click OK to return to the worksheet.

NOTE   Any cells set to the style you've just deleted are automatically reformatted using the Normal style.

WARNING   The Normal style cannot be deleted, but you can update it. Deleting any of the other styles provided with Excel can cause side effects. For example, if you delete the Comma style, Currency style, or Percent style, these will render their associated buttons on the Formatting toolbar useless.

Conditions in VBA Macros

Writing your own macros allows you the flexibility of having as many format conditions as you like. Listing 7.8 shows a macro with five conditions that sets the interior colors of cells according to the values they contain (as shown below). It uses the RGB (red-green-blue) function to compute the color values and the For loop to repeat the same code for all five cells.

Let's look first at the RGB function and how it works, then we'll move on to the For statement and then to the macro itself.

Visual Basic's *RGB* Function   The macro uses VBA's RGB function to set the color value. The RGB function requires three arguments to specify the red, green, and blue components of the color required. The RGB function uses these to calculate a number representing the color. The three arguments should all be in the range 0–255, with values greater than 255 being reduced to 255 and negative values being increased to 0.

Red is returned when RGB is called with the arguments 255,0,0; blue is returned when they are 0,0,255; and green is returned when they are 0,255,0. Black is returned if the arguments are all zero, and white if they're all assigned 255.

Looping with the *For* Statement

The For statement in Listing 7.8 loops five times to set the interior color of five cells and keeps a count of the number of times it's passed through the loop. When the For loop at Line 4 is entered for the first time, Index is initialized to 1. The Next statement at Line 20 marks the end of the For loop. Each time Next is executed, it increments Index and then loops back to the start of the For loop, which tests whether Index is less than or equal to 5. The looping continues until Index equals 6.

LISTING 7.8

```
0    Sub SetLotsOfFormatConditions()
1        '
2        'Macro to set lots of Format conditions
3        '
4        For Index = 1 To 5
5            With Worksheets("Sheet2").Cells(Index, 1)
6                If .Value < 0 Then
7                    .Interior.Color = RGB(220, 180, 255)
8                ElseIf .Value = 0 Then
9                    .Interior.Color = RGB(150, 120, 255)
10               ElseIf .Value < 10 Then
11                   .Interior.Color = RGB(200, 160, 255)
12               ElseIf .Value < 50 Then
13                   .Interior.Color = RGB(100, 80, 255)
14                   .Font.ColorIndex = 2 'set font to white
```

```
15              ElseIf .Value < 100 Then
16                  .Interior.Color = RGB(50, 40, 255)
17                  .Font.ColorIndex = 2 'set font to white
18              End If
19          End With
20      Next
21  End Sub
```

ANALYSIS

Line 4 is the start of the For loop and initializes Index to 1 the first time it's encountered. In subsequent encounters, it will increment Index before checking that Index is less than or equal to 5.

In **Line 5**, the Cells property requires two arguments to identify a cell by its row and column numbers. The Cells property of the Worksheets object (Sheet2) returns a Range object to identify the cell, so it can be used with all the Number properties and methods of the Range object, as explained in the section "VBA's Style Object" earlier in this chapter. The start of the With statement allows us to abbreviate our code by skipping the qualifier

```
Worksheets("Sheet2").Cells(Index, 1)
```

when we want to refer to the methods and properties (of the Range object it returns) in the code—that is, until the End With statement is reached at Line 19.

Line 6 is our first If condition.

Line 7 uses the RGB function to return a color value that becomes the interior color for the cell indicated at the start of the With statement.

Lines 8 through 17 have much the same features as Lines 6 and 7.

Line 14 and 17 also set the font to White for contrast to the darker interior color.

Summary

This chapter taught you all about formats and how they can be combined into a single, more easily managed style. Most of the format attributes were considered, and we looked at the relationship between the properties in VBA code and the topics in the Excel dialog boxes that allow you to specify the format settings required.

You can now

- create your own number format
- create visually pleasing worksheets (or at least make improvements to the ones you have)
- set formatting conditions manually and in macros
- use Excel's automatic features
- create your own styles
- view the `Style` and `Font` classes in the Object Browser
- merge styles from multiple workbooks
- delete styles
- write a macro with multiple formatting conditions

Your job now is to hunt down all the snazzy cells that have impressed you in the past and start building up your own library of styles.

CHAPTER
EIGHT

8

Running Macros from a Toolbar (and Getting Them Right)

This chapter describes how to create a custom toolbar and design your own icons for the buttons you place in it. You'll also see how to group buttons in the toolbar, as well as how to add functional buttons and menu item buttons. And you'll learn how to run macros from toolbar buttons and how to call the Excel Function Wizard from a macro.

After you create a macro, you can run it from a keyboard combination. However, this is not really user-friendly, since anyone who needs to run your macro has to know of the macro's existence as well as the key combination to run it. Creating a custom toolbar and running macros via toolbar buttons is an easier alternative for users. Toolbars provide visual cues to the features that are available and are one of the reasons why GUIs have proven so popular.

And you'll find Excel's extensive debugging features helpful when your macro doesn't work the way it's expected to. You can even watch the values of variables change as you step through your code line by line.

Creating Macros to Run from the Toolbar

Let's start by creating simple macros that we can run from our custom toolbar. The four macros I've created are for formatting row labels, formatting column labels, formatting headings, and restoring cells to the default format. After you've entered these macros, I'll show you how to create a toolbar containing customized buttons to run each one.

The following steps show you how to enter your macros directly into a module:

1. Create a new workbook and open the Visual Basic Editor.

2. Choose Insert ➤ Module to create `Module1`, and enter the code for the four macros as follows:

LISTING 8.1

```
0    Sub RowLabels()
1         '
2         ' RowLabels Macro
3         ' Macro to format row labels
4         '
```

```
5        With Selection
6            .HorizontalAlignment = xlLeft
7            .VerticalAlignment = xlBottom
8        End With
9        With Selection.Font
10           .Name = "Arial"
11           .FontStyle = "Bold"
12           .Size = 12
13       End With
14   End Sub
```

ANALYSIS

Line 5 starts the With statement so that the properties of the selected range of cells identified by the Selection property can be used without being fully qualified by putting Selection. in front of them.

Line 6 and **Line 7** set the HorizontalAlignment property to the constant xlLeft and the VerticalAlignment property to the constant xlBottom.

Line 9 starts the With statement so that the properties of the Font object returned by the Font property of the selected range of cells can be used without fully qualifying them by putting Selection.Font. at the front.

Lines 10 through 12 assign values to the Name, FontStyle, and Size properties of the Font object.

LISTING 8.2

```
0    Sub ColumnLabels()
1        '
2        ' ColumnLabels Macro
3        ' Macro to format column labels
4        '
5        With Selection
6            .HorizontalAlignment = xlCenter
7            .VerticalAlignment = xlBottom
8            .Orientation = 30
9        End With
10       With Selection.Font
```

```
11              .Name = "Arial"
12              .FontStyle = "Bold"
13              .Size = 14
14          End With
15  End Sub
```

ANALYSIS

Lines 5 through 14 are the same as the With statements in Listing 8.1 except that the Orientation property is set to 30 to make the text slanted and Size is set to 14 instead of 12.

LISTING 8.3

```
0   Sub Heading()
1       '
2       ' Heading Macro
3       ' Macro to format worksheet headings
4       '
5       With Selection
6           .Merge (True)
7           .HorizontalAlignment = xlCenter
8           .VerticalAlignment = xlBottom
9       End With
10      With Selection.Font
11          .Name = "Arial"
12          .FontStyle = "Bold"
13          .Size = 18
14      End With
15  End Sub
```

ANALYSIS

Lines 5 through 14 are similar to the With statements in Listing 8.1, with the Merge property set to True to merge the selected cells used for the heading.

LISTING 8.4

```
0    Sub NormalFormat()
1        '
2        ' NormalFormat Macro
3        ' Macro to return to the default format
4        '
5        With Selection
6            .HorizontalAlignment = xlGeneral
7            .VerticalAlignment = xlBottom
8            .Orientation = 0
9        End With
10       With Selection.Font
11           .Name = "Arial"
12           .FontStyle = "Regular"
13           .Size = 10
14        End With
15   End Sub
```

ANALYSIS

Lines 5 through 14 are similar to the With statements in Listing 8.1 except that all the properties are set to the default values originally assigned by Excel.

TIP

The NormalFormat macro resets the format of the selected cells back to the Excel default settings, undoing any other formatting. This is quicker than using the menu command Edit ➤ Clear ➤ Formats, and you could easily make adjustments to this macro to define your own "normal" formats.

Return to your workbook and check that your macros give the correct results by selecting a few cells and clicking the Run Macro button in the Visual Basic toolbar. When you're confident that all of your macros are working, you're ready to create the toolbar containing the buttons to run them.

Creating a New Toolbar

When you create a toolbar, it becomes an integrated part of your Excel environment. If a macro is assigned to a button in your toolbar, Excel tracks where this macro can be found and can run the macro whether or not the workbook containing the macro is open. To create a new toolbar:

1. Choose Tools ➤ Customize to open the Customize dialog box.

2. Select the Toolbars tab (shown in Figure 8.1) and click New to display the New Toolbar dialog box.

FIGURE 8.1:

Customize dialog box

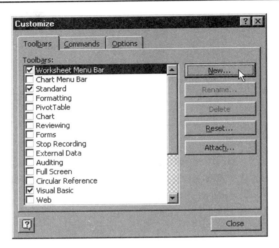

3. Replace Custom 1 with the text **Headings & Labels** in the Toolbar Name box as shown below (left) and click OK to return to the Customize dialog box. Your new toolbar's name will appear, already checked, at the end of the list in the Toolbars box, and an empty toolbar will be displayed as shown below (right).

4. Click Close to return to the worksheet.

5. Choose View ➤ Toolbars to view the drop-down list displaying your new toolbar Headings & Labels (Figure 8.2).

FIGURE 8.2:

List of toolbars including the new Headings & Labels toolbar at the end

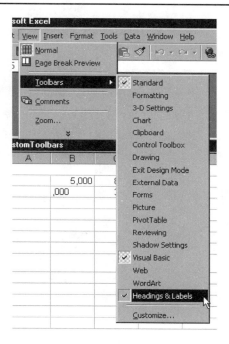

Adding Buttons to a Toolbar

Now that you've created your empty toolbar and can display it, the next thing you need to do is to place buttons into it. The following steps show you how to add the Smiley Custom Button:

1. Select the Commands tab in the Customize dialog box, then select Macros from the list in the Categories box as shown in Figure 8.3.

2. Drag and drop the Smiley Custom Button (displayed in the Commands box in Figure 8.3) into your toolbar, as shown below. The Modify Selection button will now be available for selection.

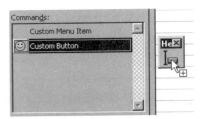

FIGURE 8.3:

Commands tab with
Macros selected

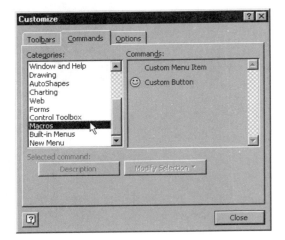

3. Click the Modify Selection button in the Customize dialog box to display the list of options shown in Figure 8.4. Overwrite "Custom Button" in the Name Box with **Column Labels** (as shown). Click Close to return to your worksheet.

4. Pause the mouse cursor over the Smiley button and the ToolTip that pops up will be Column Labels (as shown).

FIGURE 8.4:

Menu options available
when the Modify Selection
button is clicked

FIGURE 8.4:

Menu options available
when the Modify Selection
button is clicked

Designing Icons for Toolbar Buttons

Now you have a toolbar with a Smiley icon which doesn't really conjure up anything to do with formatting. There is also the fact that there are four macros to be called from the toolbar, and you can't run them all using the same Smiley icon. In this section, I'll show you how to design your own icon and save it in the format that icons require in a file with the extension .ICO. Let's redesign the icons for our buttons:

1. Right-click the Smiley button and choose Customize from the shortcut menu to display the Customize dialog box (Figure 8.3). This needs to be open so that the shortcut menu for customizing is available at the next step.

2. Right-click the Smiley button and choose Change Button Image from the shortcut menu to display the selection of existing icons shown in Figure 8.5. Since none of these reflect the functionality of the macros, I'll show you how to use the Button Editor to design your own.

3. Choose Edit Button Image from the shortcut menu to display the Button Editor dialog box, as shown in Figure 8.6. Whatever you draw in the image in the Picture box will appear as the icon in your toolbar, but the original

Smiley icon won't be changed and will still remain as the icon for new Custom Buttons. Figure 8.7 shows the picture I've designed for the icon that runs my `ColumnLabels` macro. I've made my button black and gray for printing in this book, but you might like to make the black bits red to make them stand out more.

FIGURE 8.5:

Selection of button icons available

FIGURE 8.6:

Button Editor dialog box with default Custom Button icon (Smiley face)

FIGURE 8.7:

Button Editor dialog box with image for the button icon that will run the ColumnLabels macro

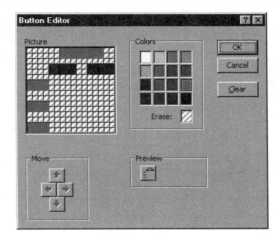

4. Click OK to close the Button Editor and display the image as the button icon in the toolbar, as shown below.

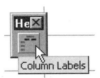

Running a Macro from a Toolbar Button

To run the ColumnLabels macro from the toolbar button:

1. Right-click the button and choose Customize to open the Customize dialog box.

2. Right-click the button again and choose Assign Macro to open the Assign Macro dialog box.

3. Select ColumnLabels from the list of macros, as shown in Figure 8.8, and click OK to return to the Customize dialog box.

4. Click Close to return to your worksheet.

5. Select the range of cells whose column labels you want to format.

FIGURE 8.8:

Assigning the macro
ColumnLabels to a
toolbar button

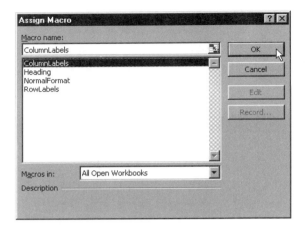

6. Click the Column Labels button in your toolbar. If your toolbar is not displayed, choose View ➤ Toolbars ➤ Headings & Labels, as shown in Figure 8.2.

The selected range of cells will now have its column labels formatted by the ColumnLabels macro.

Follow the steps given earlier in this chapter (in the section "Adding Buttons to a Toolbar") to drag and drop three more Smileys into your toolbar (as shown below). Change their Name properties to RowLabels, Headings, and Default Format for their ToolTips. Use the Button Editor (described earlier in "Designing Icons for Toolbar Buttons") to design their button icons based on the one for ColumnLabels.

Follow the steps for running a macro from a toolbar button to assign the other macros to these three new buttons in your toolbar. If my icons are as meaningful as I hope they are, then you'll have no problem in knowing which button to associate with each macro.

Adding a Functional Button to Your Toolbar

You can add any button listed in the Customize dialog box and make use of its normal functionality. For example, the Undo button allows you to backtrack by undoing things you've done recently. The following steps show you how to add the Undo button from the Edit category to your toolbar:

1. Choose Tools ➤ Customize to display the Customize dialog box.

2. Select Edit from the Categories box and drag and drop Undo from the Commands box into your toolbar (see Figure 8.9). If you right-click this button, you'll notice that the shortcut menu commands for updating the icon or assigning a macro have all been dimmed and are unavailable for selection. This makes sense, as you'd soon get into a mess if you could change the functionality of existing commands that users are familiar with.

FIGURE 8.9:

The Undo command available in the Edit category

3. Make a few changes to your worksheet and click the Down arrow in the Undo button. As shown below, this will list your changes and allow you to select individual items for undoing or to select all of the items and undo all of your actions in one hit. This button is also available in the Standard toolbar and behaves in the same way in both toolbars.

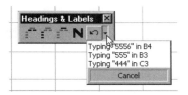
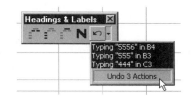

NOTE A command dragged from the Commands box of the Customize dialog box will retain its usual functionality and so cannot be used to run a macro.

Grouping Buttons on a Custom Toolbar

When you create a custom toolbar, you may want to group some of the buttons that perform similar functions. I've separated my toolbar buttons into two groups. The first group contains buttons that run macros to format the selected range of cells; the second group undoes the formatting by restoring it to the Normal formats, or undoes recent changes made to the worksheet. Groups of buttons are separated in the toolbar by vertical bars (as shown); the following steps show you how to place a vertical bar to separate groups of buttons in your toolbar.

1. Right-click the toolbar and choose Customize from the shortcut menu to open the Customize dialog box (Figure 8.9).

2. Right-click the button that runs the NormalFormat macro, which is the button that will start the second group once you have put in the vertical separator bar.

3. Choose Begin A Group from the shortcut menu. A vertical bar will be placed immediately to the left of the chosen button. (For this reason, you cannot begin a group with the first button on a toolbar.)

4. Click Close to return to the worksheet.

Adding a Menu Item Button

Your toolbar can also include buttons that contain menu commands. Let's expand our toolbar by adding one of these buttons.

1. Choose Tools ➤ Customize to open the Customize dialog box, and select the Commands tab.

2. Select New Menu from the Categories box and drag the New Menu from the Commands box to expand your toolbar, as shown below.

3. Click Modify Selection in the Customize dialog box and change "New Menu" in the Name box to **MyMacros**.

4. Click the Down arrow in the MyMacros menu item in the toolbar to display an empty drop-down list (as shown).

5. Select Macros from the Categories box in the Customize dialog box. Drag the Custom Menu Item from the Commands box over to the empty MyMacros button drop-down list, as shown in Figure 8.10.

FIGURE 8.10:

Placing an item under MyMacros

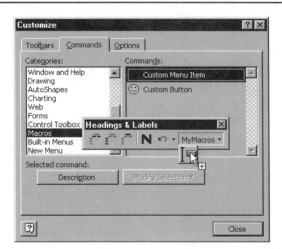

6.   Click Close to close the Customize dialog box.

Now let's write a macro to call a Visual Basic function that you can run from this new menu button. You can get help with the parameters required by the function using the Quick Info editing feature.

Using the Quick Info Editing Feature

The Quick Info editing feature in the Visual Basic Editor pops up information about the current parameter for a function or procedure call. You can have this feature pop up information on command whenever you do one of the following:

- Choose Edit ➤ Quick Info

- Enter Ctrl+I

- Click the Quick Info button on the Edit toolbar (as shown)

Alternatively, you can make the Quick Info feature generate its pop-up information automatically by:

1.   Choosing Tools ➤ Options to open the Options dialog box.

2.   Selecting the Editor tab and checking the check box for Auto Quick Info.

Before you start this next example, make sure that the Auto Quick Info check box is checked. Let's create a macro that adds the string ,000 to the contents of the active cell. I'll show you how to use the Quick Info feature to help us write the code:

1.   Enter the code opening statement shown in Figure 8.11. When you hit the Enter key at the end of this statement, the closing statement End Sub will automatically appear.

2.   Start entering the rest of the code pictured in Figure 8.12 and watch the pop-up information appear automatically when you enter the period in the second line.

FIGURE 8.11:

Entering the opening statement

FIGURE 8.11:

Entering the opening statement

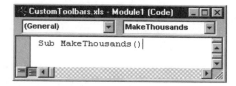

FIGURE 8.12:

Using the Quick Info editing feature to help with entering code

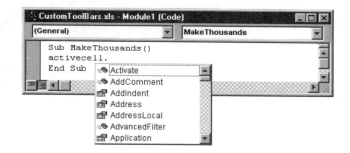

3. Start entering **value**, and as you enter each character the list will scroll and the first entry to match the string entered will be highlighted:

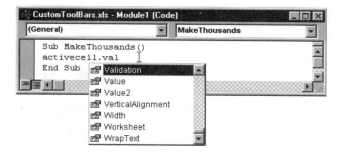

4. Continue entering the second statement. When you enter the opening parenthesis of the CVar function, the type of argument that VBA expects pops up as shown below.

5. Start off the expression by entering **activecell** followed by a period (.) and all the properties and methods for the `Range` object (which the `ActiveCell` property returns). To enter `Value`, you can either enter it via the keyboard or double-click it from the list.

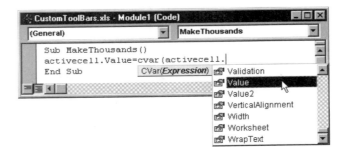

6. Complete the statement as shown in Figure 8.13.

FIGURE 8.13:

Entering a statement is best achieved using lower-case characters.

7. Click any other line in the macro and Excel will capitalize the words it recognizes and add a few spaces, as shown below.

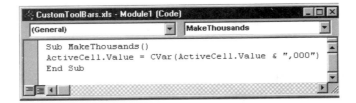

Calling a Macro from a Menu Item

Now that you've created a menu item and have a macro, MakeThousands, let's assign our macro to the menu item and change the menu item's name in the toolbar:

1. Assign your MakeThousands macro to the button in the toolbar by right-clicking the MyMacros button in your Headings & Labels toolbar and selecting Customize from the shortcut menu.

2. Click the Down arrow in the MyMacros button to display its drop-down list. Right-click the Custom Menu Item button to display the shortcut menu for customizing a toolbar button and change "Custom Menu Item" in the Name box to **Change to Thousands**.

3. Click Assign Macro from the shortcut menu to open the Assign Macro dialog box, select MakeThousands from the list, and click OK.

4. Click Close to close the Customize dialog box.

Test your new toolbar button by entering an amount into a cell and making it the active cell before clicking the Change To Thousands toolbar button.

You can call any of the functions available in Excel from your macro in the same way.

Running the Function Wizard from a Macro

The FunctionWizard method allows you to display the Paste Function dialog box in code. The code for running the Wizard to assign a function to the active cell is:

```
0    Sub FunctionWhiz()
1        ActiveCell.FunctionWizard
2    End Sub
```

I've called my macro FunctionWhiz; Line 1 shows the FunctionWizard method being called in code.

Let's assign our macro to a toolbar button so that we can run Excel's Function Wizard from our toolbar:

1. Right-click MyMacros in the toolbar and choose Customize from the short-cut menu.

2. Select the Commands tab in the Customize dialog box, select Macros from the Categories box, and drag Custom Menu Item from the Commands box to the end of the MyMacros drop-down list (as shown).

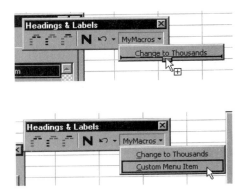

3. With the new Custom Menu Item selected, click Modify Selection and change the Name from Custom Menu Item to **Excel Function Wizard**.

4. Select Assign Macro from the shortcut menu and select FunctionWhiz from the list displayed in the Assign Macros dialog box.

5. Click OK to return to the Customize dialog box.

6. Click Close to return to your worksheet.

Let's run the FunctionWhiz macro to display the Paste Function dialog box:

1. Select the cell or range of cells that you want to apply a function to.

2. Click the Down arrow in the MyMacros button in your toolbar and click Excel Function Wizard.

An equals sign (=) will appear in the Formula bar and the Paste Function dialog box will be displayed for you to select the function required. Selecting a function opens the Formula Palette dialog box for you to enter your range or numerical information. Chapter 4 deals exclusively with formulas and functions and describes the Paste Function and Formula Palette dialog boxes in detail.

Removing a Toolbar

When you create a toolbar, it becomes part of the Excel environment until you delete it again. You can delete a toolbar even if it contains buttons.

1. Choose Tools ➤ Customize to open the Customize dialog box, and select the Toolbars tab.

2. Select the toolbar to be deleted from the Toolbars box and click Delete. The selected toolbar will have disappeared off the screen and will no longer appear in the list displayed when you choose View ➤ Toolbars.

Deleting a Button from the Toolbar

Deleting a button from a toolbar is much easier than putting it there in the first place. Just follow these two steps:

1. Choose Tools ➤ Customize to open the Customize dialog box so that the shortcut menu options for customizing become available.

2. Right-click the button you want to delete and choose Delete from the shortcut menu.

Renaming a Custom Toolbar

1. Choose Tools ➤ Customize and select the Toolbars tab.

2. Select the toolbar to be named from the list and click the Rename button to open the Rename Toolbar dialog box (Figure 8.14).

FIGURE 8.14:

Rename Toolbar dialog box

Enter the new name in the Toolbar Name box, click OK to return to the Customize dialog box, and click Close to finalize.

Debugging Features

When your macro doesn't work in the way you expect it to, you may find the debugging features supplied in the Visual Basic Editor extremely helpful. The menu options available in the Debug menu are shown in Figure 8.15.

FIGURE 8.15:

Debug menu options

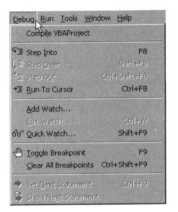

These features allow you to set a breakpoint where your code will temporarily stop executing, and to step through the code line by line while watching the values of the different variables change as you go. The debugging takes place as you run your project; when the execution stops at a breakpoint, the menu options available under the Run menu command change, as shown below.

Debug Toolbar

The Debug toolbar shown in Figure 8.16 contains shortcuts to some of the most frequently used debugging features.

Design Mode   Toggles the Design mode on or off. When it's on, event procedures can't be triggered by clicking them.

Run Sub/UserForm   Runs the Load event procedure if a UserForm is active; otherwise will run the macro or procedure where the cursor is located in the code window.

FIGURE 8.16:

Debug toolbar

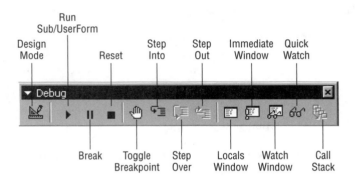

Break   Stops the code running and goes into Break mode.

Reset   Stops the project executing after resetting all of the variables and emptying any values from the stack. (Excel uses a stack to store the values of variables and arguments during procedure calls and also to store intermediate values when evaluating worksheet functions.)

Toggle Breakpoint   Sets or removes a breakpoint at the code where the cursor is.

Step Into   Executes the code line by line, jumping into any procedures as they're called.

Step Over   Executes the code line by line, processing all of the statements in any procedures in one hit as they're called.

Step Out   Completes the execution of the current procedure.

Locals Window   Displays the Locals window, containing the list of variables declared inside the current procedure with their values and types.

Immediate Window   Displays the Immediate window, where you can paste a line of code and run it immediately by pressing the Enter key.

Watch Window   Displays the Watch window, listing expressions selected for watching with their values, types, and contexts.

Quick Watch   Displays the Quick Watch window, containing the current expression with its value, type, and context.

Call Stack   Displays the Calls window, listing all of the procedures that have started to run but haven't yet finished.

Setting Breakpoints

There are four ways to set the breakpoint:

- Click the left-hand strip in the code window near the line where you want to break.

- Click anywhere in the line where you want to break and choose Debug ➢ Toggle Breakpoint.

- Click anywhere in the line where you want to break and press the F9 function key.

- Click anywhere in the line where you want to break and click the Toggle Breakpoint button in the Debug toolbar.

When a line contains a breakpoint, it's highlighted in red and a red dot appears in the left-hand strip.

When you choose Run ➢ Run Sub/UserForm, the code is executed until it reaches the line containing the breakpoint. A yellow arrow is placed inside the red dot in the left hand strip and the line becomes highlighted in yellow, as shown below.

Visual Basic can pop up values of variables when the mouse is paused over them. To turn this feature on:

1. Choose Tools ➤ Options and select the Editor tab.

2. Check the Auto Data Tips check box in the Code Settings frame.

3. Click OK to close the Options dialog box.

I selected a cell containing the value 4 before running the macro, so pausing the mouse anywhere over the string `ActiveCell.Value` gives the pop-up information shown.

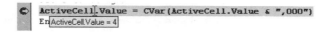

An alternative way of viewing the value is to highlight the item you want to see the value of and choose Debug ➤ Quick Watch to open the Quick Watch dialog box, as shown in Figure 8.17.

FIGURE 8.17:

Quick Watch dialog box opened for the Module1 code window

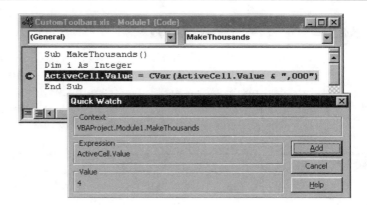

To add an item to the Watch list, click the Add button; otherwise click the Cancel button to close the list. Clicking the Add button adds the item to the list of watched expressions. If it's the first item to be watched, it also causes the Watches dialog box to be displayed. You can keep the Watches dialog box displayed while you continue your debugging process.

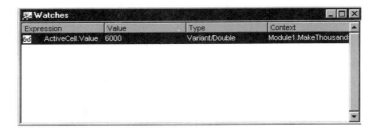

Clicking Debug ➤ Step Into (or depressing the F8 function key) executes the current line and stops at the next line, which is displayed in yellow with a yellow arrow in the left-hand strip (as shown below).

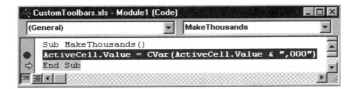

Resuming Your Macro

When you've finished debugging a section of code, you can resume running your project from that point onward by choosing the Run ➤ Continue menu option or by selecting the Continue button from the Standard toolbar or the Debug toolbar. This avoids having to start at the beginning again and allows you to see the difference your changes to statements have made to the overall application.

TIP   To debug a section of code, set a breakpoint at the first line and use the F8 function key to step through the section line by line, making changes where required. Then use the Continue button to run the remaining code and make sure your changes haven't had any adverse effects anywhere else in the application.

Summary

This chapter showed you how to

- create a new toolbar containing buttons and menu items
- design button icons using the Button Editor facility
- run macros from toolbar buttons
- add buttons that retain their normal functionality
- group buttons on the toolbar
- code macros that run Excel Wizards
- remove a button from the toolbar
- delete a toolbar

You should also be able to set and use the Quick Info editing feature that will help you code your macros.

After reading the section on debugging, you'll be able to

- set breakpoints
- run your code line by line
- watch the values of variables and expressions change as each line is completed

CHAPTER

NINE

9

Printing Your Worksheets

This chapter takes you through the facilities available in Excel and VBA for printing worksheets. It discusses the properties associated with printing worksheet images and how these can be set in the Page Setup dialog box or in VBA macro code. You'll see how you can write code to customize print macros for all your worksheets rather than printing them individually and having to remember what properties to set for each one. The Microsoft Common Dialog Control is used to display the Print dialog box that requires a response from the user, and the PrintOut method is used to print directly from a macro without user intervention.

Setting the Range of Cells to Be Printed

To avoid printing the entire worksheet each time you choose File ➢ Print, you must set up a print area to let Excel know exactly what cells you want to print. The print area is made up of one or more ranges of cells that you select before choosing File ➢ Print Area ➢ Set Print Area. This will change the solid filled border of the selected range(s) of cells to a kind of dashed effect, as shown.

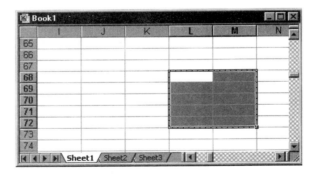

When it's not selected, the print area can be identified by the dashed line border, as shown below, to remind you of your choice. If no dashed line is displayed, you must choose File ➢ Page Setup and select the Adjust To option button in the Scaling frame. The range of cells to be printed can also be specified.

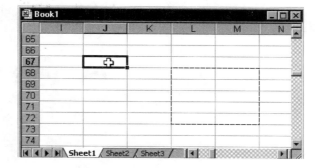

Listing 9.1 shows how to set the range of cells to be printed in a VBA macro. I'll revisit this macro later in this chapter to make it more generic after we've looked at some of the other Excel printing features.

LISTING 9.1

```
0    Sub SetPrintArea()
1        'sets the range of cells to be printed
2        ActiveSheet.PageSetup.PrintArea = "$L$68:$M$72"
3    End Sub
```

ANALYSIS

Line 2 sets the `PrintArea` property of the `PageSetup` object to the range specified by the string.

Page Settings for Printing Worksheets

The page settings allow you to control how the image of your worksheet will appear on paper when it's printed. Page settings include margins, orientation, headers and footers, print areas, whether or not to print gridlines and labels, which pages to print, and the number of copies required. These can all be set in the Page Setup dialog box (shown in Figure 9.1) and also in VBA macro code. To display the Page Setup dialog box, choose File ➤ Page Setup while in Excel and update the settings in the different tabs as required. The following sections describe some of the features available in each tab and the corresponding VBA macro code.

FIGURE 9.1:

Page tab from the Page Setup dialog box

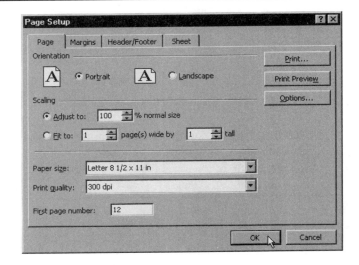

Page Tab

Select the Portrait or Landscape option button in the Orientation frame to specify which direction you want the text printed—across or down the page.

If you want to enlarge or shrink the printed image of your worksheet, then select the Adjust To option button and adjust the number in the percentage box as required.

If you want your worksheet's image printed on a specific number of pages, select the Fit To option button and enter the number of pages you'd like for the width of the worksheet (wide) and the number of pages you'd like for the height (tall). The Fit To option will scale down the printed image to fit on the number of pages requested, but won't enlarge it. The image of the worksheet's columns will be reduced to fit the number of pages wide and the image of the rows reduced to fit the number of pages tall. To see how much your image will need to be reduced, you must close the Page Setup dialog box and reopen it; the percentage now displayed in the % Normal Size box represents the greater of the width or height reduction required.

You can also specify the size of the paper being used, the print quality in dots per inch (dpi), and the page number to appear on the first page. If you click the

Options button, a dialog box will open, displaying the settings for your printer as shown in Figure 9.2.

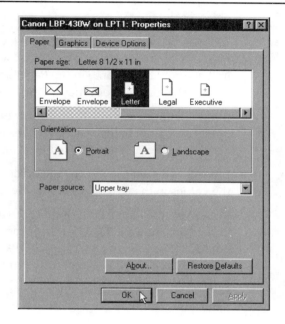

The properties available in the Page tab of the Page Setup dialog box can also be set in VBA code; Listing 9.2 shows how.

LISTING 9.2

```
0    Sub SetPagesRequired()
1        'sets the number of pages required wide and tall
2        With ActiveSheet.PageSetup
3        .Orientation = xlPortrait
4        .Zoom = False 'set to the % normal size box number
5        .FitToPagesWide = 2
6        .FitToPagesTall = 3
7        .PaperSize = xlPaperLetter
8        .PrintQuality = 300
9        .FirstPageNumber = 12
10       End With
11   End Sub
```

Line 2 uses the `With` statement to avoid having to specify the `PageSetup` object each time.

Line 3 sets the orientation using the Excel constant `xlPortrait`. The alternative is `xlLandscape` to correspond with the two option buttons available in the Orientation frame in the Page tab in either the Page Setup dialog box (Figure 9.1) or the Properties dialog box for your printer (Figure 9.2).

Line 4, setting `Zoom` to `False`, corresponds to the Adjust To option button in Figure 9.1 not being selected. If this button is selected, `Zoom` is set to the number in the % Normal Size box.

Lines 5 and 6 set the `FitToPagesWide` and `FitToPagesTall` properties to the values in the two boxes alongside the Fit To option button.

Line 7 sets the `PaperSize` property to the Excel constant `xlPaperLetter`. Other constants available for this property include `xlPaper11x17`, `xlPaperA3`, `xlPaperEnvelope10`, and `xlPaperA4`. The `PaperSize` can be set manually in either the Page Setup or Properties dialog box.

Line 8 sets the `PrintQuality` property to 300 dpi, corresponding to the value entered in the Print Quality box.

Line 9 sets the `FirstPageNumber` to 12, corresponding to the value entered in the First Page Number box.

Margins Tab

Using the features available in the Margins tab (Figure 9.3), you can set margins for the four edges of your print page. In addition, there are boxes where you can enter the position of your header and footer, which should ideally be less than the top and bottom margins, respectively.

The Horizontal and Vertical check boxes in the Center On Page frame at the bottom of this tab allow you to center your worksheet image on the page. Figure 9.4 shows what happens to the preview layout when both of these check boxes are checked.

Listing 9.3 gives the `SetMarginsRequired` macro, which shows how all these margin settings can be assigned to properties in code. After this macro is run, the Margins tab of the Page Setup dialog box will display these new values.

FIGURE 9.3:

Margins tab from the Page Setup dialog box

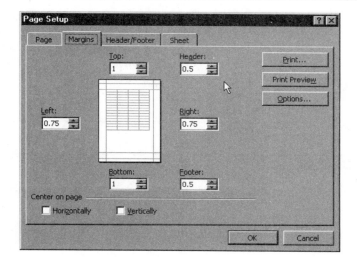

FIGURE 9.4:

Checking the Center Horizontally and Vertically check boxes updates the preview layout.

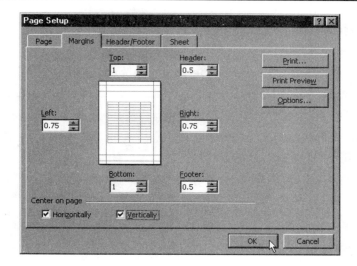

LISTING 9.3

```
0   Sub SetMarginsRequired()
1       With ActiveSheet.PageSetup
2           .LeftMargin = Application.InchesToPoints(0.75)
3           .RightMargin = Application.InchesToPoints(0.75)
```

```
4              .TopMargin = Application.InchesToPoints(1)
5              .BottomMargin = Application.InchesToPoints(1)
6              .HeaderMargin = Application.InchesToPoints(0.5)
7              .FooterMargin = Application.InchesToPoints(0.5)
8              .CenterHorizontally = True
9              .CenterVertically = True
10        End With
11   End Sub
```

ANALYSIS

Lines 2 through 7 show all the margins being set to the values shown in the boxes in Figure 9.4.

Lines 8 and 9 specify that you want to center your worksheet image horizontally or vertically.

Header/Footer Tab

The Header/Footer tab (Figure 9.5) allows you to define the text you want displayed as the header and the footer.

FIGURE 9.5:

Header/Footer tab of the Page Setup dialog box

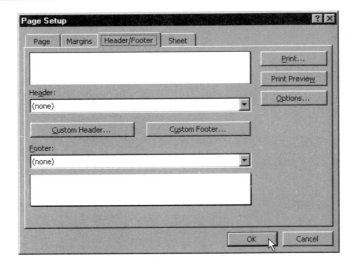

You can either select a built-in header or footer from the two drop-down lists in the Header and Footer boxes or make up your own custom ones by clicking Custom Header or Custom Footer. Figure 9.6 shows the drop-down list in the Header box.

FIGURE 9.6:

Header drop-down list

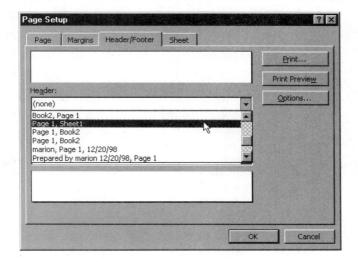

Clicking Custom Header opens up the Header dialog box, shown in Figure 9.7.

FIGURE 9.7:

Entering the header into the sections in the Header dialog box

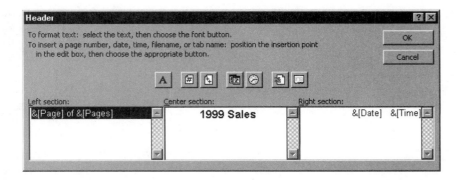

The three text boxes allow you to add heading text to the left, center, or right of the page—I've entered all three. The buttons in this dialog box allow you to add items that are commonly found in headings. The first button (with the **A** icon) displays the Font dialog box, which allows you to format your text. The other buttons (from left to right) allow you to insert a page number, total number of pages, date and time of printing, workbook name, and worksheet name.

To create the heading shown in Figure 9.8:

1. Click inside the Left section box and then on the Page Number button to enter the string &[Page].

2. Enter the string **of** (with one space character before and one after the word "of"), then click Total Pages to append &[Pages] as shown in Figure 9.7.

3. Click inside the Center section box and then on the Font button to open the Font dialog box. Select Bold from the Font Style list and 12 from the Size list. Click OK to return to the Page Setup dialog box. Enter the string **1999 Sales** as shown.

4. Click inside the Right section box and then on the Date button to enter the string &[Date]. Enter a few spaces, then click the Time button to append the string &[Time].

Click OK to close the Header dialog box. The Header/Footer tab will be updated to display the header just entered. If your headings include a date or time, this will be retrieved from the system whenever the worksheet is printed so that the current date and time of printing are always given.

FIGURE 9.8:

The Header/Footer tab showing the header assigned in the Header dialog box (Figure 9.7)

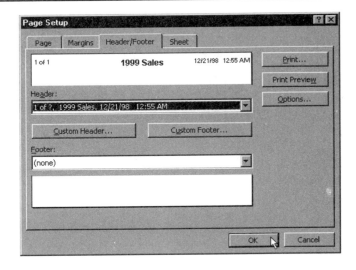

Listing 9.4 gives the `SetHeadingsAndFooters` macro that shows how to assign the above values to the three sections of the header in VBA macro code.

LISTING 9.4

```
0    Sub SetHeadingsAndFooters()
1        With ActiveSheet.PageSetup
2            .LeftHeader = "&P of &N"
3            .CenterHeader = "&""Arial,Bold""&12 1999 Sales"
4            .RightHeader = "&D    &T"
5        End With
6    End Sub
```

ANALYSIS

Line 2 sets the `LeftHeader` property to the string `"&P of &N"` where &P corresponds to clicking the Page Number button and &N the Total Pages button.

Line 3 sets the `CenterHeader` property to the string `"1999 Sales"` with the font, style, and size specified.

Line 4 sets the `RightHeader` property to the string `"&D    &T"` where &D corresponds to clicking the Date button and &T the Time button.

Sheet Tab

The Sheet tab shown in Figure 9.9 allows you to specify the area of your worksheet that you want to print, the rows or columns to print on every page, and the order in which to print the pages. It also has some general printing features, such as gridlines and print quality, that can be turned on and off.

The printing features that can be set in the Sheet tab can also be set in code. Listing 9.5 shows how this is done.

LISTING 9.5

```
0    Sub SetSheetProperties()
2        With ActiveSheet.PageSetup
```

```
 3              .PrintTitleRows = "$2:$2"
 4              .PrintTitleColumns = "$A:$A"
 5              .PrintGridlines = True
 6              .PrintHeadings = True
 7              .BlackAndWhite = True
 8              .PrintComments = xlPrintSheetEnd
 9              .PrintQuality = 300
10              .Order = xlOverThenDown
11         End With
12     End Sub
```

ANALYSIS

Lines 3 and 4 set the `PrintTitleRows` to row 2 and the `PrintTitleColumns` to column A. These two settings will appear in the two boxes in the Print Titles frame of the Sheet tab the next time you open it after running this macro.

Lines 5 through 9 set the properties that are inside the Print frame of the Sheet tab.

Line 10 sets the Order property to `xlOverThenDown`, which will display the second option button as selected. The other alternative is `xlDownThenOver`.

FIGURE 9.9:

Sheet tab in the Page Setup dialog box

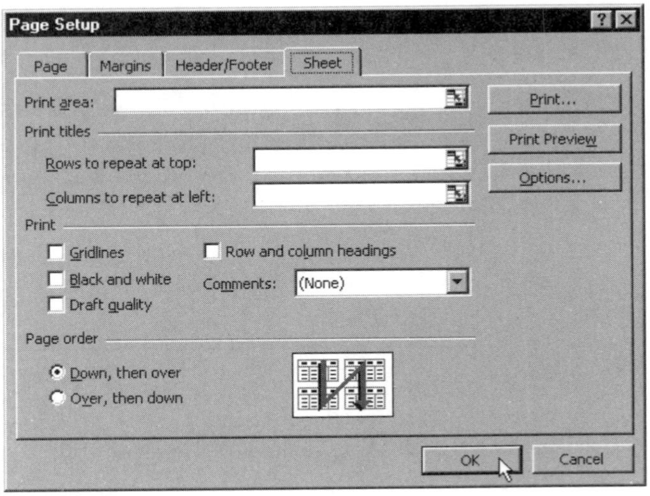

Printing Your Worksheet Using the *PrintOut* Method

The PrintOut method prints out the worksheet using the settings entered into the Page Setup dialog box or the values assigned directly to the PageSetup object. Figure 9.10 shows the PrintOut method being entered in code with the pop-up Parameter Info box listing its arguments. Listing 9.6 shows the PrintOut method being called with some of its parameters assigned values.

FIGURE 9.10:

Arguments required by the PrintOut method

```
Book1 - Module2 [Code]                                              _□×
(General)                              ▼  PrintWorkbook                ▼
    Sub PrintWorkbook()
        ActiveWorkbook.PrintOut
    End Sub          PrintOut([From], [To], [Copies], [Preview], [ActivePrinter], [PrintToFile], [Collate],
                     [PrToFileName])
```

LISTING 9.6

```
0    Sub PrintWorkBook()
1        ActiveWorkbook.PrintOut From:=3, To:=5, Copies:=4,_
         Collate:=True
2    End Sub
```

ANALYSIS

Line 1 calls the PrintOut method with arguments that will collate and print four copies of pages 3 to 5. All the arguments for the PrintOut method are optional.

Customizing Printing from a Macro

Suppose you require a macro that will print out the Sales, Purchases, and Expenses worksheets at the end of each month. Let's adapt the macros shown in

Listings 9.1 through 9.5 by passing the values of some of the properties required as arguments. Listing 9.7 shows the `EndOfMonthPrinting` calling the new versions of the macros and uses the `PrintOut` method (Listing 9.6) without any values being specified for the arguments. When this macro runs, it prints out the `Sales` worksheet on page 1, the `Purchases` worksheet on page 2, and the `Expenses` worksheet on pages 3 and 4.

LISTING 9.7

```
0    Sub EndOfMonthPrinting()
1        'print the Sales worksheet
2        Worksheets("Sales").Activate
3        SetPrintArea "A1"
4        SetPagesRequired 1, 1, 1
5        SetMarginsRequired
6        SetHeadingsAndFooters
7        SetSheetProperties
8        Selection.PrintOut
9        'print the Purchases worksheet
10       Worksheets("Purchases").Activate
11       SetPrintArea "B4"
12       SetPagesRequired 1, 1, 2
13       SetMarginsRequired
14       SetHeadingsAndFooters
15       SetSheetProperties
16       Selection.PrintOut
17       'print the Expenses worksheet
18       Worksheets("Expenses").Activate
19       SetPrintArea "C2"
20       SetPagesRequired 1, 2, 3
21       SetMarginsRequired
22       SetHeadingsAndFooters
23       SetSheetProperties
24       Selection.PrintOut
25   End Sub
26
27   Sub SetPrintArea(TopLeftCell As String)
28       'sets the range of cells to be printed
29       Range(TopLeftCell).Select
30       ActiveCell.CurrentRegion.Select
31   End Sub
32
33   Sub SetPagesRequired(PagesWide As Integer, PagesTall As Integer, _
         StartPage As Integer)
```

```
34          'sets the number of pages required wide and tall
35          With ActiveSheet.PageSetup
36              .Orientation = xlPortrait
37              .Zoom = False 'set to the % normal size box number
38              .FitToPagesWide = PagesWide
39              .FitToPagesTall = PagesTall
40              .PaperSize = xlPaperLetter
41              .PrintQuality = 300
42              .FirstPageNumber = StartPage
43          End With
44      End Sub
45
46      Sub SetMarginsRequired()
47          With ActiveSheet.PageSetup
48              .LeftMargin = Application.InchesToPoints(0.75)
49              .RightMargin = Application.InchesToPoints(0.75)
50              .TopMargin = Application.InchesToPoints(1)
51              .BottomMargin = Application.InchesToPoints(1)
52              .HeaderMargin = Application.InchesToPoints(0.5)
53              .FooterMargin = Application.InchesToPoints(0.5)
54              .CenterHorizontally = True
55              .CenterVertically = True
56          End With
57      End Sub
58
59      Sub SetHeadingsAndFooters()
60          With ActiveSheet.PageSetup
61              .LeftHeader = "&P "
62              .CenterHeader = "&""Arial,Bold""&12 " & _
                ActiveSheet.Name
63              .RightHeader = "&D    &T"
64          End With
65      End Sub
66
67      Sub SetSheetProperties()
68          With ActiveSheet.PageSetup
69              .PrintGridlines = True
70              .PrintHeadings = True
71              .BlackAndWhite = True
72              .PrintComments = xlPrintSheetEnd
73              .PrintQuality = 300
74              .Order = xlOverThenDown
75          End With
76      End Sub
```

ANALYSIS

Line 2 makes the Sales worksheet the active one.

Line 3 calls the SetPrintArea macro with the argument "A1", which references the cell in the top-left of the range required for the print area.

Line 4 calls the SetPagesRequired macro with three arguments—the number of pages wide, the number of pages tall, and the page number to start with for this worksheet.

Lines 5 through 7 call the other macros for assigning values to Page Setup settings.

Line 8 uses the PrintOut method to print the range of cells selected by the CurrentRegion property. This property references the range of cells that contains the cell passed to it by propagating out from this cell until it hits a row or column of empty cells or the edge of the worksheet.

Line 10 activates the Purchases worksheet.

Line 11 sets the print area starting from cell B4, which is the top-left cell for the Purchases data.

Line 12 calls the SetPagesRequired macro with 2 passed as the starting page.

Line 20 calls the SetPagesRequired macro with 2 as the second argument, which is the number of pages tall.

Line 27 declares the SetPrintArea macro with TopLeftCell as its one and only argument.

Line 29 selects the cell referenced by TopLeftCell to make it active.

Line 30 uses the CurrentRegion property to expand the ActiveCell in order to select the range of cells to be printed.

Line 33 declares the SetPagesRequired macro with three arguments — PagesWide, PagesTall, and StartPage. These three arguments allow the macro to be customized to meet each worksheet's requirement.

Lines 38, 39, and 42 use the values passed to the macro as arguments to set the properties required by the PageSetup object.

Line 46 declares the SetMarginsRequired macro, which remains the same as Listing 9.3.

Line 59 declares the macro `SetHeadingsAndFooters`.

Line 61, the `LeftHeader` property, now only contains the Page Number. The Total Pages part was removed, as this gives the number for each worksheet individually and these worksheets will now be printed with sequential page numbers.

Line 62, the `"1999 Sales"` string, has been replaced here by the name of the active worksheet.

Line 67 declares the `SetSheetProperties` macro. The `PrintTitleRows` and `PrintTitleColumns` properties are no longer required by this macro and have been omitted.

Customizing Dialog Boxes

This section discusses the Microsoft Common Dialog Control, which provides a set of commonly used dialog boxes with the appropriate controls already in place. In this section I'll show you how to display the Print, Color, and Font dialog boxes, which are only some of the predefined dialog boxes available.

Placing the Microsoft Common Dialog Control in a Worksheet

1. Choose View ➤ Toolbars ➤ Control Toolbox to display the Control Toolbox.

2. Click the More Controls icon in the Toolbox and select Microsoft Common Dialog Control, version 6.0, as shown in Figure 9.11. The cursor will change to a cross.

3. Position the cursor and drag it as shown below to place the Common Dialog Control in your worksheet.

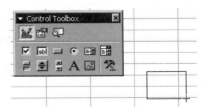

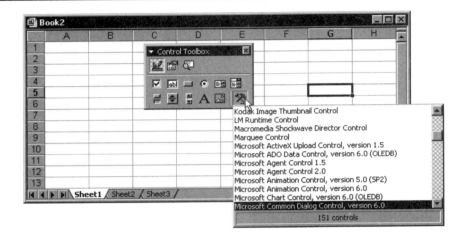

An icon for the Common Dialog Control will appear in your worksheet only when you are in Design mode. Otherwise the icon becomes invisible, though it can still be used in code to produce the type of dialog box required.

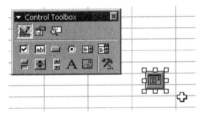

NOTE   Although the Common Dialog Control is invisible while the code is running, its properties and methods can still be referred to in code to display the type of dialog box required.

Using the Common Dialog Control in a VBA Macro

The Common Dialog Control can be used in VBA macros to specify what type of dialog box is to be shown on the screen. This section deals with three of the dialog boxes available for printing and setting the font and color properties.

Print Dialog Box   The Print dialog box is displayed to let the user know how their output will be printed. It specifies the printer, the range of pages to be printed, the number of copies to be printed, and whether or not the copies will be collated. This information can be specified in a VBA macro by assigning values to the properties of the Common Dialog Control. The code shown in Listing 9.8 sets the properties that are displayed in the Print dialog box shown in Figure 9.12.

LISTING 9.8

```
0    Sub ShowPrintDialogBox()
1        With Sheet1.CommonDialog1
2            .Flags = cdlPDPageNums
3            .Max = 6
4            .FromPage = 2
5            .ToPage = 6
6            .Copies = 4
7            .ShowPrinter
8        End With
8    End Sub
```

ANALYSIS

Line 1 starts the `With` statement so that the properties of the Common Dialog Control `CommonDialog1` in `Sheet1` can be used without being fully qualified (that is, without having to be prefixed with `Sheet1.CommonDialog1.`).

Line 2 sets the `Flags` property that determines which option buttons and check boxes will be selected. To see the list of constants available, enter the assignment statement up to `cdlPD` and then choose Edit ≻ Complete Word; this will display the drop-down list shown below. Selecting `cdlPDPage-Nums` displays the Pages option button selected. You can set several flags in this statement using the plus sign (+) to combine them. For example,

```
cdlPDPageNums + cdlPDCollate
```

will display the Pages option button selected and the Collate check box checked.

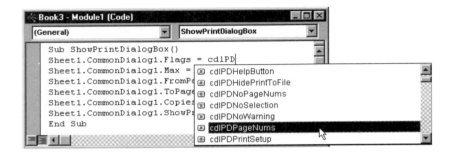

Line 3 sets the Max property, which limits the value for the print range. This needs to be at least the same as the ToPage property's value.

Line 4 and Line 5 set the limit for the print range.

Line 6 sets the Copies property of the Common Dialog Control to 4. This number will appear in the Number Of Copies box in the Print dialog box displayed when Line 6 runs.

Line 7 uses the ShowPrinter method of the Common Dialog Control placed in Sheet1 to display the Print dialog box shown in Figure 9.12.

FIGURE 9.12:

Print dialog box

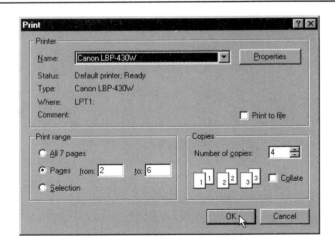

Clicking the Options button of the Print dialog box will display the Properties dialog box for the printer shown in Figure 9.2.

Color Dialog Box The Color dialog box, displayed using the ShowColor method of the Microsoft Common Dialog Control, offers a palette of colors for the application interface as shown in Figure 9.13.

FIGURE 9.13:

Color dialog box displayed fully open

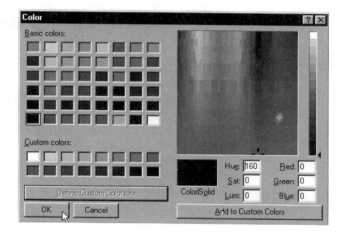

The Color dialog box can be considered as two halves. The left half shows the basic "premixed" colors available and the right half allows custom colors to be created. You can use the ShowColor control's Flags property to specify how much of the Color dialog box should be displayed; this property must be set before the ShowColor method is used to display the dialog box. The available flags and descriptions of how they affect the Color dialog box are listed in Table 9.1.

TABLE 9.1: Flags Property Settings for the ShowColor Dialog Box

Constant	Description
cdlCCRGBInit	Sets initial color value for the Color dialog box.
cdlCCFullOpen	Opens both sides of the Color dialog box. This eliminates the need for the user to click the Define Custom Colors command button.
cdlCCPreventFullOpen	Prevents users from creating their own custom colors by opening only the left-hand side of the Color dialog box and disabling the Define Custom Colors command button.
cdlCCShowHelp	Displays a Help button in the Color dialog box.

NOTE   The `Flag` property must be set before opening the Color dialog box.

The color selected from the Color dialog box is assigned to its `Color` property. This can then be used to set other color properties—for example, Listing 9.9 shows the `Color` property being assigned to the background color of a `Label` control.

LISTING 9.9

```
0    Sub UseColorDialog()
1        Sheet1.CommonDialog1.Flags = cdlCCFullOpen
2        Sheet1.CommonDialog1.ShowColor
3        Sheet1.Label1.BackColor = Sheet1.CommonDialog1.Color
4    End Sub
```

ANALYSIS

Line 1 sets the `Flags` property of the Common Dialog Control placed in `Sheet1` so that when the Color dialog box is displayed it will have both sides open, as shown in Figure 9.13.

Line 2 uses the `ShowColor` method to display the Color dialog box according to the `Flags` property.

Line 3 demonstrates the use of the `Color` property of the Common Dialog Control by assigning it to the background color of the `Label` control (which I've added to my worksheet for the sole purpose of showing how the property is used). The `Color` property is assigned the color selected by the user, or the default color if none has been selected.

Font Dialog Box   The Font dialog box is displayed to let the user adjust the features associated with fonts, such as typeface, point size, color, and style. Figure 9.14 shows some of the properties being set in the Font dialog box. Listing 9.10 shows these properties being set in VBA macro code.

LISTING 9.10

```
0    Sub UseFontDialog()
1        With Sheet1.CommonDialog1
```

```
 2              .Flags = cdlCFScreenFonts Or cdlCFPrinterFonts
 3              .ShowFont
 4              Sheet1.TextBox1.FontName = .FontName
 5              Sheet1.TextBox1.FontSize = .FontSize
 6              Sheet1.TextBox1.FontBold = .FontBold
 7              Sheet1.TextBox1.FontItalic = FontItalic
 8              Sheet1.TextBox1.FontUnderLine = .FontUnderLine
 9              Sheet1.TextBox1.FontStrikeThru = .FontStrikeThru
10          End With
11      End Sub
```

ANALYSIS

Line 1 uses the `With` statement to qualify properties in Lines 2 through 9.

Line 2 sets the `Flags` property so that screen fonts and printer fonts will both be acceptable. This property must be set first before any of the other properties are assigned values; otherwise the message "No Fonts Exist" will be displayed.

Line 3 displays the Font dialog box.

Lines 4 through 9 set the properties of the text box to the values set in the Font dialog box. (The text box was placed in the worksheet for the sole purpose of demonstrating the Font dialog box.)

FIGURE 9.14:

Font dialog box

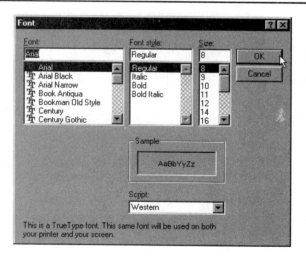

NOTE   Flags must be set to `cdlCFScreenFonts` or `cdlCFPrinterFonts` before any other properties can be assigned values.

Summary

By the end of this chapter, you should be able to do the following manually in Excel or automatically in VBA code:

- set the print area

- print across or down the page

- adjust the size of the printed image

- set the margins

- define text for headers and footers

- add page numbers and date and time of printing

- center the printed image on the page

- print your worksheet from a macro with or without user intervention

- customize macros to print worksheets, with values of their printing properties being assigned automatically in the macros

You'll also be able to display the Print, Color, and Font dialog boxes using the Microsoft Common Dialog Control.

CHAPTER
TEN

10

UserForms

This chapter describes UserForms, which are windows or dialog boxes that can be considered powerful extensions to the GUI of Excel. You've already seen in Chapters 5 and 6 how UserForms can be used to make sophisticated input boxes. In this chapter, I'll go much further and demonstrate how UserForms can contain option buttons and check boxes, placed in frames or pages, to allow you to customize printing.

UserForms are simply containers for the controls you place into them to communicate with users. Every new UserForm contains a title bar, which displays the value assigned to its Caption property (and allows the user to move the User-Form), and a Close button, which lets the user close the UserForm while the application is running. Although a border for resizing a UserForm is available while you're developing a project, it isn't available to users at runtime—this gives you full control over how your UserForm will appear to the user.

Working with UserForms

This section shows you how to

- create a UserForm
- display it as a graphical object or view its code
- view it in the Project Explorer
- view its properties

Creating a UserForm

Open the Visual Basic Editor and choose Insert ➤ UserForm to create UserForm1. This will display the UserForm as a graphical object, as shown in Figure 10.1. The UserForm's Caption and Name properties are both assigned the default string UserForm1, with the Caption property being displayed in the title bar.

FIGURE 10.1:

UserForm named User–
Form1 by default

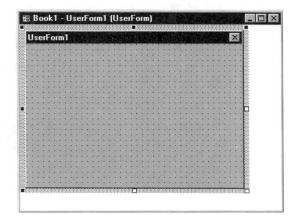

FIGURE 10.1:

UserForm named User–
Form1 by default

Viewing a UserForm

When you create a UserForm, it's initially displayed as a graphical object. A User-Form can also be viewed as code in the code window by choosing View ➤ Code or by double-clicking its graphical image. The first time the UserForm is viewed in the code window, the skeleton of the UserForm's Click event procedure—its primary event procedure—is displayed. Event procedures for each control are ordered alphabetically; subsequent viewings in the code window will display the first event procedure that has been coded for the selected control.

You can return to the graphical representation (Figure 10.1) at any time by selecting View ➤ Object.

Finding a UserForm

If no UserForm is displayed at all, you can display it by selecting it from the Project Explorer window in a similar way as you access modules: Choose View ➤ Project Explorer. Figure 10.2 shows how the UserForm just inserted appears in the list under the Forms folder.

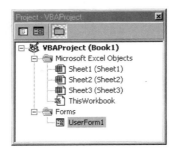

UserForm Properties

Just like controls, the UserForm object has its own set of properties. Figure 10.3 shows the Properties window for the UserForm object. To display this window, right-click UserForm1 and choose Properties from the shortcut menu.

The Properties window lists the properties that can be set during design time, but doesn't include properties that are only available during runtime. To see a complete list of the UserForm object's properties:

1.   Choose View ➤ Object Browser to open the Object Browser.

2.   Enter **userform** in the Search text box (as shown in Figure 10.4) and click the Search button.

3.   Select UserForm1 from the Search Results box and UserForm1 from the Classes box to display the list of member properties and methods in the Members Of UserForm1 box.

4.   Select ActiveControl from the members list to display the information in the bottom panel that states that this is a read-only property. Clicking the Help button will display further information about the selected item.

FIGURE 10.3:

Properties window for
UserForm1

FIGURE 10.4:

Viewing UserForm prop-
erties in the Object Browser

TIP   Properties and methods are distinguished by their icons in the Object Browser window.

The screen is considered to be the UserForm's container. Properties to define the shape of this container include the Height and Width properties to define the size of the UserForm and the Left and Top properties to define the distances from the left boundary of the screen to the left border of the UserForm and the top boundary of the screen to the top border of the UserForm. All four properties can be set at design time by updating their values in the Properties window or by dragging the borders to the size required. They can also all be set in code at runtime, but only the Left and Top properties can be changed by the user when they move the UserForm around by dragging its title bar.

The next two sections discuss these properties being set in code to provide animated sequences showing UserForm1 moving around the screen and CommandButton1 moving around UserForm1. The second sequence uses the Repaint method to avoid previous versions of CommandButton1 being displayed along with the current version.

Animating a UserForm's Position on the Screen

Animating a UserForm is easy. All it requires is making many small adjustments to the four properties defining the UserForm's position and size. When you change these properties inside your macro, the new version of the UserForm is drawn—but since Windows doesn't repaint the screen until your macro is finished, all versions of the UserForm remain on display while your macro is running (Figure 10.5). When the macro has finished and Windows has repainted the screen, only the last version is displayed. Listing 10.1 shows the code for the animated sequence with the Top, Left, Height, and Width properties being updated inside a For loop that repositions and resizes UserForm1 20 times in response to its being clicked once. Figure 10.5 shows the result of running the code shown in Listing 10.1 and taking a snapshot of the screen just before the End Sub statement in Line 8 has been executed.

LISTING 10.1

```
0    Private Sub UserForm_Click()
1        'animate UserForm1's position
2        For Counter = 1 To 20
```

```
3           UserForm1.Top = Counter * 10
4           UserForm1.Left = Counter * 15
5           UserForm1.Height = Counter * 10
6           UserForm1.Width = Counter * 15
7      Next
8   End Sub
```

ANALYSIS

Line 2 is the start of the For loop that uses the variable Counter to keep track of the number of times through the loop. (For loops are described in detail in Chapter 7.)

Lines 3 through 6 assign values to the four properties that define the position and size of UserForm1. This section has the effect of adding 10 units onto the Top and Height properties and 15 units onto the Left and Width properties as Counter is incremented each time it passes through the loop. I've chosen larger numbers for the horizontal updates to make the User-Form appear to move diagonally across the rectangular area of the screen.

FIGURE 10.5:

Result of UserForm1 being animated

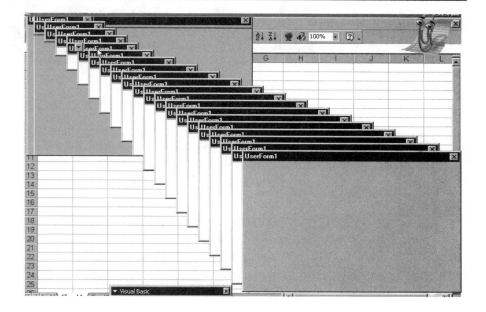

NOTE   The user can reposition the UserForm at runtime by dragging the title bar to change its **Top** and **Left** properties, but they can't resize it—so you have complete control over its size.

Me Keyword

When referring to a UserForm in an event procedure, you can use the **Me** keyword to refer to the instance of the UserForm that's currently running. In general, this is the same as UserForm#, where the UserForm referenced is the one containing the event procedure. The event procedure in Listing 10.1 could be rewritten as:

```
0    Private Sub UserForm_Click()
1        'animate UserForm1's position
2        For Counter = 1 To 20
3            Me.Top = Counter * 10
4            Me.Left = Counter * 15
5            Me.Height = Counter * 10
6            Me.Width = Counter * 15
7        Next
8    End Sub
```

The **Me** keyword not only makes the code a little more concise, it also eliminates the need to go back and change all of your code if you later decide to rename the form.

Animating a Control's Position in a UserForm

The UserForm can act as a container for controls which also have Top, Left, Height, and Width properties. The Top and Left properties in this instance are the distances from the top boundary of the UserForm to the top boundary of the control and from the left boundary of the UserForm to the left boundary of the control.

Listing 10.2 shows the code from the UserForm_Click event procedure that moves a command button from the top left corner of UserForm1 (Figure 10.6) to the bottom right and also increases its size at every move. Figure 10.7 shows the result of running this code. The Repaint method is used after the four properties have been updated to ensure that only the latest command button is displayed at any particular time.

FIGURE 10.6:

Command button in User-Form1 before the User-Form is clicked

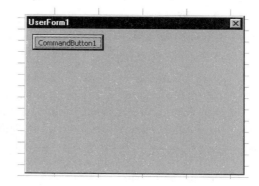

FIGURE 10.7:

Command button in User-Form1 after the UserForm is clicked

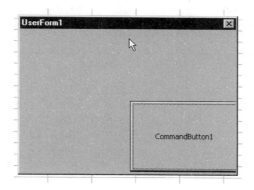

LISTING 10.2

```
0   Private Sub UserForm_Click()
1       'animate CommandButton1's position
2       For Counter = 1 To 20
3           CommandButton1.Top = Counter * 10
4           CommandButton1.Left = Counter * 15
5           CommandButton1.Height = Counter * 10
6           CommandButton1.Width = Counter * 15
7           UserForm1.Repaint
8       Next
9   End Sub
```

Lines 3 through 6 set the properties of the command button that reposition and resize it in the UserForm.

Line 7 uses the Repaint method to redraw the UserForm so that only the command button at its last position and size is displayed at any particular time. Using the Repaint method avoids having to wait until the system automatically repaints the area to paint out previous versions.

The four lines of code that assign values to the properties for positioning and resizing a UserForm or control can be streamlined into a single line of code using the Move method, which passes values as arguments to the Left, Top, Width, and Height properties. Using this method, Lines 3 through 6 in Listing 10.2 can be condensed into one line, as shown in Listing 10.3.

LISTING 10.3

```
0    Private Sub UserForm_Click()
1        'animate CommandButton1's position
2        For Counter = 1 To 20
3            UserForm1.Move Counter * 15, Counter * 10, _
             Counter * 15, Counter * 10
4            UserForm1.Repaint
5        Next
6    End Sub
```

ANALYSIS

Line 3 passes values for the Left, Top, Width, and Height properties as arguments to the Move method, which uses them to reposition and resize the UserForm.

Communicating with UserForms from a Macro

The project developed in this section uses a macro to communicate with a User-Form that allows the user to set the printing properties. The macro displays the UserForm, then waits while the user makes their selections; the UserForm is then hidden and the user's choices interpreted to set the properties for printing.

Printing Options Project

Let's start by creating the UserForm to allow the user to select the different printing options. I've used five `Frame` controls to group related items together so that the user can select their requirements from each group. Each item is represented by an `OptionButton` or `CheckBox` control. Option buttons appear as circles and exactly one must be selected from each group. One option button from each group is preselected during an initialization stage. Check boxes appear as squares that contain Xs when selected; the user can check as many check boxes as they want.

Creating the UserForm's GUI

1. Open a new Excel workbook and enter the data for the Debits and Credits (as shown).

	A	B	C	D
1	Month	Debits	Credits	Balance
2	January	3	5	2
3	February	3	4	1
4	March	2	5	3
5	April	3	6	3
6	May	4	7	3
7	June	1	8	7
8	July	2	7	5
9	August	4	6	2
10	September	6	7	1
11	October	3	8	5
12	November	4	9	5
13	December	56	67	11
14	Total	91	139	48

2. Open the Visual Basic Editor and choose Insert ➤ UserForm to display the graphical representation of UserForm1.

3. Double-click the Frame control's icon in the Toolbox (shown).

This will allow you to place multiple Frame controls in UserForm1 without having to go back to the Toolbox each time. Place five Frame controls in UserForm1 as shown in Figure 10.8 (later you'll learn an easy way to align them and make them the same size). Click anywhere in the Controls tab in the Toolbox to stop placing Frame controls.

4. If the Properties window is not already displayed, right-click UserForm1 and change the Caption properties of the UserForm and frames as shown in Figure 10.9.

FIGURE 10.8:

Five Frame controls in UserForm1

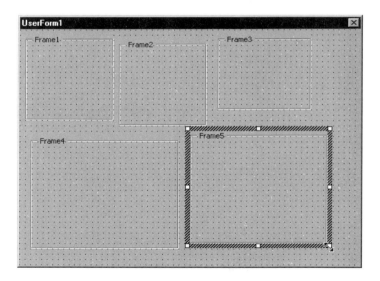

5. Double-click the OptionButton control's icon in the Toolbox and place nine OptionButton controls into the first four Frame controls, as shown in Figure 10.9.

FIGURE 10.9:

Captions set for the Frame
controls and for the added
option buttons and check
boxes

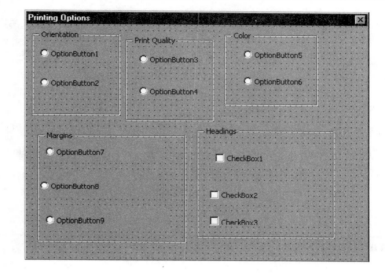

6. Double-click the CheckBox control's icon and place the three CheckBox controls into the HeadingsFrame control. Click in the Controls tab in the Toolbox to stop placing CheckBox controls.

7. Set the Name and Caption properties of the option buttons and check boxes to those shown in Table 10.1. I've used the naming conventions listed in Table 6.1 in the section "Naming Conventions for VBA Controls" in Chapter 6.

TABLE 10.1: Name and Caption Properties for Printing Options Project UserForm

Original Name	New Caption	New Name
OptionButton1	Portrait	optPortrait
OptionButton2	Landscape	optLandscape
OptionButton3	Draft	optDraft
OptionButton4	Report	optReport
OptionButton5	Color	optColor
OptionButton6	Monochrome	optMonochrome

Continued on next page

TABLE 10.1 (CONTINUED): Name and Caption Properties for Printing Options Project UserForm

Original Name	New Caption	New Name
OptionButton7	Narrow	optNarrow
OptionButton8	Standard	optStandard
OptionButton9	Wide	optWide
CheckBox1	Left (page numbers)	chkLeft
CheckBox2	Center (title)	chkCenter
CheckBox3	Right (date)	chkRight

TIP

Double-clicking an icon in the Toolbox allows you to place as many controls as you like into your UserForm without having to revert back to the Toolbox to get each one. When you're finished placing controls, click anywhere in the Controls page in the Toolbox.

Aligning and Positioning Controls

The Format menu commands enable groups of controls to be aligned and resized simultaneously. Let's adjust the OptionButton and CheckBox controls first; then we can adjust the frames to suit.

1. Hold down the Shift key and click the two option buttons in the frame captioned "Orientation." As shown in Figure 10.10, the buttons will be highlighted and surrounded by square sizing handles.

2. Choose Format ➣ Make Same Size ➣ Both (as shown below) to make the second OptionButton control the same size as the first one, which is identified by the white square sizing handles. Although the Frame control is also highlighted, its size remains unaltered.

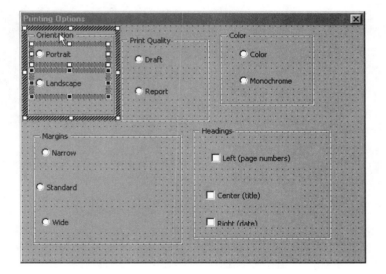

FIGURE 10.10:

Option buttons highlighted to show they've been selected

3. Choose Format ➤ Center in Form ➤ Horizontally to center the controls in the frame, then choose Format ➤ Vertical Spacing ➤ Remove to remove the spaces between the two option button controls so that they appear to become adjoined.

4. With the group of controls still selected, adjust their heights so that they appear at a reasonable distance from each other. (You'll have to remove vertical spacing

again after each height adjustment.) Figure 10.11 shows the height adjustment being carried out on the three selected check box controls simultaneously. The check box with the white sizing handles is the first one selected and will be the one that determines the size or alignment of the others.

FIGURE 10.11:

Adjusting the heights of three check boxes

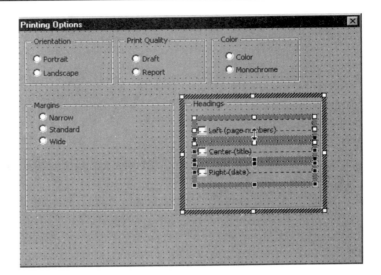

5. Click the frame to select it and adjust its size to suit the new layout of the controls it contains.

6. Repeat steps 1 through 4 for the Print Quality and Color frames.

7. Hold down the Shift key and click the Orientation frame, then the Print Quality and Color frames. Choose Format ➤ Make Same Size ➤ Both, then choose Format ➤ Align ➤ Tops and Format ➤ Horizontal Spacing ➤ Make Equal.

8. Using the grid dots as a guide, adjust the option buttons in the Print Quality and Color frames so that they sit at the same relative positions as the ones in the Orientation frame.

9. Applying the same techniques used in steps 1 through 7, adjust the Margins and Headings control groups and frames.

10. Move the Margins and Headings frames closer to the bottom of the Orientation frame.

11. Hold down the Shift key and click the Margins and Headings frames. Choose Format ➤ Align ➤ Tops and Format ➤ Make Same Size ➤ Width.

12. Click the Orientation frame; hold down the Ctrl key and click the Margins frame. Choose Format ➤ Align ➤ Lefts.

13. Click the Color frame; hold down the Ctrl key and click the Headings frame. Choose Format ➤ Align ➤ Rights.

14. Add two command buttons and change their Caption properties to OK and Cancel and their Name properties to cmdOK and cmdCancel. Set the Accelerator property of cmdOK to O and the Cancel property of cmdCancel to True. The standard Windows accelerator key for Cancel buttons is {Esc}— setting a control's Cancel property to True makes it respond to the Esc key being pressed.

15. Adjust the size of the UserForm to suit the new frame sizes.

Figure 10.12 shows the final layout of the UserForm.

FIGURE 10.12:

Final layout of the Printing Options UserForm

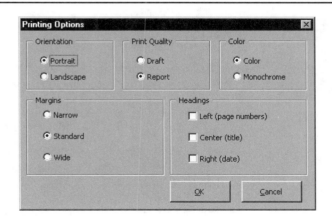

NOTE   The Center In Form menu command centers the selected controls in their container, which can be a UserForm or a frame.

To select multiple controls that are displayed adjacent to each other in the same frame, click the first one and while holding down the Shift key click the last one—all controls from first to last will be highlighted as selected. To select multiple controls that are not adjacent, click the first one and while holding down the Ctrl key click the others.

Formatting with the UserForm Toolbar

Figure 10.13 shows the UserForm toolbar, which contains shortcuts to some of the Format menu commands. If the UserForm toolbar isn't on display, access it by choosing View ➤ Toolbars ➤ UserForm.

FIGURE 10.13:

UserForm toolbar

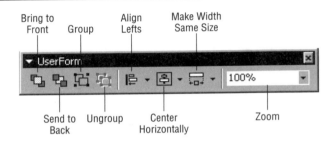

Bring To Front   Displays the selected control(s) in front of any others they overlap. This is equivalent to choosing Format ➤ Order ➤ Bring To Front.

Send To Back   Displays the selected control(s) behind any controls they overlap. This is equivalent to choosing Format ➤ Order ➤ Send To Back.

Group   Treats the selected controls as a single entity, allowing them to be moved around or formatted as a single entity. This is equivalent to choosing Format ➤ Group.

Ungroup   Splits a group of controls into separate entities. This is equivalent to choosing Format ➤ Ungroup.

Align Lefts   This is a drop-down list that allows you to align lefts, centers, rights, etc., of the selected controls. The button icon displayed in the toolbar is of the most recently used command. This is equivalent to the list of commands available when you select Format ➤ Align.

Center Horizontally   This is a drop-down list that allows you to reposition the selected control(s) in the center of the UserForm. The button icon displayed in the toolbar is of the most recently used command. This is equivalent to choosing Format ➤ Center in Form and selecting Horizontally or Vertically.

Make Width Same Size   This is a drop-down list that allows you to make the widths and heights of the selected controls the same size. The button icon displayed in the toolbar is of the most recently used command. This is equivalent to choosing Format ➤ Make Same Size and selecting Width, Height, or Both.

Zoom   Allows you to magnify or reduce the size of the selected controls. There is no menu command equivalent to this toolbar button.

You can add or remove buttons from the UserForm toolbar by clicking the Down arrow in its title bar and checking the desired check boxes in the drop-down list, as shown.

Coding the Printing Options Project

The code for the GetPrintingOptions macro is placed into a module. Choose Insert ➤ Module, which will both create Module1 and display its code window. Enter the code shown in Listing 10.4a into this module. The code shown in Listing 10.4b is a collection of event procedures and so should be entered into the skeleton procedures in the code window for the UserForm.

LISTING 10.4a

```
0    Global OKClicked as Boolean
1
2    Sub GetPrintingOptions()
3        UserForm1.Show
```

```
4         If OKClicked = True Then
5            With ActiveSheet.PageSetup
6                .CenterHorizontally = True
7                .CenterVertically = True
8                If UserForm1.optPortrait.Value = True Then _
                      .Orientation = xlPortrait
9                If UserForm1.optLandscape.Value = True Then _
                      .Orientation = xlLandscape
10               If UserForm1.optDraft.Value = True Then _
                      .PrintQuality = 300
11               If UserForm1.optReport.Value = True Then _
                      .PrintQuality = 600
12               If UserForm1.optColor.Value = True Then _
                      .BlackAndWhite = False
13               If UserForm1.optMonochrome.Value = True Then _
                      .BlackAndWhite = True
14               If UserForm1.optNarrow.Value = True Then _
                      SetMargin 0.5, 0.75, 0.25
15               If UserForm1.optStandard.Value = True Then _
                      SetMargin 0.75, 1, 0.5
16               If UserForm1.optWide.Value = True Then _
                      SetMargin 1, 1.25, 0.75
17               If UserForm1.chkLeft.Value = True Then _
                      .LeftHeader = "&P"
18               If UserForm1.chkCenter.Value = True Then _
                      .CenterHeader = InputBox(_
                      "Enter main heading.", "Worksheet Heading")
19               If UserForm1.chkRight.Value = True Then _
                      .RightHeader = "&D"
20           End With
21        End If
22     End Sub
23
24     Sub SetMargin(LeftAndRight, TopAndBottom, HeaderAndFooter)
25        With ActiveSheet.PageSetup
26           .LeftMargin = Application.InchesToPoints(LeftAndRight)
27           .RightMargin = _
             Application.InchesToPoints(LeftAndRight)
28           .TopMargin = Application.InchesToPoints(TopAndBottom)
29           .BottomMargin = _
             Application.InchesToPoints(TopAndBottom)
30           .HeaderMargin = _
```

```
        Application.InchesToPoints(HeaderAndFooter)
31      .FooterMargin = _
        Application.InchesToPoints(HeaderAndFooter)
32    End With
33 End Sub
```

ANALYSIS

Line 0 declares the OKClicked variable as a Boolean. This variable will be set to True when the OK command button is clicked and False when the Cancel command button is clicked. It will be used to determine whether or not the printer properties are assigned new values.

Line 2 starts the GetPrintingOptions macro.

Line 3 uses the Show method to display UserForm1.

Line 4 checks whether the OK button has been clicked (OKClicked = True) and will jump to Line 21 if it hasn't.

Line 5 uses the With statement to streamline setting the properties of the PageSetup object of the ActiveSheet object.

Lines 6 and 7 force the image to be printed in the center of the page.

Line 8 checks whether the value of the Portrait option button is True (i.e., has been selected). If it is, the orientation of the printed worksheet image is set to the constant xlPortrait. It's helpful to use the Auto Quick Info editing feature described in Chapter 3 for entering this line. When you enter the .opt part, a drop-down list will be displayed containing the names you've given to all the option buttons and check boxes for your project, as shown below.

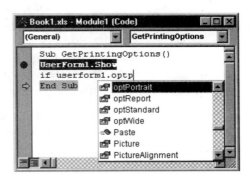

Setting the orientation to xlPortrait positions the paper vertically, as shown in Figure 10.14.

FIGURE 10.14:

Worksheet printed with Portrait orientation

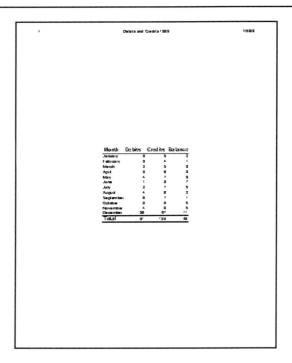

If the Landscape option button is selected, **Line 9** sets the printing orientation to xlLandscape and the paper is positioned horizontally, as shown in Figure 10.15.

Lines 10 and 11 set the print quality of the image depending on which option button was selected. I've chosen to assign the dots per inch; the other values available are -1 (draft), -2 (low resolution), -3 (medium resolution), and -4 (high resolution). The settings available are dependant on the printer driver used by your computer and the current settings of your printer. If these two statements give you an error message, comment them out by placing a single quote (') at the start of the line.

Lines 12 and 13 assign True or False to the BlackAndWhite property of the PageSetup object to reflect whether the Color or the Monochrome option button is selected.

FIGURE 10.15:

Worksheet printed with Landscape orientation

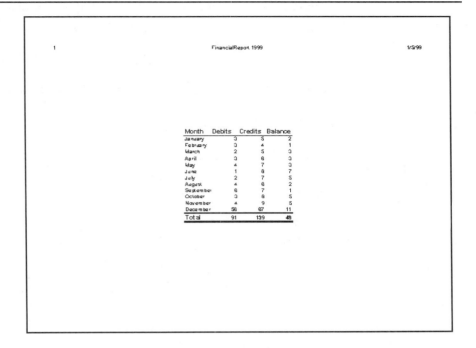

Lines 14 through 16 set the size of the margins, depending on the option selected. The `SetMargin` macro (Lines 24 through 33) is called with values (in inches) passed to its three arguments—the size of the side margins, the top and bottom margins, and the header and footer margins.

Line 17 assigns page numbers to the `LeftHeader` property.

Line 18 calls the `InputBox` function to get the heading for the worksheet from the user (as shown) and assigns it to the `CenterHeader` property.

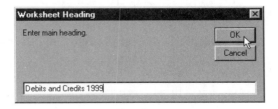

Line 19 assigns the current system date to the `RightHeader` property.

Line 24 starts the SetMargin macro with three named arguments.

Line 25 starts the With statement that allows properties of the PageSetup object of the ActiveSheet to be used without fully qualifying them (i.e., stating the objects they belong to).

Lines 26 through 31 set the six properties of the PageSetup object that pertain to margins.

LISTING 10.4b

```
0    Private Sub cmdCancel_Click()
1        UserForm1.Hide
2        OKClicked = False
3    End Sub
4
5    Private Sub cmdOK_Click()
6        UserForm1.Hide
7        OKClicked = True
8    End Sub
9
10   Private Sub UserForm_Initialize()
11       optPortrait.Value = True
12       optReport.Value = True
13       optColor.Value = True
14       optStandard.Value = True
15   End Sub
```

ANALYSIS

Line 1 hides UserForm1 from the user, but the data it contains can still be accessed by code in the project.

Because this statement is inside the Click event procedure for the Cancel command button, **Line 2** sets the OKClicked variable to False so that the printer properties will remain unchanged when the GetPrintingOptions macro has finished running.

Line 7 sets the OKClicked variable to True because it lies inside the Click event procedure for the OK command button. This ensures that the Get-PrintingOptions macro will set all the printing properties to the values required by the user according to the options they selected in UserForm1.

Line 10 starts the UserForm_Initialize event procedure, which Visual Basic runs automatically when the Show method is used to display the UserForm.

Lines 11 through 14 set the Value properties of one option button from each frame to True to select them. This is equivalent to making these choices the default.

Now that you've finished coding the Printing Options project, you can run your macro and try it out. You might want to extend the project by adding a command button to your worksheet or to a toolbar to launch the macro.

Running a Macro from a Worksheet Control

The GetPrintingOptions macro is dependent on the user knowing that the macro actually exists. It's more user-friendly to place a command button on the worksheet itself and run the macro whenever the user clicks it. This makes the macro more visible and eliminates the need for the user to memorize its existence. To run your macro from a command button placed in a worksheet:

1. Place a command button in your worksheet in a conspicuous place.

2. Change its Caption property to **Printer Options** and its Accelerator property to uppercase **P**. Because there's an uppercase and a lowercase p, the case is important here. Assigning a lowercase p to the Accelerator property would underline the second p.

3. Double-click the command button to open the Visual Basic Editor; the code window will be open and displaying the CommandButton1_Click event procedure shown in Figure 10.16. Notice how the code window's title bar displays Sheet1 to let you know that this is the event procedure of a worksheet control.

FIGURE 10.16:

Code window for Sheet1

4. Enter `GetPrinterOptions` into the `Click` event procedure.

5. Return to your worksheet and click the Exit Design Mode button in the Visual Basic toolbar.

6. Click the Printer Options command button and watch while your macro displays the UserForm. Everything else will work as before.

Printing Options UserForm with Pages

Sometimes you can update the GUI without needing to change any of the code. This section introduces pages as an alternative to frames for grouping together the printing options and uses the same code as the frames version. Pages haven't been around the Microsoft Windows environment for as long as frames and can really add that up-to-date feel to your application. Let's revisit the Printing Options project and change our dusty old frames into snazzy pages:

1. Open a new workbook and display the Visual Basic Editor.

2. Add a UserForm (choose Insert ➤ UserForm).

3. Place a `MultiPage` control (Figure 10.17) into the UserForm so that it takes up most of the UserForm's area, as shown in Figure 10.18, and add two command buttons near the bottom.

FIGURE 10.17:

The icon for the
`MultiPage` control
in the Toolbox

4. Right-click the `Page1` tab and choose Rename from the shortcut menu (as shown) to open the Rename dialog box.

FIGURE 10.18:

MultiPage control placed in a UserForm

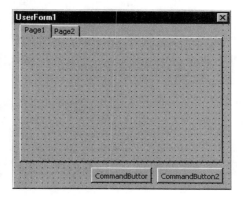

5. Change **Page1** to **Orientation** in the Caption box, insert **O** in the Accelerator Key box, and enter **Allows Portrait or Landscape Orientation** into the Control Tip Text box (as shown). Alternatively, these properties can be assigned values in the Properties window by right-clicking in the page itself and choosing Properties from the shortcut menu.

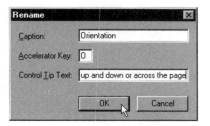

6. Add two option buttons to the Orientation page and change their Caption and Name properties to those shown in Table 10.1.

7. Right-click Page2 and change its caption to **Print Quality**. Add two option buttons and change their Caption and Name properties to those shown in Table 10.1.

8. Right-click the blank area to the right of the Print Quality tab and choose New Page from the shortcut menu. This Page3 will have the same Caption property as Frame3 (Color) in the previous Printing Options project.

9. Add another two pages, Margins and Headings, and add all the option buttons and check boxes to match those in the frames, using Table 10.1 to assign property values. Figure 10.19 shows the completed pages.

10. Change the caption of UserForm1 to **Printing Options**.

FIGURE 10.19:

Pages version of the Printing Options GUI

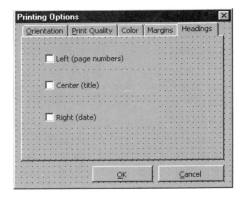

11. Since you've called all the option buttons and check boxes by the same names as before, you can cut and paste the code from the frame version in Module1 (Listing 10.4a) and UserForm1 (Listing 10.4b) to this pages version—it will work without any changes.

Dual Toolboxes

You may have already noticed that there are two Toolboxes, one for controls you can place directly onto worksheets (Figure 10.20) and another, available in the Visual Basic Editor, that contains controls you can place in UserForms (Figure 10.21).

FIGURE 10.20:

Control Toolbox containing controls for worksheets

Although they contain different sets of standard controls, these two Toolboxes are basically the same. Any missing controls can usually be accessed whenever required. Let's take a look at how a Common Dialog control can be added to a worksheet and a UserForm.

To add a Common Dialog Control to a Worksheet:

1. Click the More Tools button at the end of the Control Toolbox and select Microsoft Common Dialog Control, version 6.0 from the drop-down list (shown). This will change the mouse cursor to a cross.

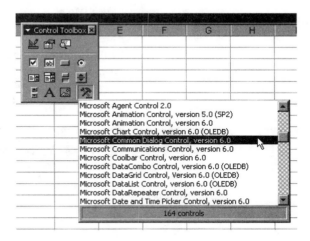

2. Place the control anywhere in the worksheet (as shown) by a drag-and-drop action of the mouse.

NOTE Using the More Controls button in the Control Toolbox (for worksheets) and selecting a control from the list doesn't add the selected control's icon to the Toolbox; rather, it allows you to place an instance of that control on your worksheet. This differs from the Toolbox in the Visual Basic Editor, which adds the icons of any additional controls to the Toolbox.

To add a Common Dialog Control to a UserForm:

1. Right-click anywhere in the Controls tab and choose Additional Controls from the shortcut menu, as shown.

2. Check the check box of the item required (Microsoft Common Dialog Control, version 6.0) in the Available Controls list in the Additional Controls dialog box, as shown. The icon will be added to the Toolbox as soon as the OK button is clicked.

FIGURE 10.22:

Selecting the Microsoft Common Dialog control

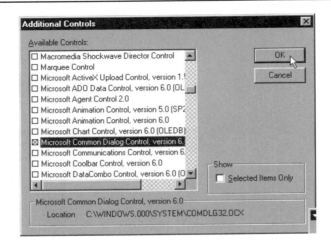

3. Place the new control in your UserForm by clicking its icon in the Toolbox then dragging and dropping it at the position required. Notice how the mouse pointer changes to a cross combined with the icon of the control selected.

Summary

When you've worked your way through this chapter you'll know how to work with UserForms, including

- creating them
- displaying them as graphical objects
- viewing their code
- viewing their properties
- repositioning and resizing them
- displaying them from a macro
- using a macro to process the information they contain
- aligning controls in frames and pages

You'll also know how to access controls that aren't included in the Control Toolbox or the Toolbox available in the Visual Basic Editor, and you'll be able to run your macros from worksheet controls.

CHAPTER

ELEVEN

Custom Command Bars

Visual Basic represents toolbars and menu bars by a single class of object—the CommandBar object. Command bars give you the best of both worlds: they can contain buttons with icons and drop-down arrows like those normally found in a toolbar, alongside menu commands like those normally found in a menu bar. Menu bars no longer need to be fixed along the top of a window but can be moved around the window in the same way as a toolbar.

This chapter describes how to customize your own menu bars and toolbars for your applications. You'll see how to do this both manually and in a macro. We'll also cover how to turn a toolbar button into a menu command.

What Is a Command Bar?

A command bar is an object that you can code to respond to a menu command or toolbar button being clicked. Command bars can be displayed as

- a button in a toolbar with an icon, caption, or both

- a shortcut menu command

- a button in a toolbar with a Down arrow and associated drop-down list

- a container for other command bars

Figure 11.1 shows the Help screen displaying the structure of the CommandBars collection, which contains all the CommandBar objects from the application. Each CommandBar object represents a menu bar or a toolbar containing CommandBar-Button, CommandBarCombobox, and CommandBarPopup objects. The CommandBar-Controls collection contains CommandBarControl objects, which contain the properties and methods for the objects contained in CommandBar objects.

FIGURE 11.1:

Help screen displaying the structure of the Command-Bars collection

Customizing the Menu Bar

The purpose of the menu bar is to provide access to the features and functionality of your application. You may want to replace the standard Excel menu bar with one more appropriate for your program. Customizing a menu bar is pretty much a mix-and-match affair, as you can customize it using bits and pieces from existing toolbars and menu commands. These bits and pieces retain their full functionality wherever they are placed, which makes them powerful blue-chip reusable features.

You can customize a command bar with buttons for the menu commands you require and use that as your new menu bar. As mentioned, any Excel menu command you include will retain its functionality, and you can add some new buttons of your own to call any macros you've created.

Creating a Hierarchical Menu Command

Creating a new menu bar is just as easy as creating a new toolbar, which was described in Chapter 8. Let's create a hierarchical menu for Accounts that contains a drop-down list item for Sheets, which in turn contains Sales, Purchases, and Expenses in its drop-down list.

1. Open a new Excel workbook and choose Tools ➤ Customize to open the Customize dialog box.

2. Click the Commands tab and select New Menu from the end of the list in the Categories box (Figure 11.2).

FIGURE 11.2:

Selecting New Menu from the Commands tab

3. Drag the New Menu item from the Commands box to the Excel menu bar and position it between File and Edit, as shown in Figure 11.3.

FIGURE 11.3:

Inserting a new menu command into the Excel menu bar

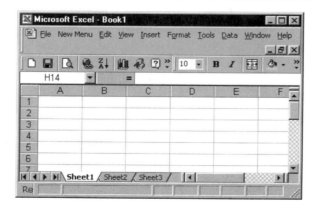

4. With the Customize dialog box still on display, right-click the New Menu item to display the shortcut menu (shown) and change the text in the Name box to **&Accounts**, finishing with the Enter key. "New Menu" will now have changed to "Accounts" in the menu bar, with the "A" underlined for keyboard access.

5. Drag another New Menu item from the Commands box to your newly created Accounts item in the menu bar, pausing over it until an empty box drops down, as shown.

Drop the dragged item there and follow step 4 to change its name to **&Sheets**. Notice how this item displays an arrow to indicate that choosing it will cause a drop-down list of further submenu commands to be displayed.

6. Click Macros in the Categories box. Drag the Custom Menu Item from the Commands box and pause it over Accounts, then over Sheets when it pops up; place it in the empty box as shown below. The vertical and horizontal

bars that appear in the drop-down lists indicate where your dragged items will be placed.

7. Release the mouse button. The Custom Menu Item will appear in the empty box, which will have stretched to fit (shown).

8. Drag another Custom Menu Item from the Commands box and pause it over Accounts, then Sheets; when the Custom Menu Item is displayed, make sure the line indicating where the new item will be placed lies along the bottom of the last menu item added (shown).

9. Repeat step 8 to add a third Custom Menu Item and then follow step 4 to enter **&Sales**, **&Purchases**, and **&Expenses** into the Name boxes for these three Custom Menu Items. Your hierarchical menu should be the same as the one shown in Figure 11.4.

10. Click Close to finish with the Customize dialog box and return to your worksheet.

FIGURE 11.4:

Hierarchical menu command containing Sales, Purchases, and Expenses menu commands

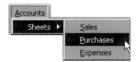

To Restore the Drop-down List of a Standard Excel Menu Command

If you delete any items available from the drop-down list on any of the menu options found in the menu bar and later need to restore them, just follow these steps:

1. Choose Tools ➤ Customize to open the Customize dialog box, which will allow you to click a menu command without activating it.

2. Right-click the standard Excel menu command you want to restore and choose Reset from the shortcut menu. The drop-down list will be restored and will now contain all the items that were available when you originally installed Office 2000.

To Add a Missing Standard Excel Menu Command

This section shows you how to restore a menu option that you've completely deleted from the menu bar.

1. Choose Tools ➤ Customize and select the Commands tab.

2. Select Built-in Menus from the Categories box to display Excel's standard menu commands (Figure 11.5).

FIGURE 11.5:

Built-in menus from Excel's standard menu bar

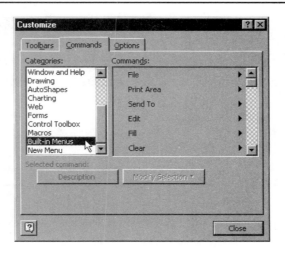

3. Drag the missing command from the Commands box and place it at the required position in the menu bar. You should try to place it in the same position it was in originally, since that's where you'll most likely look for it.

Running a Macro from a Menu Command

Now that we've built our hierarchical menu system, let's run macros to open the worksheets required when these menu commands are chosen. First, let's create the macros:

1. Open the Visual Basic Editor and choose Insert ➤ Module to open the code window for `Module1`.

2. Enter the macros shown in Listing 11.1 into `Module1`.

3. Return to Excel and rename worksheets `Sheet1`, `Sheet2`, and `Sheet3` as `Sales`, `Purchases`, and `Expenses` so that they can be selected by the macros.

4. Choose Tools ➤ Customize and click the Accounts menu command, then Sheets. Right-click Sales to display the shortcut menu.

5. Choose Assign Macro to open the Assign Macro dialog box, which will list the three macros just entered (Figure 11.6). Select `ShowSales` from the list and click OK.

FIGURE 11.6:

Assign Macro dialog box with list of macros to be run from menu commands

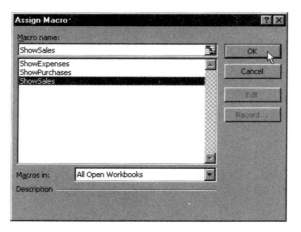

6. Repeat steps 4 and 5 to associate the other two macros with their menu commands.

7. Choose the three new menu commands in turn and watch the active worksheet change each time.

8. Click Close to close the Customize dialog box.

LISTING 11.1

```
0    Sub ShowSales()
1        Worksheets("Sales").Select
2    End Sub
3
4    Sub ShowPurchases()
5        Worksheets("Purchases").Select
6    End Sub
7
8    Sub ShowExpenses()
9        Worksheets("Expenses").Select
10   End Sub
```

ANALYSIS

Lines 1, 5, and 9 select the named worksheet from the Worksheets collection, making it the active worksheet.

Using a Toolbar Button as a Menu Command

You can place any toolbar button in your customized menu bar and it will always be available for you to use even if the toolbar it came from has been hidden. You have the choice here of placing a copy of the toolbar button in the menu bar so the toolbar stays intact or moving the button from the toolbar to the menu bar, thus removing it from the toolbar.

To Place a Copy of a Toolbar Button in the Menu Bar

1. Choose Tools ➤ Customize to display the Customize dialog box, then display the toolbar containing the button to be copied.

2. Hold down the Ctrl key and drag the button to be copied to the required position in the menu bar. Release the mouse button before releasing the Ctrl key. The button will now be available in both the menu bar and the toolbar.

To Move a Toolbar Button to the Menu Bar

1. Display the Customize dialog box, then display the toolbar containing the button to be moved.

2. Hold down the Alt key and drag the button to be moved to its required position in the menu bar. Release the mouse button before releasing the Alt key. The button will now be available only in the menu bar.

Deleting a Menu Command

Because Excel saves the latest version of its menu bar whenever you exit, any changes made will still be available next time you run it. For example, if after creating the Accounts menu option you open a new workbook or an existing workbook that has nothing to do with accounts, your Accounts menu command will come back to haunt you forever—until you delete it, that is.

Deleting a menu command is very simple and can be achieved in three different ways:

*   Choose Tools ➤ Customize, right-click the menu command to be deleted, and choose Delete from the shortcut menu.

*   With the Customize dialog box open, drag the menu command to be deleted to anywhere in the Excel window outside the menu bar.

*   Without opening the Customize dialog box, press the Alt key and drag the menu command to be deleted outside the menu bar.

NOTE   When you delete a menu command, it's removed along with any submenus lying beneath it in the hierarchy.

Customizing Menu Bars with Macros

Creating a customized menu bar in a macro allows you to recreate it at the click of a button any time it's required. This method also has the advantage that the menu bar can automatically be restored to the standard Excel menu bar immediately before the macro stops executing.

Creating a Menu Bar in a Macro

The code given in Listing 11.2 creates a menu bar with the first two menu commands taken from the standard Excel menu bar. The Normal button is equivalent to choosing View ➤ Normal and the Preview button to choosing View ➤ Page Break Preview. The next three buttons open the Expenses, Purchases, and Sales worksheets. The last button (Exit) runs the RestoreExcelMenuBar macro, which restores the standard Excel menu bar by deleting the Accounts menu bar before quitting from Excel completely. (Of course, Excel will automatically ask if you want to save any changes you've made to your worksheet.) The Excel menu bar containing these six buttons is shown in Figure 11.7.

FIGURE 11.7:

The Excel menu bar customized by the code shown in Listing 11.2

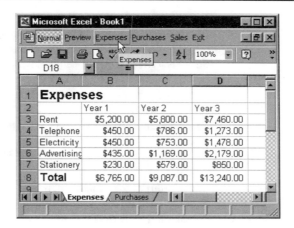

To create the Menu Bar in a macro:

1. Open a new workbook and add a new worksheet. Rename the four worksheets **Expenses**, **Purchases**, **Sales**, and **AccountsSheet**.

2. Run the Visual Basic Editor and choose Insert ➤ Module to open the code window for Module1. Enter the code shown in Listing 11.2.

3. Return to Excel and, before making the AccountsSheet worksheet active, run the CreateNewExcelMenuBar macro to create the new Excel menu bar and add the six buttons to it.

Reducing the menu commands available places restrictions on what can be done to the AccountsSheet worksheet and may make it easier for new users to work with.

TIP	Using a reduced set of menu commands is useful for training purposes where the commands from the standard Excel menu bar could be introduced gradually to the trainees.

LISTING 11.2

```
0    Sub CreateNewExcelMenuBar()
1        'the next two lines are only required during development
2        On Error Resume Next
3        CommandBars("Accounts").Delete
4
5        Dim NewMenuBar As CommandBar
6        Dim NewButton As CommandBarButton
7
8        Set NewMenuBar = CommandBars.Add("Accounts", , True)
9
10       Set NewButton = NewMenuBar.Controls.Add(_
         msoControlButton,_
         CommandBars("View").Controls("Normal").ID)
11       NewButton.Caption = "&Normal"
12       NewButton.Style = msoButtonCaption
13
14       Set NewButton = NewMenuBar.Controls.Add(_
         msoControlButton,_
         CommandBars("View").Controls("Page Break Preview").ID)
15       NewButton.Caption = "&Preview"
16       NewButton.Style = msoButtonCaption
17
18       Set NewButton = NewMenuBar.Controls.Add(msoControlButton)
19       NewButton.Caption = "&Expenses"
20       NewButton.Style = msoButtonCaption
21       NewButton.OnAction = "ShowExpenses"
22
23       Set NewButton = NewMenuBar.Controls.Add(msoControlButton)
24       NewButton.Caption = "&Purchases"
25       NewButton.Style = msoButtonCaption
26       NewButton.OnAction = "ShowPurchases"
27
28       Set NewButton = NewMenuBar.Controls.Add(msoControlButton)
29       NewButton.Caption = "&Sales"
```

```
30       NewButton.Style = msoButtonCaption
31       NewButton.OnAction = "ShowSales"
32
33       Set NewButton = NewMenuBar.Controls.Add(msoControlButton)
34       NewButton.Caption = "&Exit"
35       NewButton.OnAction = "RestoreExcelMenuBar"
36       NewButton.Style = msoButtonCaption
37
38       Worksheets("AccountsSheet").Select
39       NewMenuBar.Visible = True
40   End Sub
41
42   Sub ShowExpenses()
43       Worksheets("Expenses").Select
44   End Sub
45
46   Sub ShowPurchases()
47       Worksheets("Purchases").Select
48   End Sub
49
50   Sub ShowSales()
51       Worksheets("Sales").Select
52   End Sub
53
54   Sub RestoreExcelMenuBar()
55       CommandBars("Accounts").Delete
56       Application.Quit
57   End Sub
```

ANALYSIS

Lines 1 through 3 are required only while your macro is being developed. During the development stage, you may stop your macro prematurely, leaving the Accounts menu bar still intact, or your macro may be fully executed and the Account menu bar deleted. Because it is unknown whether or not the Accounts menu bar exists each time you start running your macro, these lines ensure that if it does exist it's deleted so that it won't cause problems when the Accounts command bar is created at Line 8. These lines can be left in the final macro, since they won't make any difference whatsoever as to how the macro operates.

Line 2 uses the On Error Resume Next statement to tell Visual Basic to simply ignore any error that may be generated in the next statement (Line 3) to prevent it from terminating the macro's execution abnormally.

Line 3 deletes the command bar named Accounts if it exists; otherwise it creates an error (in which case Visual Basic will ignore it and carry on).

Line 5 declares NewMenuBar as a CommandBar object.

Line 6 declares NewButton as a CommandBarButton object.

Line 8 uses the Add method of the CommandBars collection to create a new command bar and name it Accounts. Because the third argument (MenuBar) is set to True, Accounts will be the new and only menu bar for Excel until you restore the original menu bar at the end of the macro. (See "Adding a Command Bar" in the next section for an explanation of the MenuBar argument.)

Line 10 uses the Add method to add a new CommandBar control to the CommandBarControls collection. Its Type argument is set to msoControlButton and its Id is set to the integer assigned to the ID property of the Normal menu command in the Controls collection of the View Command Bar in the CommandBars collection. This new control will behave as if you've chosen View ➤ Normal.

Line 11 sets the Caption property to Normal. This will be displayed on the button only if the Style property is set to msoButtonCaption; otherwise, it's displayed as the ToolTip.

Line 12 sets the Style property to msoButtonCaption to display the caption on the button just like a normal menu bar command. Figure 11.8 shows the constants for setting some of the other Style properties.

Lines 14 through 16 add the Preview button to the command bar, which will behave as if you've chosen View ➤ Page Break Preview.

Line 18 uses the Add method to add a command bar, but this time only passes msoControlButton to the first argument. This adds a blank button without any associated code to the Accounts menu bar.

Line 19 sets the caption that will appear on the blank button since **Line 20** sets the Style property to msoButtonCaption.

Line 21 sets the OnAction property to ShowExpenses, which is the macro that will run when this menu command is chosen.

FIGURE 11.8:

Styles available for the
command bar

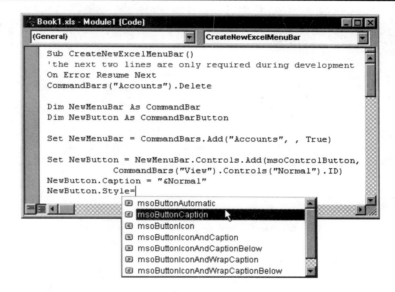

Lines 23 through 26 add the Purchases menu item to the command bar.
Line 26 uses the `OnAction` property to run the `ShowPurchases` macro each
time the `Purchases` menu command is chosen.

Lines 28 through 31 add the `Sales` menu item to the command bar. Line
31 uses the `OnAction` property to run the `ShowSales` macro each time the
Sales menu command is chosen.

Lines 33 through 36 add the Exit menu command. Line 35 uses the `OnAc-
tion` property to run the `RestoreExcelMenuBar` macro when the Exit
menu command is chosen.

Line 38 uses the `Select` method to make `AccountsSheet` the active worksheet. This will always be the first worksheet displayed every time you
run this macro.

Line 39 uses the `Visible` property to make the `NewMenuBar` command bar
(menu bar) visible to replace the standard Excel menu bar.

Lines 42 and 43 declare the `ShowExpenses` macro and use the `Select`
method to make the `Expenses` worksheet active.

Lines 46 and 47 declare the ShowPurchases macro and make the Purchases worksheet the active one.

Lines 50 and 51 declare the ShowSales macro and make Sales the active worksheet.

Lines 54 and 55 declare the RestoreExcelMenuBar macro and use the Delete method to delete the Accounts command bar (menu bar) and restore the standard Excel menu bar.

Line 56 quits from the Excel application.

WARNING   If your application replaces Excel's menu bar with a custom-built one, it needs to restore the Excel menu bar before it stops executing.

Adding a New Menu Bar with Buttons

The Add methods from two different classes of objects are used in the code shown in Listing 11.2. Both methods have the same functionality in that they both add an object to a collection. The following sections give further details about each of these methods.

Adding a Command Bar

The Add method from the CommandBars collection object creates a new command bar and adds it to the CommandBars collection. The arguments are all optional and are listed here in order:

Name is the name of the new command bar; a default name will be given if this is omitted.

Position is set to a constant from the Microsoft Office library (hence the prefix) to specify its position in the window. Available constants are msoBarLeft, msoBarRight, msoBarTop, msoBarBottom, msoBarFloating (not docked), and msoBarPopup (shortcut menu).

MenuBar is a Boolean variable set to True if the command bar being created is to replace the menu bar and False if it's to be a toolbar. In any window there's only one menu bar, but there can be oodles of toolbars.

Temporary set to True makes the command bar temporary so that it will always be deleted when you close the application.

Adding a *CommandBar* Control

The Add method from the CommandBarControls object adds a CommandBar control and returns a CommandBarButton object that's assigned to the variable NewButton. The argument list is different than the one used to add a new command bar. The arguments are all optional and are listed here in order:

Type is assigned a Microsoft Office constant to specify the type of control to be added. Constants available are msoControlButton, msoControlEdit, msoControlDropdown, msoControlComboBox, and msoControlPopup.

Id is an integer value that specifies a built-in menu command.

Parameter is used to run the built-in menu command.

Before specifies a number indicating the position for the new CommandBar control, which will be placed at this position, before any control already occupying it. If this argument is omitted, the new control is placed at the end.

Temporary set to True makes the command bar temporary so that it will always be deleted when you close the application.

Transforming a Menu Bar into a Toolbar

This is extremely easy to do in code. Let's update the CreateNewExcelMenuBar macro so that the menu bar shown in Figure 11.7 becomes the toolbar shown in Figure 11.9. Change the argument list in Line 8 of Listing 11.2 from

```
"Accounts", , True
```

to

```
"Accounts"
```

and update the macro's name from CreateNewExcelMenuBar to CreateNewToolbar.

That's all it takes! Run your macro and the toolbar shown in Figure 11.9 will appear.

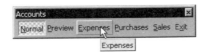

This toolbar looks more like a menu bar, so let's change some of the button styles. Changing NewButton's `Style` property in Line 12 from `msoButtonCaption` to `msoButtonIconAndCaptionBelow` and in Line 16 to `msoButtonIconAndCaption` for the Normal and Preview buttons gives the toolbar buttons shown in Figure 11.10. I've also made the Purchases button a ComboBox style.

Command Bar Button Styles

The buttons in a command bar come in different flavors, including buttons with captions, buttons with icons, and buttons with both. Buttons can also have their own drop-down lists of submenus. The toolbar in Figure 11.10 shows a variety of styles you can give to toolbar buttons. When a `CommandBar` object is displayed as a ComboBox button, it drops down a list of predefined values, with the text in the box differing according to the last item selected from the list.

LISTING 11.3

```
0    Sub CreateNewToolBar()
1        'the next two lines are only required during development
2        On Error Resume Next
3        CommandBars("Accounts").Delete
4
5        Dim NewMenuBar As CommandBar
6        Dim NewButton As CommandBarButton
7
8        Set NewMenuBar = CommandBars.Add("Accounts")
```

```
9
10      Set NewButton = NewMenuBar.Controls.Add(_
                   msoControlButton,_
                   CommandBars("View").Controls("Normal").ID)
11      NewButton.Caption = "&Normal"
12      NewButton.Style = msoButtonIconAndCaptionBelow
13
14      Set NewButton = NewMenuBar.Controls.Add(_
        msoControlButton, _
        CommandBars("View").Controls("Page Break Preview").ID)
15      NewButton.Caption = "&Preview"
16      NewButton.Style = msoButtonIconAndCaption
17
18      Set NewButton = NewMenuBar.Controls.Add(msoControlButton)
19      NewButton.Caption = "&Expenses"
20      NewButton.Style = msoButtonCaption
21      NewButton.OnAction = "ShowExpenses"
22
23      Dim NewComboboxButton As CommandBarComboBox
24      Set NewComboboxButton = _
        NewMenuBar.Controls.Add(msoControlComboBox)
25      NewComboboxButton.Caption = "&Purchases"
26      NewComboboxButton.OnAction = "ShowPurchases"
27      With CommandBars("Accounts").Controls(4)
28          .AddItem "Item 1", 1
29          .AddItem "Item 2", 2
30          .AddItem "Item 3", 3
31          .DropDownLines = 3
32          .ListIndex = 1
33      End With
34
35      Set NewButton = NewMenuBar.Controls.Add(msoControlButton)
36      NewButton.Caption = "&Sales"
37      NewButton.Style = msoButtonCaption
38      NewButton.OnAction = "ShowSales"
39
40      Set NewButton = NewMenuBar.Controls.Add(msoControlButton)
41      NewButton.Caption = "&Exit"
42      NewButton.OnAction = "RestoreExcelMenuBar"
43      NewButton.Style = msoButtonCaption
44
45      Worksheets("AccountsSheet").Select
46      NewMenuBar.Visible = True
```

```
47   End Sub
48
49   Sub ShowExpenses()
50       Worksheets("Expenses").Select
51   End Sub
52
53   Sub ShowPurchases()
54       Worksheets("Purchases").Select
55   End Sub
56
57   Sub ShowSales()
58       Worksheets("Sales").Select
59   End Sub
60
61   Sub RestoreExcelMenuBar()
62       CommandBars("Accounts").Delete
63       Application.Quit
64   End Sub
```

ANALYSIS

Line 23 declares NewComboboxButton as a CommandBarComboBox, as this name better reflects the ComboBox features that the button will adopt.

Line 24 uses the Add method to add a command bar with only the Type argument specified, using the Microsoft Office constant msoControl-ComboBox.

Line 25 sets the Caption property to Purchases.

Line 26 will run the ShowPurchases macro when the Purchases button is selected.

In **Line 27**, the With statement specifies that the fourth CommandBar control in the Accounts toolbar is to be used.

Lines 28 through 30 add three items to the drop-down list.

Line 31 sets the DropDownLines property to the number of lines in the drop-down list part of the ComboBox.

Line 32 sets the ListIndex property to 1 to display the first item in the drop-down list in the text box.

Summary

Now that you've seen how to customize your menu bars and toolbars, you know that the commands and buttons they contain are all represented by the same class of object—the CommandBar class. You should now be able to

- customize your Excel menu bar and restore it back again to the standard menu bar
- create a hierarchical menu command using items from the Customize dialog box
- copy or move a toolbar button to your menu bar
- delete a menu command
- create a menu bar in a macro
- transform a menu bar into a toolbar
- use the Style property of command bars to vary the look and functionality of your buttons

PART IV

Data Handling and Protection

CHAPTER

TWELVE

12

Handling Data in Files

This chapter describes how to code macros that will create a new workbook with a specified number of worksheets and save it to a file. You'll also see how to code macros that can rename files and copy files. There are macros to read and write data in files and to cut and paste—and when you're finished with a file, there's a macro to delete it.

Filenames and Path Names

It's much easier to find a file if all related files are placed in the same folder and the folder is given a name that reflects the contents of the files stored there. A file's name should be chosen using the same principle. The full path name for a file starts with the drive letter followed by the folder name(s) (including any subfolders) and the filename. The filename will usually include a three-letter extension that reflects the application that created it, such as .XLS for Excel workbooks and .DOC for Word documents.

Creating a New Workbook File

Let's consider creating a file containing a workbook with two worksheets. This can be achieved in three stages after you've opened Excel. I've recorded the following actions in a macro for comparison, and I'll show you later how this macro can be streamlined:

1. Select the General tab from the Options dialog box (choose Tools ➤ Options) and enter **2** in the Sheets In New Workbook box, as shown in Figure 12.1.

2. Click OK to close the Options dialog box.

3. Choose File ➤ New to create a new workbook containing two worksheets.

4. Choose File ➤ Save or File ➤ Save As to open the Save As dialog box, and enter the details of the file where you want to save your new workbook.

5. Click Save to save the file and close the Save As dialog box.

FIGURE 12.1:

General tab of the Options
dialog box

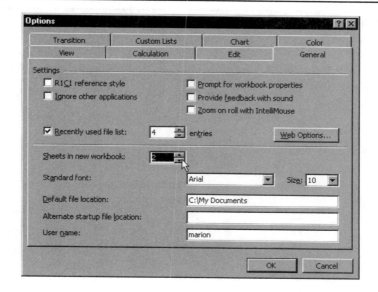

Creating a New Workbook in a Macro

You can create a new workbook from a macro. The techniques used are dependent on whether you are actually creating the workbook from scratch or are copying or moving the contents of an existing workbook to a new file.

In this section, I'll take you through the code I recorded in the steps above to create a new workbook from scratch, then I'll show you how to streamline and adjust the code. Later in the chapter, you'll see (in the "Copying Files" section) how to copy the contents of a workbook stored in a file and (in "Cutting and Pasting Data") how to move the contents of a workbook from one place to another.

The code statements in Listing 12.1 can be split into three groups that correlate with the three steps involved:

1. Set number of worksheets required (Lines 7 through 15).

2. Create a new workbook (Line 16).

3. Save the workbook to a file (Lines 17 through 21).

LISTING 12.1

```
0    Sub Macro1()
1         '
2         ' Macro1 Macro
3         ' Macro recorded 2/14/1999 by marion
4         '
5
6         '
7             With Application
8                 .UserName = "marion"
9                 .StandardFont = "Arial"
10                .StandardFontSize = "10"
11                .DefaultFilePath = "C:\My Documents"
12                .SheetsInNewWorkbook = 2
13                .EnableSound = False
14                .RollZoom = False
15            End With
16            Workbooks.Add
17            DirectoryForSaving=C:\FileHandling\RecordedCreateNewFile"
18            ChDirDirectoryForSaving
19            ActiveWorkbook.SaveAs Filename:= _
              DirectoryForSaving & "\SavedWorkbook.xls",_
              FileFormat:=xlNormal, Password:="", _
              WriteResPassword:="", ReadOnlyRecommended:=False, _
              CreateBackup:=False
20            ActiveWindow.WindowState = xlNormal
21            ActiveWindow.Close
22            ActiveWorkbook.Save
23   End Sub
```

ANALYSIS

Lines 7 through 15 contain the code statements written in response to the actions taken at step 1. These statements assign values to some of the properties in the Application object, which represents the Microsoft Excel application itself. (See sidebar below for more information about the Application object.)

Line 16, the code recorded in response to choosing File ➣ New (step 2), creates a new workbook containing two worksheets and adds it to the Workbooks collection.

Line 17 sets the variable `DirectoryForSaving` to the long path name of the directory where we're going to save our file. This avoids having the even longer path names required at Lines 18 and 19.

Line 18 is the code for the actions I made when selecting the directory for the new workbook file, except that I've used the `DirectoryForSaving` variable as the path name for conciseness.

Line 19 uses the `SaveAs` method of the object returned by the `ActiveWorkbook` property to save the file assigned to the `FileName` argument. The filename is constructed from the directory selected in the Save As dialog box (`DirectoryForSaving`) followed by the text from the File Name box, which together make up the full path name for the file the workbook is being saved to. The file will be saved in the format assigned to the `FileFormat` property and other properties shown in Line 19. All the arguments for the `SaveAs` method are described later in this chapter in the "Saving a New Workbook" section.

Line 20 uses the `ActiveWindow` property to return the `Window` object for the active window, which is the one on top—with a blue title bar if you're using one of the Windows standard display settings from the Control Panel. Line 20 then sets the `WindowState` property of this window to `xlNormal`. (The other settings available are `xlMaximized` and `xlMinimized`.)

Line 21 calls the `Close` method to close the active window, which is the Save As dialog box.

Line 22 calls the `Save` method to save the active workbook to the selected file.

Streamlining the Recorded Macro

This section will streamline the recorded macro in three parts that coincide with the three steps that created it:

- specify the number of worksheets
- create the workbook
- save the workbook

The *Application* Object

The Application object contains many of the property settings made in the Options dialog box, along with methods that return what are considered top-level objects, such as the ActiveWorkbook, ActiveSheet, and ActiveCell objects. Most of the time, the Application qualifier for these objects is omitted for brevity.

The Help facility in the Visual Basic Editor provides a great way to view the hierarchical structure of the objects available in Excel VBA: you can see how everything fits together. Below you can see the screen for the Microsoft Excel Objects.

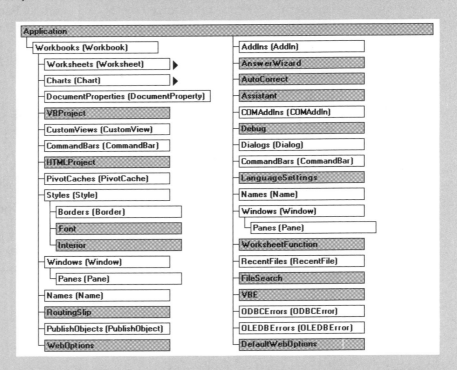

The yellow, or light, rectangles in the graphic contain collections of objects, with individual objects from the collection in parentheses. In general, accessing an object from a collection is achieved using the string assigned to the collection's Name property followed by either the name assigned to that individual object enclosed in parentheses and double quotes, or the index number for that object enclosed in parentheses. The blue, or dark, rectangles contain objects that don't belong to any collection.

Clicking any of the colored areas opens the Help screen for that object. Below you can see the Help screen displayed when the area containing the `Application` object is clicked.

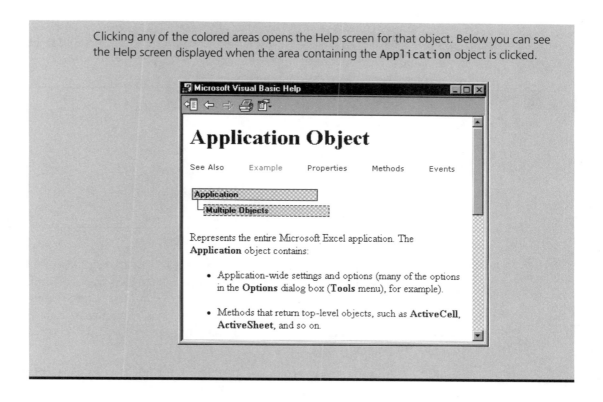

Specifying the Number of Worksheets in Code

Excel's `Application` object has a property called `SheetsInNewWorkbook` that can be set in code and has the same effect as manually entering a value into the Sheets In New Workbook box in the General tab of the Options dialog box (Figure 12.1).

The code statements in Lines 7 through 15 in the recorded macro (Listing 12.1) set up the number of worksheets to be inserted in any new workbook (step 1). Since only the `SheetsInNewWorkbook` property actually changes, these nine statements can be streamlined into the single statement shown in Listing 12.2. This lists the `GetNumberOfWorksheetsRequired` macro, which uses the `InputBox` function to prompt the user to enter a number. That number is then assigned to the `SheetsInNewWorkbook` property of the `Application` object. Every new workbook will be allocated the specified number of worksheets from that point onward until this property is changed again.

Giving the user control over the number of worksheets to be added makes this macro more useful than Listing 12.1, where the number was hard-coded in by the statement `Application.SheetsinNewWorkbook = 2`.

LISTING 12.2

```
0    Sub GetNumberOfWorksheetsRequired()
1        On Error GoTo EndOfMacro
2        Application.SheetsInNewWorkbook = _
         InputBox("How many worksheets do you require?", _
         "Worksheets Required")
3        EndOfMacro:
4    End Sub
```

Specifying the Number of Worksheets for One Workbook   Suppose you only want to apply the new number of worksheets to one workbook and then set it back to what it was before. You can easily expand the macro shown in Listing 12.2 to do this for you automatically and save you from having to remember what the previous setting was and from having to reset it manually or run the GetNumberOfWorksheetsRequired macro again.

Listing 12.3 shows this new expanded GetNumberOfWorksheetsRequiredAnd-CreateNewWorkbook macro (hope you like the name), which also creates a workbook containing the number of worksheets specified by the user.

Notice how the macro uses the variable Temp to capture the value assigned to the SheetsInNewWorkbook property before it's set to the new value entered by the user. Temp is used again after the new workbook has been created to restore the value back to what it was previously.

LISTING 12.3

```
0    Sub GetNumberOfWorksheetsRequiredAndCreateNewWorkbook()
1        Temp = Application.SheetsInNewWorkbook
2        On Error GoTo EndOfMacro
3        Application.SheetsInNewWorkbook = _
         InputBox("How many worksheets do you require?", _
         "Worksheets Required")
4        Workbooks.Add
5        Application.SheetsInNewWorkbook = Temp
```

```
6        EndOfMacro:
7    End Sub
```

In **Line 1**, Temp captures the current setting for the number of sheets that are inserted into a new workbook. This will be used in Line 5 to restore the SheetsInNewWorkbook property to this current setting.

Line 2 uses the On Error statement to jump to the EndOfMacro label at Line 6.

Line 3 sets the SheetsInNewWorkbook property to the value entered by the user into the input box generated using the InputBox function.

Line 4 creates a new workbook and adds it to the Workbooks collection, and inserts the number of worksheets entered by the user.

Line 5 restores the number of sheets to be added to new workbooks back to its original setting before it was changed at Line 3.

Line 6 contains the EndOfMacro label used by the On Error statement in Line 2.

Creating a Workbook in Code

As you've already seen in Line 16 of the recorded macro (Listing 12.1) and Line 4 of Listing 12.3, to create a new workbook all you need to do is add a new workbook to the Workbooks collection. The Add method for this collection creates a new workbook and makes it the active workbook. The Add method can be called with one optional argument:

```
Workbooks.Add(TemplateRequired)
```

The TemplateRequired argument can be passed the filename or path name of an existing Microsoft Excel template file, which will then be used to create the new workbook. You'll see later in Chapter 18 how to create template files. The Template-Required argument can also be passed an Excel constant, which will create a workbook containing a single sheet of the type specified by one of the xlWBATemplate constants. The constants available and the worksheet created by passing each one are given in Table 12.1.

TABLE 12.1: xlWBATemplate Constants

Constant	Sheet Created
xlWBATChart	Worksheet containing a chart; also displays the Chart Toolbox
xlWBATExcel4IntlMacroSheet	Microsoft Excel 4.0 international macro sheet
xlWBATExcel4MacroSheet	Microsoft Excel 4.0 macro sheet
xlWBATWorksheet	Worksheet (default)

Microsoft Excel 4.0 Macro Sheets and International Macro Sheets

Excel 4.0 macro sheets (US English) and Excel 4.0 international macro sheets (for numerous languages) are from workbooks created using Excel version 4.0. Excel 2000 allows you to open and edit these macro sheets. Excel 4.0 had two kinds of macros:

- Command macros that contain the sequence of commands recorded as you do a particular task

- Function macros that calculate a value and return it to a cell or cells in the worksheet(s)

Excel 2000 VBA provides the Excel4MacroSheets property to return macro sheets and the Excel4ExecuteExcel4Macro method to run a macro sheet and return the result.

Saving a Workbook to a File

There are two methods you can choose when you need to save a workbook: the Save method and the SaveAs method. The Save method is used to save changes to a workbook that's been saved before. The SaveAs method is used to save a workbook for the first time. However, if you call the Save method for a new workbook, Visual Basic will automatically convert this into a call to the SaveAs method.

Saving a New Workbook   The SaveAs method serves two purposes: to save a workbook that's never been saved before and to save an existing workbook to a different file. This method has lots of arguments, as you can see from Figure 12.2.

FIGURE 12.2:

List of arguments required by the SaveAs method

Although the sheer number of these arguments may seem daunting at first glance, they're really all quite straightforward and they're all optional. A brief description of each argument follows.

Filename is passed the filename of the file to be saved if it's in the current folder; otherwise a path name is specified.

FileFormat allows you to save the file in one of the many formats available. These include various versions of each database format, Excel workbooks, Excel templates, Unicode, HTML, and many more.

Password allows you to protect a workbook by specifying a password of up to 15 case-sensitive characters. If this argument is assigned a value, the workbook can't be opened without the correct password being entered.

WriteResPassword allows you to set a password that needs to be entered before the file can be updated. A file can still be opened without giving this password, but it will be opened as read-only.

ReadOnlyRecommended allows you to stipulate that on opening the file a message recommending that the file be opened as read-only will be displayed.

CreateBackup when assigned True will create a backup copy of the file so that you can resort to it if required.

AccessMode allows you to specify the access mode as xlShared, xl-Exclusive, or xlNoChange (default). Occasionally you'll need to open up a shared file exclusively—this is done using the ExclusiveAccess method. The following code uses the MultiUserEditing property to test whether the active workbook is opened in shared access mode:

```
If ActiveWorkbook.MultiUserEditing Then
ActiveWorkbook.ExclusiveAccess
End If
```

After the `ExclusiveAccess` method has been called and another user opens the same workbook file, the File In Use dialog box is displayed.

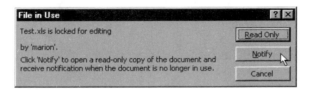

Clicking Notify in this dialog box lets Excel know that you want to be notified when the other user is finished, at which time the File Now Available dialog box will be displayed.

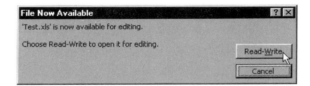

ConflictResolution only works for workbooks opened in shared access mode. It allows you to pass an Excel constant to specify how any conflicts should be resolved. The three constants available and the effect of passing each one are:

- `xlUserResolution` will display the Resolve Conflicts dialog box (default) shown in Figure 12.3. When you've clicked one of the Accept buttons, the Office Assistant will display an appropriate message. The one shown below is in response to clicking the `Accept Other` button.

- `xlLocalSessionChanges` will accept any changes made by the local user.

- `xlOtherSessionChanges` will accept any changes except those made by the local user.

FIGURE 12.3:

Resolve Conflicts dialog
box

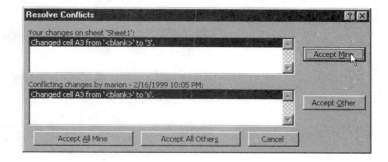

AddToMru when set to True will add the workbook to the list of recently accessed files.

TextCodePage is not used if the application language is set to US English.

TextVisualLayout is not used if the application language is set to US English.

Saving a Workbook Again   To save a workbook that's been saved previously, you use the Save method. For example, the code for saving the active workbook is simply

```
ActiveWorkbook.Save
```

You can name an open workbook that you want to save (or use its **Workbooks** collection index number, if known):

```
Workbooks("Accounts").Save
```

You can also save all the open workbooks to the files they were originally read from:

```
Workbooks.Save
```

> **NOTE**   If you use the Save method to save a workbook that's never been saved before, Excel will automatically respond as if you'd used the SaveAs method.

Renaming a Workbook's File   To rename an open workbook in a macro, all you've got to do is save it to a file with the new filename using the SaveAs method, as follows:

```
ActiveWorkbook.SaveAs "c:\Accounts\Expenses.xls"
```

If any part of the path name is inaccessible, a runtime error dialog box will result:

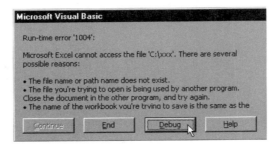

When you rename a file in this way, the original file will still exist, containing the data last saved. The renamed version of the file will contain the same data plus any updates made since the last save of the original file.

Copying Files

The FileCopy method in the VBA library allows you to copy a source file to a destination file. The FileCopyMethod macro shown in Listing 12.4 demonstrates how the FileCopy method is implemented.

LISTING 12.4

```
0    Sub FileCopyMethod()
1        FileCopy  "C:\My Documents\Test.xls", _
         "C:\My Documents\TestNew.xls"
2    End Sub
```

Copying Multiple Files

The CopyFile method of the FileSystemObject copies one or more files from a specified source to a single file that's been specified as the destination. Source and Destination are both arguments of this method. The Source argument is passed a string that can include wildcards in the filename to identify one or more files. The Destination argument is passed a string that must uniquely identify a file, so it can't contain any wildcards. The Source and Destination arguments for obvious reasons are both required. A third argument, Overwrite, is optional and is set to True whenever you want to overwrite the contents of an existing file.

Normally the source file will exist and the destination file will need to be created or overwritten—but sometimes things can go wrong, such as:

- The source file doesn't exist.

- The destination file exists, but its access mode has been set to read-only.

- The destination file exists, but the Overwrite argument has been assigned False.

The CopyFilesMethod macro in Listing 12.5 shows the CopyFile method in action. A FileSystemObject must be created first using the CreateObject function, then you can use its CopyFile method to do the copying.

LISTING 12.5

```
0    Sub CopyFilesMethod()
1        Set Newfilesystemobject = _
         CreateObject("Scripting.FileSystemObject")
2        Newfilesystemobject.copyfile "C:\My Documents\Test.xls", _
         "C:\My Documents\TestNew.xls", True
3    End Sub
```

Cutting and Pasting Data

Copying data by cutting and pasting is achieved using the Cut method, which copies the selected data into the Clipboard and clears it from the worksheet, then pastes the contents of the Clipboard into the worksheet at the specified range. Listing 12.6 shows the Cut method in action.

LISTING 12.6

```
0    Sub CutAndPaste()
1        Worksheets("Sheet1").Range("a1:b5").Cut _
2        Worksheets("Sheet1").Range("C1")
3    End Sub
```

When cutting data, the range of cells specified for the destination should have the same dimensions as the range copied to the Clipboard. Otherwise you'll get a runtime error:

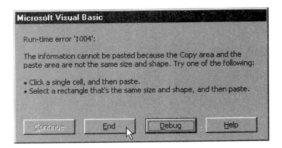

This error can be avoided by specifying only the upper-left cell of the destination range.

Opening Files

This section looks at opening files for reading and writing. You must, of course, open a file before you can read data from it or write data to it. VBA provides the Open statement to do this. Let's look at a simplified version of the Open statement that's capable of handling all the input and output required by Excel VBA. The syntax of this Open statement is

    Open *pathname* For *mode* As *#filenumber*

where the path name uniquely identifies a file and the mode can be Input, Output, or Append. In Input mode you input data to your application from a file, in Output mode you output data from your application to a file, and in Append mode you output data from your application to the end of a file.

NOTE   Opening a file in Output mode deletes any data in the named file when it's opened. Opening a file in Append mode preserves any data already in the file.

The #filenumber is also known as the *file handle* and can range from #1 through #511, inclusive. After the file is opened, its name is never referred to again—it's the magic filenumber that's used to identify the open file in the rest of the code.

If the path name is hardwired into the code and someone accidentally deletes or moves the file, the macro will no longer work if the file is opened for input. Hardwiring also makes a macro less flexible, since it is then only able to open one particular file. Your code will be more useful if you allow the user to select the file to be opened in the same way that choosing File ➤ Open does.

Displaying the Save As Dialog Box from a Macro

In VBA the Save As dialog box can be displayed by calling the GetSaveAsFile-name function that gets the file selected by the user but doesn't actually save it.

```
FilenameRequired = Application.GetSaveAsFilename
```

This function has the following optional arguments:

InitialFilename allows you to name the file path that will initially be displayed when the Save As dialog box is first opened.

FileFilter allows you to specify the list items for the Save As Type drop-down list.

FilterIndex allows you to define the default file filter using its position (index) in the drop-down list of items you specified for the FileFilter argument (above).

Title allows you to replace the Save As in the title bar with your own text.

Listing 12.7 shows the GetSaveAsFilename function being called; note that two of its properties have been assigned values. Figure 12.4 shows the Save As dialog box when it's first opened by this GetSaveAsDialogBox macro.

LISTING 12.7

```
0    Sub GetSaveAsDialogBox()
1        SavedName = Application.GetSaveAsFilename(_
2        Initialfilename:="C:\My Documents\Text.xls", _
3        FileFilter:="Workbooks (*.xls), *.xls,Word _
         Documents (*.doc),*.doc")
4    End Sub
```

FIGURE 12.4:

Save As dialog box opened
from the macro shown in
Listing 12.7

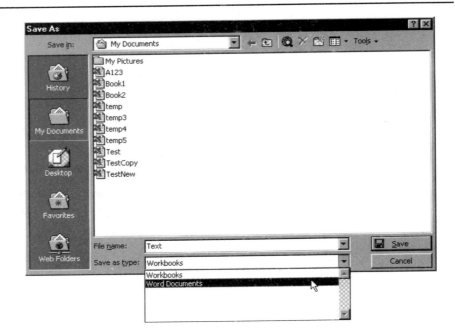

Displaying the Open Dialog Box from a Macro

The Open dialog box can be displayed by calling the GetOpenFilename function,
as shown in Listing 12.8. The GetOpenFilename function has five arguments, all
of them optional. The first three arguments are FileFilter, FilterIndex, and
Title, the same as the ones for the GetSaveAsFilename function. The other two
arguments are ButtonText, which is for Macintosh only, and MultiSelect,
which is set to True to allow more than one file to be selected at a time.

LISTING 12.8

```
0   Sub GetOpenDialogBox()
1       OpenFilename = Application.GetOpenFilename
2   End Sub
```

Writing Data to a File

Writing data to a file is done using the Write statement. Before you can write to a file, it must have been opened using the Open method. Listing 12.9 shows the Open method being used to open a data file and assign it the handle #1. The Write statement uses this handle to send the string "Hello" to the file, and the Close method uses it to close the file.

LISTING 12.9

```
0    Sub WriteToFile()
1        Open "C:\My Documents\DataFile1.dat" For Output As #1
2        Write #1, "Hello"
3        Close #1
4    End Sub
```

The Write statement sends text to files so that you can read the data file using any application that can read text, such as Notepad, WordPad, or Word.

Reading Data from a File

Reading data from a file is done using the Input statement. Listing 12.10 shows the string written in Listing 12.9 being retrieved and displayed in a message box as shown.

LISTING 12.10

```
0    Sub ReadFromFile()
1        Open "C:\My Documents\DataFile1.dat" For Input As #2
2        Input #2, InputString
3        MsgBox "The input was " & InputString
4        Close #2
5    End Sub
```

Several items can be read from a file in the same statement, with the variables being assigned input values separated by commas—for example, Input #4, InputValue1, InputValue2, InputValue3.

Saving Changes Automatically

Before you close a file, you may want to verify that no updates have taken place since it was last saved. This is simple to do using the Saved property, which is True if no changes have been made since the last save. Saved is a property of the Workbook object and is coded as follows:

```
If ActiveWorkbook.Saved = False Then
ActiveWorkbook.Save
End If
```

Testing whether a File Exists

If you try to open a file that doesn't actually exist, your application will grind to a stop with a runtime error. If you have any doubt about a file's existence, it's much better to search for the file before you try to open it. The macro shown in Listing 12.11 prompts the user to enter the name of a file, then checks to see whether the file is stored on the system. If it isn't, a message box informs the user that the file entered doesn't exist.

LISTING 12.11

```
0    Sub FileExists()
1        Dim DataFile As String, TestData As String
2        DataFile = InputBox("Enter the name of the file", _
         "Data File")
3        TestData = Dir(DataFile)
4        If Len(TestData) = 0 Then MsgBox "Error - the file " + _
         DataFile + " doesn't exist!", , "Error"
5    End Sub
```

ANALYSIS

Line 1 uses the `Dim` statement to declare the variables `DataFile` and `TestData` as String types. Several variables can be declared on the same line even if they are different types. If the `as type` part is skipped, the variable is assumed to be the `Variant` type, which can be assigned just about anything.

Line 2 calls the `InputBox` function to get a file's path name from the user.

Line 3 uses the `Dir` function to search for the file specified by the path name stored in the variable `DataFile`. Users can enter multiple character (*) and single character (?) wildcards in their path names and `Dir` will return the first file it finds that matches. If no matching files are found, `Dir` returns the empty string (`""`). The variable `TestFile` is assigned the returned string.

Line 4 uses the `Len` function to find the length of the string assigned to `TestData`. If the length is 0, no matching file was found and the `MsgBox` function is called to inform the user.

When you save data to a file that doesn't already exist, Visual Basic will create a new file and place the data into it. When you save data to a file that already exists, Visual Basic will clear any data currently in the file before placing the new data into it. Before allowing users to save data to a file from your macro, you may want to warn them that a file already exists to avoid their destroying the contents in the file by mistake. You can find out whether or not a file exists using the `Dir` function (Line 3, Listing 12.11).

Deleting Folders and Files

The `RmDir` (remove directory) statement deletes the folder passed to it as an argument, provided it's empty. If the folder contains files or other folders, the runtime error message "Path/File access error" will be displayed. The `Kill` statement deletes the file passed to it, provided it's closed—otherwise you'll get an error message. A single `Kill` statement can be used to delete several files if wildcards are employed to specify the filename or path name. The wildcard * replaces multiple characters and ? replaces single characters. For example, if you have several workbooks all starting with Book followed by a number, Kill Book* will delete them all.

The Kill and RmDir statements are often used together to remove all the files from a folder and then to delete the folder itself.

Summary

After reading this chapter, you'll know how to create a new workbook containing a specified number of worksheets from a macro and how to save it. You'll be able to

- rename files
- copy complete files or cut and paste bits and pieces from one file to another
- display the Save As and Open dialog boxes and retrieve the path names for the selected files
- read data from and write data to files
- test whether a file exists before opening it
- delete folders and files

Visualizing Data with Charts

Presenting your data in charts can make it more interesting and visually appealing than it would be as a collection of numbers in a worksheet. Excel has a powerful wizard for producing charts, making the creation of awesome-looking charts extremely simple and efficient. Charts provide a visual means for presenting your information that can be much easier to interpret than rows and columns of numbers, especially when the data is spread over several worksheets and workbooks.

What Is a Chart?

A chart is a way of visually representing the values assigned to a range of cells in your worksheet. Charts provide an easy way for users to interpret the numerical information and to see trends and patterns that might be present in the data. Charts also allow you to compare sets of data—even from different worksheets—and see immediately, for example, whether actual sales are keeping up with the sales forecast or have increased or decreased from previous years.

Figure 13.1 shows the hierarchical relationship of the objects involved with charts.

FIGURE 13.1:

Objects involved with charts

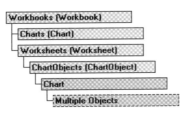

- The Charts collection object contains a collection of all Chart objects in the active workbook that represent chart sheets (a chart that is created in its own worksheet), but it doesn't contain any Chart objects that represent embedded charts.

- The ChartObjects collection object contains a collection of all ChartObject objects in the active chart sheet or worksheet.

- The ChartObject object can represent an embedded chart and can also act as a container for a Chart object, which in turn can represent a chart sheet.

- The Chart object can represent either an embedded chart (ChartObjects collection) or a chart in a chart sheet (Charts collection).

- "Multiple Objects" in Figure 13.1 refers to the different objects that make up a chart, such as the ChartTitle, Axis, ChartArea, PlotArea, and Legend objects.

Embedded Charts and Chart Sheets

Two types of charts exist in Excel: charts that are embedded into existing worksheets and charts that are created in separate worksheets, called chart sheets.

An embedded chart is attached to a worksheet and is displayed whenever that worksheet is open; it is also printed with the data every time you print the worksheet. This type of chart is part of the worksheet, in the same way as the data it represents.

Chart sheets are separate sheets that are created and added to a workbook for the sole purpose of containing a single chart.

The points plotted in both types of charts are linked to the data at selected cells of a worksheet, so they will be automatically updated whenever any of the data values change.

Embedded charts are most often used for a quick analysis of the data. Normally, the readability of an embedded chart isn't good enough for a printed presentation; in those instances, a chart sheet is preferred.

Creating an Embedded Chart

Creating an embedded chart is easy to do using the Chart Wizard. Before you run the Chart Wizard you'll need to create the data to be plotted in your worksheet, so enter the row and column labels and the data values shown in Figure 13.2.

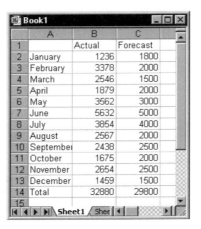

Creating a Chart with the Wizard

The Chart Wizard consists of a series of dialog boxes that allow you to set the various options you want for your chart. These dialog boxes provide a selection of numerous chart styles for you to choose from. The Chart Wizard provides an excellent tool for designing a new chart the way you'd like it! Once you know what the Chart Wizard's features actually do, you'll be able to design charts that won't need any readjusting later. The following steps show you how to set some of the options available. I recorded my actions in a macro as I went along, and we'll review them in Listing 13.1.

1. Select cells in the range A1:C4 to include in our chart. I've selected the row and column labels as well so that they'll also appear in the chart. I've included only a few data samples in this step to keep the chart simple while we experiment with chart types; we'll add the rest further on in the process.

2. Choose Insert ➤ Chart (or click the Chart Wizard button in the Standard toolbar) to display the first Chart Wizard dialog box, shown in Figure 13.3.

3. Click and hold the mouse button down on the Press And Hold To View Sample button (as shown in Figure 13.4) to view the selected data as a chart. The Chart type used will be the one highlighted in the Chart Type box and the subtype used will be the one that was highlighted in the Chart Sub-type

box immediately before this button was held down (Figure 13.3). Let go of the button when you've finished looking at the chart.

FIGURE 13.3:

Chart Wizard–Step 1 of 4: Standard Types tab of the first Chart Wizard dialog box

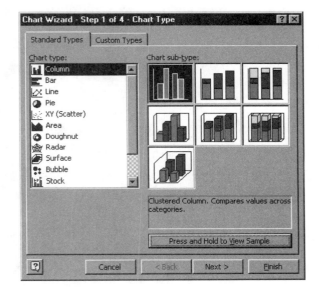

FIGURE 13.4:

Chart Wizard–Step 1 of 4: Standard Chart Types tab showing Press And Hold To View Sample button pressed

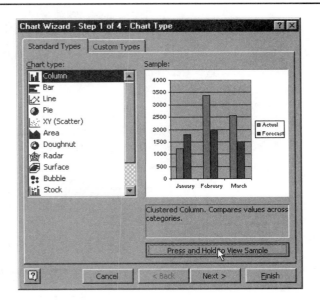

4. Select the Custom Types tab and click the Cones item from the Chart Type list, as shown in Figure 13.5. This will change the type of chart displayed in the Sample box. You may want to pause here to explore what the other chart types look like—there are some pretty fantastic ones. (My two favorites are Cones and Tubes.)

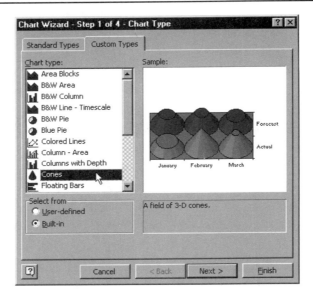

5. For a preliminary view of our charted data, click Next to open the second Chart Wizard dialog box with its Data Range tab selected, as shown in Figure 13.6.

6. Our chart compares the actual sales figures with those forecast for each of the three months. Figure 13.6 shows the series formatted in columns; select the Series In Rows option button to reformat the data with the series in rows, as shown in Figure 13.7.

7. Now we'll include the rest of our sales data in the chart. Click the Collapse Dialog button at the end of the Data Range box to reduce the dialog box to the one shown below and select cells in the range A1:C13. The new selection will appear in your dialog box.

FIGURE 13.6:

Chart Wizard–Step 2 of 4: Data Range tab in the second Chart Wizard dialog box

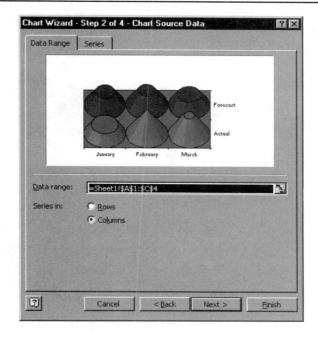

FIGURE 13.7:

Chart Wizard–Step 2 of 4: Rows selected in the Chart Source Data Range tab

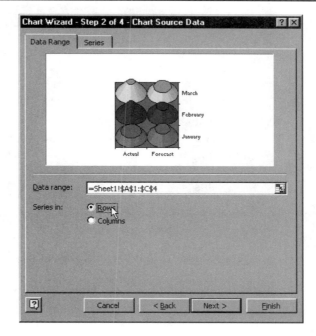

8. Click the Expand Dialog button at the end of the box to restore the dialog box to its full size. The chart will now represent the new expanded data selection, as shown in Figure 13.8.

FIGURE 13.8:

Chart Wizard–Step 2 of 4: Second Chart Wizard dialog box updated to chart the expanded data set

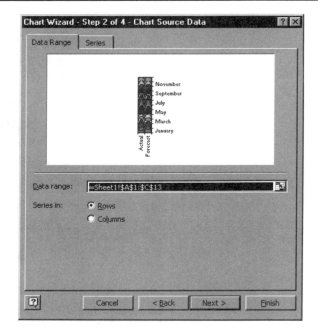

9. It's time to give a title to our chart. Click Next to display the third Chart Wizard dialog box, enter the title **Sales Results** into the Chart Title box as shown in Figure 13.9, and watch as Excel adds it to the top of the chart.

10. Click Next to display the fourth (and last) Chart Wizard dialog box. This is where you've got to decide between placing your chart into a chart sheet or embedding it as an object into a worksheet. I've opted for the chart sheet alternative by selecting the As New Sheet option button in the Chart Location dialog box, as shown in Figure 13.10.

11. And that's it! Click Finish to return to your workbook, which will now display the new chart sheet shown in Figure 13.11.

FIGURE 13.9:

Chart Wizard–Step 3 of 4: Entering a chart's title in the Titles tab of the third Chart Wizard dialog box

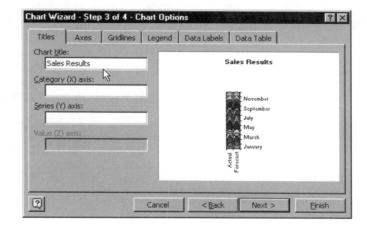

FIGURE 13.10:

Chart Wizard–Step 4 of 4: Creating a new sheet to display your chart

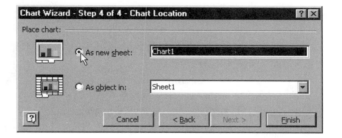

FIGURE 13.11:

Chart1 created by the Chart Wizard

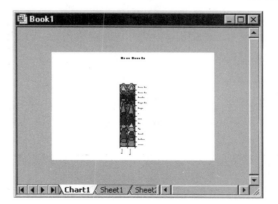

Recorded Macro for Using the Wizard

Listing 13.1 shows the macro recorded while using the Chart Wizard to create a chart.

LISTING 13.1

```
0    Sub Macro1()
1        '
2        ' Macro1 Macro
3        ' Macro recorded 2/27/1999 by marion
4        '
5        '
6        '
7        Range("A1:C4").Select
8        Charts.Add
9        ActiveChart.ApplyCustomType ChartType:=xlBuiltIn,_
         TypeName:="Cones"
10       ActiveChart.SetSourceData_
         PlotBy:=xlRows,Source:=Sheets("Sheet1").Range("A1:C13")
11       ActiveChart.Location Where:=xlLocationAsNewSheet,_
         Name:="Chart1"
12       With ActiveChart
13           .HasTitle = True
14           .ChartTitle.Characters.Text = "Sales Results"
15           .Axes(xlCategory).HasTitle = False
16           .Axes(xlSeries).HasTitle = False
17           .Axes(xlValue).HasTitle = False
18       End With
19   End Sub
```

ANALYSIS

Lines 0 through 6 are the opening statement and description.

Line 7, recorded at step 1, makes the range A1:C4 both selected and active.

Line 8, recorded at step 2, creates a new chart object representing a new chart sheet and adds it to the `Charts` collection object. Since there are no other chart sheets in the workbook, this will be the only `Chart` object in this collection.

Line 9, recorded at step 4, first uses the `ActiveChart` property to return the active `Chart` object. It then uses the `Chart` object's `ApplyCustomType` method to apply the specified chart type (`xlBuiltIn`) in the `ChartType` argument and the name of the chart type (`"Cones"`) in the `TypeName` argument. Other chart types available include `xlColumnStacked`, `xlBarClustered`, `xlLine`, `xlPie`, `xlAnyGallery`, and `xlUserDefined`.

Line 10, recorded during steps 5 through 8, uses the `SetSourceData` method to set the source data range for the active chart. The `PlotBy` argument is set to `xlRows` in response to the Rows option button being selected at step 6. The `Source` argument is set to the new extended range that was selected when the Collapse button at the end of the Data Range box was clicked in step 7.

Line 11, recorded at step 10 (I'll go back to step 9 when I get to Lines 13 through 17), uses the `Location` method to move the chart to its new location. In this case, the `Where` argument is assigned `xlLocationAsNewSheet` to make the location a new chart sheet in response to my selecting the As New Sheet option button, and the `Name` argument is assigned `"Chart1"`, which was the default entry in the Chart Location dialog box.

Line 12 starts the `With` statement.

Lines 13 through 17 set the properties of the active chart in response to the actions taken or not taken at step 9. Lines 13 and 14 were recorded in response to entering "Sales Results" in the Chart Title box. Lines 15 through 17 were recorded in response to clicking Finish while the Category (X) Axis and Series (Y) Axis boxes were empty.

Instant Chart Sheets

Chart sheets can be created instantly at the click of a key—the F11 function key, to be precise! All you need is some data to plot; then you can either chart the data of an entire table that contains a selected cell or, if you require only part of the data to be plotted, you can select the range of cells required and then create a chart based on that selection.

Charting Data in a Table

The following steps show you how to create a chart based on all the data in a table and place it in its very own chart sheet with just one key press:

1. Open a new workbook and enter the table of data shown in Figure 13.2.

2. Select a single cell within the table and Excel will search for and include data from adjacent cells automatically.

3. Press F11 to produce the chart sheet Chart1, shown in Figure 13.12, which will have the data plotted in a chart that uses all the default settings.

FIGURE 13.12:

Chart created by selecting one cell from the table shown in Figure 13.2

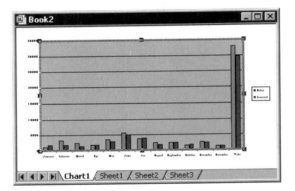

Charting Data in a Range

To chart data that makes up only part of a table, you must select the cells you want to chart. For example, repeat the above three steps for charting data in a table, but instead of selecting only one cell at step 2, select the range of cells A1:C4. The chart sheet Chart2, shown at Figure 13.13, will be created.

You can quickly create a chart in a chart sheet using the default settings by clicking the F11 function key with the data selected.

FIGURE 13.13:

Chart created by selecting a range of cells from the table shown in Figure 13.1

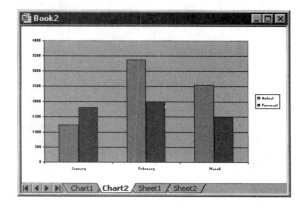

Recorded Macro for Instant Chart Sheets

Macro1 (Listing 13.2) was recorded while creating the chart shown in Figure 13.12; Macro2 (Listing 13.3) was recorded while creating the chart shown in Figure 13.13. Notice that there's no difference between the two macros except for the range of cells assigned to the Source argument of the SetSourceData method in Line 8.

LISTING 13.2

```
0    Sub Macro1()
1        '
2        ' Macro1 Macro
3        ' Macro recorded 2/24/1999 by marion
4        '
5
6        '
7        Charts.Add
8        ActiveChart.SetSourceData _
         Source:=Sheets("Sheet1").Range("A1:C14")
9        ActiveChart.Location Where:=xlLocationAsNewSheet
10   End Sub
```

ANALYSIS

Line 7 creates a Chart object that represents a new chart sheet, which will be given the default name Chart1.

Line 8 uses the SetSourceData method of the active chart sheet (the one you've just created) to set the range of cells that will be used as the data source for plotting the chart. The range of data required—cells A1:C14 in our table of data—is assigned to the Source argument. Although we selected only one cell in the "Charting Data in a Table" exercise, Excel searches adjacent cells for data when a single cell is selected, and this is reflected in the recording of the steps.

Line 9 uses the Where argument of the Location method to stipulate that the chart is to be placed in the new chart sheet Chart1.

LISTING 13.3

```
0    Sub Macro2()
1        '
2        ' Macro2 Macro
3        ' Macro recorded 2/24/1999 by marion
4        '
5        '
6        '
7        Charts.Add
8        ActiveChart.SetSourceData _
         Source:=Sheets("Sheet1").Range("A1:C4")
9        ActiveChart.Location Where:=xlLocationAsNewSheet
10   End Sub
```

ANALYSIS

The analysis of the lines of code in Listing 13.3 is the same as the analysis for Listing 13.2 except for **Line 8**, where Excel plots the data at the selected range of cells without searching adjacent cells for more data values.

Resizing Charts

Embedded charts can be resized easily by dragging the sizing handles to the size required—but charts placed in chart sheets can't! Chart sheets are best resized using menu commands: they can be resized by zooming in and out, or they can be resized to fit in the window exactly. You can also drag the sizing handles of the plot area of a chart to resize it, but you'll have to adjust the size of the title and legend separately.

Resizing a Chart Sheet

The following steps show you how to resize a chart in a chart sheet:

1. Select the tab of the chart sheet containing the chart you want to resize.

2. Choose View ➢ Zoom to open the Zoom dialog box or click the Zoom button in the Standard toolbar (both shown below).

3. Choose whatever magnification you want, or select Custom and enter your own.

You must take care when resizing chart sheets not to make them too small or too large. Figure 13.14 shows a chart sheet that's too small for the window containing it; notice the large border area that's redundant because it doesn't contribute anything to the interpretation of the data.

Figure 13.15 shows a chart sheet that's too large for its window—parts of the chart have disappeared.

FIGURE 13.14:

Chart sheet that hasn't been sized with its enlarged window

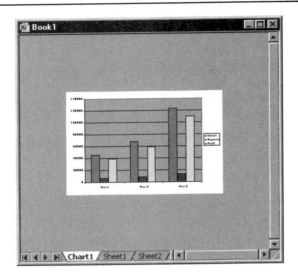

FIGURE 13.15:

Chart sheet inside a window that's been reduced

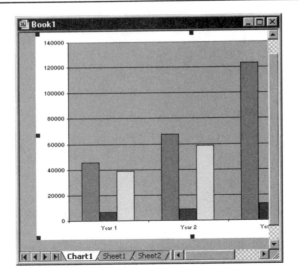

Resizing a Chart with a Macro

To resize a chart using a macro you set the Zoom property, which controls the size of the chart displayed in a window. The macro shown in Listing 13.4 animates the zoom from 26% to 65%.

LISTING 13.4

```
0    Sub AnimateZoom()
1        ' animates the chart being resized
2        For Count = 1 to 40
3            ActiveWindow.Zoom = 25 + Count
4        Next
5    End Sub
```

ANALYSIS

Line 2, the For loop, makes sure the zoom is done 40 times.

Line 3, the ActiveWindow property, is used to return the Window object that represents the active window. The Zoom property is a member of the Window object class and displays the chart at whatever percentage is assigned to it.

Resizing a Chart Sheet to Fit in the Window

You can have the chart area sized automatically to fit snugly inside the window by choosing View ➤ Sized With Window, as shown below.

This sets the SizeWithWindow property of the Chart object to True, which means that the chart area's size will be adjusted to fit the window. Figure 13.16 shows a chart sheet that's been sized with the window by turning on the Sized With Window option in the View menu.

FIGURE 13.16:

Chart sheet adjusted to fit inside the window

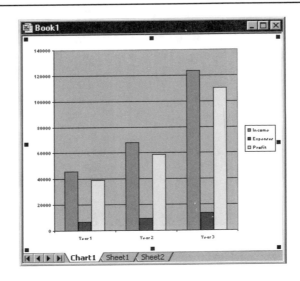

Turning on the Sized With Window option from a macro can be done in a single statement. Listing 13.5 shows this statement in the SizeChartWithWindow macro, which sets the SizeWithWindow property of the active chart sheet.

LISTING 13.5

```
0   Sub SizeChartWithWindow()
1       Answer = MsgBox("Do you want chart sized with window?", _
        vbYesNo, "Sized with Window")
2       If Answer = vbYes Then
3           ActiveChart.SizeWithWindow = True
4       Else
5           ActiveChart.SizeWithWindow = False
6       End If
7   End Sub
```

ANALYSIS

Line 0 starts the SizeChartWithWindow macro.

Line 1 uses the MsgBox function to display a message box (shown below) to ask the user if they want the chart sized with the window, and then assigns their response to the variable Answer.

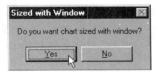

Line 2 tests whether the answer is equal to the constant vbYes. If so, it executes Line 3; if not, execution jumps to Line 4.

Line 3 sets the SizeWithWindow property of the active chart sheet to True.

Line 4 starts the Else part of the If statement, which will be executed if the condition in Line 2 is False.

Line 5 sets the SizeWithWindow property of the active chart sheet to False.

Line 6 ends the If statement.

NOTE   When a chart sheet has been sized with the window, you can't change its size using the Zoom menu command.

Moving an Embedded Chart to a Chart Sheet and Back Again

This section shows you how to move an embedded chart from a worksheet to a chart sheet and how to move it back again. Before you can start this example, you'll need to have a worksheet available that contains an embedded chart to use for the move.

Moving an Embedded Chart to a Chart Sheet

1. Select the embedded chart to be moved. The chart will display its sizing handles to show that it's been selected.

2. Choose Chart ➤ Location to open the Chart Location dialog box, shown in Figure 13.17. Notice the similarity between this dialog box and the last Chart Wizard dialog box (Figure 13.10).

FIGURE 13.17:

Moving the embedded chart in Sheet1 to chart sheet Chart1 using settings in the Chart Location dialog box

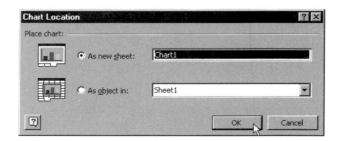

3. Select the As New Sheet option button and make sure that Chart1 appears in the box beside it.

4. Click OK to return to sheet Chart1 in the workbook. The embedded chart will now be displayed in chart sheet Chart1 and will no longer appear in the worksheet.

Moving an Embedded Chart to a Chart Sheet with a Macro

The macro code for moving an embedded chart to a chart sheet requires only one line of code. However, this is one of these dicey situations that depends on the user running the macro only if there is a chart embedded in the worksheet. I've taken care of this dilemma by using an On Error statement at Line 2 in Listing 13.6.

LISTING 13.6

```
0   Sub MoveEmbeddedChartToChartSheet()
1       'This macro moves a chart to a chart sheet
2       On Error Resume Next
3       ActiveChart.Location Where:=xlLocationAsNewSheet,_
        Name:="NewChart"
4       If Err > 0 Then
5           MsgBox "Error-no chart in worksheet!"
6           Err.Clear
7       End If
8   End Sub
```

Line 2 uses the On Error Resume Next form of the On Error statement. This form instructs Excel that if there is an error on the next line, it should resume execution at the following line (Line 4).

Line 3 moves the embedded chart from the current worksheet to the chart sheet named NewChart.

Line 4 uses the Err object returned by the On Error statement to test whether an error has occurred. Err used on its own is equivalent to Err.Number.

Line 5 is executed only if Line 3 has resulted in an error. This gives a message to the user to alert them that the move couldn't take place because there was no chart in the worksheet.

Line 6 reinitializes the properties of the Err object back to their non-error values.

On Error Statement

The On Error statement enables you to handle what would otherwise be fatal errors—that is, errors that would normally cause your macro to grind to a halt. If you know that a macro may be prone to crash if the user runs it at the wrong time, you should take steps within the macro to recover gracefully. The On Error allows you to do this! In the case of an error, an Err object is assigned a number to its Number property and a description of the error is assigned to its Description property. The description is very general and probably won't mean very much to the user of your application, so you may want to give your users a more appropriate message. For example, changing Line 5 in Listing 13.6 to

```
MsgBox Err.Number & "-" & Err.Description
```

would present the following message box to the user:

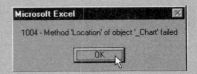

Moving a Chart from a Chart Sheet to a Worksheet

This section shows you how to move a chart from a chart sheet to a worksheet. Listing 13.7 (following) shows how this can be achieved in a macro.

1. Select the chart in chart sheet Chart1.

2. Choose Chart ➤ Location to open the Chart Location dialog box.

3. Select the As Object In option button and make sure that Sheet1 appears in the box beside it.

4. Click OK to return to worksheet Sheet1 in the workbook. The chart will now be embedded in worksheet Sheet1.

Moving a Chart from a Chart Sheet to a Worksheet with a Macro

LISTING 13.7

```
0    Sub MoveChartToWorksheet()
1        'This macro moves a chart to Sheet1
2        On Error Resume Next
3        ActiveChart.Location Where:=xlLocationAsObject,_
         Name:="NewSheet"
4        If Err > 0 Then
5            MsgBox "Error—need to open a chart sheet!"
6            Err.Clear
7        End If
8    End Sub
```

ANALYSIS

Most of these lines are the same as (or similar to) those given in Listing 13.6, so refer to the Analysis for that listing if you need to.

Line 3 uses the Location method to move the chart from the chart sheet to the worksheet named Sheet1.

Parts of a Chart

A chart is made up of several different parts. Figure 13.18 shows the parts that make up a 2-D chart.

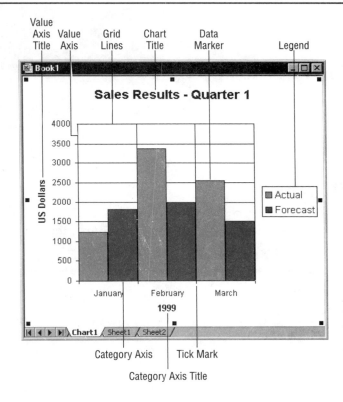

Figure 13.19 shows parts that are found only in 3-D charts. Six of the corners are shown highlighted—the far bottom-left corner is displayed in light gray, visible in the foremost January column.

Parts found in a 3-D chart

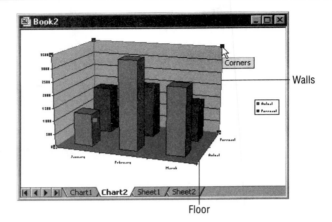

Plot Area

The plot area, enclosed within the chart area, is where all the data markers such as the lines, columns, and bars representing the data values are displayed. Figure 13.20 shows this area selected.

FIGURE 13.20:

The plot area of a chart

Formatting the Plot Area

The plot area can be formatted by adding a color, a pattern, or even a picture to the background, or by changing the font. Let's add a picture to a chart:

1. Create a new chart.

2. Double-click inside the plot area to open the Format Plot Area dialog box, shown in Figure 13.21.

FIGURE 13.21:

Format Plot Area
dialog box

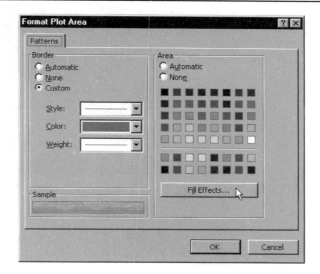

3. Click Fill Effects to open the Fill Effects dialog box (shown in Figure 13.22) and select the Picture tab.

4. Click Select Picture to open the Select Picture dialog box, shown in Figure 13.23, and select a picture from your PC (I've selected Globe). Click Insert to return to the Fill Effects dialog box (Figure 13.24).

5. Click OK to return to the Format Plot Area dialog box, then click OK to return to your chart, which will now have the picture as a background. Mine is shown in Figure 13.25.

FIGURE 13.22:

The Fill Effects dialog box

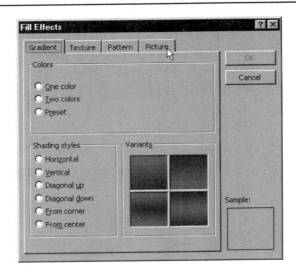

FIGURE 13.23:

The Select Picture dialog box

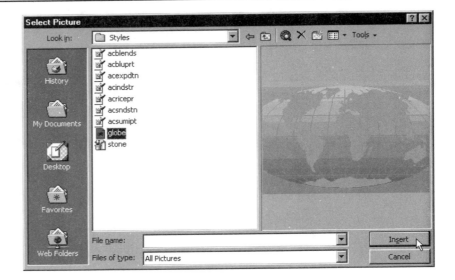

FIGURE 13.24:

The Fill Effects dialog box showing the picture selected in the Select Picture dialog box

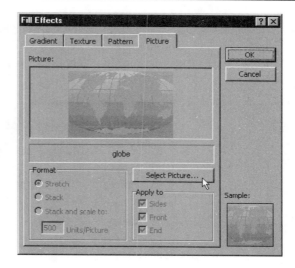

FIGURE 13.25:

The Globe picture displayed as the background

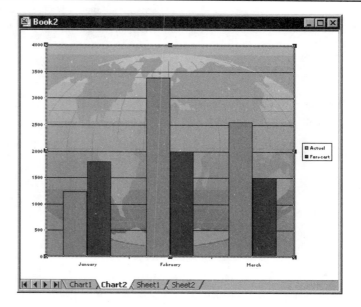

The Chart Area

Figure 13.26 shows the chart area containing several elements that relate to a chart, including the data values, axis label and titles, chart title, and legend. It's the chart area that you would select if you wanted to copy a chart to a different location.

Formatting the Chart Area

In Figure 13.27, the chart area is selected in a chart produced by the Chart Wizard using the original (as installed) default settings with the values 7, 9, and 5.

Let's change the color of the chart area:

1. Double-click the chart area somewhere near its boundaries outside the plot area to display the Format Chart Area dialog box, shown in Figure 13.28.

2. Click Fill Effects to open the Fill Effects dialog box and select the From Corner option button in the Shading Styles frame; select the top-right pane from the Variants frame, as shown in Figure 13.29. Click OK to return to the Format Plot Area dialog box.

FIGURE 13.27:

Chart with chart area
selected

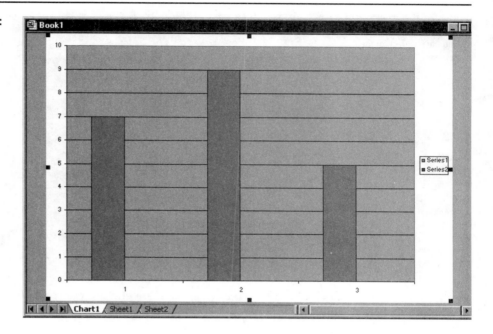

FIGURE 13.28:

Format Chart Area dialog
box

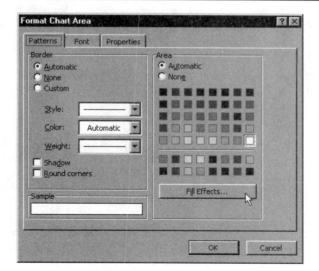

FIGURE 13.29:

Setting the fill effect for the chart area

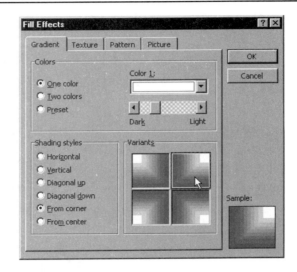

3. Click OK to return to your chart sheet. Your chart will now probably look something like the one shown in Figure 13.30.

FIGURE 13.30:

Chart1 with colored chart sheet and white plot area

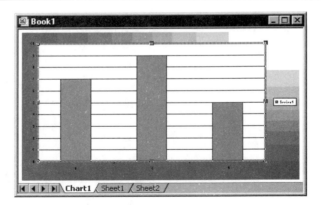

4. Double-click the plot area to open the Format Plot Area dialog box shown in Figure 13.21. Check the None option buttons in both the Border and Area frames—this will make the plot area transparent. Click OK to return to your chart sheet, which will now look more like the one in Figure 13.31.

FIGURE 13.31:

Chart1 with colored chart sheet and transparent plot area

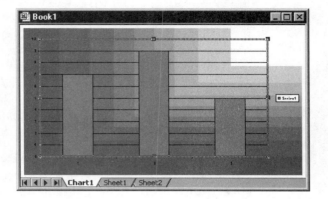

Formatting the Chart Area and Plot Area with a Macro

Listing 13.8 shows how the formatting for the chart area and plot area is achieved in a macro. Running a macro is much easier than going through the steps required every time you want to get the same effect.

LISTING 13.8

```
0   Sub FormatPlotAndChartAreas()
1       ' formats the Plot and Chart Areas
2       With ActiveChart.ChartArea
3           .Fill.OneColorGradient Style:=msoGradientFromCorner,_
                Variant:=2, Degree:=0.25
4           .Fill.ForeColor.SchemeColor = 2
5       End With
6       With ActiveChart.PlotArea
7           .Border.LineStyle = xlNone
8           .Interior.ColorIndex = xlNone
9       End With
10  End Sub
```

ANALYSIS

Line 2 uses the With statement to refer to the chart area returned by the ChartArea property of the active chart returned by the ActiveChart property.

Line 3 uses the Fill property to return a FillFormat object containing all formatting properties of the active chart. It uses the OneColorGradient method of this object to assign msoGradientFromCorner as the Style (the one selected from the Shading Styles frame in step 2) and 2 as the Variant (the one selected from the Variants frame). The third argument is Degree, which represents the level set in the Dark/Light scroll bar in the Colors frame. The Degree argument can have values from 0.0 (darkest) to 1.0 (lightest). We didn't set this value manually in the above exercise; in the macro I've set it to 0.25.

Line 4 assigns color number 2 from the Excel color scheme to the Scheme-Color property of the ColorFormat object. This object is returned by the ForeColor property of the FillFormat object returned by the Fill property of the active chart. Changing the 2 to another number will provide a different color but the gradation of the color will remain the same.

Line 6 uses the With statement to refer to the plot area of the active chart.

Line 7 sets the border's LineStyle to xlNone, which is equivalent to checking None in the Border frame of the Format Plot Area dialog box.

Line 8 sets the interior area's ColorIndex to xlNone, which has the same effect as checking the None in the Area frame of the Format Plot Area dialog box.

Figure 13.32 shows the result of running the macro with a line chart.

FIGURE 13.32:

Line chart with colored chart area and transparent plot area

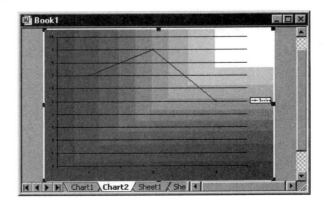

Creating Charts with Numerical Labels

In the previous example, Excel interpreted the values in the first column as being row labels. The situation is different when the first column contains numerical data values, as these could be either row labels or part of the data you want plotted. Excel will initially interpret them as values to be plotted, but you can easily change them to labels after the chart has been plotted. The following example shows how this can be done:

1. Open a new workbook and enter the data shown in Figure 13.33.

FIGURE 13.33:

Workbook containing
Annual Sales data

2. Highlight cells A1 through B7 and click the Chart Wizard button.

3. Click Next in the first Chart Wizard dialog box to open the second dialog box, which will display a bar chart representing data from the selected cells. As you can see from the chart shown in Figure 13.34, the year has been included in the values charted.

4. Select the Series tab, highlight the Annual Sales Year item from the list in the Series box, and click the Remove button. This will immediately remove values in the first column from the chart as shown in Figure 13.35.

5. Click the Collapse button at the end of the Category (X) Axis Labels box, select the A3:A7 range of cells, and click the Expand button to return to the second dialog box, which will now have years along the x-axis as shown in Figure 13.36. Click Next to proceed to the third Chart Wizard dialog box.

6. To polish off your corrected chart, update the title in the Chart Title box and watch it appear immediately in the chart, as shown in Figure 13.37.

FIGURE 13.34:

Initial result of charting
numerical row labels

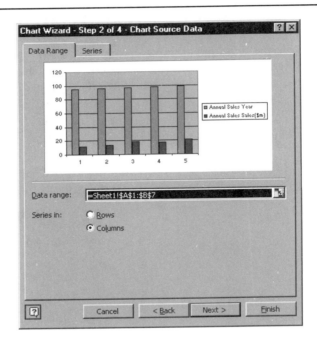

FIGURE 13.35:

Result of removing the year
values from the chart

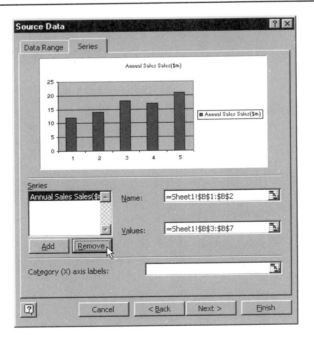

FIGURE 13.36:

Result of changing the Category axis labels

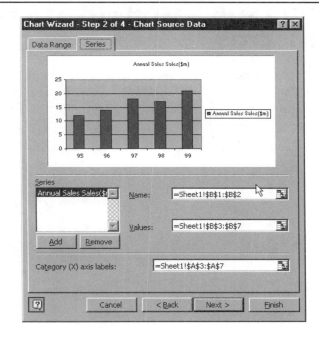

FIGURE 13.37:

Result of changing the chart title to Annual Sales

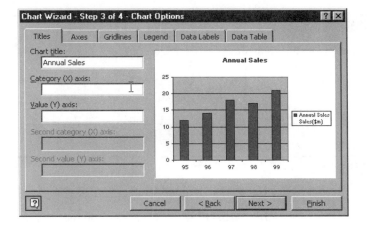

Applying the Different Types of Charts from Macros

There are many different kinds of charts available in the lists in the first dialog box of the Chart Wizard. Let's take a look at some of these charts and how they can be selected within macros. Figure 13.38 is a column chart, which is probably about the most common chart you'll see.

FIGURE 13.38:

Column chart

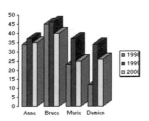

This chart was selected from the Chart Type box in the Custom Types tab in the first dialog box of the Chart Wizard. Listing 13.9 shows how you can create a chart of this type in a macro.

LISTING 13.9

```
0   Sub CreateColumnChart()
1       Charts.Add
2       ActiveChart.ApplyCustomType ChartType:=xlBuiltIn, _
        TypeName:= "Columns with Depth"
3   End Sub
```

ANALYSIS

Line 1 creates a new chart sheet and makes it active.

Line 2 calls the ApplyCustomType method to the Chart object to apply a type from the Custom Types tab. Its ChartType argument is set to xlBuiltIn, as one of the built-in types is being used. Its TypeName argument is set to the name in the Chart Type box.

The charts available from the Chart Type box in the Standard Types tab are accessed in a different way than Custom Types are. Listing 13.10 shows how the doughnut chart (Figure 13.39) from the standard types of charts is generated from a macro.

FIGURE 13.39:

Doughnut chart

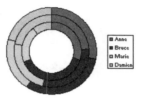

LISTING 13.10

```
0    Sub CreateDoughnutChart()
1        Charts.Add
2        ActiveChart.ChartType = xlDoughnut
3    End Sub
```

ANALYSIS

Line 1 creates a Chart object representing a chart sheet and adds it to the Charts collection object.

Line 2 sets the ChartType argument of the active chart to xlDoughnut. There are many types available and all are assigned using Excel constants, which include xlLine, xlArea, xl3DbarStacked, and xl3Dpie.

Figures 13.40 to 13.44 show some of the interesting charts available that will add a touch of class to your worksheets.

FIGURE 13.40:

A B&W Area custom type chart

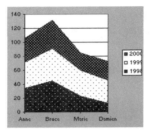

FIGURE 13.41:

A Pie Explosion custom type chart

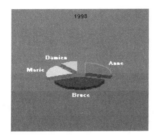

FIGURE 13.42:

A Tubes custom type chart

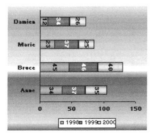

FIGURE 13.43:

A Cones custom type chart

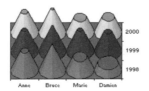

FIGURE 13.44:

A standard chart represented in macros by the constant x1Bubble3DEffect

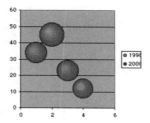

Making Your Charts Sparkle!

The chart shown in Figure 13.11 leaves a lot to be desired, but with a little bit of formatting here and there you can make it into something that's visually delightful. A chart is made up of several parts that are all formatted as separate entities. This section describes how you can

- change the font on text items
- add borders and colors to titles and legends
- change gridlines
- change the color and shape of data markers such as columns and bars

In general, to format any part of a chart you first double-click it to display the formatting dialog box for that part.

Formatting the Title

Double-click the title part of a chart to open the Format Chart Title dialog box, shown in Figure 13.45. On the Font tab, change the size in the Size box to 16 and click OK to return to your chart.

To format the title in a macro

```
ActiveChart.ChartTitle.Font.Size = 16
```

It's easy to interpret this assignment statement as setting the size of the active chart's title font to 16.

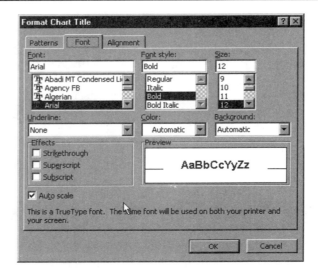

Formatting the Legend

Double-click the legend to open the Format Legend dialog box, shown in Figure 13.46. Select the Placement tab and check the Left option button to move the legend box to the left side of the chart.

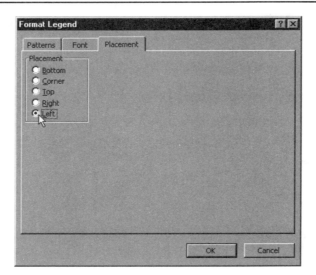

To format the legend in a macro

```
ActiveChart.Legend.Position = xlLeft
```

This assignment statement sets the `Position` of the active chart's legend to `xlLeft`.

Formatting a Data Point

Click the data marker you want to isolate from the rest, then click it again—making two separate clicks rather than a double-click. Once it's been isolated and has its sizing handles displayed, double-click it to display the Format Data Point dialog box (shown in Figure 13.47). Select a color from the palette and click OK to return to the chart.

To change the color of a single data point in a macro

```
ActiveChart.SeriesCollection(1).Points(1).Interior.ColorIndex = 6
```

This assignment statement sets the `ColorIndex` of the `Interior` of the first data marker in the first series of the collection in the active chart. To set the `ColorIndex` of other data markers, change the number in parentheses following `Points`; to set it for other series, change the number following `SeriesCollection`.

FIGURE 13.47:

Changing the color of a data marker in the Format Data Point dialog box

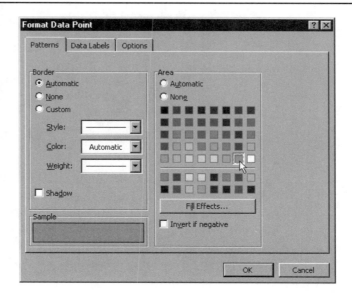

Replacing a Data Marker with a Picture

You can replace a data marker with a picture so that it really jumps out from the chart. This is simple to do:

1. Click that data point on the chart to select all the data points in that category, then click again to select the individual data point. (You can tell from the selection handles when you've isolated the one required.)

2. Either double-click the marker or choose Format ➤ Selected Data Point to open the Format Data Point dialog box, shown in Figure 13.48, and select the Patterns tab.

FIGURE 13.48:

The Patterns tab of the Format Data Point dialog box

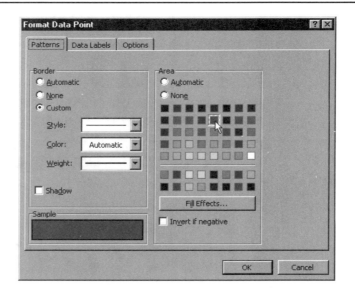

3. Click Fill Effects to open the Fill Effects dialog box, shown in Figure 13.49. On the Picture tab, click Select Picture to open the Select Picture dialog box (shown in Figure 13.50) and choose a picture to replace the bar for the desired data point. I've chosen my picture from the ClipArt directory, but most picture formats (such as BMP, JPEG, and GIF) are acceptable. Click Insert to return to the Fill Effects dialog box. Click OK to return to the Format Data Point dialog box.

FIGURE 13.49:

The Picture tab in the
Fill Effects dialog box

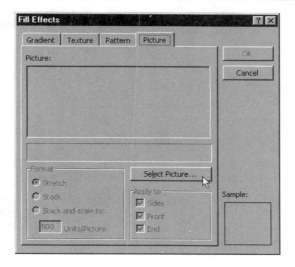

FIGURE 13.50:

The Select Picture
dialog box

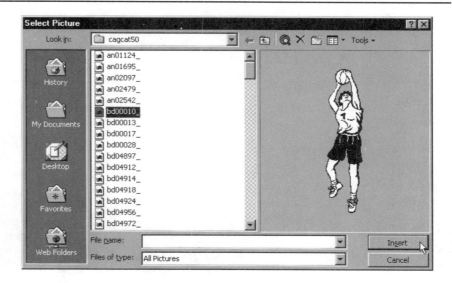

4. Click OK to return to your chart, which, as shown in Figure 13.51, will now display a picture where the selected bar used to be.

Data marker replaced by a
picture in 2-D

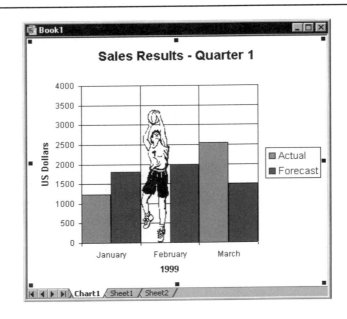

The effect is even more incredible in 3-D, as you can see in the example in
Figure 13.52.

FIGURE 13.52:

Data marker replaced by a
picture in 3-D

To change a marker to a picture in a macro:

```
ActiveChart.SeriesCollection(1).Points(2).Fill.UserPicture _
PictureFile:= "C:\Program Files\Clipart\cagcat50\bd00010_.wmf",_
PictureFormat := xlStretch, PicturePlacement := xlAllFaces
```

This uses the UserPicture method to assign the picture passed to its Picture-File to fill the second data marker in the first series of the active chart. The PictureFormat argument is set to xlStretch to make sure that the picture matches the height of the data marker it replaces. The PicturePlacement is set to xlAll-Faces so that it appears on all faces in the 3-D version.

Formatting a Data Series

The following steps show you how to change a series of data markers to marble.

1. Click a data marker in the series you want to change; a selection handle will be displayed on each data marker in the series. Double-click one of the markers to open the Format Data Series dialog box, shown in Figure 13.53.

FIGURE 13.53:

Format Data Series dialog box

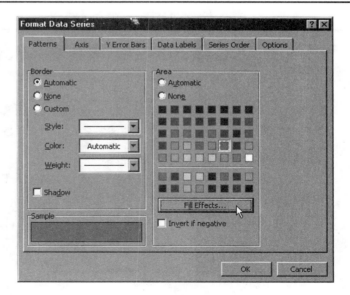

2. Click Fill Effects to open the Fill Effects dialog box, and select the Texture tab, shown in Figure 13.54. Select a marble effect and click OK to return to

the Format Data Series dialog box. Click OK to return to the chart, which will now show the series selected in marble (Figure 13.55).

FIGURE 13.54:

The Texture tab in the Fill Effects dialog box

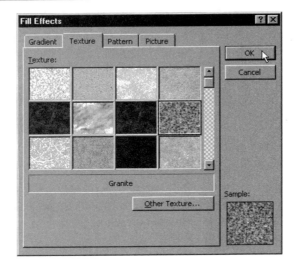

FIGURE 13.55:

Chart with marble columns

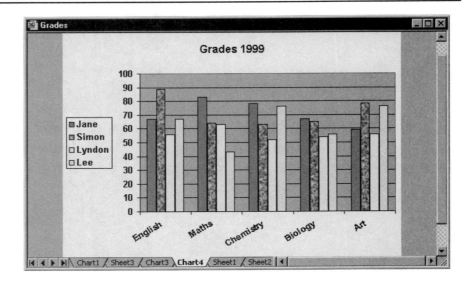

To format a data series in a macro

```
ActiveChart.SeriesCollection(1).Fill.PresetTextured _
PresetTexture := msoTextureGranite
```

This uses the `PresetTextured` method to set the fill format to a preset texture, which is specified in the `PresetTexture` argument as `msoTextureGranite`. The fill is applied to all of the points in the first series of the active chart.

Formatting an Axis

1. Select an axis and choose Format ➤ Selected Axis (or double-click the axis) to open the Format Axis dialog box, shown in Figure 13.56.

2. Select the Alignment tab and adjust the degrees to 30. Click OK to return to your chart, which will draw the axis labels at the angle specified.

To format an axis in a macro

```
ActiveChart.Axes(xlCategory).TickLabels.Orientation = 30
```

This uses the Excel constant `xlCategory` to identify the axis to be updated. The `Orientation` property is set to 30 degrees, which will rotate the tick labels of the category axis (X–axis). (Ticks are the little lines placed at regular intervals along the axis to split it up into sections.)

FIGURE 13.56:

The Alignment tab in the Format Axis dialog box

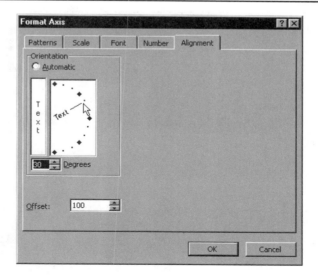

Setting the Default Chart Type

If you've got a favorite chart type that you prefer to the default type, you can make it the default type by choosing Chart ➤ Chart Type to open the Chart Type dialog box, selecting the chart type that you want as a default, and then clicking Set As Default Chart. You'll be asked to confirm that that's what you want to do before it's set in stone—or at least until you set another type.

Saving Your Chart Type for Reusability

If you've spent a long time creating the most amazing chart you've ever created, you're probably wishing you'd kept a note of how you did it so that you could use it for other charts. Weep not—you can save all of these settings as a user-defined chart type, and then it will be as easy to access as any of the types provided by Excel. The procedure is very simple; just refer to the following steps.

1. Select your amazing chart and choose Chart ➤ Chart Type to open the Chart Type dialog box.

2. Select the Custom Types tab and check the User-defined option button (Figure 13.57).

FIGURE 13.57:

Adding a chart type to the custom types

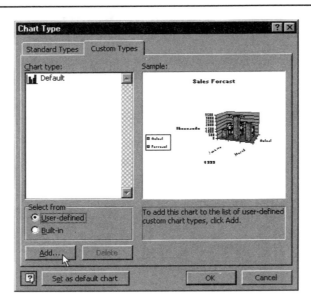

3. Click Add and in the Name box enter a name for your amazing chart's type, as shown below. Enter a description in the Description box so that it'll be easy to find among the other amazing charts you'll be adding in the future. Click OK to return to the Chart Type dialog box, which will now have the new type listed.

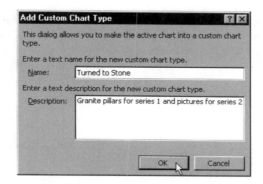

4. Click OK to return to your worksheet.

5. Enter some data in Sheet2 and select it.

6. Click the Chart Wizard button to open the first dialog box of the Chart Wizard and select the Custom Types tab. Select the User-Defined option button to display the list of user-defined types.

7. Select your new type and click Finish—and you've just created another amazing chart, as brilliant as the first one!

Printing a Chart

Before you print a chart, you may need to adjust its size and orientation. By default, charts are printed in landscape orientation and sized to fit the full page. These can both be adjusted irrespective of whether the chart is in a chart sheet or is embedded in a worksheet. The first thing to do is to view your chart using the Print Preview option from the drop-down menu under File. Previewing a chart in a chart sheet always fits it to the printed page, but there are two ways to preview an embedded chart:

- You can preview an embedded chart along with the data values from the same worksheet by choosing File ➤ Print Preview—but make sure the chart isn't selected before you start (Figure 13.58).

FIGURE 13.58:

Previewing printing the data with the embedded chart

- You can preview an embedded chart by itself if you select the chart before choosing File ➤ Print Preview. The chart will be resized to fit on the printed page, as shown in Figure 13.59.

FIGURE 13.59:

Previewing an embedded chart without the data

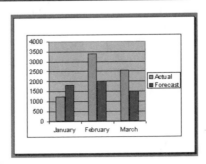

The preview window provides a number of features that let you make adjustments to the size and shape of your charts until you get the look you want to print. Notice the formatting buttons in the Microsoft Excel preview window shown below, which has an embedded chart being previewed along with its data.

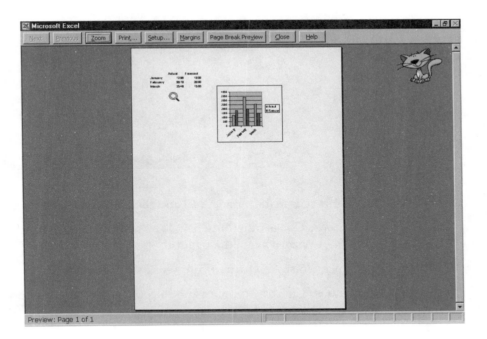

Formatting 3-D Charts

There are several parts specific to some types of 3-D charts that you can format separately. These include walls, floor, perspective, rotation, height, and elevation. There are three categories of 3-D charts:

- The basic 3-D chart, which represents the plotted data with a Category axis (X-axis) and a Value axis (Y-axis) and uses three-dimensional data markers

- The 3-D perspective chart, which plots the data using an additional axis—the Series axis (Z-axis)

- The 3-D pie chart, which represents the data as a round disc without axes, floors, and walls that the other two have

Let's open a new workbook and create a 3-D chart based on the simple table shown in Figure 13.60. We can then format the floors and walls and view the chart from different angles.

FIGURE 13.60:

Grades data for representing in 3-D

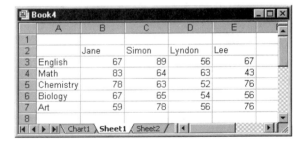

1. Select cells in the range A2:E7 and click the Chart Wizard button in the toolbar.

2. Choose Cones from the Chart Type box in the Custom Types tab of the Chart Wizard's first dialog box.

3. Click Finish to return to your workbook.

4. Choose Chart ➤ Location and select the As A New Sheet option to move your chart to a chart sheet.

Now you're ready to start formatting!

Formatting the Floor

Double-click an area of the floor that hasn't any data markers and is not an axis lying along the edge of the floor. The ToolTip will let you know if your mouse cursor is pointing at the floor. This will open the Format Floor dialog box, which—except for the title—is exactly the same as the Format Plot Area dialog box shown in Figure 13.21. I've changed my floor to a lighter color.

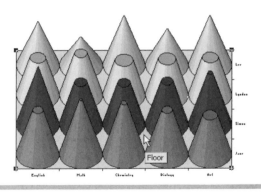

Formatting the Walls

To find the walls, click just above the data markers, as shown below.

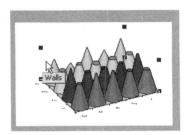

When the ToolTip lets you know that you've selected the walls, double-click in the same area above the data markers to open the Format Walls dialog box, which, again, is the same as the Format Plot Area dialog box (Figure 13.21) except for the title. I've clicked Fill Effects and selected the Denim texture from the Texture tab for my walls, as shown below.

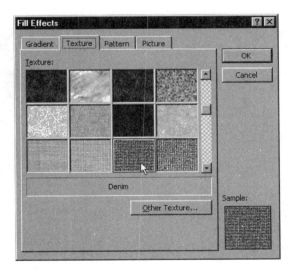

Viewing from Different Angles

Viewing your chart from different angles can be achieved by dragging the mouse or by making changes in the 3-D View dialog box. First let's take a look at how the corners are dragged.

Select a wall, then select one of the corners of the chart (the ToolTip will let you know when you've selected a corner). While holding down the mouse button, move the mouse around and watch the skeleton view of your chart move with you (Figure 13.61).

FIGURE 13.61:

Skeleton view of the chart displayed while readjusting the viewing position

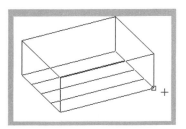

When the chart is at the required angle, let the mouse button go and your chart will be redisplayed (Figure 13.62).

FIGURE 13.62:

The chart viewed from the new viewing position

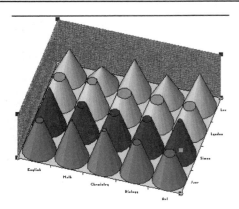

TIP   By holding down the Control key while performing the actions above, an outline of the data markers will be displayed so that you can visualize the position of the markers as you change the orientation.

3-D View Dialog Box

Select Chart ➢ 3-D View to open the 3-D View dialog box, shown in Figure 13.63.

FIGURE 13.63:

3-D View dialog box

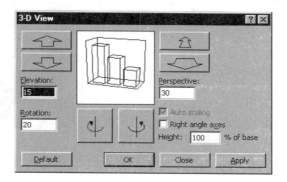

The skeleton chart in the white pane moves as you make selections, thus providing some feedback as to how your chart will be viewed. Clicking either of the two boxes below this will rotate your chart in the direction of the arrows.

Clicking the arrows above the Elevation box allows you to move your viewing position up and down and changes the number in the box to suit. The arrows above the Perspective box allow you to change the perspective, which causes your axes not to meet at right angles anymore. If you check the Right Angle Axes check box, the perspective features will all become invisible. Changing the height in the box will increase or decrease the height of your data markers.

If you're using the 3-D View dialog box to adjust the view of a pie chart, changing the height setting will increase or decrease the thickness of your pie and the elevation arrows will let you view your pie chart from above. The chart drawn in the white pane will, of course, be a pie chart (Figure 13.64).

FIGURE 13.64:

3-D View dialog box for adjusting a pie chart

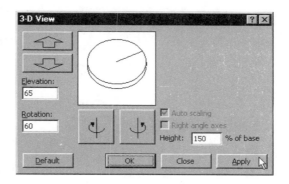

Figure 13.65 shows the final pie chart.

FIGURE 13.65:

Pie chart after the adjustments made in the 3-D View dialog box have been applied

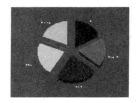

Summary

By the end of this chapter, you'll be able to

- create charts embedded in worksheets
- create charts in chart sheets
- move a chart from a worksheet to a chart sheet and back again
- resize charts
- assign a chart's type with a macro
- format parts of charts with a macro
- create a new chart type for reuse
- print a chart
- format a 3-D chart
- view a 3-D chart from different viewing positions
- change the height of data markers in columns charts and pie charts

CHAPTER

FOURTEEN

14

Data Security

Data security involves protecting data against accidental loss or alteration and restricting access to sensitive data. This chapter describes how to make workbooks read-only, how to use passwords to restrict access, how to hide data, and how to use Excel's auditing features to graphically track relationships between cells.

Levels of Security

There are several levels of security that can be used to secure the data stored in a workbook.

- At the highest level, you can prevent unauthorized users from accessing the file itself by requiring all users to enter the correct password before the workbook can be opened.

- At the next level, you can allow users to open the workbook and view the data as read-only to prevent any unauthorized editing.

- You can allow users to open the workbook and make changes, but require them to enter a password if they want to save these changes.

- You can simply have a backup copy of the workbook created every time any user's changes are saved.

Password Requirement

Files that have been secured using passwords require authorized users to enter a correct password before the file can be opened or modified. Passwords can be up to 15 characters in length and can contain a combination of letters (case sensitive), numbers, and symbols. To set up the password protection:

1. Choose File ➤ Save As to display the Save As dialog box.

2. In the Save As dialog box, choose Tools ➤ General Options to display the Save Options dialog box, shown in Figure 14.1.

3. Check the Always Create Backup check box to save a backup copy of the workbook every time you save the workbook.

FIGURE 14.1:

Save Options dialog box

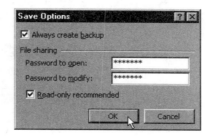

4. Enter a password in the Password To Open box (Figure 14.1) to stop any unauthorized users from opening the workbook.

5. Enter a password in the Password To Modify box to prevent read-only users from overwriting it. This doesn't prevent a user who can open the file from saving it to a different file.

6. Check the Read-Only Recommended check box (Figure 14.1). This recommends that other users be restricted to opening the workbook as read-only.

7. Click OK, and the Confirm Password dialog box shown in Figure 14.2 will be displayed. Re-enter your password for opening the file in the Confirm Password dialog box and click OK. The Confirm Password dialog box will be displayed again; re-enter your password for modifying the file and click OK to return to the Save Options dialog box.

FIGURE 14.2:

Confirm Password dialog box

8. Click OK to return to the Save As dialog box, then click Save to save the workbook. Close the workbook, and then you can test whether the passwords actually work.

9. Re-open the workbook to display the Password dialog box (shown), enter your password in the box provided, and click OK.

10. A second Password dialog box (shown) will be displayed. Enter your password for modifying the worksheet and click OK.

11. Because you checked the Read-Only Recommended check box, the information message box shown in Figure 14.3 will be displayed.

FIGURE 14.3:

Message box for read-only files

- Clicking Yes displays the workbook and allows you to make changes to it and to save it to a different file. You won't be allowed to overwrite the original file with the new information. Even when you get desperate and turn off the Read-Only Recommended check box, you still can't save your work in the same file.

- Clicking No opens the workbook and allows full access. The Read-Only text doesn't appear in the menu bar, and you can save any changes to the same file.

12. Click No and make a few changes, then save and close your workbook. Your changes will be included in the workbook.

Entering a new password to protect a workbook will display the Confirm Password dialog box. Here you need to re-enter the new password to double-check that you have entered it correctly.

Setting the Password Requirement from a Macro

The SetPasswordProtection macro shown in Listing 14.1 has the same effect as the 12 steps given in the previous section.

LISTING 14.1

```
0    Sub SetPasswordProtection()
1        'set the password for workbook testPassword.xls
2        ActiveWorkbook.SaveAs
         Filename:="C:\My Documents\testPassword.xls", _
         Password:="xyz123", WriteResPassword:="abc123", _
         ReadOnlyRecommended:=True, CreateBackup:=True
3    End Sub
```

ANALYSIS

Line 0 starts the SetPasswordProtection macro.

Line 2 uses the SaveAs method to save the file specified by the Filename argument with password protection, requiring users to enter the passwords assigned to the Password and WriteResPassword arguments. It also sets the ReadOnlyRecommended and CreateBackup arguments to True, which has the same effect as checking the two check boxes in the Save Options dialog box.

WARNING Make a note of any passwords you set for workbooks, as you can't open password-protected workbooks without them.

Protection when Opening a Workbook

When opening a workbook, you have three choices:

- Open with full access permission
- Open as read-only
- Open a copy of the workbook

Opening a workbook with full access permission should really only be done when the user needs to update existing data or insert new data.

Opening a workbook as a copy is useful for viewing data that never changes, and prevents data in the original workbook from being accidentally modified. It allows the user to make changes to the workbook, but when they save it the words Copy of are automatically added in front of the original file's name. In fact, you can open the Copy Of file as a copy and this will be saved with the words Copy of Copy of preceding the original filename.

To view the list of access choices available when you open a workbook:

1. Choose File ➤ Open to display the Open dialog box.
2. Select the file containing the workbook you want to open.
3. Click the Down arrow on the right side of the Open button, as shown in Figure 14.4.

NOTE   Opening a workbook as read-only will display the words Read-only in brackets after its name in the title bar.

NOTE   Opening a workbook as a copy will add the words Copy of in front of its name in the title bar.

FIGURE 14.4:

List of access modes available from the Open dialog box

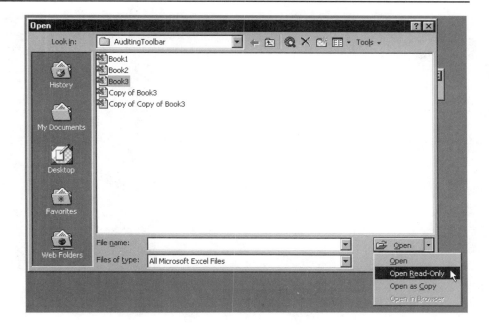

Making a Workbook Read-only

You can make a workbook read-only rather than just recommending it to be read-only. The following steps show you how:

1. Open the Windows Explorer application and select the workbook you want to make read-only.

2. Choose File ➢ Properties to open the file's Properties dialog box, as shown in Figure 14.5.

3. Select the General tab and check the Read-Only check box in the Attributes frame, as shown. Click OK to return to the workbook. Click OK again to return to Windows Explorer.

FIGURE 14.5:

General tab of the Properties dialog box

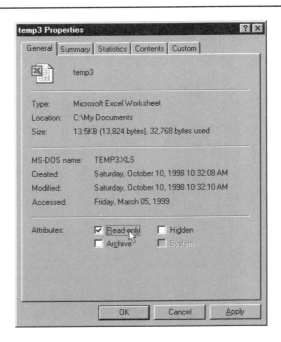

When you open the workbook in Excel and try to save it again, the message box shown below will be displayed to instruct you to give the workbook a new name.

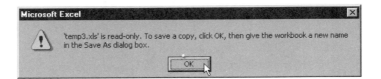

TIP

When a workbook is read-only, you can still make changes to it provided you save them to a different file.

Opening a Workbook as Read-only from a Macro

The OpenWorkbookAsReadOnly macro shown in Listing 14.2 opens the testnew.xls workbook as read-only.

LISTING 14.2

```
0    Sub OpenWorkbookAsReadOnly()
1        Workbooks.Open Filename:="C:\My Documents\testnew.xls", _
         ReadOnly:=True
2    End Sub
```

ANALYSIS

Line 0 starts the OpenWorkbookAsReadOnly macro.

Line 1 uses the Open method of the Workbooks collection to open the file specified in the Filename argument as read-only, as specified by the ReadOnly argument being set to True.

Hiding Data in Workbooks and Worksheets

Suppose you have critical data in a workbook (or worksheet) that you don't want modified accidentally, but it's referenced by formulas in a workbook that needs to be updated on a regular basis. Since the workbook with the critical data is referenced in formulas, it must be opened to allow its data to be accessed. As an alternative to opening the workbook as read-only, you can hide it from the user—out of sight, out of mind! Hiding workbooks and worksheets also serves the purpose of keeping sensitive data confidential.

Hiding Workbooks

Let's look at an example that has four workbooks, Book1...Book4, where Book1 contains a formula that references cells in the other three workbooks. All four workbooks are shown in Figure 14.6.

1. Open four new workbooks. Enter the data shown in Figure 14.6 into Book2, Book3, and Book4 and the formula into Book1.

2. Select Book2 and choose Window ≻ Hide. Book2 will disappear from display, but the formula in Book1 will still be able to access it.

3. Repeat Step 2 to hide Book3 and Book4.

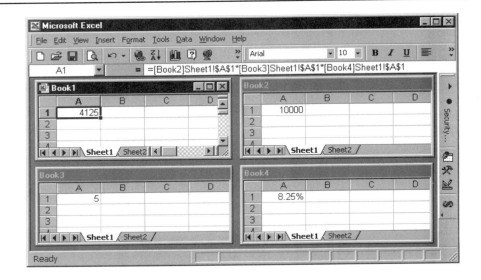

TIP   Hiding workbooks that don't need to be updated allows the user to focus on the workbooks that do! Hiding them also reduces the chance that a user could update or enter data into the wrong workbook.

Hiding Workbooks Using a Macro

The HideWorkbook macro shown in Listing 14.3 shows how to hide a workbook by setting its Visible property.

LISTING 14.3

```
0    Sub HideWorkbooks()
1        'hide workbooks 2 through 4
2        Windows("Book2.xls").Activate
3        ActiveWindow.Visible = False
```

```
4        Windows("Book3.xls").Activate
5        ActiveWindow.Visible = False
6        Windows("Book4.xls").Activate
7        ActiveWindow.Visible = False
8    End Sub
```

ANALYSIS

Line 0 starts the HideWorkbooks macro.

Line 2 uses the Activate method of the Window object to make Book2 the active window.

Line 3 sets the Visible property of the active window that's represented by the Window object returned by the ActiveWindow property. Setting the Visible property to False makes it invisible.

Lines 4 and 5 and **Lines 6 and 7** set the Visible properties of Book3 and Book4 in the same way as Lines 2 and 3 set Book2's to make it invisible.

Saving a Hidden Workbook

Suppose you've made changes to a workbook before hiding it. When you choose File ➤ Exit, the usual message box, shown below, will be displayed to ask if you want to save your changes.

Unhiding Workbooks

Choosing Window ➤ Unhide displays the Unhide dialog box that lists all of the workbooks that are currently hidden. Figure 14.7 shows the Unhide dialog box after the three workbooks were hidden in the last example.

FIGURE 14.7:

Unhide dialog box listing hidden workbooks

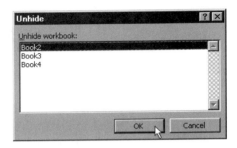

Unhiding Workbooks in a Macro

Listing 14.4 lists the code for the UnhideWorkbooks macro, which allows hidden workbooks to be displayed again.

LISTING 14.4

```
0    Sub UnhideWorkbooks()
1        'unhide workbooks 2 through 4
2        Windows("Book2.xls").Activate
3        ActiveWindow.Visible = True
4        Windows("Book3.xls").Activate
5        ActiveWindow.Visible = True
6        Windows("Book4.xls").Activate
7        ActiveWindow.Visible = True
8    End Sub
```

ANALYSIS

Line 0 starts the UnhideWorkbooks macro.

Line 2 uses the Activate method of the Window object to make Book2 the active window.

Line 3 sets the Visible property of the active window that's represented by the Window object returned by the ActiveWindow property. Setting the Visible property to True makes it visible.

Lines 4 and 5 and **Lines 6 and 7** set the Visible properties of Book3 and Book4 in the same way as Lines 2 and 3 set Book2's to make it visible.

Opening a Workbook with Links to Hidden Workbooks

When you open a workbook that contains links to other workbooks, a message box is displayed to give you the opportunity to keep existing information or to update the linked information.

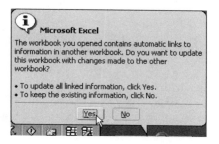

Clicking Yes displays the File Not Found dialog box with one of the workbooks selected. Click OK. This will open it as Hidden if it was saved as Hidden. The File Not Found dialog box is repeatedly displayed until all the required workbooks have been opened.

Hiding and Unhiding Worksheets

To hide a worksheet, make it the active worksheet and choose Format ➤ Sheet ➤ Hide. To unhide a worksheet, choose Format ➤ Sheet ➤ Unhide to open the Unhide dialog box. This dialog box is the same as the Unhide dialog box for workbooks shown in Figure 14.7 except that it lists hidden worksheets from the active workbook.

Hiding a worksheet with a macro is achieved the same way as hiding a workbook: by setting its Visible property to False. The following line of code hides all of the selected worksheets:

```
ActiveWindow.SelectedSheets.Visible = False
```

This uses the SelectedSheets property of the Window object returned by the ActiveWindow property to return all of the selected sheets. The Visible properties of all Sheet objects for the selected sheets are set to False to hide them.

NOTE   A workbook must contain at least one visible worksheet, so you cannot hide all the worksheets in a workbook.

Hiding Rows and Columns of Data

If you don't want users to be able to view the contents of a specific row or column in a worksheet, choose Format ➤ Row ➤ Hide or Format ➤ Column ➤ Hide and that row or column will no longer be displayed.

Listing 14.5 shows the HideRowAndColumn macro, which hides row 5 and column B.

LISTING 14.5

```
0    Sub HideRowAndColumn()
1        'hide row 5 and column B
2        Columns("B:B").Hidden = True
3        Rows("5:5").Hidden = True
4    End Sub
```

ANALYSIS

Line 0 starts the HideRowAndColumn macro.

Line 2 uses the Columns property to return a Range object containing column B. The Hidden property of this Range object is set to True, which hides column B.

Line 3 uses the Rows property to return a Range object containing row 5; the Hidden property is set to True to make it invisible.

Hiding the Formula in a Cell

To hide the formula in a specific cell:

1. Select the cell you want to hide and choose Format ➤ Cells to display the Format Cells dialog box.

2. Choose the Protection tab, shown in Figure 14.8.

3. Check the Hidden check box and click OK to return to your worksheet.

4. If the formula is still displayed in the formula bar, you'll have to protect the worksheet. Choose Tools ➤ Protection ➤ Protect Sheet to display the Protect

Sheet dialog box. If a password is desired, enter a password first; otherwise, click OK to protect the worksheet and hide the formula in the formula bar (Figure 14.9).

FIGURE 14.8:

Hiding a cell in the Format Cells dialog box

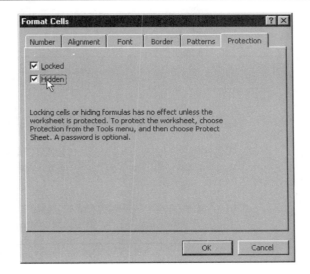

FIGURE 14.9:

Formula hidden in cell A1

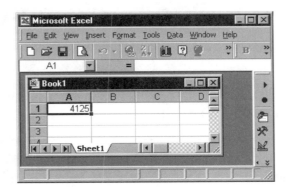

Hiding a Formula with a Macro

Listing 14.6 shows how to hide a formula using the HideWorksheetFormula macro.

LISTING 14.6

```
0    Sub HideWorksheetFormula
1        'hide the formula in the selected cell
2        Selection.FormulaHidden = True
3        ActiveSheet.Protect
4    End Sub
```

ANALYSIS

Line 0 starts the HideWorksheetFormula macro.

Line 2 uses the Selection property to return the Range object containing the selected cell, then sets its FormulaHidden property to True to hide the formula it contains.

Line 3 uses the ActiveSheet property to return the Worksheet object, then calls its Protect method to protect it against change.

Protecting Workbooks and Worksheets

After you've hidden items in a workbook, you've got to protect the workbook to prevent other users from undoing your good work.

1. Choose Tools ➢ Protection ➢ Protect Workbook (Figure 14.10) to open the Protect Workbook dialog box.

FIGURE 14.10:

Menu commands for protecting data in a workbook

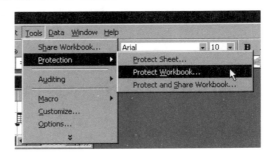

2. In the Protect Workbook For... frame, check the Structure check box and the Windows check box. Enter a password in the Password box before clicking OK to return to your workbook.

Features of the Protect Workbook Dialog Box

The Protect Workbook dialog box shown in Figure 14.11 provides security features in three important areas.

FIGURE 14.11:

Protect Workbook
dialog box

The **Structure** check box allows you to protect the structure of your workbook so that unauthorized users can't add or remove, hide or unhide, move, or rename any of the worksheets.

The **Windows** check box protects how your workbook is displayed in a window by stopping unauthorized users from moving or resizing, hiding or unhiding, or closing the window displaying the workbook.

The **Password** box allows you to enter the password required for authorized users to remove or alter the workbook protection that you've applied in this dialog box.

Protecting Worksheets

A worksheet can be protected in isolation from the rest of the workbook by choosing Tools ➤ Protection ➤ Protect Sheet to open the Protect Sheet dialog box, as shown below.

The **Contents** check box allows you to stop unauthorized users from making changes to the worksheet or any charts it contains.

The **Objects** check box allows you to stop unauthorized users from changing graphic objects in a worksheet or in a chart sheet.

The **Scenarios** check box allows you to prevent definitions of scenarios from being changed. (Scenarios are handled later in Chapter 21.)

The **Password** box allows you to specify the password required before the sheet protection features you've set in this dialog box can be removed or altered.

Unlocking Ranges of Cells in a Protected Worksheet

When you choose Tools ➢ Protection ➢ Protect Sheet, all of the cells in that worksheet are automatically locked against change, provided the worksheet's contents were protected (the Contents check box was checked). You may want to unlock some of them to allow the data to be updated. The following steps show you how this is done.

1. Open the worksheet containing the range of cells you want to unlock and choose Tools ➢ Protection ➢ Unprotect Sheet. If Unprotect Sheet isn't listed, then you don't have to do anything—your worksheet wasn't protected in the first place.

2. Select the range of cells you want to unlock, choose Format ➢ Cells, and uncheck the Locked check box on the Protection tab. Click OK to return to the workbook.

3. Choose Tools ➢ Protection ➢ Protect Sheet, provide a password if desired, and click OK.

You'll be able to enter new data in the unlocked cells, but if you try to enter data in cells outside the range of unlocked cells, a message box will be displayed:

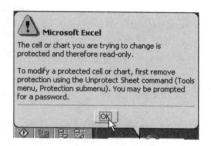

Protecting Shared Resources

When a workbook is shared, more than one person has read and write permission to it at any one time. (Shared workbooks are described in the section "Shared Workbooks" in Chapter 2.) You can protect a shared workbook by performing the following steps:

1. Choose Tools ➤ Protection ➤ Protect And Share Workbook to open the Protect Shared Workbook dialog box shown below.

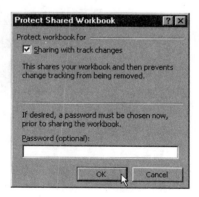

2. Check the Sharing With Track Changes check box to prevent the Sharing and Change History tracking from being turned off.

3. Enter a password to stop unauthorized users from altering workbook protection. Click OK to return to your workbook.

Auditing Features

One of the hard tasks in Excel is to keep tabs on which cells are related to each other through references in formulas. Lacking this information, you may innocently change a cell in one worksheet with disastrous effects in another worksheet or workbook. Trying to keep track of all these interrelationships can be time-consuming and difficult to monitor, especially when the data model is complex.

Luckily, Excel provides some clever auditing features to assist you in getting back on track! Figure 14.12 shows the features available from the Auditing menu options—all these features and more are available via buttons in the Auditing toolbar.

FIGURE 14.12:

Features of the Auditing menu option

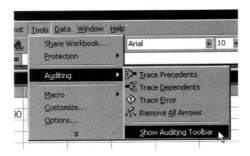

Auditing Toolbar

If the Auditing toolbar isn't displayed, choose Tools ➣ Auditing ➣ Show Auditing Toolbar (Figure 14.12). This toolbar is pictured in Figure 14.13.

FIGURE 14.13:

Auditing toolbar

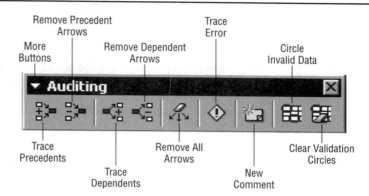

If your Auditing toolbar has fewer buttons than the one shown here, then:

1. Select the More Buttons arrow and click Add Or Remove Buttons to display the shortcut menu shown below.

2. Choose Reset Toolbar to add any missing buttons or check any unchecked buttons.

NOTE   Before using the Auditing toolbar, check the Show All or Show Placeholders option button in the View tab in the Options dialog box (Tools ➢ Options). Otherwise, only the last three buttons will be selectable.

Let's take a look at what the auditing features available from this toolbar can do to help you.

Tracing Dependent and Precedent Cells

In Excel it's important to be able to trace the source of the data in a cell or to see whether a cell is referenced by any formulas. The Trace Precedents and Trace Dependents buttons in the Auditing toolbar allow you to see all of these interdependencies at a glance.

When data in one cell is referenced by a formula in another cell, the cell containing the data is known as the *precedent* cell and the cell containing the formula is known as the *dependent* cell. When you select the dependent cell and click the Trace Precedents button, an arrow emanates from the precedent cell and points to the selected cell. The same arrow is displayed when you select the precedent cell and click the Trace Dependents button.

Let's take a look at these features in action.

1. Create a new workbook and enter the values shown in the Loan Payment Calculator worksheet (Figure 14.14).

FIGURE 14.14:

Worksheet with interde-
pendencies

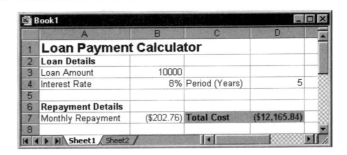

The formula in cell B7 is =PMT(B4/12, D4*12,B3); you can use the Formula Wizard to help you enter it, as shown below. The formula in cell D7 is B7*D4*12.

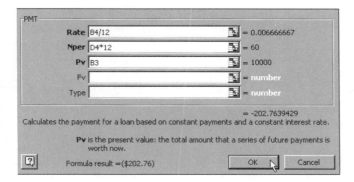

2. Select cell B3 and click the Trace Precedents toolbar button. A beep will sound (if your PC can beep), because cells containing constants can't have precedents!

3. With cell B3 still selected, click the Trace Dependents button to display a blue arrow, which will start in cell B3 and point to cell B7 to denote the direct dependency.

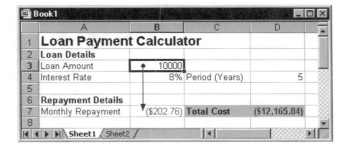

4. Click Trace Dependents again to draw another blue arrow denoting the next level of dependency:

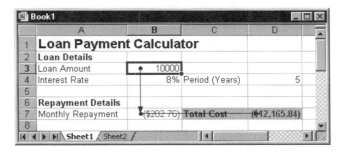

5.   Keep clicking Trace Dependents until Excel beeps and no more arrows are displayed, indicating that there are no more levels of dependency.

Using the Trace Precedent and Trace Dependent Menu Commands

If you select a cell containing a constant and then choose Tools ➤ Auditing ➤ Trace Precedents, Excel will give you the following warning message:

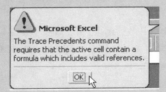

When you reach the last cell in a chain of traces and then choose Tools ➤ Auditing ➤ Trace Dependents, Excel will give you this message:

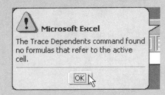

Tracing All Dependent Cells with a Macro

Listing 14.7 provides the code for starting up a chain reaction by finding the range containing all the cells that are directly dependent on the selected cell, and then finding the range containing their direct dependents' dependents... and so on, drawing arrows as it goes. This macro could be run from a toolbar button and would require only one click.

LISTING 14.7

```
0    Sub TraceAllLevelsOfDependency()
1        'draws trace arrows for all levels of dependency
2        Do
```

```
3          On Error GoTo AllArrowsShown
4          Selection.ShowDependents
5          Selection.Dependents.Select
6      Loop
7      AllArrowsShown:
8  End Sub
```

ANALYSIS

Line 0 starts the TraceAllLevelsOfDependency macro.

Line 2 starts the Do loop, which will continue until an error occurs when the end of the dependency trail is reached.

In Line 3, the On Error statement causes execution to jump to the label AllArrowsShown (Line 7) when an error occurs.

Line 4 uses the ShowDependents method to draw tracer arrows to the direct dependents of the selected range.

Line 5 uses the Dependents property to return the range containing all dependents of a range, not just the direct dependents. This line returns an error when the Select method is called and there are no direct dependent cells left to select.

Line 6 is the end of the Do statement, which sends execution back to Line 2 with a new range selected.

Line 7 contains the label AllArrowsShown to enable the On Error statement to jump to it when the end of the chain is reached and there are no more dependent cells to be traced.

Tracing All Precedent Cells with a Macro

Listing 14.8 shows the code to trace all the cells precedent to the selected cell.

LISTING 14.8

```
0  Sub TraceAllLevelsOfPrecedency()
1      'draws trace arrows for all levels of precedency
2      Finished = False
3      While Not Finished
```

```
4              On Error GoTo AllArrowsShown
5              Selection.ShowPrecedents
6              Selection.Precedents.Select
7          Wend
8          AllArrowsShown:
9      End Sub
```

ANALYSIS

Line 0 starts the TraceAllLevelsOfPrecedency macro.

Line 2 sets the variable to be tested in the While loop.

Line 3 starts the While loop, which will end only when there are no more precedent cells to be found.

Line 4 uses the On Error statement to go to the AllArrowsShown label at Line 8 outside the loop.

Line 5 uses the ShowPrecedents method to draw tracer arrows to the direct precedents of the selected range.

Line 6 uses the Precedents property to return the range containing all precedents of a range of cells, not just the direct precedents. The Select method of the Range object returned by this property gives an error when no Range object is returned due to there being no precedents left to trace.

Line 7 marks the end of the While loop.

Line 8 uses the label AllArrowsShown as the line to jump to when all precedent cells have been traced.

Tracing All Precedent and Dependent Cells with a Macro

Listing 14.9 calls both the TraceAllLevelsOfPrecedency and TraceAllLevelsOfDependency to show all direct and indirect precedents and dependents of the selected cell. Running this macro from a toolbar button can avoid repeated clicks of both buttons. Figure 14.15 shows the result of running this macro with cell D7 selected.

FIGURE 14.15:

All levels of precedent and dependent cells on cell B7

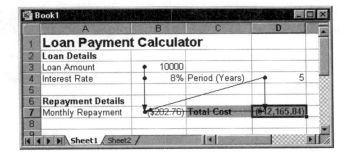

LISTING 14.9

```
0    Sub TraceAllInterdependencies()
1        TraceAllLevelsOfPrecedency
2        TraceAllLevelsOfDependency
3    End Sub
```

ANALYSIS

Lines 1 and 2 call the TraceAllLevelsOfPrecedency and TraceAll-LevelsOfDependency to draw trace arrows for all related cells.

Tracing Precedents and Dependents in Other Worksheets

When a precedent or dependent cell is located in another worksheet, the tracer arrow points to or from a worksheet icon, as shown in Figure 14.16 and Figure 14.17. Cell A1 in Sheet2 contains the constant 1001 and cell A1 in Sheet1 refers to the constant in the formula =Sheet2!A1/10*112%.

FIGURE 14.16:

Dependent tracer arrow emanating from the data and pointing to the work-sheet icon to indicate that a cell in another worksheet is a dependent

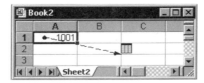

FIGURE 14.17:

Precedent tracer arrow emanating from the work-sheet icon and pointing to the cell containing the for-mula that uses the data in the other worksheet

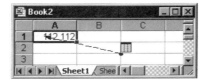

Following the Tracer Arrow

These steps show you how to follow the tracer arrow to the other worksheet:

1. Double-click the arrow shown in Figure 14.16 to display the Go To dialog box (shown), which will contain references to all the precedence traces available—even those in different workbooks.

2. Click the reference you need in the Go To list to copy it into the Reference box and click OK to change to Sheet1.

WARNING   If the precedent or dependent cell is located in another workbook, you must ensure that the other workbook is open before attempting the trace. Otherwise, you'll get the warning message "Reference is not valid" and your attempt will fail.

Removing Tracer Arrows

The Auditing toolbar has three buttons for removing arrows: Remove Precedent Arrows, Remove Dependent Arrows, and Remove All Arrows. The Remove Precedent Arrows and Remove Dependent Arrows buttons remove individual arrows from a selected cell. If you want to remove a chain of arrows, select the cell at the beginning of the chain and repeatedly click the Remove Dependent Arrows button—or select the cell containing the end of the chain and repeatedly click the Remove Precedent Arrows button—until all the arrows you want to remove have been deleted.

Click the Remove All Arrows button to delete all the arrows in a workbook in one click.

Removing All Arrows with a Macro

Listing 14.10 shows the ClearArrows method being used to clear all tracer arrows from a worksheet.

LISTING 14.10

```
0   Sub ClearAllArrows()
1       'clears all arrows from the active worksheet
2       ActiveSheet.ClearArrows
3   End Sub
```

ANALYSIS

Line 2 uses the ClearArrows method of the Worksheet object to remove all tracer arrows from the current worksheet.

Summary

When you have finished this chapter, you'll be able to

- set passwords for opening workbooks and saving workbooks
- protect a workbook by opening it as read-only, or by opening a copy of it
- make a workbook read-only
- hide workbooks, worksheets, rows and columns of cells, and individual cells
- unlock a range of cells in a locked workbook
- use the auditing features to trace chains of dependent and precedent cells and remove tracer arrows

PART V

Web Publishing

CHAPTER

FIFTEEN

15

Hyperlinks

A hyperlink is underlined text or a graphic object that, when selected, will connect you to some other location in a file on your computer, on the network, or on the Internet. This is a very powerful tool, as the destination can be just about anywhere. It can be to a cell or worksheet in the same workbook or in another workbook, or to a local file or shared file on a network system—it can even be to information on the World Wide Web or on your company's intranet. I'm sure you're already familiar with hyperlinks in help facilities and on the World Wide Web.

Creating a Hyperlink

Creating a hyperlink is extremely easy to do using the Hyperlink menu command, available under Insert. In this section, you'll see how to set up the following three types of hyperlinks:

- cell text
- a graphic object
- another hyperlink

WARNING   You can't have a macro and a hyperlink attached to the same text, graphic, or link location since it wouldn't be clear what you were actually wanting to do when you clicked it—run the macro or follow the hyperlink.

Using Cell Text as a Hyperlink

When you enter text into a cell or range of cells and convert it to a hyperlink, all hyperlink text appears as blue (default) underlined characters that cause a jump to the link's destination file or location whenever that text is clicked. Let's create a new workbook with a hyperlink to the TaxRates worksheet created in Chapter 4.

1. Create a new workbook, select cell A1, and either choose Insert ➤ Hyperlink (Figure 15.1) or click the Insert Hyperlink toolbar icon (shown below) to display the Insert Hyperlink dialog box (Figure 15.2).

FIGURE 15.1:

Choosing Insert ➤
Hyperlink menu
commands

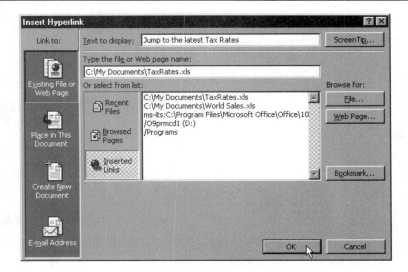

FIGURE 15.2:

Insert Hyperlink dialog box

2. Enter the string **Jump to the latest Tax Rates** into the Text To Display box. This string will be displayed as blue underlined text at cell A1 in the worksheet (Figure 15.3).

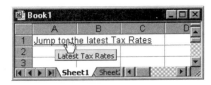

3. Click the ScreenTip button (in the upper-right corner of the Insert Hyperlink dialog box, as shown in Figure 15.2) to open the Set Hyperlink ScreenTip dialog box, and enter **Latest Tax Rates** into the ScreenTip Text box, as shown in Figure 15.4.

FIGURE 15.4:

Set Hyperlink ScreenTip
dialog box

If the ScreenTip text is not specified, the path name pops up in its place, as shown in Figure 15.5.

FIGURE 15.5:

ScreenTip defaulted to the
path name

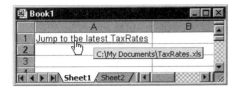

4. Click OK to return to the Insert Hyperlink dialog box.

5. Click File to open the Link To File dialog box and select the file containing the TaxRates workbook (Figure 15.6). I copied my TaxRates file into the My Documents folder to keep my hyperlink's filename to a reasonable length so that it would easily fit on the page of this book.

FIGURE 15.6:

Link To File dialog box

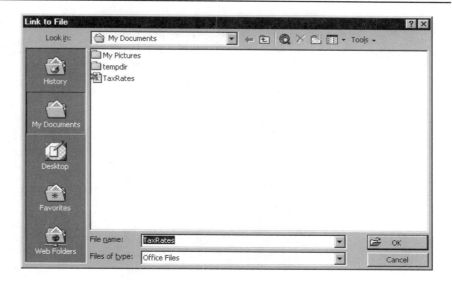

6. Click OK to return to the Insert Hyperlink dialog box, which now displays your file's path name in the Type The File Or Web Page Name box (see Figure 15.2).

7. Click OK to return to your worksheet. The text for the hyperlink will be displayed as blue underlined text, as shown in Figure 15.3.

To Test the Hyperlink Text

Expand the width of cell A1 so that the hyperlink text fits in it, then click it to open the `TaxRates` workbook.

Link To File Dialog Box

The Link To File dialog box, shown in Figure 15.6, contains five large buttons down the left side. Here's what happens when you click them:

History: All the links to folders from your `C:\Windows\Application Data\ Microsoft\Office\Recent` folder are displayed to help you select the file required.

Continued on next page

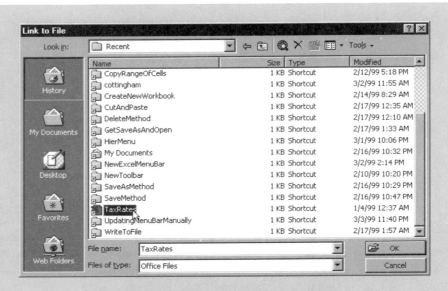

My Documents: All files and folders in the C:\My Documents folder are listed.

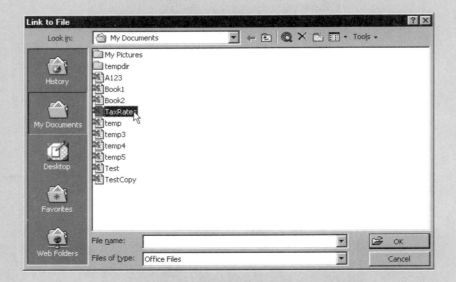

Desktop: The items on your desktop are listed. The example below shows the items I have on my desktop—these will vary among computers.

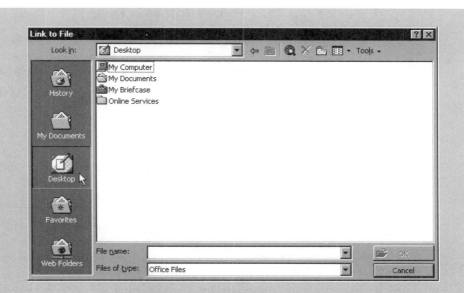

Favorites: The items from your C:\Windows\Favorites folder are listed; these results are also dependent on what you have installed in your PC.

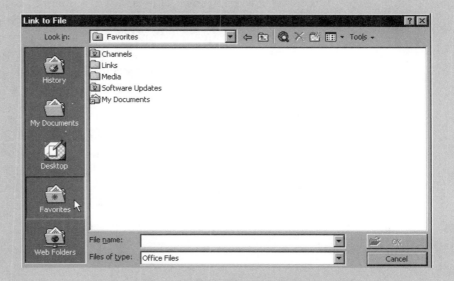

Web Folders: These will vary depending on how you've set up your PC and whether you can access the Web.

Inserting a Text Hyperlink in a Macro

Listing 15.1 shows you how to insert a text hyperlink from a macro named `InsertHyperlinkInActiveCell`. Once you've created the macro, all you will need to do to insert the link is select the cell where you want the hyperlink to go and run the macro.

LISTING 15.1

```
0    Sub InsertHyperlinkInActiveCell()
1        'inserts a hyperlink to TaxRates into the active cell
2        ActiveSheet.Hyperlinks.Add Anchor:=ActiveCell, _
         Address:="C:\My Documents\TaxRates.xls", _
         ScreenTip:="Latest Tax Rates", _
         TextToDisplay:="Jump to the latest Tax Rates"
3    End Sub
```

ANALYSIS

Line 2 uses the Add method in the Hyperlinks collection to add a hyperlink to the specified range. The Anchor argument is assigned the location for the hyperlink, which is assigned the active cell. The Address argument is the hypertext destination, which is assigned the path name to jump to. The ScreenTip argument is assigned the text that will pop up as the ScreenTip, and the TextToDisplay is the hyperlink text, which will normally be colored blue and underlined.

The disadvantage when using this macro is that the destination will always be the TaxRates workbook. You can increase the usefulness of the macro by adjusting the code to display the Open dialog box (described in Chapter 12). The user can then select the file containing the destination workbook and assign its path name to the Address argument. Listing 15.2 shows how this is achieved.

LISTING 15.2

```
0    Sub InsertHyperlinkInActiveCell()
1        'inserts a hyperlink to TaxRates into the active cell
2        OpenFileName = Application.GetOpenFilename
```

```
3        ActiveSheet.Hyperlinks.Add Anchor:=ActiveCell, _
         Address:=OpenFileName, _
         ScreenTip:="Latest Tax Rates", _
         TextToDisplay:="Jump to the latest Tax Rates"
4    End Sub
```

ANALYSIS

Line 0 starts the `InsertHyperlinkInActiveCell` macro.

Line 2 uses the `GetOpenFilename` function to display the Open dialog box, which returns the file selected by the user; the path name is then assigned to the `Address` argument in Line 3.

Using a Graphic as a Hyperlink

A graphic can be placed on a worksheet and made into the hyperlink object. Clicking the graphic then causes the jump to the link's destination file or Web site. In this example, you'll learn how to use one of your existing workbooks as the destination for the hyperlink—this will not change the workbook in any way. The hyperlink will be placed in a Shape object created from the Drawing toolbar.

To Place the *Shape* Object in the Workbook:

1. If the Drawing toolbar isn't already on display, choose View ➢ Toolbars ➢ Drawing to display it.

2. Click the Oval button (shown below) from the Drawing toolbar and place an oval on your workbook.

3. With the oval graphic still selected (sizing handles still displayed), choose Insert ➢ Hyperlink. The Insert Hyperlink dialog box (Figure 15.2) will appear.

4. Click File to open the Link To File dialog box shown in Figure 15.6 and select any workbook of your choice as the destination for the hyperlink to jump to. Click OK to return to the Insert Hyperlink dialog box. The path name for the file you selected will be displayed in the Type The File Or Web Page Name box.

5. Click ScreenTip to open the Set Hyperlink ScreenTip dialog box (Figure 15.4) and enter **This jumps to a workbook.** Click OK to return to the workbook.

6. Test your hyperlink by pausing the mouse pointer over the graphic and watch the ScreenTip appear in the pop-up box. Click anywhere on the oval, and the workbook you selected will open.

Listing 15.3 shows the macro recorded while this hyperlink was being set up.

NOTE A graphic is any picture that's available in a file. VBA supports all of the common graphical file formats.

LISTING 15.3

```
0   Sub Macro1()
1   '
2   ' Macro1 Macro
3   ' Macro recorded 5/5/1999 by Marion Cottingham
4   '
5   '
6   '
7       ActiveSheet.Hyperlinks.Add _
        Anchor:=Selection.ShapeRange.Item(1), Address:= _
        "C:\My Documents\Project1.xls", _
        ScreenTip:="This jumps to a workbook."
8       Range("C3").Select
9   End Sub
```

ANALYSIS

Line 7 adds a hyperlink to the shape that jumps to the file assigned to its Address argument and assigns the ScreenTip text to the ScreenTip argument.

Adding the Map Button

Let's create a World Sales workbook with an appropriate graphic that we'll use as the hyperlink. Before starting this application, you'll need to create an empty workbook called World Sales that will be used as the destination to jump to from the hyperlink. You'll also need to place the Map button in a toolbar so that you can generate the map that we'll use as the graphic. (If the button isn't already in your toolbar, you'll need to add it.)

Adding the Map Button to a Toolbar

The Map button runs Microsoft Map, which is a small application that's provided with the Microsoft Office suite of applications. If Map isn't available on your PC, you'll need to install it by running Setup from the Office 2000 CDs and selecting Microsoft Map when given the choice of applications you want to install.

To Place the Map Icon in a Toolbar:

1. Choose Tools ➣ Customize to open the Customize dialog box.

2. Select the Commands tab and select Insert from the Categories list, as shown below.

3. Drag the Map item from the Commands list to any toolbar you have on display.

4. Open a new Workbook and click the Map icon in the toolbar, as shown below.

Continued on next page

5. Place the map in Sheet1. Make the map quite large by dragging its sizing handles. This will cause the Unable To Create Map dialog box shown below to be displayed until you select a region.

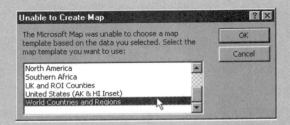

6. Select World Countries And Regions from the list in the Unable To Create Map dialog box (as shown above) and click OK to return to the worksheet, which will now display a map of the world.

7. The menu bar will toggle between containing the normal Excel menu options and the Map menu options. To change from Excel to Map options, click anywhere inside the map to select it, right-click it, and select Microsoft Map Object ➢ Edit from the shortcut menu (as shown).

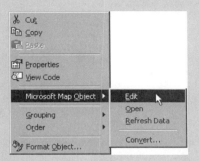

The menu bar will change to the one shown below.

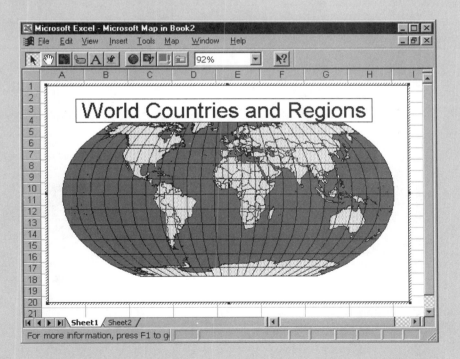

Continued on next page

8. Double-click anywhere in the World Countries And Regions title to open the Edit Text Object input box. Enter **World Sales 1999** into the box, as shown:

9. Click OK to return to Microsoft Map, then click anywhere on `Sheet1` outside the area taken up by the graphic to return to the Excel menu bar.

10. Select the graphic so that it has the focus (as can be seen by the sizing handles being displayed). Choose Insert ➤ Hyperlink to open the Insert Hyperlink dialog box shown in Figure 15.2.

11. Click File to open the Link To File dialog box shown in Figure 15.6, click the large My Documents button, and select World Sales. Click OK to return to the Insert Hyperlink dialog box.

12. Click ScreenTip to open the Set Hyperlink ScreenTip dialog box (Figure 15.4) and enter **World Sales** in the ScreenTip Text box. Click OK to return to the Insert Hyperlink dialog box.

13. Click OK to return to the worksheet. Click the worksheet outside the graphic area so that the map is no longer selected and the Excel menu options are displayed.

To Test the Hyperlink Graphic

Move the mouse cursor over the rectangular area containing the graphic and watch it change into a hand. The ScreenTip "World Sales" will also pop up, as shown. Clicking the mouse causes the jump to the hyperlink's destination file and opens `World Sales.xls`.

Recorded Macro for Using a Graphic as a Hyperlink

Listing 15.4 shows the macro recorded during the last section while we created a workbook containing the `Map` object that became the hyperlink location.

LISTING 15.4

```
0    Sub Macro1()
1        '
2        ' Macro1 Macro
3        ' Macro recorded 3/3/1999 by marion
4        '
5        '
6        '
7        ActiveSheet.OLEObjects.Add(ClassType:="MSMap.8", _
         Link:=False,DisplayAsIcon:=False, Left:=11.25, _
         Top:=8.25, Width:=11.25, Height:=8.25).Activate
8        Application.CutCopyMode = False
9        ActiveWindow.ScrollRow = 1
10       Range("J7").Select
11       ActiveSheet.Shapes("Object 1").Select
12       ActiveSheet.Hyperlinks.Add _
         Anchor:=Selection.ShapeRange.Item(1), Address:= _
         "C:\My Documents\World Sales.xls", _
         ScreenTip:="World Sales"
13       Range("K16").Select
14   End Sub
```

ANALYSIS

Line 7 adds a new OLE object to the active worksheet. OLE objects (see below) are linked or embedded in worksheets. The ClassType argument is assigned the programmatic identifier that identifies the Map object by the name that Excel recognizes. The Link argument is set to False; therefore the OLE object is copied (embedded) rather than a link being created to the original Map. The DisplayAs-Icon argument is set to False so that the OLE object is displayed in its usual form. The Left, Top, Width, and Height arguments define the OLE object's position and size.

Line 8 sets the CutCopyMode of the Application object to False so that the application isn't in Cut or Copy mode.

Line 9 uses the ScrollRow property to specify that row 1 will appear at the top of the active window.

Line 11 selects the Map object, which is Object 1 in the Shapes collection.

Line 12 adds a hyperlink to the map with the Address argument assigned the destination file and the ScreenTip argument assigned the ToolTip.

Continued on next page

OLE—Object Linking and Embedding

OLE allows objects from one application to be linked or embedded into other applications. When an object is linked, both applications must be open so that the latest information is available to the OLE object. A link to an application that's not open will provide the information that appeared the last time the link was refreshed, which may be out of date. When an object is embedded, a copy of the information is taken at the time the OLE object is created; it is then not necessary for the other application to be open, as the copy is never updated.

Using a Toolbar Button as a Hyperlink

A toolbar button can also be used as a hyperlink. In this example, we'll create a new toolbar with one button to provide a direct link to a workbook. To create the toolbar, follow the instructions in the section "Creating a New Toolbar" in Chapter 8, but instead of entering Headings & Labels in the Toolbar Name box, enter **Links**. Place a button in the toolbar by following the instructions in the section "Adding Buttons to a Toolbar" in Chapter 8, but drag the Custom Menu Item instead of the Smiley Custom Button. Your new toolbar should look the same as the one shown in Figure 15.7.

FIGURE 15.7:

Links toolbar containing the Custom Menu Item button

Now let's assign a hyperlink to the button:

1. Right-click the Custom Menu Item button in your toolbar and choose Customize from the shortcut menu to open the Customize box.

2. Click the button again to select it and to activate the Modify Selection button. Click Modify Selection and choose Assign Hyperlink ➤ Open from the shortcut menu, as shown in Figure 15.8. This opens the Assign Hyperlink: Open dialog box shown in Figure 15.9.

FIGURE 15.8:

Shortcut menu available by clicking Modify Selection

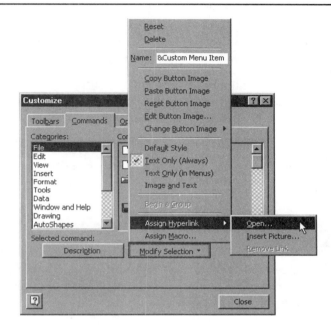

FIGURE 15.9:

Assign Hyperlink: Open dialog box

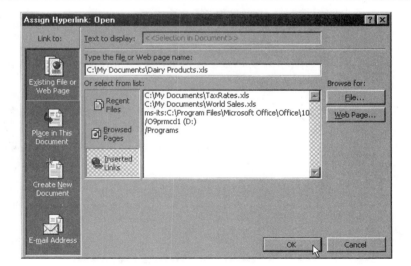

3. Click File to open the Link To File dialog box and select the worksheet you want to jump to. Click OK to return to the Assign Hyperlink: Open dialog box, which will now display the path name for the destination file you selected. Click OK to return to the workbook.

4. Use the Modify Selection button to access the shortcut menu shown in Figure 15.8 and update the Name from &Custom Menu Item to &Dairy-Products. Click Close to return to your worksheet.

5. Close the Customize dialog box.

6. Test your toolbar button by closing any open workbooks and clicking your new button.

Using a Hyperlink as a Hyperlink

Let's make the World Sales example (see sidebar, above) more interesting by creating hyperlinks for the countries your company does business with. In essence, you're placing a graphic object containing hyperlinks on top of a larger graphic that also contains a hyperlink.

Before you begin this example, save an empty workbook as US Sales. We will continue our World Sales application by adding a hyperlink for sales in the US.

1. If the Drawing toolbar isn't displayed, choose View ➤ Toolbars ➤ Drawing to display it.

2. Right-click the map to select it and to avoid jumping to the destination workbook.

3. Use the Oval button to place a circle somewhere in the US and the Fill Color button to fill it with color.

4. Right-click the circle you've just drawn and choose Hyperlink from the shortcut menu.

5. Click the File button, select US Sales.xls as the Type Of File and set the ScreenTip to **US Sales**. Click OK, then click OK again to return to the workbook.

To Test Your Hyperlink's Hyperlink

Pause the mouse cursor over the circle placed in the US, and the ScreenTip shown below will be displayed.

Clicking the circle will open the US Sales workbook.

Coding a macro to create a hyperlink in a hyperlink requires only one line of code—Line 12 from Listing 15.4.

```
ActiveSheet.Hyperlinks.Add _
Anchor:=Selection.ShapeRange.Item(1), Address:= _
"C:\My Documents\World Sales.xls", ScreenTip:="World Sales"
```

Using the *HYPERLINK* Worksheet Function

Excel's HYPERLINK worksheet function creates a hyperlink for you. This function is available from the drop-down list of functions displayed when you click the Edit Formula button (=) and then on the Down arrow, as shown below.

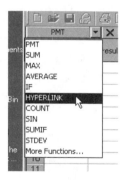

This function requires two pieces of information. Excel calls these the link_location and the friendly_name. The syntax of this function is

```
HYPERLINK(link_location, friendly_name)
```

The link_location can be

- the path and filename of the document to be opened as a result of the link being instigated

- a cell containing the path and filename as a text string

- a specific place in a document, such as a cell or named range in a worksheet or workbook

- a file stored on a hard disk drive

- a path on a server or a URL path on your company's intranet or the World Wide Web

The `friendly_name` is what is displayed as underlined blue text and can be

- the jump text, enclosed in quotation marks

- a cell containing the jump text

- a numeric value that is displayed in the cell

- omitted—in this case, the `friendly_name` is assigned the same text string as the `link_location`

TIP
    To select a cell containing a hyperlink without making the jump, click an adjoining cell and use the arrow keys to maneuver to the cell.

When you enter a HYPERLINK function with the `link_location` and `friendly-_name` entered in the boxes in the Formula Palette (shown in Figure 15.10), the following text will appear in the Formula Bar:

`=HYPERLINK("c:\My Documents\TaxRates.xls","Click here for tax rates!")`

FIGURE 15.10:

Formula palette for the HYPERLINK function

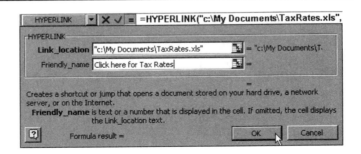

Figure 15.11 shows the hyperlink that will appear in the worksheet along with the ToolTip, which is the same as the `link_location`.

FIGURE 15.11:

Worksheet hyperlink, including friendly_name

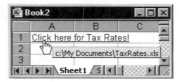

If you call the HYPERLINK function with only the link_location specified, as follows:

```
=HYPERLINK("c:\My Documents\TaxRates.xls")
```

then the text entered for the link_location is used for both the hyperlink and the ToolTip (Figure 15.12).

FIGURE 15.12:

Worksheet hyperlink with only the link_location specified

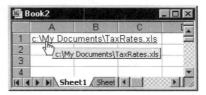

If you enter the HYPERLINK function with a cell reference as the friendly_name, such as

```
=HYPERLINK("c:\My Documents\hierarchy.xls",H1)
```

then the hyperlink will be displayed as the value at that cell. For example, Figure 15.13 shows the hyperlink displayed when the value at cell H1 is 0.

FIGURE 15.13:

Worksheet hyperlink with cell reference as the friendly_name

This may not appear very useful at first sight, but if you enter another HYPERLINK function into the cell reference assigned to the friendly_name, you can set up a string of jumps. For example, you can specify a cell in a worksheet as the link_-location. The following example creates a hyperlink in cell B3 of worksheet

Sheet1 in the TaxRates workbook. The hyperlink text is stored in cell E1 of the active workbook and is displayed at the hyperlink location (B3).

```
=HYPERLINK("[c:\TaxRates.xls]Sheet1!B3",E1)
```

The name of cell B3 (i.e., TaxBand1) can be used here instead of its cell reference.

Updating a Hyperlink

If you move a destination file to a different folder, you'll have to update your hyperlink to connect with its new location. You may also want to change the string displayed at the text hyperlink to something more appropriate. For example, the text hyperlink Jump to New Tax Rates is a likely candidate for updating—at some stage these tax rates will no longer be considered new, so it would make sense to remove the New from the text. Updating a hyperlink is as easy as creating one. These steps show you how:

1. Open the World Sales workbook and right-click anywhere in the map to give it the focus.

2. Click the Insert Hyperlink button in the toolbar to display the Edit Hyperlink dialog box shown in Figure 15.14. This is almost identical to the Insert Hyperlink dialog box shown in Figure 15.2 except for an extra button with the caption Remove Link.

FIGURE 15.14:

Edit Hyperlink dialog box

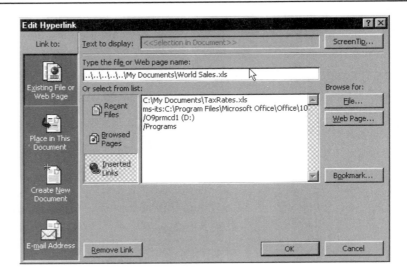

3. Make the required new entries in the Text To Display box and the Type The File Or Web Page Name box and click OK.

Updating a Hyperlink from a Macro

A hyperlink's destination and ToolTip can be updated from a macro by assigning the Address and ScreenTip arguments, as shown in Listing 15.5.

LISTING 15.5

```
0    Sub UpdateSelectedHyperlink()
1        'update the destination or ToolTip of the selected _
         'hyperlink
2        Selection.ShapeRange.Item(1).Hyperlink.Address = _
         "My Documents\World Sales.xls"
3        Selection.ShapeRange.Item(1).Hyperlink.ScreenTip = _
         "World Sales"
4    End Sub
```

ANALYSIS

Line 2 uses the Item method to return the first Shape in the ShapeRange object of the selected item identified by the Selection property to return the hyperlink, and then updates its destination to a new file.

Line 3 updates the ScreenTip for the selected hyperlink.

Removing a Hyperlink

There are two ways to remove a hyperlink—the hard way and the easy way. Let's start with the hard way:

1. Select a cell by clicking it and holding down the mouse button briefly before releasing it.

2. Choose Insert ➤ Hyperlink to open the Insert Hyperlink dialog box and, near the bottom of the Edit Hyperlink dialog box, click Remove Link (see Figure 15.14).

The easy way is to do step 1 to select the hyperlink cell and then simply hit the Delete key.

Formatting All Hyperlink Styles in a Workbook

You can change how a hyperlink will look both before it's been clicked and after it's been clicked. The following steps will change the style of all hyperlinks in your current workbook.

Changing the Before-Click Appearance   The following steps show you how to change the look of a hyperlink before it has been clicked:

1. Open the workbook you created in the section "Using Cell Text as a Hyperlink" early in this chapter, or any other workbook of your choice that contains a hyperlink.

2. Choose Format ➤ Style to open the Style dialog box and select Hyperlink in the Style Name box list.

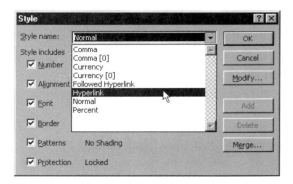

3. Click Modify to open the Format Cells dialog box and select Bold Italic from the list of Font Styles in the Font tab. Click OK to return to the Style dialog box.

4. Click OK to return to your worksheet, which will now show the hyperlink in bold italic text.

Changing the After-Click Appearance   Repeat steps 1 through 4, but at step 2 select Followed Hyperlink from the list instead of Hyperlink, and at step 3 choose the modification you want to make.

All hyperlinks associated with the same workbook—whether or not they existed when you changed the style—will have the before-click appearance of bold italic text and whatever style you adopted for the after-click look. The appearance of hyperlinks in other workbooks and in any new workbooks will revert to the previous before-click and after-click styles.

> **NOTE**   The Hyperlink style will be listed in the Style Name box only if the active workbook contains a text hyperlink. The Followed Hyperlink style will appear in the Style Name box if the text hyperlink exists, jumps to another file, and returns to the workbook when that file is closed.

Summary

When you've completed this chapter, you'll know how to create a hyperlink in a worksheet using

- cell text
- a graphic object
- an OLE object
- a toolbar button
- a hyperlink in a hyperlink
- the HYPERLINK worksheet function

You'll also be able to

- update your hyperlink's destination and ScreenTip manually and in a macro
- remove a hyperlink
- format all hyperlinks in a workbook

CHAPTER
SIXTEEN

16

Publishing Worksheets on the Web

This chapter looks at the many features that Excel provides to make publishing data in your Excel workbooks extremely easy. In this chapter, you'll see how to convert an Excel workbook into an HTML document without having to learn the HTML lingo, and how to turn Excel workbooks into the start page in your Web browser. You'll also see how to download data from a Web site into a worksheet, and how to connect to an FTP site to transmit and receive data.

Web Applications

Web applications is the jargon used for applications that have Web-based clients (or users). This is a booming area, with personal, corporate, and government Web sites joining the World Wide Web at a mind-boggling rate. This pace will quicken when users find out just how easy it is to create a Web page using the Microsoft Office 2000 suite of applications. For help turning your Microsoft Word 2000 documents into Web pages, see *Word 2000 Developer's Handbook* by Guy Hart-Davis (ISBN 0-7821-2329-5, Sybex, 1999) and *Microsoft FrontPage 2000: No Experience Required* by Gene Weisskopf (ISBN 0-7821-2482-8, Sybex, 1999).

Excel's Web Jargon

Excel's powerful Web publishing features make it extremely easy for you to change data from existing workbooks into HTML documents without needing to learn the specialized HTML command language. (See the sidebar "HTML" later in this chapter for a sample of how Excel worksheets translate into HTML.) After your document has been converted into HTML format, you can place it on a Web server where it can be retrieved using either HTTP or FTP. A Web server is a computer that has all of the Web server software and hardware necessary to connect to the World Wide Web. It is set up with the TCP/IP network addresses necessary to make the Web connection. The HTTP and FTP protocols can be described as follows:

- **HTTP (Hypertext Transfer Protocol)**: This Internet communications protocol is used to connect to servers on the World Wide Web and to transmit Web pages written in HTML.

- **FTP (File Transfer Protocol)**: This communications protocol is used to connect to TCP/IP networks, which include UNIX and the Internet. FTP allows connections to be established at FTP sites throughout the world where you can log in and download files from that site to your own computer. This protocol is one of the older protocols and is generally harder to use than the newies since it is command based. It's still heavily used because of the efficient way it passes the files requested by users around the Web.

Web Browsers

Web browsers are software applications that interpret HTML pages, Gopher pages, and FTP directories, thus enabling you to view the various kinds of information available on the Web without having to lift a finger! Browsers can transfer files, follow hyperlinks, and execute programs. Some even allow you to play video clips that are embedded in Web pages.

Excel 2000, in combination with Microsoft's Internet Explorer browser, lets you choose to save your data so that users can interact with it in a similar way as they interact with a workbook, a PivotTable, or a chart sheet in their own PCs—they can make changes to the data locally within their Web browsers without actually modifying the source. Alternatively, you can save your data in a non-interactive form so that it can't be changed.

HTML

HTML stands for Hypertext Markup Language, a formatting language used by World Wide Web servers that contains *tags* (or commands) that are placed strategically within the text to specify how it will appear on a Web page. These tags are composed of the character <, the characters representing the tag, and then the character >. For example, <b> turns boldface on and </b> turns it off again. So the text

```
Now is the <b>time</b> for <u>all</u> to unite.
```

will be displayed on the Web page as

```
Now is the time for all to unite.
```

HTML documents are really just unformatted text documents. When a workbook is saved as a Web page, Excel inserts these tags into a file with the data you want to publish, alleviating

Continued on next page

the need for you to learn how to write HTML tags. The HTML document required to store an Excel workbook's data and reproduce it on the Web is very long and complicated. The following sample of an HTML document was taken from the beginning of an HTML file that contains the workbook `OneCell` containing cell A1 with value 123 saved as a Web page with the title `Cell A1 as Web Page`.

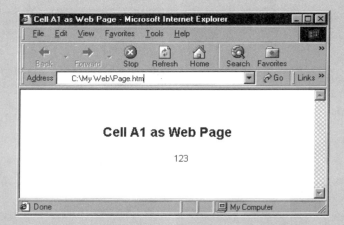

This sample is only a fraction of the HTML document, which has to store all information about the state Excel was in when the page was created. Some of this code is actually *XML*, which is used to store and describe the information in the workbook—HTML is used only to describe how to present or format the data.

```
<html xmlns:o="urn:schemas-microsoft-com:office:office"
xmlns:x="urn:schemas-microsoft-com:office:excel"
xmlns="-//W3C//DTD HTML 4.0//EN">

<head>
<meta http-equiv=Content-Type content="text/html; charset=windows-
    1252">
<meta name=ProgId content=Excel.Sheet>
```

```
<meta name=Generator content="Microsoft Excel 9">
<link rel=File-List href="./OneCell_files/filelist.xml">
<link rel=Edit-Time-Data href="./OneCell_files/editdata.mso">
<link rel=OLE-Object-Data href="./OneCell_files/oledata.mso">
<title>Cell A1 as Web Page</title>
<!-[if gte mso 9]><xml>
 <o:DocumentProperties>
  <o:Author>marion</o:Author>
  <o:LastAuthor>marion</o:LastAuthor>
  <o:Created>1999-03-08T11:23:24Z</o:Created>
etc...
```

Preparing Data for the Web

The first thing you need to do is create your Excel data and save it as a Web page. Then you can dress it up with more text and graphics, using Excel or, if you prefer, Microsoft FrontPage 2000, a stand-alone Web publishing application that is also included in the Microsoft Office 2000 Premium suite.

Let's create a simple school timetable, with all of the required information entered using Excel's default settings.

1. Create the worksheet shown in Figure 16.1.

FIGURE 16.1:

Simple school timetable

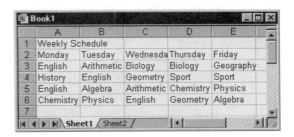

2. Choose File ➢ Web Page Preview to see the data in your Web browser, as shown in Figure 16.2, then close the Web Page Preview window again before continuing.

FIGURE 16.2:

Simple school timetable in
Web browser

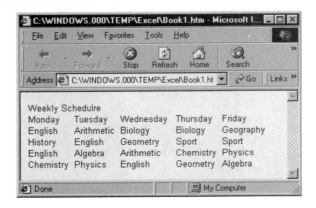

3. Select cell A1 and format it as Bold font style and 36 font size (this is most quickly done using the buttons in the toolbar). Select A1:E1 and click the Merge and Center toolbar button (shown below).

4. Select A2:E2 and format the text to Bold and the font size to 16. Adjust the width of the columns by selecting columns A through E and dragging the right boundary of column C to the width required to see all of the characters in "Wednesday." All selected columns will be adjusted to the same width (Figure 16.3). Select row 2 and drag the bottom border down to make the height around 40 pixels—a ToolTip will let you know the current height (as shown).

FIGURE 16.3:

Timetable worksheet with formatting so far

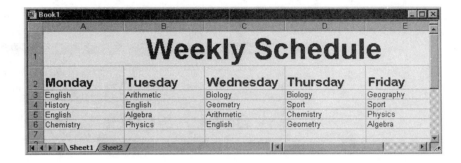

5. Select cells A3 through E6 and format the text to Arial Narrow font, size 16, and Bold.

6. Select A1:E6, click Fillcolor from the toolbar, and choose Light Turquoise from the bottom of the palette.

7. Select A2:E2 and fill these cells with Turquoise.

8. Display the Drawing toolbar and click Insert WordArt to display the Word-Art Gallery dialog box, shown in Figure 16.4. Choose a WordArt style for your worksheet title—I've chosen the fourth style in the second column of the gallery samples.

FIGURE 16.4:

WordArt styles available from the gallery

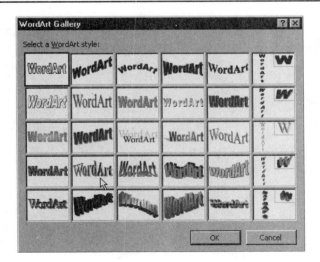

9. Click OK to open the Edit WordArt Text dialog box and enter the text **Weekly Schedule** (as shown). Click OK to return to your workbook.

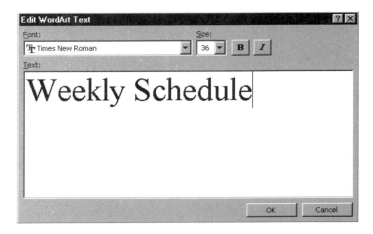

10. Delete the old Weekly Schedule text from cell A1 and drag your hot, new graphic version into position at the top. Your workbook is now ready for publishing.

11. Choose File ➢ Web Page Preview to see the results, which should look like Figure 16.5. (See Chapter 24, "That's Entertainment," for more WordArt formatting features.)

FIGURE 16.5:

Formatted Web page for timetable

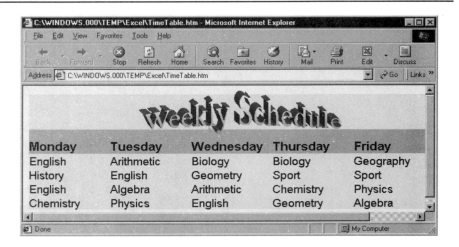

Considerations for Web Pages

Before you convert an Excel worksheet into an HTML page, you should:

- Increase the font size. Small text often becomes harder to read after it undergoes the conversion process. Remember that not everyone has high-resolution, state-of-the-art displays.

- Keep your worksheet simple and avoid cluttering it with too many bits and pieces of unrelated information.

- Avoid having too many long lines of text. It's difficult to move from the end of one line of text to the start of the next one if there are more than five or six lines.

- Avoid large areas of saturated blue color. Our eyes need to refocus more when we look at blue after looking at other colors, and after a while this leads to eye fatigue. If you really must have blue, add red and green to lighten it and reduce this effect.

One excellent resource for Web page design is Molly Holzschlag's *Web by Design: The Complete Guide* (ISBN 0-7821-2201-9, Sybex, 1998).

Web Toolbar

Figure 16.6 shows the buttons available in the Web toolbar. They may already be familiar to you, as they are also part of the Microsoft Internet Explorer Web browser.

FIGURE 16.6:

Web toolbar

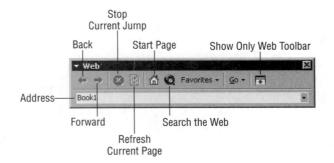

Back and **Forward**   Allows you to jump backward and forward among workbooks and other files that have been accessed via hyperlinks or by entering a URL in your Web browser.

Stop Current Jump   Allows you to stop loading a page. This is useful if a page that's being loaded is taking a long time to display and you don't want to wait.

Refresh Current Page   Ensures that you've got the latest version of the current document.

Start Page   Displays the start page for your local Web site. The start page is the first Web page displayed when you start up your browser application. The start page can be any Web site of your choice or it can be a document on your PC. You can place hyperlinks in your start page to take you to other documents located anywhere on the World Wide Web or on your PC.

Search the Web   Runs your Web browser application and downloads your Search page to allow you to start searching the Web immediately.

Favorites   Displays a drop-down list of your favorite documents and Web sites/URLs that you like to access frequently.

Go   Allows you to run a program by entering its name in the Address bar and clicking Go. You can also use this button to search the Web.

Show Only Web Toolbar   Hides all toolbars that are on display and places the Web toolbar under the Excel menu bar, allowing it to behave like a browser (Figure 16.7). Clicking this button again redisplays all of the hidden toolbars and restores the standard Excel toolbar to its privileged place under the menu bar.

Address   Allows you to specify where you want to go today!

FIGURE 16.7:

Excel with the Web toolbar

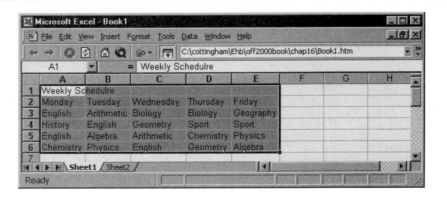

Starting Up in Excel

You can easily make an Excel workbook the start page for your Web browser. The following steps show you how:

1. Open the workbook that you want to make your start page.

2. Click Go in the Web toolbar and select Set Start Page from its drop-down list (shown below) to open the Set Start Page dialog box (Figure 16.8). Changing the start page in Excel changes it in all of your applications—make a note of your original start page filename so that you can restore it at the end of this example.

FIGURE 16.8:

Set Start Page dialog box

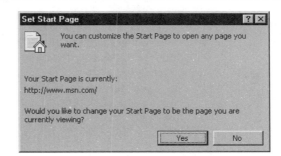

3. Click Yes to make your active workbook the start page.

4. Test the new start page by closing your workbook and running your Web browser—your workbook should open inside your browser's window, as the World Sales workbook does in Figure 16.9.

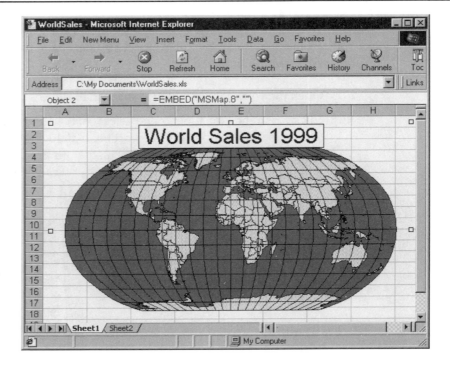

5. Now you're ready to restore your original start page. This can be done in two ways:

   • Since you already have your Web browser open, you can set it there. With Internet Explorer, this means choosing Tools ➤ Internet Options and entering the original start page in the Address box in the Home Page frame in the General tab.

   or

   • Choose Start ➤ Settings ➤ Control Panel to open the Control Panel dialog box. Double-click the Internet or Internet Options button to open the Internet Properties dialog box, shown in Figure 16.10. Enter the original start page filename (the one that was shown in the Set Start Page dialog box in step 2) into the Address box.

6. Close Excel and open your Web browser, which should now go to your original start page.

Restoring the start page in
the Internet Properties dialog box

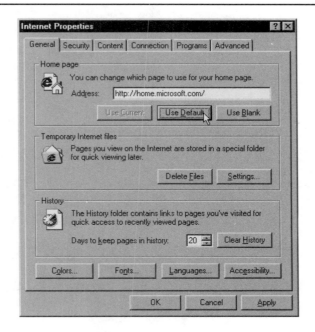

Previewing Your Web Page

To preview and make changes to your Web page before saving it or publishing it:

1. Open the Excel worksheet you want to make your Web page and choose
   File ➢ Web Page Preview. Figure 16.11 shows the result of previewing the
   World Sales worksheet in this way.

2. Click the US hyperlink (the colored circle on the west coast of the United
   States) to jump to the US Sales.xls location. Make some changes and click
   the Back button at the top of your browser window. The message box
   shown below will prompt you about saving these changes.

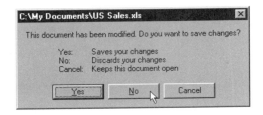

FIGURE 16.11:

World Sales work-
sheet previewed in
the Web browser

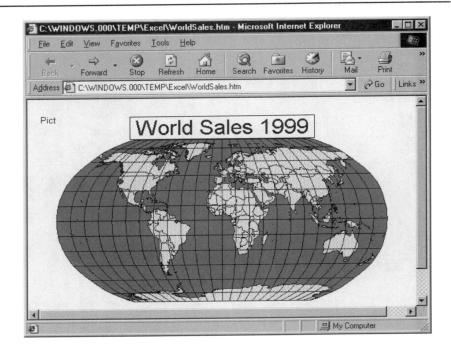

3.   Click No and the map will be displayed again.

Previewing Your Web Page from a Macro

The following `PreviewWorkbook` macro allows you to preview your Web page
from a macro:

```
Sub PreviewWorkbook()
    ActiveWorkbook.WebPagePreview
End Sub
```

Creating a Web Page from a Worksheet

You can publish the data from your workbooks on the World Wide Web or on your company's intranet as easily as clicking a button. Ranges of cells are published as tables and all of your hyperlinks are published as HTML links. Let's publish our `World Sales` worksheet from Chapter 15:

1. Open the `World Sales` workbook with `Sheet1` (containing your map) active.

2. Choose File ➤ Save As Web Page to display the Save As dialog box, shown in Figure 16.12. Enter the Folder in the Save In box and enter the filename in the File Name box.

FIGURE 16.12:

Save As dialog box for saving a workbook as a Web Page

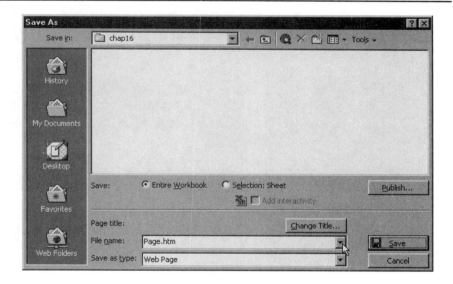

3. Make sure the Entire Workbook option button is selected. Click Change Title to open the Set Page Title dialog box, shown in Figure 16.13. Enter a new title and click OK to return to the Save As dialog box, which will now display the new title in the Page Title frame. This title will be displayed in the title bar of your Web browser when this page is opened.

4. In the Save As dialog box, click Publish to open the Publish As Web Page dialog box, shown in Figure 16.14.

FIGURE 16.13:

Set Page Title dialog box for specifying the title to be displayed in the Web browser's title bar

FIGURE 16.14:

Publish As Web Page dialog box

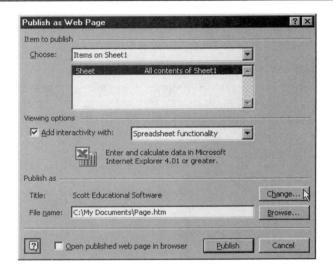

5. Click the Down arrow in the Choose box to see the list of items available; this list allows you to select individual sheets, a range of cells, or previously published items. Selecting Items On Sheet1 will make the Publish button at the bottom available for selection and will highlight all of the cells in Sheet1 to show they've been selected. The tip at the end of this section provides a faster way to choose a whole worksheet.

6. Make sure that the Add Interactivity With check box hasn't been selected (we don't want to give users the ability to interact with our worksheet just yet).

7. Click Change to open the Set Title dialog box shown in Figure 16.15. By default this title is the same as the one entered for the title bar, but a Web page title can be specified separately. Enter a new title and click OK to return to the Publish As Web Page dialog box, which will now display the

new title in the Publish As frame. This title will be displayed above the Excel data when you open this page in your Web browser.

FIGURE 16.15:

Set Title dialog box for specifying the title that will appear centered over the Excel data

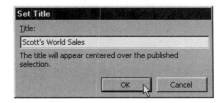

8. Click Publish to create the Web page and return to your workbook.

TIP   To select the active worksheet in its entirety, click the Selection: Sheet option button in the Save As dialog box (Figure 16.12). If the active worksheet has been published previously, the caption of this option button will be Republish: Sheet.

Viewing Your Web Page in the Browser

Open the Windows Explorer application and double-click your new Web page to open the Web browser displaying your worksheet. The title will be displayed in two places—on the title bar of the Web browser and on the Web page itself, as shown in Figure 16.16.

Transferring Web Page Data to Your Worksheet

You may want to download data from a Web page to your worksheet. The following example demonstrates how to download information stored about Microsoft stocks:

1. Open a new workbook and select cell A1. Choose Data ➤ Get External Data ➤ Run Saved Query to display the Run Query dialog box listing all of the query format files (.IQY) in the Queries folder (the default folder where Excel looks for query files). Microsoft Excel provides the query files shown in Figure 16.17.

FIGURE 16.16:

New Web page created as a result of following the steps in the last section

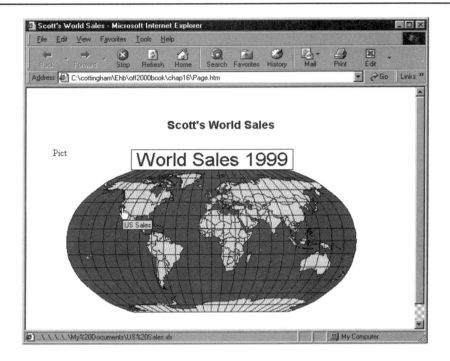

FIGURE 16.17:

Run Query dialog box showing a list of query files from the Queries folder

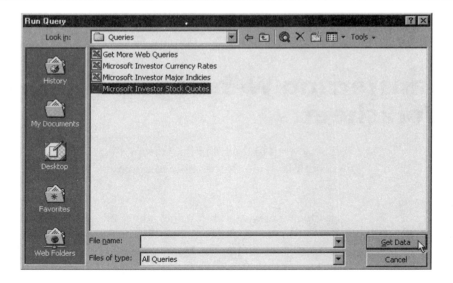

Contents of Query Files

The Query format files contain URL information as well as what text to display in the Enter Parameter Value dialog box. The following text provides an example:

```
WEB

1

http://webservices.pcquote.com/
cgi-bin/excelget.exe?
TICKER=["TICKER","Enter your stock symbol for a detailed quote."]
```

2. Select Microsoft Investor Stock Quotes, which will be used later in this example to download the detailed stock quote figures. Click Get Data to display the Returning External Data to Microsoft Excel dialog box.

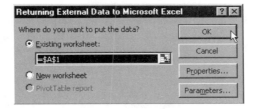

3. Ensure that the Existing Worksheet option button is selected and that =$A$1 appears in the box, or change the cell reference if you want to return the data to a new location. Click OK to display the Enter Parameter Value dialog box.

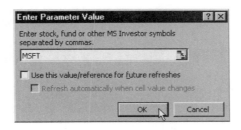

4. Enter **MSFT** as the stock symbol in the box, as shown. Click OK to return to your worksheet. Figure 16.18 shows the message that will appear at the selected cell while the data is being downloaded. Figure 16.19 shows the worksheet after the downloading has been completed.

FIGURE 16.18:

Text displayed temporarily while data is being downloaded from the Web

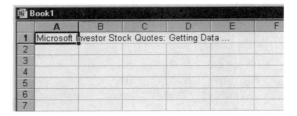

FIGURE 16.19:

Downloaded data placed in the worksheet

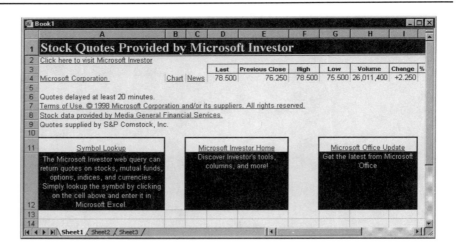

Downloading Web Data with a Macro

The `DownloadDataFromWeb` macro shown in Listing 16.1 shows how to code a macro that downloads data from the Web and places it into your worksheet, with the active cell being the top-left corner of the range of cells that the data is loaded into.

LISTING 16.1

```
0    Sub DownloadDataFromWeb()
1        'downloads data from the Web to the range based
2        'on the active cell
3        With ActiveSheet.QueryTables.Add(Connection:= _
             "FINDER;C:\Program Files\Microsoft Office\_
             Office \Queries\Microsoft Investor Stock Quotes"_
             , Destination:=Range("A1"))
4            .Name = "Microsoft Investor Stock Quotes"
5            .FieldNames = True
6            .RowNumbers = False
7            .FillAdjacentFormulas = False
8            .PreserveFormatting = False
9            .RefreshOnFileOpen = False
10           .BackgroundQuery = True
11           .RefreshStyle = xlInsertDeleteCells
12           .SavePassword = False
13           .SaveData = True
14           .AdjustColumnWidth = True
15           .RefreshPeriod = 0
16           .WebSelectionType = xlAllTables
17           .WebFormatting = xlWebFormattingAll
18           .WebPreFormattedTextToColumns = False
19           .WebConsecutiveDelimitersAsOne = True
20           .WebSingleBlockTextImport = False
21           .WebDisableDateRecognition = False
22           .Refresh BackgroundQuery:=False
23       End With
24   End Sub
```

ANALYSIS

Line 0 starts the DownloadDataFromWeb macro.

Line 3 uses the Add method of the QueryTables collection to create a new query table in a new QueryTable object. The Connection and Destination arguments are required; the Connection argument is assigned the path name of a query format file and the Destination argument is assigned the selected cell(s).

> Lines 4 through 22 set the various properties of the new `QueryTable` object. The `Name` property at Line 4 is set to the name of the query file.

Opening HTML Documents in Excel

You can open HTML documents in Excel the same way you open workbooks on your PC. (This feature is not yet available for Macintosh users.) HTML documents are saved in files with the extension .HTM.

- If the HTML document was originally created by saving an Excel worksheet containing values as a Web page, you'll be able to change these values just as you do in a normal workbook.

- If the HTML document was created by saving an Excel worksheet containing a chart as a Web page, the chart has been saved as a picture. This means that when you open the document again you won't be able to access any of the chart's components, such as its title or axis labels.

- If the HTML document was saved by another Office application (such as Word or FrontPage), opening the document from within Excel will automatically start the application it was saved from.

TIP You can force Excel to open by right-clicking on the file in the Open dealog box and choosing Open In Microsoft Excel from the shortcut menu.

Connecting to an FTP Site

You may need to connect to an FTP site to transmit or receive data. This is as easy as opening and saving a local file on your PC. The following steps show how to connect to the FTP site to receive data from Excel:

1. Open Excel and choose File ➤ Open to display the Open dialog box.

2. Click the Down arrow at the end of the Look In box and select FTP Locations from the list, as shown in Figure 16.20. This will display FTP Locations in the Look In list with Add/Modify FTP Locations as a subcategory beneath it.

FIGURE 16.20:

Opening a link to a file on the Web

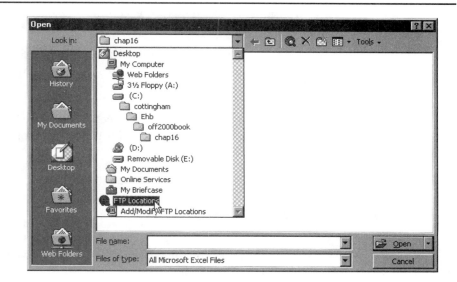

3. Select Add/Modify FTP Locations and click Open to display the Add/Modify FTP Locations dialog box, shown in Figure 16.21.

FIGURE 16.21:

Add/Modify FTP Locations dialog box

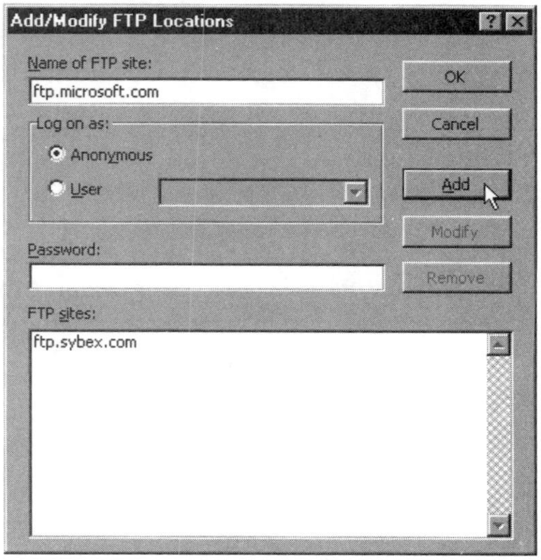

4. Enter the name of an FTP site that you can access (or click one if there are any in the FTP Sites list) and supply your password. Click Add to display your entry in the FTP site box. Click OK to return to the Open dialog box, which will now display the FTP location you've added. Just like files, your FTP locations will be displayed each time you select the FTP Locations folder.

5. Select the FTP site and click Open. The connection to the FTP site will be made and the list of folders at that site will be displayed for you to select the one you want to open.

To transmit data to an FTP site, all you need to do is use the Save As menu command and follow the same procedure as for the Open command. Any FTP sites previously added will still be available.

Formatting a Web Page

Web pages should be colorful and well laid out. With Excel's powerful HTML authoring capabilities, you can quickly and easily format a few cells here and there to develop a Web page that looks quite snazzy. Let's run through an example that demonstrates how Excel need not be restricted to holding numerical information. We'll give our Web page the title Success in Business:

1. Open a new Workbook and select A1:B3, choose Format ➤ Cells, and select the Borders tab.

2. Select the red color for your line and click on a thick line in the Style box. Choose the four buttons for the outside borders.

3. Select the Patterns tab and choose a pale yellow color. Click OK to return to your workbook.

4. Select B3:E6, choose Format ➤ Cells, and select the Borders tab. This time, set the outside border to a cyan and then set the fill color to a pale cyan in the Patterns tab. Click OK to return to your worksheet, which will now look like the one shown in Figure 16.22.

5. Select cell A1 and select the Font tab of the Format Cells dialog box. Set the font style to Bold Italic and the font size to 28. Click OK to return to the worksheet and enter an uppercase **A** into cell A1.

FIGURE 16.22:

Initial formatting for the
Success in Business
worksheet

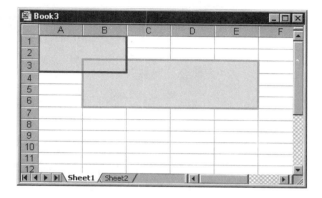

6. Select cell D5 and set the font size to 18; adjust the widths and heights as shown.

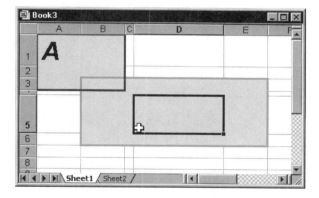

7. Select cells A1:E6 and drag-copy down to E29. You'll need to make adjustments to some of the row heights.

8. Enter the textual values shown in Figure 16.23 and Figure 16.24 into columns A and D.

9. Select the range A1:F31 and choose File ➤ Save As Web Page to open the Save As dialog box (shown in Figure 16.12). This time, the Selection: Sheet option button will read Selection: $A$1:$F$31.

10. Click Publish to display the Publish As Web Page dialog box (shown in Figure 16.14). This time, Range Of Cells will appear in the Choose box and =Sheet1!$A$1:$F$31 will appear in the box below it.

FIGURE 16.23:

The first half of the FormattedWorksheet worksheet

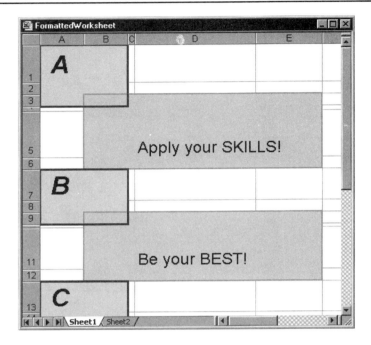

FIGURE 16.24:

The second half of the FormattedWorksheet worksheet

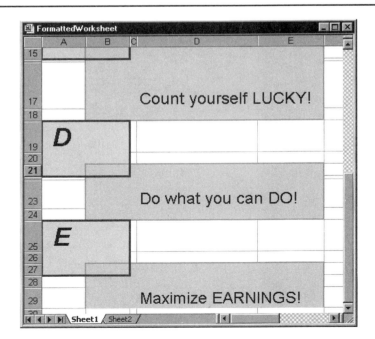

11. Click Publish to display the page in your browser, as shown in Figure 16.25.

FIGURE 16.25:

The Success in Business worksheet displayed in the browser

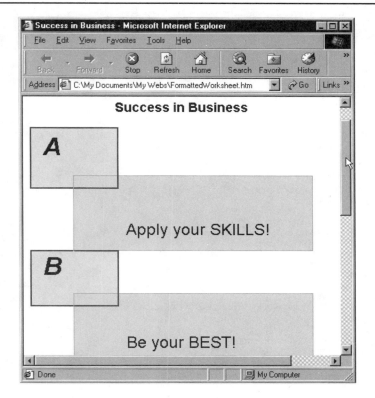

Summary

By the end of this chapter, you'll be able to

- prepare data for the Web
- start your Web browser application in Excel
- make a worksheet your start page
- open an HTML page in Excel
- format a page for the Web
- connect to an FTP site to transmit and receive data

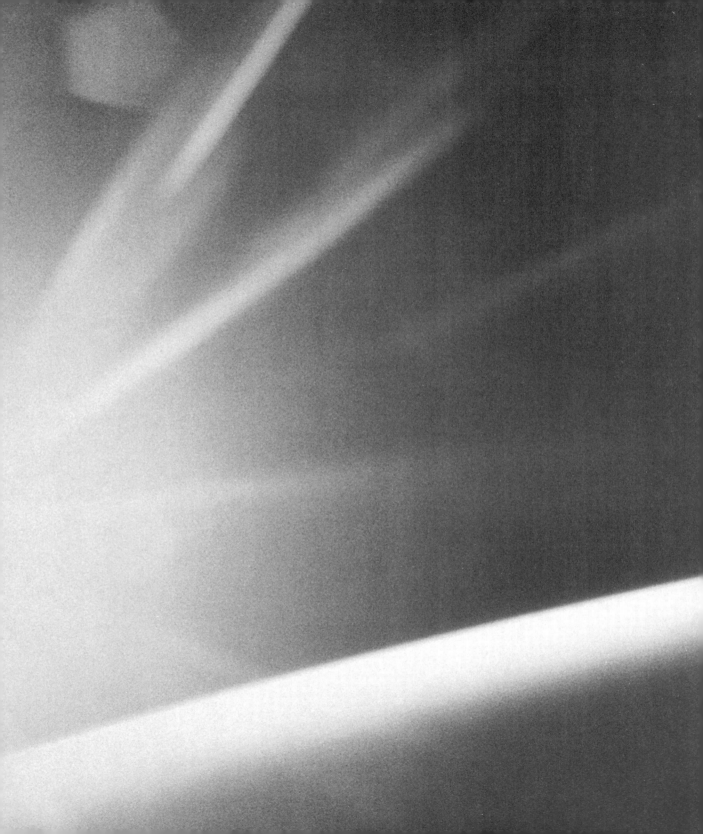

CHAPTER SEVENTEEN

Publishing Charts on the Web

This chapter shows you how to put your charts on the Web. Publishing a chart as a Web page (or, more commonly, as part of a Web page) enables you to show off your artistic talents in full color instead of being restricted to the sterile monochrome limitations of paper. The Color Scheme for Bars application developed in this chapter gives you a starting point for developing automatic color schemes for your charts and lets you make use of the thousands of colors your PC is capable of displaying.

Pages for the Internet and Intranets

There are two reasons for wanting to create snazzy Web pages using charts produced by Microsoft Excel—the explosion of Internet sites and the expected continuing proliferation of intranet sites.

In recent years, the Internet has become the most powerful marketing and commerce tool for many companies around the world. Indeed, lots of companies only do business on the Internet, so the all-important first impression is created by their home pages.

Many companies are now realizing that they can mimic the Web in their own internal networks (*intranets*), which are used to circulate information for internal use only between different departments and offices. An intranet can gain access to the powerful search engines provided on the Internet. It eliminates the need for photocopying and circulating paper copies of documents and makes information instantly accessible as soon as it becomes available. This is where dressing up your charts becomes increasingly important. No longer can you make the excuse that black, white, and gray are sufficient for the printed page—managers will be viewing your work in full color!

Publishing a Chart on the Web

Publishing a chart on the Web has never been easier. You can give a chart interactive functionality or make it static just as you did with your worksheets in the last chapter—by checking the Add Interactivity With check box that was shown in Figure 16.14 of Chapter 16.

Unfortunately, when you save your chart with interactive functionality some of its features may be diminished. Figure 17.1 shows a chart saved with interactive functionality; Figure 17.2 shows the same chart saved without interactive functionality.

FIGURE 17.1:

Chart saved with interactive functionality; note the loss of some formatting features

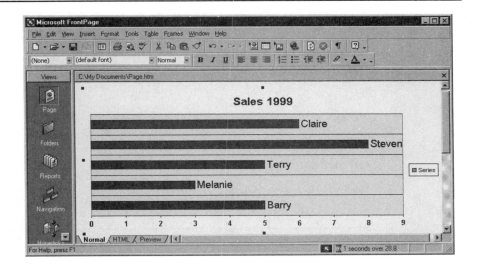

FIGURE 17.2:

Chart saved without interactive functionality

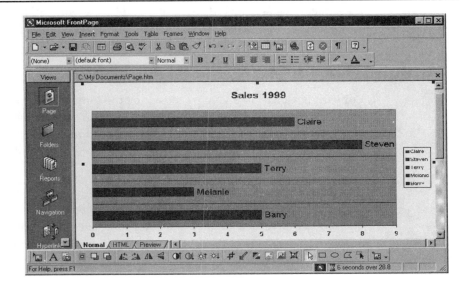

You should therefore avoid making your chart interactive unless that's absolutely necessary to make your Web page appear really whiz-bang! Table 17.1 provides a list of some of the features that are visually diminished in an interactive chart and how each will affect the appearance of your chart in a Web page.

TABLE 17.1: Chart Features and How Their Appearance Is Affected When Made Interactive on the Web

Feature	Displayed Effect
Auto Scale fonts	Default font size
3-D Chart	2-D Chart
Surface Chart	Column Chart
Series Lines	Lost
Text Boxes and Pictures	Lost
Drawing Objects and Shadows	Lost
Semi-transparent Fill	Lost

When you publish a chart (or workbook), the .HTM file created by Excel is associated with certain supporting files. These files are placed in a folder that has the same name as the Web page followed by the word `files`. Supporting files contain elements such as background textures and graphic objects.

Publishing a Chart in a Web Page

Publishing a chart in a Web page is done the same way as publishing a workbook. Charts are automatically scaled when you save them as Web pages; normally, they end up too big for the window. Although you can usually view the whole chart bit by bit using the horizontal and vertical scroll bars as shown in Figure 17.3, this is not the ideal situation!

Charts placed on existing Web pages frequently need to be resized to fit into some layouts, but charts saved in HTML format can't be resized using Excel. Therefore, I've turned to the Microsoft FrontPage 2000 application, which can resize charts stored in HTML. I've split the procedure for publishing a chart on the Web into three stages.

1. Formatting the chart

2. Saving it as a Web page

3. Resizing it inside the HTML file using Microsoft FrontPage 2000

WARNING   Protected workbooks or charts cannot be published in a Web page.

FIGURE 17.3:

Sales 1999 chart saved as a Web page in Excel then displayed using the Microsoft Internet Explorer

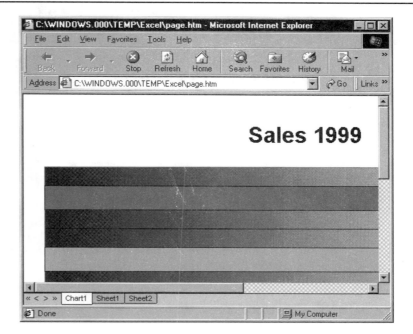

Microsoft FrontPage 2000

Microsoft FrontPage is one of the Office 2000 applications and one of the world's leading creation and management programs for Web site design. It provides seamless integration with all of the other Office applications, including Excel. For thorough coverage of FrontPage 2000, see *Microsoft FrontPage 2000: No Experience Required* by Gene Weisskopf (ISBN 0-7821-2482-8, Sybex, 1999).

Formatting a Chart for the Web

Let's create a Sales 1999 chart showing the sales made by our company's representatives and format it into something flashy that we can publish in a Web page:

1. Open a new workbook and enter the data shown in Figure 17.4.

FIGURE 17.4:

Worksheet with data for our Sales 1999 chart

2. Select cells A1:B5 and click the Chart button to open the first dialog box of the Chart Wizard. All four dialog boxes of the Chart Wizard are shown in Figures 13.3 through 13.10 of Chapter 13. Select Bar from the Chart Type list and be sure that the top-left chart is highlighted in the Chart Sub-type list.

3. Click Next twice (slowly rather than a double-click) to display the Chart Wizard's third dialog box. Select the Titles tab and enter **Sales 1999** in the Chart Title box.

4. Select the Gridlines tab and check the Category (X) Axis Major Gridlines check box; leave all the other check boxes clear.

5. Select the Data Labels tab and select the Show Label option button.

6. Select the Axes tab and clear the Category (X) axis check box.

7. Click Next and select the As New Sheet option button, ensure that Chart1 appears in the box alongside, and click Finish.

8. Choose View ➤ Size with Window. Figure 17.5 shows the resulting Sales 1999 chart.

FIGURE 17.5:

The Sales 1999 chart formatted with the selected settings

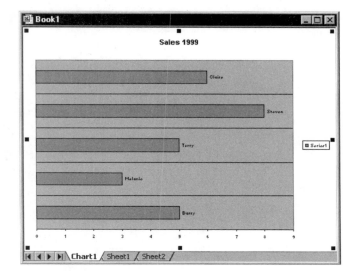

9. Next, we'll choose colors for our chart, beginning with the data bars. Click the top bar (labeled "Claire") to select the series and click again on any bar to select only that bar. Right-click the bar and choose Format Data Point from the shortcut menu to open the Format Data Point dialog box (Figure 17.6). Select a fill color from the palette to fill that single bar. Click OK to return to the worksheet.

10. Repeat step 9 to fill the other bars, selecting different colors each time. I've chosen Autumn colors to blend in with the background that I'll be setting in steps 11 through 14.

11. Right-click in the plot area and choose Format Plot Area from the shortcut menu to open the Format Plot Area dialog box, shown in Figure 17.7.

12. Click Fill Effects to open the Fill Effects dialog box (shown in Figure 17.8) and select the Two Colors option button.

13. Click the Down arrow in the Color 1 box and select a light color. Click the Down arrow in the Color 2 box and choose a dark color that contrasts with the first color you selected. I've chosen Light Yellow and Brown.

14. Select the Vertical option button and the second Variant, as shown in Figure 17.8. Click OK to return to the Format Plot Area dialog box.

Selecting a color for the
current bar from the Format
Data Point dialog box

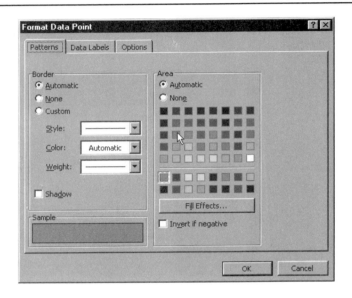

FIGURE 17.7:

Format Plot Area
dialog box

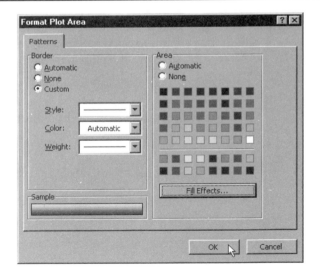

FIGURE 17.8:

Fill Effects dialog box

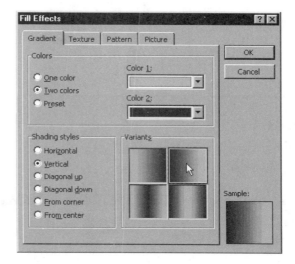

15. Click OK to return to the chart sheet, which will now look like the chart shown in Figure 17.9.

FIGURE 17.9:

Formatted Sales 1999 chart

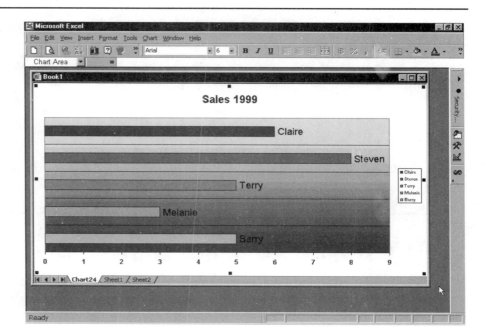

16. Click one of the Data Labels to select them all, and change the font size to 14 in the toolbar.

17. Click the title and change its font size to 16.

18. Save your workbook.

Fill Effects

The Fill Effects dialog box provides many visually appealing options, including gradient fills (shown in Figure 17.8) and texture fill (shown below).

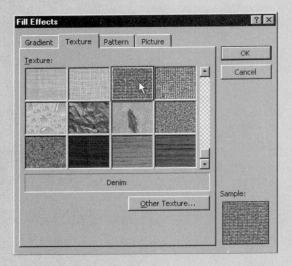

The Fill Effects button that opens this dialog box becomes available when you try to format any 2-D or 3-D area. The gradient fill is achieved by specifying one or two colors that gradually change. The texture fill allows you to select from a range of textures that you want to map onto the selected area.

Macro-izing Formatting a Chart for the Web

Let's develop a macro that creates a chart and does much the same formatting as we've just done manually to our five sales figures. Then we can generalize it to be able to cope with different sizes of data plots and various color schemes.

LISTING 17.1

```
0    Sub CreateBarChart()
1        ' create a bar chart
2        Charts.Add
3        With ActiveChart
4            .ChartType = xlBarClustered
5                'set data to be plotted
6            .SetSourceData Source:=Sheets("Sheet1").Range("A1:B5")
7            .Location Where:=xlLocationAsNewSheet
8                'Y-axis settings
9            .HasAxis(xlCategory, xlPrimary) = False
10           With .Axes(xlCategory)
11               .HasMajorGridlines = True
12               .HasMinorGridlines = False
13           End With
14               'X-axis settings
15           With .Axes(xlValue)
16               .HasMajorGridlines = False
17               .HasMinorGridlines = False
18               .TickLabels.Font.Size = 16
19               .TickLabels.Font.Bold = True
20           End With
21               'Data labels settings
22           .ApplyDataLabels Type:=xlDataLabelsShowLabel
23           .SizeWithWindow = True
24           .SeriesCollection(1).DataLabels.Font.Size = 14
25               'Data bars settings
26           With .SeriesCollection(1)
27               .Points(5).Interior.ColorIndex = 53
28               .Points(4).Interior.ColorIndex = 46
29               .Points(3).Interior.ColorIndex = 45
30               .Points(2).Interior.ColorIndex = 44
31               .Points(1).Interior.ColorIndex = 40
32           End With
33               'Plot area settings
34           With .PlotArea.Fill
35               .TwoColorGradient Style:=msoGradientHorizontal, _
                 Variant:=1
36               .ForeColor.SchemeColor = 36
37               .BackColor.SchemeColor = 53
38           End With
```

```
39                 'Title settings
40              .HasTitle = True
41              .ChartTitle.Characters.Text = "Sales 1999"
42              .ChartTitle.Font.Size = 16
43              .ChartArea.Deselect
44           End With
45   End Sub
```

ANALYSIS

Line 2 uses the Add method to create a new Chart object and add it to the Charts collection.

Line 3 uses the With statement so that the ActiveChart properties and methods can be referred to in the With statement without having to qualify them.

Line 4 sets the ChartType property to the Excel constant xlBarClustered. Other constants available include xlBarStacked, xlColumnClustered, xlLine, xlBarOfPie, and xlBubble. There is a constant for each subtype; these can all be viewed in the Object Browser by entering any one of them in the search box.

The **Line 5** comment indicates that the next few lines of code deal with the data to be plotted.

Line 6 uses the SetSourceData method with its Source argument (required) set to the range of the data selected for the chart. This method has another argument, PlotBy, that can be set to xlColumns or xlRows.

Line 7 uses the Location method with its Where argument set to xlLocationAsNewSheet to create a new chart sheet. The alternative is to set it to xlLocationAsObject to embed the chart in the active worksheet.

The **Line 8** comment indicates that the next few coding statements deal with Y-axis settings.

Line 9 assigns False to the HasAxis property, with the xlCategory constant specifying the axis type and the xlPrimary specifying the axis group.

Line 10 starts the With statement so that the properties of the Category axis can be set without fully qualifying them.

Lines 11 and 12 set the major and minor gridline properties.

The **Line 14** comment indicates that the next few statements deal with the X-axis.

Line 15 uses the `With` statement so that the properties of the `Value` axis can be used without fully qualifying them.

Lines 16 and 17 set the major and minor gridline properties.

Line 18 and 19 set the `Value` axis labels to size 16 and bold.

The **Line 21** comment marks the start of setting up the data labels that appear at the tip of each bar.

Line 22 uses the `ApplyDataLabels` method with the argument `Type` set to `xlDataLabelsShowLabel` to display the data labels. The other constants that this argument can be assigned to are `xlDataLabelsShowNone`, `xlDataLabelShowValue` (default), `xlDataLabelShowPercent`, or `xlDataLabelsShowLabelAndPercent` (pie charts and doughnut charts only).

Line 23 sets the `SizeWithWindow` property so that the size of the chart is adjusted to fit inside the window.

Line 24 uses the `SeriesCollection` method to return the one and only series in the collection and sets the font size of its data labels to 14.

The **Line 25** comment marks the start of handling data bar settings.

Line 26 uses the `With` statement so that the properties of the series returned by the `SeriesCollection` method can be used without fully qualifying them.

In **Lines 27 through 31**, each coding statement assigns the required index value of the color palette to an `Interior` object's `ColorIndex` property. The `Interior` object is returned by the `Interior` property of the `Point` object specified from the `Points` collection of the current series.

The **Line 33** comment marks the start of the plot area settings.

Line 34 uses the `With` statement so that `PlotArea.Fill` options can be set without having to fully qualify them.

Line 35 uses the `TwoColorGradient` method with the `Style` argument set to `msoGradientHorizontal`. Other `Style` argument constants are msoGradientDiagonalDown, msoGradientDiagonalUp, msoGradient-FromCenter, msoGradientFromCorner, and msoGradientVertical. (The mso prefix indicates that these constants belong to the Microsoft Office library.) This time, we'll assign 1 to the Variant argument. The Variant argument can be set from 1 through 4, representing the four squares in the Variants frame in the Fill Effects dialog box (Figure 17.8). If the style is to start from the center (xlGradientFromCenter), this argument can only be set to 1 or 2 to specify which color should be in the center.

Lines 36 and 37 set the foreground color and background color of the plot area to index numbers into the current color palette.

The **Line 39** comment begins the title settings.

Line 40 sets the HasTitle property to True to state that a title is required.

Line 41 sets the Text property of the Characters object of the ChartTitle object to a text string. The Characters object can be used to format the characters in a string.

Line 42 sets the font size of the ChartTitle object returned by the Chart-Title property to 16.

Line 43 serves no other purpose but to prevent the ChartTitle from being the selected object.

To extend this macro into a more general one, you need to resolve any unexpected errors that the user makes as they enter cell references. This could be handled by extending the Masked Edit box code given in Chapter 5, which checked whether a cell reference entered into an input box was correct. Or you could just give a general error message if an invalid range (including no entry) has been entered. You would also need to be able to handle different numbers of bars representing the selected data values instead of exactly five as used here.

Color Scheme for Bars Application

The Color Scheme for Bars application adapts the CreateBarChart macro to make it more general so that it will create a chart for the currently selected range of cells and will automatically create your color scheme for you. The color scheme for both the bars and the background goes from light at the top to dark at the bottom (Figure 17.10).

FIGURE 17.10:

Result produced by the
Color Scheme for Bars
application

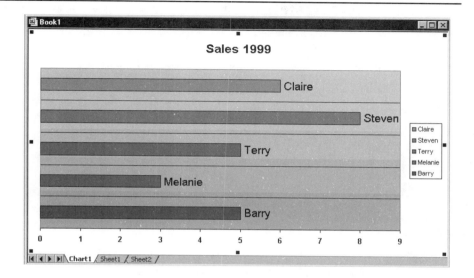

Creating the GUI for the Color Scheme for Bars Application

Figure 17.11 shows the GUI for the Color Scheme for Bars application, and the following steps show you how to build it:

1. Open a new workbook and enter the data shown in Figure 17.4.

2. Run the Visual Basic Editor and choose Insert ➣ UserForm to create an empty UserForm. Change its `Caption` property to **Color Scheme for Bars**.

3. Place a `Label` control near the top and set its `Caption` property to **Enter cell reference:**.

4. Place a Masked Edit box to the right of the `Label` control. (You'll need to add the `Masked Edit` control to your Toolbox, if you didn't do so in Chapter 5. If you don't have the `Masked Edit` control on your PC, you can use a `TextBox` control instead.)

5. Add a `Frame` control with caption **Color Scheme**, then insert three check boxes into it and change their `Caption` strings to Red, Green, and Blue (as shown below) and their `Name` properties to chkRed, chkGreen, and chkBlue.

6. Add two `CommandButton` controls at the bottom and change their `Caption` and `Accelerator` properties as shown below.

Macro-izing the Color Scheme for Bars Application

Now that you've created the GUI, you'll need to add a new module (choose Insert ➤ Add Module) and enter the code shown in Listing 17.2 into it.

This listing contains two macros. The first one, `StartBarApplication`, displays the UserForm shown in Figure 17.11 to the user, who is expected to enter a cell reference, select a color scheme, and click OK. Clicking OK runs the second macro `ColorBarChart` from this listing.

LISTING 17.2

```
0    Sub StartBarApplication()
1        UserForm1.Show
2    End Sub
3
4    Sub ColorBarChart()
5        ' create a bar chart
6        Charts.Add
7        With ActiveChart
8            .ChartType = xlBarClustered
9                'set data to be plotted
10           On Error GoTo EndOfMacro
11           .SetSourceData Source:=Sheets("Sheet1") _
                 .Range(UserForm1.MaskEdBox1.Text)
12           .Location Where:=xlLocationAsNewSheet
```

```
13                  'Y-axis settings
14              .HasAxis(xlCategory, xlPrimary) = False
15              With .Axes(xlCategory)
16                  .HasMajorGridlines = True
17                  .HasMinorGridlines = False
18              End With
19                  'X-axis settings
20              With .Axes(xlValue)
21                  .HasMajorGridlines = False
22                  .HasMinorGridlines = False
23                  .TickLabels.Font.Size = 16
24                  .TickLabels.Font.Bold = True
25              End With
26                  'Data labels settings
27              .ApplyDataLabels Type:=xlDataLabelsShowLabel
28              .SizeWithWindow = True
29              .SeriesCollection(1).DataLabels.Font.Size = 14
30                  'Data bars settings
31              If UserForm1.chkRed Then RedComponent = 1
32              If UserForm1.chkGreen Then GreenComponent = 1
33              If UserForm1.chkBlue Then BlueComponent = 1
34              With .SeriesCollection(1)
35                  For Counter = 1 To .Points.Count
36                      ActiveWorkbook.Colors(Counter) = _
                        RGB(RedComponent * (100 + Counter * 150 _
                                            / .Points.Count), _
                            GreenComponent * (100 + Counter * 150 _
                                            / .Points.Count), _
                            BlueComponent * (100 + Counter * 150 _
                                            / .Points.Count))
37                  Next
38                  'two colors for gradient fill
39                  ActiveWorkbook.Colors(49) = RGB(_
                        150 + RedComponent * 50,_
                        150 + GreenComponent * 50,_
                        150 + BlueComponent * 50)
40                  ActiveWorkbook.Colors(50) = RGB(_
                        150 + RedComponent * 250,_
                        150 + GreenComponent * 250,_
                        150 + BlueComponent * 250)
41                  For Counter = .Points.Count To 1 Step -1
42                      .Points(Counter).Interior.ColorIndex = Counter
43                  Next
```

```
44              End With
45                  'Plot area settings
46              With .PlotArea.Fill
47                  .TwoColorGradient Style:=msoGradientHorizontal, _
                    Variant:=1
48                  .ForeColor.SchemeColor = 50
49                  .BackColor.SchemeColor = 49
50              End With
51                  'Title settings
52              .HasTitle = True
53              .ChartTitle.Characters.Text = "Sales 1999"
54              .ChartTitle.Font.Size = 16
55              .ChartArea.Deselect
56          End With
57          GoTo PassedEndOfMacro
58          EndOfMacro: MsgBox _
            "You need to enter the cells to be charted (eg A1:B4)!"
59          PassedEndOfMacro:
60      End Sub
```

ANALYSIS

Line 0 declares the `StartBarApplication` macro, which is the startup macro for the application.

Line 1 displays the `UserForm1` shown in Figure 17.11.

Line 4 declares the `ColorBarChart` macro that's called when the OK command button is clicked.

Lines 5 through 9 are the same as Lines 1 through 5 in Listing 17.1.

Line 10 uses the `On Error` statement to jump to the `EndOfMacro` label if any of the following statements are wrong. The type of action that causes an error here is the user entering an invalid cell reference or not entering anything in the Masked Edit box.

Line 11 uses the `SetSourceData` method with its `Source` argument set to the range of data assigned to the `Text` property of the `Masked Edit` control. Notice how the `Text` property needs to be fully qualified, with both its control and its container specified before the value can be returned from the `Masked Edit` control.

Lines 12 through 30 are the same as Lines 7 through 25 in Listing 17.1.

Lines 31 through 33 set the red, green, and blue components according to whether or not the associated check boxes have been checked.

Line 34 is the same as Line 26 in Listing 17.1.

Lines 35 through 37 compose a single-statement For loop that sets up the colors to be used for the bars. Line 35 uses the Count property of the Points collection to provide the maximum value for the Counter variable. The Count property is assigned the number of points (or bars) required to represent the data items selected. Line 36 calls the RGB function (see the section "Visual Basic's RGB Function" in Chapter 7) to reset the values controlling the colors in the active workbook's color palette, which you can view in the Color tab of the Options dialog box (Tools ➤ Options).

Lines 38 through 40 set the two colors in the active workbook's color palette that will be used for the two-color gradient fill for the chart's background.

Lines 41 through 43 compose a single-statement For loop that allocates the colors set in the active workbook's color palette to the ColorIndex of the Interior property of each Point object (Bar) in the Points collection. Notice how the For loop's step size is negative and Counter starts at its maximum value and is decremented until it reaches one. This For loop replaces Lines 27 through 31 in Listing 17.1 and is more general, as it can cope with any number of bars instead of being limited to five as Listing 17.1 is.

Lines 45 through 56 are the same as Lines 33 through 44 in Listing 17.1, but with different SchemeColor settings.

Line 57 uses the GoTo statement to skip Line 58, which is executed only if there is an error with the cell reference entered, and to jump to the label PassedEndOfMacro in Line 59.

Line 58 contains the EndOfMacro label that will be executed only in the event of an error occurring at Line 10. The error message is very general. You could reset the Mask property of the Masked Edit control to force the input characters to be within a set range, thus ensuring that they are compatible with the mask string. Chapter 5 describes this control in more detail.

Line 59 contains the PassedEndOfMacro label.

Coding the Event Procedures for the Color Scheme for Bars Application

Now that you've developed the GUI and you've entered the two macros (Listing 17.2) that perform the bulk of the work, you're ready to code the event procedures that will react to the command buttons being clicked. Open the code window for UserForm1 and enter the two single lines of code for both skeleton event procedures shown in Listing 17.3.

LISTING 17.3

```
Private Sub CommandButton1_Click()
    ColorBarChart
End Sub

Private Sub CommandButton2_Click()
    Unload Me
End Sub
```

ANALYSIS

Clicking the OK button runs the Click event procedure for Command-Button1 that calls the ColorBarChart macro.

Clicking the Exit button runs the Click event procedure for Command-Button2 that calls the Unload Me function to stop the macro running.

The Color Scheme for Bars application can be launched by clicking the Run Macro button from the Visual Basic toolbar and selecting StartBarApplication from the Macro Name list in the Macro dialog box.

Sizing a Web Page Using Microsoft FrontPage 2000

A workbook or chart sheet saved as a Web page is automatically sized to take up the whole area of the page and can't be adjusted in Excel. Normally, the chart representation of the data is accompanied by a textual description alongside—so it's absolutely essential that you can resize and position the chart to achieve the layout you want for your Web page.

The following steps show you how to create a Web page using Microsoft Front-Page 2000 and how to position an Excel chart on the page:

1. Run Microsoft FrontPage and choose File ➤ New ➤ Web (as shown below) to display the New dialog box shown in Figure 17.12.

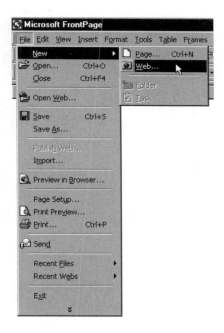

2. Choose the One Page Web option and enter the path name for the folder that is to contain all the files associated with your new Web page, then click OK to return to FrontPage. If you included an existing folder in the path name, your newly created blank Web page will be displayed, with the path name in the title bar (Figure 17.13). If you entered a new folder, the Create New Web dialog box (shown below) will be displayed with an animated arrow while your new Web page is being created.

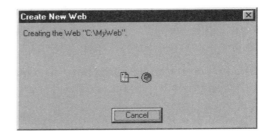

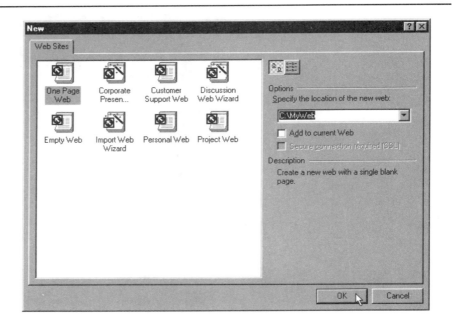

3. While still running FrontPage, open Excel and select the chart sheet you want to insert into your Web page. Choose File ➤ Save As Web Page (Excel) to open the Save As dialog box (Figure 17.14). Choose the folder you specified in step 2 and check the Selection: Chart option button; the filename will automatically change to the default page name `Page.htm`. Click Save to return to your chart.

4. Return to FrontPage, select the top folder from the Folder list, and choose View ➤ Refresh to display the file containing your page. Double-click the `Page.htm` file in the Folder list to display the chart in the Normal tab of the

Page panel. Because you haven't saved your chart as an interactive Web page, it should have the same appearance as it did in Excel (Figure 17.2). To see the HTML document for your chart sheet, select the HTML tab (Figure 17.15).

FIGURE 17.13:

Developing a Web page using Microsoft FrontPage 2000

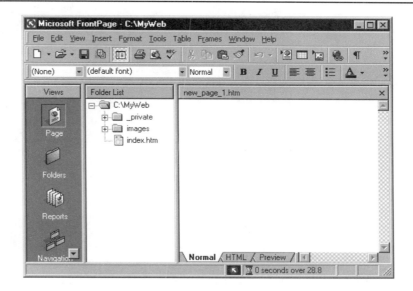

FIGURE 17.14:

Save As dialog box for saving a Web page

FIGURE 17.15:

HTML tab from Microsoft FrontPage

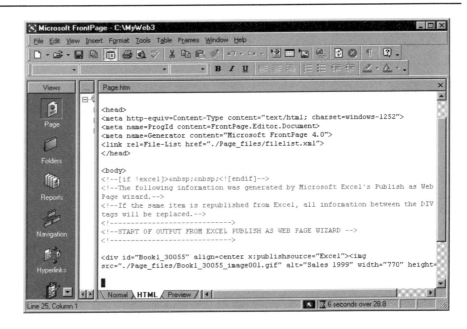

5. Resize your chart by dragging the sizing handles, as shown in Figure 17.16.

FIGURE 17.16:

Chart resized in the Front-Page window

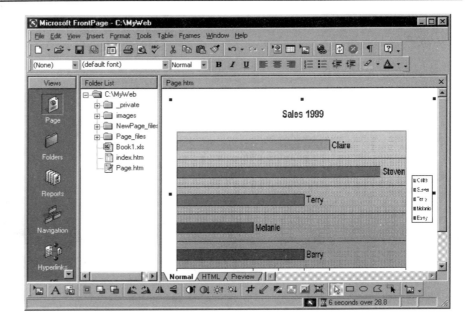

Summary

When you've finished this chapter, you'll be able to

- publish a chart as a Web page
- publish a chart as part of a Web page
- resize and reposition a chart saved in an HTML-format file using Microsoft FrontPage
- code a macro to format a chart for the Web
- change the color palette using a macro

PART VI

Automating Blueprints and Scenarios

Templates for Blueprint Workbooks

Templates are blueprints for reproducing workbooks and worksheets with identical formats, headings, and labels. Templates allow you to create new workbooks or new worksheets electronically, just like going to the stationery cabinet for a new ledger book or a fresh ledger sheet in years gone by. Imagine if all you had to do was open up a new workbook and start entering the data! This chapter will show you how to do exactly that.

What Are Templates?

Templates automate the task of reproducing a workbook, saving you time and ensuring that everything is set up exactly the way you want it. You've probably already realized that you use a template every time you run Microsoft Excel. A template is used as the blueprint for new workbooks. Your original template (Book.xlt) will be based on the default settings that are assigned values when you install Excel. With this template, all new workbooks you create will contain three blank worksheets, have no labels, and have gridlines displayed. If your workbooks need to have a different format, you can create your own templates to help you automate whatever is required.

A template is created just like an ordinary workbook, but its sole purpose is to act as a blueprint for the creation of other workbooks or worksheets. The template will contain all the characteristics of the workbook that you want duplicated, such as row and column labels and headings with any color schemes you've developed. You normally wouldn't include any data items unless they are the same from workbook to workbook. Templates can be set up to reproduce a single worksheet or a whole workbook containing a complete set of worksheets all formatted as required.

Templates for Saving Time

It's easy to fall into the trap of spending more time manually setting up workbooks than you spend actually entering new data. If you find yourself fumbling your way through workbooks you only use once in a while, or copying a worksheet and deleting the old data to make way for the new—then it's time you thought seriously about automation. Templates are becoming even more important as the pressure increases to present worksheets that have a pleasant visual appearance as well as correct data.

In Chapter 7, you saw how to bundle a collection of formats into a single style. Templates work at a higher level than styles; as mentioned above, they are used to automate the creation of whole workbooks and worksheets, not just selected elements, to save you even more time. Templates can contain styles too!

Settings Saved in a Template

The settings that Excel saves in a template determine how workbooks and worksheets based on that template are reproduced. The types of settings include

- formatting and styles
- text for headings and labels
- macros and worksheet formulas
- graphical items such as company logos
- colors and patterns set for borders and filling cells
- custom command bars
- hyperlinks
- protected and hidden areas for security purposes

Workbook Template Types

Excel has three types of templates that are used for reproducing workbooks and worksheets:

- autotemplates for workbooks with default settings
- autotemplates for worksheets with default settings
- custom templates for workbooks with custom settings

A template starts out just like an ordinary workbook or worksheet. The type of template it becomes will be determined by the name that's assigned to it combined with the name and location of the folder where it's saved.

Autotemplates

An *autotemplate* is an ordinary template that has the super status of being the default template for each new workbook or worksheet you create if you don't specify that another template be used.

To make a template into an autotemplate, you simply give it a special name and save it in a special folder known as the *startup* folder. Excel comes with one autotemplate for workbooks and one for worksheets; the templates with this super status are Book.xlt for workbooks and Sheet.xlt for worksheets.

When you open Excel, the Book.xlt template is used to create a new workbook. When you choose File ➤ New, the New dialog box is displayed with the Workbook icon preselected, but there's actually no template named "Workbook"—selecting the Workbook icon uses the settings in the Book.xlt autotemplate. When you choose Insert ➤ Worksheet, the Sheet.xlt template is used to create a new worksheet; Excel adds it to the active workbook immediately in front of the currently active worksheet and then makes the new sheet the active worksheet.

Custom Templates

Not all templates have the special autotemplate status. Those that don't are called *custom* templates. You can create as many custom templates as you want and use them for reproducing the occasional workbook. Custom templates for workbooks are saved as follows:

1. Create a workbook containing everything you want reproduced, then choose File ➤ Save As to open the Save As dialog box. Select Template from the drop-down list in the Save As Type box, as shown in Figure 18.1. This will automatically display the folder containing templates in the Save In box at the top.

2. Enter a name for your template into the File Name box. You can't name it Book1, as that has special significance in Excel—you'll find out why in the next section. I've named mine AnnualSales. Choose names that are easy to remember, since the Templates folder will probably end up containing a library full of useful templates.

3. Click Save to save all of your workbook's attributes in the specified file and to return to your workbook. The saved file will automatically have an .XLT extension.

FIGURE 18.1:

Saving a workbook as a template

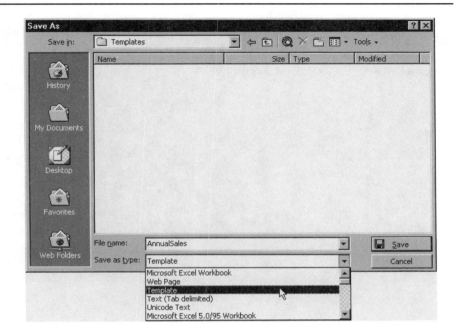

Creating Your Own Template Folder

You can collect all of your templates together in a separate folder and designate it as the alternate startup folder. When you choose File ➤ New to create a new work-book, Excel displays the icons for templates in this folder alongside icons for the templates stored in the official startup folder in the New dialog box. The following steps show how to designate a folder as the alternative startup folder:

1. Choose Tools ➤ Options and select the General tab in the Options dialog box.

2. Enter the full path name for your templates folder into the Alternate Startup File Location box (Figure 18.2).

FIGURE 18.2:

Entering the name of the folder containing your collection of templates

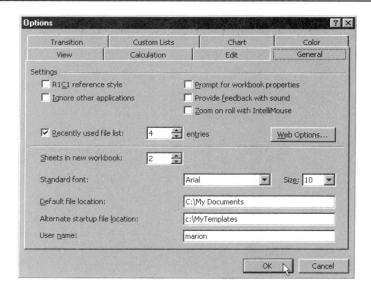

3. Because this adjustment is made at the application level, you'll have to close Excel and reopen it again before the templates in the Alternate Startup File will become available.

4. Choose File ➤ New. Icons for templates in the folder entered at step 2 will now be displayed alongside the icon for the default Workbook template (Figure 18.3).

You can create your own tab containing all of your customized templates in the New dialog box by creating a subdirectory in `Windows\Application Data\Microsoft\Templates` and then placing your templates into that directory. Figure 18.4 shows the template that I've placed in the `MyTemplates` folder in that directory.

FIGURE 18.3:

The New dialog box displaying the new Annual-Sales template

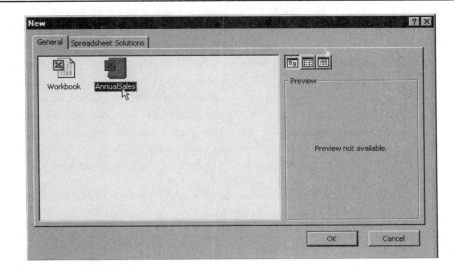

FIGURE 18.4:

The MyTemplates tab containing my customized template

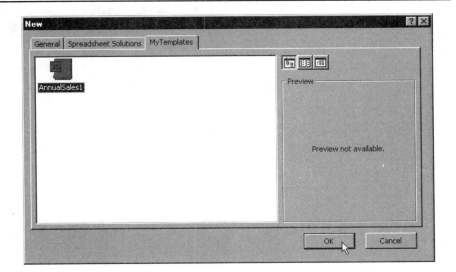

Creating a Workbook Template

Let's create a new workbook and spend time entering labels, formulas, and formats. Then I'll show you how to code a macro that fills the cells with different colors. Finally, I'll show you how to store all this information in a template so that you can later use it as a blueprint for reproducing as many of the same workbooks as you need. Figure 18.5 shows the finished template that we're going to develop, but it looks much jazzier in color with shades of green along the top, slowly blending into shades of pink at the bottom. This color scheme would be virtually impossible to set up manually without using a VBA macro.

1. Open a new workbook and enter the title and the row and column labels shown in Figure 18.5.

FIGURE 18.5:

The AnnualSales template that will be used for reproducing the final sales figures at the end of every year

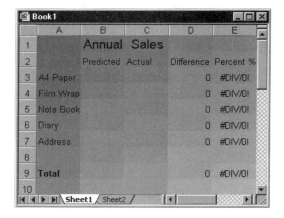

2. Enter the formula =**C3-B3** into cell D3 and drag-copy it down to D9, then delete the formula from D8 since it's not required there.

3. Enter the formula =**D3/B3**% into cell E3 and drag-copy it down to E9, then delete the formula from E8.

4. Open the Visual Basic Editor and choose Insert ➤ Module. Enter the code shown in Listing 18.1.

LISTING 18.1

```
0    Sub ColorAnnualSalesCells()
1        ' colors the cells containing annual sales figures
2        For ColumnNumber = Asc("A") To Asc("E")
3            For Counter = 1 To 10
4                Temp = ColumnNumber - Asc("A")
5                ActiveWorkbook.Colors(Counter + Temp * 10) = _
                 RGB(100 + 10 * Counter + Temp * 10, _
                 150 + Temp * 10, 100 + 10 * Counter + Temp *
                 10)
6                Range(Chr(ColumnNumber) & Counter).Interior_
                 .ColorIndex = Counter + Temp * 10
7            Next
8        Next
9    End Sub
```

ANALYSIS

Line 2 is the start of the outer For loop that sets the `ColumnNumber` variable to the values in the range of 65 to 69 to represent columns A through E.

Line 3 is the start of the inner For loop that sets the `Counter` variable to the values in the range of 1 through 10 to represent the first ten rows in the worksheet.

Line 4 assigns the `Temp` variable a number denoting the column, with A being 1, B being 2, etc.

Line 5 sets the first 50 colors in the `ActiveWorkbook` to the colors required, which are specified using the RGB function. The red and blue components have 100 added and the green has 150 added to create pastel shades of color. Figure 18.6 shows the color palette created by the macro.

Line 6, the string representing the cell reference for the `Range` property, is constructed from the `ColumnNumber` concatenated (joined sequentially) to the `Counter` value. The `Interior` property of the `Range` object returned is then assigned the index number constructed from the `Counter` (row number) value and the `Temp` (column number) value multiplied by 10.

FIGURE 18.6:
Color palette updated by the macro

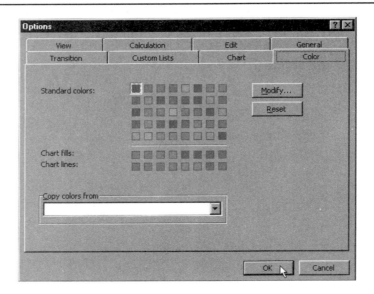

TIP   If you have several worksheets that you always create as a set, such as forms for ordering, delivery, and invoicing, place them in the same workbook template.

RGB Function

The RGB function has three arguments to allow you to specify the relative intensities of red, green, and blue that you want to add to the color being created. Intensities are in the range 0–255, with RGB(255,0,0) displayed as red, RGB(0,255,0) displayed as green, and RGB(0,0,255) displayed as blue. When the red, green, and blue intensities are all zero, black is displayed; when all three intensities are 255, white is displayed. To create pastel colors all intensities must be reasonably high. To create dark colors the intensities must be reasonably low, but you'll find that setting only one intensity to 80 results in a color that's hard to distinguish from black.

New Workbooks Based on Custom Templates

Now that we have developed the AnnualSales template, we can use it to produce a new workbook that has the same features. The following steps show you how.

1. Choose File ➣ New to display the New dialog box shown in Figure 18.3.

2. Select the AnnualSales icon and click OK to return to Excel with the new workbook active.

3. This first workbook created is named `AnnualSales1`, which is the number "1" appended to the name of the template it was based on (Figure 18.7). The second workbook created will have a 2 appended, and so on, in the same way as the default workbooks you create are named `Book1`, `Book2`... after the `Book.xlt` template they were based on.

FIGURE 18.7:

The first workbook based on the AnnualSales template is automatically given the name `AnnualSales1`.

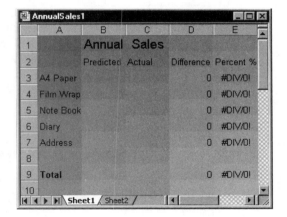

The new workbook will have all the formatting characteristics of the template and will include any macros, hyperlinks, and other items associated with the template.

Changing a Workbook Template

The following steps show you how to update the features contained in a template.

1. Choose File ➤ Open menu command and select your template from the Open dialog box. This loads the contents of the actual template file into memory.

2. Make the necessary updates and choose File ➤ Save to overwrite your template with the new information.

NOTE Because a template is used simply to create a workbook and isn't actually associated with the workbook, changing the template doesn't affect the existing workbooks that were created using that template.

New Templates from Old

This section shows you a safe way to create a new template based on an existing one without the danger of actually overwriting the original template.

1. Run Excel and choose File ➤ New to display the New dialog box.

2. Select the template you want as the basis for your new template. As usual, Excel will use this template to create a new workbook with the same attributes and assign it the same name as the template followed by a 1 (or the next number in the sequence). This new filename safeguards against your accidentally overwriting other files created from the same template file, as choosing File ➤ Save will save the new workbook in a file with the new name.

3. Update the features you want in your new template.

4. Choose File ➤ Save As, give your workbook a different name than that of the original template file, and save it as the Template type (Figure 18.1). You will now have two templates to choose from. The results will be the same as those achieved by following the steps in the previous section, "Changing a Workbook Template."

TIP You can make use of the number appended to the end of the template's name if you're trying out different versions—the number appended to the end acts as a sequential version number.

> **NOTE**   Because you can add new features and update old ones in a template without ever having to start from scratch, over time your template will evolve into one capable of creating visually outstanding and functionally complex workbooks.

Summary

After you've finished this chapter, you will know

- what a template is and how it can save you time
- how to create a new workbook template
- the difference between a custom template and an autotemplate
- how to save a workbook as a custom template and as an autotemplate
- how to update the active workbook's color palette in a macro using the RGB function
- how to update a workbook template by overwriting it or creating a second file

CHAPTER

NINETEEN

19

PivotTable and PivotChart Reports

PivotTable and PivotChart reports add interactive data analysis capability to your worksheets and charts that allows you to view subsets of the data in isolation. This chapter describes how to create PivotTable and PivotChart reports using a Wizard and how to view your data in the different ways available. You'll also see how to filter data in your worksheet lists.

What Is a PivotTable Report?

A PivotTable report provides a means of taking data from your worksheet and adding interactive features that allow you to analyze the data by viewing it in different ways. The PivotTable report can be used to

- select subsets of data that you want to analyze more closely or view in isolation

- filter data and place results on different pages

- summarize your data

- sort your data

- automatically provide totals for your data

Let's take a look at a simple example. Figure 19.1 shows the data items that we'll use as the basis for our PivotTable.

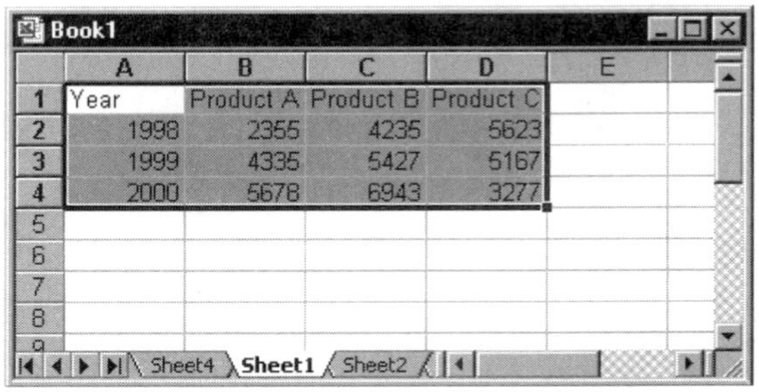

FIGURE 19.1:

Data items arranged in labeled columns suitable for building the PivotTable

Excel finds the fields in the range of cells that you specify and provides the Layout dialog box (shown in Figure 19.2) containing buttons for these fields.

FIGURE 19.2:

The Layout dialog box containing buttons for the fields Excel found in the range of cells shown in Figure 19.1

FIGURE 19.2:

The Layout dialog box containing buttons for the fields Excel found in the range of cells shown in Figure 19.1

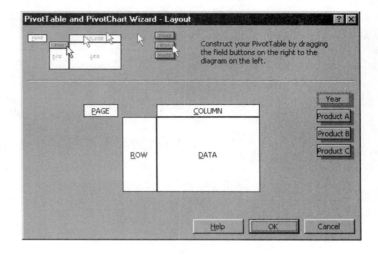

The field buttons can be dragged onto different areas of the PivotTable to create the table required (Figure 19.3).

FIGURE 19.3:

Drag and drop the field buttons to create the PivotTable required

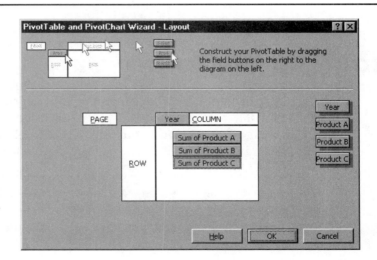

Figure 19.4 shows the PivotTable created from the data items shown in Figure 19.1 and the layout shown in Figure 19.3. The Grand Total has been calculated automatically for you; you'll see later how you can switch this option off if you don't want the automatic total.

FIGURE 19.4:

PivotTable created from the
layout shown in Figure 19.3

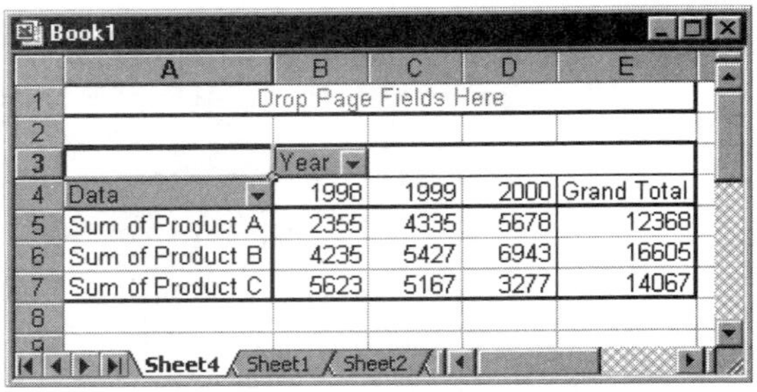

As you can see, the PivotTable itself consists of fields (one per column) that can be arranged in various layouts to allow you to view items of data in different ways. PivotTable reports can be generated from one or more Microsoft Excel lists, from another PivotTable report, or from several other applications, including Microsoft Access, dBase, FoxPro, and Oracle.

NOTE   A worksheet can contain as many PivotTables as you require.

Setting Up the Source Data

The source data for a PivotTable report must be organized as a list with every row containing the same categories of information listed in the same order. The first row in the list must contain column labels that Excel can use to create the Pivot-Table fields and to identify individual data items whenever required.

Avoid having more than one list in the same worksheet, as this can confuse Excel when it's filtering, sorting, or inserting totals. Make sure the list is separated from other data in the worksheet by blank rows and columns, but avoid using these in the list itself. If you need to separate the row or column labels from the data, set a distinctive border in between them rather than leaving a row or column blank or filling a row with underscore characters.

For example, in the Excel list in Figure 19.5, every cell in column B contains the name of a student and every cell in column G contains a mark (grade) for Physics.

FIGURE 19.5:

Data to be used in the
PivotTable report

	A	B	C	D	E	F	G	H	I	J	K
1					Examination Marks						
2	Year	Student	Study Group	Tutor	Eng	Math	Phys	Chem	Geo	Hist	Average
3	97	James	A	David	78	85	75	68	77	75	76.3
4	99	Peter	A	Suzanne	67	70	62	58	66	68	65.2
5	98	Mary	A	Mark	65	78	64	57	64	69	66.2
6	97	John	B	Marie	87	92	90	78	86	89	87.0
7	98	Louise	B	David	68	74	62	59	63	67	65.5
8	97	Matilda	C	Mark	98	89	91	89	89	93	91.5
9	98	Scott	C	Suzanne	76	83	74	67	74	70	74.0
10	99	Anne	B	Marie	56	51	49	48	60	58	53.7
11	98	Colin	D	Suzanne	78	74	74	67	79	80	75.3
12	97	Steven	D	David	95	92	91	87	95	92	92.0
13	98	Alan	E	Mark	68	73	72	57	69	69	68.0
14	98	Janet	F	David	37	67	29	27	40	40	40.0
15	98	Rita	G	Marie	82	95	73	73	83	60	77.7
16	99	Elizabeth	C	Suzanne	64	63	57	56	67	67	62.3
17	99	Joan	D	Marie	68	70	63	51	69	68	64.8
18	99	Jeffrey	E	Mark	74	72	78	63	80	78	74.2
19	99	Barry	F	David	74	68	71	61	78	77	71.5
20	97	Thomas	E	Suzanne	79	77	72	64	70	80	73.7
21	98	Warren	F	Marie	73	69	69	68	71	78	71.3

Sheet1 Sheet2

Data Form Dialog Box

After creating the column labels for a list, you can display a complete row of data
fields in a Data Form dialog box. This provides a convenient way to update, add,
and delete data and to search for items in the list that meet some criteria. Select a cell
within the list and choose Data ➤ Form to open the dialog box shown in Figure 19.6.

You can move down the column row by row by clicking the Find Next button,
or jump ahead by using the scroll bar. The numbers "*n* of *n*" in the top-right corner of the box (above the New button) give the position of the row displayed with
respect to the rest of the list.

Fields and Items

Fields in PivotTable reports are automatically created from the column labels in
the list being analyzed. Items are the individual entries in the fields—they are the
data values copied from this list. A field is said to be a category of data and an
item is said to be a subcategory. Considering the list shown in Figure 19.5, Year is
a field and 98 is an item.

FIGURE 19.6:

Data Form dialog box
for the list shown in
Figure 19.5

Although fields are based on columns, they can be placed in either rows or columns in the PivotTable report. Figure 19.7 shows the PivotTable report containing the average marks for each tutor's study groups over three years. Notice how the three fields are filled to distinguish them from items.

FIGURE 19.7:

PivotTable report showing
the average marks associ-
ated with the four tutors
over three years

	A	B	C	D	E
1					
2					
3	Sum of Average	Year			
4	Tutor	97	98	99	Grand Total
5	David	168	106	72	345
6	Marie	87	149	119	355
7	Mark	92	134	74	300
8	Suzanne	74	149	128	351
9	Grand Total	421	538	392	1350
10					

The row and column labels in a PivotTable report are the items assigned to fields. For example, in Figure 19.7 the column labels are 97, 98, and 99, which are the three different subcategories (items) assigned to the Year field. The rows are labeled David, Marie, Mark, and Suzanne, which are the four items assigned to the Tutor field.

Page Fields

Page fields allow you to split your PivotTable report over several pages so that you can isolate individual items. For example, Figure 19.7 shows the averages for all study groups for each tutor over three years. You could choose to view the average marks of students in Study Group B who had both David and Marie for tutors during different years by assigning the Study Group field button to the Page field, as shown in Figure 19.8.

FIGURE 19.8:

Study Group field assigned to the Page field to allow data to be viewed for each study group in separate pages

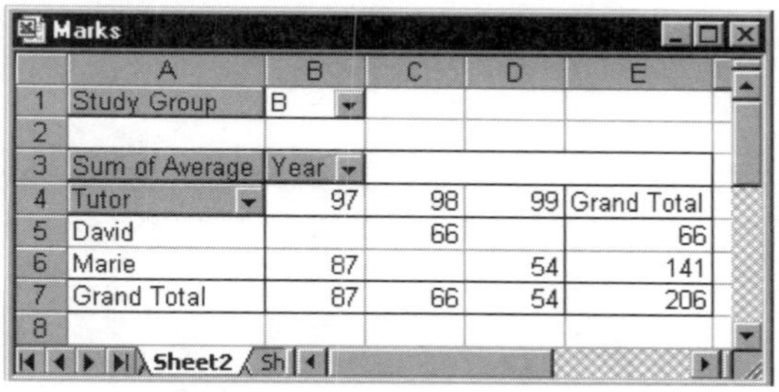

You can click the Down arrow and select one or all of the study groups from the drop-down list. I've selected Study Group B in the PivotTable report shown.

NOTE   Your PivotTable can contain as many row or column fields as you like, limited only by the number of fields (or columns) in the source list. Page and data fields, however, are limited to 256.

Creating a PivotTable Report Using the Wizard

Excel provides a PivotTable And PivotChart Wizard, which is a set of three dialog boxes that take you through the steps of building your report. The Wizard helps you to select the source data, choose between creating a PivotTable or a Pivot-Chart, decide where to place the results, and create the layout for the report. There are lots of options to choose from along the way, among them changing the PivotTable's name and layout and deciding whether or not to include totals.

We will use this Wizard to create a PivotTable report that gives us the average marks of the students in all study groups.

1. Create a new workbook and enter the data shown in Figure 19.5. You may want to add items to the worksheet list using Data Forms (see Figure 19.7) after initially entering the column labels.

2. Select any cell in the list and choose Data ➤ PivotTable And PivotChart Report (as shown) to display the first dialog box of the PivotTable And PivotChart Wizard, shown in Figure 19.9. You can also use the PivotTable toolbar to access this Wizard. The toolbar is described later in this chapter in the section "PivotTable Toolbar."

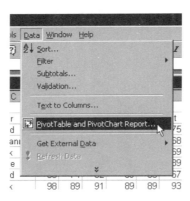

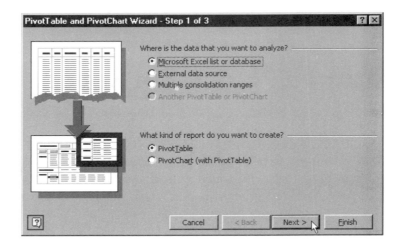

FIGURE 19.9:

First dialog box of the PivotTable And PivotChart Wizard

3. Ensure that the Microsoft Excel List Or Database and the PivotTable option buttons are selected. Click Next to display the second dialog box of the Pivot-Table And PivotChart Wizard, shown in Figure 19.10.

FIGURE 19.10:

Second dialog box of the PivotTable And PivotChart Wizard

4. Ensure that the range of cells containing your list appears in the Range box—Excel automatically calculates this range for you by propagating outward from the cell you selected at Step 2. Click Next to display the third dialog box, shown in Figure 19.11.

FIGURE 19.11:

Third dialog box of the PivotTable And PivotChart Wizard

5. Ensure that the New Worksheet option button is selected. Click Finish to return to your worksheet, which will now display a toolbar with field buttons and areas for you to drag and drop the buttons into (Figure 19.12).

6. Drag and drop field buttons as follows:

    *   the Study Group button to the Drop Row Fields Here area
    *   the Student button to the Drop Column Fields Here area
    *   the Year button to the Drop Page Fields Here area
    *   the Average button to the Drop Data Items Here area

The items of data will appear in the PivotTable as soon as you drop the button. If you're using a large data set, this may take a while depending on the speed of your PC. The next section describes a way around this.

FIGURE 19.12:

Empty PivotTable report awaiting field button positioning

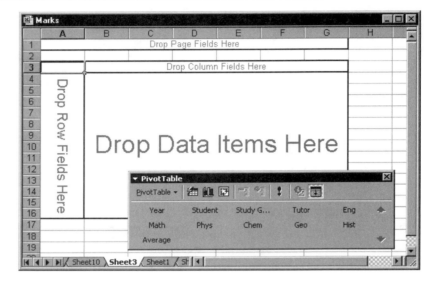

7. Select the table, click the Down arrow in the PivotTable button in the toolbar, and choose the Select ➢ Data command (Figure 19.13) to select the range of cells displaying the Average data. If you don't select the entire table, the Data menu command will not be available.

FIGURE 19.13:

Selecting the range of cells that contain data

8. Click the Down arrow in the PivotTable button again and choose Field Settings to open the PivotTable Field dialog box (shown).

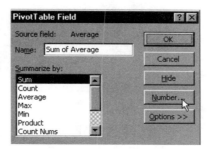

9. Click Number to open the Format Cells dialog box and view the Number tab, as shown in Figure 19.14.

FIGURE 19.14:

Number tab of the Format Cells dialog box

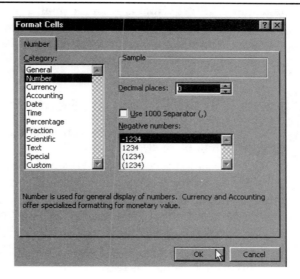

10. Select Number from the list in the Category box and enter **0** in the Decimal Places box. Click OK to return to the PivotTable Field dialog box, then click OK to return to your PivotTable report, which should now look like the one shown in Figure 19.15.

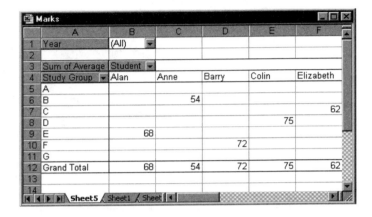

Placing field buttons in a PivotTable in your worksheet gives you the advantage that WYSIWYG and is great for small amounts of data, but for large data sets this can mean a long wait. The next section shows you how to switch over to the Wizard's layout feature, which merely drops the buttons in the Data Items area without maneuvering the data.

Using the Wizard's Layout Feature

The PivotTable And PivotChart Wizard has a layout feature that's quicker than placing field buttons directly onto a PivotTable on the worksheet when you have a large data set to move around. When you place a button directly into the Data Item area of your worksheet, all the data associated with that button has to be moved too. The Wizard is used to position only the buttons, not the data associated with those buttons. You can change over to the layout feature in the Wizard if your data is taking a while to appear after you place a field button in the Data Item area. The following steps show how to make this changeover and lay out your PivotTable using this feature:

1. Click the PivotTable Wizard button on the PivotTable toolbar to display the third dialog box of the Wizard (Figure 19.11). Click Layout to display the Pivot-Table And PivotChart Wizard - Layout dialog box, as shown in Figure 19.16.

2. Drag and drop the Year field button into the Row area and the Tutor field button into the Column area. Drag and drop the Math field button into the Data area and watch it automatically change to Sum Of Math (Figure 19.17).

FIGURE 19.16:

PivotTable And PivotChart
Wizard - Layout dialog box

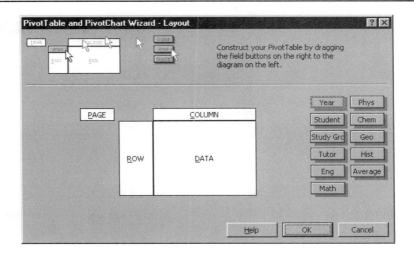

FIGURE 19.17:

Constructing the PivotTable
report layout by dragging
the field buttons derived
from the Marks list

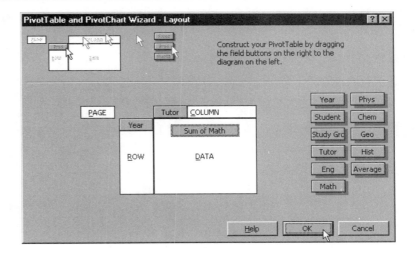

3. Click OK to return to the Wizard, and click Finish to return to your worksheet. Figure 19.18 shows the PivotTable, created with the Tutor and Year field buttons containing drop-down lists for you to use to set filters.

4. Drag and drop the Tutor field button to the same column as the Year field button; the report's layout will immediately change to accommodate the adjustment (Figure 19.19).

FIGURE 19.18:

PivotTable based on the Marks list

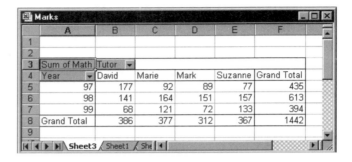

FIGURE 19.19:

New layout of PivotTable report as a result of dragging the Tutor field button over to the same column as the Year field button

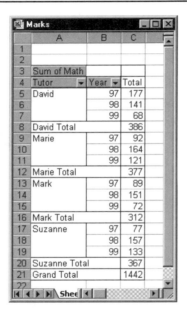

Creating a PivotTable Report in a Macro

Creating a PivotTable report in a macro is achieved using the `PivotTableWizard` method of the active worksheet. Although this does much the same thing as the PivotTable And PivotChart Wizard, it doesn't display any of the Wizard's dialog boxes. The macro shown in Listing 19.1 shows how this method is called in code.

Let's build an application that creates a PivotTable report based on the list containing the active cell. The application will prompt the user to include or exclude fields based on column labels from the list. Two macros are used, one for creating the PivotTable report and the other for prompting the user for the fields they want to include. The following steps show you how to build this application.

1. Open the workbook containing the examination marks shown in Figure 19.5 and make sure that Sheet1 is selected.

2. Open the Visual Basic Editor, choose Insert ➤ Module to open Module1's code window, and enter the code shown in Listing 19.1. Click the View Microsoft Excel button (first button in the toolbar) to return to Excel.

3. Select any cell in your list and click the Run Macro button from the Visual Basic toolbar to open the Macro dialog box. Choose CreatePivotTable and click Run.

4. The message box shown below will be displayed with the first field, Year, and the command buttons Yes and No.

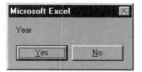

Click Yes to the Year, Student, and Math fields and No to the others. Watch as the field buttons appear in the PivotTable report, as shown in Figure 19.20.

FIGURE 19.20:

Field buttons added to the row fields of the PivotTable by the macro

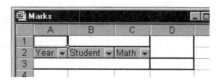

5. Drag and drop the Math field button to cell A1 to make it the source data field, and adjust the width of column A to fit the field buttons. Your PivotTable report will change as shown in Figure 19.21.

FIGURE 19.21:

PivotTable report using the
Math field as the data field

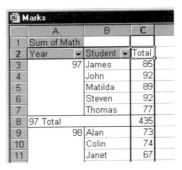

PivotTableWizard Method

The PivotTableWizard method has many arguments that are all optional. The ones you are likely to use are listed below, each with a brief description.

SourceType is the type of source data, which is specified using an Excel constant—for example, xlDatabase for an Excel list and xlPivotTable for another PivotTable report.

SourceData specifies where the source data is; this is typically a range of cells.

TableDestination indicates where the report is to be placed in the worksheet; the default is to place it at the active cell.

TableName is the name of the new report.

RowGrand must be set to True if grand totals are required for rows.

ColumnGrand must be set to True if grand totals are required for columns.

SaveData must be set to True if the data is to be saved with the report.

HasAutoFormat must be set to True if you want Excel to apply automatic formatting whenever fields are moved or refreshed.

OptimizeCache must be set to True to optimize the PivotTable cache when it's built. The cache contains all the potential layouts for the PivotTable so that they can be generated quickly whenever required.

LISTING 19.1

```
0    Sub CreatePivotTable()
1        'create a PivotTable report
2        ActiveSheet.PivotTableWizard TableName:="New Pivot Table"
3        ShowTheFieldNames
4    End Sub
5
6    Sub ShowTheFieldNames()
7        'show the field names for user to choose
8        With ActiveSheet.PivotTables("New Pivot Table")
9            For Index = 1 To .PivotFields.Count
10               Response = MsgBox(.PivotFields(Index).Name, _
                 vbYesNo)
11               If Response = vbYes Then
12                   .AddFields _
                     RowFields:=.PivotFields(Index).Name, _
                     AddToTable:=True
13               End If
14           Next
15       End With
16   End Sub
```

ANALYSIS

Line 0 starts the CreatePivotTable macro.

Line 2 uses the PivotTableWizard method of the active worksheet to create a PivotTable object and assigns "New Pivot Table" to its TableName argument. This name will become the name for the new PivotTable report.

Line 3 calls the ShowTheFieldNames macro.

Line 6 starts the ShowTheFieldNames macro.

Line 8 uses the With statement so that properties of the PivotTable "New Pivot Table" can be used without qualifying them.

Line 9 begins the For loop that's used to loop around all the column labels from the worksheet list that Excel has identified as fields. The Count property of the PivotFields collection returns the number of PivotField objects in the collection.

Line 10 sets the variable `Response` to the value returned by the `MsgBox` function that is either the constant `vbYes`, which means "Add this field to my PivotTable," or `vbNo`, which means "Ignore this field."

The **Line 11** `If` statement tests whether `Response` is set to `vbYes`. If so, it continues with Line 12; otherwise it jumps to Line 14.

Line 12 uses the `AddFields` method of the `PivotTable` object to add the Name property of the current `PivotField` object identified by its position (`Index`) in the list of row fields. The `AddToTable` argument is set to `True` so that each field button is added to the table. Omitting this argument or setting it to `False` has the effect of overwriting the last field button with the new one—you'd always end up with only one field button in the Pivot-Chart after all the field buttons have been added.

Automatic Totaling Option

In the PivotTable reports you've seen so far, all of the subtotals and totals have automatically been included. Totaling is controlled by the values of check boxes in the PivotTable Options dialog box, which can be displayed by clicking the Options button in the third dialog box of the PivotTable And PivotChart Wizard (Figure 19.11).

Figure 19.22 shows the PivotTable Options dialog box with the various format options and data source options you can choose from.

The two top check boxes in this dialog box control whether or not totals are automatically calculated and included in the PivotTable report. The two bottom check boxes allow you to set how frequently to refresh your PivotTable data from the source data.

FIGURE 19.22:

PivotTable Options
dialog box

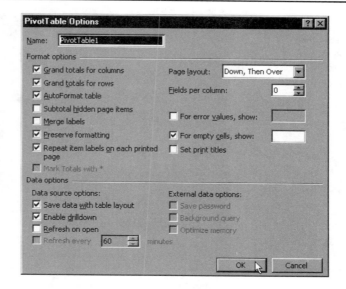

Creating a PivotChart Report Using the Wizard

Creating a PivotChart report using the Wizard is achieved much the same way as creating a PivotTable report, described in the last section. Let's create a Pivot-Chart based on the same list as our PivotTable.

1. Using the workbook containing the list shown in Figure 19.5 (created in the last section), select any cell in the list and choose Data ➤ PivotTable And PivotChart Report to display the first dialog box of the Wizard. Ensure that the Microsoft Excel List Or Database option button is selected from the top set of options and select the PivotChart (With PivotTable) option button from the bottom set. The image on the dialog box will change to the one shown in Figure 19.23.

2. Click Finish to return to your worksheet, which will display a toolbar with field buttons and the areas for you to drag and drop the buttons into. Choose View ➤ Sized With Window so that you can adjust the size of your Pivot-Chart (Figure 19.24).

FIGURE 19.23:

First dialog box of the Wizard when the PivotChart option box is selected

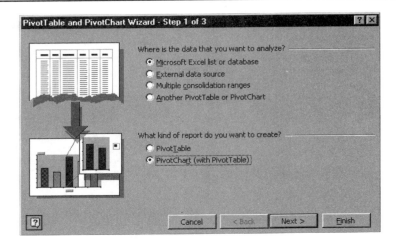

FIGURE 19.24:

PivotChart report showing areas to hold field buttons

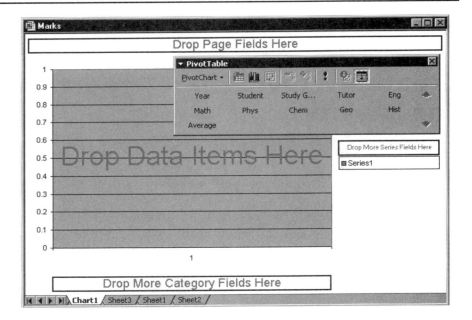

3. Drag and drop field buttons as follows:

   • the Year button to the Drop Page Fields Here area

- the Study Group button to the Drop More Category Fields Here area

- the Average button to the Drop Data Items Here area

- the Tutor button to the Drop More Series Fields Here area

This will display the PivotChart report shown in Figure 19.25, with field buttons containing drop-down lists for you to use to filter the data further.

FIGURE 19.25:

PivotChart report showing the study group averages for each tutor

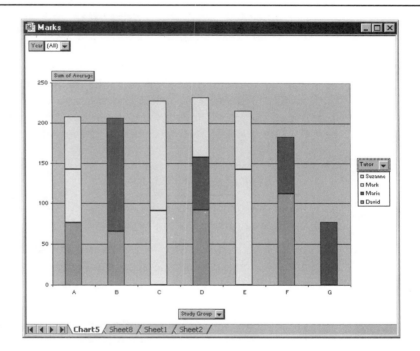

Creating a PivotChart Report in a Macro

Let's create an Excel application that uses a UserForm as its GUI to guide the user through creating a PivotChart report. The UserForm will prompt the user for the field names that they want to include in the report and will allow them to set the placement of the field buttons in the chart. Figure 19.26 shows the UserForm with four `Label` controls with their `Caption` properties set to the areas where the field buttons are placed in the PivotChart report.

FIGURE 19.26:

The GUI for the application that runs a macro to create PivotChart reports

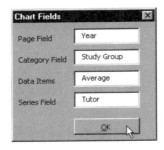

The four text boxes allow the user to enter column labels to specify the fields they want and where in the chart to put them. The command button at the bottom has its `Click` event procedure coded to create the PivotChart report to the user's specifications. The following steps show you how to create this application. For this example, we will duplicate the report shown in Figure 19.25.

1. Open the workbook containing the Marks data shown in Figure 19.5 and select a cell in the list.

2. Open the Visual Basic Editor, insert a Module (Insert ➤ Module), and enter the code shown in Listing 19.2.

3. Insert a UserForm (Insert ➤ UserForm) and add four labels, four text boxes, and a command button, as shown in Figure 19.26. Change the `Caption` properties of the `Label` controls, the command button, and the UserForm to those shown.

4. Double-click the command button to open the code window displaying the `CommandButton1_Click` event procedure and enter the code shown in Listing 19.3.

5. Click the View Microsoft Excel button to return to your worksheet from the Visual Basic Editor and click the Run Macro button in the Visual Basic toolbar. Select `CreatePivotChart` in the Macro dialog box and click Run. The PivotChart report shown in Figure 19.25 will be created.

LISTING 19.2

```
0   Sub CreatePivotChart()
1       ' create a PivotChart report
2       ActiveSheet.PivotTableWizard _
        TableName:="New PivotChart Report"
```

```
3        UserForm1.Show
4    End Sub
```

ANALYSIS

Line 0 starts the CreatePivotChart macro.

Line 2 uses the PivotTableWizard method to create a new PivotTable object for our PivotChart report. The string assigned to the TableName argument will become the new PivotChart report's name when it has been created.

Line 3 displays the UserForm that is the GUI for the application.

LISTING 19.3

```
0    Private Sub CommandButton1_Click()
1        Charts.Add
2        With ActiveChart.PivotLayout
3            .PivotFields(TextBox1.Text).Orientation =_
             xlPageField
4            .PivotFields(TextBox3.Text).Orientation =_
             xlDataField
5            .PivotFields(TextBox4.Text).Orientation =_
             xlColumnField
6            .PivotFields(TextBox2.Text).Orientation =_
             xlRowField
7        End With
8        UserForm1.Hide
9    End Sub
```

ANALYSIS

Line 0 is the start of the command button's Click event procedure.

Line 1 creates a Chart object and adds it to the Charts collection.

Line 2 starts the With statement, which uses the PivotLayout property to return the PivotLayout object that represents the placement of axes in the PivotChart report.

Lines 3 through 6 use the `PivotFields` collection of the `PivotLayout` object to set the fields in the PivotChart report to the fields entered by the user into the text boxes. Each statement sets a different field in the Pivot-Chart report. These fields are specified using the Excel constants `xlPage-Field`, `xlDataField`, `xlColumnField`, and `xlRowField`.

Line 8 hides the UserForm used for the GUI, leaving the user looking at the PivotChart report just created.

PivotTable Toolbar

The PivotTable toolbar (Figure 19.27) allows you to format your PivotTable report, or recall the PivotTable Wizard to make changes to your report. Among other options, you can refresh your source data, show or hide report details, and create a new chart without the drag-and-drop field buttons.

TIP   If the PivotTable toolbar is not on display, choose View ➤ Toolbars ➤ PivotTable to display it.

FIGURE 19.27:

PivotTable toolbar

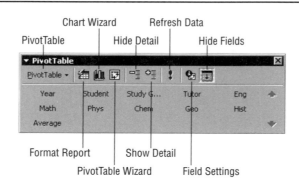

PivotTable has a drop-down list containing the other buttons in this tool-bar with a few additional commands. Figure 19.28 shows the list of commands available. I've shown the Select item expanded, as this is a quick way of highlighting the different areas in a PivotTable.

FIGURE 19.28:

Drop-down list for the
PivotTable button

Format Report displays the AutoFormat dialog box (shown in Figure 19.29),
which contains a list of the built-in formats for PivotTable reports.

FIGURE 19.29:

AutoFormat dialog box displaying built-in formatted
PivotTables

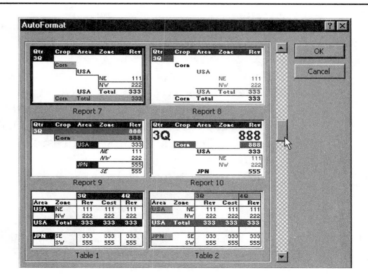

Chart Wizard creates a new chart sheet and generates a chart for the Pivot-
Table without the field buttons (Figure 19.30).

PivotTable Wizard starts the PivotTable And PivotChart Wizard at its
third dialog box, since the source list for the PivotTable has already been
established.

FIGURE 19.30:

Chart sheet containing a chart of the PivotTable report's data

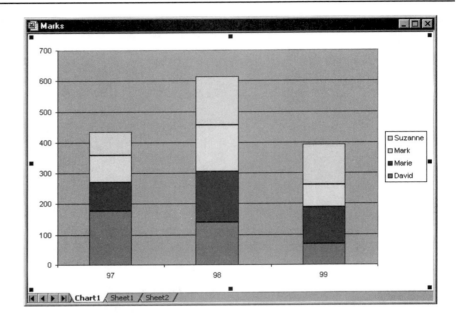

FIGURE 19.30:

Chart sheet containing a chart of the PivotTable report's data

Show Detail displays the Show Detail dialog box (shown below) and adds the field you select to the active PivotTable. Figure 19.31 shows the Pivot-Table before requesting the extra details and Figure 19.32 shows the result of selecting cell A5 before clicking Show Details from the toolbar and selecting Chem from the drop-down list of fields. This adds the Chem field button to the PivotTable, along with any data relating to Chem such as marks and the tutor called Mark.

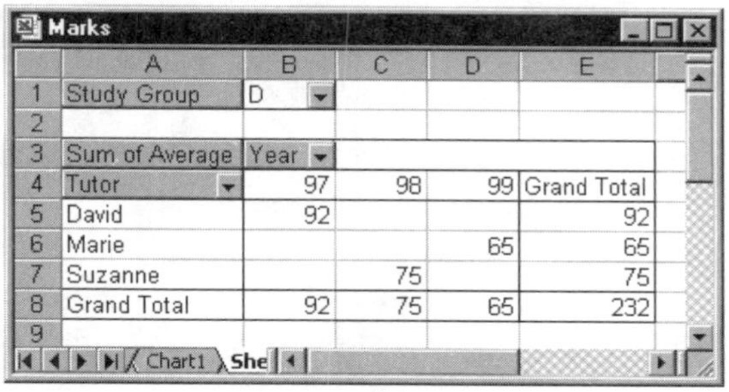

	A	B	C	D	E
1	Study Group	D			
2					
3	Sum of Average	Year			
4	Tutor	97	98	99	Grand Total
5	David	92			92
6	Marie			65	65
7	Suzanne		75		75
8	Grand Total	92	75	65	232
9					

FIGURE 19.31:

PivotTable before clicking the Show Detail button

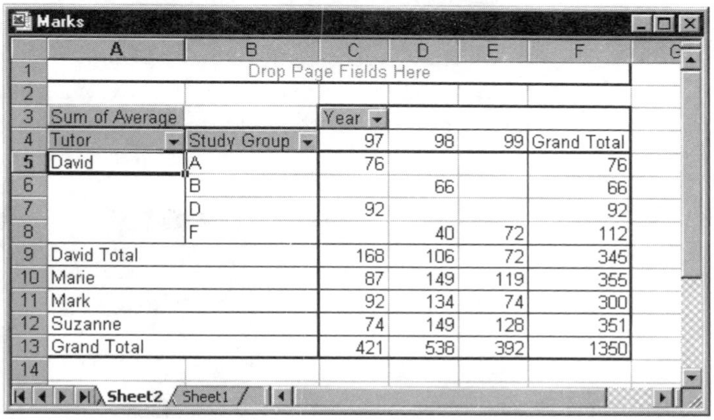

	A	B	C	D	E	F
1	Drop Page Fields Here					
2						
3	Sum of Average		Year			
4	Tutor	Study Group	97	98	99	Grand Total
5	David	A	76			76
6		B		66		66
7		D	92			92
8		F		40	72	112
9	David Total		168	106	72	345
10	Marie		87	149	119	355
11	Mark		92	134	74	300
12	Suzanne		74	149	128	351
13	Grand Total		421	538	392	1350
14						

FIGURE 19.32:

PivotTable after selecting cell A5 (David), clicking Show Detail, and selecting `Chem` from the list of fields

Hide Detail is used to hide the extra details that were added in your PivotTable when you clicked the Show Detail button. Before clicking the Hide Detail button, choose one of the field buttons that were selected before you clicked the Show Detail button. For example, select the cell containing the Chem field button shown in Figure 19.32 and click on Hide Detail; the extra detail will disappear, leaving behind the PivotTable shown in Figure 19.33.

Refresh Data refreshes the data in your PivotTable report from the source list. You can also have Excel do this automatically by choosing Tools ➢ Options to open the PivotTable Options dialog box and checking the Refresh On Open check box, by checking the Refresh Every check box and setting the minutes, or by checking both.

FIGURE 19.33:

PivotTable shown in Figure 19.32 after the extra details have been removed

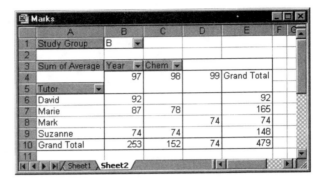

Field Settings displays the PivotTable Field dialog box for you to select formatting, sorting, and other options. If the selected cell contains a field button, the version shown in Figure 19.34 appears; if the selected cell contains data values, the version shown in Figure 19.35 appears.

FIGURE 19.34:

PivotTable Field dialog box for row and column fields

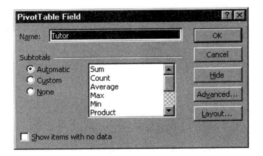

FIGURE 19.35:

PivotTable Field dialog box for the source field

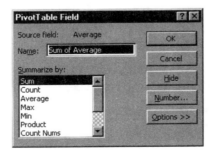

Clicking Options expands this dialog box to the one shown in Figure 19.36.

FIGURE 19.36:

PivotTable Field dialog box extended as a result of clicking Options

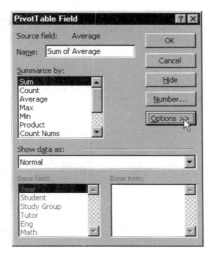

Hide Fields/Display Fields hides or displays the fields that are in the group below the line in the PivotTable toolbar. Figure 19.37 shows the list displayed and Figure 19.38 shows the result of the list being hidden.

FIGURE 19.37:

PivotTable toolbar with list of fields displayed

FIGURE 19.38:

PivotTable toolbar with list of fields hidden

Changing the Layout of a PivotTable

How fields and items are placed in a PivotTable is called the *layout*. This can easily be changed using the mouse. Let's update the layout of the PivotTable report shown in Figure 19.18 by changing the Sum Of Math button to a Sum Of Ave (Average) button and adding the Student field button beside the Tutor field button.

1. Click anywhere inside the PivotTable report to display the PivotTable toolbar (shown in Figure 19.27).

2. Drag and drop the Sum Of Math button anywhere outside the PivotTable report. You can easily see when it's outside the report, as the mouse cursor will change to an "X" (as shown). All of the items will disappear from the PivotTable report, as shown in Figure 19.39.

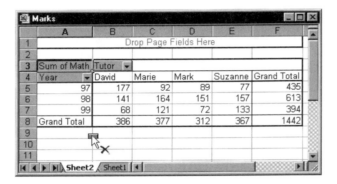

FIGURE 19.39:

PivotTable report without any items

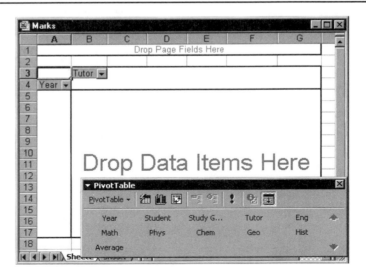

3. Drag and drop the Average field button from the toolbar to cell A3. The Pivot-Table report will now display numerical data.

4. Drag and drop the Student field button from the toolbar to cell C3 to provide a wide PivotTable report that gives information on all the students tutored by each tutor (Figure 19.40).

FIGURE 19.40:

PivotTable report containing information about all of the students tutored by each tutor

	A	B	C	D	E	F	G	H
1								
2								
3	Sum of Average	Student ▾	Tutor ▾					
4		Alan	Alan Total	Anne	Anne Total	Barry	Barry Total	Colin
5	Year ▾	Mark		Marie		David		Suzanne
6	97							
7	98	68	68					75.33333333
8	99			53.66666667	53.66666667	71.5	71.5	
9	Grand Total	68	68	53.66666667	53.66666667	71.5	71.5	75.33333333
10								
11								

Marks — Chart1 \ Sheet3 / Chart2 / Chart4

5. Click the Down arrow on the Tutor field button and uncheck all of the tutors except Marie, as shown. Click OK to return to the reduced Pivot-Table report, shown in Figure 19.41.

You can move a field button around in a PivotTable report by dragging it from its position at the head of a column to a row. Figure 19.42 shows the PivotTable report when the Tutor field button was moved from its column field position (Figure 19.41) to a row field position.

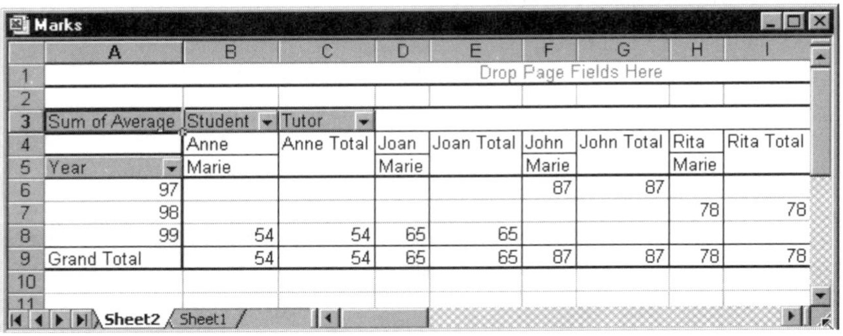

	A	B	C	D	E	F	G	H	I
1	Drop Page Fields Here								
2									
3	Sum of Average	Student	Tutor						
4		Anne	Anne Total	Joan	Joan Total	John	John Total	Rita	Rita Total
5	Year	Marie		Marie		Marie		Marie	
6	97					87	87		
7	98							78	78
8	99	54	54	65	65				
9	Grand Total	54	54	65	65	87	87	78	78

FIGURE 19.41:

PivotTable report displaying only the information associated with Marie

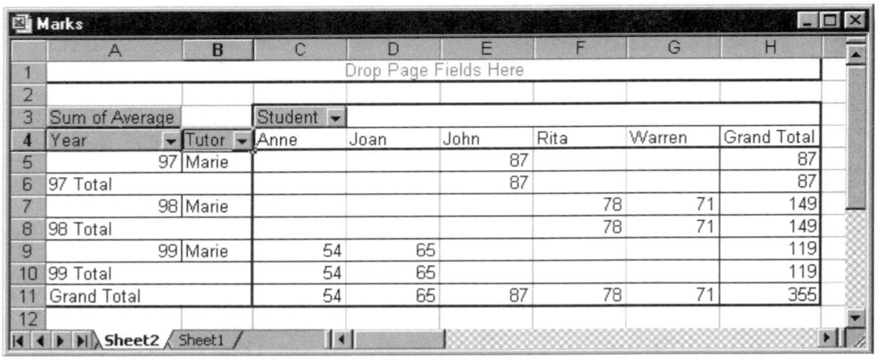

	A	B	C	D	E	F	G	H
1	Drop Page Fields Here							
2								
3	Sum of Average		Student					
4	Year	Tutor	Anne	Joan	John	Rita	Warren	Grand Total
5	97	Marie			87			87
6	97 Total				87			87
7	98	Marie				78	71	149
8	98 Total					78	71	149
9	99	Marie	54	65				119
10	99 Total		54	65				119
11	Grand Total		54	65	87	78	71	355

FIGURE 19.42:

The PivotTable created as a result of moving the Tutor field button from the column field position to the row field position

Filtering Data in a List

You can filter the data in a worksheet list without creating a PivotTable report using the AutoFilter feature available in Excel. The `AutoFilter` command is used with a worksheet list to place Down arrows at each column label, as shown in Figure 19.43.

Clicking a Down arrow lists all the items in the list without duplication and provides three other choices:

- **All** to cancel the filter set for that column

- **Top 10** to display the Top 10 AutoFilter dialog box with the highest or lowest values of items in that field or to change the number of items required

- **Custom** to apply your own criteria to the data items in the column

FIGURE 19.43:

Down arrows placed at
each column label by the
AutoFilter command

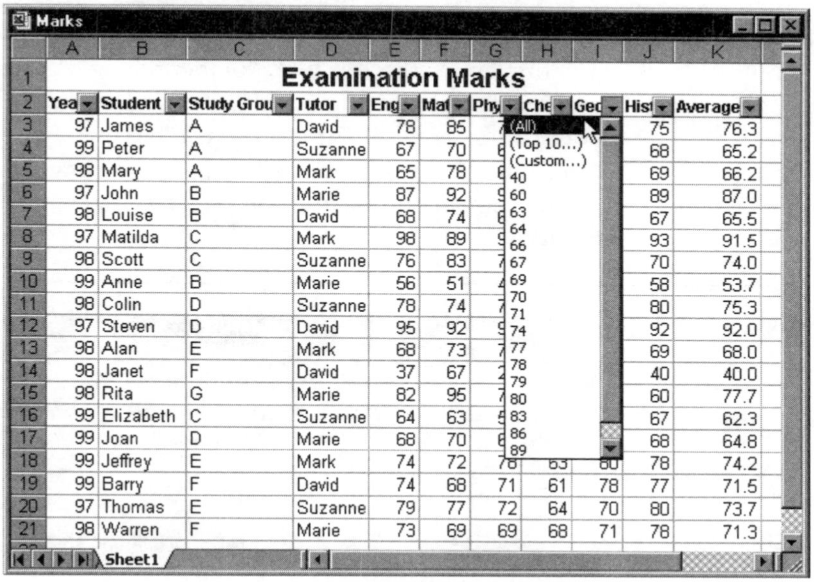

Year	Student	Study Group	Tutor	Eng	Mat	Phy	Che	Geo	Hist	Average
										Examination Marks
97	James	A	David	78	85	7	(All)		75	76.3
99	Peter	A	Suzanne	67	70	8	(Top 10...)		68	65.2
98	Mary	A	Mark	65	78	8	(Custom...) 40		69	66.2
97	John	B	Marie	87	92	9	60		89	87.0
98	Louise	B	David	68	74	8	63		67	65.5
97	Matilda	C	Mark	98	89	9	64 66		93	91.5
98	Scott	C	Suzanne	76	83	7	67		70	74.0
99	Anne	B	Marie	56	51	4	69		58	53.7
98	Colin	D	Suzanne	78	74	7	70 71		80	75.3
97	Steven	D	David	95	92	9	74		92	92.0
98	Alan	E	Mark	68	73	7	77		69	68.0
98	Janet	F	David	37	67	2	78 79		40	40.0
98	Rita	G	Marie	82	95	7	80		60	77.7
99	Elizabeth	C	Suzanne	64	63	5	83		67	62.3
99	Joan	D	Marie	68	70	6	86 89		68	64.8
99	Jeffrey	E	Mark	74	72	76	63	60	78	74.2
99	Barry	F	David	74	68	71	61	78	77	71.5
97	Thomas	E	Suzanne	79	77	72	64	70	80	73.7
98	Warren	F	Marie	73	69	69	68	71	78	71.3

Using the Top 10 Criteria

The Down arrows displayed when the AutoFilter mechanism is switched on are used to set criteria (or filters). Let's create a filter that hides everything except the four top-scoring students in geography:

1. Open the worksheet containing your list and select a cell in the list.

2. Choose Data ➤ Filter ➤ AutoFilter to display Down arrows beside the column labels in the first row of your list.

3. Click the Down arrow for Geo to see the list shown in Figure 19.43.

4. Select Top 10 from the list to display the Top 10 AutoFilter dialog box, shown below.

5. The first box in the Top 10 AutoFilter dialog box can be set to Top or Bottom; make sure that Top is selected. The middle box can be set to the number of your choice; enter **4**. The last box can be set to Items or Percent; select Items. Click OK to return to your worksheet, which will now contain only the information about the four top-scoring Geography students, as shown in Figure 19.44.

FIGURE 19.44:

Items meeting the criteria of being the four top-scoring geography students

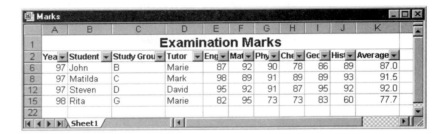

You can apply additional filters by repeating Steps 3 through 5 for other columns. Excel displays only those items that match all criteria, so every time you add a new filter the amount of data is likely to decrease. For example, if I continued with my example and added the filter for the top two English students, my list would be reduced to Matilda and Steven. If I changed that filter to the bottom two English students, the list would be empty.

Creating a Custom Filter

Excel gives you the freedom of creating your own filters using the Custom Auto-Filter dialog box. The following steps show you how this is done.

1. Click the Down arrow in the Geo field button and select Custom from the drop-down list to display the Custom AutoFilter dialog box, shown in Figure 19.45.

FIGURE 19.45:

Custom AutoFilter
dialog box

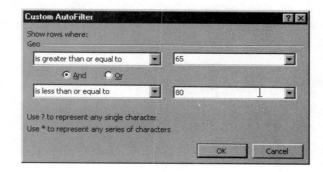

2. Choose Is Greater Than Or Equal To from the top-left drop-down list, and enter **65** into the top-right box. Ensure that the And option button is selected. Choose Is Less Than Or Equal To from the bottom-left drop-down list and enter **80** in the bottom-right box. Click OK to return to your list, which will now display the 11 items that meet the criteria.

Removing All AutoFilters from a List

If the Down arrows are displayed beside the column labels in your worksheet list, choosing Data ➤ Filter ➤ AutoFilter will toggle the AutoFilter feature off and the Down arrows will simply disappear.

Summary

By the end of this chapter, you'll be able to

- create worksheet lists for use as source data for PivotTable and PivotChart reports

- use data forms for entering data items into a list

- drag and drop field buttons into PivotTables and PivotCharts

- use the PivotTable And PivotChart Wizard to create reports

- create PivotTable and PivotChart reports from a macro

- control whether or not totals are included automatically
- control how frequently your PivotTable or PivotChart report is refreshed from the source data
- use the Wizard's layout feature
- change the layout in a PivotTable
- set criteria to filter data in your list

Data Tables and Goal Seek Features for "What-if" Analysis

This chapter looks at Excel's data table feature that allows you to see *what* the results would be *if* different values were used to calculate a formula. You'll see how to produce one-input and two-input data tables before going on to automating the whole shooting match with a macro that can do both.

It also describes the Goal Seek feature that tells you *what* value is required *if* you want to achieve a desired goal. You'll see how to use the Goal Seek feature with worksheet data and with charts, and how to develop an application that animates interactive changes to a bar chart.

Data Tables

The Excel data table feature creates a data table by taking a cell containing a formula with a cell reference to a cell that's been specified as an input box (the *input cell*) and by including a list of *input values,* which are placed in the input box one by one to produce a list of results. If you have one or more formulas and you would like to see *what* the results would be *if* one or two values used by each formula were to vary over a range of values—use a data table.

There are two varieties of data tables: the one-input data table, which allows you to change the value at one cell reference used by a formula, and the two-input data table, which allows you to change the values at two cell references.

Although you can achieve similar results by copying formulas, a data table offers additional security that the drag-and-drop operation cannot provide: values in cells belonging to a data table cannot be updated.

The One-Input Data Table

The one-input data table is used to calculate results that can be placed in a single column or row—for example, the amounts of interest paid for a set of different interest rates (input values).

A one-input data table is a table with a list of input values in the first row (or column) that are substituted for one particular value in a formula with the results given in the next row (or column). You can also see the what-if results for the same input values substituted into several different formulas, with each set of results listed in separate rows (or columns).

Structure of the One-Input Data Table

There are two structures that one-input data tables can be based on, one with the input values entered down a column of cells (Figure 20.1) and one with input values entered across a row of cells (Figure 20.2).

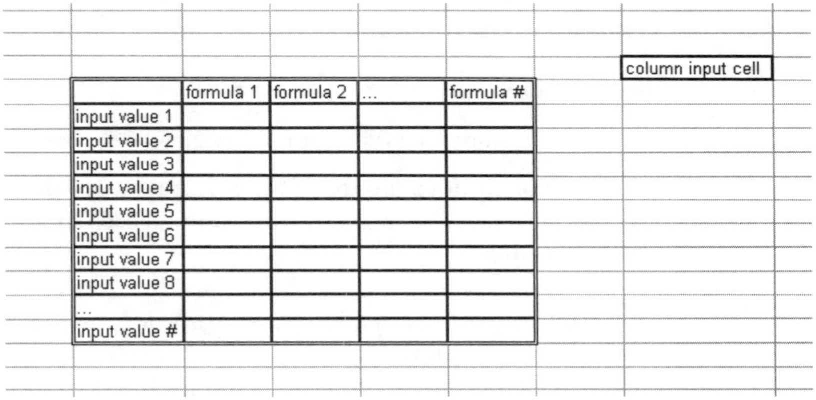

FIGURE 20.1:

Structure of a one-input data table with column input values

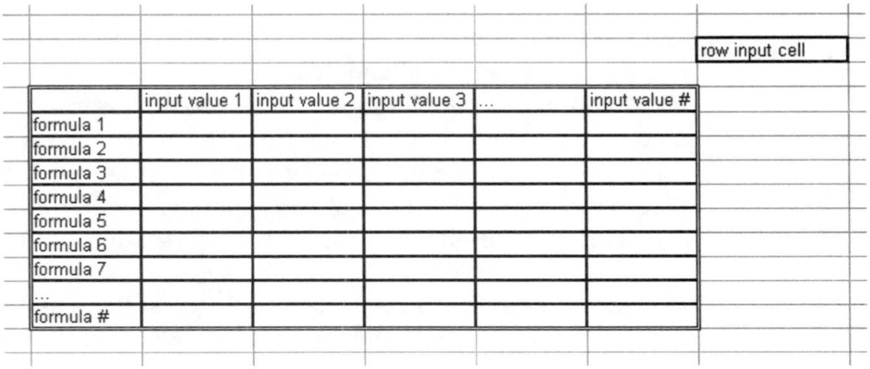

FIGURE 20.2:

Structure of a one-input data table with row input values

In both cases, the top-left cell in the row or column containing the list of input values is left free of input values—the first formula is entered into the next cell as the first entry in the row or column to be assigned the results. The formula should include a reference to the input cell; otherwise, all the results will end up the same. The cell that's designated the input cell can be located anywhere in the same worksheet.

Components of a One-Input Data Table

As you can see from Figure 20.1 and Figure 20.2, three components are required to build any one-input data table:

- an input cell

- one or more formulas containing a cell reference to the input cell

- a list of input values that Excel's data table feature will place one by one into the input cell, recalculating the formula each time and placing the result in the data table

The input values to be used in the substitution and the formula must be placed in adjacent cells, as shown. These are selected before calling on Excel to create the data table, which will then prompt you for the input cell.

Creating a One-Input Data Table

The following example creates a column-style one-input data table using only one formula. (We will extend this to two formulas later in the chapter, in the section "Adding Another Formula.") The table in this example shows the interest paid for a variety of interest rates (input values) which are entered in column A. The formula is placed in cell B5, with the input cell at B2. Notice here that I've designated an input cell that already contains a value, but this needn't be the case. Let's get started in our DataTables application.

1. Open a new workbook, name it **Interest Paid**, and enter the values shown in Figure 20.3 with the formula =A2*B2 at cell B5. Cells in the range A6:A11 contain the *input values* that will be substituted for the value in the *input cell* B2.

2.   Format the input cell and the cells containing the input values (A6:A11) as Percentage with two decimal places. This is done in the Number tab from the Options dialog box (Format ➤ Cells). Click on OK to return to the worksheet.

FIGURE 20.3:

Setting up a one-input data table

3.   Select the range A5:B11, which encompasses both the formula (B5) and the input cells (A6:A11). These are the values that will be substituted in the input cell (B2) referenced by the formula.

4.   Choose Data ➤ Table to display the Table dialog box shown in Figure 20.4.

FIGURE 20.4:

Table dialog box

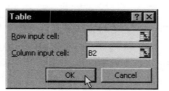

5.   Enter the input cell **B2** in the Column Input Cell box and click OK to return to your worksheet, which will now display the results of calculating the "what-if" values (Figure 20.5).

NOTE   When entering input values and formulas into a one-input data table, the top-left cell should be left blank.

FIGURE 20.5:

One-input data table
(Interest Paid) with
the results calculated

Input Values   Input Cell

Formula

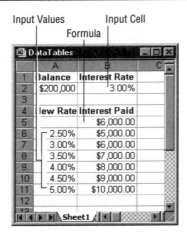

Creating a One-Input Data Table from a Macro

Let's create a Discount Ready Reckoner application that calls a macro to create the entire one-input data table. This macro calculates the bulk purchase discount, which is zero for buying one item, 2% for buying two, 4% for buying three, and so on until a maximum discount of 20% is reached for buying 11 or more items.

The OneInputTable macro for automatically creating this table is listed in Listing 20.1. The data table produced by this macro is shown in Figure 20.6. The macro uses the CalculateDiscount function listed in Listing 20.2 by calling it with the quantity (input values); this function calculates and returns the discount. For more information about functions, see the section "Creating Your Own Function" in Chapter 4.

FIGURE 20.6:

Discount Ready
Reckoner data table

LISTING 20.1

```
0   Sub OneInputTable()
1       'set the range where the table will be placed
2       Set DataTableCells = Worksheets("Sheet1").Range("A1:P2")
3
4       'set the row input cell
5       Set RowInputCell = Worksheets("Sheet1").Range("A12")
6
7       'assign the formula that calls the CalculateDiscount
8       'macro into cell A1
9       Worksheets("Sheet1").Range("A1").Formula = _
        "=CalculateDiscount(A12)"
10
11      'assign input values
12      For i = 2 To 16
13          Worksheets("Sheet1").Cells(1, i) = i - 1
14      Next i
15
16      'create the table
17      DataTableCells.Table RowInputCell
18
19      'format the cells containing the table
20      With Worksheets("Sheet1").Range("A1").CurrentRegion
21          .Columns.AutoFit
22          .Rows(1).Font.Bold = True
23          .Columns(1).Font.Bold = True
24          .Rows(1).Borders(xlEdgeBottom).Weight = xlMedium
25          .Columns(1).Borders(xlEdgeRight).Weight = xlMedium
26      End With
27  End Sub
```

ANALYSIS

Line 0 starts the OneInputTable macro.

Line 2 uses the Set statement to assign the Range object referencing A1:P2 to the variable DataTableCells.

Line 5 uses the Set statement to assign the Range objects containing A12 to the variable RowInputCell.

Line 9 assigns the formula `"=CalculateDiscount(A12)"` to A1. Notice how the formula contains a call to a macro (shown in Listing 20.2) developed in this application.

Lines 12 through 14 assign the input values to cells along the first row of `Sheet1`.

Line 17 uses the `Table` method of the `Range` object assigned to the variable `DataTableCells` with the arguments `RowInputCell`, which was set to A12 in Line 5.

Line 20 uses the `With` statement so that the properties assigned to the `CurrentRegion` in Lines 21 through 25 don't need to be fully qualified.

Line 21 adjusts the columns to fit the values created by the `Table` method in Line 17.

Line 22 and Line 23 make the font of the first row and column bold.

Line 24 sets the bottom-edge border of cells in the first row to medium width so that they appear as a dark horizontal line separating the row labels from the data values.

Line 25 sets the right-edge border of the first column to medium width so that it will appear as a dark vertical line separating the column labels from the data values.

LISTING 20.2

```
0   Function CalculateDiscount(Quantity)
1       'calculate discounts for purchasing two or more products _
        'rising in 2% steps up to a maximum of 20%
2       If Quantity > 10 Then
3           CalculateDiscount = 20
4       Else
5           If Quantity <= 1 Then
6               CalculateDiscount = 0
7           Else
8               CalculateDiscount = (Quantity - 1) * 2
9           End If
10      End If
11  End Function
```

Line 0 starts the function `CalculateDiscount`, which has one argument—`Quantity`.

Line 2 and Line 3 check whether the quantity is greater than 10; if so, the maximum discount of 20% is returned.

Line 4 starts the `Else` part, which will be executed only if the quantity is 10 or fewer.

Line 5 and Line 6 check whether the quantity is 1; if so, the discount is set to 0.

Line 7 starts the `Else` part, which will be executed only if the quantity is in the range 2 through 10.

Line 8 assigns a discount of 2% when the quantity is 2, and rises in 2% increments up to a maximum of 18%.

Line 9 ends the inner `If` statement that started at Line 5.

Line 10 ends the outer `If` statement that started at Line 2.

Adding Another Formula

You can have as many formulas as you like in your data table. Each one should directly or indirectly reference the input cell; otherwise, all the values in the associated list of results will be exactly the same. Additional formulas are placed in cells immediately to the right of existing formulas.

Let's add another formula to the data table in Figure 20.5 that calculated the interest paid for different interest rates. This new formula will be used to calculate the monthly payments required for the different interest rates.

1. Continuing with the `Interest Paid` data table created earlier, enter **Years** at cell C1, **25** at cell C2, and **Payments** at cell C4. Enter the formula **=PMT(B2/12,C2*12,-A2)** at cell C5.

2. Select the range A5:C11 and choose Data ➢ Table to display the Table dialog box (Figure 20.4). Enter the input cell **B2** in the Column Input Cell box and

click OK to return to your worksheet, which will now display the results of calculating the extra values (Figure 20.7).

FIGURE 20.7:

Resulting Interest
Paid data table
using two formulas

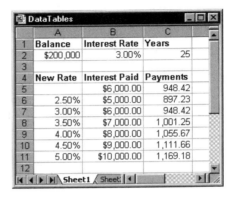

	A	B	C
1	Balance	Interest Rate	Years
2	$200,000	3.00%	25
3			
4	New Rate	Interest Paid	Payments
5		$6,000.00	948.42
6	2.50%	$5,000.00	897.23
7	3.00%	$6,000.00	948.42
8	3.50%	$7,000.00	1,001.25
9	4.00%	$8,000.00	1,055.67
10	4.50%	$9,000.00	1,111.66
11	5.00%	$10,000.00	1,169.18
12			

The Two-Input Data Table

The two-input data table is used to calculate results that can be placed in a table containing several columns and rows. The one-input data table example could be extended into a two-input data table by making the first set of input values interest rates and the second set different loan periods. Each column (or row) would contain the monthly repayments for the different interest rates for each particular loan period.

Structure of the Two-Input Data Table

There is only one structure for the two-input data table, which is shown in Figure 20.8. You could, however, swap the row and column input values to give two different results.

The two-input data table can have only one formula. This is placed in the cell at the top-left corner of the table—the one that was left empty in the one-input data table.

FIGURE 20.8:

Structure of a two-input data table

	column input cell					
					row input cell	
formula	row input 1	row input 2	row input 3	...	row input #	
column input 1						
column input 2						
column input 3						
column input 4						
column input 5						
column input 6						
column input 7						
column input 8						
...						
column input #						

Components of a Two-Input Data Table

Figure 20.8 shows the five components required to build a two-input data table:

- a row input cell that will be used in the substitution of row input values

- a column input cell that will be used to contain each of the column input values

- a list of row input values

- a list of column input values

- one formula that contains cell references to the designated column and row input cells

Creating a Two-Input Data Table

The two-input data table is a "square" table in that it takes up the same number of rows as columns. The row and heading labels are the values from the two input lists; this feature allows you to update the value of two cell references in the same formula simultaneously by taking the next values from the two lists of input data.

Creating a Two-Input Data Table from a Macro

The macro for creating a two-input data table is almost identical to the macro for creating the one-input data table (the Discount Ready Reckoner macro) shown in

Listing 20.1. Let's create a Price Ready Reckoner macro that figures the discounted price for different quantities of items purchased. The original prices will be listed down column A and the number of items purchased will be listed across the first row. We'll use the CalculateDiscount function shown in Listing 20.2 to calculate the discounted bulk purchase price.

The TwoInputTable macro is shown in Listing 20.3 and the data table it produces is shown in Figure 20.9. Most of the code statements in this macro are the same as the code for the OneInputTable macro (Listing 20.1); I've highlighted the differences in bold to show you just how alike these macros are.

FIGURE 20.9:

Price Ready Reckoner data table

Price Ready Reckoner

	A	B	C	D	E	F	G	H	I	J	K	L	M	N	O	P
1	0	1	2	3	4	5	6	7	8	9	10	11	12	13	14	15
2	10	10	19.6	28.8	37.6	46	54	61.6	68.8	75.6	82	88	96	104	112	120
3	15	15	29.4	43.2	56.4	69	81	92.4	103.2	113.4	123	132	144	156	168	180
4	20	20	39.2	57.6	75.2	92	108	123.2	137.6	151.2	164	176	192	208	224	240
5	25	25	49	72	94	115	135	154	172	189	205	220	240	260	280	300
6	30	30	58.8	86.4	112.8	138	162	184.8	206.4	226.8	246	264	288	312	336	360
7	35	35	68.6	100.8	131.6	161	189	215.6	240.8	264.6	287	308	336	364	392	420
8	40	40	78.4	115.2	150.4	184	216	246.4	275.2	302.4	328	352	384	416	448	480
9	45	45	88.2	129.6	169.2	207	243	277.2	309.6	340.2	369	396	432	468	504	540
10	50	50	98	144	188	230	270	308	344	378	410	440	480	520	560	600
11	55	55	107.8	158.4	206.8	253	297	338.8	378.4	415.8	451	484	528	572	616	660
12	60	60	117.6	172.8	225.6	276	324	369.6	412.8	453.6	492	528	576	624	672	720
13	65	65	127.4	187.2	244.4	299	351	400.4	447.2	491.4	533	572	624	676	728	780
14	70	70	137.2	201.6	263.2	322	378	431.2	481.6	529.2	574	616	672	728	784	840
15	75	75	147	216	282	345	405	462	516	567	615	660	720	780	840	900
16	80	80	156.8	230.4	300.8	368	432	492.8	550.4	604.8	656	704	768	832	896	960
17																

Sheet1 / Sheet2

LISTING 20.3

```
0    Sub TwoInputTable()
1        'set the range of cells to hold the data table
2        Set DataTableCells = Worksheets("Sheet1").Range("A1:P16")
3        'set the row and column input cells
4        Set RowInputCell = Worksheets("Sheet1").Range("A17")
5        Set ColumnInputCell = Worksheets("Sheet1").Range("A18")
6        'assign to A1 the formula that calculates the price _
         'taking the high volume discount into account
```

```
7        Worksheets("Sheet1").Range("A1").Formula = _
         "=(A17*A18)*(100-CalculateDiscount(A17))/100"
8        'assign input values
9        For i = 2 To 16
10           Worksheets("Sheet1").Cells(i, 1) = i * 5
11           Worksheets("Sheet1").Cells(1, i) = i - 1
12       Next i
13       'create the table
14       DataTableCells.Table RowInputCell, ColumnInputCell
15       'format the data table by adjusting the column widths _
         'to suit the values, bold the row and column labels and _
         'separate from the values by creating dark lines using _
         'borders.
16       With Worksheets("Sheet1").Range("A1").CurrentRegion
17           .Columns.AutoFit
18           .Rows(1).Font.Bold = True
19           .Columns(1).Font.Bold = True
20           .Rows(1).Borders(xlEdgeBottom).Weight = xlMedium
21           .Columns(1).Borders(xlEdgeRight).Weight = xlMedium
22       End With
23   End Sub
```

ANALYSIS

Rather than repeat the analysis given after Listing 20.1, I've described only the differences here.

Line 0 starts the TwoInputTable macro that creates a table of prices for volume sales.

Line 2 requires that the range be square (same number of rows and columns), whereas the one-input data table requires only two rows (or columns).

Line 7 requires that both the row and column input cells be referenced in the formula.

The For loop in **Lines 9 through 12** requires that both row and column labels be set.

Automating and Editing Data Tables

Application for Building Data Tables

The `OneInputTable` macro in Listing 20.1 could create only one-input data tables, and the `TwoInputTable` macro in Listing 20.3 could create only two-input data tables. Both of these macros were hard-coded to always place their data tables at the same position, and the tables they produced always contained the same amount of information.

In this section, we'll build a more general Ready Reckoner application for pricing that will give the user a choice of what type of data table to build, how many input values should be included, and where to place the data table in the worksheet. A UserForm will be developed for the GUI that will allow the user to have control over the data table that's generated.

The application will include the `CreateDataTable` macro shown in Listing 20.5 that is based on the `OneInputTable` and the `TwoInputTable` macros but is more flexible. This macro is able to create a one-input or a two-input data table wherever the user requests it to be and at whatever size. Figure 20.10 gives a sample of the output from this application.

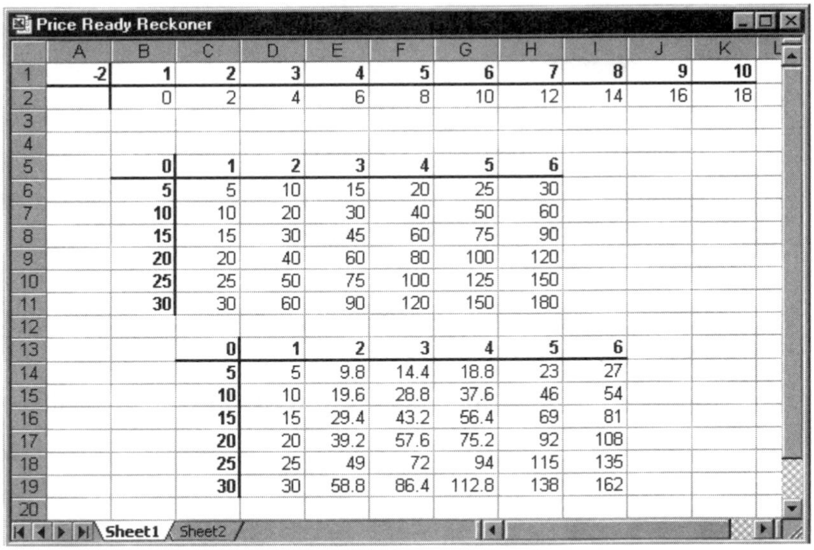

	A	B	C	D	E	F	G	H	I	J	K
1	-2	1	2	3	4	5	6	7	8	9	10
2		0	2	4	6	8	10	12	14	16	18
3											
4											
5		0	1	2	3	4	5	6			
6		5	5	10	15	20	25	30			
7		10	10	20	30	40	50	60			
8		15	15	30	45	60	75	90			
9		20	20	40	60	80	100	120			
10		25	25	50	75	100	125	150			
11		30	30	60	90	120	150	180			
12											
13			0	1	2	3	4	5	6		
14			5	5	9.8	14.4	18.8	23	27		
15			10	10	19.6	28.8	37.6	46	54		
16			15	15	29.4	43.2	56.4	69	81		
17			20	20	39.2	57.6	75.2	92	108		
18			25	25	49	72	94	115	135		
19			30	30	58.8	86.4	112.8	138	162		
20											

FIGURE 20.10:

Sample of data tables created by the Ready Reckoner application

The GUI for this application is shown in Figure 20.11.

FIGURE 20.11:

GUI for the Ready Reckoner
application

Let's start by developing the GUI:

1. Open a new workbook and save it as **Price Ready Reckoner**, which will be
    displayed in the title bar. Open the Visual Basic Editor and choose Insert ➤
    UserForm to create UserForm1, then change its Caption property to **Ready
    Reckoner**.

2. Add three OptionButton and two Label controls and change their Caption
    properties, as shown in Figure 20.11. Add the two TextBox controls that will
    allow the user to enter the information needed by the application to build
    the data table to the user's specifications.

3. Add two CommandButton controls, placing the first one (CommandButton1)
    on the right. Change the Caption properties of the command buttons to
    those shown in Figure 20.11. Change the Cancel property of the Cancel but-
    ton to True so that it will respond to users pressing the Esc key.

Now you're ready to start coding:

1. Choose Insert ➤ Module to open the code window for Module1 and enter
    the code shown in Listing 20.4. This will display the GUI for the application.

2. Add the code for the CalculateDiscount function shown in Listing 20.2 to
    this module.

3. Open the code window for UserForm1 and enter the code for the event pro-
    cedures in Line 50 onward in Listing 20.5. The skeleton first and last lines

for these event procedures will already be there; you only need to enter the statements inside them.

4. Enter Lines 1 through 53 in the General section, which is always at the start of the UserForm code window.

LISTING 20.4

```
0    Sub GenerateTable()
1        UserForm1.Show
2    End Sub
```

ANALYSIS

Line 0 starts the GeneralTable macro; its only function is to display the UserForm (GUI) for the application.

Line 1 uses the Show method to display the UserForm so that the user can provide the information needed to create the data table. If the UserForm isn't already loaded, the Show method will need to load it into memory before displaying it. When the UserForm is loaded it can be manipulated by the code, but the user can't interact with it until it's on display.

LISTING 20.5

```
0    Dim OneInputCellOnly As Boolean
1
2    Sub CreateDataTable()
3        'split the top-left and bottom-right cell references _
         'into row and column components
4        LengthCellReference = Len(TextBox1.Text)
5        TopLeftCellColumn = Left(TextBox1.Text, 1)
6        TopLeftCellRow = Right(TextBox1.Text, _
         LengthCellReference - 1)
7        'set the row and column input cell references
8        If OneInputCellOnly = True Then
9            RowInputCellReference = TopLeftCellColumn & _
             (TopLeftCellRow + 2)
10           ColumnInputCellReference = TopLeftCellColumn & _
             (TopLeftCellRow + 3)
```

```
11      Else
12          RowInputCellReference = TopLeftCellColumn & _
            (Int(TopLeftCellRow) + TextBox2.Text + 1)
13          ColumnInputCellReference = TopLeftCellColumn & _
            (Int(TopLeftCellRow) + TextBox2.Text + 2)
14      End If
15      'set the formula according to the option button checked
16      If OptionButton1.Value = True Then
17          CurrentFormula = "=(" & RowInputCellReference & "*" _
            & ColumnInputCellReference & ")"
18      ElseIf OptionButton2.Value = True Then
19          CurrentFormula = "=CalculateDiscount(" & _
            RowInputCellReference & ")"
20      ElseIf OptionButton3.Value = True Then '
21          CurrentFormula = "=(" & RowInputCellReference & "*" _
            & ColumnInputCellReference & ")" & _
            "*(100-CalculateDiscount(" & RowInputCellReference & _
            "))/100"
22      End If
23      If OneInputCellOnly = True Then
24          Set DataTableCells = _
            Worksheets("Sheet1").Range(TextBox1.Text & ":" & _
            Chr$(Asc(UCase(TopLeftCellColumn)) + _
            Int(TextBox2.Text)) & _
            Format(Int(Right(TextBox1.Text, _
            LengthCellReference - 1) + 1)))
25      Else
26          Set DataTableCells = _
            Worksheets("Sheet1").Range(TextBox1.Text & ":" & _
            Chr$(Asc(UCase(TopLeftCellColumn)) + _
            Int(TextBox2.Text)) & _
            Format(Int(Right(TextBox1.Text, _
            LengthCellReference - 1) + Int(TextBox2.Text))))
27      End If
28      Set RowInputCell = _
        Worksheets("Sheet1").Range(RowInputCellReference)
29      Set ColumnInputCell = _
        Worksheets("Sheet1").Range(ColumnInputCellReference)
30      Worksheets("Sheet1").Range(TextBox1.Text).Formula = _
        CurrentFormula
31      'assign input values
32      Count = 1
33      For i = 2 To TextBox2.Text + 1
```

```
34              If OneInputCellOnly = False Then
35                  Worksheets("Sheet1").Cells(Int(TopLeftCellRow) _
                    + Count, Asc(UCase(TopLeftCellColumn)) - 64) = _
                    Count * 5
36              End If
37              Worksheets("Sheet1").Cells(Int(TopLeftCellRow), _
                Asc(UCase(TopLeftCellColumn)) - 64 + Count) = Count
38              Count = Count + 1
39          Next i
40          DataTableCells.Table RowInputCell, ColumnInputCell
41          With _
            Worksheets("Sheet1").Range(TextBox1.Text).CurrentRegion
42            .ColumnWidth = 6
43            .Rows(1).Font.Bold = True
44            .Columns(1).Font.Bold = True
45            .Rows(1).Borders(xlEdgeBottom).Weight = xlMedium
46            .Columns(1).Borders(xlEdgeRight).Weight = xlMedium
47          End With
48      End Sub
49
50      Private Sub CommandButton1_Click()
51          If TextBox1.Text = "" Then
52              MsgBox "Please enter the location for the table!", _
                vbOKOnly, "Position for Table"
53          ElseIf TextBox2.Text = "" Then
54              MsgBox _
                "Please enter the number of items to be calculated!",_
                vbOKOnly, "Items in Table"
55          Else
56              UserForm1.Hide
57              CreateDataTable
58              Unload Me
59          End If
60      End Sub
61
62      Private Sub CommandButton2_Click()
63          Unload Me
64      End Sub
65
66      Private Sub OptionButton1_Click()
67          OneInputCellOnly = False
68      End Sub
69
```

```
70    Private Sub OptionButton2_Click()
71        OneInputCellOnly = True
72    End Sub
73
74    Private Sub OptionButton3_Click()
75        OneInputCellOnly = False
76    End Sub
77
78    Private Sub UserForm_Initialize()
79        OptionButton1.Value = True
80    End Sub
```

ANALYSIS

Line 0, the Dim statement, is used to declare the OneInputCellOnly variable as type Boolean so that it can be used by the CreateDataTable macro and the Click event procedures of the three OptionButton controls. Declaring a variable outside any procedure makes it accessible to all the procedures in the UserForm.

Line 2 starts the CreateDataTable macro.

Lines 4 through 6 split the text representing the top-left cell into its row number and column letter. Line 4 uses the Len function to find the length of the string entered by the user as the position for the top-left corner of the table. Line 5 uses the Left function to assign the column letter to the variable TopLeftCellColumn. Line 6 uses the Right function to assign the row number to the variable TopLeftCellRow— notice how the length is used to throw away the first letter of the string. The Left and Right functions were described earlier in the analysis of Listing 5.12 in Chapter 5.

Line 8 through 10 make up the If part of the If...Then...Else... statement, which tests whether the data table is a one-input or two-input style. If it is a one-input table, the table will be placed along the specified row. The row and column input cells can be allocated to two cells below the table by adding 2 and 3 to the row part of the position specified for the top-left corner; the column part can remain the same.

Lines 11 through 13 make up the Else part of the If...Then...Else... statement, which is executed if a two-input data table is required. The cell references for the row and column input cells start with the same letters as the top-left cell. The number representing the row is calculated from the position of the top-left corner plus the number of items the user entered into the second `TextBox` control with 2 and 3 added on.

Lines 16 through 22 set the formula according to the option button selected by the user. Notice how Line 20 tests whether `OptionButton3` has been selected, even though it's obvious that if this `ElseIf` is reached it must have been. This line has been included to make the code easier to read and understand; the alternative would be to replace the line with `Else`. `CurrentFormula` is assigned the string that would normally be entered in the Formula bar if the data table was being constructed manually. Here the formula string is pieced together using the concatenation operator (&).

Lines 23 through 27 set the variable `DataTableCells` to the range of cells specified by the user in the two text boxes. Again, the cell reference for the range of cells is pieced together using the concatenation operator (&).

Line 28 and Line 29 set the variables `RowInputCell` and `ColumnInput-Cell` to the `Range` objects containing the row and column input cells.

Line 30 assigns the current formula to the top-left cell.

Lines 31 through 39 assign the list(s) of input values to cells in the worksheet. Notice how the variable `Count` is used to allocate the number of items to cells (Line 37) and also to allocate the price if a two-input data table is required (Line 35).

Line 40 uses the `Table` method of the `Range` object assigned to the variable `DataTableCells` to create all of the results and place them in the cells of the data table.

Lines 41 through 47 use the `With` statement to set the properties of the current region without having to fully qualify them. All of the properties are set in the first row or column of the data table (rather than the first row or column in the worksheet). The row and column labels are made bold and the cells in the first row have their bottom edges made thicker to separate the column labels from the data with a black line. Similarly, the cells in the first column have their right edges made thicker to separate the row labels from the data values with a black line.

Line 50 is the `CommandButton1_Click` event procedure that will be executed whenever the user clicks the command button captioned Create Table.

Line 51 tests whether the user has specified a cell reference for the top-left corner of the data table.

Line 52 uses the `MsgBox` function to inform the user that they haven't entered the location for the table.

Line 53 tests whether the user has specified the number of items they want calculated in the table.

Line 54 uses the `MsgBox` function to tell the user to enter the number of items required.

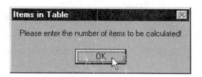

Line 56 uses the `Hide` method to make the UserForm invisible. This doesn't remove it from memory, so the code can still access the values in its text boxes and option buttons.

Line 57 calls the macro `CreateDataTable` (Lines 2 through 48) to create and display the data table.

Line 62 starts the `Click` event procedure for the command button captioned Cancel.

Line 63 uses the `Unload Me` statement to stop the application running and to unload the UserForm from memory.

Lines 67, 71, and 75 assign `True` or `False` to the variable `OneInputCell-Only`.

Line 79 assigns `True` to the `Value` property of `OptionButton1`. This means that the top button will be displayed as selected when the UserForm is displayed for the first time upon starting the application.

Updating a Data Table

You can edit only the input values and the formula(s) in a data table; you cannot change any of the results. This makes the data table more secure than if you had dragged and dropped a formula across the results cells. If you click any of the values calculated by Excel for a data table, the Formula Bar will display

```
{=TABLE(,B2)}
```

or

```
{=TABLE(B12,B13)}
```

where the cell references are the input cells.

Copying a Data Table

When a data table is copied to another location in the workbook (or to another workbook), it loses its data table status. Any formulas it contains are copied as formulas with their cell references updated to reflect their new positions in the usual way, but all of its result values become common old garden gnome worksheet constants even though they were originally evaluated from the formulas.

Deleting All Results from a Data Table

If you want to delete all of the results from a data table, you must select all cells contained in the table and choose Edit ➤ Clear ➤ All. If you don't select all of the cells, Excel will give you the message that you cannot change part of a data table.

Deleting One Formula's Results from a Data Table

If you want to remove a formula and its results from a data table, you really have to delete all cells containing the results and do some cut–and-paste work. The following steps show you one way of doing this:

1. Open the worksheet containing the data table, select the cell containing the formula, and press the Delete key. The formula cell will become empty and the cells containing the results for that formula will all display a zero value.

2. Select all of the cells in the data table that contain results, being careful not to include any input values or formulas, and press the Delete key to make all of the result cells empty.

3. Make your formula cells continuous by moving (copying) formulas into cells whose values were deleted, thus filling any gaps.

4. Rebuild the table by selecting the range of cells that include all of the input values and the formulas, choosing Data ➤ Table, and entering the cell reference of the input cell when requested.

Goal Seek Feature

The Goal Seek feature allows you to state the desired value that you would like a particular formula to produce and the cell reference you want to change to achieve this value (goal). The Goal Seek feature will then attempt to find a solution.

Structure of the Goal Seek Feature

This feature requires two cell references, one for the location of the formula and the other for the cell that's to change its value so that the goal may be achieved. Figure 20.12 shows the simple structure of the Goal Seek feature.

FIGURE 20.12:

Structure of the Goal Seek feature

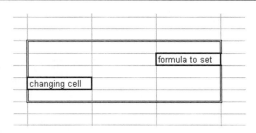

Seeking Your Goal

In this example, we'll use the Goal Seek feature to change the value at cell B2 in order to reach the desired value of 1,000 for the formula at cell C5, which contains a reference to the changing cell. The following steps show how this is done:

1. Open a new workbook and name it **GoalSeek**. Copy the data in the range A1:C5 from the worksheet containing the `Interest Paid` data table shown in Figure 20.7. Cell C5 should contain the formula `=PMT(B2/12,C2*12,-A2)`.

2. Select cell C5 and choose Tools ➤ Goal Seek to display the Goal Seek dialog box with cell C5 already in the Set Cell box, as shown in Figure 20.13. Enter the value **1000** into the To Value box and the cell reference **B2** into the By Changing Cell box.

FIGURE 20.13:

Setting values in the Goal Seek dialog box

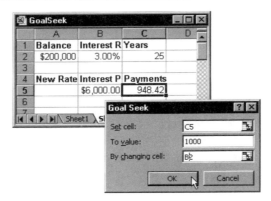

3. Click OK to start the goal seeking and to display the Goal Seek Status dialog box shown in Figure 20.14. The interest rate at cell B2 will have been changed to the value required by the formula in cell C5 to evaluate to the value specified in the To Value box at step 2.

FIGURE 20.14:

Goal Seek Status dialog box giving the information that a solution was found

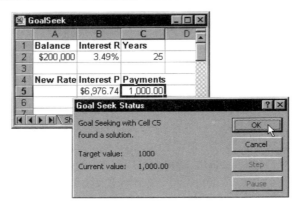

4. Click OK to return to your workbook.

Seeking the Impossible

Using the same worksheet, let's see what happens if we specify a changing cell that isn't referenced by the formula:

1. Using the same GoalSeek workbook as in the previous example, select cell C5 and choose Tools ≻ Goal Seek to display the Goal Seek dialog box (Figure 20.13).

2. Enter **1200** into the To Value box and the cell reference **D5** into the By Changing Cell box.

3. Click OK to start the Goal Seek feature, and watch cell D5 change values as a solution is sought. When this process has finished, the Goal Seek Status dialog box shown in Figure 20.15 will be displayed to inform you that the Goal Seek feature may not have found a solution.

FIGURE 20.15:

Goal-seeking the impossible

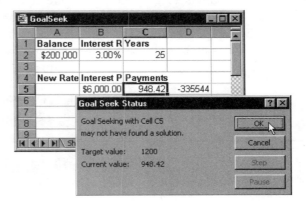

Macro-izing Goal Seeking

Listing 20.6 shows how simple the Goal Seeking feature is to implement in a macro.

LISTING 20.6

```
0    Sub SeekingAGoal()
1        Range("C5").GoalSeek Goal:=1000, ChangingCell:=Range("B2")
2    End Sub
```

ANALYSIS

Line 0 starts the `SeekingAGoal` macro.

Line 1 uses the `GoalSeek` method to calculate the new value for the cell assigned to the `ChangingCell` argument. The new value in this cell will be changed to achieve the amount assigned to the `Goal` argument if a solution is found.

Goal Seeking with Charts

The Goal Seek feature also works with charts. In this example, we'll return to academia and set a goal for an Average mark by changing the Math grade. We'll add a bar chart to our worksheet, adjust the height of the Average bar interactively using the mouse, and watch Excel change the height of the Math bar to meet the goal. We will expand this example in the "Interactively Seeking Your Goal Using a Macro" section coming up next.

1. Open a new workbook, save it as **GoalSeekFromMacro**, and enter the values shown in Figure 20.16, with the formula **=AVERAGE(B1:B4)** at cell B6.

FIGURE 20.16:

Changing the height of the bar representing the result of the formula at cell B6

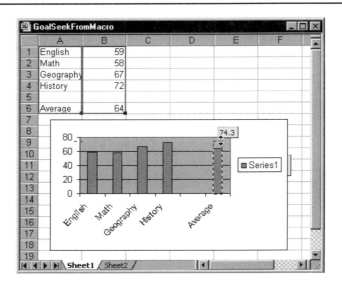

Click the Chart Wizard from the toolbar and accept all the default values in the Chart Wizard by clicking Next in every dialog box. Make sure that the As Object In option button is selected in the fourth dialog box.

2. Click twice (once to select the series and a second time to select the bar from the series) on the last bar, which represents the Average, and increase its height by dragging the sizing handles, as shown in Figure 20.16.

3. When the bar has reached the required height, release the button and the Goal Seek dialog box (Figure 20.17) will open. The Set Cell box will display B6 and the To Value box will contain 74.3, which was the last value displayed in the ToolTip. The Enter cursor should already be displayed in the By Changing Cell box, so all you have to do is enter **B2**, as shown in Figure 20.17.

FIGURE 20.17:

Adjusting the height of the bar representing the value of the formula at cell B6

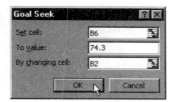

4. Click OK to display the Goal Seek Status dialog box (shown below), which will let you know that a solution meeting your goal has been found.

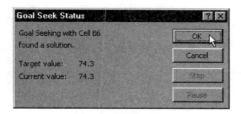

5. Click OK to return to your worksheet. Cells B2 and B6 will now contain their new values and the bars representing Math and Average will be adjusted to their new heights (Figure 20.18).

FIGURE 20.18:

Result of Goal Seeking by adjusting the chart

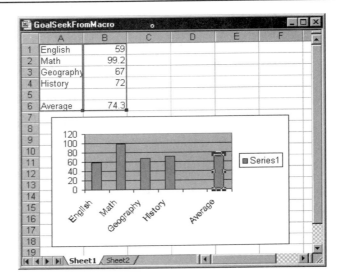

Interactively Seeking Your Goal Using a Macro

Let's develop the GoalSeekFromMacro workbook into an application that allows you to select the subject to be changed and to specify the desired Average grade using a SpinButton control. The SpinButton control allows you to change the Average gradually and to watch the bars grow and shrink at your command. The subject bar changes faster than the Average bar because a grade-point difference in a subject is divided by four to give the new Average.

SpinButton Control

The SpinButton control is used to increment or decrement numbers according to the arrow clicked. Clicking on this control changes only its Value property, but its event procedures can be programmed to update values elsewhere. The two most useful events are the SpinUp and SpinDown events. The SpinUp event procedure is executed when the user clicks the Up or Right arrow, and the SpinDown event procedure is executed when the user clicks the Down or Left arrow.

Let's start our GoalSeekFromChart application by developing the GUI shown in Figure 20.19.

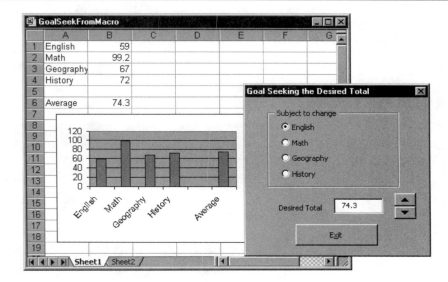

1. Continuing with the GoalSeekFromMacro workbook, open the Visual Basic Editor and choose Insert ➢ UserForm to create UserForm1. Change its Caption property to **Goal Seeking the Desired Total**.

2. Add a Frame control and place four option buttons inside it. Change the Caption properties of all four controls as shown in Figure 20.19.

3. Add a Label control and give it the caption shown. Add a TextBox control and place a SpinButton control beside it. Add a CommandButton control and change its Caption property to **Exit** and its Accelerator property to **x** to make it keyboard selectable.

Now we're ready to start entering code:

1. From the Visual Basic Editor, choose Insert ➢ Module and enter the code shown in Listing 20.7. This GoalSeekFromChart macro displays the GUI that allows the user to interact with the application.

2. Open the code window for UserForm1 and enter the code shown in Listing 20.8. The Dim statement should be placed in the General section, and

the statements inside the event procedures should be placed inside the skeleton event procedures created by Visual Basic.

3. Return to Excel and run the GoalSeekFromChart macro to display the User-Form shown in Figure 20.19. Check a subject, then depress the mouse button on an arrow in the SpinButton control and watch the height of the bars representing the subject and the Average respond. Figure 20.20 shows the result after the option buttons for several subjects have been used to set the changing cell.

FIGURE 20.20:

Holding down the Spin-Button control animates changes to the bars representing the selected subject and the Average.

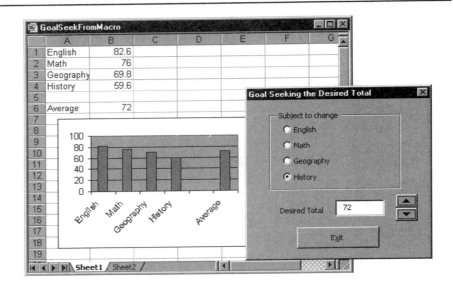

LISTING 20.7

```
0    Sub GoalSeekFromChart()
1        UserForm1.Show
2    End Sub
```

ANALYSIS

Line 0 starts the GoalSeekFromChart macro.

Line 1 displays UserForm1, which allows the user to interactively set whatever goal they require.

LISTING 20.8

```
0    Dim ChangingCellReference As String
1
2    Private Sub CommandButton1_Click()
3        Unload Me
4    End Sub
5
6    Private Sub OptionButton1_Click()
7        ChangingCellReference = "B1"
8    End Sub
9
10   Private Sub OptionButton2_Click()
11       ChangingCellReference = "B2"
12   End Sub
13
14   Private Sub OptionButton3_Click()
15       ChangingCellReference = "B3"
16   End Sub
17
18   Private Sub OptionButton4_Click()
19       ChangingCellReference = "B4"
20   End Sub
21
22   Private Sub SpinButton1_SpinDown()
23       TextBox1.Text = TextBox1.Text - 0.1
24       Range("B6").GoalSeek Goal:=TextBox1.Text, _
         ChangingCell:=Range(ChangingCellReference)
25   End Sub
26
27   Private Sub SpinButton1_SpinUp()
28      TextBox1.Text = TextBox1.Text + 0.1
29       Range("B6").GoalSeek Goal:=TextBox1.Text, _
30       ChangingCell:=Range(ChangingCellReference)
31   End Sub
32
33   Private Sub UserForm_Initialize()
34       OptionButton1.Value = True
35       TextBox1.Text = Range("B6").Value
36   End Sub
```

ANALYSIS

Line 0 uses the `Dim` statement to declare the variable `ChangingCellReference` as a `String` type. This is declared here so that it can be used by the four option buttons' `Click` event procedures and by the spin button's `SpinUp` and `SpinDown` event procedures.

Lines 2 through 4 make up the code for the `Click` event procedure of `CommandButton1`. This event procedure uses the `Unload Me` statement to stop the application running and return to the worksheet, which will display the latest values.

Lines 6 through 20 contain the `Click` events for the four `OptionButton` controls that set the cell reference for the changing cell.

Lines 22 through 31 contain the `SpinUp` and `SpinDown` event procedures for the `SpinButton` control. The `SpinUp` event adds 0.1 to the value in the text box and the `SpinDown` event deducts 0.1. Line 24 and Line 29 use the `GoalSeek` method to calculate the new value for the changing cell to achieve the new goal in the text box.

Lines 33 through 36 contain the `Initialize` event for the UserForm, to be executed as soon as the UserForm is loaded and before it's displayed. This event procedure also causes the first option button to be initially displayed as selected and assigns the `Average` value to the text box

Summary

After you have read this chapter, you'll be able to

- create one-input row and column data tables
- create two-input data tables
- create data tables from a macro that fully automates the operation
- update a data table

- use the Goal Seek feature to achieve goals
- goal-seek interactively using a chart
- goal-seek from a macro

CHAPTER

TWENTY-ONE

The Scenario Manager and the Solver

This chapter describes how to use Excel's powerful Scenario Manager feature to create Scenario Summary tables showing the results of different scenarios and the values used to achieve them. It also describes the Solver command that will help you find a solution when you need to maximize, minimize, or meet some target value.

The Scenario Manager

The Scenario Manager is another "What-if" feature of Excel. This feature allows you to specify several different sets of values for *changing cells* (cells to be modified using the sets of values), then calculates the results for each set and places them in a Scenario Summary report.

A *scenario* is one set of these values. Several scenarios can be applied to the same worksheet, each producing a different outcome. This is a useful tool if you are trying to plan ahead, especially if you already have best-case and worst-case scenarios; these can both be applied, along with others in between these extremes.

Exploring Alternatives with the Scenario Manager

Assume you're planning for your retirement and want to know the end results of four different scenarios. You want to know the difference in savings at the time of retirement if you save between $400 and $700 per month, with interest averaging 4% or 5% over the years, and retire in 10 to 20 years' time. The Scenario Manager in Excel can help you plan your retirement by working out what the results of the different scenarios are.

Before you can create any scenarios, you need to build a workbook model. The Scenario Manager will then modify your model by substituting the different sets of values (a set for each scenario) into cells you designate to be changing cells. Let's create our retirement plan now.

1. Create a new workbook and save it as **Retirement Plan**. Select cells A1:F1 from Sheet1, choose Format ➤ Cells, and check the Wrap Text box in the Alignment tab to spread the text for the column labels over two lines. Select Bold in the Font tab and click OK to return to the worksheet.

2. Enter the labels shown in Figure 21.1 into cells A1:F1. Choose Format ➤ Column ➤ Width to display the Column Width dialog box and enter **11** in the Column Width box. Click OK to return to the worksheet. Expand the first row using a drag-and-drop action so that all the column labels can be seen.

FIGURE 21.1:

Retirement Plan
workbook

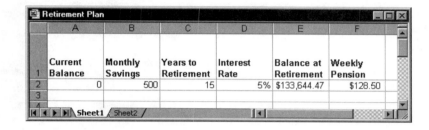

3. Enter the values shown into cells A2:D2 and name these cells "Balance," "Savings," "Years," and "Interest" by selecting them one by one and typing their names in the Name box to the left of the Formula Bar. (Remember to hit Enter each time to finalize the entry.) It is necessary to name these cells because their names will be used later to customize the dialog box where you enter values for the scenarios.

4. Enter the formula **=FV(Interest/12,Years*12,-Savings,-Balance,0)** into cell E2 and **=E2*Interest/52** into cell F2. Your worksheet should now contain the same values as the one shown in Figure 21.1.

5. Select cells B2:D2 and choose Tools ➤ Scenarios to display the Scenario Manager dialog box shown in Figure 21.2. The Scenario Manager will now regard the selected cells to be the ones designated as changing cells.

6. Click Add to display the Add Scenario dialog box shown in Figure 21.3.

7. Enter **Five Hundred for Fifteen Years** into the Scenario Name box. The cell reference for the selected cells should appear automatically in the Changing Cells box. (If it doesn't, click the Collapse Dialog button found at the right of the Changing Cells box to display the Add Scenario - Changing Cells dialog box, shown in Figure 21.4. Select cells B2:D2 and click the Collapse Dialog button again to expand the Add Scenario dialog box and continue.) The Scenario Manager will update the Comment box, showing your name as the creator of the scenario and the date the scenario was created.

FIGURE 21.2:

Scenario Manager dialog box

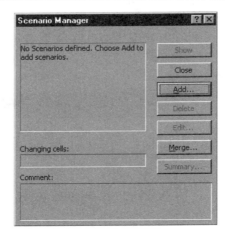

FIGURE 21.3:

Add Scenario dialog box

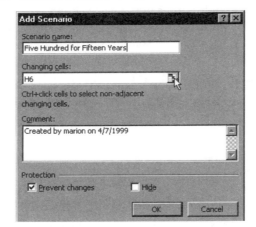

FIGURE 21.4:

Selecting cells using the Add Scenario - Changing Cells dialog box

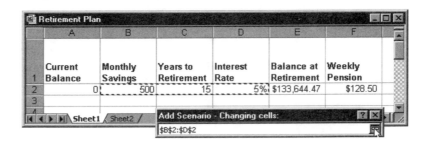

8. Click OK to display the Scenario Values dialog box, shown in Figure 21.5. Notice that the dialog box has been customized with the names of the selected cells as the captions for each box, and the values selected from the worksheet have been copied into the boxes for the first scenario.

FIGURE 21.5:

Scenario Values dialog box

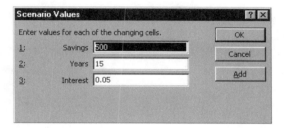

9. Click Add to add the new scenario and to display the Add Scenario dialog box, which will enable you to set up the next scenario. The selected changing cells will already be displayed in the Changing Cells box.

10. Add the last three scenarios shown in Table 21.1 by repeating steps 7 through 9, changing the name in the Add Scenario dialog box and the values in the Scenario Values dialog box for each one.

TABLE 21.1: Retirement Scenarios

Scenario Name	Savings	Years	Percent
Five Hundred for Fifteen Years	500	15	5
Four Hundred for Twenty Years	400	20	5
Four Hundred Fifty for Eighteen Years	450	18	5
Seven Hundred for Ten Years	700	10	4

Click Add from the Scenario Values dialog box after the second and third scenario to display the Add Scenarios dialog box. When you've entered the values for the fourth scenario, click OK instead of Add to return to the Scenario Manager dialog box, which will now display a list of the scenarios that you've just added (Figure 21.6).

FIGURE 21.6:

Scenario Manager dialog box showing the list of scenarios

11. Choose the name of a scenario from the list and click Show to change the values in the worksheet to those of the selected scenario.

12. Click Summary to display the Scenario Summary dialog box, shown in Figure 21.7. Ensure that the Scenario Summary option button has been selected, and delete the contents of the Result Cells box. Click OK to create a new worksheet, `Scenario Summary`, containing the summary information.

FIGURE 21.7:

Specifying where to place the results in the Scenario Summary dialog box

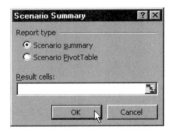

Figure 21.8 shows a formatted version of the Scenario Summary report just created. Because the Result Cells box was left empty, only the changing cells for each scenario are actually included.

13. Format your report the same way as you made the adjustments to `Sheet1` in steps 1 and 2: Choose columns D through H, check the Wrap Text box in the

Alignment tab of the Format dialog box, and adjust the Widths to 11 in the Column Width dialog box. Adjust the height of row 3 so that the whole of each scenario name is displayed. Click OK to return to the workbook.

FIGURE 21.8:

Scenario Summary created without specifying result cells

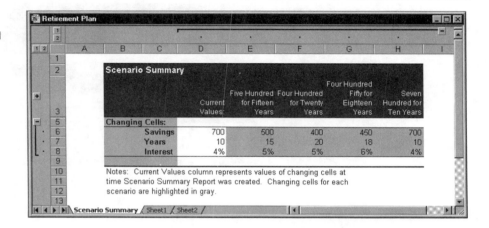

Let's create a second Scenario Summary report, this time with cell references entered into the Result Cells box so that the results from the different scenarios are actually shown.

1. Continuing with the same workbook, select Sheet1 and choose Tools ➤ Scenario to open the Scenario Manager (shown in Figure 21.6.)

2. Click Summary to open the Scenario Summary dialog box (shown in Figure 21.7) and enter **E2,F2** in the Result Cells box, or select these two cells using the Collapse Dialog button, as explained above in step 7.

3. Click OK to create a new worksheet, Scenario Summary 2, displaying the results; format it the same way as you formatted the first Scenario Summary worksheet. Figure 21.9 shows my worksheet after the formatting.

NOTE   Result cells are any cells in your worksheet that have been evaluated for each new scenario. Normally, a result cell will contain a formula that directly or indirectly refers to the changing cells.

FIGURE 21.9:

Scenario Summary created with result cells specified

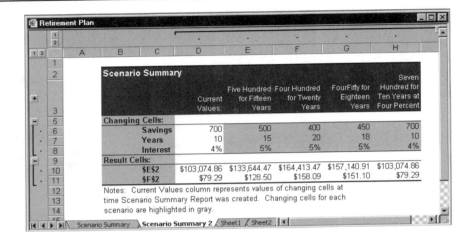

Editing Values in a Scenario

Suppose you would like to change the interest rate for the Four Hundred for Twenty Years scenario in the Retirement Plan workbook from 5% to 6%. The following steps show you how:

1. Open worksheet Sheet1 of the Retirement Plan workbook. Choose Tools ➤ Scenarios to display the Scenario Manager dialog box, which will contain a list of all scenarios associated with Sheet1.

2. Select Four Hundred for Twenty Years in the Scenario Manager dialog box and click Edit to display the Edit Scenario dialog box shown in Figure 21.10. Notice how the Scenario Manager is keeping track of any changes made to the scenario by adding the name of the person making the modification and the modification date to the Comment box.

3. Click OK to display the Scenario Values dialog box with the values for the current scenario displayed. Change the Interest box to **0.06** and click OK to return to the Scenario Manager dialog box.

4. Click Show to see the consequences of your edit. Click Close to finalize the edit and return to your worksheet.

FIGURE 21.10:

Edit Scenarios dialog box

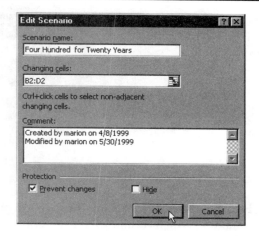

Deleting a Scenario

To delete a scenario, choose Tools ➤ Scenarios to display the Scenario Manager. Select the name of the scenario you want to delete from the list and click Delete; the named scenario will immediately be removed from the worksheet and will disappear from the list. You can also delete a scenario by renaming it in the Edit Scenario dialog box by overtyping the text in the Scenario Name box.

Scenario Manager Macro

In this section, we'll develop an application that takes scenario-building further. It will display a UserForm for the user to enter the initial values of the changing cells and then will create a scenario named Plan and call on the Scenario Manager to create a Scenario Summary sheet. The user can then make adjustments to these from a UserForm. We'll base the application on our Retirement Plan.

Let's start by designing the UserForm shown in Figure 21.11 to allow the user to adjust values in the text boxes using the SpinButton control. The event procedures belonging to these SpinButton controls will respond to the changes by updating the Scenario and the Scenario Summary sheet.

FIGURE 21.11:

GUI for the Macro-ized
Retirement Plan application

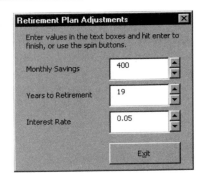

The following steps take you through the processes involved in creating the workbook, which contains the user's original Retirement Plan, and the User-Form, which allows the user to make adjustments to the original plan:

1. Open a new workbook and call it **Macro-ized Retirement Plan**. Copy values and formulas from the Retirement Plan workbook shown in Figure 21.1—we'll use these as a basis for our new application.

2. Open the Visual Basic Editor and choose Insert ➤ UserForm to create a new UserForm and display its graphical representation. Set the UserForm's Caption property to **Retirement Plan Adjustments**, as shown in the title bar in Figure 21.11.

3. Place four Label controls at similar positions to those shown in Figure 21.11 and set their Caption properties.

4. Add three TextBox controls and change their names to **txtSavings**, **txtYears**, and **txtInterestRate**.

5. Add three SpinButton controls alongside the text boxes. Add a command button at the bottom and change its Name property to **cmdExit**, its Caption property to **Exit,** and its Accelerator property to **x**.

Now we're ready to start entering the code:

1. Create a new Module (Insert ➤ Module) and enter the CreateRetirement-Plan macro, shown in Listing 21.1, which displays the GUI for the application so that the user can revise the plan.

2. Open the code window for your UserForm and enter the code into the procedures as shown in Listing 21.2. The code in one of the event procedures will run each time a spin button's arrow is clicked to update the scenario.

The time has come: Run your application and try clicking an arrow on any of the SpinButton controls to create a new scenario. Your Scenario Summary will be recreated based on the new values.

Figure 21.12 shows the Scenario Summary after a few adjustments have been made.

FIGURE 21.12:

Scenario Summary displaying new figures that reflect the adjustments made to the changed values

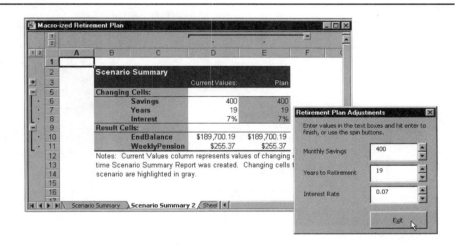

LISTING 21.1

```
0    Sub CreateRetirementPlan()
1        Answer = MsgBox("You are required to enter your monthly" _
         & vbCrLf & "savings, years to retirement and the" _
         & vbCrLf & "estimated average interest rate into cells" _
         & vbCrLf & "B2:D2 of Sheet1. These figures are used as" _
         & vbCrLf & "the starting point for your retirement plan" _
         & vbCrLf & "and can be revised later." & vbCrLf & vbLf &
         "Do you want to proceed with the current values?", _
         vbYesNo, "Retirement Plan - Information Required")
2        If Answer = vbYes Then UserForm1.Show
3    End Sub
```

ANALYSIS

Line 0 starts the `CreateRetirementPlan` macro that displays `UserForm1`, the GUI for the application.

Line 1 displays the message box that reminds the user to enter the values they want into `Sheet1` for the application to use as a basis for the retirement plan.

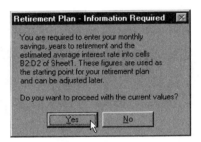

Line 2 checks whether the user wants to proceed; if they do, `UserForm1` is loaded into memory (if it isn't already loaded) and becomes visible, allowing the user to interact with its controls.

LISTING 21.2

```
0    Private Sub UpdateScenarioSummary()
1        Sheets("Sheet1").Select
2        ActiveSheet.Scenarios("Plan").ChangeScenario _
         ChangingCells:=Range("B2:D2"), _
         Values:=Array(txtSavings.Text, _
         txtYears.Text, txtInterestRate.Text)
3        Worksheets("Scenario Summary").Select
4        Application.DisplayAlerts = False
5        ActiveWindow.SelectedSheets.Delete
6        Application.DisplayAlerts = True
7        Worksheets("Sheet1").Scenarios.CreateSummary _
         ReportType:=xlStandardSummary, ResultCells:=Range("E2:F2")
8    End Sub
9
10   Private Sub cmdExit_Click()
```

```
11      Unload Me
12   End Sub
13
14   Private Sub SpinButton1_SpinDown()
15       txtSavings = txtSavings - 50
16       Sheet1.Range("B2").Value = txtSavings
17       UpdateScenarioSummary
18   End Sub
19
20   Private Sub SpinButton1_SpinUp()
21       txtSavings = txtSavings + 50
22       Sheet1.Range("B2").Value = txtSavings
23       UpdateScenarioSummary
24   End Sub
25
26   Private Sub SpinButton2_SpinDown()
27       txtYears = txtYears - 1
28       Sheet1.Range("C2").Value = txtYears
29       UpdateScenarioSummary
30   End Sub
31
32   Private Sub SpinButton2_SpinUp()
33       txtYears = txtYears + 1
34       Sheet1.Range("C2").Value = txtYears
35       UpdateScenarioSummary
36   End Sub
37
38   Private Sub SpinButton3_SpinDown()
39       txtInterestRate = txtInterestRate - 0.01
40       Sheet1.Range("D2").Value = txtInterestRate
41       UpdateScenarioSummary
42   End Sub
43
44   Private Sub SpinButton3_SpinUp()
45       txtInterestRate = txtInterestRate + 0.01
46       Sheet1.Range("D2").Value = txtInterestRate
47       UpdateScenarioSummary
48   End Sub
49
50   Private Sub UserForm_Initialize()
51       'assign changing values to text boxes
52       txtSavings = Sheet1.Range("B2")
```

```
53      txtYears = Sheet1.Range("C2")
54      txtInterestRate = Sheet1.Range("D2")
55      On Error GoTo JumpToHere
56      ActiveWorkbook.Worksheets("Scenario Summary").Delete
57  JumpToHere:
58      If Worksheets("Sheet1").Scenarios.Count > 0 Then
59          Worksheets("Sheet1").Scenarios("Plan").Delete
60      End If
61      Sheets("Sheet1").Select
62      ActiveSheet.Scenarios.Add Name:="Plan", _
        ChangingCells:=Range("B2:D2"), _
        Values:=Array(Format(txtSavings), Format(txtYears), _
        Format(txtInterestRate))
63      ActiveSheet.Scenarios.CreateSummary _
        ReportType:=xlStandardSummary, ResultCells:=Range("E2:F2")
64  End Sub
```

ANALYSIS

Line 0 starts the UpdateScenarioSummary sub procedure. This is declared as Private to make it available to all the event procedures within this UserForm. Any sub or function within a UserForm is Private by default, so including the word "Private" is optional.

Line 1 makes Sheet1 the active sheet.

Line 2 calls the ChangeScenario method of the Scenario object named Plan, with the ChangingCells argument assigned cells B2:D2 and the Values argument assigned the contents of the text boxes. The Values argument expects a string value for each changing cell inside an array structure; the Format function is used to ensure that the values in the text boxes are in the string format required.

Line 3 selects the Scenario Summary sheet, making it active.

Line 4 sets the DisplayAlerts property of the Application object to False so that the message box containing the warning message routinely displayed by Excel when you delete a worksheet is no longer displayed.

Line 5 uses the Delete method to remove the selected sheets (Scenario Summary) in the window returned by the ActiveWindow property.

Line 6 sets the DisplayAlerts property back to True so that Excel will once again display warning messages when required.

Line 7 uses the CreateSummary method of the Scenarios collection, which includes all of the Scenario objects that are associated with Sheet1. This method is called with the ReportType argument set to the Excel constant xlStandardSummary. (The other constant available for use here is xlSummaryPivotTable.) The second argument, ResultCells, is assigned E2:F2, which is where the outcome of the scenario is to be displayed.

Lines 10 through 12 make up the cmdExit_Click event procedure, which executes when the command button is clicked and uses the Unload Me statement to stop the application running.

Lines 14 through 18 contain the SpinButton1_SpinDown event procedure, which is executed in response to the Down (or the Right) arrow being clicked. Line 15 deducts 50 from the amount in the Savings text box and Line 16 assigns the new value to cell B2 in Sheet1 so that it can be used by the scenario named Plan. Line 17 calls the UpdateScenarioSummary, which updates the scenario named Plan and uses it to recreate the Scenario Summary sheet.

Lines 20 through 24 contain the SpinUp event procedure. They are the same as Lines 14 through 18 except that 50 is added onto the amount in the Savings text box in response to the Up (or Left) arrow being clicked.

Lines 26 though 48 contain the SpinDown and SpinUp event procedures for the other two SpinButton controls. The code is more or less the same as the code in Lines 14 through 24 except for the values of the increase or decrease and the cell that the new text box values are assigned to.

Line 50 starts the UserForm_Initialize event procedure, which is executed when the UserForm is first loaded into memory. The code in this section will be executed when the Show method is initially used to display the UserForm (Line 2 of Listing 21.1).

Lines 52 through 54 assign the values from the Changing Cells argument (B2:D2) into the text boxes in the UserForm.

Lines 55 to 57 delete the Scenario Summary sheet that may exist in the workbook from previous runs of the application. Because Excel will give an error if you try to delete something that doesn't actually exist, we use the On Error statement.

Lines 58 through 60 check whether the Scenarios collection contains any Scenario objects; if it does, the Scenario named Plan is deleted.

Line 61 selects Sheet1 to make it the active sheet.

Line 62 uses the Add method to create a new Scenario object and adds it to the Scenarios collection. It assigns B2:D2 to the ChangingCells argument, and assigns the contents of the three text boxes to the Values argument. These values will be placed in the ChangingCells argument to find the outcome of the scenario.

Line 63 uses the CreateSummary method to create a new Scenario Summary sheet. The ReportType argument is xlStandardSummary and the ResultCells are E2 and F2. (The analysis for Line 7 gives more detail.)

The Solver

The Microsoft Excel Solver makes adjustments to values in one or more changing cells to meet a targeted objective. The aim of the Solver is to minimize, maximize, or make the target cell (objective) equal to a specific value by adjusting changing cells, subject to one or more *constraints*, until a solution is found. A constraint on a cell restricts its value to lying within specified limits; constraints can be placed on any cell in your model, including any of the changing cells and the target cell.

TIP   To find the value for a particular cell by adjusting only one other cell, you may prefer to use the Goal Seek feature described in the previous chapter.

Structure of the Solver

Figure 21.13 shows the structure of the Solver with one constraint. The Solver finds solutions by adjusting values at changing cells until the target cell contains the value required. In finding these solutions, the Solver must take into account one or more constraints, such as that a changing cell must contain nonzero values or values that are within some range.

FIGURE 21.13:

Structure of the Solver with one constraint

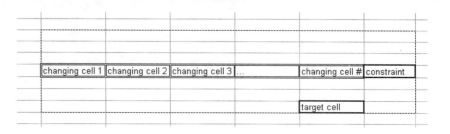

Installing the Solver

The Excel Solver command is not automatically installed when you install Excel. To find out if the Solver has been installed on your machine, check whether the Solver menu command is listed in the Tools menu drop-down list. If it isn't listed, follow these steps to install it:

1. Choose Tools ➢ Add-Ins to open the Add-Ins dialog box (shown in Figure 21.14) and check the Solver Add-In check box.

FIGURE 21.14:

Selecting the Solver Add-In command from the Add-Ins dialog box

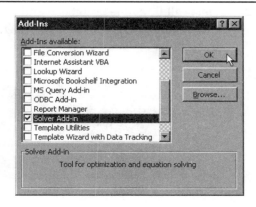

2. Click OK to display the message box (shown below) asking if you'd like to install the Solver add-in. Click Yes to start the installation process and follow the instructions on the screen.

3. When the installation is finished, check that the Solver command has been added to the drop-down list for the Tools menu item.

Targeting a Result with the Solver

Suppose you're planning for your retirement in the distant future and want to know how much to save monthly over the next 22 years so that you can have a weekly pension of $300. You have decided to keep a constant interest rate of 5%. Why not let the Solver produce the solution for you? The following steps show you how.

1. Open a new workbook and copy the contents of cells A2:F2 from the Retirement Plan workbook shown in Figure 21.1. Save the new workbook as Retirement Solution.

2. Select cell F2 as the target cell and choose Tools ➤ Solver to display the Solver Parameters dialog box (shown in Figure 21.15), which should already display cell F2 in the Set Target Cell box.

FIGURE 21.15:

Solver Parameters dialog box

3. As shown in Figure 21.15, check the Value Of option button and enter **300** into the box, and enter **B2:C2** into the By Changing Cells box.

4. Click Add to open the Add Constraint dialog box shown in Figure 21.16. Enter **C2** in the Cell Reference box, choose <= as the relationship, and enter **22** in the Constraint box.

5. Click OK to return to the Solver Parameters dialog box, which will now display the constraint.

6. Click Solve to display the Solver Results dialog box, shown below. Ensure that the Keep Solver Solution option button is checked and click OK to return to the worksheet. The Solver solution will be displayed as shown in Figure 21.17.

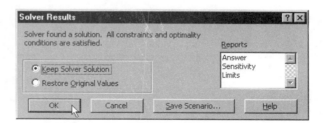

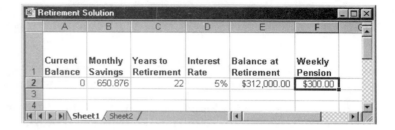

	Current Balance	Monthly Savings	Years to Retirement	Interest Rate	Balance at Retirement	Weekly Pension	
1							
2	0	650.876	22	5%	$312,000.00	$300.00	
3							
4							

NOTE   When you keep a Solver solution, all the settings are saved to the worksheet and will be displayed the next time you open the Solver Parameters dialog box.

Macro-izing the Solver

The steps taken in the preceding section can easily be coded in a macro. Listing 21.3 shows just how easy this is to do in the SolvingRetirementProblem macro.

WARNING   Before you can run this macro, you must establish a reference to the Solver Add-In (see sidebar below). If you don't, you'll get an error message that tells you that the SolverReset function is not found.

LISTING 21.3

```
0    Sub SolvingRetirementProblem()
1        'this macro uses the Solver command to solve
         'the retirement problem
2        SolverReset 'clear all Solver settings to default values
3        SolverOk SetCell:="$F$2", MaxMinVal:=3, ValueOf:="300", _
         ByChange:="$B$2:$C$2"
4        SolverAdd cellref:=Range("B2"), relation:=1, _
         formulatext:=300
5        SolverSolve
6    End Sub
```

ANALYSIS

Line 0 starts the SolvingRetirementProblem macro, which uses several functions from Excel's Solver facility.

Line 2 uses the SolverReset function to reset any previously modified cells, values, and constraints back to their original default settings, ready for you to enter the new problem's settings.

Line 3 uses the SolverOk function to define the problem, assigning the values set in the Solver Parameters dialog box to its arguments.

Line 4 uses the SolverAdd function to add a constraint to the problem. The values assigned to the arguments are those found in the Add Constraint dialog box (shown in Figure 21.16). The Relation argument is given a number corresponding to the arithmetic relationship required; Table 21.2 lists the relationships available.

Line 5 uses the SolverSolve function to run the Solver to find a solution.

Establishing a Reference to the Solver Add-In

Establishing a reference to the Solver Add-In is easy to do. Simply choose Tools ➤ References to open the References dialog box (shown below), check the SOLVER check box, and choose OK. The next time you run the macro, all of the Solver functions will be available and the macro will find a solution (if there is one) and display the Solver Results dialog box.

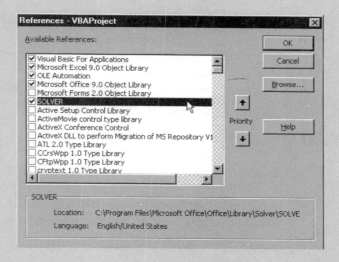

The reference you've established will be stored with your Visual Basic application so that you don't need to reestablish it every time you want to run your macro. If you choose Project ➤ Explorer, you'll see the reference displayed as a component of the project, as shown here.

TABLE 21.2: Relationships Available for Constraints

Value of Relation	Relationship
1	<=
2	=
3	>=
4	Cell reference with integer value
5	Cell reference with value of 0 or 1

Summary

After reading this chapter, you'll be able to

- create scenarios by specifying changing cells and sets of values to be substituted in changing cells, and by controlling where the results will be placed

- create Scenario Summary sheets manually and update them interactively from a macro

- edit and delete scenarios

- use the Solver functions, both manually and from macros, to set target cells, changing cells, and constraints

- install the Solver add-in

- establish a reference to the Solver from Visual Basic

PART VII

Help

CHAPTER
TWENTY-TWO

Excel Visual Basic's OnLine Help Facility

In this chapter you'll learn all about the Visual Basic Help facility, which includes a goldmine of information for you to explore. It is useful for learning all about the Visual Basic programming environment, including the Visual Basic language and objects with their properties, methods, and events. The Help facility also includes lots of code examples that you can copy and run from your computer. You'll see how the Help facility can be accessed through the Office Assistant, by clicking a menu command, or, more directly, by pressing a function key.

Office Assistant

Help is at hand with the Office Assistant, who is always ready and willing to answer questions about anything to do with Excel or VBA (Figure 22.1). You can also get the Assistant to automatically provide you with helpful suggestions and tips while you work. There are several versions of the Office Assistant; you'll see later what these are and how to change the Assistant on your PC.

FIGURE 22.1:

Getting help from the Office Assistant

Enter a question in the Office Assistant's balloon and you'll be presented with a list of topics to choose from. You can even ask the Office Assistant about itself by entering **Office Assistant** as the question and clicking Search (or hitting the Enter key) to list the topics shown in Figure 22.2.

Clicking any of the topics displays the Help window containing information on that topic. If you need more help, you can select another topic from the balloon or you can explore the Help facility—you'll see how in the section "Exploring the Help Facility" later in this chapter.

FIGURE 22.2:

Office Assistant displaying help topics about itself

What would you like to do?

- Show, hide, or turn off the Office Assistant
- Get Help without using the Office Assistant
- Ways to get assistance while you work
- Turn the Office Assistant sound on or off
- Troubleshoot the Office Assistant
▼ See more...

office assistant

Options   Search

NOTE   Once you've selected a topic from the Office Assistant's topic list, the text will change color (until you end your current session in Excel) to let you know that you've already selected it. If you surf the Web, you'll already be familiar with this technique.

Turning the Office Assistant On and Off

The Office Assistant can be turned on and off within any of the Microsoft Office applications. This section describes how to do this within Excel. Turning the Office Assistant off allows you to get help without using the Assistant. This differs from hiding it, as the hidden Assistant will pop up the next time you use the Help facility. When you turn the Assistant off it's still available on your PC and can easily be turned on again; the next sections show how this is done.

Turning the Office Assistant On

Follow these steps to turn the Office Assistant on:

1. If you are in the Visual Basic Editor, click the View Microsoft Excel toolbar button to return to the Excel window.

2. Choose Help ➤ Show The Office Assistant, and the last version of the Office Assistant prior to turning this feature off will appear.

Turning the Office Assistant Off

Follow these steps to turn the Office Assistant off:

1. Choose Help ➤ Microsoft Visual Basic Help to display the Office Assistant shown in Figure 22.1 if it isn't already on display.

2. If the Office Assistant's balloon isn't displayed, click the Assistant to make it appear. Click Options from the balloon and select the Options tab of the Office Assistant dialog box, shown in Figure 22.3.

FIGURE 22.3:

Options tab of the Office Assistant dialog box

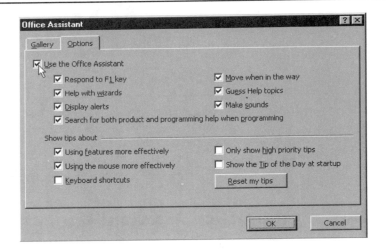

3. Uncheck the check box labeled Use The Office Assistant. All of the check box options will become unavailable (dimmed). Click OK to return to the Visual Basic Editor minus the Office Assistant.

Showing and Hiding the Office Assistant

You can show the Office Assistant by choosing Help ➤ Microsoft Visual Basic or clicking the toolbar button (shown below).

You can hide the Office Assistant by right-clicking it and choosing Hide from the shortcut menu (shown). The Assistant will remain hidden until the next time you use the Help facility.

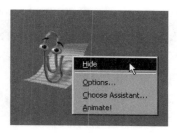

Showing and Hiding the Balloon

Often, the Office Assistant balloon will obscure information that you want to view—but at the same time, you may not want to lose the contents of the balloon in case you need to read it again. Showing and hiding the balloon only changes its visibility and not its contents and is achieved simply by clicking the Office Assistant to toggle between showing it and hiding it.

Getting Tips Automatically While You Work

You don't need to ask the Office Assistant a question to receive help. The Office Assistant can be set up so that it gives you useful information while you work. The following steps show you how to turn on and off the different tips and suggestions available.

1. Display the Office Assistant with its balloon, click Options to display the Office Assistant dialog box, and select the Options tab (Figure 22.3).

2. Check the boxes for the suggestions and tips that you'd like to see while you work. Following is a list of the check box captions with a brief summary of the sorts of tips and suggestions you can expect by checking each one:

Using Features More Effectively: Tells you about features you may not already know and suggests ways to make effective use of features you do know.

Using The Mouse More Effectively: Gives tips on how to work faster using the mouse.

Keyboard Shortcuts: Displays the shortcut keys for commands.

Only Show High Priority Tips: Gives tips that are valuable and will save you significant amounts of time.

Show The Tip Of The Day At Startup: Shows the Tip of the Day dialog box containing a tip every time you open Microsoft Excel.

Employing a New Office Assistant

There are several cartoon-like representations of the Office Assistant to choose from. The following steps show you how easy it is to employ a new one.

1.   Display the Office Assistant, complete with balloon. Click Options to display the Office Assistant dialog box and select the Gallery tab, as shown in Figure 22.4.

FIGURE 22.4:

Gallery tab of the Office Assistant dialog box

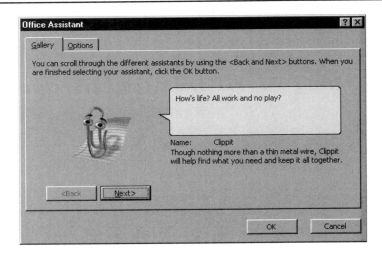

2.   Repeatedly click Next to view the Office Assistants shown below, who will each perform a delightful animated sequence just for you.

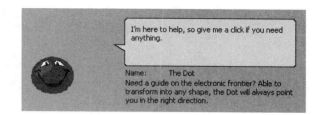

I'm here to help, so give me a click if you need anything.

Name: The Dot
Need a guide on the electronic frontier? Able to transform into any shape, the Dot will always point you in the right direction.

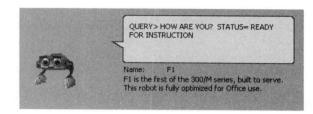

QUERY> HOW ARE YOU? STATUS= READY FOR INSTRUCTION

Name: F1
F1 is the first of the 300/M series, built to serve. This robot is fully optimized for Office use.

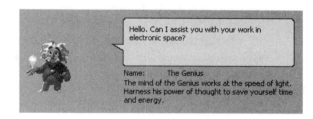

Hello. Can I assist you with your work in electronic space?

Name: The Genius
The mind of the Genius works at the speed of light. Harness his power of thought to save yourself time and energy.

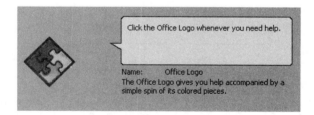

Click the Office Logo whenever you need help.

Name: Office Logo
The Office Logo gives you help accompanied by a simple spin of its colored pieces.

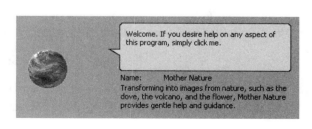

Welcome. If you desire help on any aspect of this program, simply click me.

Name: Mother Nature
Transforming into images from nature, such as the dove, the volcano, and the flower, Mother Nature provides gentle help and guidance.

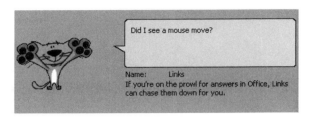

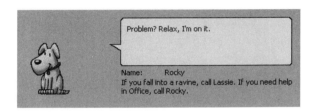

3. Use the Back and Next buttons to access the Office Assistant of your choice (I've selected Links the cat) and click OK to return to the Visual Basic Editor with your new Office Assistant ready and waiting. If the selected Office Assistant is not available on your machine, you'll be prompted to install it.

Because the Office Assistant is shared by all the Microsoft Office suite of programs, your choice of Assistant will apply to these other programs too.

NOTE   If the Office Assistant you want to employ is not available on your computer, you'll be asked to follow the steps required to install it.

Getting Help without the Office Assistant

You can turn off the Office Assistant and get help using the Help window's Contents, Answer Wizard, and Index tabs, as discussed in the next section.

To bypass the Office Assistant, do the following:

1. If the Office Assistant is displayed, you must turn it off (see "Turning the Office Assistant On and Off" earlier in this chapter).

2. Choose Help ➢ Microsoft Visual Basic Help to display the Visual Basic Help window, similar to the one shown in Figure 22.5.

FIGURE 22.5:

Microsoft Visual Basic Help window displaying information about the Options dialog box

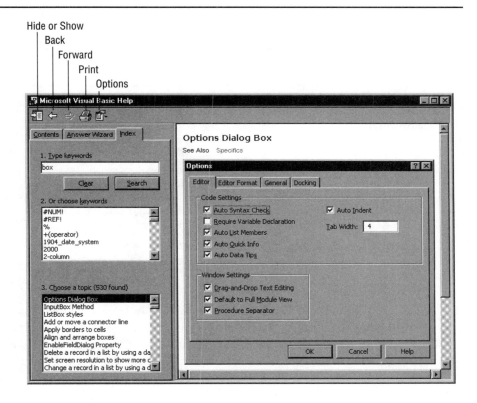

The Help window is split into two panes. The left pane can be displayed on its own or you can expand the window to include the right pane, which displays the results for the topic you select from the Choose A Topic box. Expansion of the Help window is controlled by the Hide or Show button in the top-left corner of the window.

Exploring the Help Facility

Excel provides three tabs to help you explore the Help facility. The Contents tab allows you to select a topic from the contents list, or you can use the Answer Wizard tab to ask a question, or you can search for keywords in the Index tab. The

Contents and Index tabs serve the same purpose as the contents and index sections of a book.

Help from the Contents Tab

The Contents tab displays a list of high-level topics, each displayed with a book icon as shown in Figure 22.6.

FIGURE 22.6:

Contents tab displaying
high-level topics

The contents list is a hierarchical structure, and clicking a book icon will display a list of subtopics that may also have book icons. The lowest level of subtopics will be displayed with question mark icons; clicking one of these will display information in the right pane of the Help window. The layout of the Help window resembles a table of contents showing chapters and subsections in a book. Figure 22.7 shows the different levels of topics that need to be selected to view help on a Visual Basic function.

Asking the Answer Wizard Questions

Figure 22.8 shows the Answer Wizard tab ready for you to enter your question.

Let's ask for help on the Asc Visual Basic function that was discussed in the section "Validating Input to a Text Box" in Chapter 6:

1.   Enter **asc function** in the What Would You Like To Do? box and click Search. A list of topics that contain your search term will be displayed in the Select Topic To Display box, shown in Figure 22.9.

FIGURE 22.7:

Accessing help on Visual Basic functions using the Contents tab

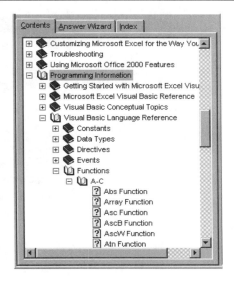

FIGURE 22.8:

Answer Wizard tab waiting for your question

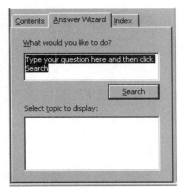

Select the **Asc Function** topic from the list to display the help information in the right half of the Help window, as shown in Figure 22.10.

FIGURE 22.9:

List of topics displayed in response to entering **asc function** in the What Would You Like To Do? box

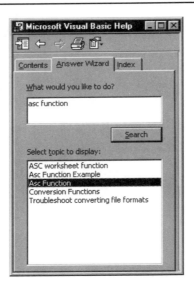

FIGURE 22.10:

Information on the Asc function

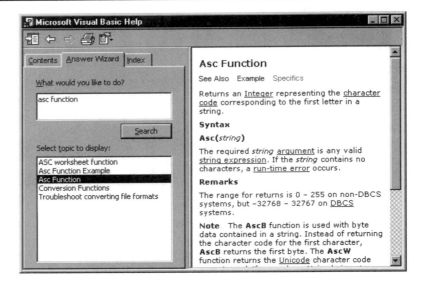

Getting Help Using the Index

Using the Index tab is like using the index of a book—you need to know the keyword(s) for the topic you want help on. Start entering the keyword in the Type Keywords box and watch as the Help facility tries to complete the word for you (Figure 22.11). The letters Help adds are highlighted so that the next letter you enter will overwrite them. When the required word is reached, click Search to display the information about that topic in the right pane of the Help window.

FIGURE 22.11:

Entering a topic using the Index tab

Context-Sensitive Help

The context-sensitive help feature in Visual Basic provides direct access to information dependant on current circumstances. For example, to get help on any control, simply select it and press F1; to get help on a reserved word (see Note below) in a code window, click it to place the insertion point on it and press F1. This is much faster than asking the Office Assistant to help you or accessing the Help facility and searching for the item required.

Context-sensitive help can be accessed from many different items, including

- all windows, including the Help window, code window, Properties window, Object Browser window, etc.
- controls in the Toolbox
- objects on a UserForm and the UserForm itself
- properties in the Properties window

- event procedures
- all reserved words in the Visual Basic language

NOTE   Reserved words are those words that are part of the programming language and by default are displayed as blue text in the code window.

Figure 22.12 shows the Help window displayed when the F1 key is depressed with a UserForm selected.

FIGURE 22.12:

Help window containing information about the UserForm object

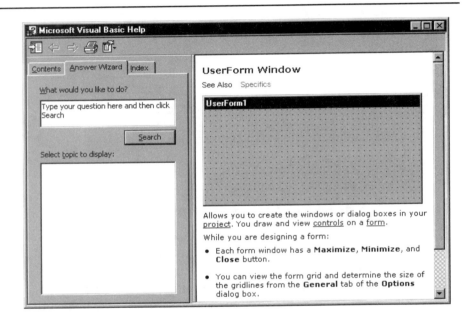

Help Facility Code Examples

The Visual Basic Help facility contains numerous examples of how language items can be implemented in code. Some examples provide a few statements while others provide complete macros and procedures.

The example for the Asc function shown in Figure 22.13 demonstrates how Asc is used in code, with the comments following each assignment statement giving the value it returns.

FIGURE 22.13:

Example code for the Asc function

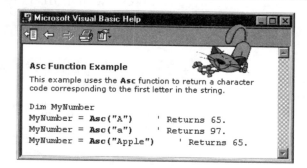

The example for the SheetCalculate event shown in Figure 22.14 contains the complete Workbook_SheetCalculate event procedure that you can copy into ThisWorkbook's code window and run.

FIGURE 22.14:

Example code for the SheetCalculate event

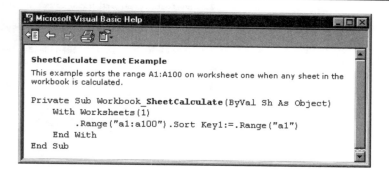

Sometimes a small application is given as an example, preceded by a brief description of what the code does and a list of any controls that must be placed on the UserForm for the application to run without any errors, as shown in Figure 22.15. The code can be copied into the clipboard and pasted into the Declarations section of the UserForm.

The event sub procedure in this example code overwrites the sub procedure of the same name, so as soon as the code is pasted into the Declarations section it disappears from that section and becomes accessible in the usual way, using the control's name from the Object list and the event from the Proc list. Figure 22.15 shows the Help window containing three event procedures that you'll have to scroll to see—UserForm_Initialize, ToggleButton1_Click, and `ToggleButton2_Click`—with instructions about creating the GUI, copying the code, and running the application.

FIGURE 22.15:

Help window for the Bor-
derStyle and Special-
Effect properties

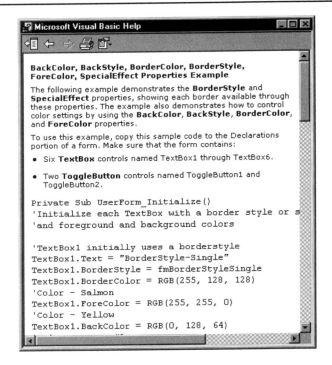

Summary

This chapter will enable you to

- turn the Office Assistant on and off

- hide and show the Office Assistant

- customize the Office Assistant

- set up the Office Assistant to provide suggestions and tips automatically while you work

- access the Help facility without going through the Office Assistant
- explore the Help facility using the Contents, Answer Wizard, and Index tabs
- use context-sensitive help
- access and use code examples

CHAPTER

TWENTY-THREE

23

Customizing Help for Your Users

In this chapter, you'll learn how to build a help facility for your application. You may want to stop at providing ToolTips or you may want to provide a full online help facility that will have all of the features found in help facilities of other Microsoft Windows applications. To develop a full-blown help facility, you'll need access to a help compiler.

Creating an Application

Let's develop a simple New Color Scheme application for filling a range of cells with new colors. Then I can show you how to develop the online help facility and link it to your application. New Color Scheme will be developed in three stages:

1. Create the GUI.

2. Develop the code, including the macro that will display the GUI to start the application.

3. Develop the online help facility.

Creating the GUI

Figure 23.1 shows the GUI for our New Color Scheme application. The GUI facilitates the entry of the red, green, and blue color components for the top-right and bottom-left cells in the selected range. When the user then clicks Change Color, the cells will be filled with graduated colors and the `Caption` property will be changed to `Clear`.

Figure 23.2 shows the result of entering the values shown in Figure 23.1 and clicking Change Color to run the `CommandButton1_Click` event procedure.

The following steps show you how to create this GUI:

1. Open a new workbook and run the Visual Basic Editor.

2. Choose Insert ➤ UserForm to add `UserForm1` to your application. Use the sizing handles to resize the UserForm so that everything will fit in. Change the `Caption` property to **New Color Scheme**.

3. Place two `Frame` controls into the UserForm as shown in Figure 23.1, and set their `Caption` properties to **Top-Right Corner** and **Bottom-Left Corner**.

FIGURE 23.1:

GUI for the New Color Scheme application

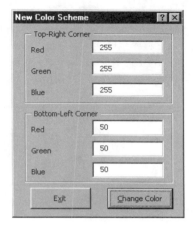

FIGURE 23.2:

Result of entering the numbers shown in Figure 23.1 and clicking Change Color

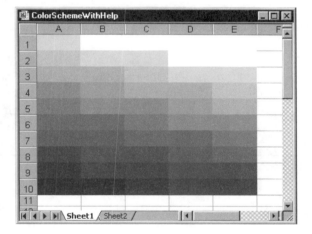

4. Place three Label controls and three TextBox controls into each frame and change the Caption properties of the Label controls to match those shown.

5. Place a command button at the bottom-right corner of the UserForm. Change its Caption property to Change Color, and change its Accelerator property to C to display the caption text with the first letter underlined.

6. Place a command button at the bottom-left corner and change its Caption property to Exit and its Accelerator property to x.

Coding the New Application

Listing 23.1 shows the code that displays the GUI for the New Color Scheme application. Here the UserForm is made available so the user can enter the numbers denoting the colors they want for their range of cells. Enter this code into a module (choose Insert ➤ Module).

LISTING 23.1

```
0    Sub StartApplication()
1        UserForm1.Show
2    End Sub
```

ANALYSIS

Line 1 uses the Show method to load UserForm1, if it isn't already loaded, and to make it visible to the user.

Listing 23.2 shows the code for the ColorRangeOfCells procedure that runs to provide the results. This procedure is entered into the General section of the code window for UserForm1. The other two procedures are the Click event procedures for the two CommandButton controls; their code is entered into the skeleton procedures that already exist in UserForm1's code window.

LISTING 23.2

```
0    Sub ColorRangeOfCells()
1        ' colors the cells containing annual sales figures
2        If TextBox1.Value = "" Then TextBox1.Value = 0
3        If TextBox2.Value = "" Then TextBox2.Value = 0
4        If TextBox3.Value = "" Then TextBox3.Value = 0
5        If TextBox4.Value = "" Then TextBox4.Value = 0
6        If TextBox5.Value = "" Then TextBox5.Value = 0
7        If TextBox6.Value = "" Then TextBox6.Value = 0
8        For ColumnNumber = Asc("A") To Asc("E")
9        For Counter = 1 To 10
10           Temp = ColumnNumber - Asc("A")
11           ActiveWorkbook.Colors(Counter + Temp * 10) = _
                 RGB((10 - Counter) * TextBox1.Value / 10 + Counter _
```

```
                  * TextBox4.Value / 10 + Temp * 10, _
                  (10 - Counter) * TextBox2.Value / 10 + Counter _
                  * TextBox5.Value / 10 + Temp * 10, _
                  (10 - Counter) * TextBox3.Value / 10 + Counter _
                  * TextBox6.Value / 10 + Temp * 10)
12                Range(Chr(ColumnNumber) & _
                  Counter).Interior.ColorIndex = Counter + Temp * 10
13                Next
14        Next
15    End Sub
16
17    Private Sub CommandButton1_Click()
18        If CommandButton1.Caption = "Change Color" Then
19            ColorRangeOfCells
20            CommandButton1.Caption = "Clear"
21            CommandButton1.ControlTipText = "Clears Colors"
22        Else
23            Range("A1:E10").Clear
24            CommandButton1.Caption = "Change Color"
25            CommandButton1.ControlTipText = "Changes Colors"
26        End If
27    End Sub
28
29    Private Sub CommandButton2_Click()
30        End
31    End Sub
```

ANALYSIS

Line 0 starts the ColorRangeOfCells macro.

Lines 2 through 7 ensure that if any of the text boxes are empty, their Value properties are assigned zeros.

Line 8 starts the For loop that will jump from column A to column E. This statement uses the Asc function to convert letters A and E to their ASCII character codes (see Appendix A).

Line 9 starts the For loop that handles rows 1 through 10.

Line 10 sets the Temp variable to the numbers 1 through 5 to represent the column numbers.

Line 11 sets the colors in the active workbook's palette using the RGB function to come up with values. The entries in all six text boxes are used to calculate the values passed to the Red, Green, and Blue arguments of this function.

Line 12 assigns the number of the color in the palette to the current cell's interior color index.

Lines 13 and 14 mark the end of the two For loops.

Line 17 starts the Click event procedure for CommandButton1.

Line 18 starts the If...Then...Else... statement by testing whether the Caption property of the CommandButton1 control is currently set to Change Color.

Line 19 runs the ColorRangeOfCells macro to fill the range of cells with color.

Line 20 sets the Caption property to Clear.

Line 21 sets the ControlTipText to Clears Colors so that the tip matches the new caption on the command button.

Line 22 starts the Else part of the If...Then...Else... statement, which will be executed if the caption isn't Change Color.

Line 23 uses the Clear method to restore the worksheet by removing the interior colors.

Line 24 assigns the Caption property Change Color.

Line 25 assigns Changes Colors to the ControlTipText property to make the ToolTip match the command button's new caption.

Line 29 starts CommandButton2's Click event procedure.

Line 30 uses the End statement to stop the application running.

Providing Help with ToolTips

A ToolTip is the information that pops up when you pause the mouse cursor over a control. ToolTips provide instant help by giving a (very brief) description of the purpose of that control.

ToolTips are the lowest level of help and are the easiest to implement: Simply set the ControlTipText property of the control in the Properties window and it will appear to the user while the code is running. Let's provide ToolTips for our New Color Scheme application. Table 23.1 lists the controls and the text assigned to the ControlTipText property of each.

TABLE 23.1: ToolTips Assigned to Controls in the GUI of the New Color Scheme Application

Control	ControlTipText Setting
TextBox1	Enter 0-255 for Red
TextBox2	Enter 0-255 for Green
TextBox3	Enter 0-255 for Blue
TextBox4	Enter 0-255 for Red
TextBox5	Enter 0-255 for Green
TextBox6	Enter 0-255 for Blue
Frame1	Set color for top-right cell
Frame2	Set color for bottom-left cell
CommandButton1	Change color scheme
CommandButton2	Exit from the Application

Figure 23.3 shows the text assigned to the ControlTipText property of Frame1 being displayed as a ToolTip.

The ControlTipText can be set in code too, giving the additional advantage of being able to change the text to suit the situation. Lines 21 and 25 of Listing 23.2 show the ControlTipText property of CommandButton1 being assigned new text to suit its changing Caption property.

NOTE By default, the ControlTipText is set to the empty string and does not show a ToolTip.

FIGURE 23.3:

ToolTip being displayed for
`Frame1`

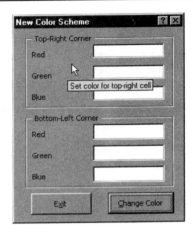

Creating the Help Facility

I'm sure that you'll agree that the online help facility plays an important role in how user-friendly your application seems to its users. Can you imagine using Microsoft Excel without its online help?

The online help facility increases the usability of an application and should be made as comprehensive as possible to provide appropriate help any time the user requests it. Help may be required with data entry or with responding to message boxes, as well as with technical aspects of the application.

There are three common access methods in a Windows help facility that experienced users will expect to find in your application:

- the F1 function key
- the What's This button
- the Contents and Index buttons in the Help window

We will include all of these access methods in the online help facility for the New Color Scheme application.

The online help information in our application will be contained in help pages that include not only the text displayed to the user, but also the control codes that support these access methods. The codes permit direct access via the What's This button or the F1 function key, determine what's displayed in the Find Topics list and index entries, and allow jumps from a topic in one page to a topic in another.

The help facility for the New Color Scheme application consists of three files. The first file contains all of the information displayed to the user, with each topic placed on a separate help page accompanied by the control codes to specify the topic and its index entries and context name. Although we're going to place all of our help pages into this one file, it may be more convenient for the help pages of a large application to be split between several files.

The second file contains a list of all context names from the help pages and allocates them the numbers assigned to the `HelpContextId` properties of the controls. When you ask for help on a particular control, its HelpContextId number is used to look up the list of context names to find the required help page, which is then displayed to the user. Context names are also used for the jump text strings. This information can be placed directly into the help project file, but I think it's more practical to keep it in its own separate file.

The third required file is the help project file. This file tells the help compiler where to find the first two files and where to place the compiled executable help file, which it creates and gives the extension .HLP.

The full-blown help facility is developed in seven stages:

1. Create the help file in Rich Text Format and add control codes to identify context names, index entries, and topics to be used by the Find feature.

2. Create the file containing context names and HelpContextId numbers.

3. Assign the numbers to the `HelpContextId` properties of the controls.

4. Create the help project file and specify the two filenames.

5. Compile the help project file.

6. Update the application so that it can call help.

7. Test and debug the help facility.

Creating the Help Pages

In creating your help pages, you'll want to write the information for each topic on a separate page. Instructions can include

- how to use the application
- what particular controls do
- useful information related to the topic
- what interaction is expected by a control placed on the form

Keep information as brief and concise as possible and use short paragraphs, since reading from the screen causes eyestrain faster than reading from a printed page does. Long topics should be structured hierarchically, enabling different subtopics to be accessed.

Help files must be created using a text editor—such as Microsoft Word—that can save files in Rich Text Format (.RTF), the format required by the control codes. Let's enter the help information for our New Color Scheme application into a file. Open the editor application and enter the help pages shown in Listing 23.3, with a hard page break between each page where stated.

LISTING 23.3

```
Color Scheme - Help

Help topics for Color Scheme have the same structure as the menu
topics.

Topics appearing as green underlined text can be selected by position-
ing the mouse cursor over the topic and clicking the mouse button.

To learn how to use Help, choose Help and press F1.

To return to this screen at any time, select the Contents button at the
top of the Help screen.

General Information on the Color Scheme software!

Red

Blue
```

<u>Green</u>

<u>Help</u>

<u>Continue</u>

<u>Exit</u>

------------Page Break------------
General Information on the Color Scheme software

The Color Scheme software is based on a simple model for providing the colors of your choice for the top-left and bottom-right corners. Colors elsewhere are interpolated between these two.

------------Page Break------------
Red Entry

The Red entry can be in the range 0 through 255 depending on the level of red you want in your color. When all three color components are 0 the color is black and when all three color components are 255 the color is white.

------------Page Break------------
Blue Entry

The Blue entry can be in the range 0 through 255 depending on the level of blue you want in your color.

------------Page Break------------
Green Entry

The Green entry can be in the range 0 through 255 depending on the level of green you want in your color.

------------Page Break------------
Continue Button

The **Continue Button** displays the Color Scheme for the colors specified in the text boxes.

Keyboard shortcut: Alt + C

————————Page Break————————
Exit Button

The **Exit** button closes the Color Scheme application.

Keyboard shortcut: Alt + X

Adding Control Codes

Now it's time to add the control codes to our help pages to allow the user to access them in different ways. The Table 23.2 shows the control codes for each access method.

T A B L E   2 3 . 2 : Access Method Control Codes

Control Code	Control Name	Access Method
footnote $	Topic in Find list	Used to search for a topic.
footnote #	Context Name	User presses F1 or uses the What's This button.
solid underlined text	Jump	Jumps to other help pages using the context name.
footnote K	Keyword in Index	User enters keyword or selects one from the list of Index entries.

Keywords in Index

Keywords appear as an index entry when the Index button is clicked. Figure 23.4 shows the index list for the New Color Scheme application.

The following steps show how to set the index entries for the New Color Scheme when Microsoft Word is used to create the help pages:

1. Open Microsoft Word and display the first help page and place the insertion point before the first character in the topic heading.

2. Select Insert ➤ Footnote to display the Footnote and Endnote dialog box shown in Figure 23.5.

FIGURE 23.4:

List of index entries in the Index tab of the Help Topics dialog box

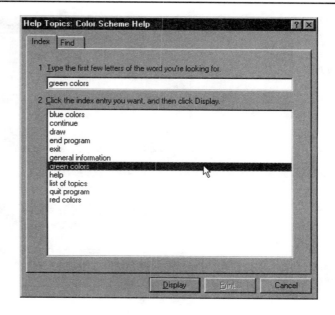

FIGURE 23.5:

Making text an index entry using the Footnote And Endnote dialog box

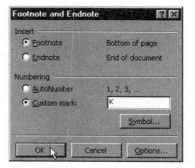

3. Check the Footnote and Custom Mark option buttons and enter the upper-case letter **K** into the box, as shown.

4. Click the OK button.

5. The letter K will appear as a superscript footnote mark against the topic heading, as shown in Figure 23.6. A K will also appear as the start of the footnote with the entry cursor alongside it, as shown in Figure 23.7.

FIGURE 23.6:

Result of entering a footnote prior to the first character in the topic heading

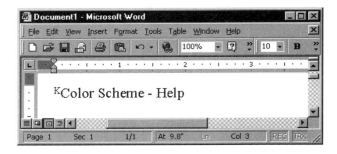

FIGURE 23.7:

The letter K at the footnote is followed by the entry cursor waiting for you to enter the text that will become an index entry.

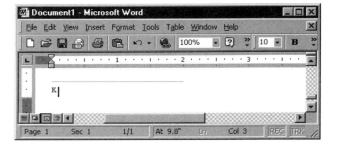

Specifying text as a footnote with the letter K immediately forces the cursor to the bottom of the current page so that the text for the index can be entered. Enter the text **Help;list of topics**. This will appear as two entries in the Index list. Make sure that only a single space separates the K and the index entries—Excel enters this space for you and positions the cursor to allow you to start entering the index text right away.

6. Repeat steps 1 through 5 for the other help pages, giving them the following index entries:

```
general information
red colors
blue colors
green colors
continue;draw
exit;quit program;end program
```

NOTE If more than one index entry is required for the same help page, separate them with a semicolon.

Context Strings

Each topic in the help file is uniquely identified by a context name. Context names are inserted in much the same way as index entries are, but the # symbol is used instead of the letter K. The following steps show you how to enter context strings:

1. Display the first help page and place the insertion point before the first character in the first line of text. It doesn't matter whether you place it before or after the K.

2. Select Insert ➤ Footnote from the menu bar, as you did in the previous section.

3. Ensure that Footnote and Custom Mark are selected, and enter # in the box. Click OK. A small # symbol will appear as a superscript against the topic heading; another will appear at the bottom of the page at the start of the footnote.

4. Enter **HELP** as the context string for the footnote, making sure that only a single space separates the # and the first letter of the context string.

NOTE Valid context strings can contain alphabetic and numeric characters, the period character, and the underscore character. They can be up to 255 characters in length, although short strings may be preferable since they require less typing and are easier to get right.

Jump Text

Now that you have created context names, you can jump to the location represented by a context name using jump text. This enables you to jump from one help page to another that contains the help required; it serves the same purpose as cross-references in books. A jump is specially coded text that's displayed to the user as underlined green text that, if clicked, causes a jump to the topic it references. The reference is a context name, which is hidden from the user when the jump text is displayed. The following steps show how to set up the jump text and its reference for the first help page in the New Color Scheme's online help facility

1. Open the file containing your help pages. Add **GENERAL** onto the end of the General Information on the Color Scheme Application! jump text without leaving any spaces in between.

2. Select the jump text General Information on the Color Scheme Application! and choose Format ➢ Font to open the Font dialog box. Select the double underline feature from the Underline Style drop-down list (Figure 23.8) and click OK to return to your help page (Figure 23.9).

FIGURE 23.8:

Selecting the double underline style from the Font dialog box

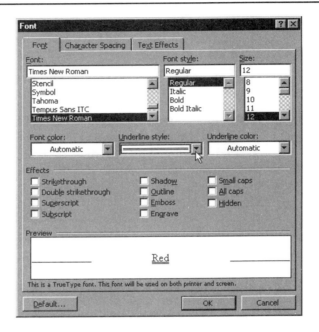

FIGURE 23.9:

Entering the context string that will be used to determine the destination in the jump

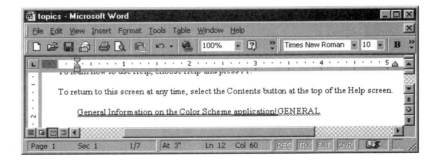

3. Select GENERAL and choose Format ➢ Font to display the Font dialog box again. Make sure that the Underline box is set to None and check the Hid-

den check box in the Effects options. Click OK to return to Microsoft Word, which now won't display the reference GENERAL.

4. Repeat steps 1 through 3 again for the other jump strings by adding shortened references to the strings. Using uppercase for your jump references is helpful, as is using words that are related to the string concerned.

TIP

Entering jump references in uppercase only makes them easier to distinguish from jump texts. The help compiler does not distinguish between uppercase and lowercase characters, so you could have the jump reference and the destination help page specified using different cases.

WARNING

Where more than one help file exists and you want to enable jumping between files, the files' path names must be included as part of the hidden context string. The format is *context_string@c:\dir1\file3.hlp*.

Topics in Find List

Help applications have a Find feature that lets the user search for a topic by entering or selecting a word or phrase to be searched for. Specifying a topic to be included in the Find list is achieved with the following actions:

1. Display the first help page again and position the mouse cursor immediately before the first character.

2. Choose Insert ➤ Footnote. Ensure that Footnote and Custom Mark are selected, and enter a $ symbol in the box.

3. Click OK. A small $ will appear against the topic heading and at the bottom of the page at the start of the footnote. Enter **ColorScheme - Help** as the keyword phrase in the footnote. Only a single space is allowed between the $ and the first keyword character, and that space will already have been entered by Excel.

Figure 23.10 shows the three footnote symbols entered so far in front of the title on the first help page, and Figure 23.11 shows the footnote entries.

The same "find" word can be used in more than one help page. When the user enters a keyword to search the topics in the help files, a list of all of the topics associated with that word are displayed. Figure 23.12 shows the result of selecting "color" as a search word.

The three footnote symbols placed against the title in the first help page

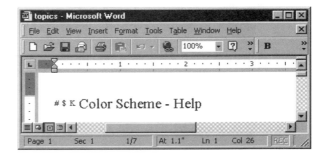

FIGURE 23.11:

The three footnote entries for the help page

Linking Help Pages with Context Numbers

Context-sensitive help provides direct access to the help page required. The user needs to select a control to give it the focus, and then depress the F1 key. Alternatively, the user can click the What's This button and click the control. The help page for the selected control will be displayed.

In order to implement context-sensitive help in your application, you must associate controls with their help pages. These associations are achieved by listing the context numbers of controls (the HelpContextId property) with the context names of their help pages.

FIGURE 23.12:

Selecting "color" as the word to be searched displays a list of three topics

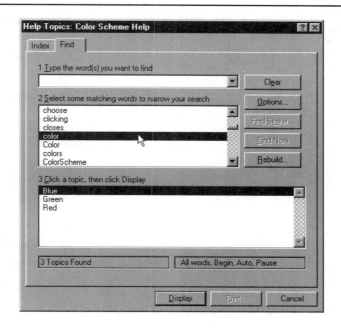

Let's continue developing the New Color Scheme help facility. Open a new file in Microsoft Word and save it as **HelpContextIds.h**. Enter the following information in the file with a tab character separating context names and HelpContextId numbers:

```
#define HELP        10
#define GENERAL     20
#define RED         30
#define BLUE        40
#define GREEN       50
#define CONTINUE    60
#define EXIT        70
```

Assigning Context Numbers to Controls

The HelpContextId numbers must be entered into the Property window for each control. Assign the numbers listed in Table 23.3 to the controls shown.

TABLE 23.3: Controls and the Numbers Assigned to the HelpContextId

Control	HelpContextId number
TextBox1	30
TextBox2	50
TextBox3	40
TextBox4	30
TextBox5	50
TextBox6	40
CommandButton1	60
CommandButton2	70

Creating the Help Project File

All of the files that make up the help facility must be listed in a specific way in the help project file, which has the extension .HPJ. The help compiler uses this file to compile and link all required files into a binary source file of the same name with the extension .HLP.

The help project file is split into several sections with section names enclosed in brackets. Listing 23.4 shows the contents of the project file for the New Color Scheme.

LISTING 23.4

```
[OPTIONS]
LCID=0x409 0x0 0x0 ; English (United States)
REPORT=Yes
TITLE=Color Scheme Help
HLP=.\CompiledHelp.hlp

[FILES]
Topics.rtf
```

```
[MAP]
#include <HelpContextIds.h>

[WINDOWS]
main="Color Scheme",(0,0,1023,1023),0,,(r12632256)
```

ANALYSIS

The **OPTIONS** section allows you to specify the language required for your help facility. Setting REPORT to Yes tells the help compiler to report on its progress. TITLE is set to the caption you want displayed on the title bar. HLP is used to specify the file where the executable code produced by the help compiler is to be written.

The **FILE** section contains one or more help files (.rtf) listed one per line.

The **MAPS** section includes the file that associates the context names that are stored in help pages with the context numbers that are assigned to the HelpContextID properties of the controls. Note how #include is used here with the filename enclosed in angle brackets. This is carried over from the C programming language and allows the compiler to replace this single line with the contents of the specified file.

The **WINDOWS** section enables the attributes of the help window to be specified.

WARNING   Project files must be saved as Text Only (ASCII) format.

Compiling the Help Project File

There are several help compilers available and they all do much the same thing. Some run under DOS and others, like the help compiler from the Microsoft Help Workshop that's used here, are Windows applications. The Help Workshop application is included with the Microsoft Visual Studio 6.0 suite of applications. The Web page at http://www.luhsd.k12.ca.us/lhs/rtfprog.html gives details about some programs that are available for creating help files and has a link to a Microsoft Help Compiler you can download.

To create your executable help file using Help Workshop:

1. Run `Hcrtf.exe` to display the Microsoft Help Workshop window and choose File ➤ Compile, as shown in Figure 23.13, to open the Compile A Help File dialog box.

FIGURE 23.13:

Choosing the `Compile` command in the Microsoft Help Workshop application

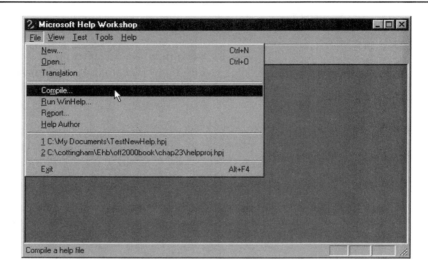

2. Enter the name of your help project file into the Project File box, as shown in Figure 23.14.

FIGURE 23.14:

Entering the name of the help project file in the Compile A Help File dialog box

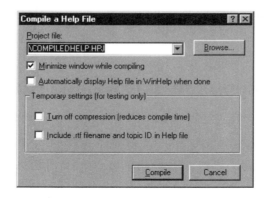

3. Click Compile to make your help files into an executable help facility. When the compilation is complete, the compiler will provide a report on its findings, as well as warnings and error messages (if requested in the OPTIONS section of the help project file). Figure 23.15 shows the report generated for the New Color Scheme application.

FIGURE 23.15:

Report generated by the help compiler after compiling the New Color Scheme help facility

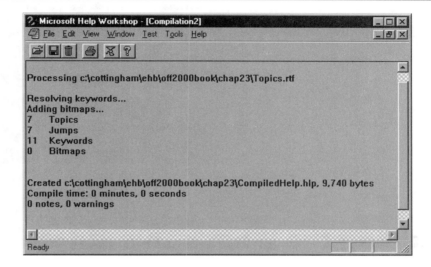

If the compilation is successful, the binary resource file that the compiler generates is given the same name as the help project file but will have an extension of .HLP.

Specifying the Help File for a Project

You need to tell Visual Basic the name of the executable help file that you want to use for your application. The following steps show you how:

1. Run Excel, open the New Color Scheme application, and open the Visual Basic Editor.

2. Choose Tools ➤ VBAProject Properties to display the VBAProject - Project Properties dialog box, shown in Figure 23.16. Enter the compiled help file-name into the Help File box and **10** in the Project Help Context Id box. (We assigned the HelpContextId number "10" to the #defineHELP context name earlier in the "Linking Help Pages with Context Numbers" section.) Click OK to return to your New Color Scheme application.

FIGURE 23.16:

Specifying the help file to
be used for the New Color
Scheme application

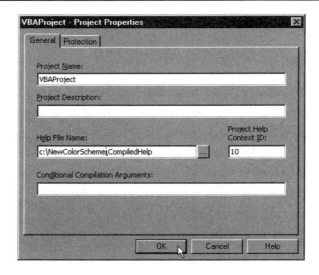

Adding the What's This Button

To place a What's This button on the title bar, all you need to do is set the `Whats-ThisButton` property of the UserForm to `True`. The button containing a question mark icon will then appear (as shown below) and will already have its `Control-TipText` property set to `Help`.

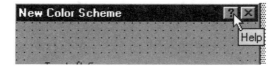

When you change the `WhatsThisButton` property to `True` in the Property window, the `WhatsThisHelp` property will also change to `True` if it isn't `True` already. Setting the `WhatsThisHelp` property to `True` allows Windows Help to be used to display the help pages in your application.

The What's This button allows the user to get help on controls that respond when clicked. These controls cannot be selected by clicking before using the F1 key. The only way to select them is by tabbing until the required control has the focus and then pressing the F1 key. For example, Figure 23.17 shows the help page contents for the Change Color command button in the New Color Scheme application.

FIGURE 23.17:

Using the What's This button to get help on the Change Color command button

Testing and Debugging the Help Facility

The help facility can be easily tested by running the New Color Scheme application and using the context-sensitive help feature. Test each control that you've supplied help for, pressing F1 each time and checking that the correct help topic is displayed. Figure 23.18 shows the help page displayed by clicking on the top text box ("Red") to give it the focus and then pressing the F1 function key.

FIGURE 23.18:

Help page displayed as the result of clicking TextBox1 and pressing the F1 function key

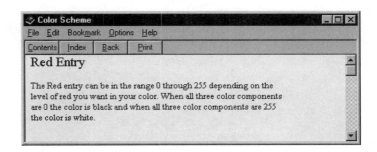

Accessing Contents in the Online Help

The Contents help page in the online help facility provides an overview of the application, much as the contents section of a book gives an overview of sections and chapters. To view the Contents help page:

1. Run the New Color Scheme application and click the What's This button. Move the mouse cursor—now accompanied by a question mark icon—to anywhere inside the UserForm but outside the text boxes and command buttons.

2. Click the mouse to open the online help window, which will display the first help page, as shown in Figure 23.19. This was the help page specified when you entered 10 in the Project Help Context ID box (Figure 23.16).

3. Click each underlined topic from the list in turn and check that the help page jumped to is the correct one. Click Back or Contents to redisplay the contents list after each jump.

FIGURE 23.19:

Help page displayed to the user when they access the online help facility

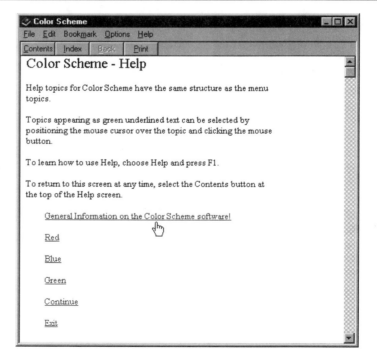

Accessing Topics Using the Index

The Index option provides keyword lists and index entries as navigational aids that provide the same facility as an index in a book. Figure 23.20 shows the list of topics in the Index in the New Color Scheme application.

FIGURE 23.20:

Index entries for the New Color Scheme application

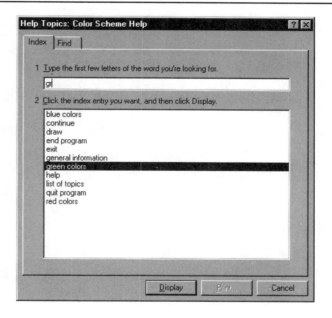

Selecting an item from the list or entering a keyword in the box enables direct access to the help page required. As you begin entering a keyword, the first index entry starting with the text entered so far is highlighted. When you've identified the entry you would like help on, click Display. Figure 23.21 shows the help page displayed when the General Information entry was selected.

FIGURE 23.21:

General Information
help page

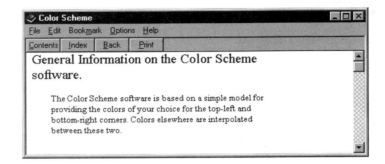

Summary

After completing this chapter, you'll be able to

- provide users of your applications with ToolTip text
- create help pages and add control codes
- provide help via the F1 function key
- provide help using the What's This button
- create the help project file
- compile the help facility
- specify the help file that the application is to use and define the first help page to be displayed
- test and debug your facility
- provide jumps to the help pages required from the Contents page
- provide index entries for users to find help

CHAPTER
TWENTY-FOUR

24

That's Entertainment

Add some spice to your applications and let the Office Assistant dance to amuse and entertain your users—you'll have fun too! In this chapter, you'll see how to specify the animated sequence that you want the Office Assistant to perform and how to use callouts to communicate with the user. You'll also see how to dress up a worksheet using WordArt objects by specifying attributes such as the path for their characters to follow and whether or not a shadow is required.

Dancing with the Office Assistant

In this example, you'll see how to make the Office Assistant dance and display text in a callout bubble.

1. Open a new workbook and save it as **Dancing Office Assistant**.

2. Move the Office Assistant to where you want it to dance on your worksheet.

3. Choose View ➤ Toolbars ➤ Drawing to display the Drawing toolbar. Click AutoShapes, select Callouts from the drop-down list, and click Cloud Callout, as shown in Figure 24.1

FIGURE 24.1:

Choosing the Cloud Callout drawing object from the Drawing toolbar

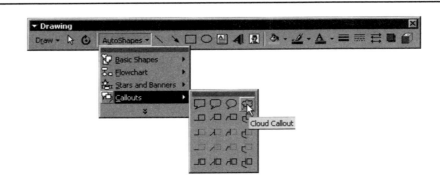

4. Place the callout on your worksheet above the Office Assistant. The entry cursor will immediately appear in the callout, as shown below.

5. Open the Visual Basic Editor and choose Insert ➤ Module to add `Module1` to your project. Enter the code shown in Listing 24.1 into `Module1`'s code window. This code controls the actions of the Office Assistant by setting its `Animation` property to a Microsoft Office constant. Figure 24.2 shows some of these constants listed in the Help window.

FIGURE 24.2:

Constants available for setting the `Animation` property of the Assistant

6. Run your Dance macro and watch while the Office Assistant entertains you! The following images provide you with frames from some of the clips you'll see.

LISTING 24.1

```
0   Sub Dance()
1       'prepare balloon
2       ActiveSheet.Shapes("AutoShape 1").Visible = True
3       ActiveSheet.Shapes("AutoShape 1").Select
4       Selection.Characters.Text = "Hi!"
5       With Selection.Characters(Start:=1, Length:=4).Font
6           .Name = "Arial"
7           .FontStyle = "Bold"
8           .Size = 12
9       End With
10      'prepare assistant
11      With Assistant
12      OrigAssistant = .Filename
13          .Filename = _
            "C:\Program Files\Microsoft Office\Office\OffCat.acs"
14          WaitABit
15          DoRoutine
16          .Filename = OrigAssistant
17      End With
18      ActiveSheet.Shapes("AutoShape 1").Visible = False
19  End Sub
20
21  Sub WaitABit()
22      Start = Timer
23      Do While Timer < Start + 4
24          DoEvents
25      Loop
26  End Sub
27
28  Sub DoRoutine()
29      With Assistant
30          Selection.Characters.Text = "Look left!"
31          .Animation = msoAnimationGestureLeft
32          WaitABit
33          Selection.Characters.Text = "Look right!"
34          .Animation = msoAnimationGestureRight
35          WaitABit
36          Selection.Characters.Text = "Now let me see!"
37          .Animation = msoAnimationWritingNotingSomething
38          WaitABit
39          Selection.Characters.Text = "Need my glasses!"
```

```
40          .Animation = msoAnimationWorkingAtSomething
41          WaitABit
42          Selection.Characters.Text = _
            "Let's keep the place tidy."
43          .Animation = msoAnimationSaving
44          WaitABit
45          Selection.Characters.Text = "Let's dance!"
46          .Animation = msoAnimationEmptyTrash
47          WaitABit
48          .Animation = msoAnimationSearch
49          WaitABit
50          Selection.Characters.Text = "La! La! La!"
51          .Animation = msoAnimationGetAttentionMinor
52          WaitABit
53          Selection.Characters.Text = "Purrrrrrrr! That's nice."
54          .Animation = msoAnimationCharacterSuccessMajor
55          WaitABit
56          Selection.Characters.Text = "Play it again Sam!"
57          .Animation = msoAnimationEmptyTrash
58          WaitABit
59          .Animation = msoAnimationGetAttentionMinor
60          WaitABit
61          Selection.Characters.Text = "Purrrrr, lovely"
62          .Animation = msoAnimationCharacterSuccessMajor
63          WaitABit
64          .Animation = msoAnimationAttentionMinor
65          WaitABit
66          Selection.Characters.Text = "Bye!"
67          .Animation = msoAnimationGoodbye
68          WaitABit
69      End With
70  End Sub
```

ANALYSIS

Line 0 starts the Dance macro.

Line 2 sets the Visible property of the Cloud Callout to True.

Line 3 makes the Cloud Callout Shape object the selected object.

Line 4 assigns "Hi!" to the Text property of the selected shape, which immediately displays it in the callout.

Line 5 uses the `With` statement to enable the properties of the `Font` object in Lines 6 through 8 to be set without needing to fully qualify them.

Lines 6 through 8 set some `Font` properties.

Line 11 uses the `With` statement to allow the Assistant's properties to be set in Lines 13 and 16, and to be used in Line 12 without the need to qualify them.

Line 12 assigns the value of the current Assistant's `Filename` property to the variable `OrigAssistant`; this variable is used in Line 16 to restore the Assistant back to what it was before running this macro. The next section, "Assigning the Office Assistant," provides further information on how to find out which Assistants are installed on your computer.

Line 13 sets the `Filename` property of the Assistant to the name of the file containing Links the cat. Table 24.1 lists a few of the Office Assistants available and their Microsoft Agent Character filenames (.ACS). Use the Windows Explorer to find the .ACS files available on your PC. If you don't have `OffCat.acs`, then use one of the other .ACS files that you have available.

Line 14 calls the `WaitABit` macro to slow things down so that the first animated sequence has time to finish.

Line 15 calls the `DoRoutine` macro that makes the Office Assistant perform all of the actions.

Line 16 sets the `Filename` property of the `Assistant` object back to the Assistant that was current before running this macro.

Line 18 sets the `Visible` property of the Cloud Callout to `False` to make it invisible.

Line 21 starts the `WaitABit` macro, causing a delay to allow the current action of the Assistant time to finish before performing the next action.

Line 22 sets the variable `Start` to the value returned by the `Timer` function.

Line 23 uses the condition in the `While` statement to loop for four seconds from now.

Line 24 uses the `DoEvents` function to process any Microsoft Windows events that are waiting for a response. The events in this case are displaying frames from the animated sequence of the Office Assistant.

Line 28 starts the `DoRoutine` macro that displays several animated sequences of the Office Assistant.

Line 29 uses the With statement so that the Assistant object's properties can be used without being qualified. There is only one Assistant object that represents the Microsoft Office Assistant.

Line 30 uses the Characters method of the Cloud Callout (which was selected in Line 3 of the Dance macro) to set the characters in the Shape object's text. The text reflects the action being performed.

Line 31 sets the Animation property of the Assistant object to a Microsoft Office constant that determines what action the Office Assistant will perform.

Line 32 calls the WaitABit macro to delay jumping to the next action to enable the current action to finish.

Lines 33 through 68 repeat Lines 30 through 32 to perform a sequence of different actions.

NOTE   The Timer function returns the number of seconds since midnight.

Assigning the Office Assistant

The Assistants available with Microsoft Office 2000 and the names of the files containing their details are shown in Table 24.1. All files are installed in the folder C:\Program Files\Microsoft Office\Office. You may have other Assistants on your PC depending on what other applications you have installed. The dancing example in the previous section used the Links Assistant; the full pathname for OffCat.acs was assigned to the Filename property to change the Office Assistant to Links.

T A B L E 2 4 . 1: Microsoft Office 2000 Assistants

Assistant	Filename
Clippit	Clippit.acs
Links	OffCat.acs
Rocky	Rocky.acs
Office.Logo	Logo.acs

Continued on next page

TABLE 24.1 CONTINUED: Microsoft Office 2000 Assistants

Assistant	Filename
The Dot	Dot.acs
Mother Nature	Mnature.acs
F1	F1.acs

WordArt Text Enhancement

WordArt provides a great way to enhance the text in your workbooks. The artistic text strings are WordArt objects that can be stored in templates with all of the other information required for reproduction. WordArt objects can be updated using the WordArt toolbar.

The WordArt Toolbar

The WordArt toolbar, shown in Figure 24.3, can be displayed in either of the following ways:

- Click Insert WordArt in the Drawing toolbar, choose a special effect, and enter the text required. The WordArt toolbar will then appear and let you add or change the effects.

- Choose View ➤ Toolbars ➤ WordArt.

FIGURE 24.3:

WordArt toolbar

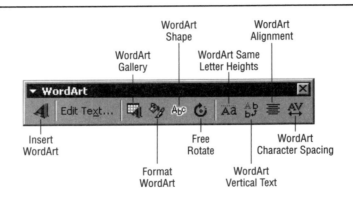

Insert WordArt opens the WordArt Gallery dialog box (Figure 24.4), which displays a selection of WordArt styles that you can choose from.

WordArt Gallery dialog box

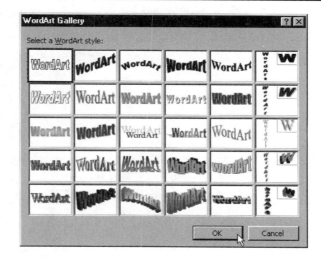

When you've made your choice, the Edit WordArt Text dialog box (Figure 24.5) is displayed to allow you to personalize your text.

Edit WordArt Text dialog box

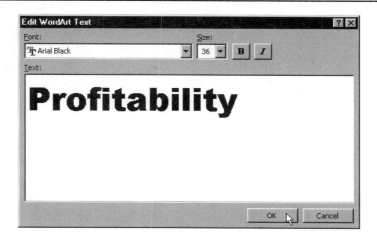

Edit Text opens the Edit WordArt Text dialog box (Figure 24.5), which allows you to enter new text or to change the text in the selected WordArt object.

WordArt Gallery opens the WordArt Gallery dialog box (Figure 24.4), which allows you to change the art style of the selected `WordArt` object.

Format WordArt displays the Format WordArt dialog box (Figure 24.6), which allows you to specify the size, fill, and outline colors for the lettering.

FIGURE 24.6:

Format WordArt dialog box

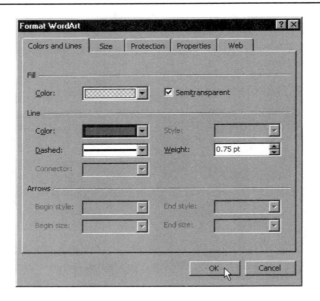

If your `WordArt` object is to be included inside a Web page, you can select the Web tab (Figure 24.7) and specify the Alternative Text you want displayed while the Web page containing the object is being loaded. By default, the text in the `WordArt` object is used. This text is important, as Web search engines will use it when trying to find Web pages containing requested information.

WordArt Shape allows you to choose a shape for the path of your `WordArt` object from the list of shapes shown in Figure 24.8.

FIGURE 24.7:

The Web tab from the Format WordArt dialog box

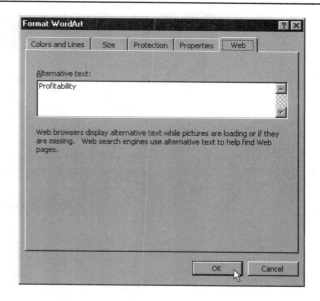

FIGURE 24.8:

Shapes available for WordArt objects

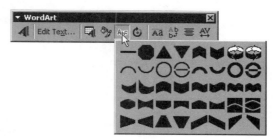

Examples of some of the shapes available for WordArt objects are shown below; in order, they are Arch Up (curve), Circle (curve), Ring Inside, Wave 1, and Inflate Top.

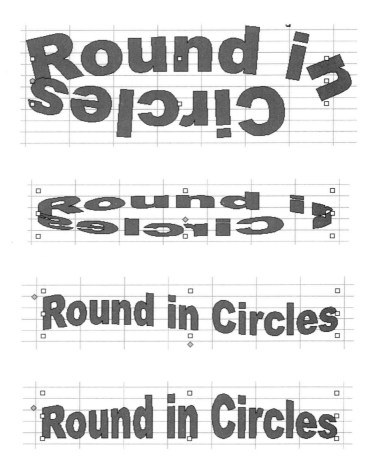

Free Rotate changes the squares that denote the sizing handles to small green circles and turns the mouse cursor into four arrows in a circle when it's positioned over a green circle, as shown below.

Dragging the sizing handle around rotates the dashed lines that show where the WordArt object will be positioned. Releasing the mouse button displays the WordArt text at its rotated position, as shown below.

WordArt Same Letter Heights makes lowercase and uppercase letters have the same height while still preserving the WordArt object's shape:

WordArt Vertical Text toggles between displaying the text vertically and displaying it horizontally while trying to preserve the WordArt object's shape. This example shows the text being displayed vertically.

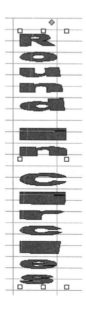

WordArt Alignment displays a list of choices for aligning text within the area allocated to a `WordArt` object (Figure 24.9).

The Word Justify option changes space between words without adjusting spacing between characters. The Letter Justify option adjusts spaces between characters. The Stretch Justify option adjusts characters instead of spaces.

WordArt Character Spacing displays a list that allows you to set the spacing between characters (Figure 24.10).

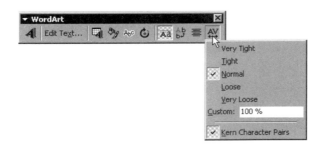

The last option, Kern Character Pairs, changes the amount of space between pairs of characters where normal spacing would make them appear too close or too far apart. The other options all have to do with *tracking*, which refers to the amount of space uniformly applied between characters. Figure 24.11 shows the WordArt text when the Very Tight option is selected, and Figure 24.12 shows the same object when the Very Loose option is selected.

Figure 24.13 shows an additional feature that's displayed with the sizing handles to make the text slant forward or backward according to the direction you move the yellow diamond.

FIGURE 24.11:

WordArt text when the Very Tight option for character spacing is selected

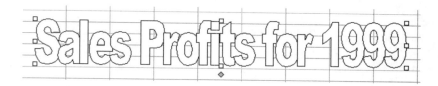

FIGURE 24.12:

WordArt text when Very Loose option for character spacing is selected

FIGURE 24.13:

Moving the diamond to the left makes the text slant forward.

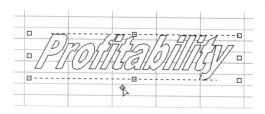

Enhancing a Workbook

Let's add formatting to a new worksheet. First we'll add the title artwork, using commands from the WordArt and Drawing toolbars; then we can color it, add shadows, and format the text to make a snazzy title for Sheet2.

Adding a *WordArt* Object

1. Choose File ➢ New, click the AnnualSales icon in the New dialog box to open workbook AnnualSales1, and click OK.

2. Select the Sheet2 tab.

3. Choose View ➤ Toolbars ➤ WordArt to display the WordArt toolbar (Figure 24.3). Choose the Insert WordArt button (sloping **A** icon) from the toolbar to open the WordArt Gallery dialog box (Figure 24.4).

4. Select the top-left style in the WordArt Gallery and click OK to open the Edit WordArt Text dialog box (Figure 24.5). This style will provide a good basic WordArt object that we can dress up. Enter **Profitability** and click OK to return to your worksheet, which will now display your WordArt object, as shown in Figure 24.14. Because a WordArt object is selected, the WordArt toolbar is now on display to allow you to make adjustments—the toolbar will disappear if you click anywhere else in your worksheet.

FIGURE 24.14:

WordArt object with the text "Profitability"

5. Drag your WordArt graphic to cells A2:D5 of Sheet2, leaving row 1 clear to accommodate a shadow, which we will add below.

Adding Color to a *WordArt* Object

1. Click the Format WordArt button on the WordArt toolbar to open the Format WordArt dialog box (Figure 24.6) and select the Colors and Lines tab. Click the Down arrow in the Color box to display the color palette and click More Colors to open the Colors dialog box.

2. Select the Custom tab and choose a bright shade of green, as shown in Figure 24.15, by doing one of the following:

    •   Move the cross within the Colors box and the triangle down the right side until you achieve the color you want.

    •   Adjust the values for hue, saturation, and luminosity in the boxes labeled Hue, Sat, and Lum. I've set these to 87, 185, and 139, respectively.

- Adjust the values in the Red, Green, and Blue boxes. I've set these to 55, 223, and 63, respectively.

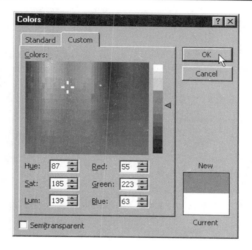

3.   Click OK to return to the Format WordArt dialog box; the Color box will be filled with the selected color. Click OK to return to your worksheet, which will now display your letters filled with bright green.

Applying Shadows to a *WordArt* Object

Applying a shadow to a WordArt object is simply a matter of clicking a button. The Shadow button is the second button from the end of the Drawing toolbar. Click it to display the selection of shadow formats available, then click Shadow Settings at the bottom of the shadow formats list, as shown, to display the Shadow Settings toolbar.

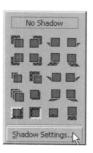

Figure 24.16 identifies the commands on the Shadow Settings toolbar.

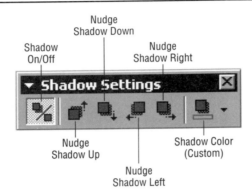

Shadow On/Off toggles between displaying the shadow and omitting it.

Nudge Shadow Up, Nudge Shadow Down move the shadow upward and downward.

Nudge Shadow Left, Nudge Shadow Right move the shadow left and right.

Shadow Color (Custom) allows you to change the color and transparency effect for the shadow.

Let's make our WordArt object even more impressive by adding a shadow.

1. Select your WordArt object and click the Shadow On/Off button to display a default shadow.

2. Repeatedly click any of the four Nudge Shadow buttons shown in Figure 24.16 to move the shadow in your WordArt object to the position required.

3. Click Shadow Color to display the colors available and choose More Shadow Colors from the bottom (as shown below). Choose a dark green color (the color I've chosen is 3, 39, 8 in terms of red, green, and blue). Click OK to return to your worksheet.

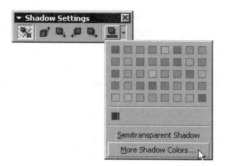

4. Select cells A1:E5 and choose Format ➤ Cells to display the Format Cells dialog box. Select the Patterns tab and the dark green color from the bottom-right corner of the palette to contrast with the text and shadow in your WordArt graphic.

5. Use the yellow diamond to make your WordArt text slant forward slightly—the shadow will follow, too.

Formatting the Text of a *WordArt* Object

Now that we've completed the artwork for the title, let's complete the rest of the formatting. Figure 24.17 shows the WordArt object after all of the formatting has been completed.

FIGURE 24.17:

Final version of the worksheet to be saved as a template

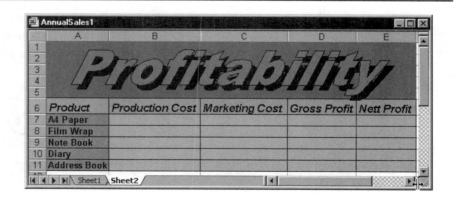

1. Enter the text shown into column A and into row 6.

2. To format the worksheet labels, first select A6:E6 and choose Format ➢ Cells to open the Format Cells dialog box. Click the Patterns tab and select the color in the second column of the second row. Click the Font tab and choose Arial from the Font list, Bold Italic from the Font Style list, and 12 from the Size list. Click OK to return to the worksheet.

3. To add shading to the Product column, select A7:A11 and choose Format ➢ Cells. Click the Patterns tab and select the bottom-left color immediately above "Pattern." Click the Font tab and select Arial from the Font list, Bold from the Font Style list, and 10 from the Size list. Click OK to return to the worksheet.

4. To add shading to the other data columns, select cells B7:E11 and choose Format ➢ Cells. Click the Patterns tab and select the fifth color in the top row. Click OK to return to your worksheet.

5. Finally, to add a border around the data area, select A6:E11 and choose Format ➢ Cells. Click the Border tab and select the thin line at the bottom of the left column in the Style box. Ensure that the Outline and Inside buttons are both selected in the Presets area. Click OK to return to your worksheet.

Now that we've completed dressing up our worksheet, we could save it as a template by overwriting the old version of the AnnualSales template. The following steps show you how this is done:

1. Choose File ➢ Save As and enter the name of the template in the File Name box.

2. Choose Template from the list in the Save As Type box. Click Save to save your workbook as a template file with the extension .XLT before returning to your worksheet.

NOTE   Templates that appear in the New dialog box can be stored in either the xlstart folder (to appear in the General tab) or your designated alternative startup folder (to appear in a tab with the folder's name).

Macro for Creating a Title

The TitleDesign macro shown in Listing 24.2 takes the WordArt object you've inserted in a worksheet and sets the fill color and the shadow color. If a WordArt object has a two-color fill effect, only the first color is changed. If it doesn't have a shadow effect, a shadow will be added at an incremental distance of five units downward and five to the right—this means that the shadow grows further away from the text each time the macro is run.

Figure 24.18 shows a WordArt object added to Sheet2 before the macro was called. Figure 24.19 shows the visual effects added as a result of running the macro. The WordArt object then needs to be positioned as required by physically dragging it. If the WordArt object is always to appear in the same place, you could set its Top and Left properties in a macro. For example, the following two lines could be added after Line 4 in the TitleDesignMacro macro shown in Listing 24.2 if you always want the WordArt placed in the top-left corner of the worksheet:

```
.Top = 0
.Left = 0
```

To make the macro more general, I have avoided setting the position here.

FIGURE 24.18:

WordArt object before running the TitleDesign macro

FIGURE 24.19:

WordArt object with the visual effects added by the TitleDesign macro

LISTING 24.2

```
0    Sub TitleDesignMacro()
1        ' Macro for designing titles
2        ' requires a WordArt object
3        ActiveSheet.Shapes.SelectAll
4        With Selection.ShapeRange
5            .IncrementLeft -5
6            .Fill.ForeColor.RGB = RGB(55, 223, 63)
7            'deal with shadow
8            .Shadow.IncrementOffsetX 5#
9            .Shadow.IncrementOffsetY 5#
10           .Shadow.Visible = msoTrue
11           .Shadow.ForeColor.RGB = RGB(3, 39, 8)
12           .Adjustments.Item(1) = 0.4812
13       End With
14       Range("A1:E5").Select
15       With Selection.Interior
16           .ColorIndex = 54
17           .Pattern = xlSolid
18           .PatternColorIndex = xlAutomatic
19       End With
20   End Sub
```

ANALYSIS

Line 0 starts the TitleDesignMacro macro.

Line 3 uses the SelectAll method to select all of the Shape objects in the Shapes collection associated with the active worksheet. Shape objects include WordArt objects in addition to other graphical objects, such as pictures and AutoShapes.

Line 4 uses the With statement so that the methods and properties of the selected ShapeRange object (WordArt object) can be used without being fully qualified.

Line 5 passes −5 to the IncrementLeft method, which moves the WordArt object horizontally 5 points to the left. Passing a positive number moves it to the right.

Line 6 sets the fill color using the RGB function.

Line 8 and **Line 9** set the `IncrementOffsetX` and `IncrementOffsetY` methods of the shadow on the selected shape to 5 points each.

Line 10 makes the shadow on the selected object visible.

Line 11 sets the fill color for the shadow using the RGB function.

Line 12 causes the WordArt shadow to be moved from its current position toward the lower-right corner. This code uses the `Item` property of the `Adjustments` object with an index of **1** to assign the first adjustment value associated with this movement. Any value between 0 and 1 is valid here.

Lines 14 through **18** set the color for cells A1:E5.

Summary

By the end of this chapter, you'll be able to

- specify the animated sequence to be performed by the Office Assistant from a macro
- add callouts to your worksheet and assign text to them in a macro
- change the Office Assistant's appearance
- add WordArt text to your worksheets
- alter the path the text follows in a `WordArt` object
- specify color for your `WordArt` object
- make the characters in your `WordArt` object cast a shadow
- write a macro to set the properties of a `WordArt` object

APPENDIX

A

A

ASCII Character Set

TABLE A.1: ASCII Character Set (0–127)

0	[null]	32	[space]	64	@	96	`
1	[start of heading]	33	!	65	A	97	a
2	[start of text]	34	"	66	B	98	b
3	[end of text]	35	#	67	C	99	c
4	[end of transmission]	36	$	68	D	100	d
5	[enquiry]	37	%	69	E	101	e
6	[acknowledge]	38	&	70	F	102	f
7	[bell]	39	'	71	G	103	g
8	[backspace]	40	(	72	H	104	h
9	[horizontal tab]	41	)	73	I	105	i
10	[line feed]	42	*	74	J	106	j
11	[vertical tab]	43	+	75	K	107	k
12	[form feed]	44	,	76	L	108	l
13	[carriage return]	45	-	77	M	109	m
14	[shift out]	46	.	78	N	110	n
15	[shift in]	47	/	79	O	111	o
16	[data link escape]	48	0	80	P	112	p
17	[device control 1]	49	1	81	Q	113	q
18	[device control 2]	50	2	82	R	114	r
19	[device control 3]	51	3	83	S	115	s
20	[device control 4]	52	4	84	T	116	t
21	[negative acknowledge]	53	5	85	U	117	u
22	[synchronous idle]	54	6	86	V	118	v
23	[end transmission block]	55	7	87	W	119	w
24	[cancel]	56	8	88	X	120	x
25	[end of medium]	57	9	89	Y	121	y

TABLE A.1 CONTINUED: ASCII Character Set (0–127)

26	[substitute]	58	:	90	Z	122	z
27	[escape]	59	;	91	[	123	{
28	[file separator]	60	<	92	\	124	|
29	[group separator]	61	=	93	]	125	}
30	[record separator]	62	>	94	^	126	~
31	[unit separator]	63	?	95	_	127	[delete]

Nonprinting characters are described within brackets.

ASCII code characters 0–7, 11, 12, and 14–31 are not supported by Microsoft Windows.

TABLE A.2: ASCII Character Set (128–255)

128	¤	160	[space]	192	À	224	à
129	¤	161	¡	193	Á	225	á
130	¤	162	¢	194	Â	226	â
131	¤	163	£	195	Ã	227	ã
132	¤	164	¤	196	Ä	228	ä
133	¤	165	¥	197	Å	229	å
134	¤	166	¦	198	Æ	230	æ
135	¤	167	§	199	Ç	231	ç
136	¤	168	¨	200	È	232	è
137	¤	169	©	201	É	233	é
138	¤	170	ª	202	Ê	234	ê
139	¤	171	«	203	Ë	235	ë
140	¤	172	¬	204	Ì	236	ì
141	¤	173	-	205	Í	237	í
142	¤	174	®	206	Î	238	î

TABLE A.2 CONTINUED: ASCII Character Set (128–255)

143	¤	175	‾	207	Ï	239	ï
144	¤	176	°	208	Ð	240	ð
145	¤	177	±	209	Ñ	241	ñ
146	¤	178	²	210	Ò	242	ò
147	¤	179	³	211	Ó	243	ó
148	¤	180	´	212	Ô	244	ô
149	¤	181	µ	213	Õ	245	õ
150	¤	182	¶	214	Ö	246	ö
151	¤	183	·	215	×	247	÷
152	¤	184	¸	216	Ø	248	ø
153	¤	185	¹	217	Ù	249	ù
154	¤	186	º	218	Ú	250	ú
155	¤	187	»	219	Û	251	û
156	¤	188	¼	220	Ü	252	ü
157	¤	189	½	221	Ý	253	ý
158	¤	190	¾	222	þ	254	þ
159	¤	191	¿	223	ß	255	ÿ

¤These characters are not supported by Microsoft Windows.

The values in the table are the Windows default. However, values in the ANSI character set above 127 are determined by the code page specific to your operating system.

APPENDIX

B

Objects, Collections, Properties, Events, and Methods

This appendix contains a brief description of objects used throughout the book, the collections they belong to, and some of their properties, events, and methods.

Objects

In VBA, an object represents a specific item such as a cell, worksheet, chart, or control.

Application object represents the application itself—in our case, Microsoft Excel—and all of its application-wide settings, including those that can be set in the Options dialog box.

Axis object contains everything related to one of the axes in a chart and is a member of the `Axes` collection. This object includes properties that specify the axis title, border, and tick labels.

Border object represents one of the four borders of a cell (or range of cells), or the complete border of a chart area or plot area. The `Border` object belongs to the `Borders` collection object.

Character object represents the characters in an object containing text. You can make changes to the font properties for any substring within the text.

Chart object contains all of the details about a chart embedded in a worksheet or in a chart sheet. The `Chart` object is a member of the `Charts` collection object.

ChartArea object contains details about the chart area of the specified chart, including attributes of the border font and interior color and pattern.

ChartObject object is a container for a chart embedded in a worksheet and controls the appearance and size of the chart it contains.

ChartTitle object contains details about the attributes of a chart title, including the text it contains, the font to be used to display it, its border attributes, and the interior color or pattern.

ColorFormat object represents the color of an object. This object is returned by several properties including `BackColor` and `ForeColor`.

CommandBar object represents a command bar in an application. A command bar can represent either a menu bar or a toolbar. The `CommandBar` object is a member of the `CommandBars` collection.

CommandBarButton object contains details about a button on a custom command bar. This object uses the properties and methods of the `CommandBarControl` object.

CommandBarComboBox object includes details about a combo box with a drop-down list on a custom command bar. This object uses the properties and methods of the `CommandBarControl` object.

CommandBarControl object represents a command bar control. The properties and methods of this object are used by the `CommandBarButton`, `CommandBarComboBox`, and `CommandBarPopup` objects.

CommandBarPopup object represents a pop-up control on a custom command bar. This object uses the properties and methods of the `CommandBarControl` object.

Comment object represents a worksheet comment attached to a range of cells. The `Comment` object belongs to the `Comments` collection object.

Control object contains information about a toolbox control placed on a UserForm. This control is a member of the `Controls` collection object.

Err object contains information, such as a number, about a runtime error to uniquely identify the problem that caused the error.

FillFormat object contains the details of how a shape or chart is to be filled. These details include solid, gradient, texture, or picture.

Font object contains information about how text is to be displayed on a UserForm or control.

FormatCondition object contains a conditional format for a specified cell or range of cells. This object is a member of the `FormatConditions` collection object.

Hyperlink object represents a hyperlink in a worksheet or range of cells.

Interior object represents the interior color or pattern for an object.

Legend object contains details about the legend in a chart. There is only one `Legend` object for each chart.

Name object represents the name defined for a cell (or range of cells). The Name object belongs to the Names collection object.

Point object contains details about a point in a series or chart. The Point object is a member of the Points collection.

PageSetup object represents all of the page setup details required to print values from a worksheet.

PlotArea object contains details about the area of a chart where the data is plotted. The details included are dependent on whether the chart is 2-D or 3-D.

Range object identifies one or more cells that you want to collectively refer to, which don't need to be adjacent to each other on the workbook.

Shape object represents a drawing object, such as a picture or an Auto-Shape. This object is a member of the Shapes collection object.

Style object contains properties for all of the components of a style, such as font, size, and alignment, that's applied to a range of cells.

Walls object represents all of the walls of a 3-D chart as a single item.

Window object represents a window in Microsoft Excel or in a workbook. The Window object is a member of the Windows collection.

Workbook object contains all of the details about a Microsoft Excel workbook and is a member of the Workbooks collection.

Worksheet object represents a Microsoft Excel worksheet and is a member of the Worksheets collection. Worksheet objects are returned by the Active-Sheet and Worksheet properties.

Collections

Several objects that are usually of the same type are often grouped together in a collection object called by the plural of the type of object it contains. Collections can contain generic (universally available) objects, as well as objects specifically related to open workbooks.

Axes collection contains all of the Axis objects representing axes from the same chart.

Borders collection contains four Border objects representing the four borders of a cell or range of cells.

ChartObjects collection contains all of the ChartObject objects that represent the embedded charts on a worksheet.

Charts collection includes all of the Chart objects associated with a specified (or active) workbook.

CommandBars collection object contains all of the CommandBar objects that represent the command bars in the application.

CommandBarControls collection object contains all of the CommandBar-Control objects that represent the command bar controls on a command bar you've added to an application.

Comments collection contains the Comment objects representing all of the comments associated with the specified or active worksheet.

Controls collection contains all of the Control objects associated with an object.

FormatConditions collection contains up to three FormatCondition objects that each represent a single conditional format. The maximum is three to match the three conditions you are allowed to specify in the Conditional Formatting dialog box.

Hyperlinks collection represents all of the Hyperlink objects for a worksheet or range of cells.

Names collection contains all of the Name objects associated with an application or a workbook.

Points collection contains all of the Point objects in one series.

Shapes collection represents all of the Shape objects on a selected worksheet.

ShapeRange collection represents a selection of one or more shapes (drawing objects) on a worksheet.

Sheets collection represents all of the sheets in a specified or active workbook. The Sheets collection can contain Chart or Worksheet objects and allows you to retrieve sheets of either type.

Windows collection can be contained in the Application object and include all of the Window objects in Microsoft Excel, or it can be contained in the Workbook object and include all of the Window objects contained in the specified workbook.

Workbooks collection is all of the Workbook objects associated with the workbooks that are currently open in Microsoft Excel.

Worksheets collection contains all of the Worksheet objects associated with a specified or active workbook.

Properties

Each object contains properties that can be considered its attributes. Properties can represent objects as well as numerical or textual values. Properties that return an object have the same name as the object being returned. You can use any method or property of the returned object just as if you'd named the object itself.

Accelerator property is set to one of the letters in a control's Caption property to allow it to be accessed using the keyboard. The accelerator letter is displayed in the control's caption as an underlined character.

ActiveCell property returns the Range object representing the active cell. You can make a cell the active cell using the Activate method.

ActiveChart property returns a Chart object representing the active chart embedded in a worksheet or in a chart sheet.

ActiveSheet property returns an object representing the active sheet, which can be in the active workbook or in a specified workbook or window.

ActiveWindow property returns the Window object containing the active window.

ActiveWorkbook property returns an object representing the active workbook.

Application property returns an Application object representing the application—in our case, Microsoft Excel.

AutoSize property resizes a control automatically so that its Caption property can be displayed in full.

BackColor property defines the background color.

BackStyle property determines whether a label appears transparent or opaque.

BlackAndWhite property is set to `True` to print worksheet values in black and white.

BorderColor property determines the color for the border of a cell or range of cells.

Borders property returns a `Borders` collection containing four `Border` objects representing borders of a cell or range of cells.

BorderStyle property can be set to either `fmBorderStyleNone` or `fmBorderStyleSingle` to determine whether or not a border is displayed. If the border is required, it's drawn as a single line.

Calculation property belongs to the Microsoft Excel `Application` object and determines whether formulas are calculated automatically if a value they reference changes.

Caption property is assigned the text to be displayed to the user. The text is read-only, so it can't be changed while the program is running.

Cells property belongs to the `Application`, `Range`, and `Worksheet` objects and returns the `Range` object containing all of the cells in the active worksheet.

ChartArea property returns a `ChartArea` object that contains details about the chart area in the specified chart.

ChartTitle property returns the `ChartTitle` object representing the title of the specified chart.

Color property represents the color of an object such as the border, font, or interior fill.

Colors property refers to the 56 colors in the color palette for a workbook; each color is specified by an RGB value.

ColorIndex property acts as an index to the color palette for a workbook.

ControlTipText property is assigned the text to be displayed as a ToolTip for a control.

Count property contains the number of objects in a collection.

CurrentRegion property returns a Range object that contains the current region, which is the range containing the current cell bounded by blank rows and columns.

Dependents property returns the Range object that contains all of the cells that are dependent on the current cell.

Description property returns text that gives a description of the problem that caused an error.

DropDownLines property determines the number of lines displayed in the drop-down list of a combo box.

Enabled property determines whether a control is available for the user to select.

FileSystem property returns the type of file system that's being used by the specified drive. Systems include FAT, NTFS, and CDFS.

Fill property returns a FillFormat object describing how the specified shape or chart is to be filled.

FilterMode property is set to True if a worksheet contains a filtered list.

FitToPagesTall property is set to the number of pages tall that the worksheet will be scaled to fit onto when it's printed. If this property is set to False, the FitToPagesWide property is used for the scaling.

FitToPagesWide property is set to the number of pages wide that the worksheet will be scaled to fit onto when it's printed. If this property is set to False, the FitToPagesTall property is used for the scaling.

Font property returns a Font object containing details of the attributes for displaying text on a control or UserForm.

ForeColor property belongs to the ChartFillFormat object or the ColorFormat object and represents the color of the foreground fill or solid color.

Formula property is assigned the string representing a worksheet formula, with any references defined in the A1 style.

FormulaR1C1 property is assigned the string representing a worksheet formula, with any references defined in the R1C1 style.

HasTitle property determines whether a title is displayed along an axis or in a chart.

Height property contains the height of the control, which can also be set by dragging and dropping its selection handles.

HelpContextId property is assigned a number that can be used to identify a page in the help file.

Interior property returns an `Interior` object that contains details about the interior color or pattern of an object.

Left property contains the distance between the left edge of the control and the worksheet containing it.

ListCount property applies to the `ComboBox` and `ListBox` controls and contains the current number of items in the list.

ListIndex property applies to the `ComboBox` and `ListBox` controls and is assigned the index value denoting the position of the current item in a list. It can be reset in code to make any item in the list the new current item. It can be reset at runtime in response to the user clicking on a list item, which becomes the new current item with the `ListItem` property automatically being updated to the new index value.

Max property determines the maximum value that a scroll bar or spin button can be assigned. This must be greater than the value assigned to the `Min` property.

Min property determines the minimum value that a scroll bar or spin button can be assigned, which must be less than the value of the `Max` property.

MousePointer property defines the type of mouse cursor displayed when the mouse is paused over the control.

MultiLine property determines whether or not a control can display text on multiple lines.

MultiUserEditing property is set to `True` if the workbook is open in Shared mode.

Name property is assigned the name of the specified object.

Number property belongs to the `Err` object and is assigned a number identifying the problem that caused the error.

OnAction property is assigned the name of a macro that will be executed whenever a specified object, such as a control or toolbar button, is clicked.

Order property belongs to the `PageSetup` object and determines the order for printing pages.

Orientation property determines how a chart or range of values from a worksheet is printed (horizontally or vertically).

PaperSize property is assigned a constant that defines the size of the paper when a worksheet or chart sheet is being printed.

Picture property allows you to specify a picture to place on a control.

Placement property defines the way a `Worksheet` object is attached to the cells beneath it.

Precedents property returns a `Range` object containing all of the precedents of a cell.

PrintArea property defines the range to be printed in the A1 referencing style.

Range property returns a `Range` object that represents a cell (or range of cells).

RemoveItem method removes items from the list in a `ListBox` or `ComboBox` object and shifts all of the subsequent items up one to fill the blank space.

Rows property can belong to an `Application`, `Range`, or `Worksheet` object. The `Rows` property of the `Application` object returns all of the rows in the active worksheet; the `Rows` property of the `Range` object returns all of the rows in a specified range; and the `Rows` property of the `Worksheet` object returns all of the rows in a specified worksheet.

Saved property can be used to determine whether any changes have been made to a specified workbook since it was last saved. You can set this property to `True` to avoid displaying the message box prompt about saving, in which case any changes are simply discarded without warning.

ScrollBars property defines whether a control or UserForm has vertical or horizontal scroll bars or both.

Selection property belongs to the `Application` object and returns the selected object from the active window.

Shadow property is set to `True` or `False` depending on whether or not an object has a shadow.

Sheets property can belong to the Application object or the Workbook object. When it belongs to the Application object, it returns the Sheets collection object containing all of the worksheets in the active workbook. When it belongs to the Workbook object, the Sheets collection it returns contains all of the worksheets in the specified workbook.

SheetsInNewWorkbook property belongs to the Application object and determines the number of sheets that Excel creates for new workbooks.

SizeWithWindow property belongs to the Chart object and when set to True will resize a chart in a chart sheet as the window containing it is resized.

SpecialEffect property determines the appearance of an object, including giving it a flat, sunken, or raised look.

StatusBar property applies to the Application object and is assigned the text that appears in the status bar.

Style property applies only to the CommandBarButton and CommandBar-ComboBox objects and determines how they are displayed.

Text property is assigned the contents of the current item in a list box or combo box, or the text in a text box.

Top property specifies the distance between the top of the object and the UserForm, window, or screen containing it, depending on the object involved.

Value property is assigned different types of values depending on what object it belongs to. For example, the Application object's value is the string "Microsoft Excel"; the value for a Range object is the value at the specified cell, or an array of values if the Range object represents several cells. A text box has a value of type Variant, which allows it to contain a string or a number.

Visible property determines whether or not a control is displayed.

Walls property returns a Walls object representing all of the walls of a 3-D chart.

WhatsThisButton property determines whether or not the What's This button appears on a UserForm's title bar.

Width property defines the width of a UserForm or control; it can be assigned values in code or can be set by dragging the selection handles.

WindowState property determines whether a window is displayed as normal, maximized to cover the screen, or minimized to an icon.

WordWrap property determines whether the text is wrapped down to the next line. If a control has its `AutoSize` property set to `True`, the `WordWrap` property determines whether the control should be expanded horizontally or vertically. If `WordWrap` is set to `True`, then the expansion is done vertically by wrapping the text down to the next line. If `WordWrap` is `False`, then the expansion is done horizontally and the text is displayed as a single line.

Workbooks property returns the `Workbooks` collection object that contains the `Workbook` objects for all of the currently open workbooks in the Microsoft Excel application.

WorkSheet property belongs to the `Range` object and returns the worksheet that contains the specified cells.

Zoom property determines how much a worksheet will be scaled for printing and is assigned a percentage between 10 and 400.

Events

An event provides the response to the user when they perform some specific action that triggers that event.

Change event occurs when the user changes the `Value` property of a control.

Click event happens when the user clicks a control with the mouse or selects the control using the accelerator key.

Initialize event occurs immediately after an object is loaded but before it is displayed.

KeyPress event takes place when the user presses a keyboard key. This event has a `KeyAscii` argument that contains the integer ASCII representation of the key pressed.

Load statement loads into memory all of the information required to display and run an object, but doesn't display the object. In this state, the program can refer to the object and change its properties.

NewSheet event occurs when a new worksheet is added to the workbook.

SelectionChange event happens when new cells are selected from the worksheet.

Methods

Methods can be considered to be the actions of an object.

Activate method is applied to an object to make it the active object. This method can make the `Cell`, `Range`, `Worksheet`, `Workbook`, and `Chart` objects active.

Add method is applied to a collection object; it creates a new object of the same type represented in the collection and adds it to the collection.

AddComment method adds a worksheet comment to a range of cells.

ApplyCustomType method changes a chart's type to the one specified.

ApplyDataLabels method applies data labels to a point in a chart, or to one (or all) series in a chart.

ApplyNames method creates names for cells in the specified range.

AutoFill method automatically fills the cells in the specified range as if you had filled them by dragging.

BorderAround method draws a border around the specified cell or range of cells, in the color, thickness, and linestyle assigned to its arguments.

Calculate method calculates all of the formulas in the cells of the object it belongs to. For example, if it belongs to the `Application` object, it will calculate any formulas in all open workbooks; if it belongs to a `Worksheet` object, it will calculate formulas in the specified worksheet; and if it belongs to the `Range` object, it will calculate formulas in the specified range of cells.

Clear method deletes all values in a range of cells, or clears a chart area or legend.

ClearArrows method removes the tracer arrows from a worksheet.

Close method closes the `Window` or `Workbook` object that it's applied to.

ConvertFormula method converts a formula between the A1 and R1C1 reference styles and between the relative and absolute modes.

CreateNames method creates names for cells in the specified range based on row and column labels.

Delete method removes an object from its collection.

ExclusiveAccess method gives exclusive access to the current user of a workbook that's open in Shared mode.

FunctionWizard method belongs to the Range object and runs the Function Wizard for the top-left cell in the specified range.

Hide method makes an object invisible to the user but doesn't delete it from memory. In this state, it can still be manipulated by the program.

Item method belongs to any collection object and retrieves the member identified by an index number or a string expression.

Location method belongs to the Chart object and moves a chart to a different location.

Move method moves a specified file to another location.

OneColorGradient method belongs to the FillFormat and ChartFill-Format objects and sets the specified fill to a one-color gradient fill.

Open method opens the file containing the specified workbook.

Paste method pastes the contents of the clipboard to the area required. The area can be a range of cells or a wall in a 3-D chart.

PrintOut method sends output to the printer and allows you to specify settings such as which pages to print, how many copies to print, and whether to collate the output.

Protect method prevents a chart or worksheet from being updated.

RemoveItem method deletes items from the lists in list boxes or combo boxes.

Save method saves a specified workbook to the file it was retrieved from using the Open method.

SaveAs method saves a workbook to a different file than the one it was retrieved from.

Select method selects an object, which could be a cell or range of cells or a component of a chart.

SeriesCollection method returns an object that contains one or more series in a chart.

SetFocus method gives a Control object the focus that will display it in a special way to let the user know that it's special. For example, a TextBox control with the focus will contain the blinking entry cursor, or a Command-Button control will have its Caption property enclosed in a box with dashed lines.

SetSourceData method belongs to the Chart object and sets the range containing the data to be used to generate a chart.

Show method is used to display a UserForm object. If the UserForm is being used for the first time, it will be loaded into memory so that it can be displayed.

ShowDependents method belongs to the Range object and shows tracer arrows to the cells that are direct dependents of the specified range.

ShowPrecedents method belongs to the Range method and shows tracer arrows to the cells that are direct precedents to the specified range.

TwoColorGradient method belongs to the FillFormat and ChartFill-Format objects and sets the specified fill to a two-color gradient fill.

UserPicture method belongs to the FillFormat and ChartFillFormat objects and fills the specified shape with a picture.

INDEX

Note to the Reader: Throughout this index **boldfaced** page numbers indicate primary discussions of a topic. *Italicized* page numbers indicate illustrations.

SYMBOLS

(%) percent operator, 134–136
(') single quote, 71, 140
(*) wildcard character, 443–444
(.) period character, 89
(/) division operator, 136
(=) equals sign, 126

NUMBER

2-D charts, *469*
3-D charts, *470*, **497–502**
   3-D View dialog boxes, **499–502**, *501*
   formatting floor of, 498
   formatting walls of, 499
   viewing from different angles, 499–500
3-D comment boxes, **51–52**, *52*
3-D references, **22–23**
3-D View dialog boxes, **499–502**, *501*

H

I

K

O

P

S

T

W

X

SYBEX BOOKS ON THE WEB

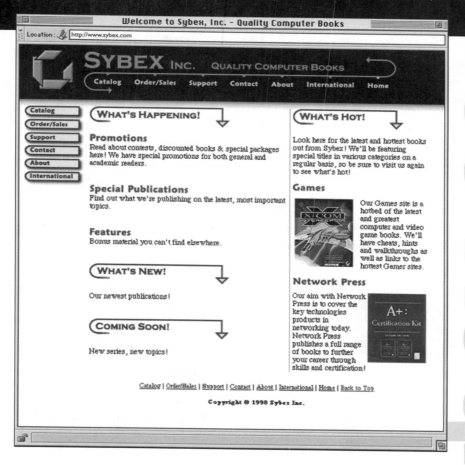

At the dynamic and informative Sybex Web site, you can:

- view our complete online catalog
- preview a book you're interested in
- access special book content

- order books online at special discount prices
- learn about Sybex

www.sybex.com

SYBEX Inc. • 1151 Marina Village Parkway, Alameda, CA 94501 • 510-523-8233

About the CD

The companion CD-ROM contains the code from many of the examples in this book. It also contains various evaluation demos, documentation, tags, a JavaScript reference, and an electronic version of the book.

Source code and Access MDB database from the book chapters

Evaluation Version of Cold Fusion Application Server 4: A fully-functional, time-limited evaluation version of the software used to run the applications developed in this book

Evaluation Version of Cold Fusion Studio 4: A fully-functional, time-limited evaluation version of the integrated development tool for ColdFusion

Evaluation version of Cold Fusion Forums: A fully-functional, time-limited evaluation of an extension to ColdFusion Application Server that provides Web-based discussion forum capabilities

Allaire documentation for evaluation versions

Allaire Alive Presentations: A collection of multimedia tutorials about various aspects of ColdFusion from Allaire, the developer of ColdFusion

Custom Tags from the Developer's Exchange: a collection of custom tags you can use to extend the functionality of ColdFusion

Apache: A freely-available Web server you can use to run ColdFusion Server for development purposes and for production Web servers

"Comparing Javascript and JScript," used by permission from *Mastering JavaScript and JScript* by James Jaworski (Sybex, 1999, ISBN# 0-7821-2492-5)

Electronic PDF version of *Mastering ColdFusion 4*

FusionChat from http://www.aylo.com/development.htm: A ColdFusion application for creating a Web-based chat system

Appendices:

1. ColdFusion Tag Reference

2. ColdFusion Function Reference

3. Using ColdFusion Studio

4. Creating Databases and Tables

5. Differences between ColdFusion and Traditional Server-Side Programming

6. ColdFusion for Solaris

7. Large-Scale FuseBox Applications

8. Additional Resources

9. ColdFusion Administration